CITY IN THE DESERT

THE COMPLETE EDITION

BY MORO ROGERS

LETTERING BY DERON BENNETT
ORIGINAL DESIGN BY FAUN LAU

WWW.NAKRAPRESS.COM

PRINTED IN SOUTH KOREA
FIRST PRINTING, 2015
ISBN 978-0-692-57146-0
NAKRA PRESS
WWW.NAKRAPRESS.COM

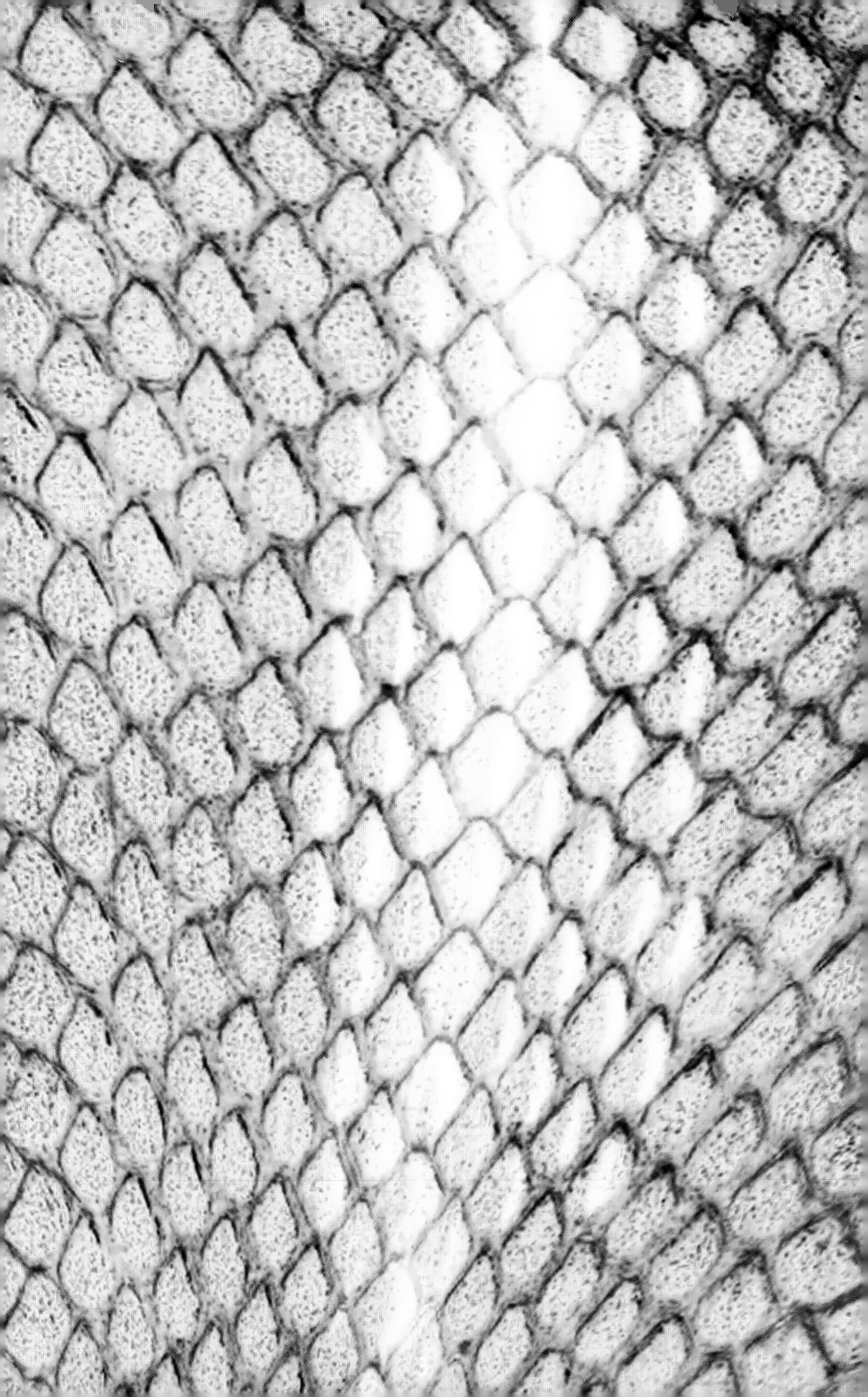

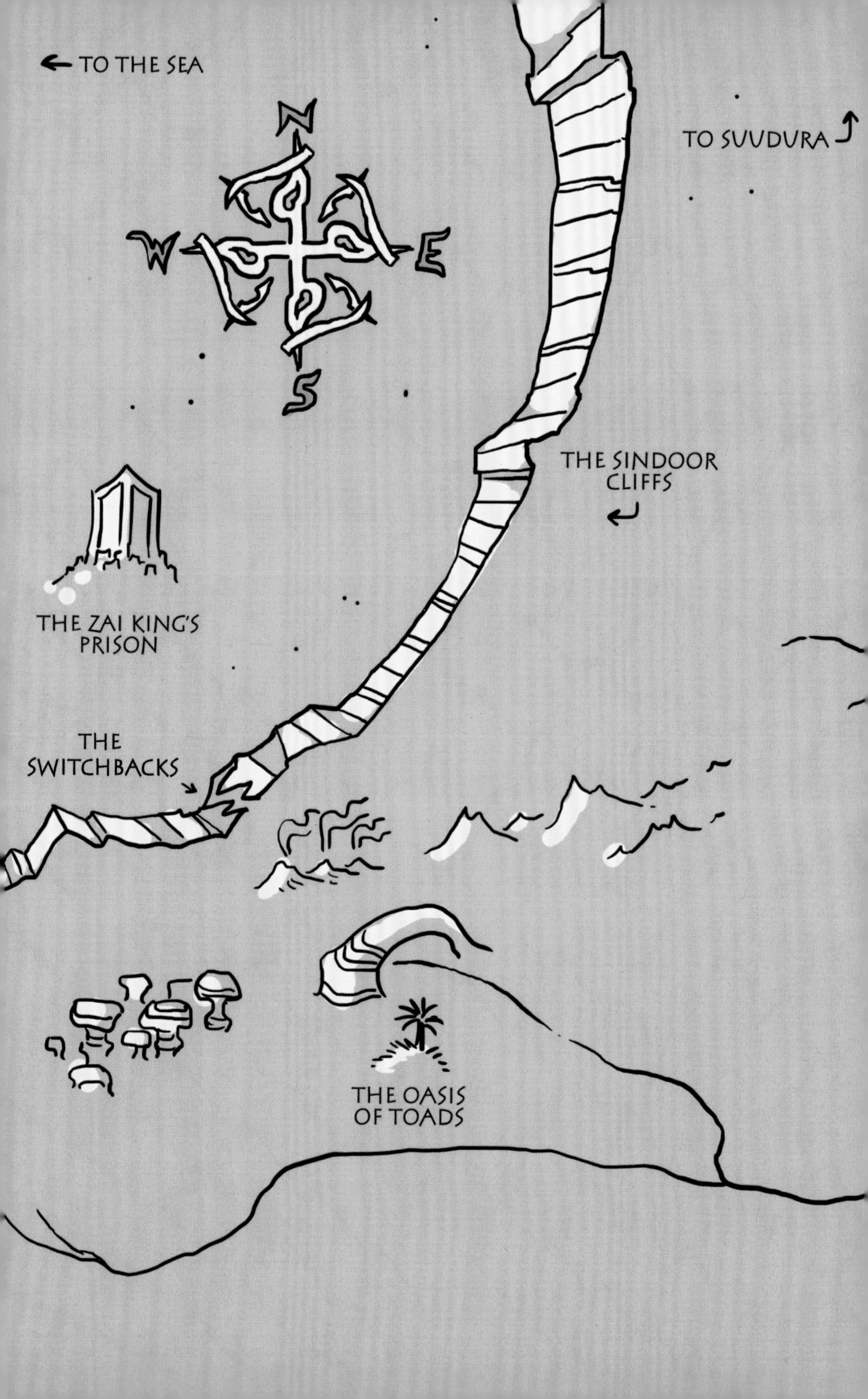

← TO THE SEA
N
W
E
S
TO SUUDURA
THE SINDOOR CLIFFS
THE ZAI KING'S PRISON
THE SWITCHBACKS
THE OASIS OF TOADS

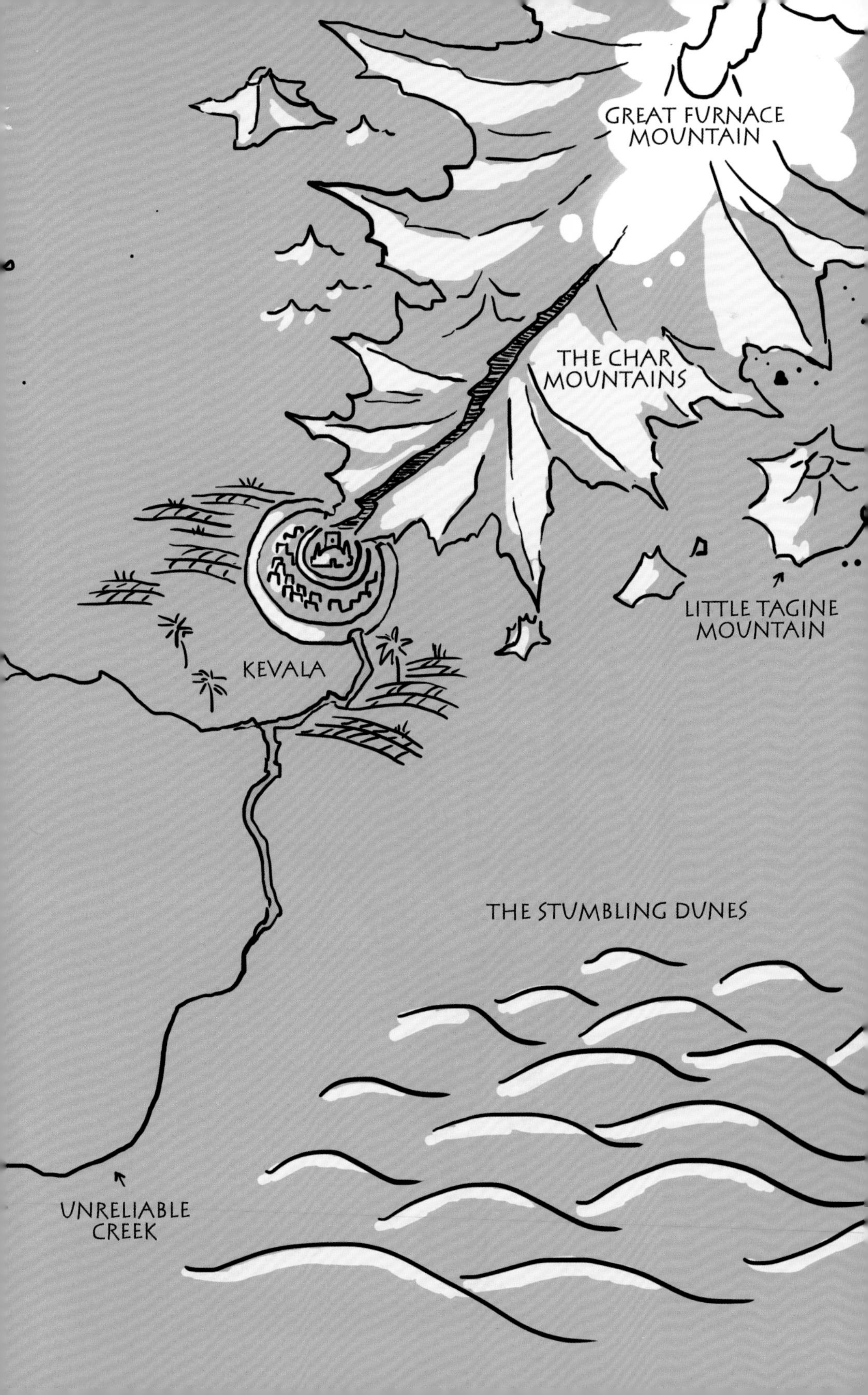
GREAT FURNACE MOUNTAIN
THE CHAR MOUNTAINS
LITTLE TAGINE MOUNTAIN
KEVALA
THE STUMBLING DUNES
UNRELIABLE CREEK

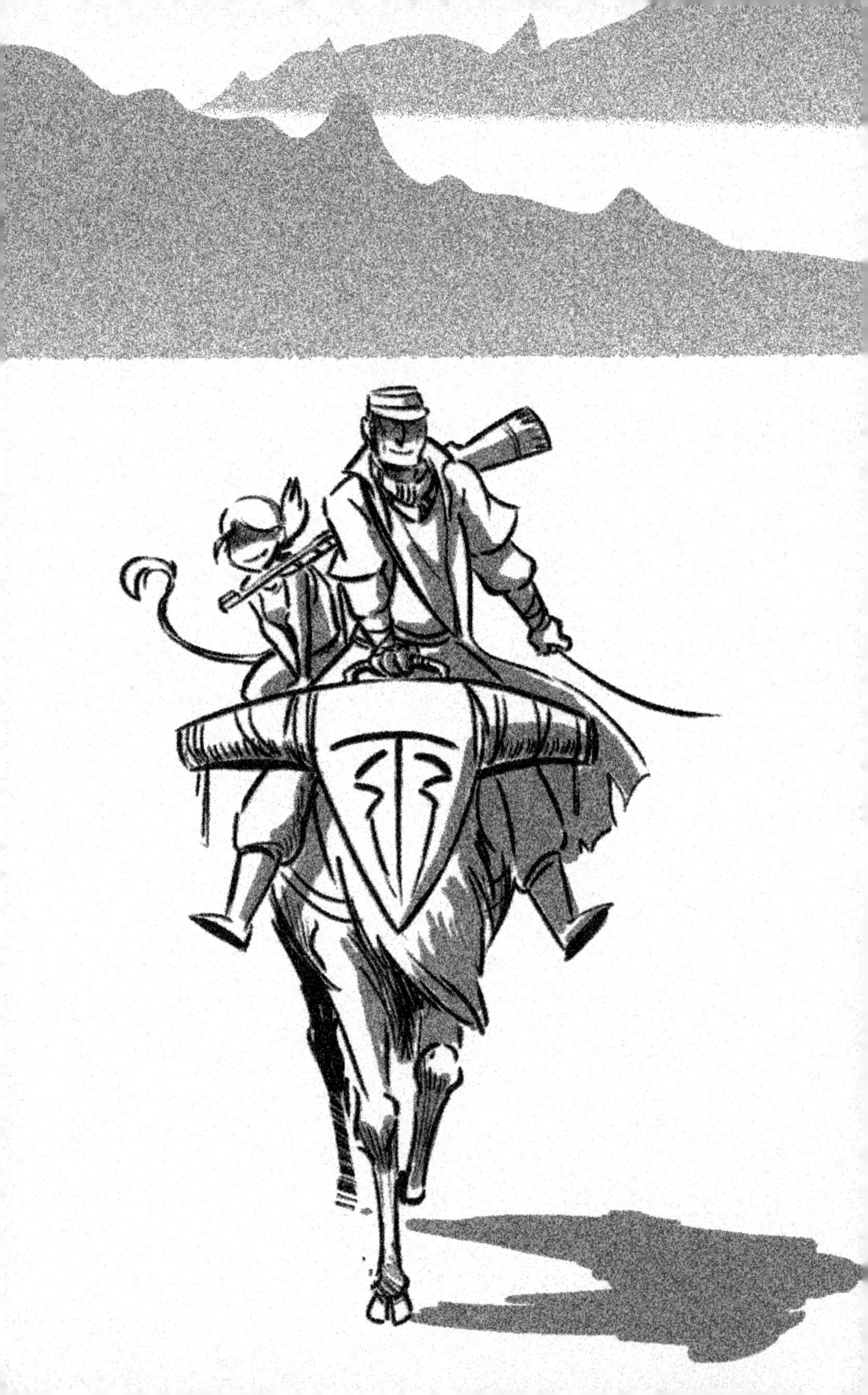

PART 1-
THE MONSTER PROBLEM
WRITTEN AND DRAWN
BY
MORO ROGERS

LETTERING BY
DERON BENNETT

FOR MY DAD, WHO TOLD ME TO

"KEEP WATCHING THIS MOVIE, THERE'S GOING TO BE A MONSTER."

SPECIAL THANKS

TO MY HUSBAND AND PARENTS FOR
THEIR LOVE AND SUPPORT, THE FOLKS AT
ARCHAIA, AND TO MY FRIEND MINKYU LEE
FOR HIS MUCH-NEEDED ADVICE AND CRITS.

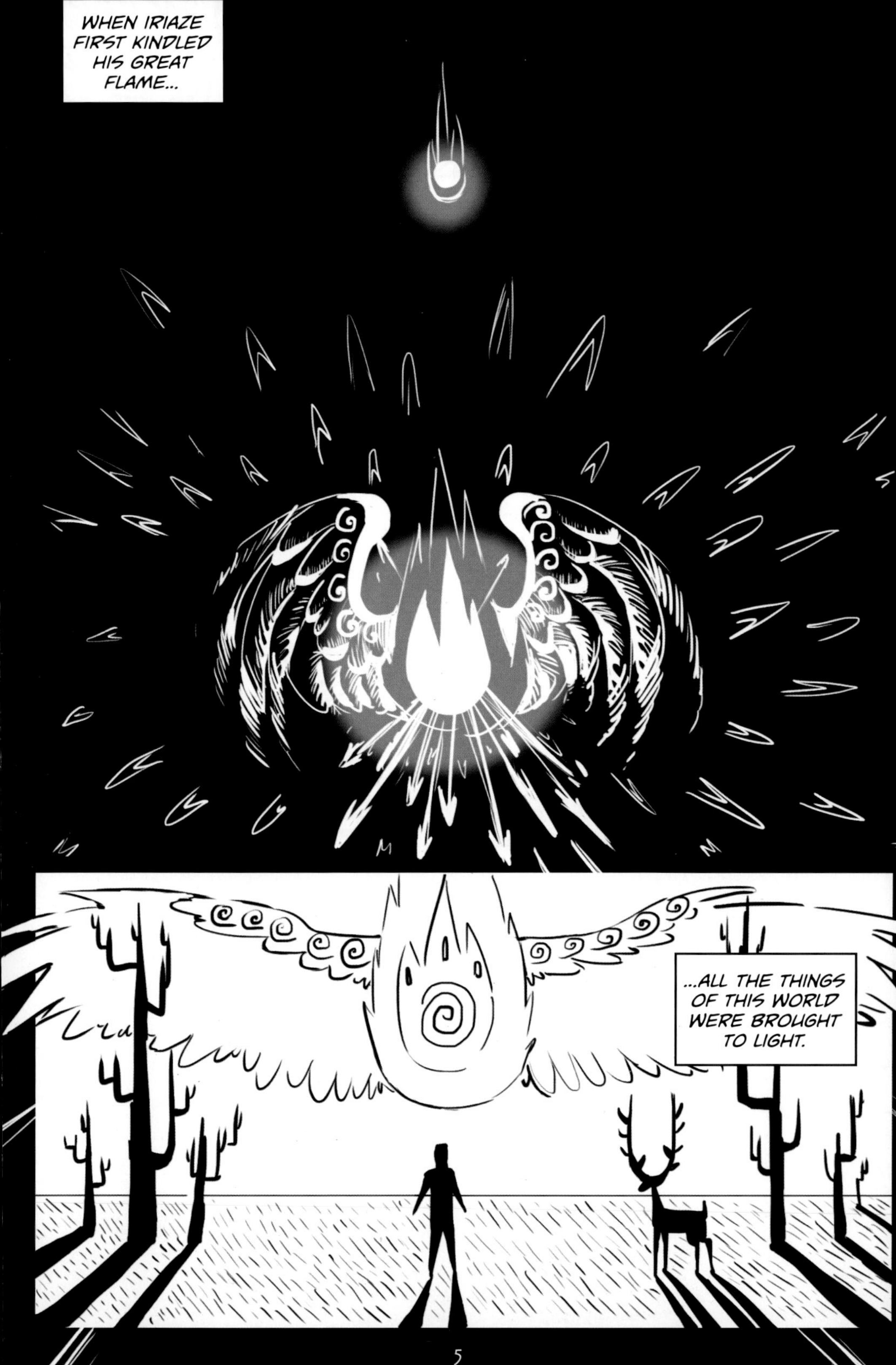
WHEN IRIAZE FIRST KINDLED HIS GREAT FLAME...
...ALL THE THINGS OF THIS WORLD WERE BROUGHT TO LIGHT.

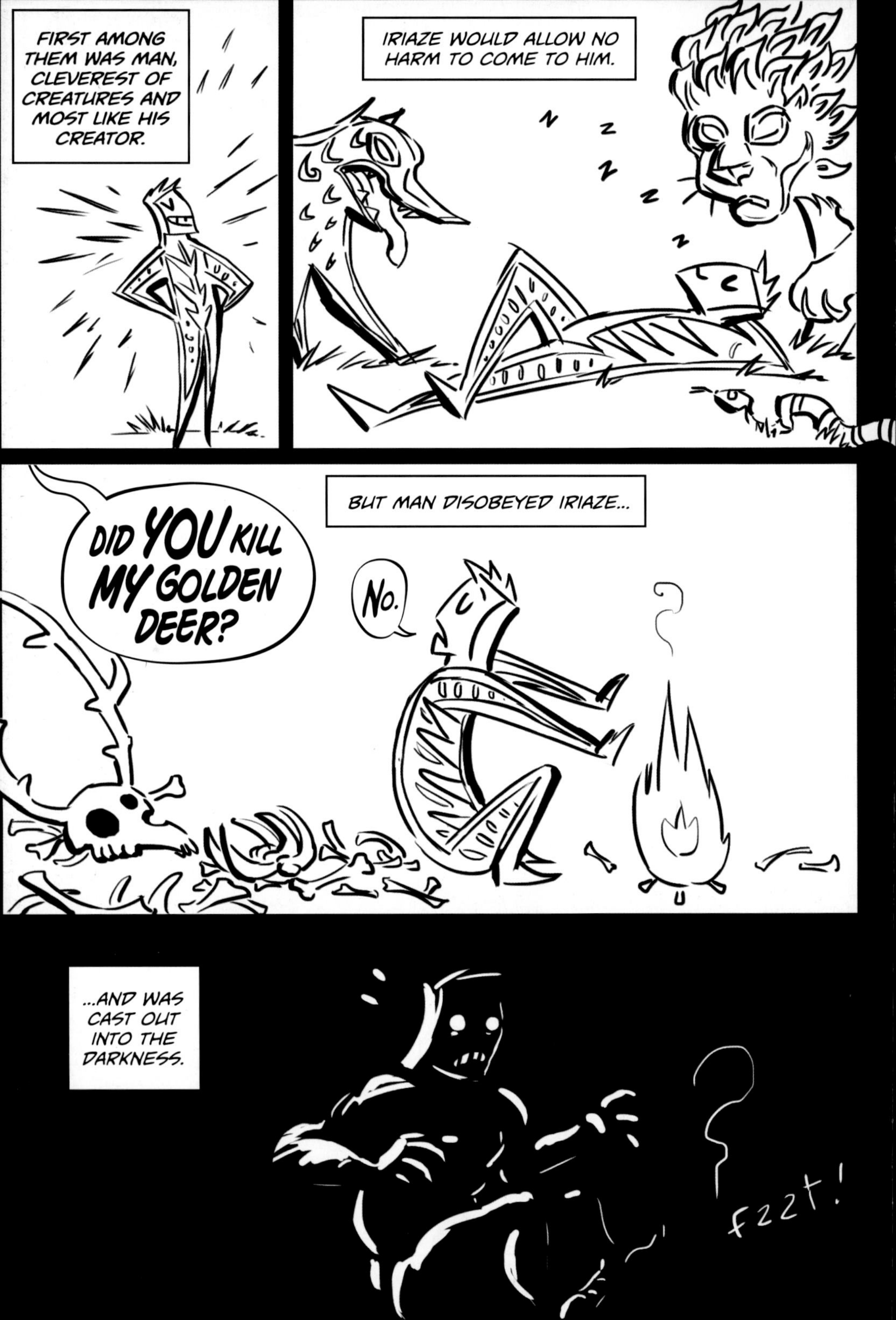
FIRST AMONG THEM WAS MAN, CLEVEREST OF CREATURES AND MOST LIKE HIS CREATOR.
IRIAZE WOULD ALLOW NO HARM TO COME TO HIM.
Z Z Z Z Z
BUT MAN DISOBEYED IRIAZE...
DID YOU KILL MY GOLDEN DEER?
No.
...AND WAS CAST OUT INTO THE DARKNESS.
?
FZZT!

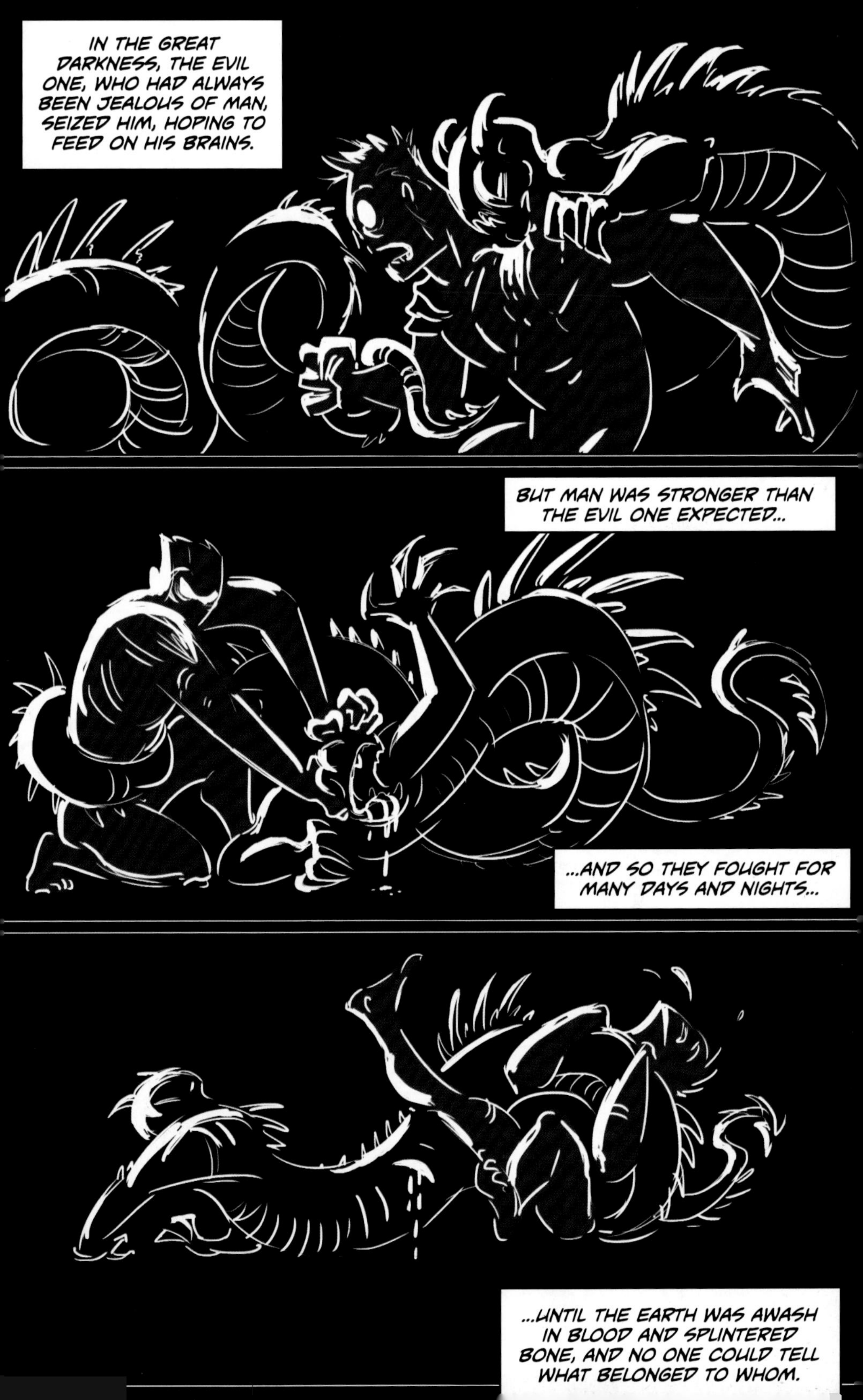
IN THE GREAT DARKNESS, THE EVIL ONE, WHO HAD ALWAYS BEEN JEALOUS OF MAN, SEIZED HIM, HOPING TO FEED ON HIS BRAINS.
BUT MAN WAS STRONGER THAN THE EVIL ONE EXPECTED...
...AND SO THEY FOUGHT FOR MANY DAYS AND NIGHTS...
...UNTIL THE EARTH WAS AWASH IN BLOOD AND SPLINTERED BONE, AND NO ONE COULD TELL WHAT BELONGED TO WHOM.

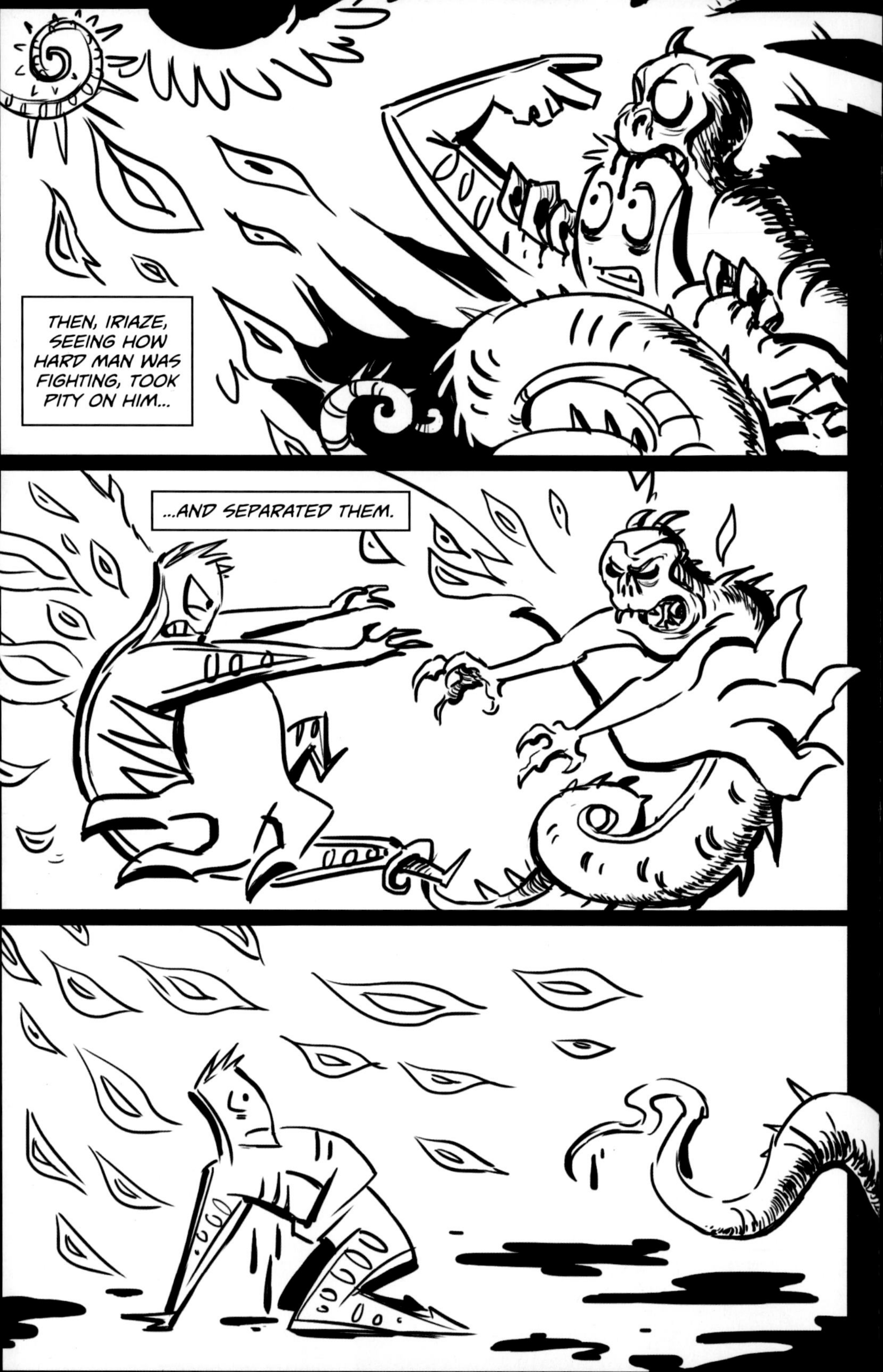
THEN, IRIAZE, SEEING HOW HARD MAN WAS FIGHTING, TOOK PITY ON HIM...
...AND SEPARATED THEM.

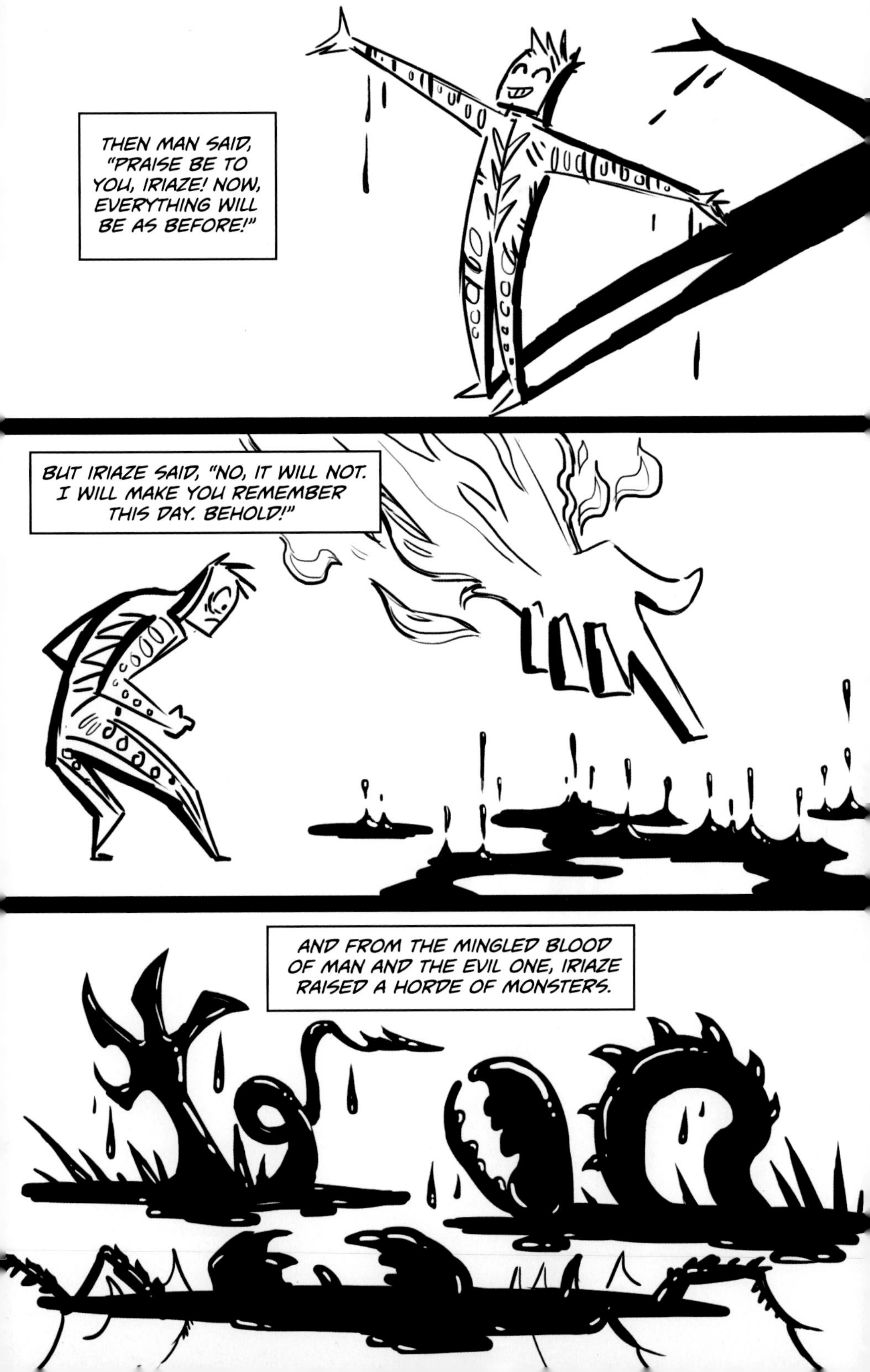
THEN MAN SAID, "PRAISE BE TO YOU, IRIAZE! NOW, EVERYTHING WILL BE AS BEFORE!"
BUT IRIAZE SAID, "NO, IT WILL NOT. I WILL MAKE YOU REMEMBER THIS DAY. BEHOLD!"
AND FROM THE MINGLED BLOOD OF MAN AND THE EVIL ONE, IRIAZE RAISED A HORDE OF MONSTERS.

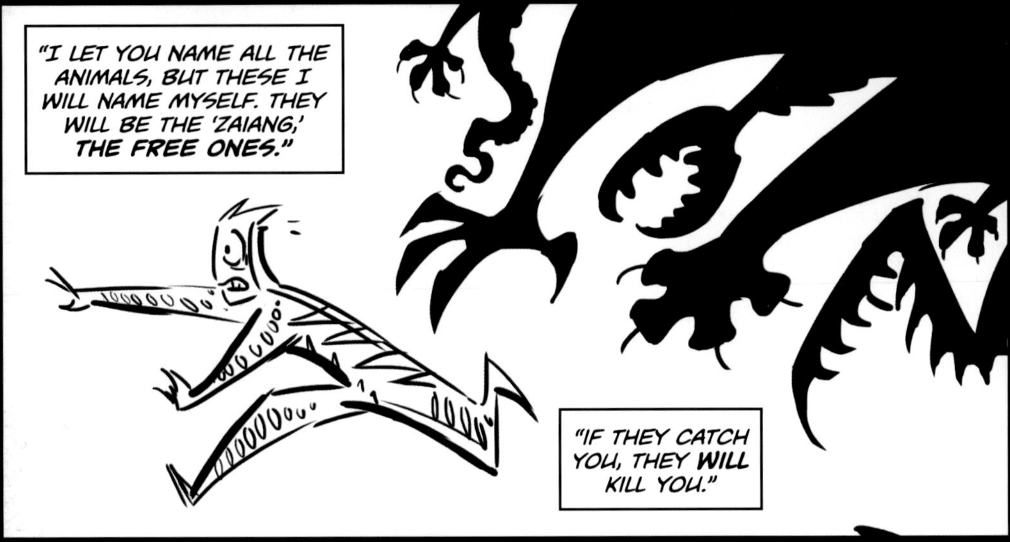
"I LET YOU NAME ALL THE ANIMALS, BUT THESE I WILL NAME MYSELF. THEY WILL BE THE 'ZAIANG,' THE FREE ONES."
"IF THEY CATCH YOU, THEY WILL KILL YOU."

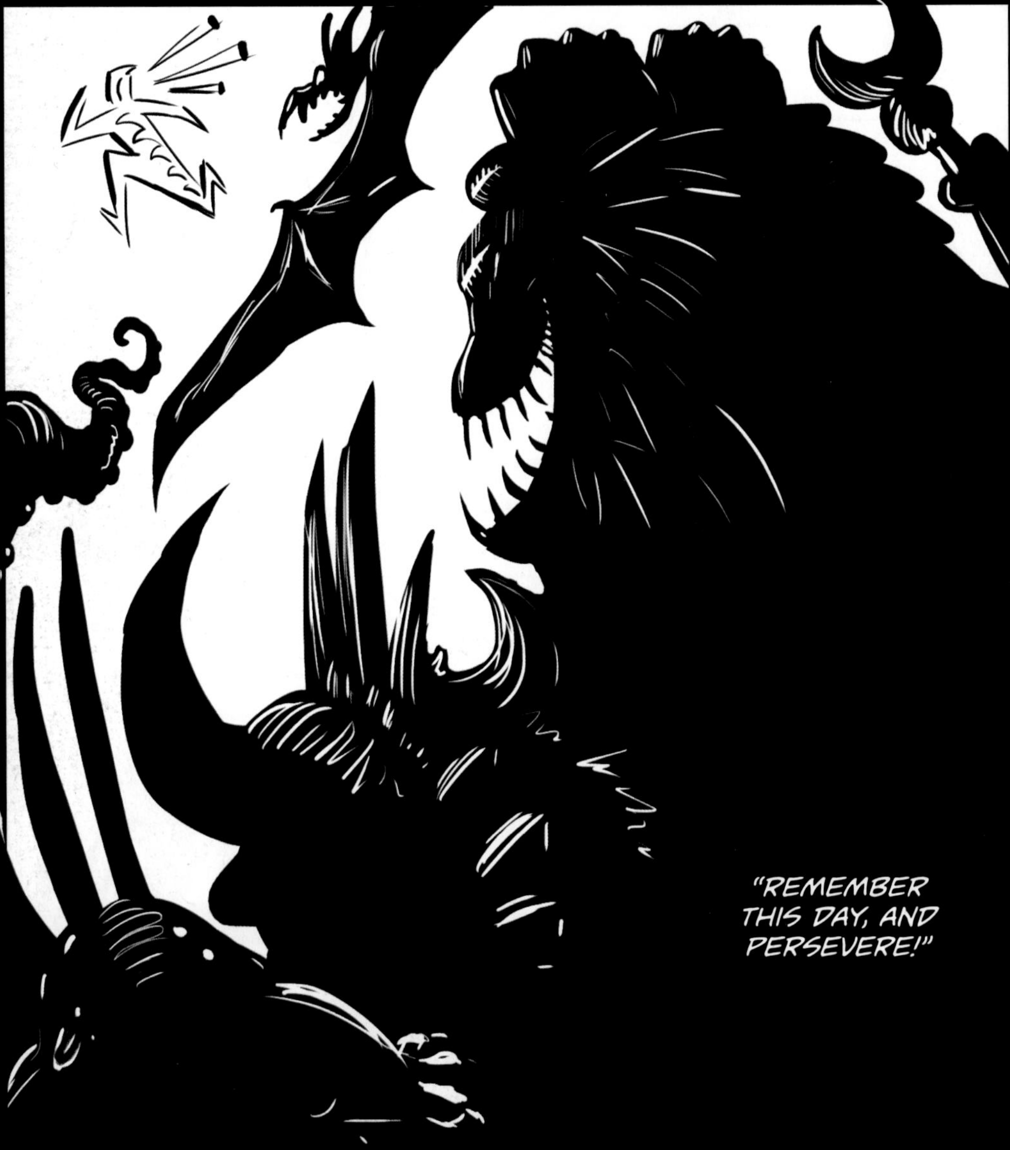
"REMEMBER THIS DAY, AND PERSEVERE!"

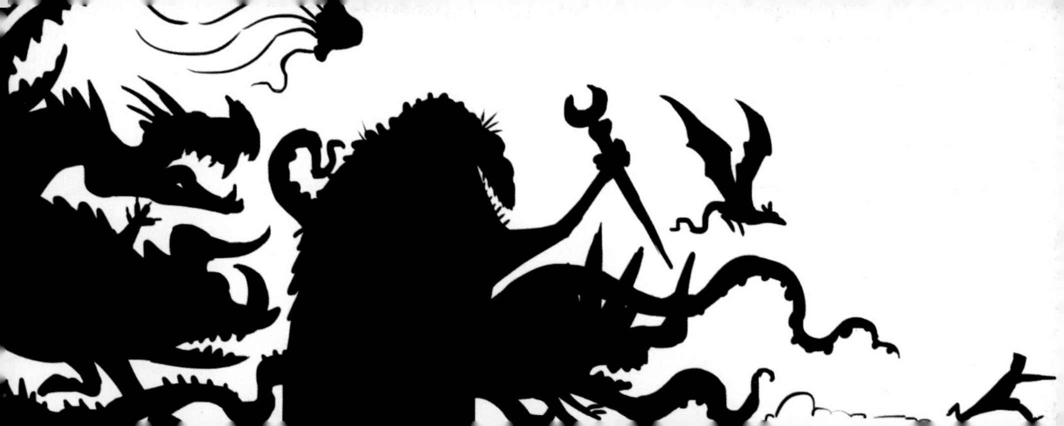

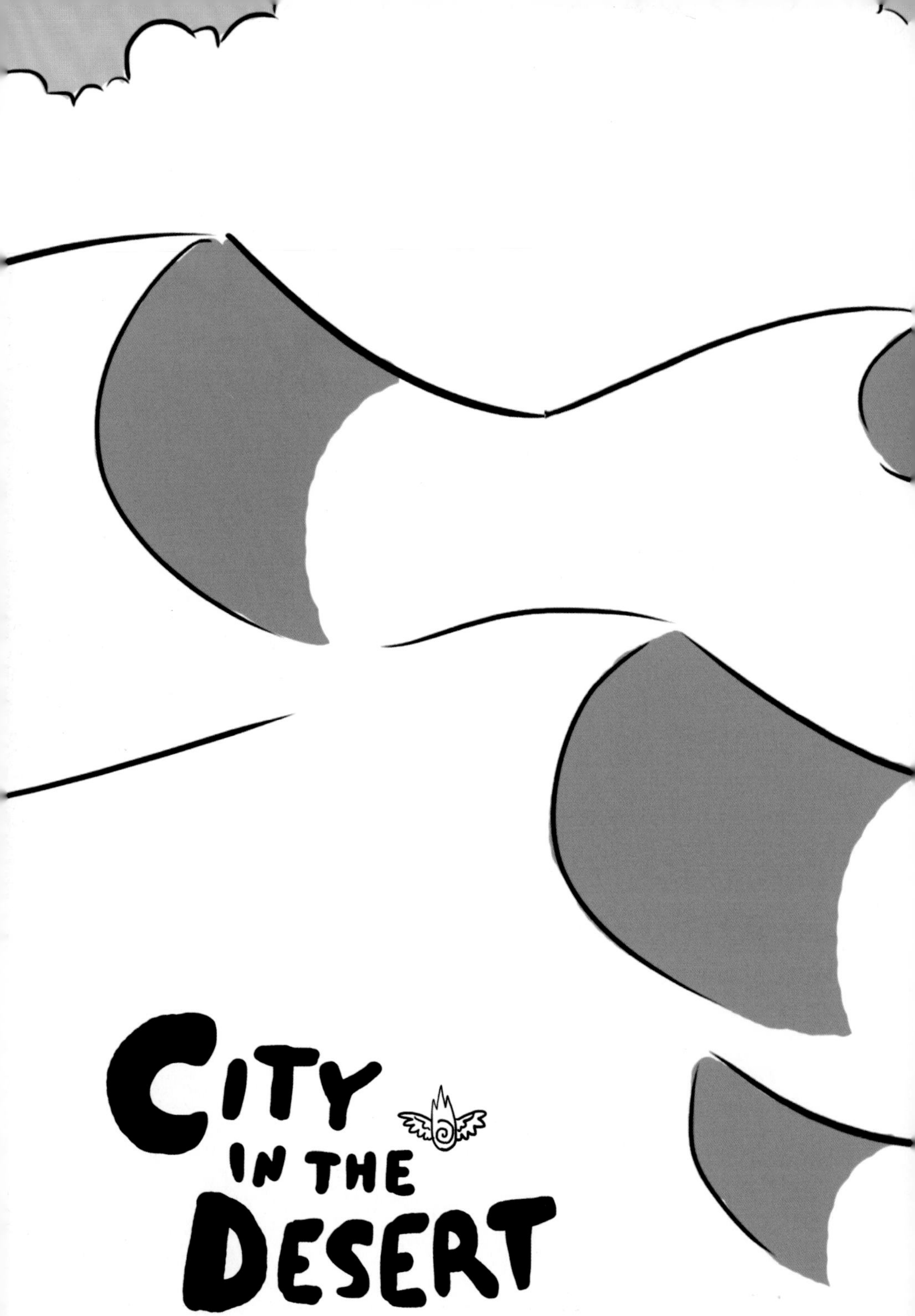

CITY IN THE DESERT

THE MONSTER PROBLEM

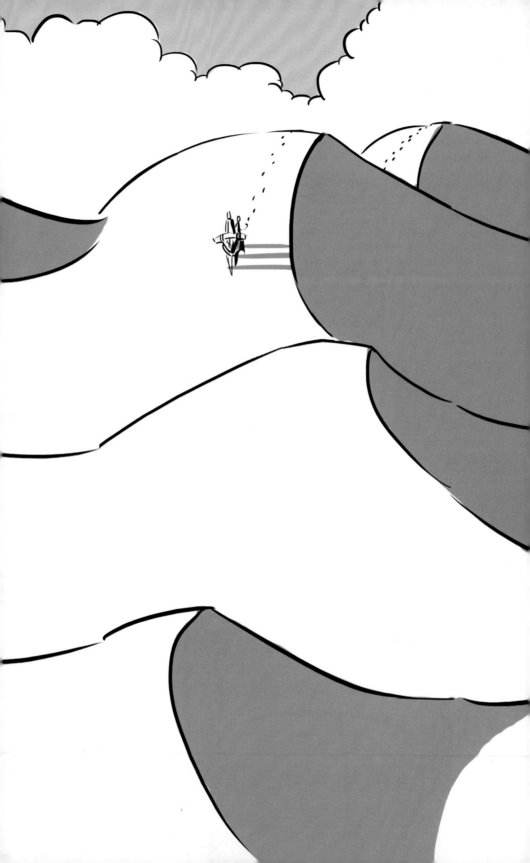

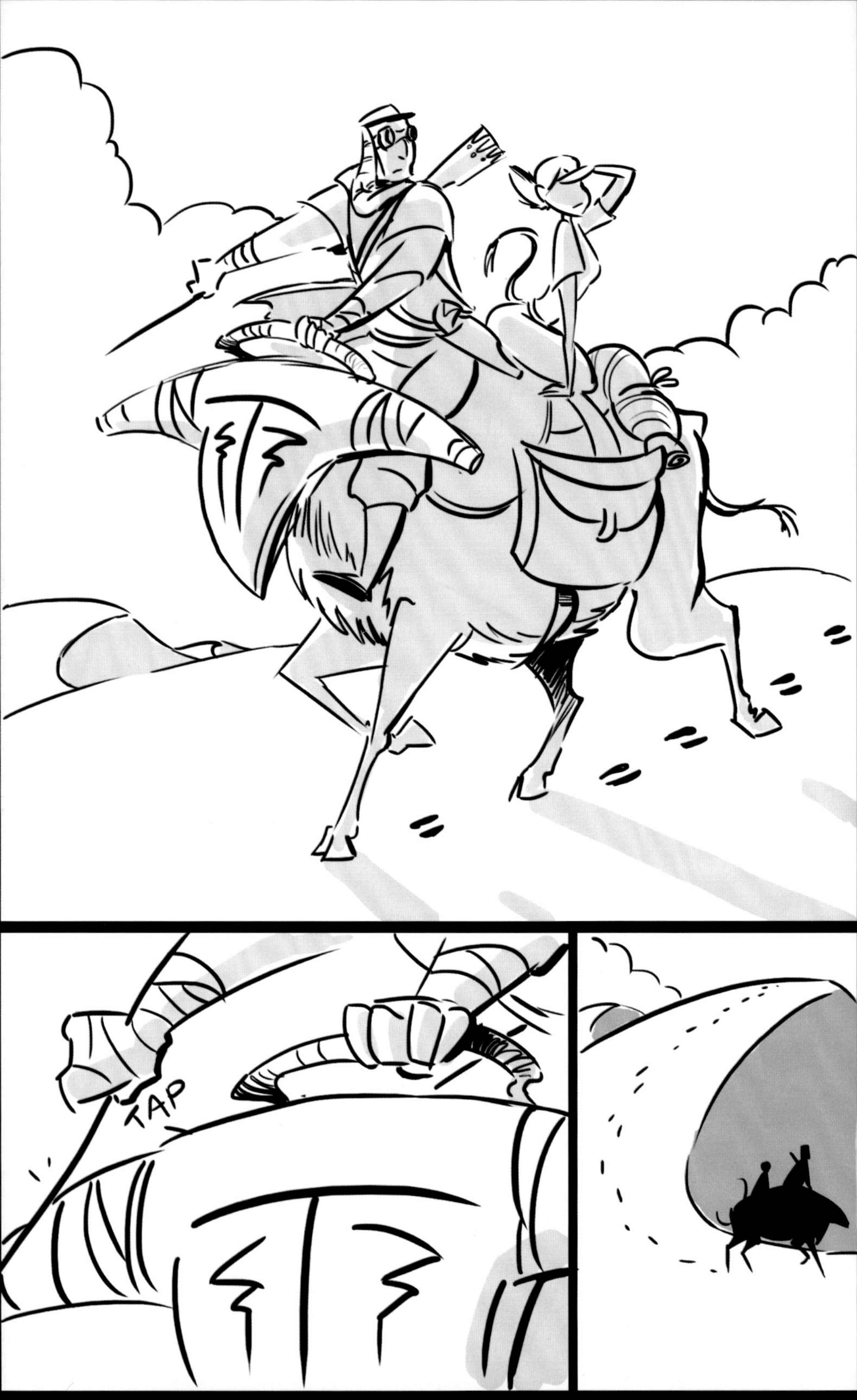
TAP

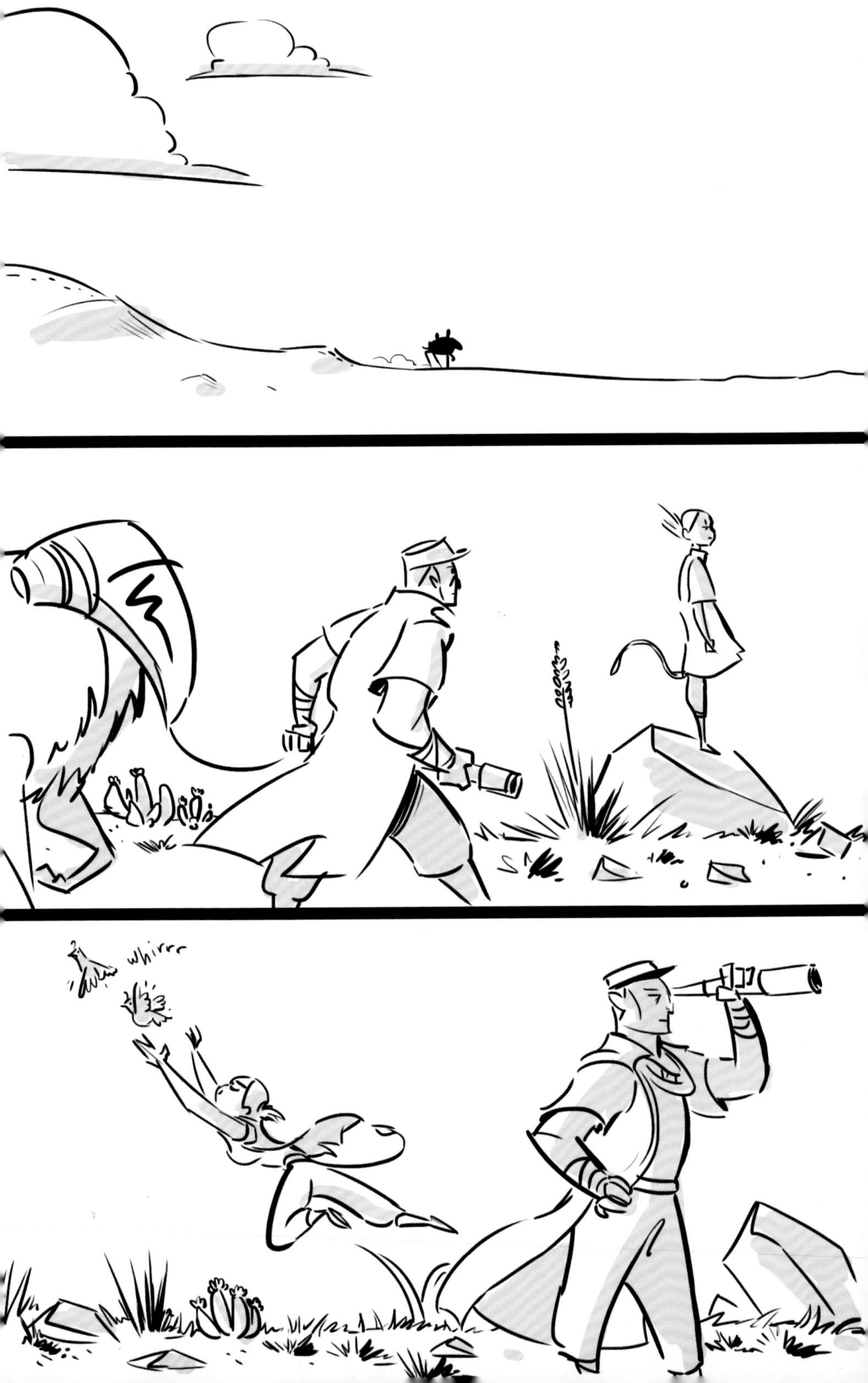
whirrr

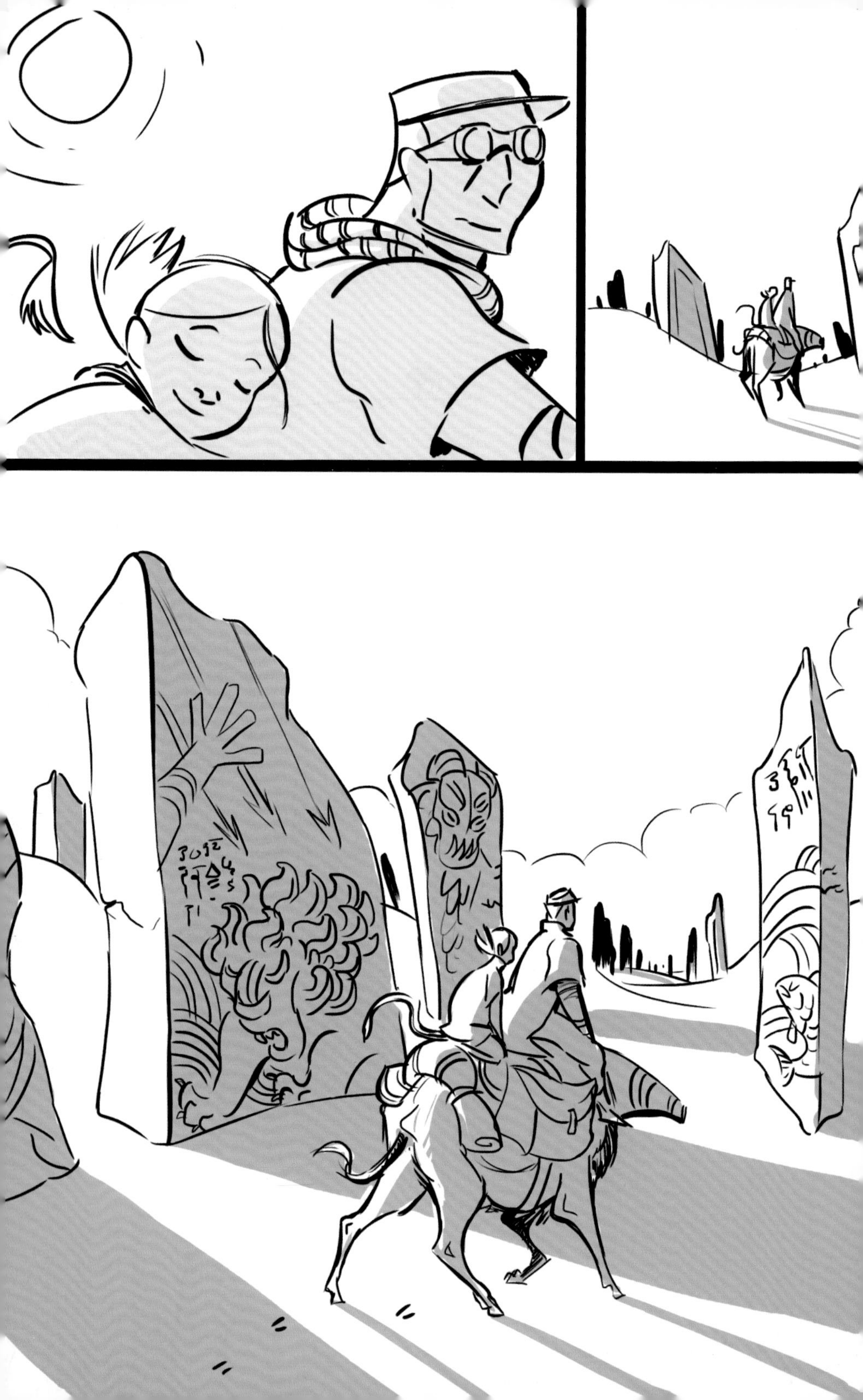

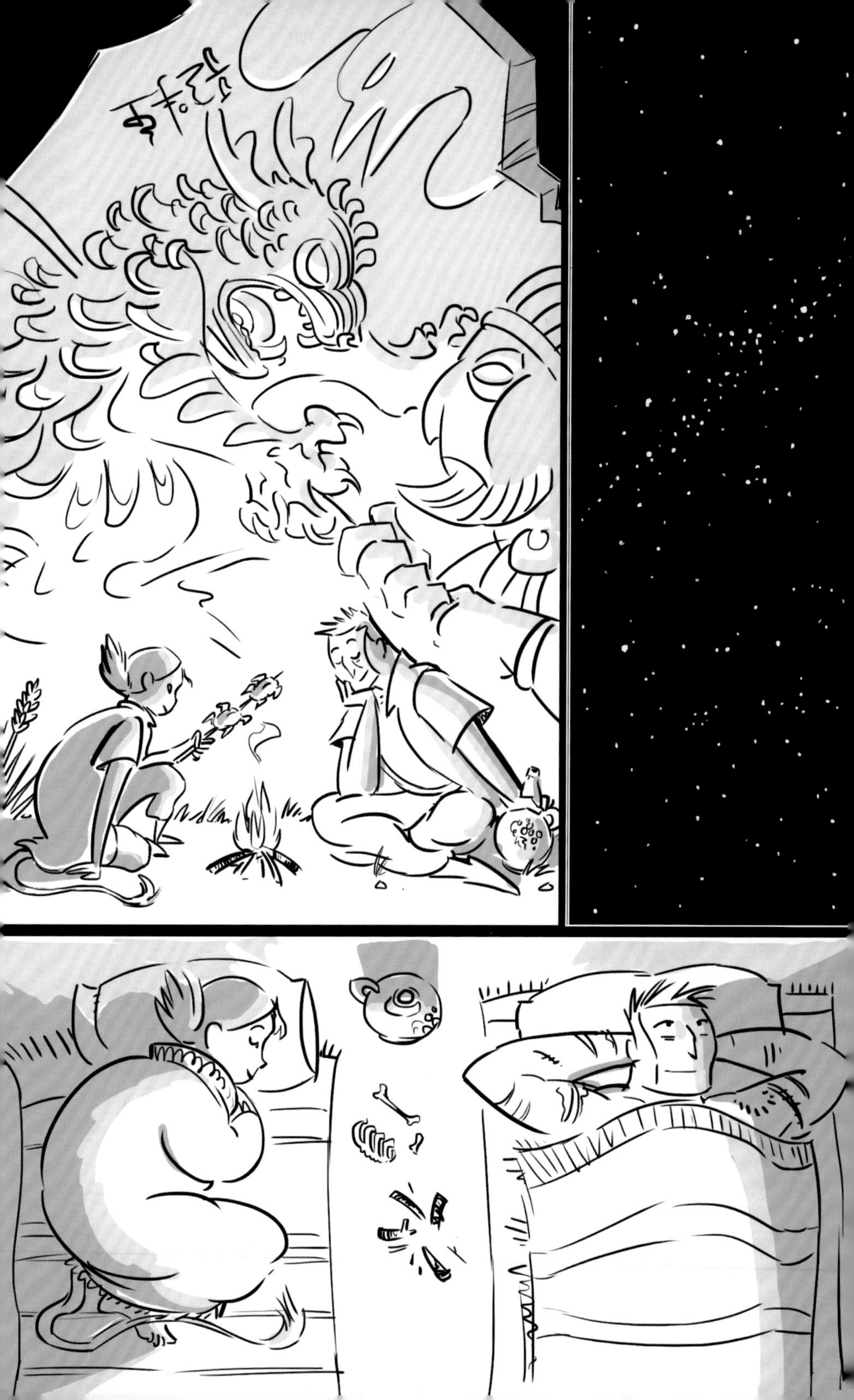

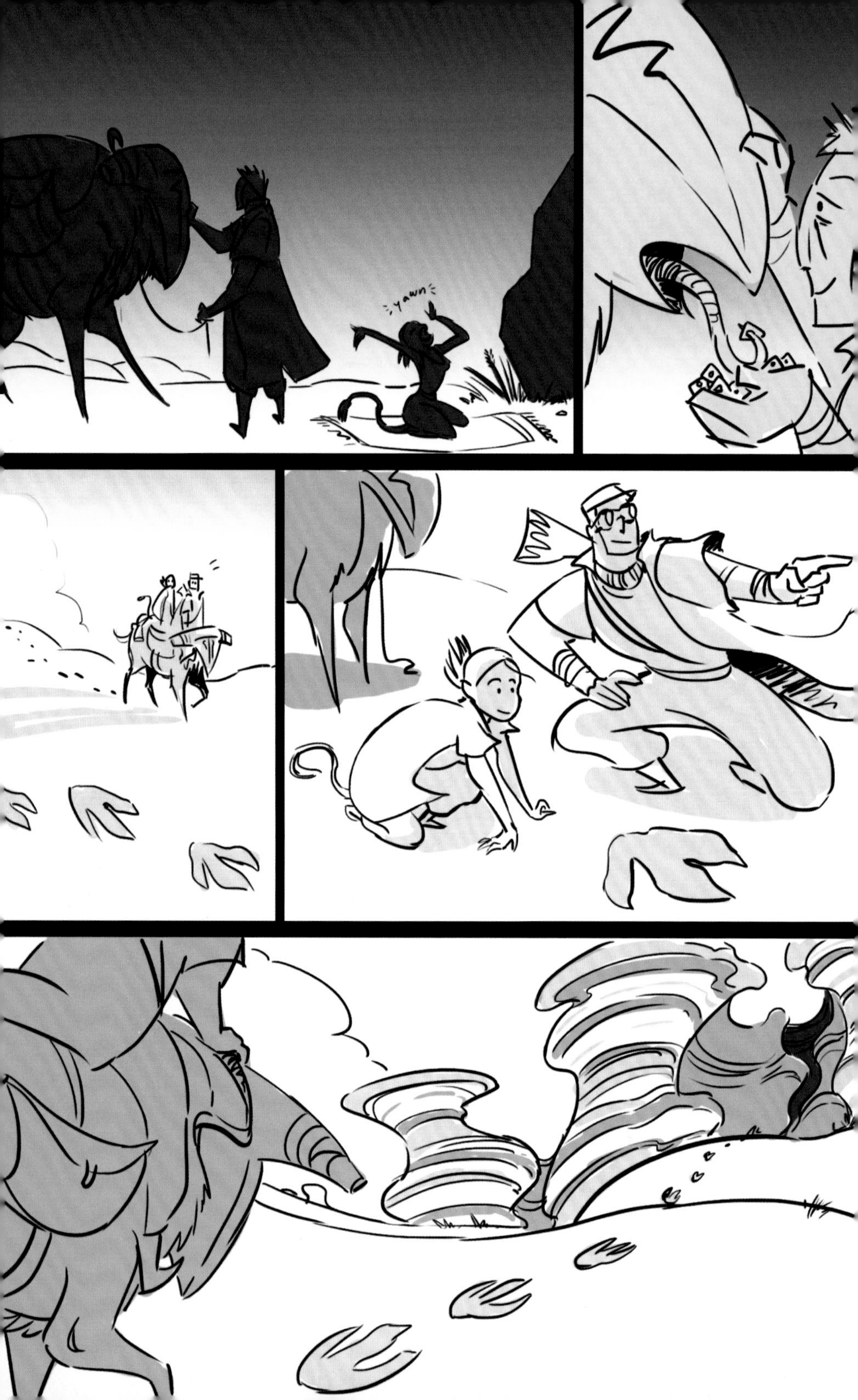
yawn

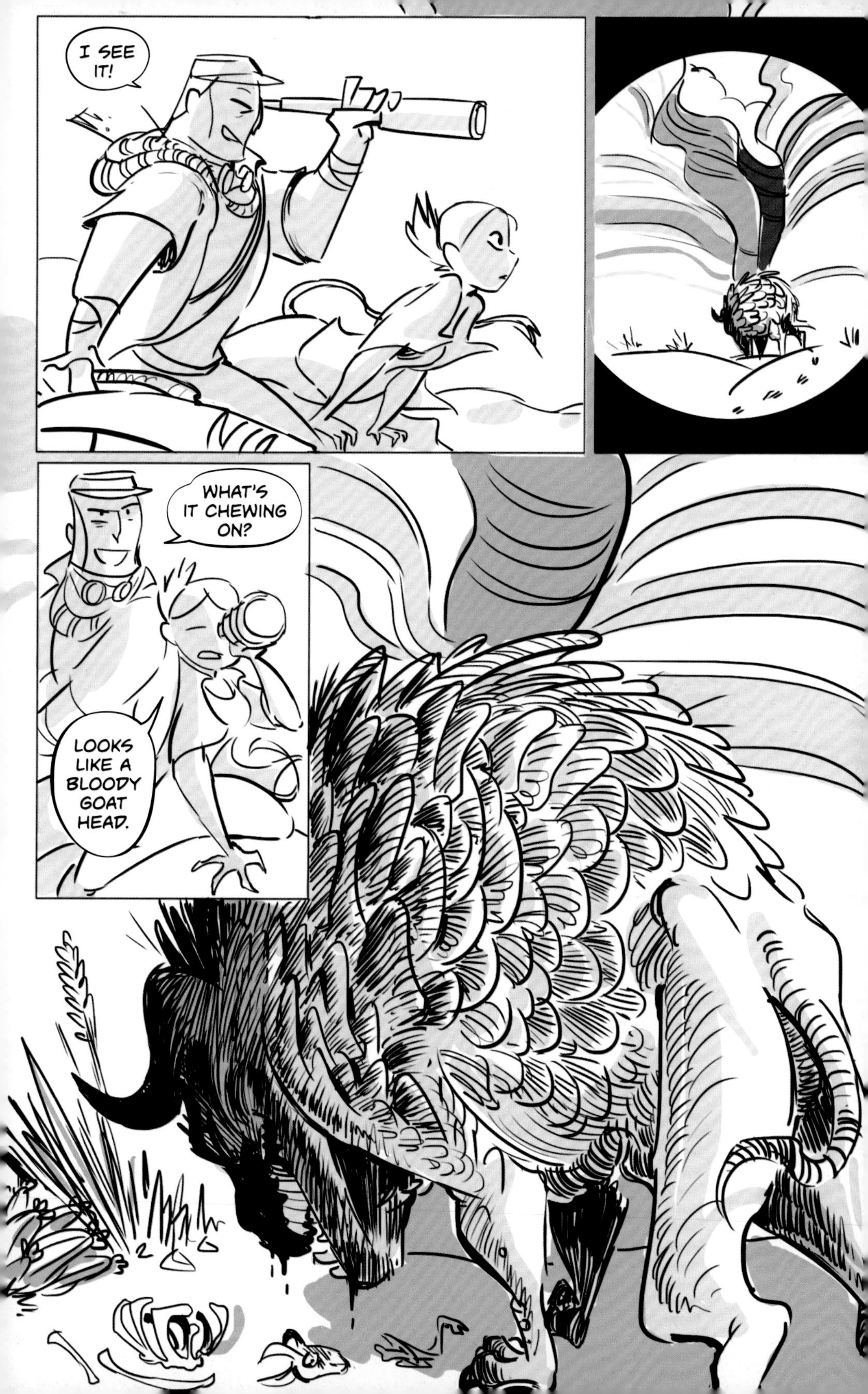
I SEE IT!
WHAT'S IT CHEWING ON?
LOOKS LIKE A BLOODY GOAT HEAD.

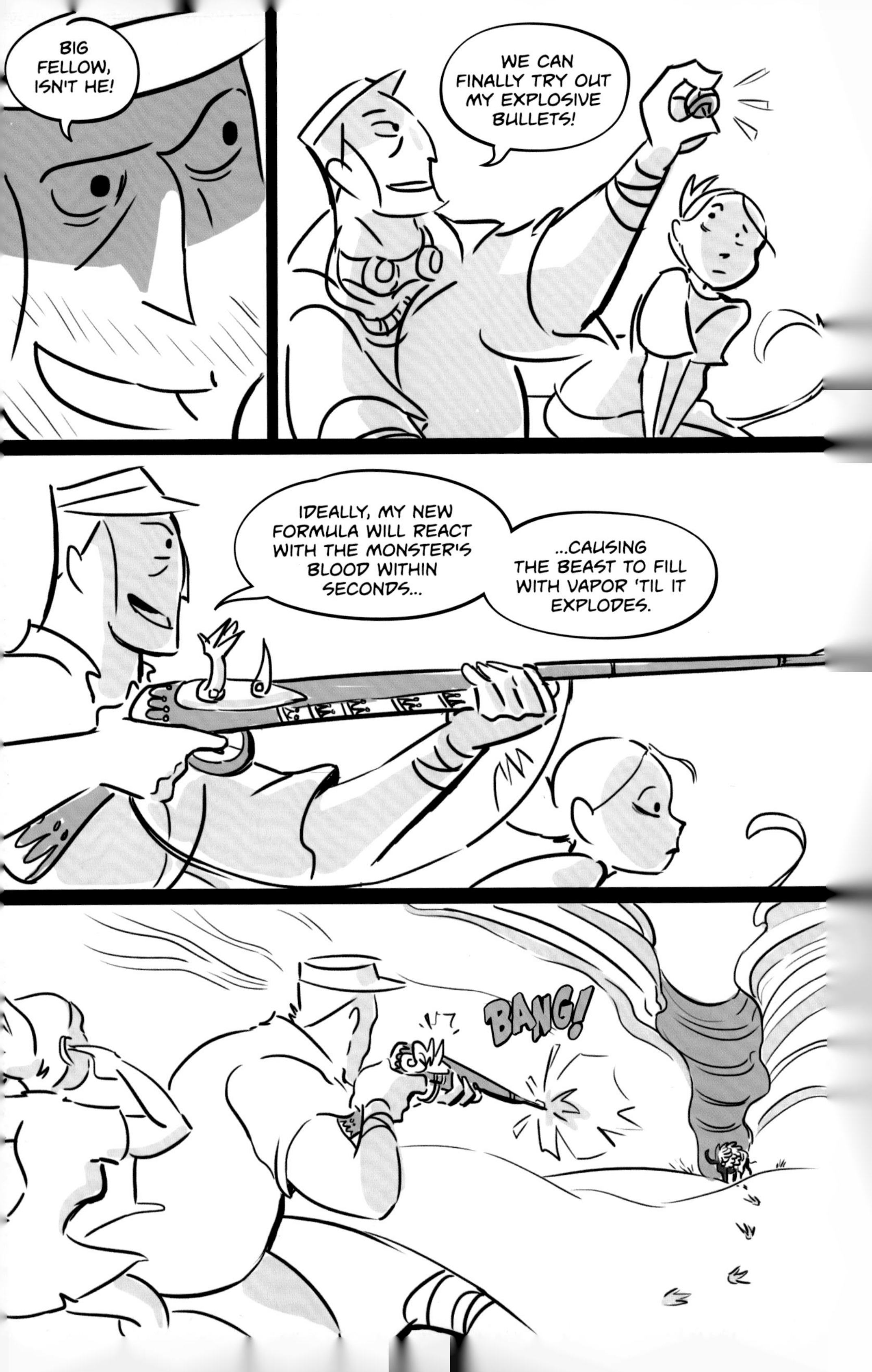
BIG FELLOW, ISN'T HE!
WE CAN FINALLY TRY OUT MY EXPLOSIVE BULLETS!
IDEALLY, MY NEW FORMULA WILL REACT WITH THE MONSTER'S BLOOD WITHIN SECONDS...
...CAUSING THE BEAST TO FILL WITH VAPOR 'TIL IT EXPLODES.
BANG!

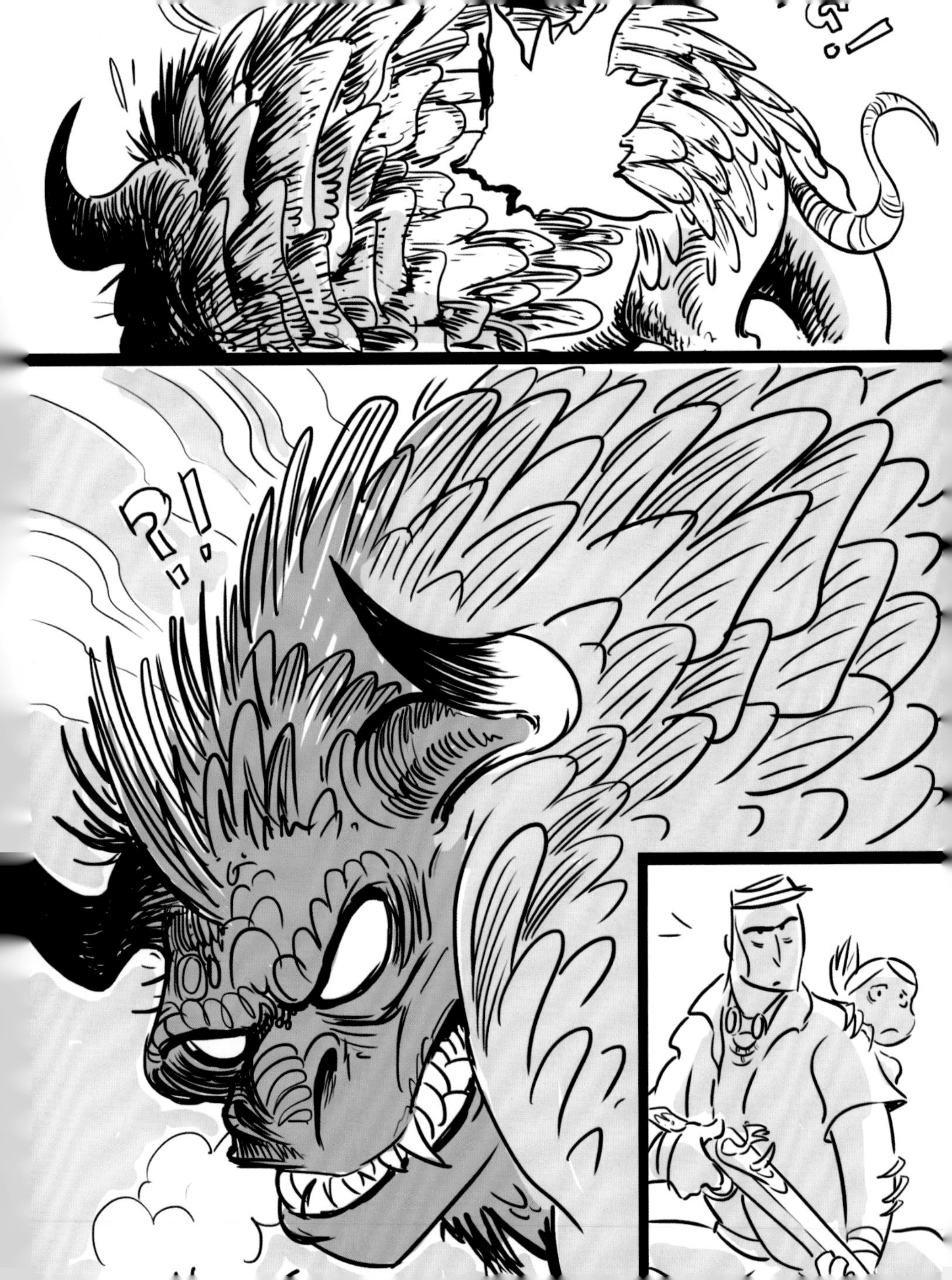
?!
?!!

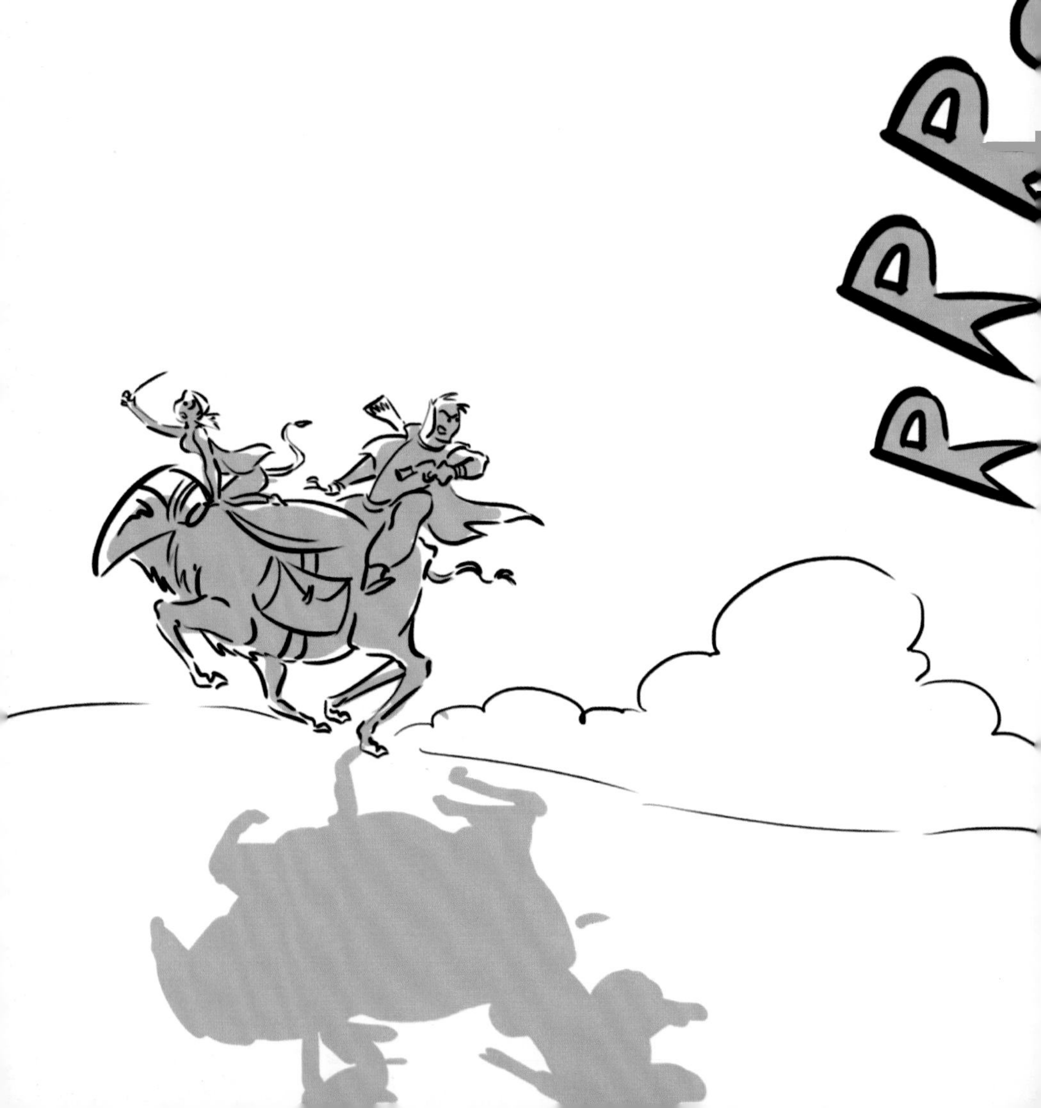

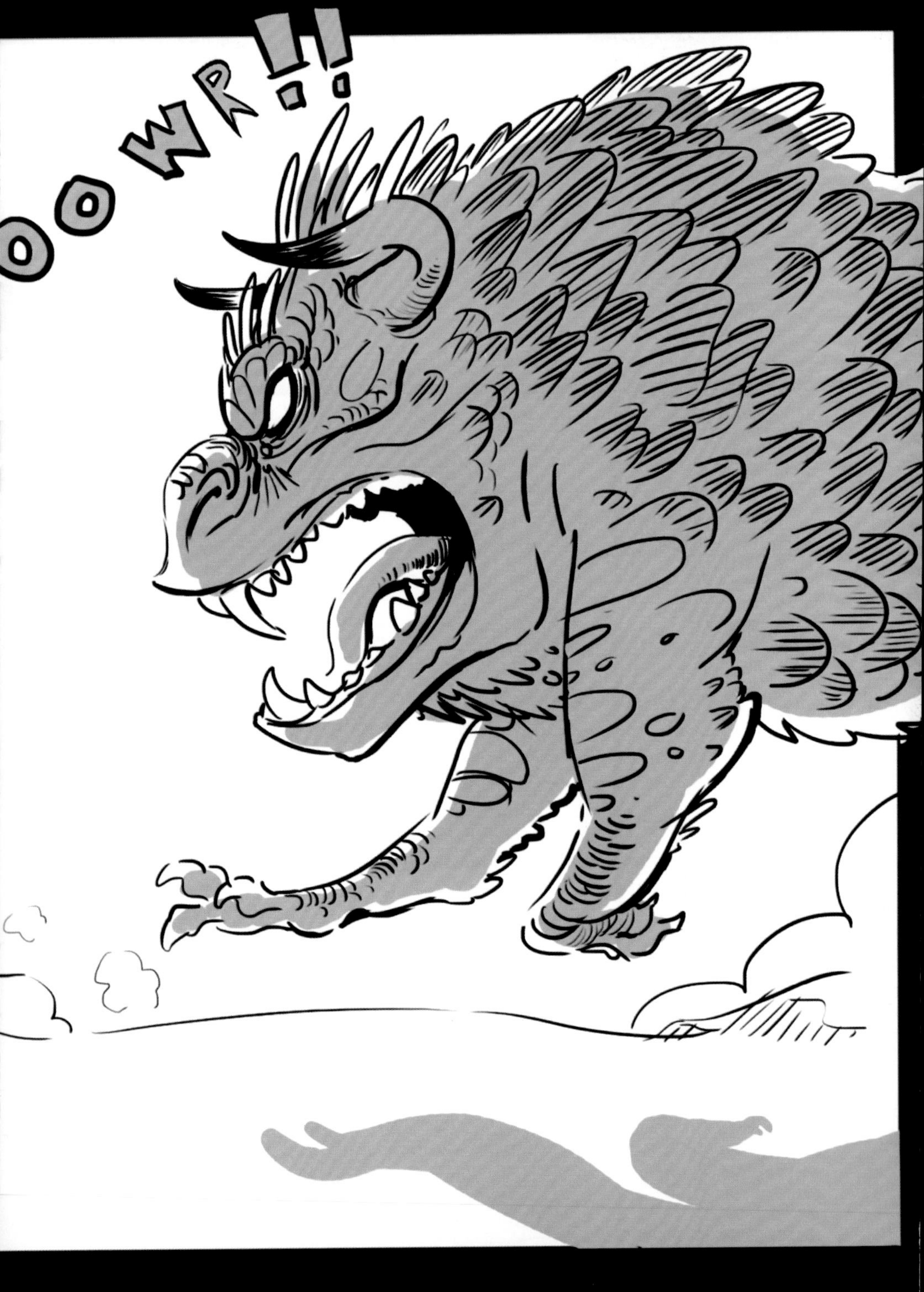
OOWR!!

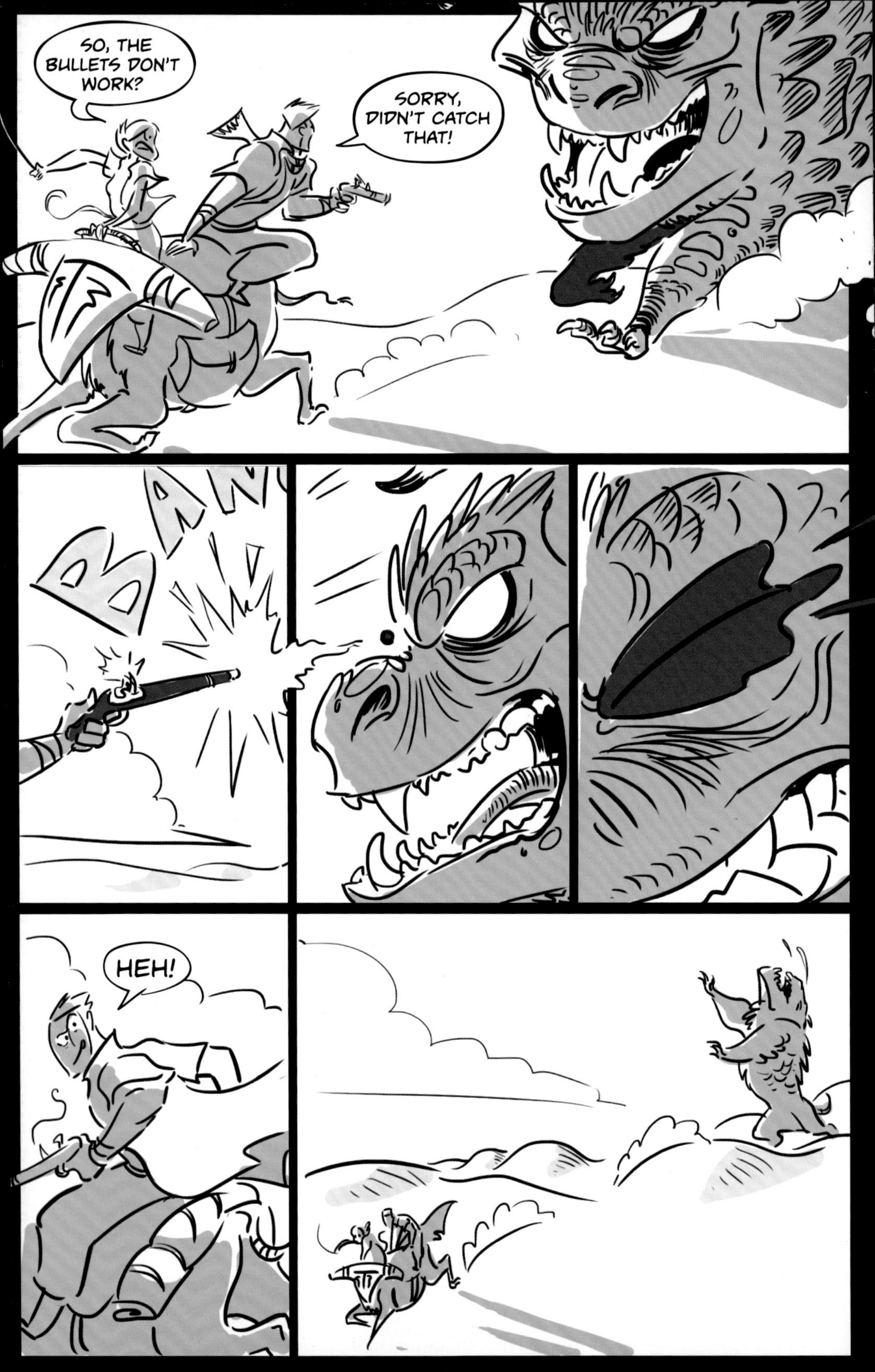
SO, THE BULLETS DON'T WORK?
SORRY, DIDN'T CATCH THAT!
BAM
HEH!

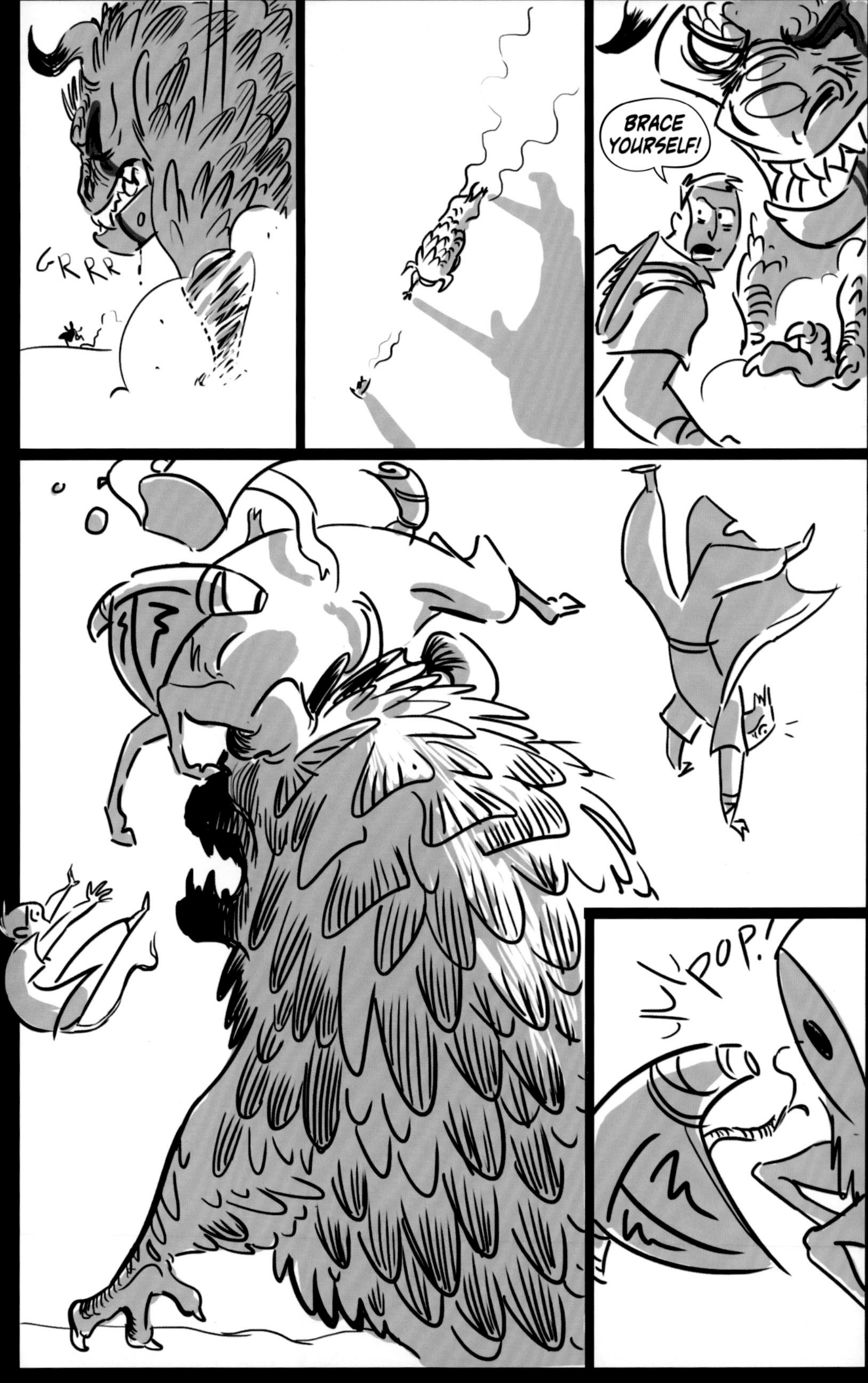
GRRR!
BRACE YOURSELF!
POP!

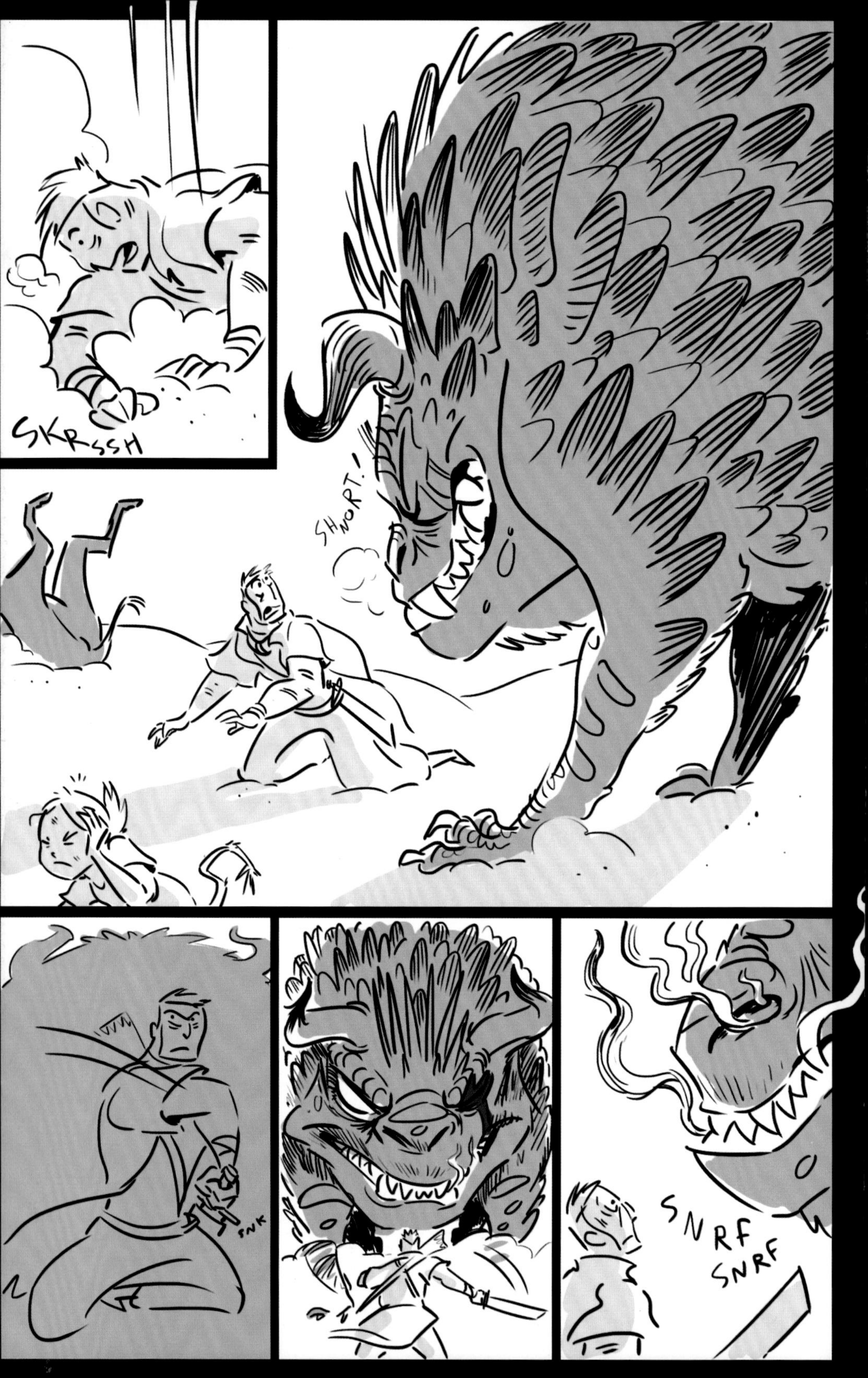
SKRSSH
SHNORT!
SNK
SNRF
SNRF

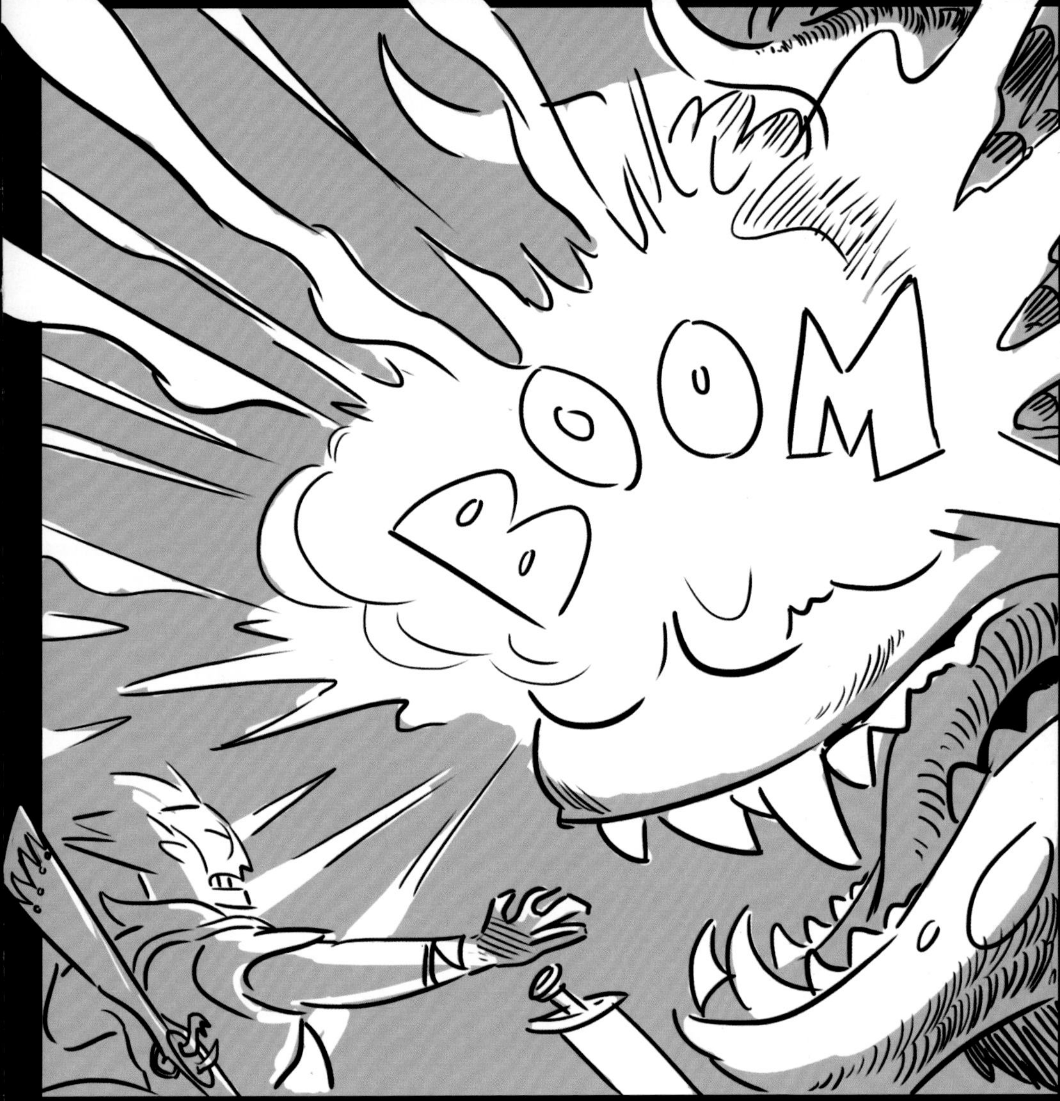
BOOM
!!!

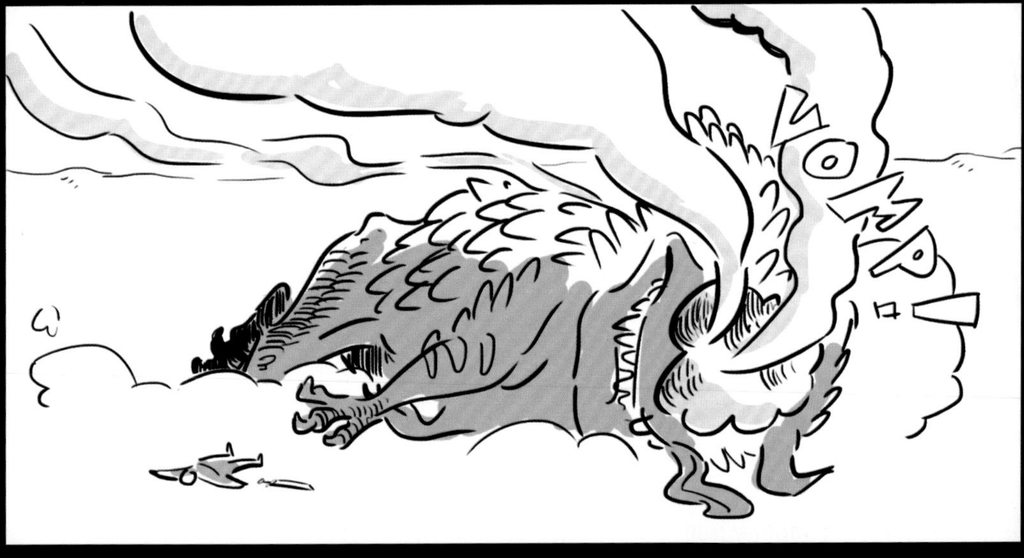
WOMP!!

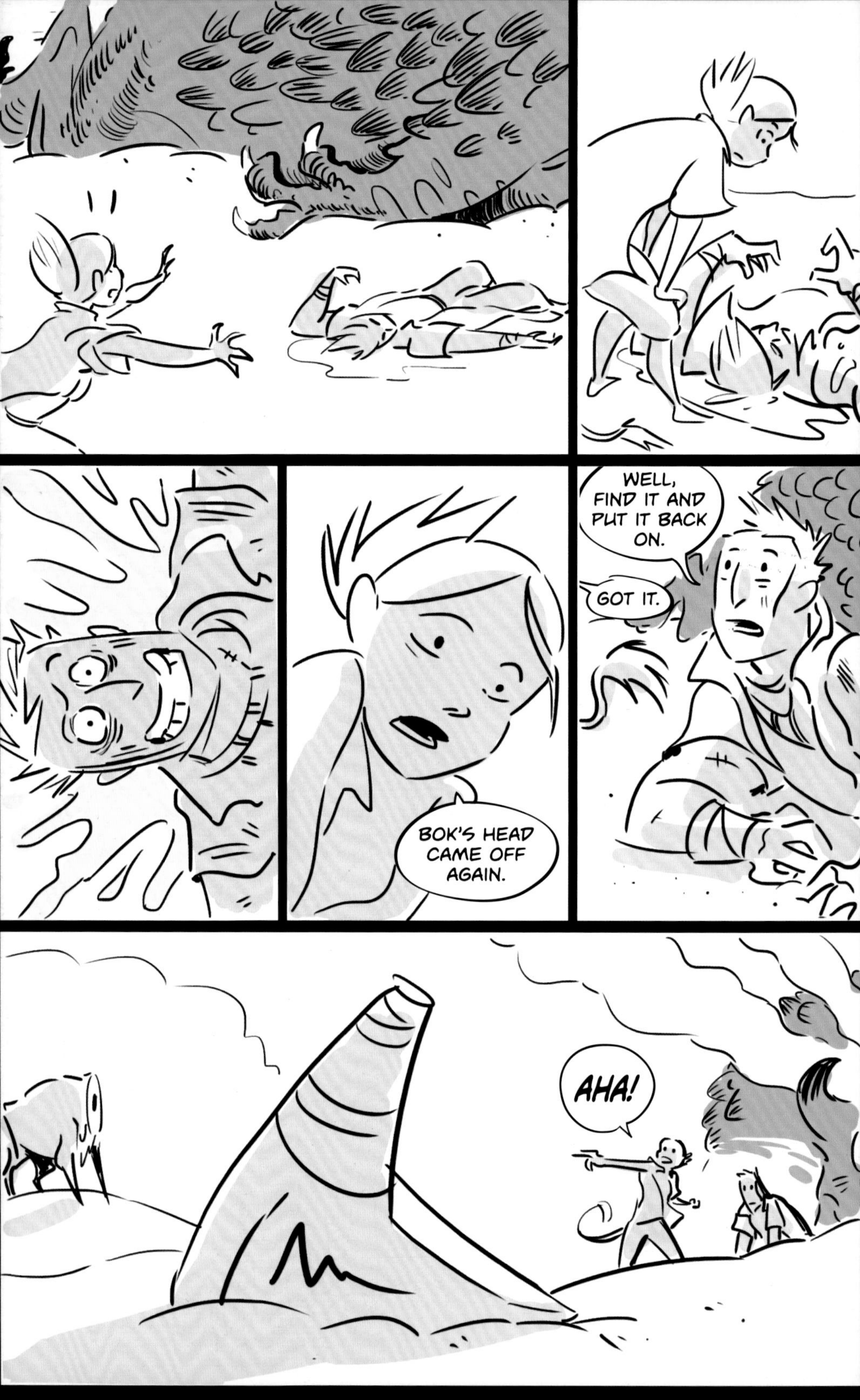
BOK'S HEAD CAME OFF AGAIN.
WELL, FIND IT AND PUT IT BACK ON.
GOT IT.
AHA!

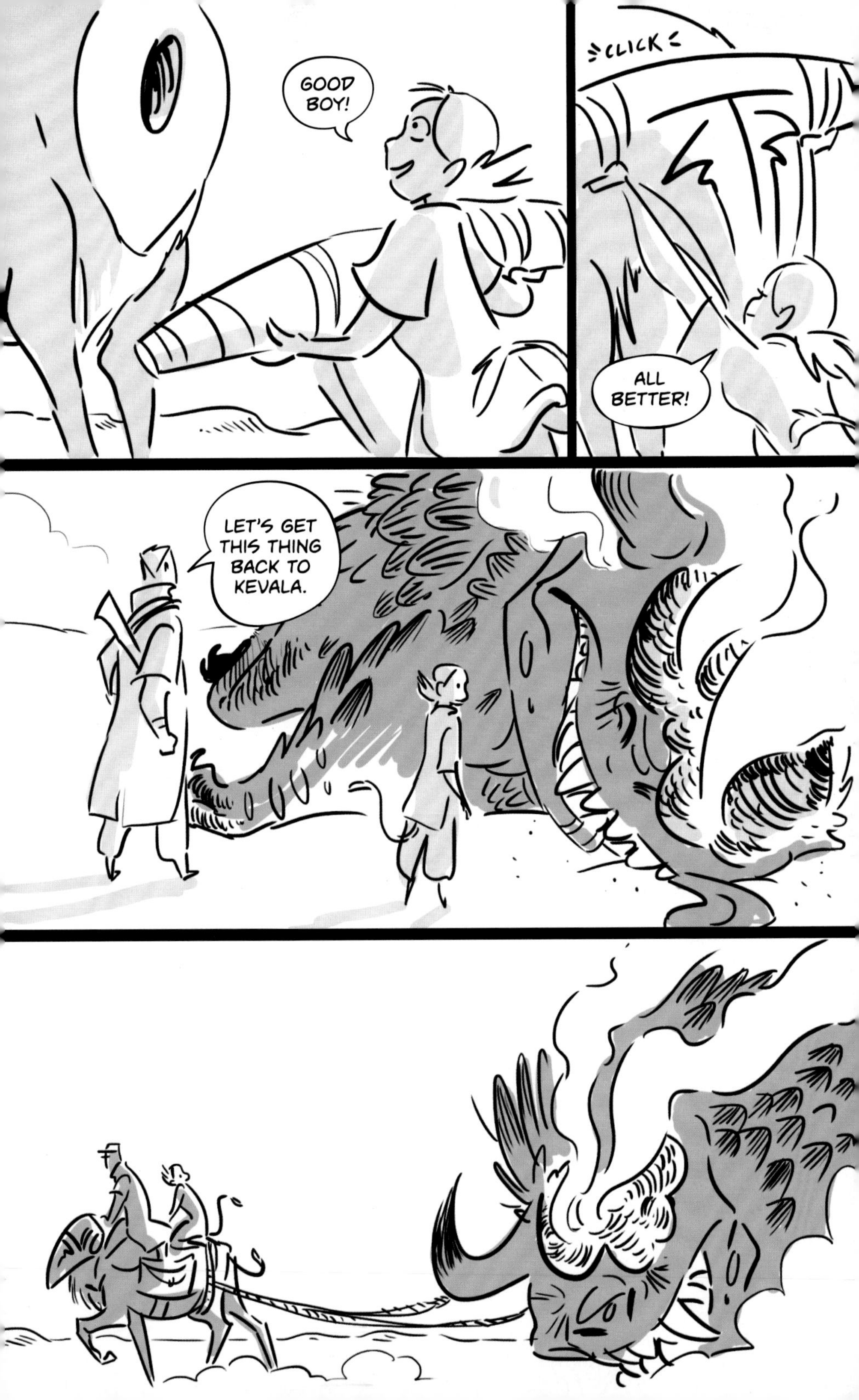
GOOD BOY!
CLICK
ALL BETTER!
LET'S GET THIS THING BACK TO KEVALA.

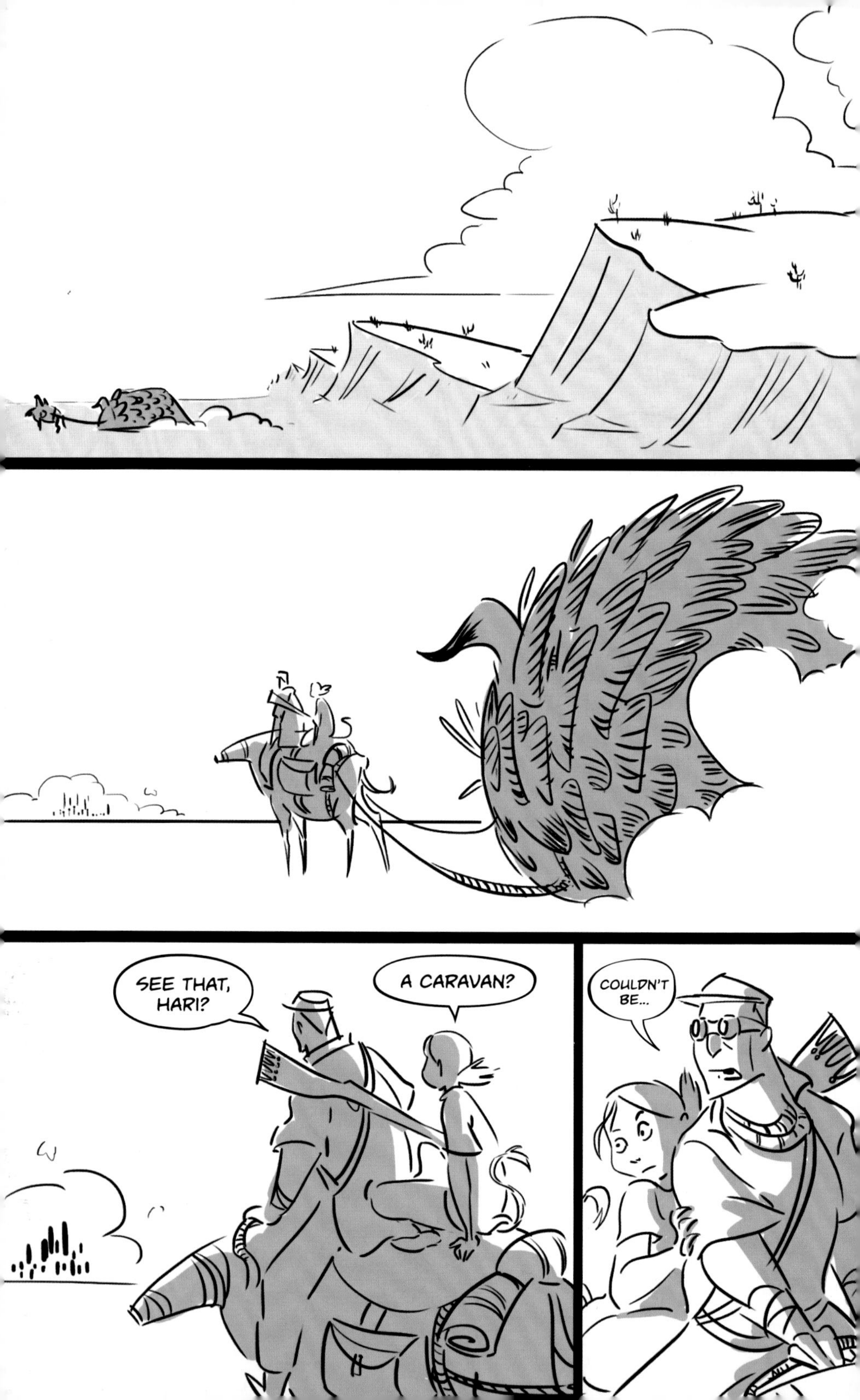
SEE THAT, HARI?
A CARAVAN?
COULDN'T BE...

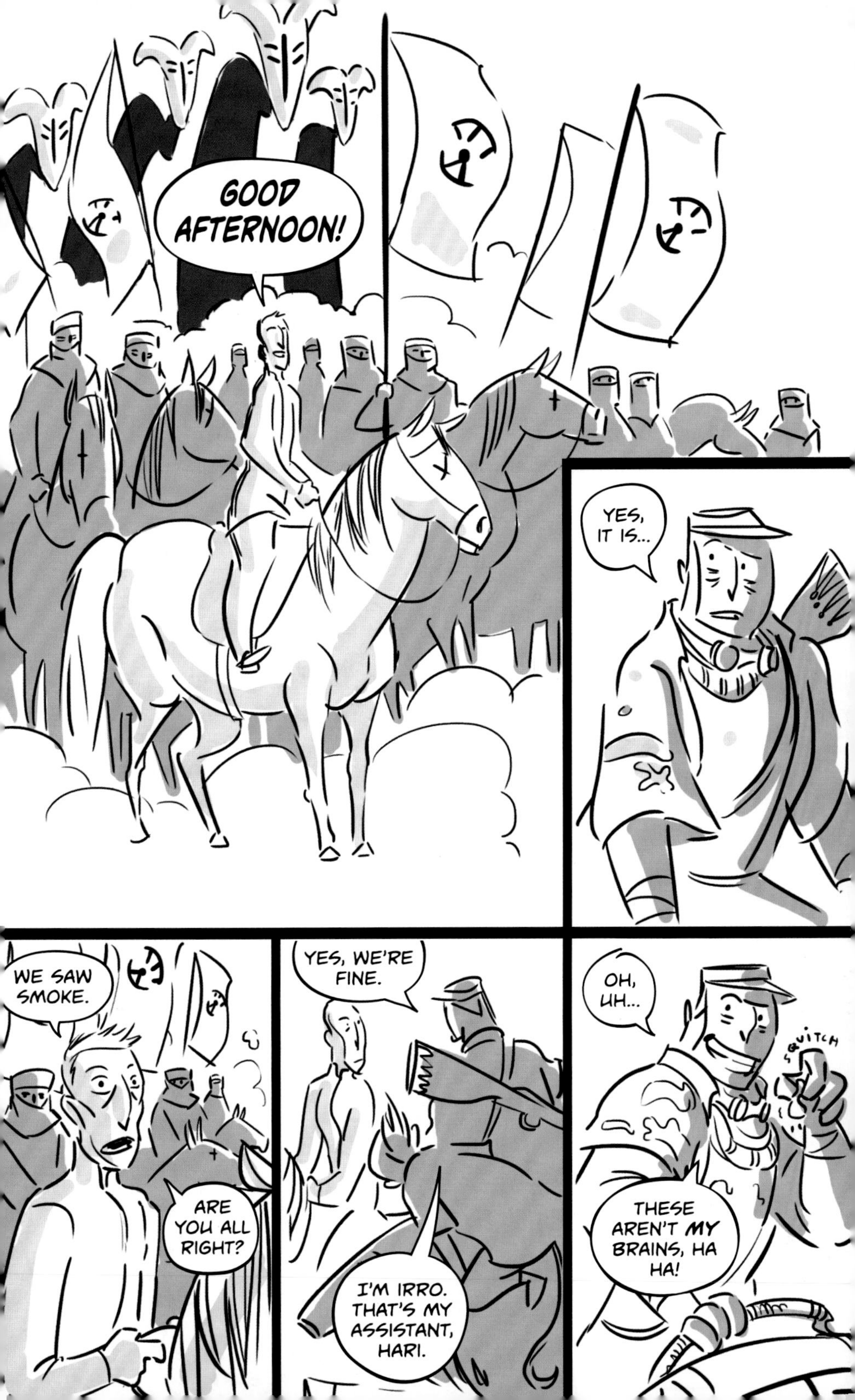
GOOD AFTERNOON!
YES, IT IS...
WE SAW SMOKE.
ARE YOU ALL RIGHT?
YES, WE'RE FINE.
I'M IRRO. THAT'S MY ASSISTANT, HARI.
OH, UH...
SQUITCH
THESE AREN'T MY BRAINS, HA HA!

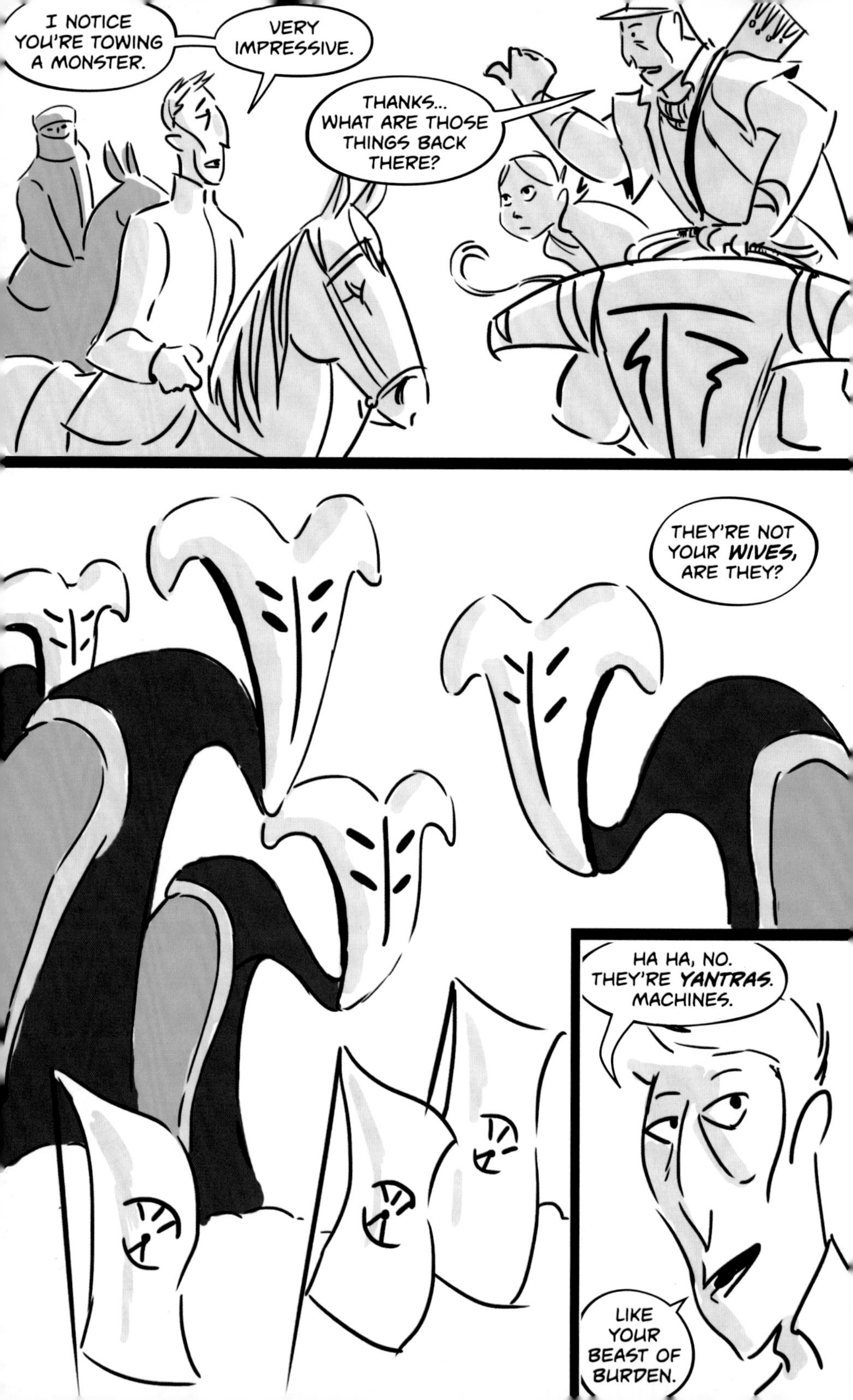
I NOTICE YOU'RE TOWING A MONSTER.
VERY IMPRESSIVE.
THANKS... WHAT ARE THOSE THINGS BACK THERE?
THEY'RE NOT YOUR ***WIVES,*** ARE THEY?
HA HA, NO. THEY'RE ***YANTRAS.*** MACHINES.
LIKE YOUR BEAST OF BURDEN.

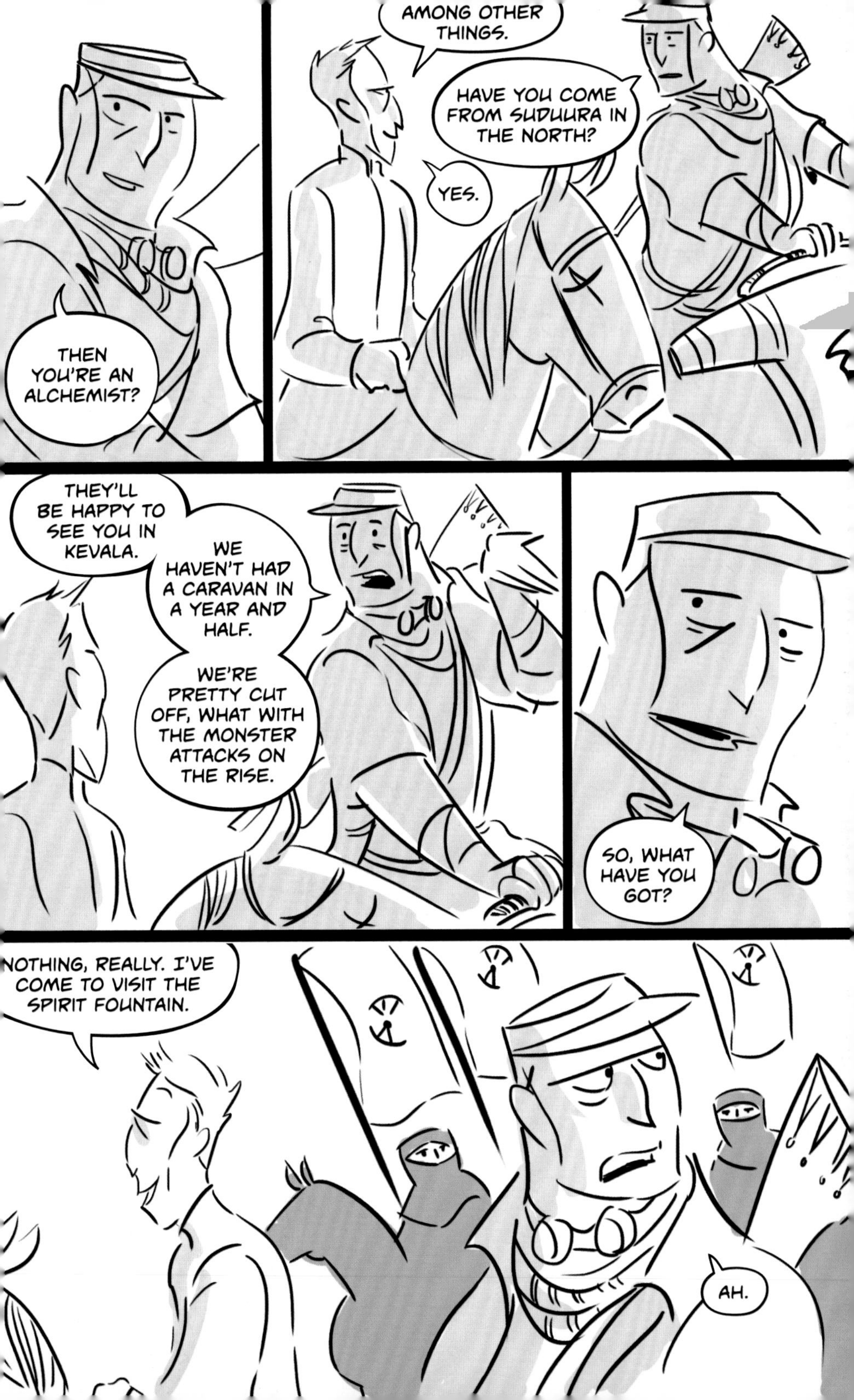
THEN YOU'RE AN ALCHEMIST?
AMONG OTHER THINGS.
HAVE YOU COME FROM SUDUURA IN THE NORTH?
YES.
THEY'LL BE HAPPY TO SEE YOU IN KEVALA.
WE HAVEN'T HAD A CARAVAN IN A YEAR AND HALF.
WE'RE PRETTY CUT OFF, WHAT WITH THE MONSTER ATTACKS ON THE RISE.
SO, WHAT HAVE YOU GOT?
NOTHING, REALLY. I'VE COME TO VISIT THE SPIRIT FOUNTAIN.
AH.

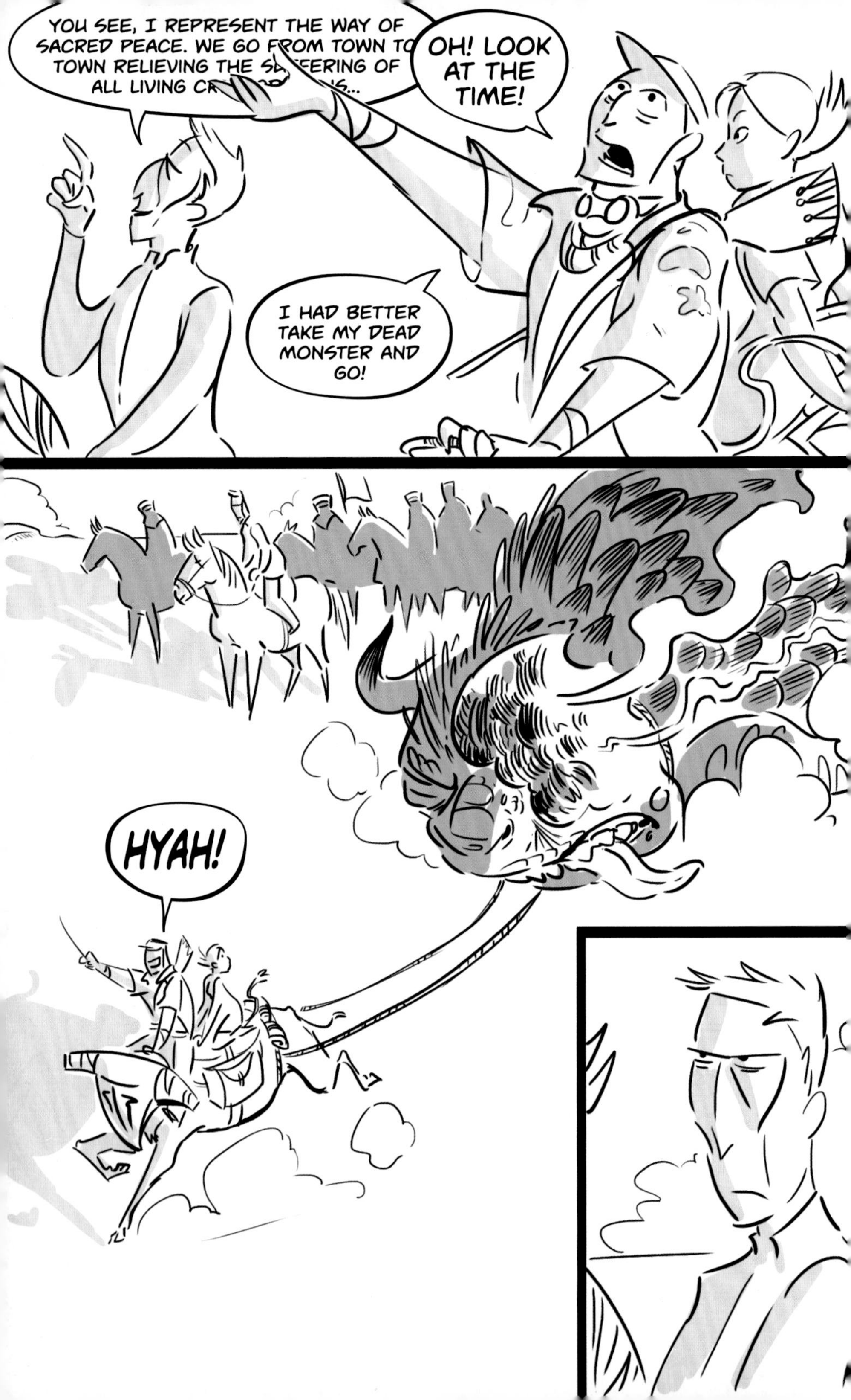
YOU SEE, I REPRESENT THE WAY OF SACRED PEACE. WE GO FROM TOWN TO TOWN RELIEVING THE S FFERING OF ALL LIVING CR S...
OH! LOOK AT THE TIME!
I HAD BETTER TAKE MY DEAD MONSTER AND GO!
HYAH!

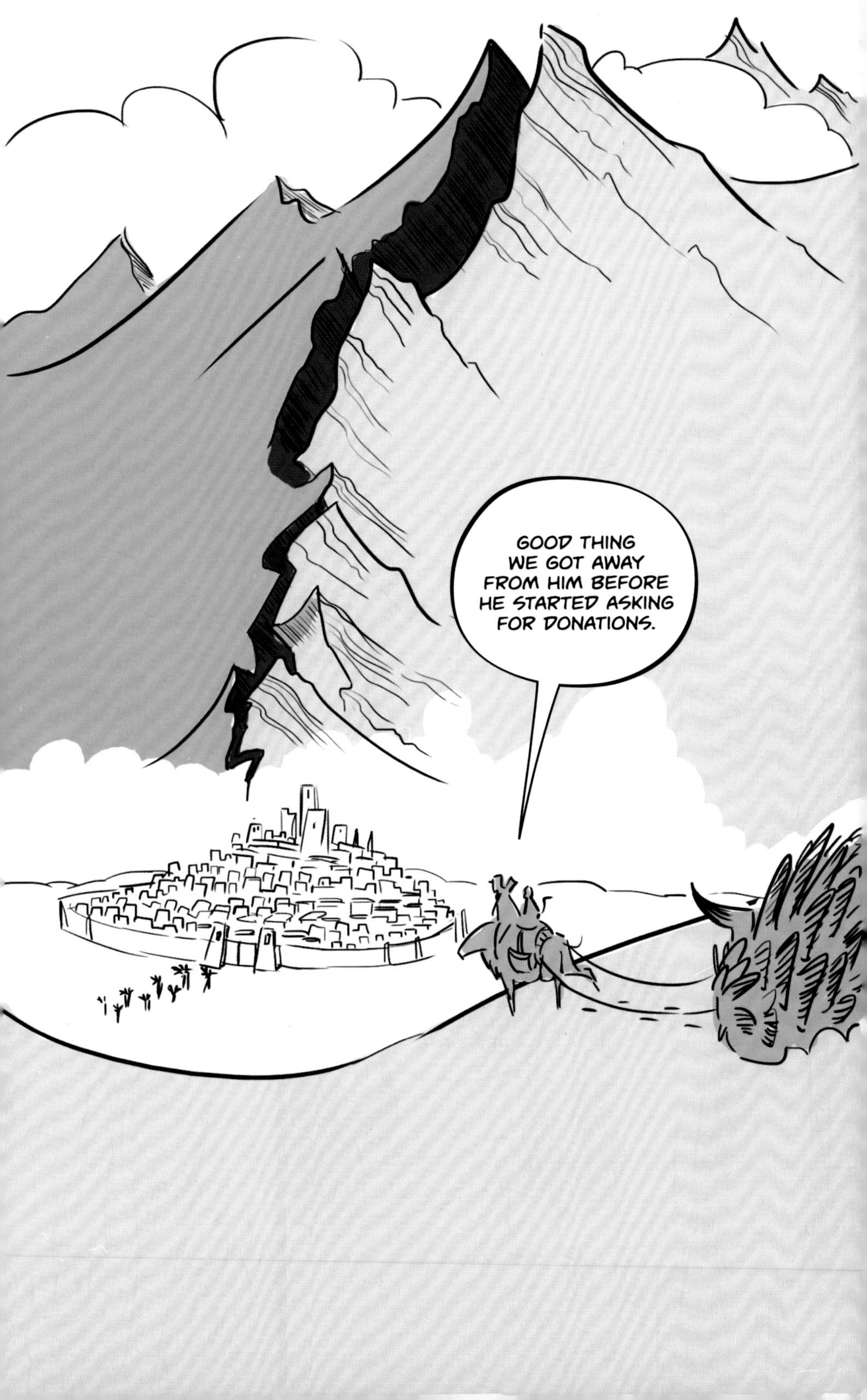
GOOD THING WE GOT AWAY FROM HIM BEFORE HE STARTED ASKING FOR DONATIONS.

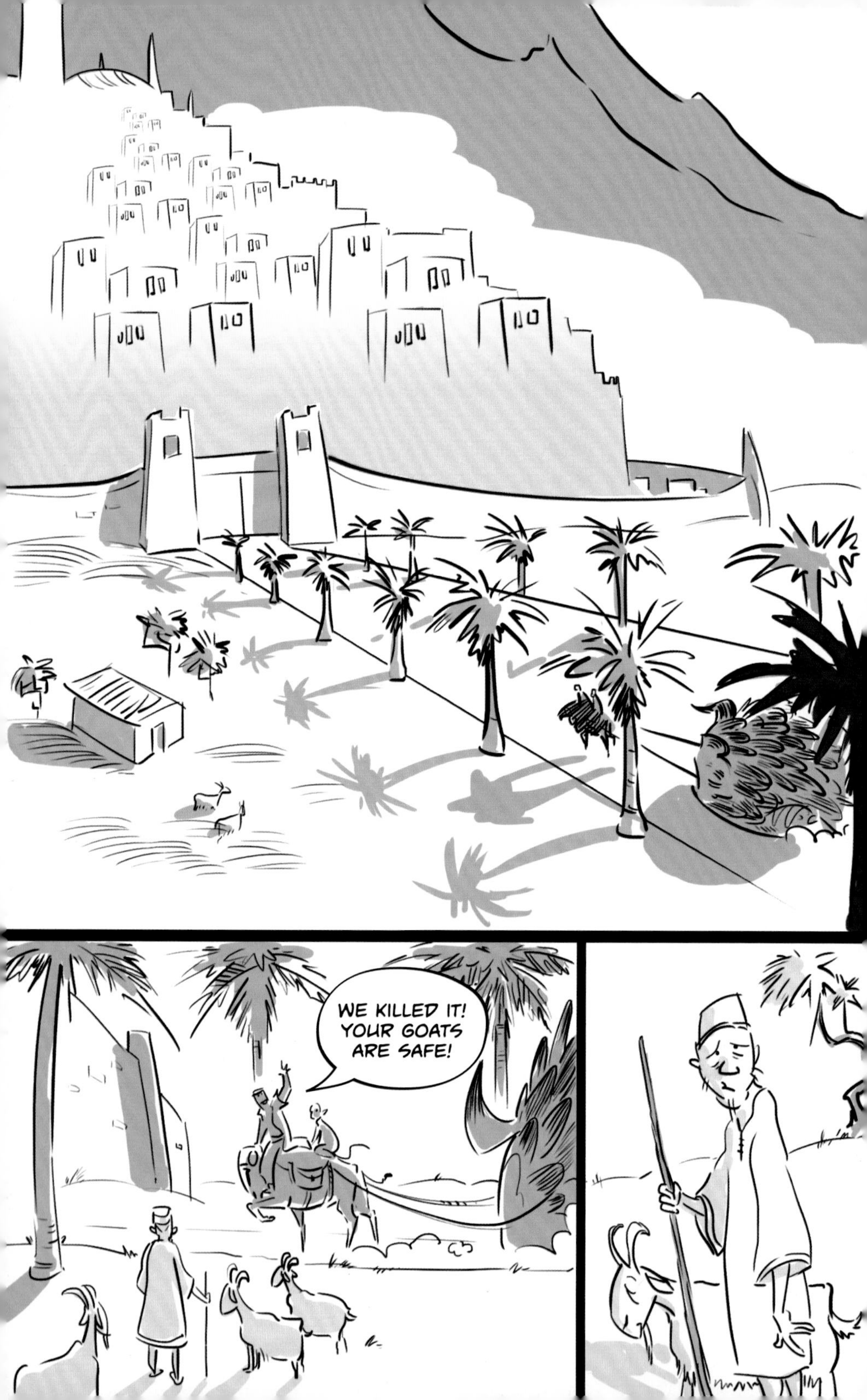
WE KILLED IT! YOUR GOATS ARE SAFE!

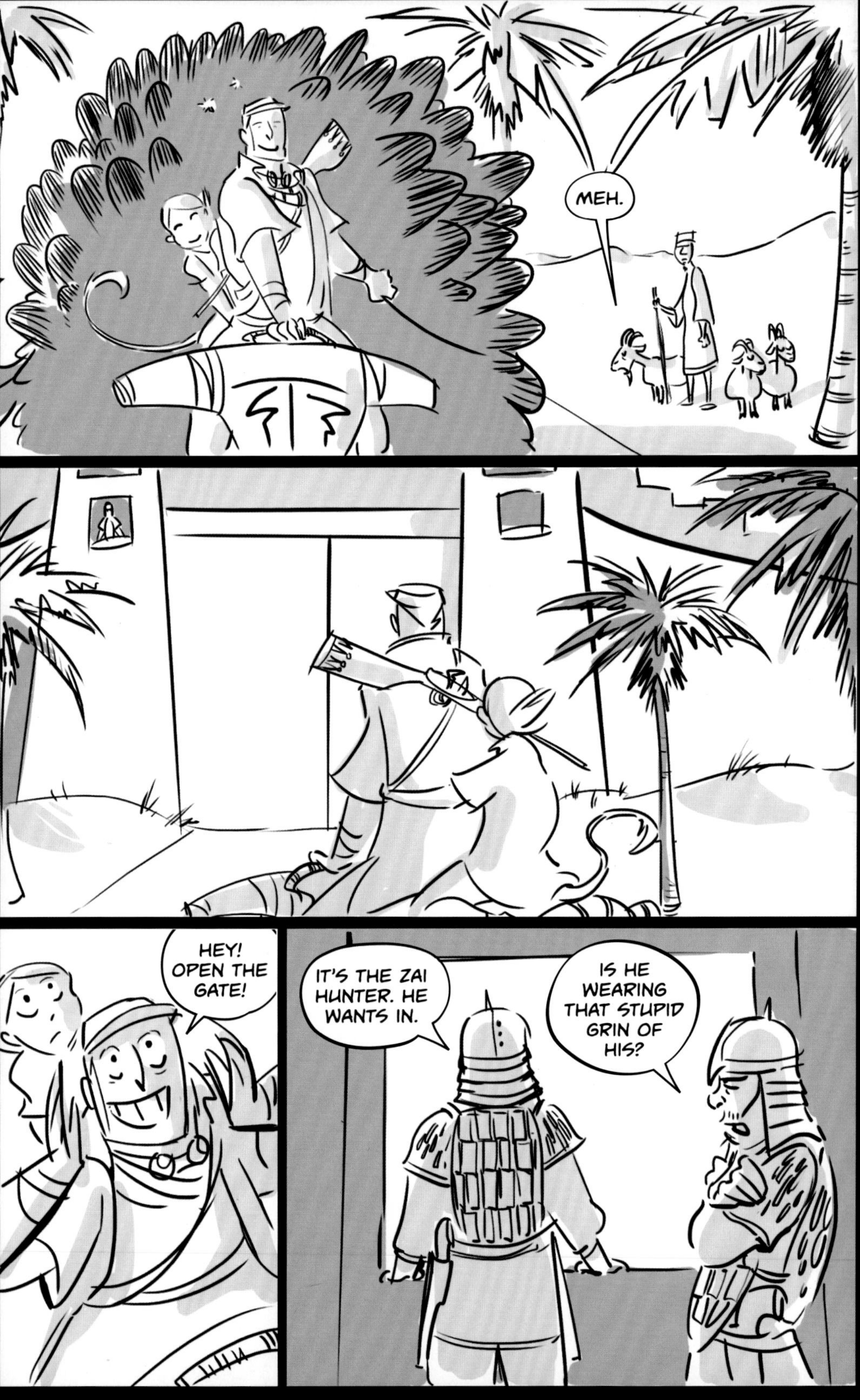
MEH.
HEY! OPEN THE GATE!
IT'S THE ZAI HUNTER. HE WANTS IN.
IS HE WEARING THAT STUPID GRIN OF HIS?

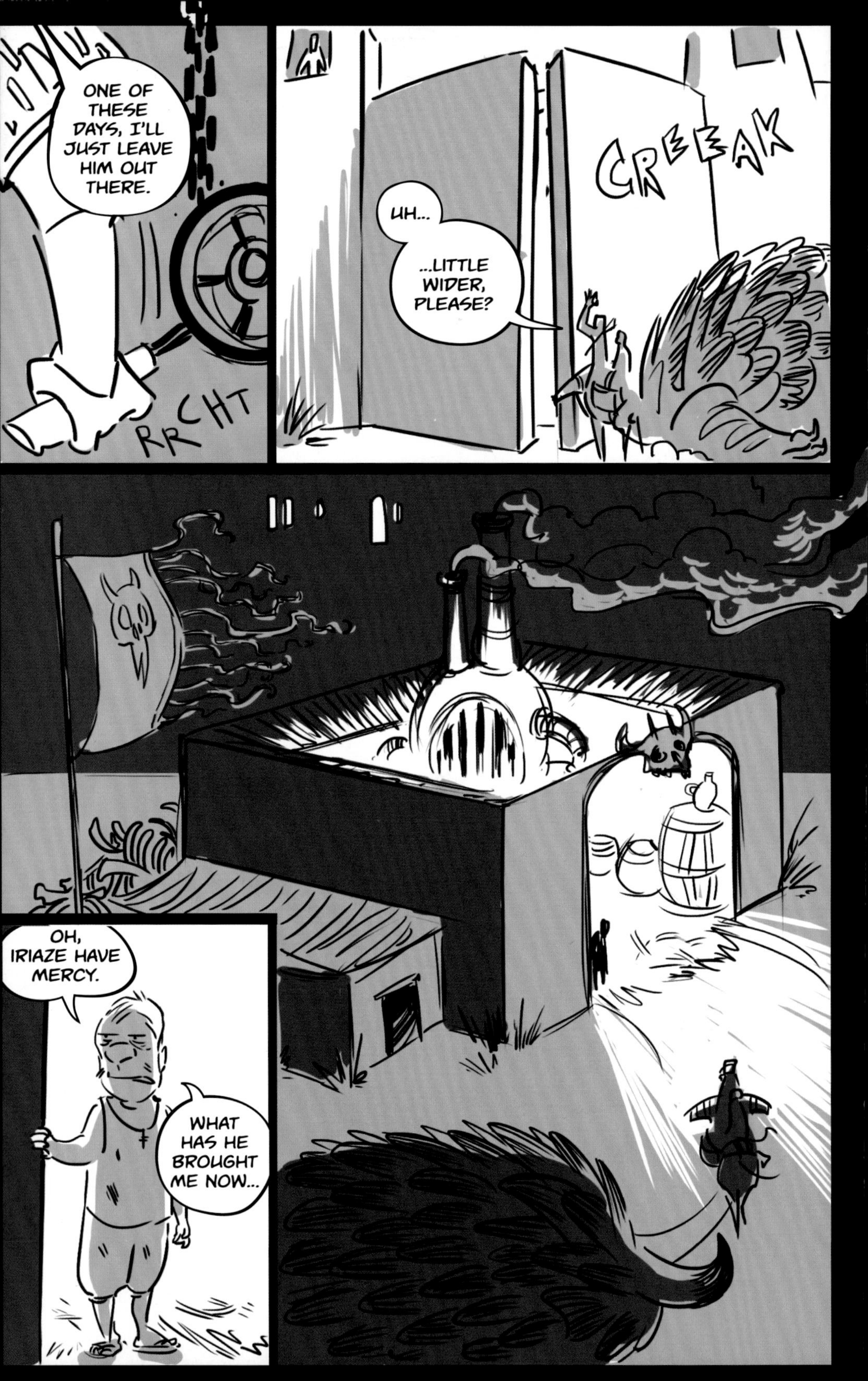
ONE OF THESE DAYS, I'LL JUST LEAVE HIM OUT THERE.
RRCHT
UH...
...LITTLE WIDER, PLEASE?
CREEAK
OH, IRIAZE HAVE MERCY.
WHAT HAS HE BROUGHT ME NOW...

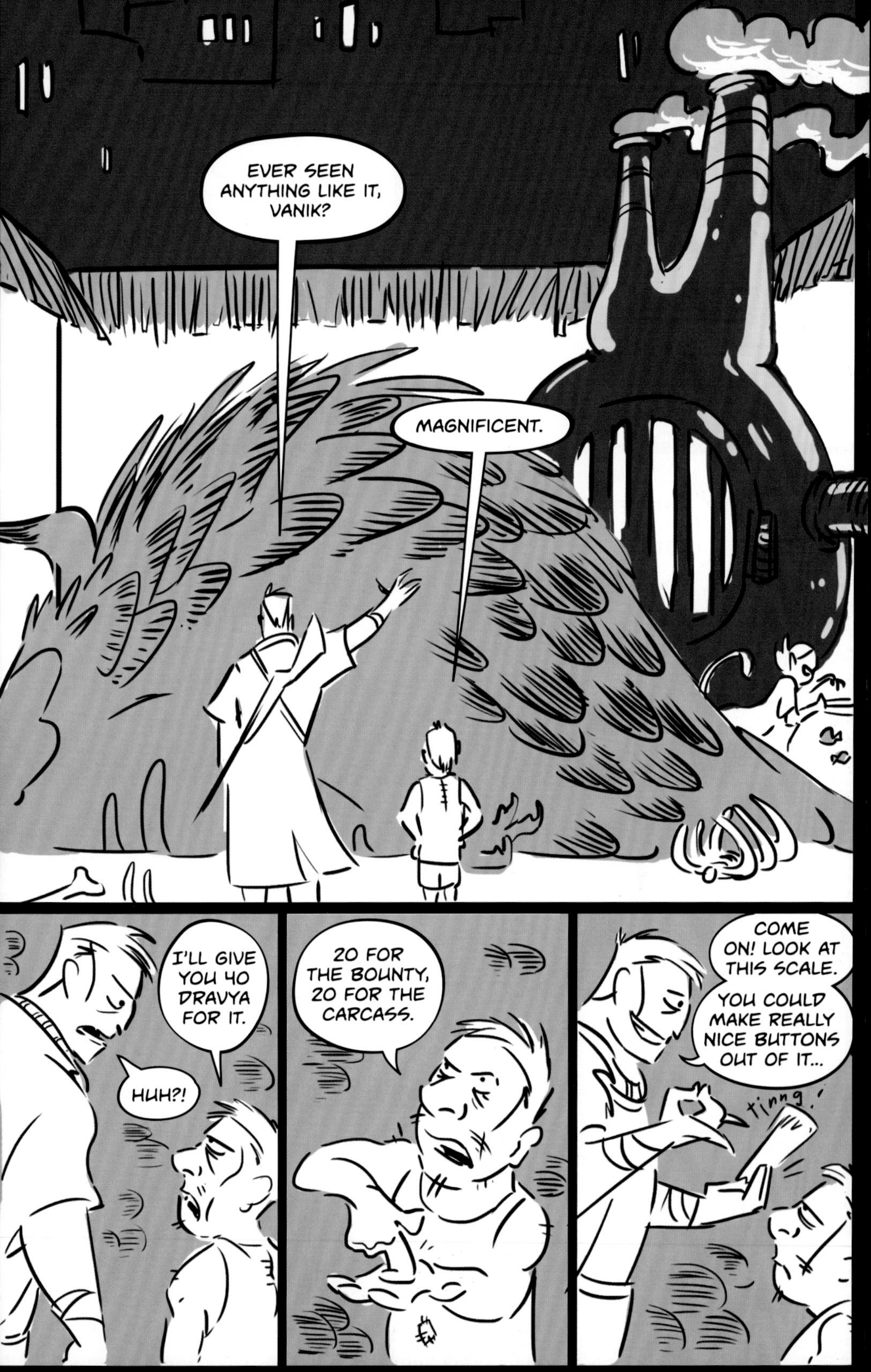
EVER SEEN ANYTHING LIKE IT, VANIK?
MAGNIFICENT.
I'LL GIVE YOU 40 DRAVYA FOR IT.
HUH?!
20 FOR THE BOUNTY, 20 FOR THE CARCASS.
COME ON! LOOK AT THIS SCALE.
YOU COULD MAKE REALLY NICE BUTTONS OUT OF IT...
tinng!

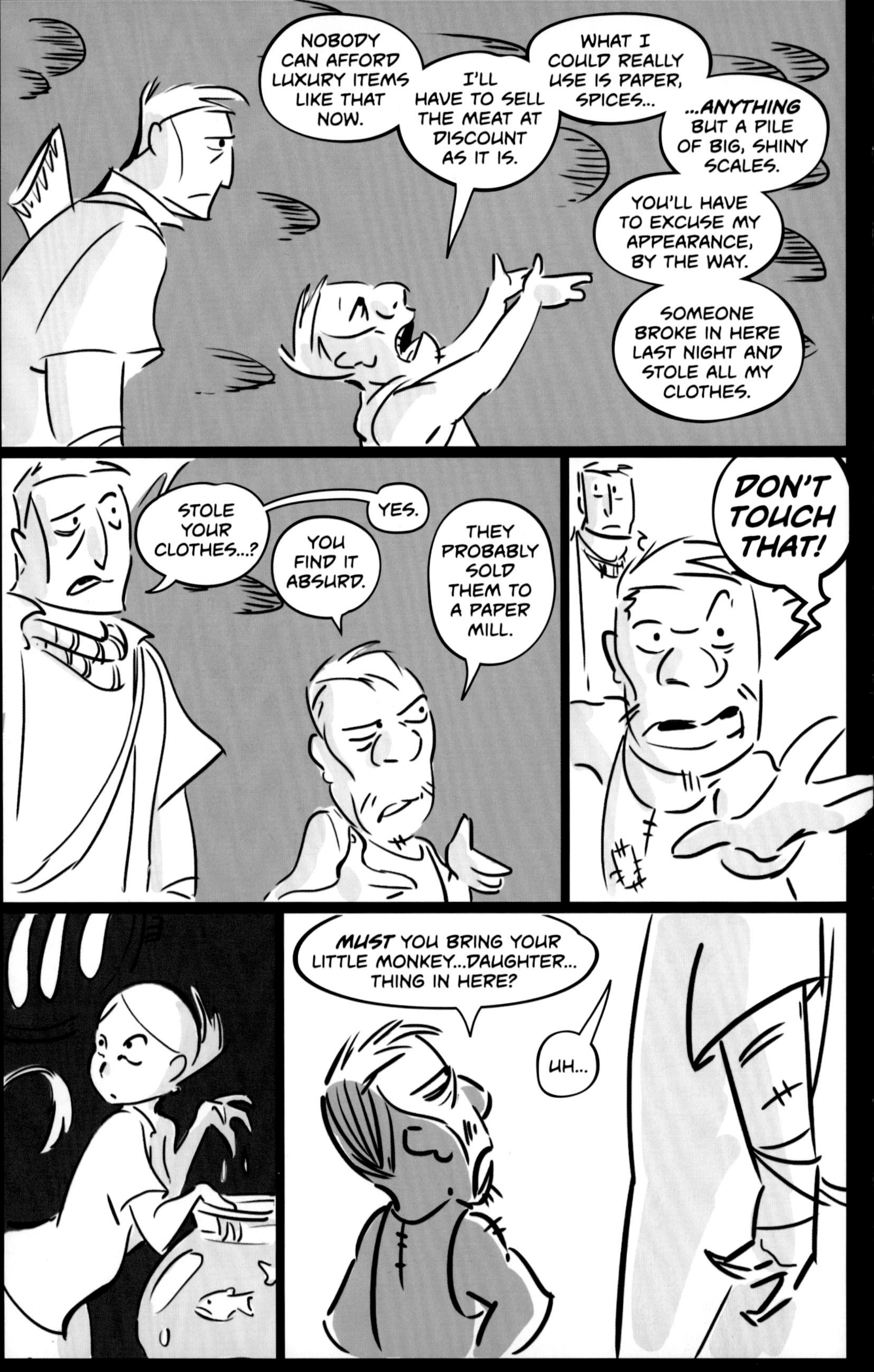
NOBODY CAN AFFORD LUXURY ITEMS LIKE THAT NOW.
I'LL HAVE TO SELL THE MEAT AT DISCOUNT AS IT IS.
WHAT I COULD REALLY USE IS PAPER, SPICES...
...*ANYTHING* BUT A PILE OF BIG, SHINY SCALES.
YOU'LL HAVE TO EXCUSE MY APPEARANCE, BY THE WAY.
SOMEONE BROKE IN HERE LAST NIGHT AND STOLE ALL MY CLOTHES.
STOLE YOUR CLOTHES...?
YES.
YOU FIND IT ABSURD.
THEY PROBABLY SOLD THEM TO A PAPER MILL.
DON'T TOUCH THAT!
MUST YOU BRING YOUR LITTLE MONKEY...DAUGHTER... THING IN HERE?
UH...

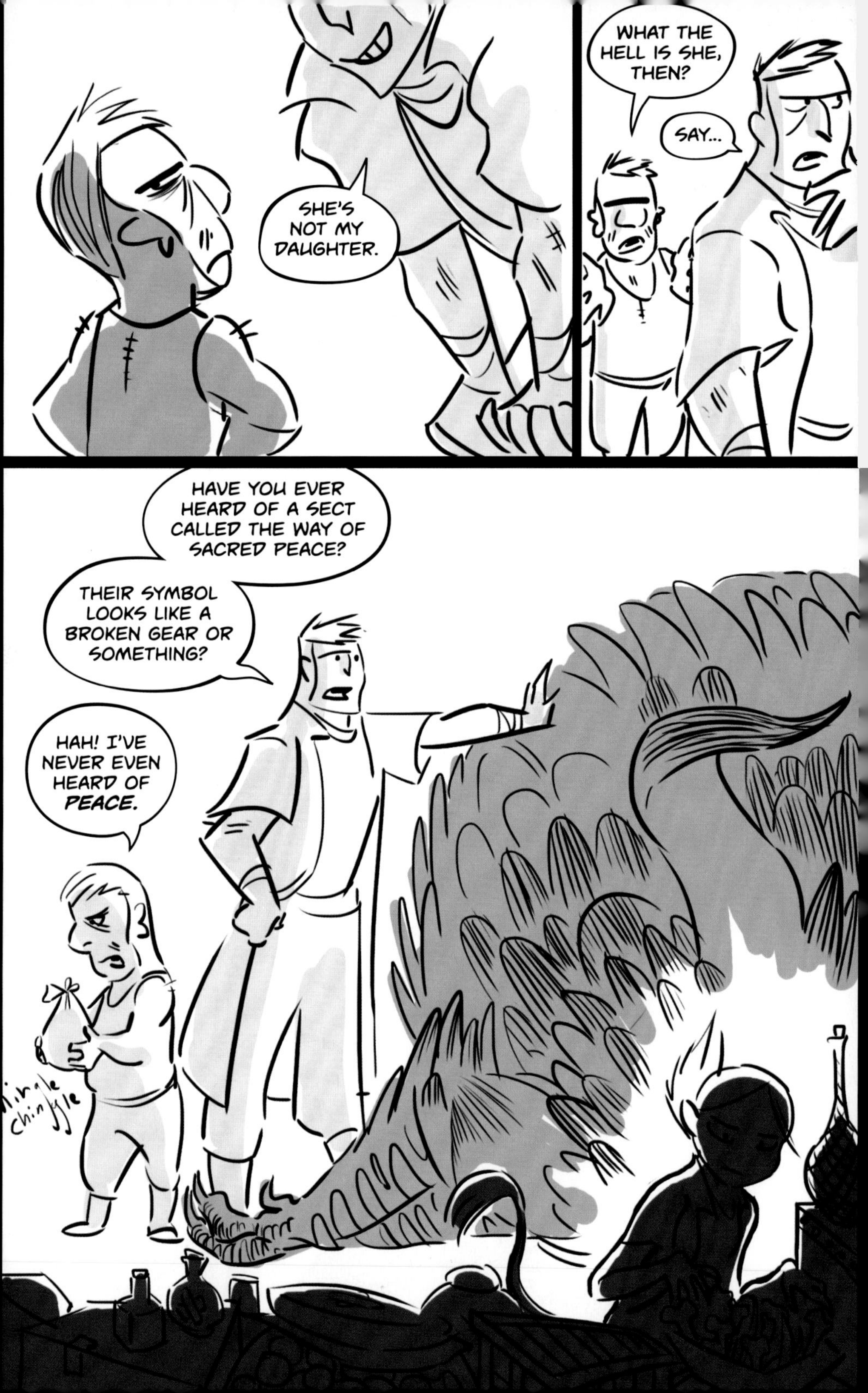
SHE'S NOT MY DAUGHTER.
WHAT THE HELL IS SHE, THEN?
SAY...
HAVE YOU EVER HEARD OF A SECT CALLED THE WAY OF SACRED PEACE?
THEIR SYMBOL LOOKS LIKE A BROKEN GEAR OR SOMETHING?
HAH! I'VE NEVER EVEN HEARD OF *PEACE.*
chingle chingle

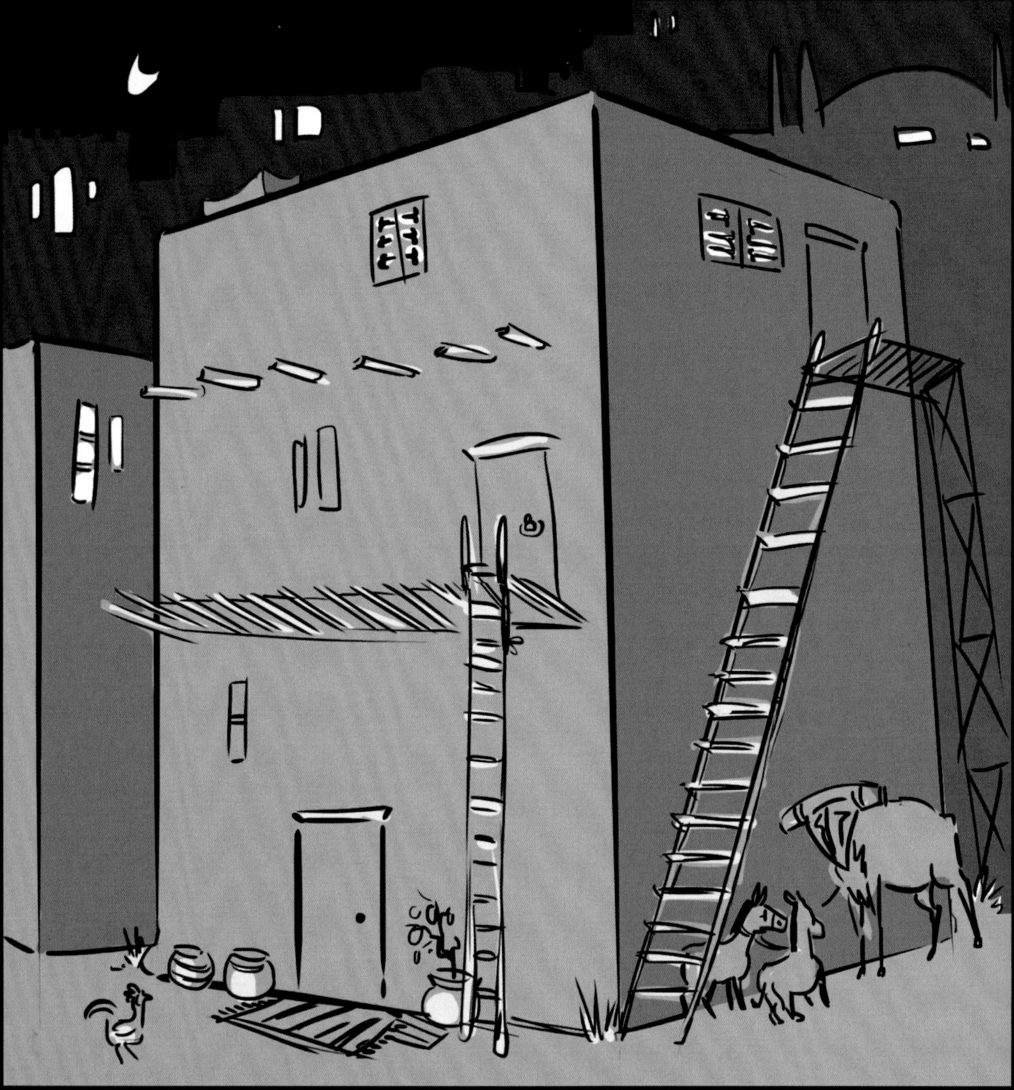

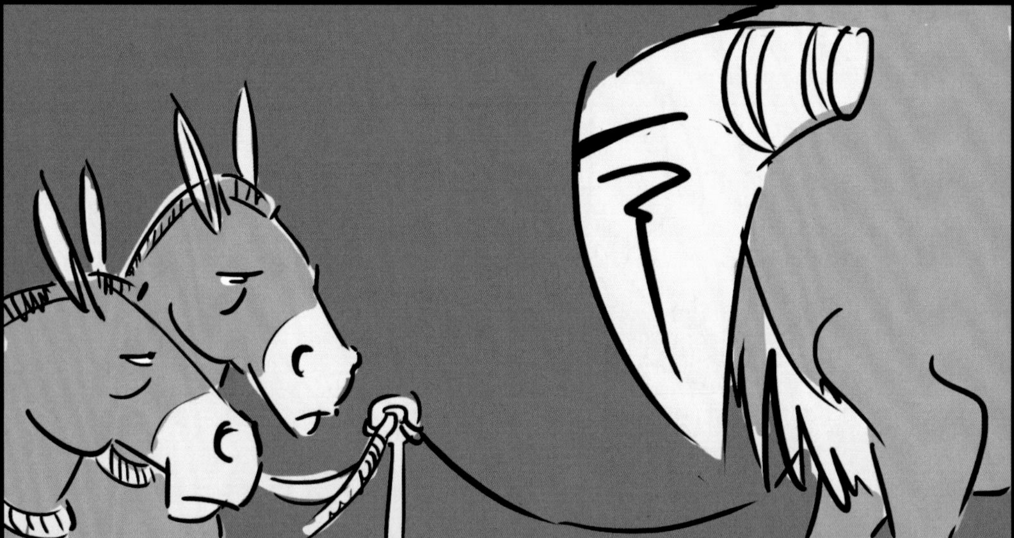

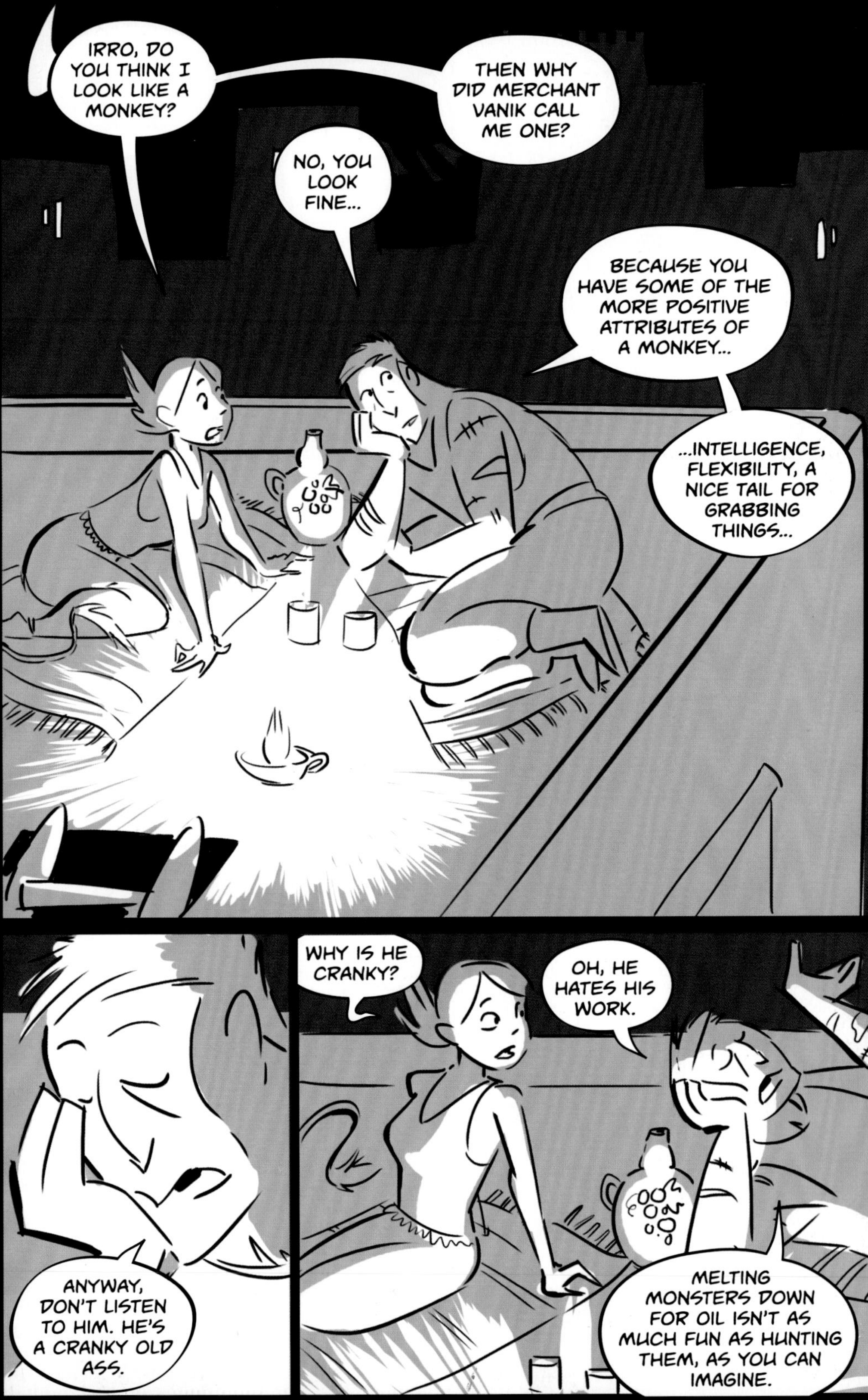
IRRO, DO YOU THINK I LOOK LIKE A MONKEY?
NO, YOU LOOK FINE...
THEN WHY DID MERCHANT VANIK CALL ME ONE?
BECAUSE YOU HAVE SOME OF THE MORE POSITIVE ATTRIBUTES OF A MONKEY...
...INTELLIGENCE, FLEXIBILITY, A NICE TAIL FOR GRABBING THINGS...
ANYWAY, DON'T LISTEN TO HIM. HE'S A CRANKY OLD ASS.
WHY IS HE CRANKY?
OH, HE HATES HIS WORK.
MELTING MONSTERS DOWN FOR OIL ISN'T AS MUCH FUN AS HUNTING THEM, AS YOU CAN IMAGINE.

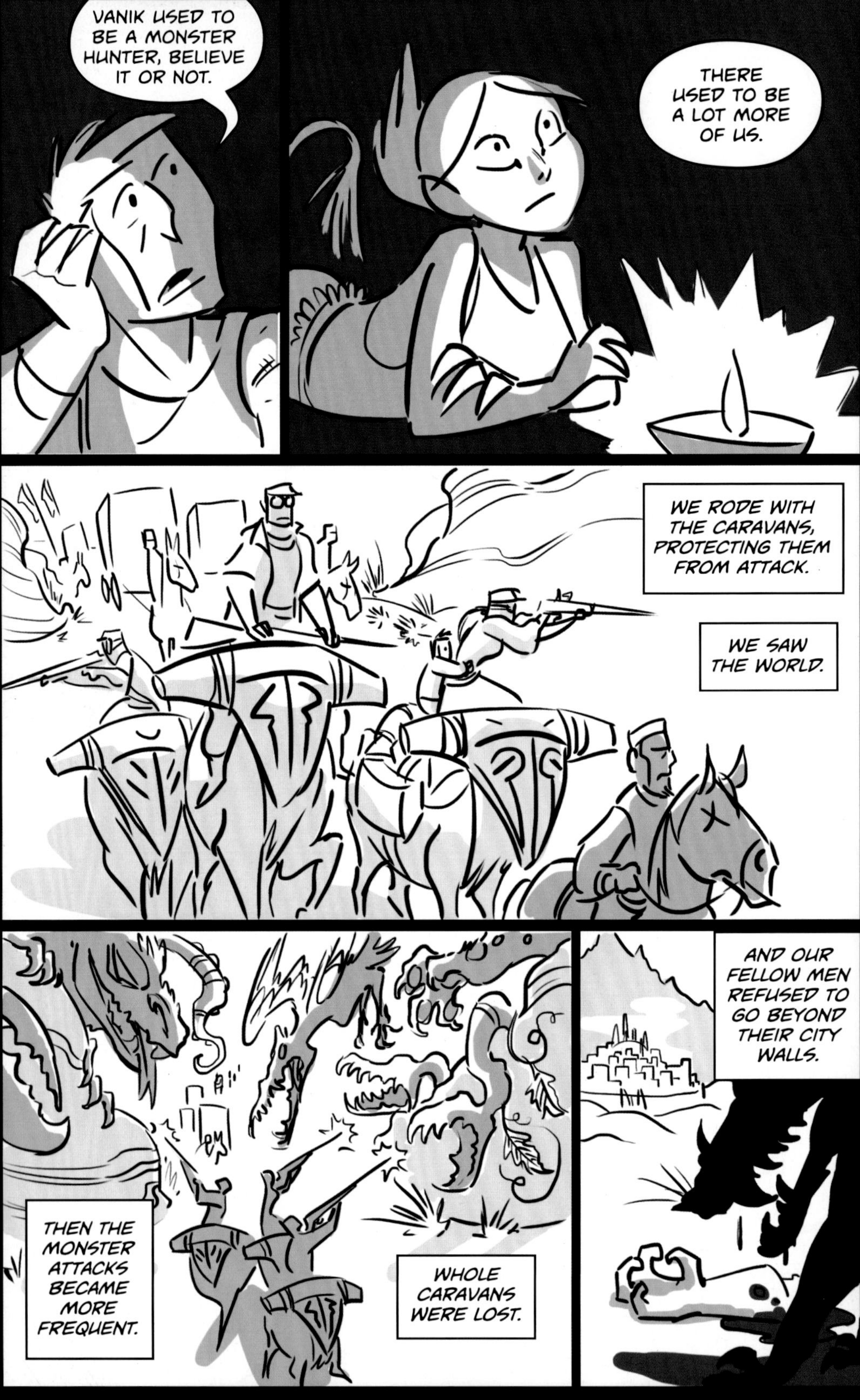
VANIK USED TO BE A MONSTER HUNTER, BELIEVE IT OR NOT.
THERE USED TO BE A LOT MORE OF US.
WE RODE WITH THE CARAVANS, PROTECTING THEM FROM ATTACK.
WE SAW THE WORLD.
THEN THE MONSTER ATTACKS BECAME MORE FREQUENT.
WHOLE CARAVANS WERE LOST.
AND OUR FELLOW MEN REFUSED TO GO BEYOND THEIR CITY WALLS.

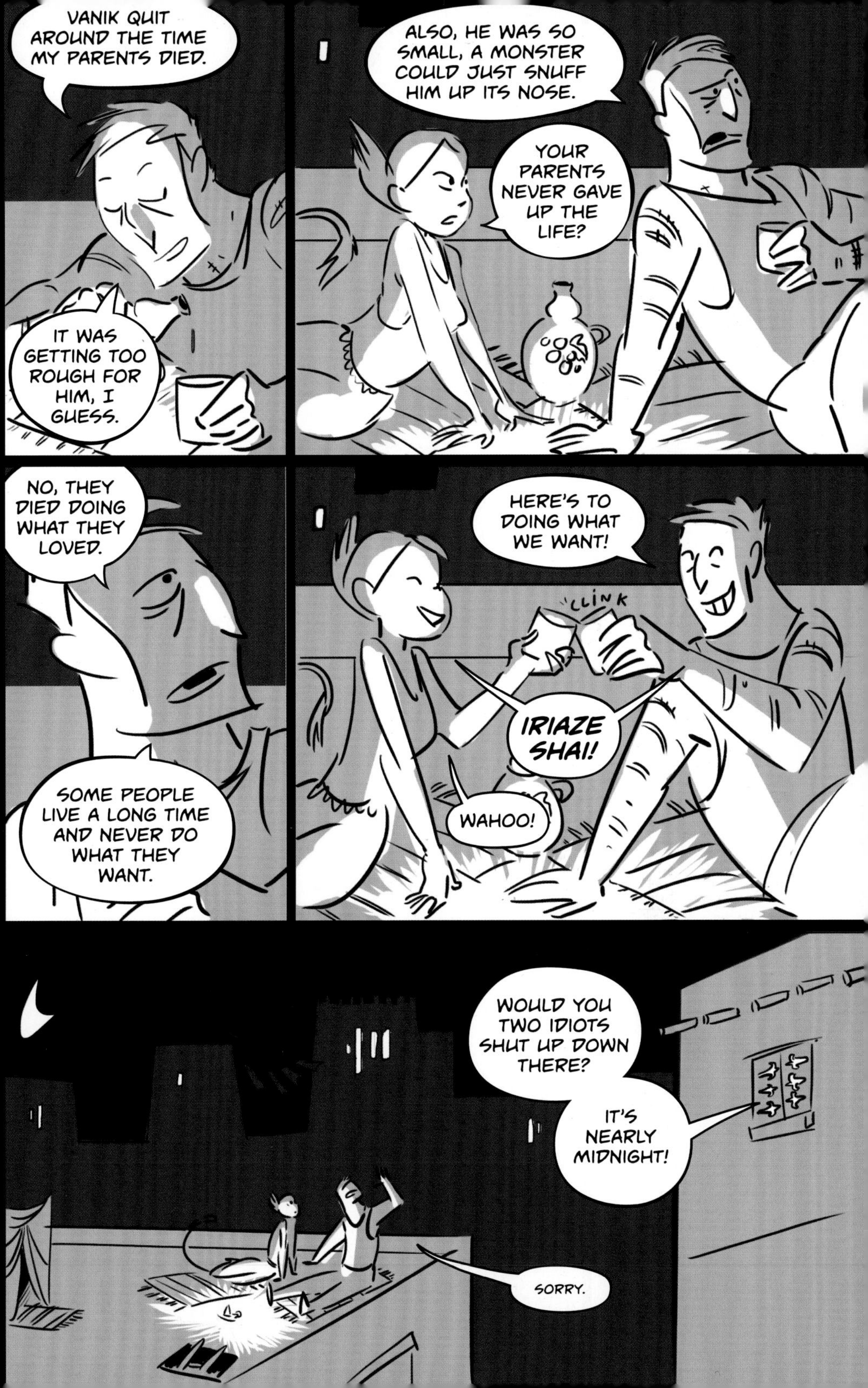
VANIK QUIT AROUND THE TIME MY PARENTS DIED.
IT WAS GETTING TOO ROUGH FOR HIM, I GUESS.
ALSO, HE WAS SO SMALL, A MONSTER COULD JUST SNUFF HIM UP ITS NOSE.
YOUR PARENTS NEVER GAVE UP THE LIFE?
NO, THEY DIED DOING WHAT THEY LOVED.
SOME PEOPLE LIVE A LONG TIME AND NEVER DO WHAT THEY WANT.
HERE'S TO DOING WHAT WE WANT!
CLINK
IRIAZE SHAI!
WAHOO!
WOULD YOU TWO IDIOTS SHUT UP DOWN THERE?
IT'S NEARLY MIDNIGHT!
SORRY.

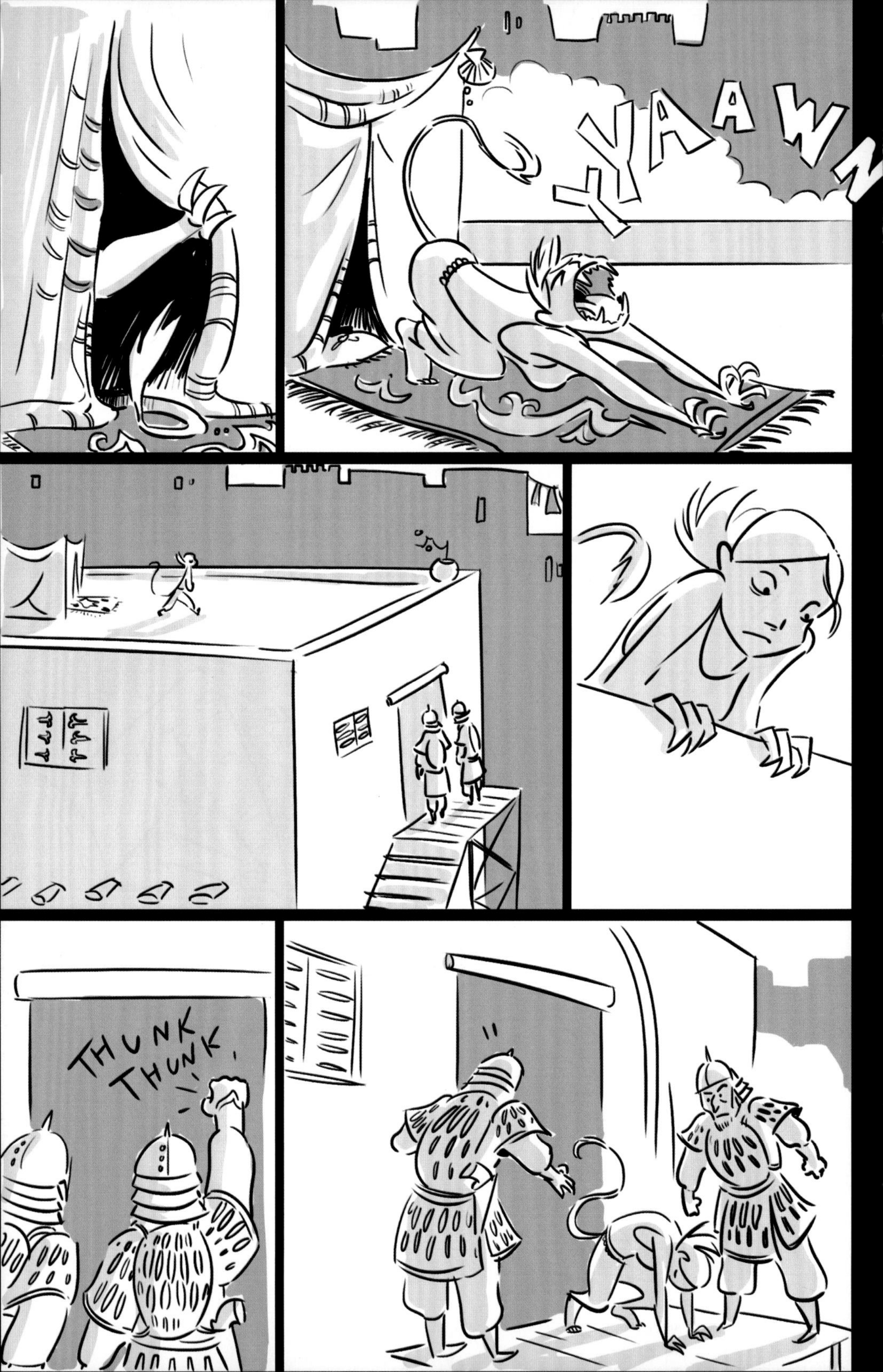
YAAWN
THUNK
THUNK

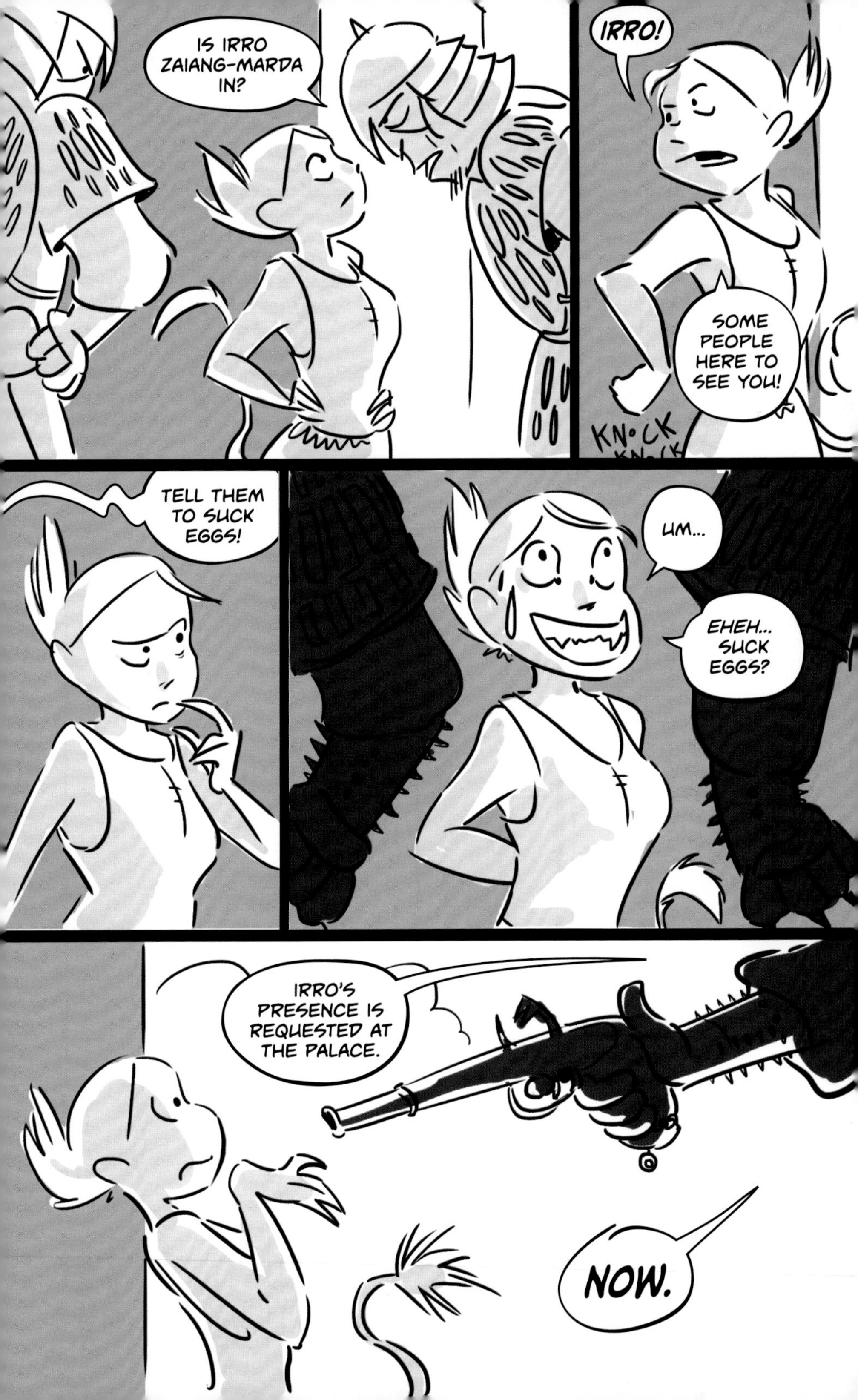
IS IRRO ZAIANG-MARDA IN?
IRRO!
SOME PEOPLE HERE TO SEE YOU!
KNOCK
TELL THEM TO SUCK EGGS!
UM...
EHEH... SUCK EGGS?
IRRO'S PRESENCE IS REQUESTED AT THE PALACE.
NOW.

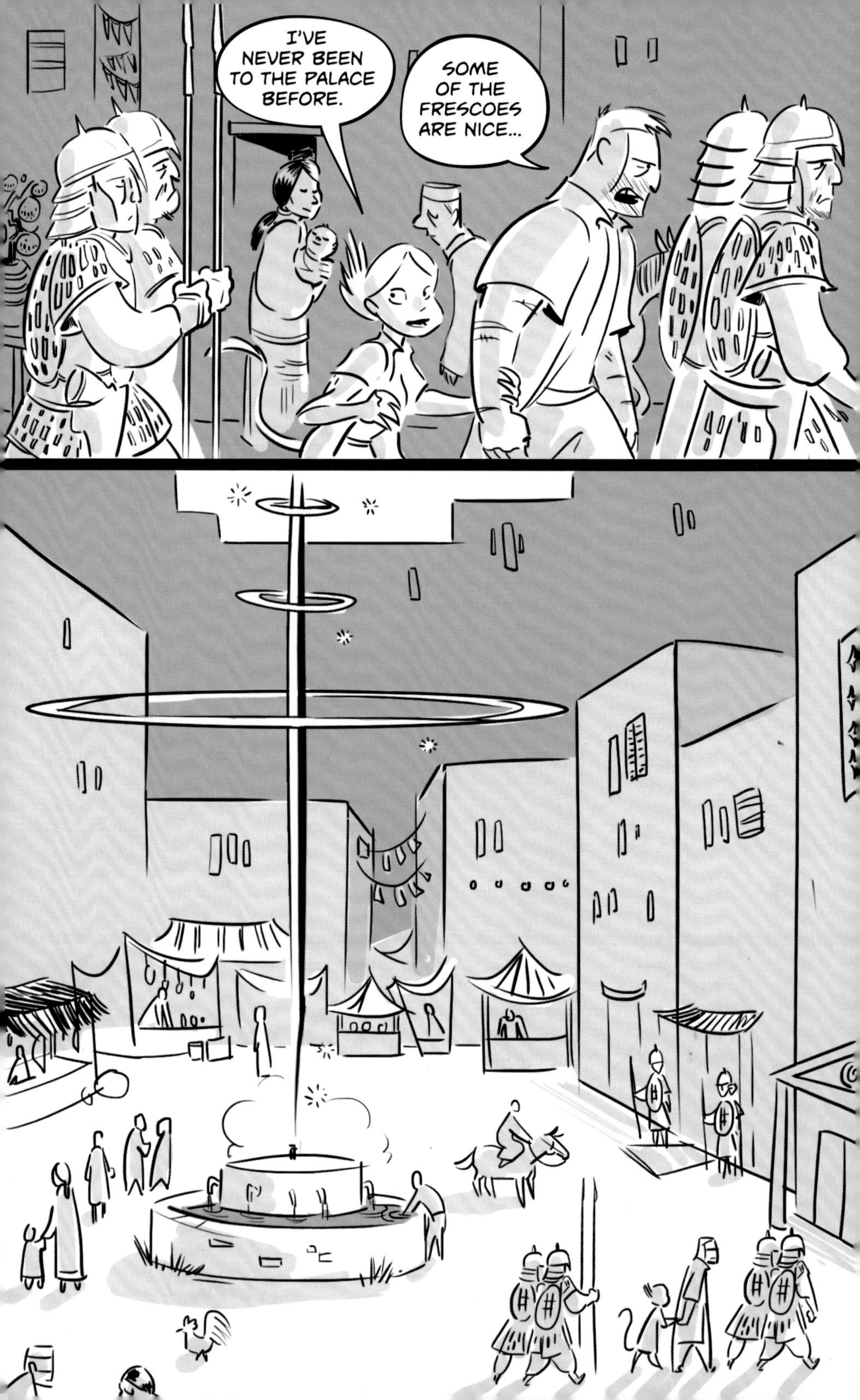
I'VE NEVER BEEN TO THE PALACE BEFORE.
SOME OF THE FRESCOES ARE NICE...

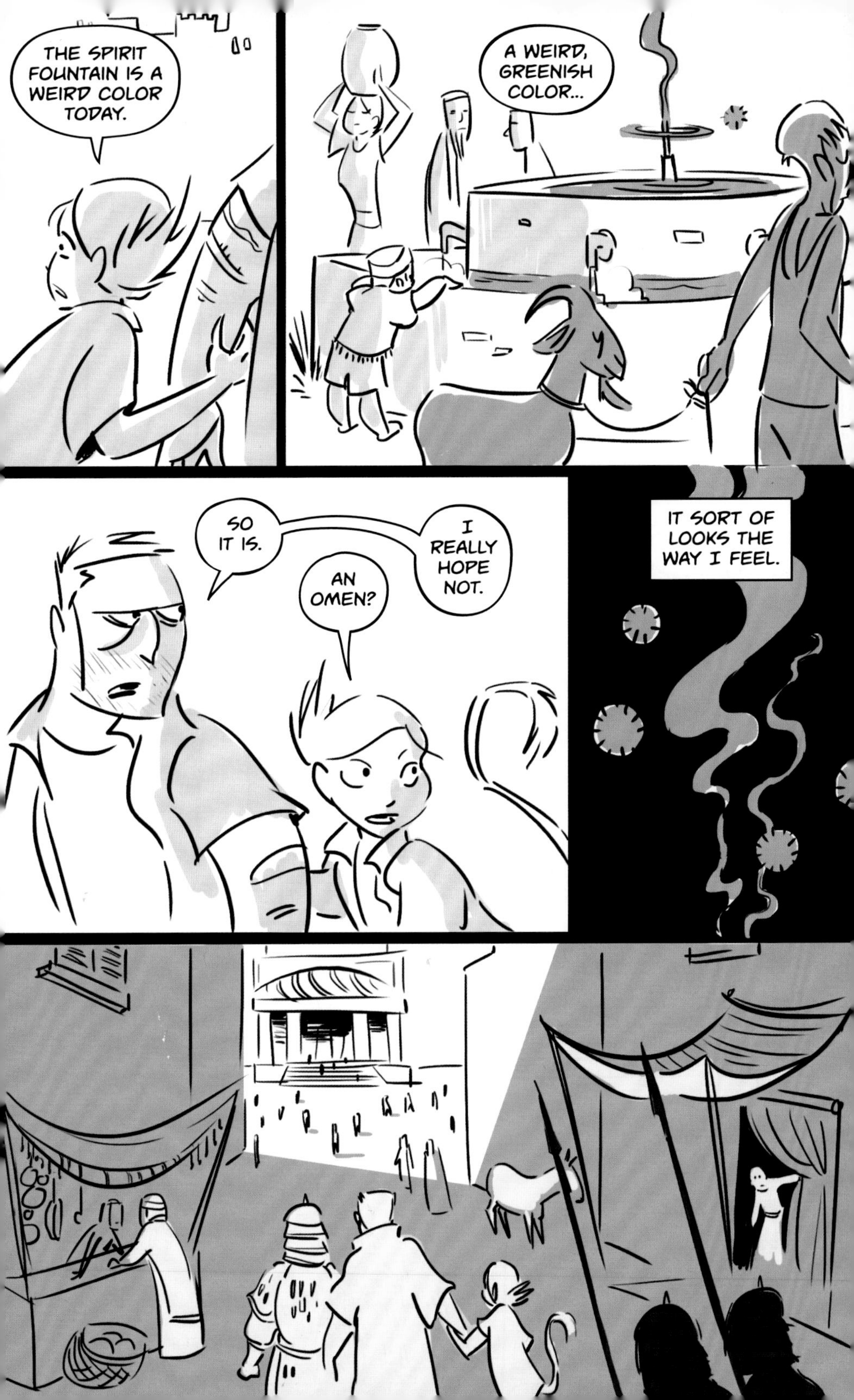
THE SPIRIT FOUNTAIN IS A WEIRD COLOR TODAY.
A WEIRD, GREENISH COLOR...
SO IT IS.
AN OMEN?
I REALLY HOPE NOT.
IT SORT OF LOOKS THE WAY I FEEL.

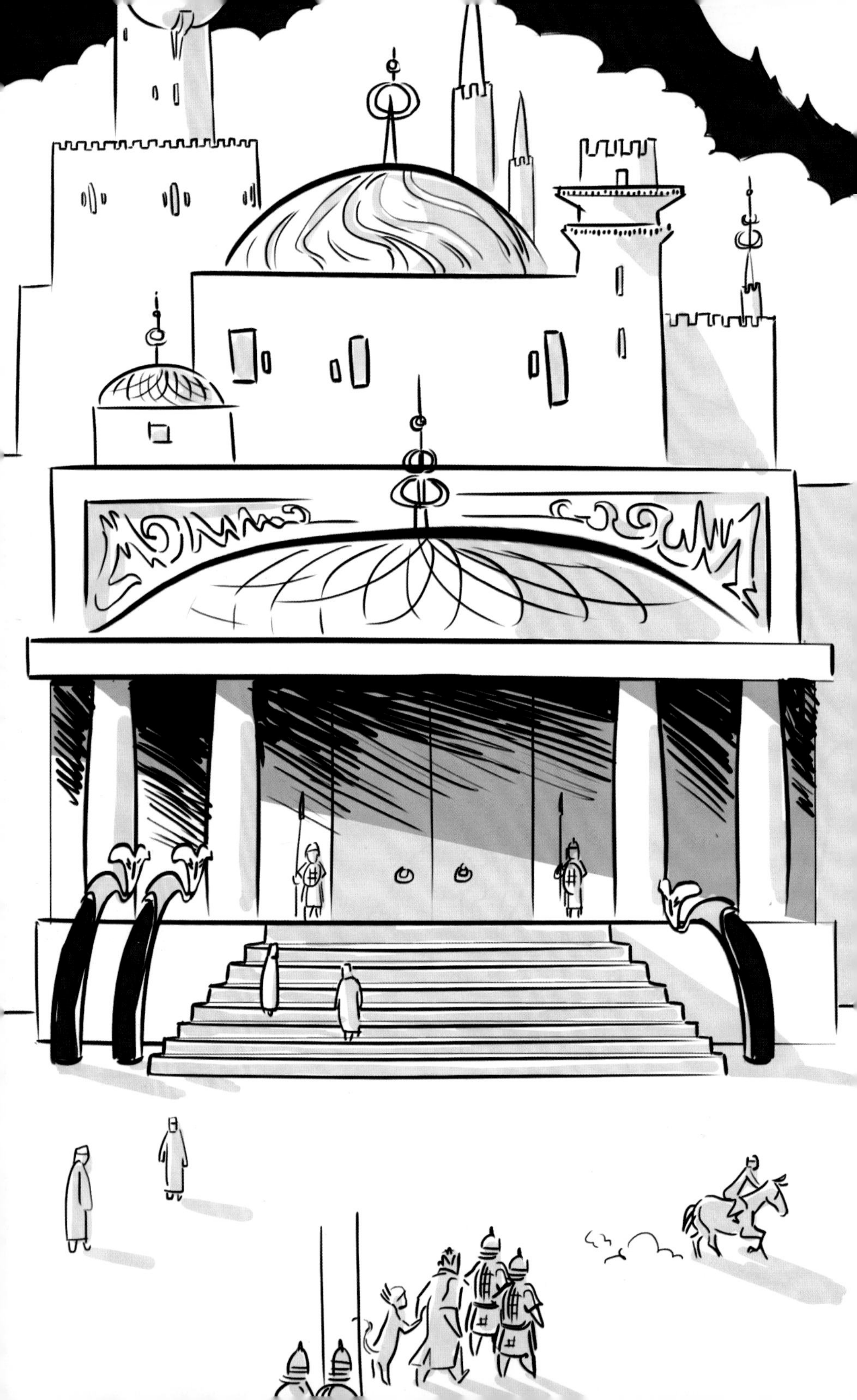

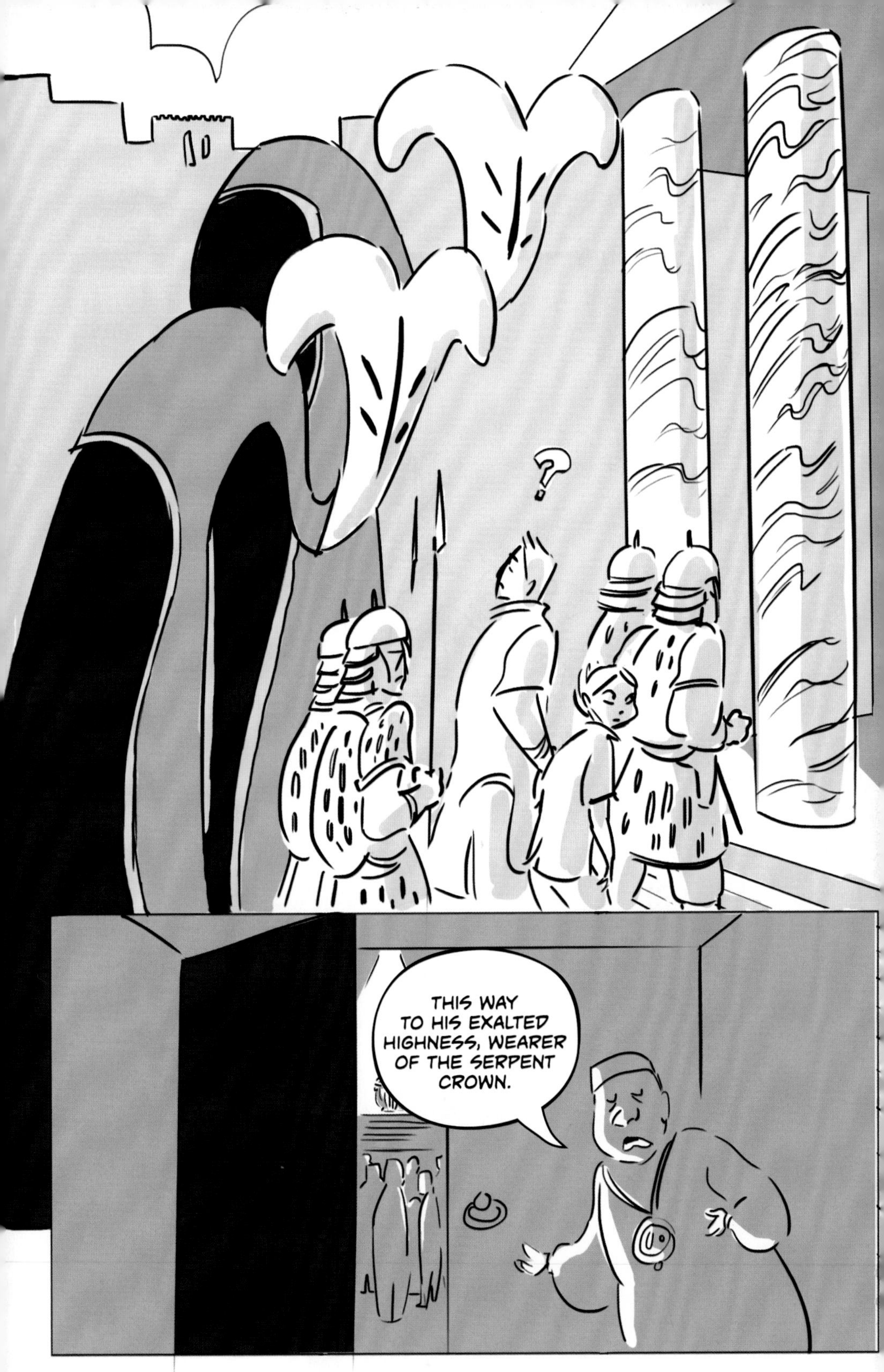
?
THIS WAY TO HIS EXALTED HIGHNESS, WEARER OF THE SERPENT CROWN.

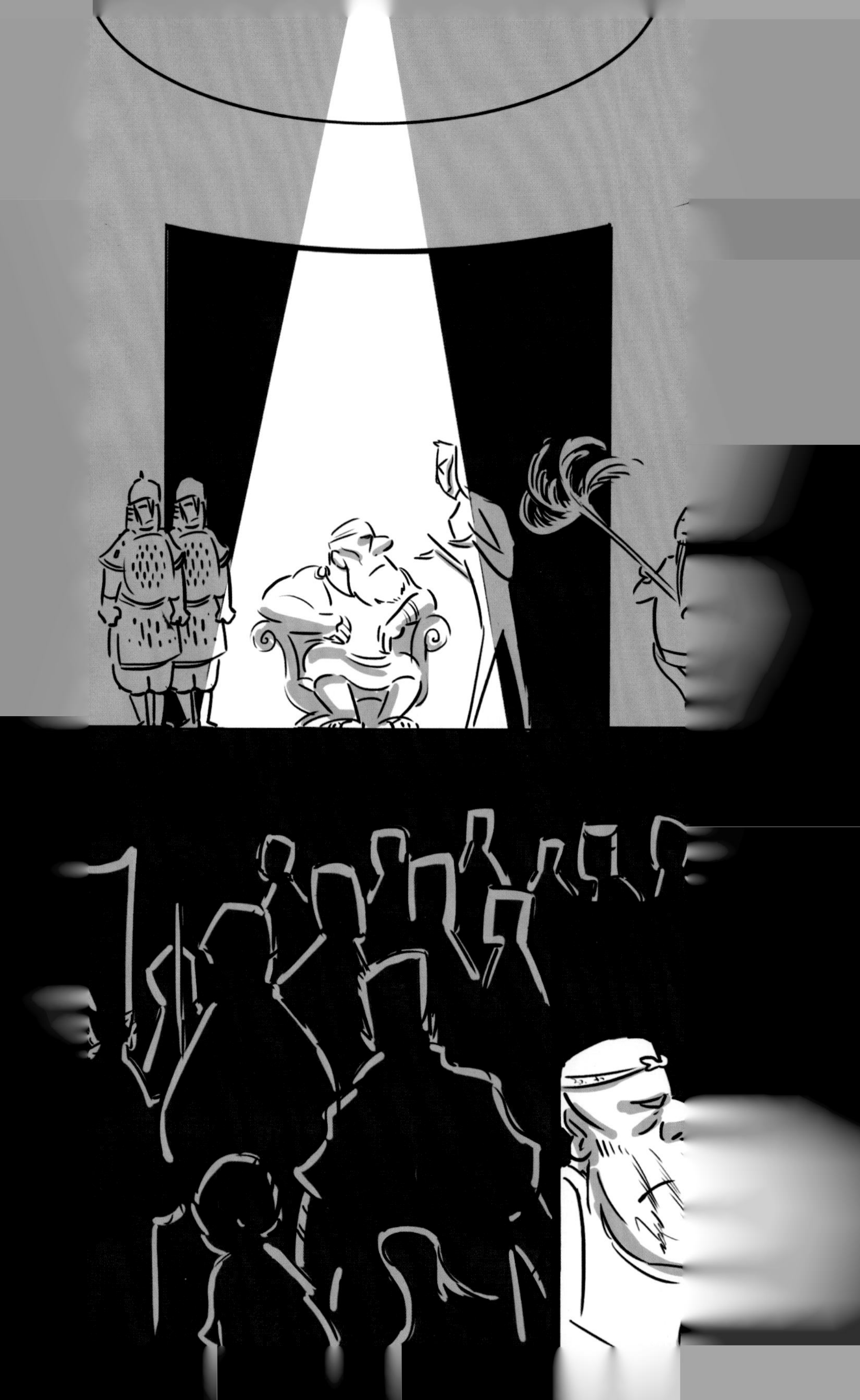

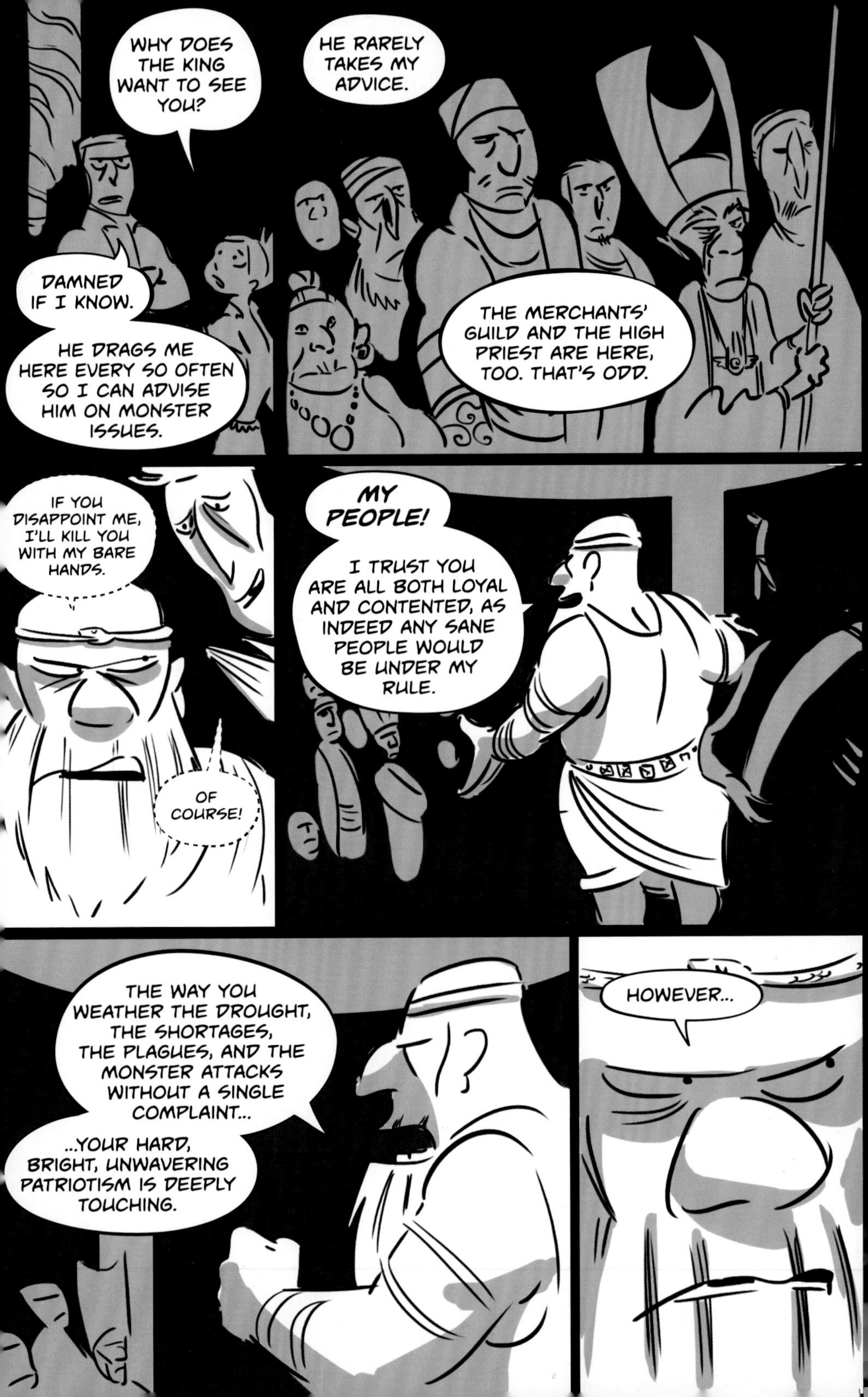
WHY DOES THE KING WANT TO SEE YOU?
DAMNED IF I KNOW.
HE DRAGS ME HERE EVERY SO OFTEN SO I CAN ADVISE HIM ON MONSTER ISSUES.
HE RARELY TAKES MY ADVICE.
THE MERCHANTS' GUILD AND THE HIGH PRIEST ARE HERE, TOO. THAT'S ODD.
IF YOU DISAPPOINT ME, I'LL KILL YOU WITH MY BARE HANDS.
OF COURSE!
MY PEOPLE!
I TRUST YOU ARE ALL BOTH LOYAL AND CONTENTED, AS INDEED ANY SANE PEOPLE WOULD BE UNDER MY RULE.
THE WAY YOU WEATHER THE DROUGHT, THE SHORTAGES, THE PLAGUES, AND THE MONSTER ATTACKS WITHOUT A SINGLE COMPLAINT...
...YOUR HARD, BRIGHT, UNWAVERING PATRIOTISM IS DEEPLY TOUCHING.
HOWEVER...

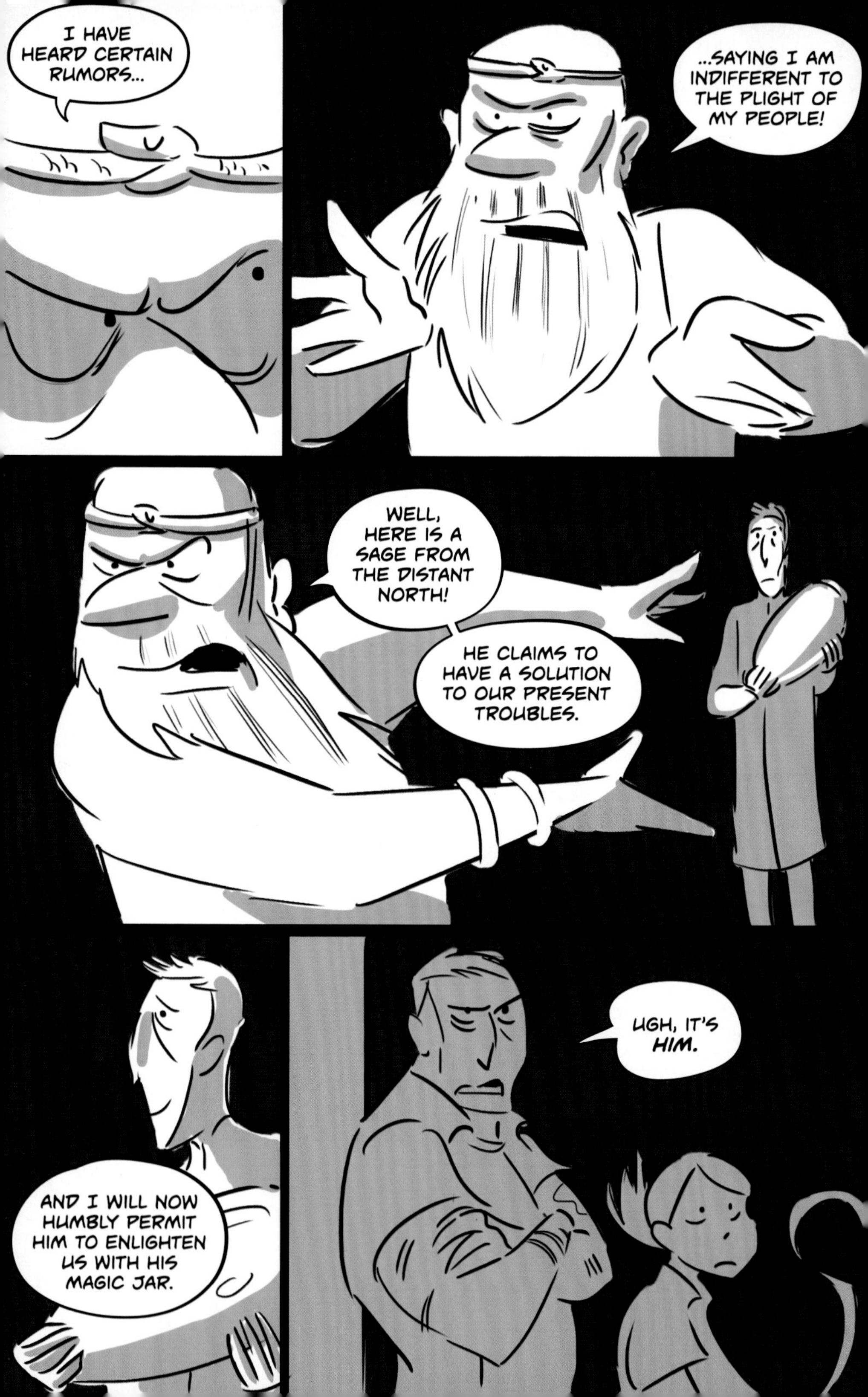
I HAVE HEARD CERTAIN RUMORS...
...SAYING I AM INDIFFERENT TO THE PLIGHT OF MY PEOPLE!
WELL, HERE IS A SAGE FROM THE DISTANT NORTH!
HE CLAIMS TO HAVE A SOLUTION TO OUR PRESENT TROUBLES.
AND I WILL NOW HUMBLY PERMIT HIM TO ENLIGHTEN US WITH HIS MAGIC JAR.
UGH, IT'S *HIM*.

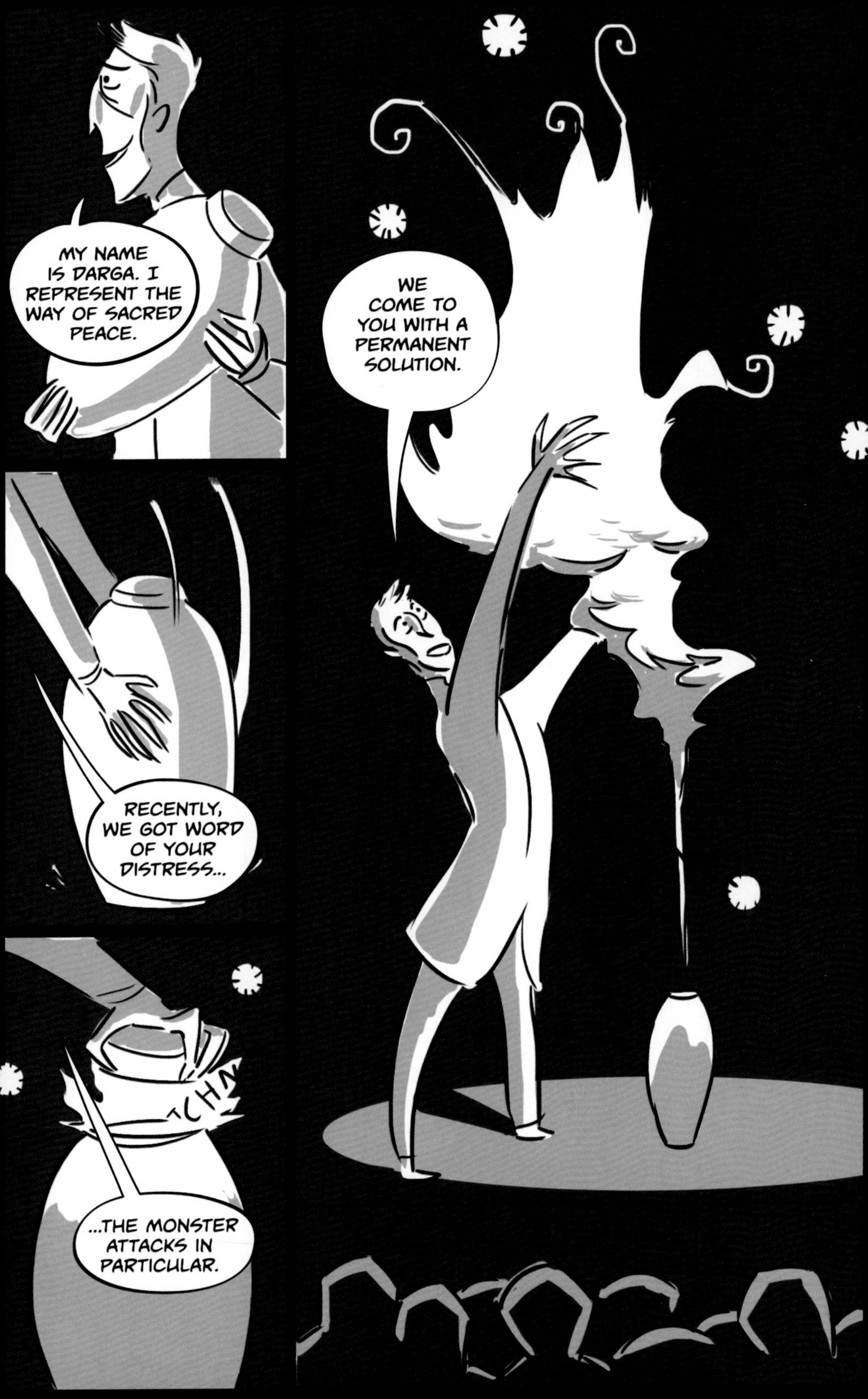
MY NAME IS DARGA. I REPRESENT THE WAY OF SACRED PEACE.
WE COME TO YOU WITH A PERMANENT SOLUTION.
RECENTLY, WE GOT WORD OF YOUR DISTRESS...
...THE MONSTER ATTACKS IN PARTICULAR.

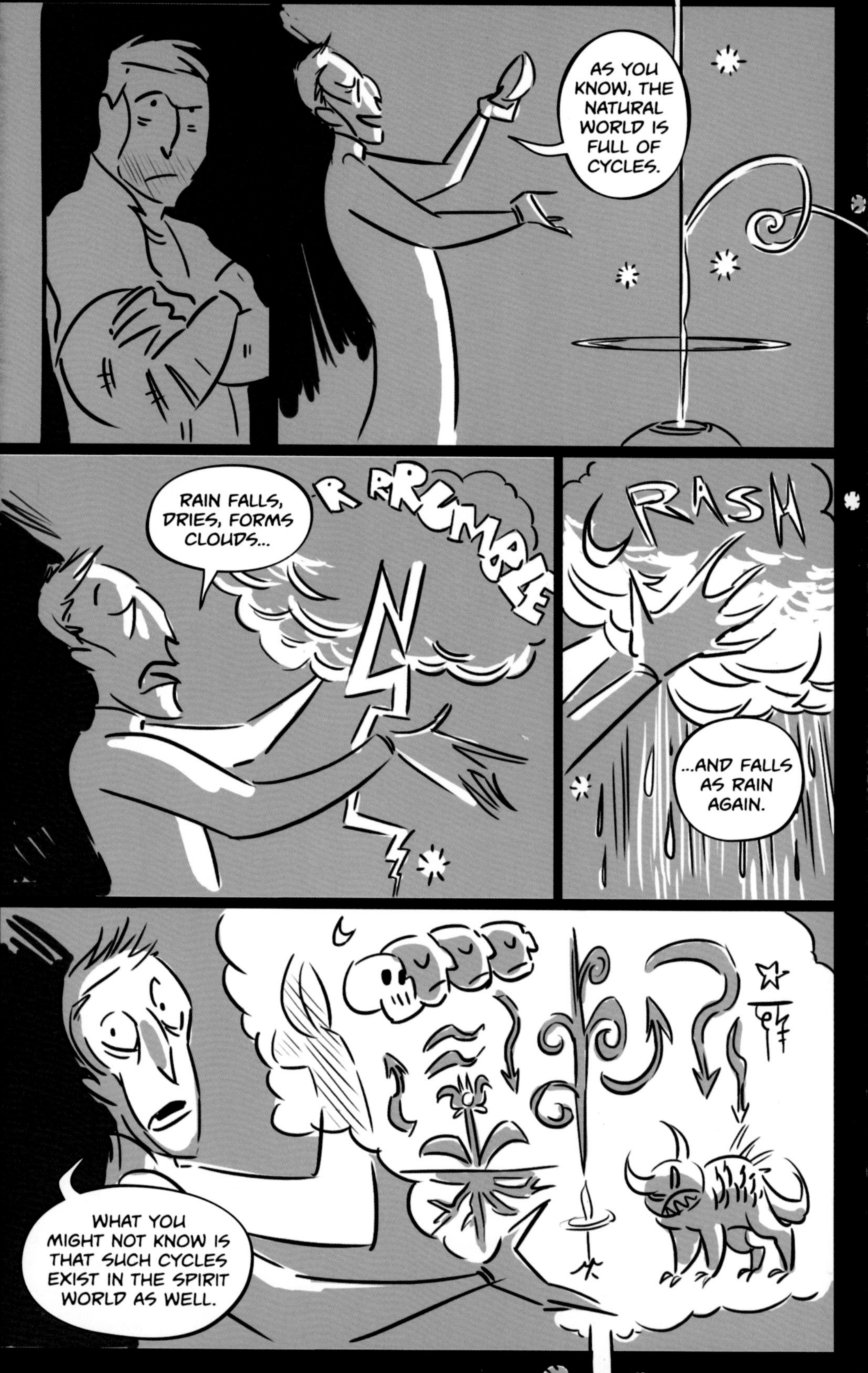
AS YOU KNOW, THE NATURAL WORLD IS FULL OF CYCLES.
RAIN FALLS, DRIES, FORMS CLOUDS...
R RRUMBLE
CRASH
...AND FALLS AS RAIN AGAIN.
WHAT YOU MIGHT NOT KNOW IS THAT SUCH CYCLES EXIST IN THE SPIRIT WORLD AS WELL.

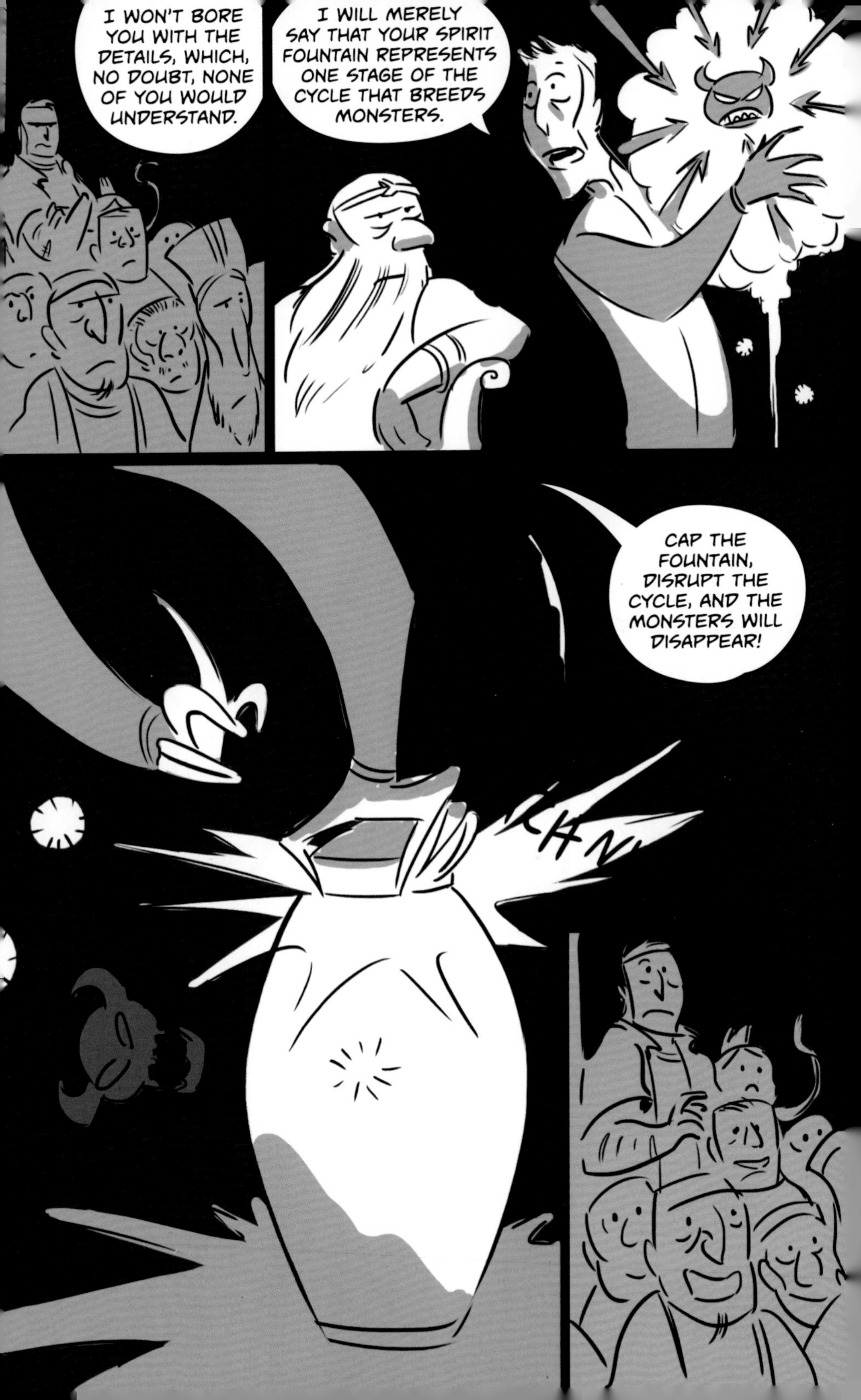
I WON'T BORE YOU WITH THE DETAILS, WHICH, NO DOUBT, NONE OF YOU WOULD UNDERSTAND.
I WILL MERELY SAY THAT YOUR SPIRIT FOUNTAIN REPRESENTS ONE STAGE OF THE CYCLE THAT BREEDS MONSTERS.
CAP THE FOUNTAIN, DISRUPT THE CYCLE, AND THE MONSTERS WILL DISAPPEAR!
KHN

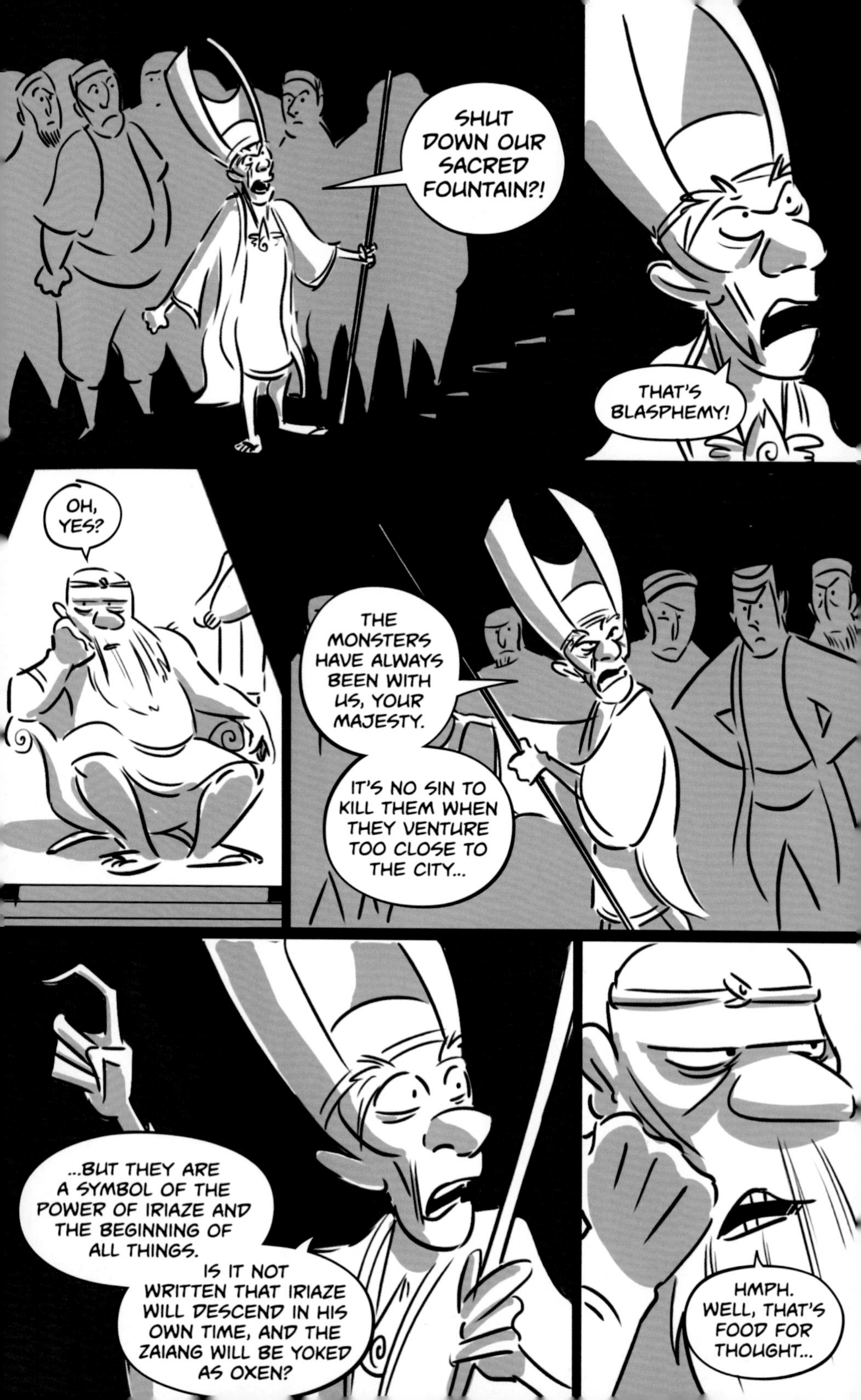
SHUT DOWN OUR SACRED FOUNTAIN?!
THAT'S BLASPHEMY!
OH, YES?
THE MONSTERS HAVE ALWAYS BEEN WITH US, YOUR MAJESTY.
IT'S NO SIN TO KILL THEM WHEN THEY VENTURE TOO CLOSE TO THE CITY...
...BUT THEY ARE A SYMBOL OF THE POWER OF IRIAZE AND THE BEGINNING OF ALL THINGS.
IS IT NOT WRITTEN THAT IRIAZE WILL DESCEND IN HIS OWN TIME, AND THE ZAIANG WILL BE YOKED AS OXEN?
HMPH. WELL, THAT'S FOOD FOR THOUGHT...

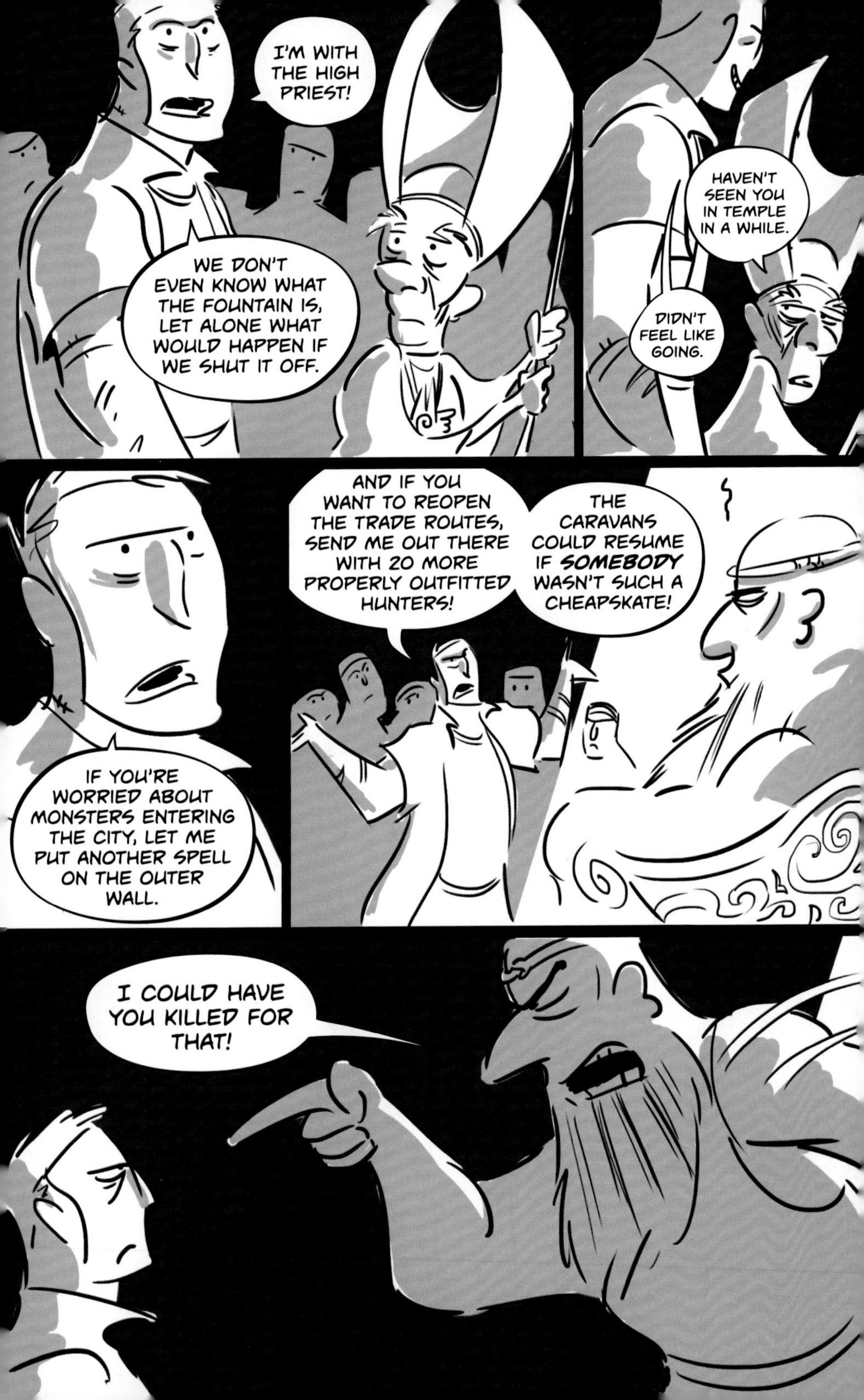

I'M WITH THE HIGH PRIEST!
WE DON'T EVEN KNOW WHAT THE FOUNTAIN IS, LET ALONE WHAT WOULD HAPPEN IF WE SHUT IT OFF.
HAVEN'T SEEN YOU IN TEMPLE IN A WHILE.
DIDN'T FEEL LIKE GOING.
IF YOU'RE WORRIED ABOUT MONSTERS ENTERING THE CITY, LET ME PUT ANOTHER SPELL ON THE OUTER WALL.
AND IF YOU WANT TO REOPEN THE TRADE ROUTES, SEND ME OUT THERE WITH 20 MORE PROPERLY OUTFITTED HUNTERS!
THE CARAVANS COULD RESUME IF SOMEBODY WASN'T SUCH A CHEAPSKATE!
I COULD HAVE YOU KILLED FOR THAT!

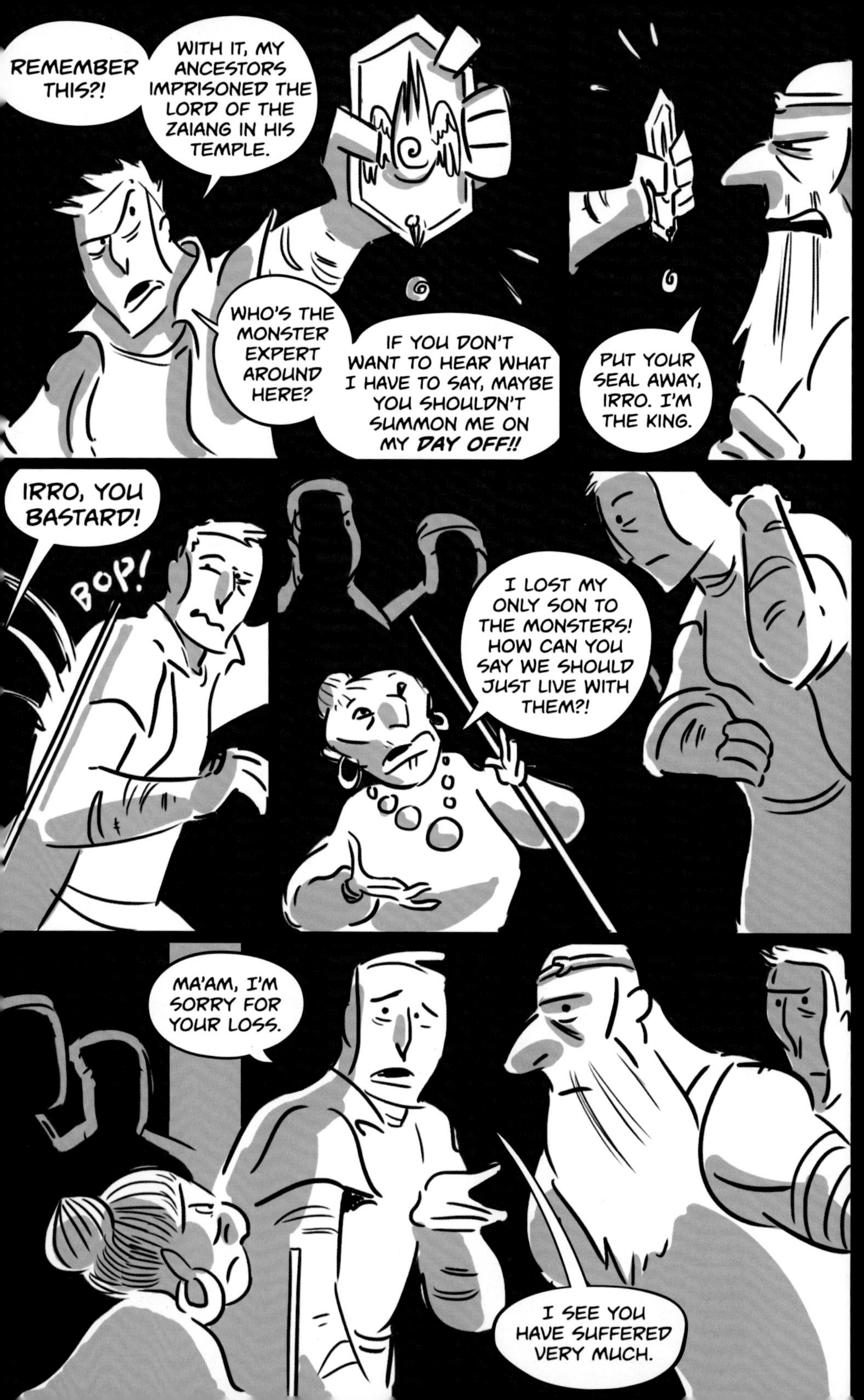
REMEMBER THIS?!
WITH IT, MY ANCESTORS IMPRISONED THE LORD OF THE ZAIANG IN HIS TEMPLE.
WHO'S THE MONSTER EXPERT AROUND HERE?
IF YOU DON'T WANT TO HEAR WHAT I HAVE TO SAY, MAYBE YOU SHOULDN'T SUMMON ME ON MY DAY OFF!!
PUT YOUR SEAL AWAY, IRRO. I'M THE KING.
IRRO, YOU BASTARD!
BOP!
I LOST MY ONLY SON TO THE MONSTERS! HOW CAN YOU SAY WE SHOULD JUST LIVE WITH THEM?!
MA'AM, I'M SORRY FOR YOUR LOSS.
I SEE YOU HAVE SUFFERED VERY MUCH.

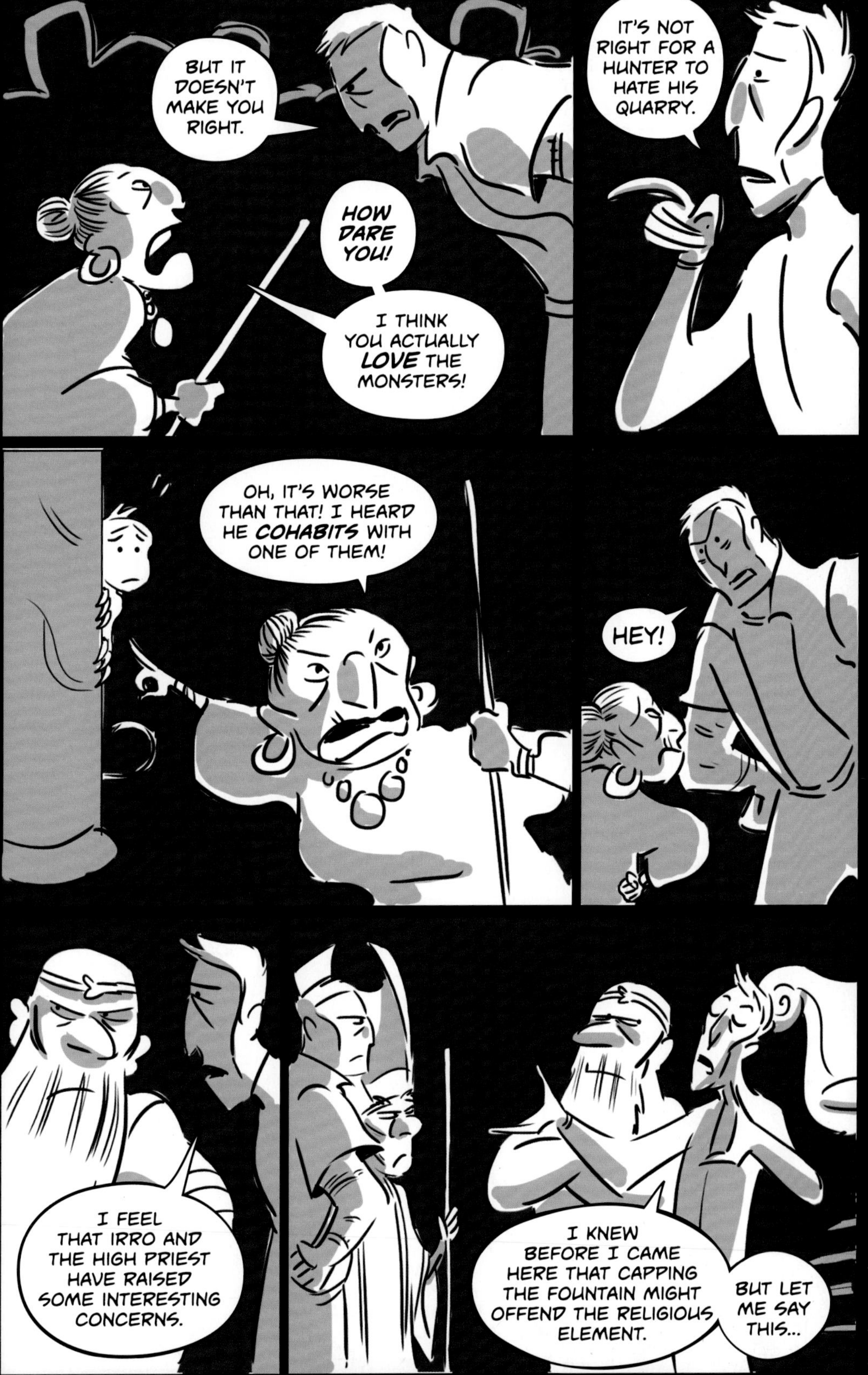
BUT IT DOESN'T MAKE YOU RIGHT.
HOW DARE YOU!
I THINK YOU ACTUALLY LOVE THE MONSTERS!
IT'S NOT RIGHT FOR A HUNTER TO HATE HIS QUARRY.
OH, IT'S WORSE THAN THAT! I HEARD HE COHABITS WITH ONE OF THEM!
HEY!
I FEEL THAT IRRO AND THE HIGH PRIEST HAVE RAISED SOME INTERESTING CONCERNS.
I KNEW BEFORE I CAME HERE THAT CAPPING THE FOUNTAIN MIGHT OFFEND THE RELIGIOUS ELEMENT.
BUT LET ME SAY THIS...

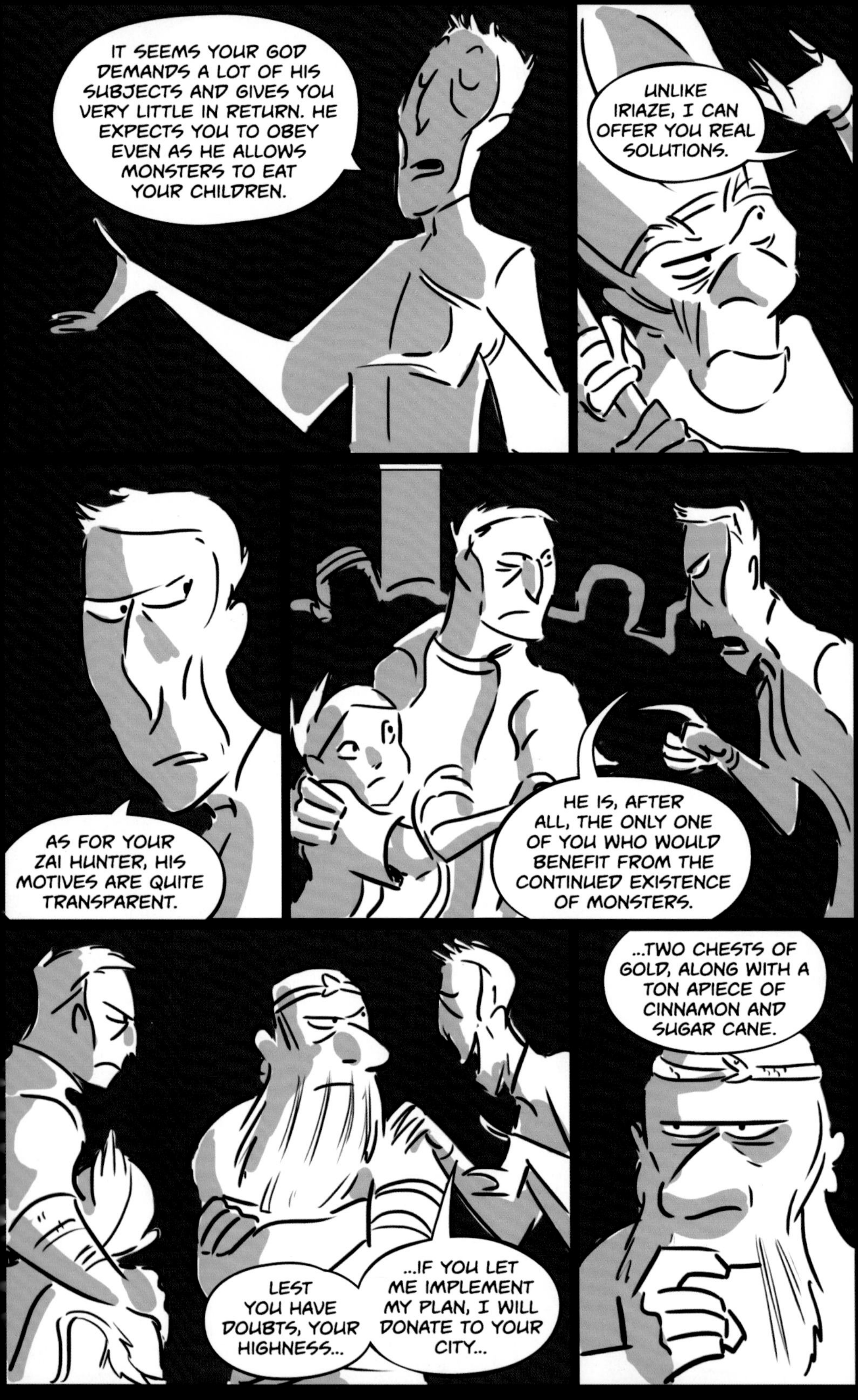
IT SEEMS YOUR GOD DEMANDS A LOT OF HIS SUBJECTS AND GIVES YOU VERY LITTLE IN RETURN. HE EXPECTS YOU TO OBEY EVEN AS HE ALLOWS MONSTERS TO EAT YOUR CHILDREN.
UNLIKE IRIAZE, I CAN OFFER YOU REAL SOLUTIONS.
AS FOR YOUR ZAI HUNTER, HIS MOTIVES ARE QUITE TRANSPARENT.
HE IS, AFTER ALL, THE ONLY ONE OF YOU WHO WOULD BENEFIT FROM THE CONTINUED EXISTENCE OF MONSTERS.
LEST YOU HAVE DOUBTS, YOUR HIGHNESS...
...IF YOU LET ME IMPLEMENT MY PLAN, I WILL DONATE TO YOUR CITY...
...TWO CHESTS OF GOLD, ALONG WITH A TON APIECE OF CINNAMON AND SUGAR CANE.

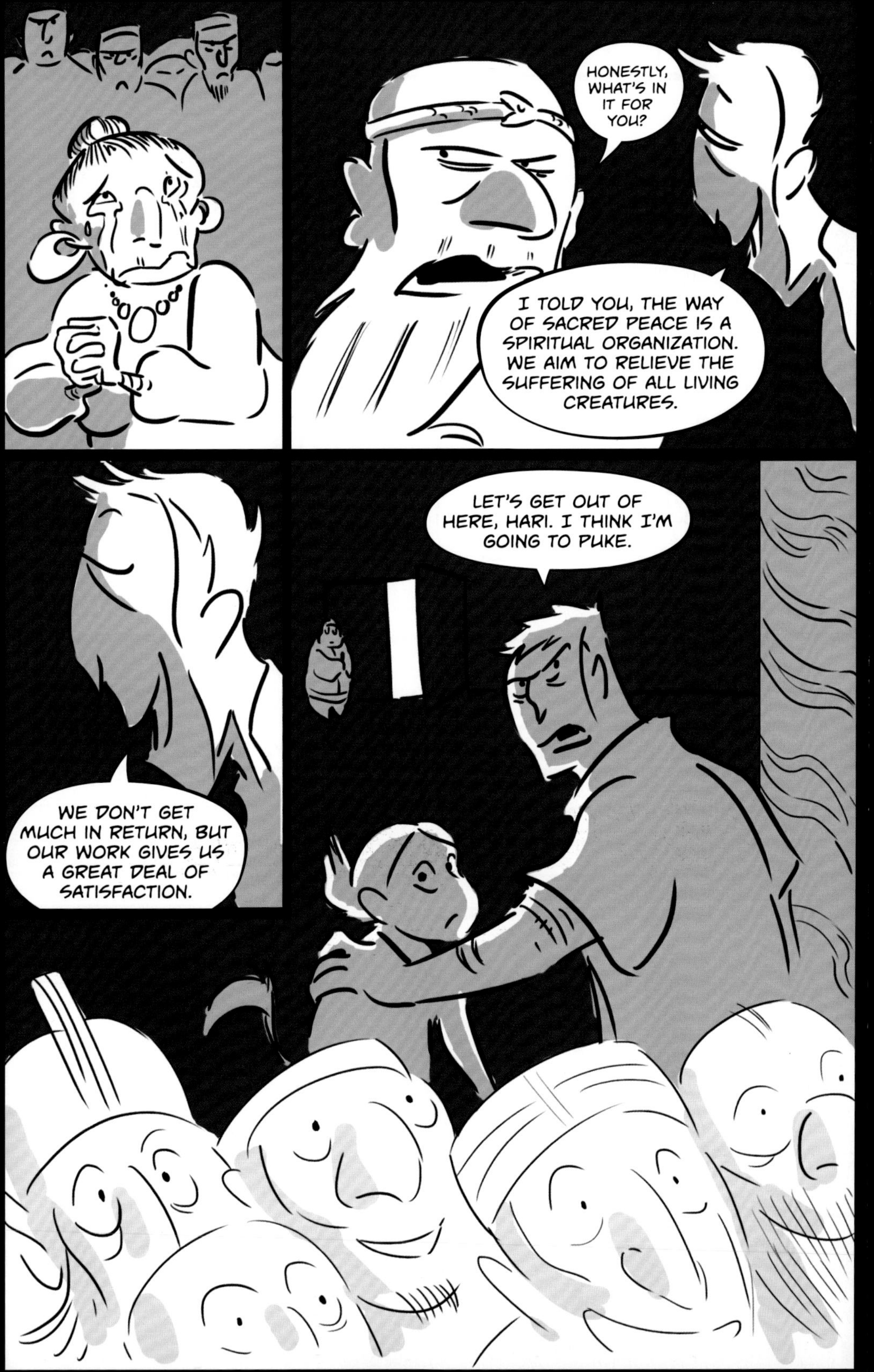
HONESTLY, WHAT'S IN IT FOR YOU?
I TOLD YOU, THE WAY OF SACRED PEACE IS A SPIRITUAL ORGANIZATION. WE AIM TO RELIEVE THE SUFFERING OF ALL LIVING CREATURES.
WE DON'T GET MUCH IN RETURN, BUT OUR WORK GIVES US A GREAT DEAL OF SATISFACTION.
LET'S GET OUT OF HERE, HARI. I THINK I'M GOING TO PUKE.

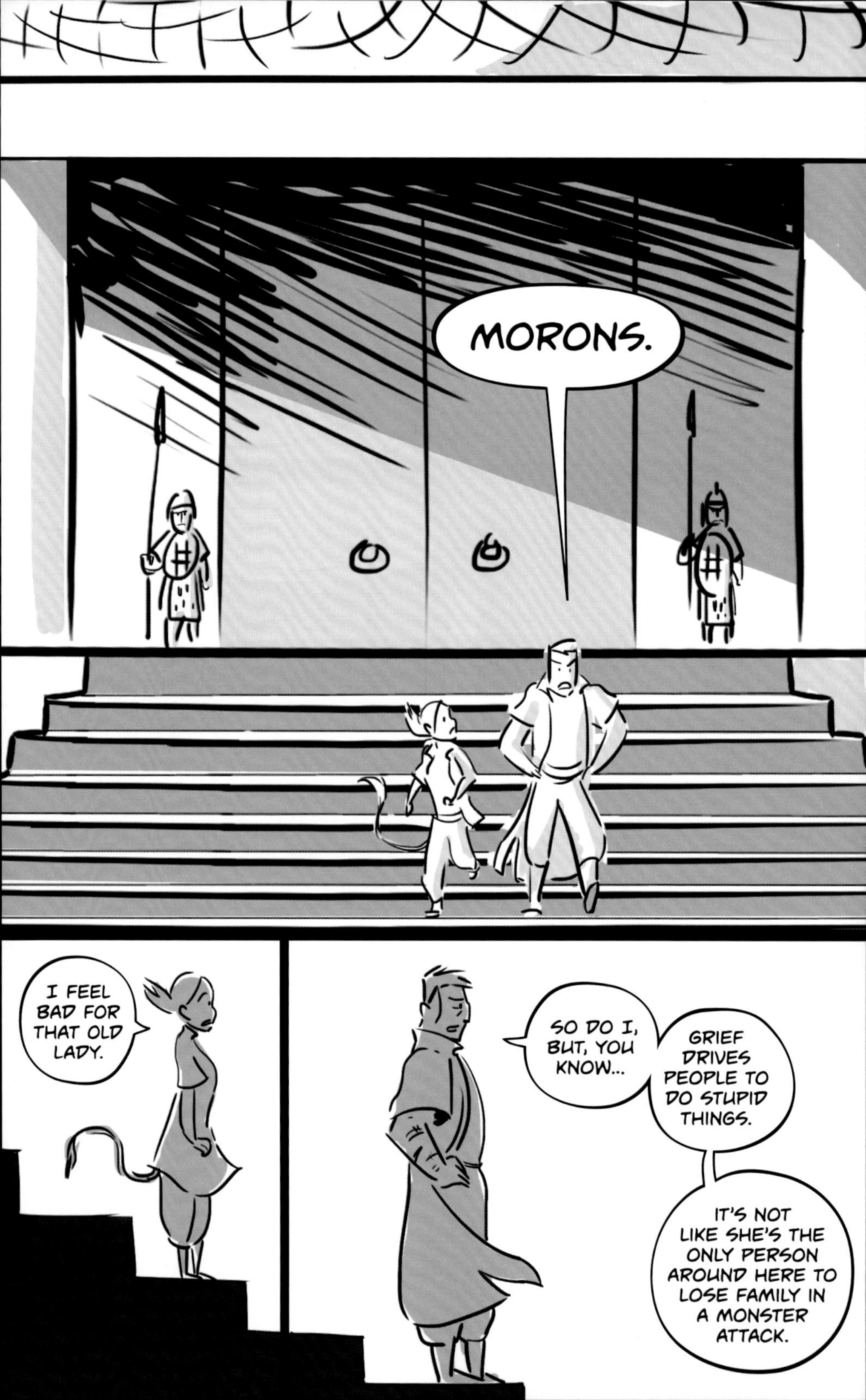
MORONS.
I FEEL BAD FOR THAT OLD LADY.
SO DO I, BUT, YOU KNOW...
GRIEF DRIVES PEOPLE TO DO STUPID THINGS.
IT'S NOT LIKE SHE'S THE ONLY PERSON AROUND HERE TO LOSE FAMILY IN A MONSTER ATTACK.

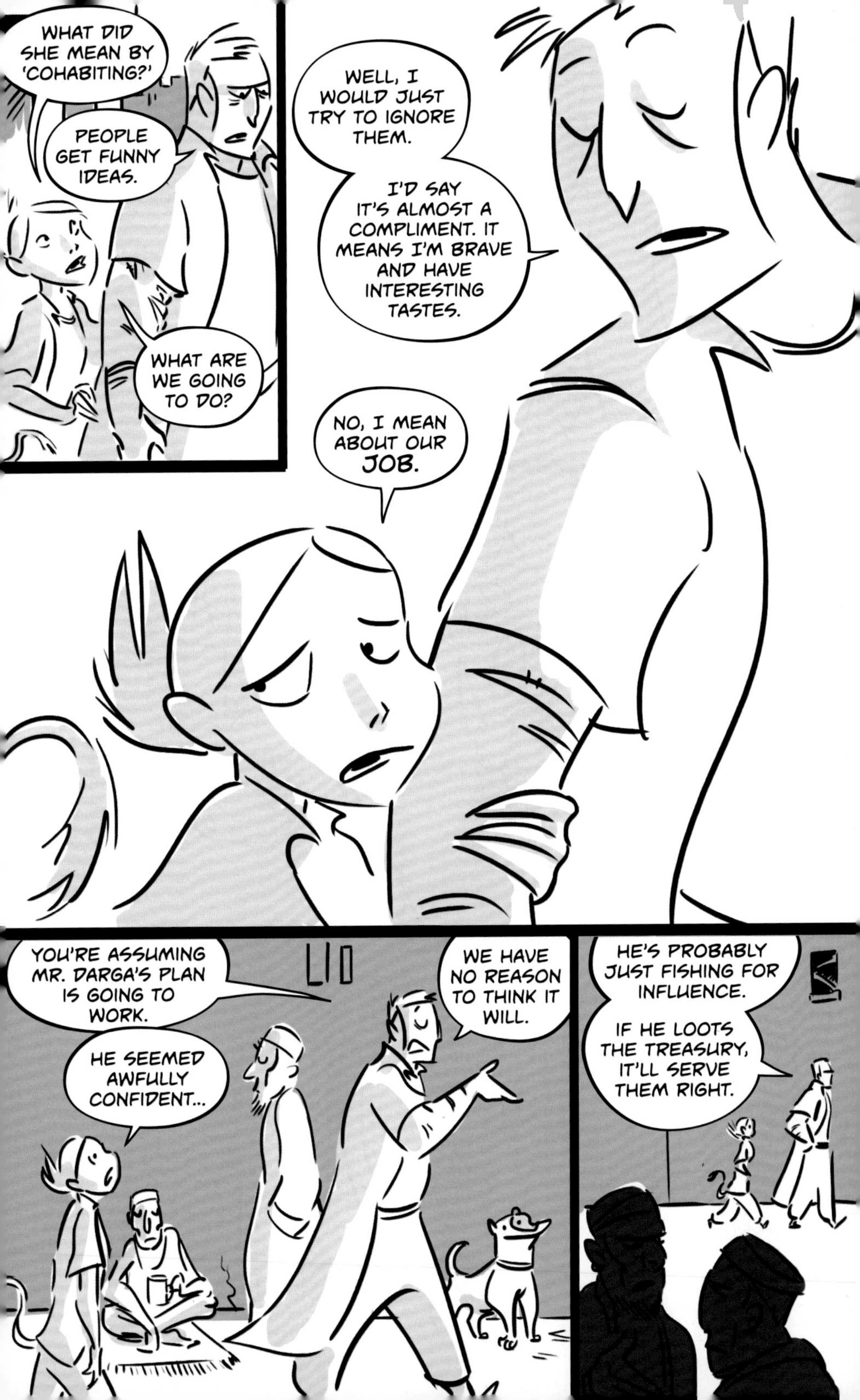
WHAT DID SHE MEAN BY 'COHABITING?'
PEOPLE GET FUNNY IDEAS.
WELL, I WOULD JUST TRY TO IGNORE THEM.
I'D SAY IT'S ALMOST A COMPLIMENT. IT MEANS I'M BRAVE AND HAVE INTERESTING TASTES.
WHAT ARE WE GOING TO DO?
NO, I MEAN ABOUT OUR JOB.
YOU'RE ASSUMING MR. DARGA'S PLAN IS GOING TO WORK.
HE SEEMED AWFULLY CONFIDENT...
WE HAVE NO REASON TO THINK IT WILL.
HE'S PROBABLY JUST FISHING FOR INFLUENCE.
IF HE LOOTS THE TREASURY, IT'LL SERVE THEM RIGHT.

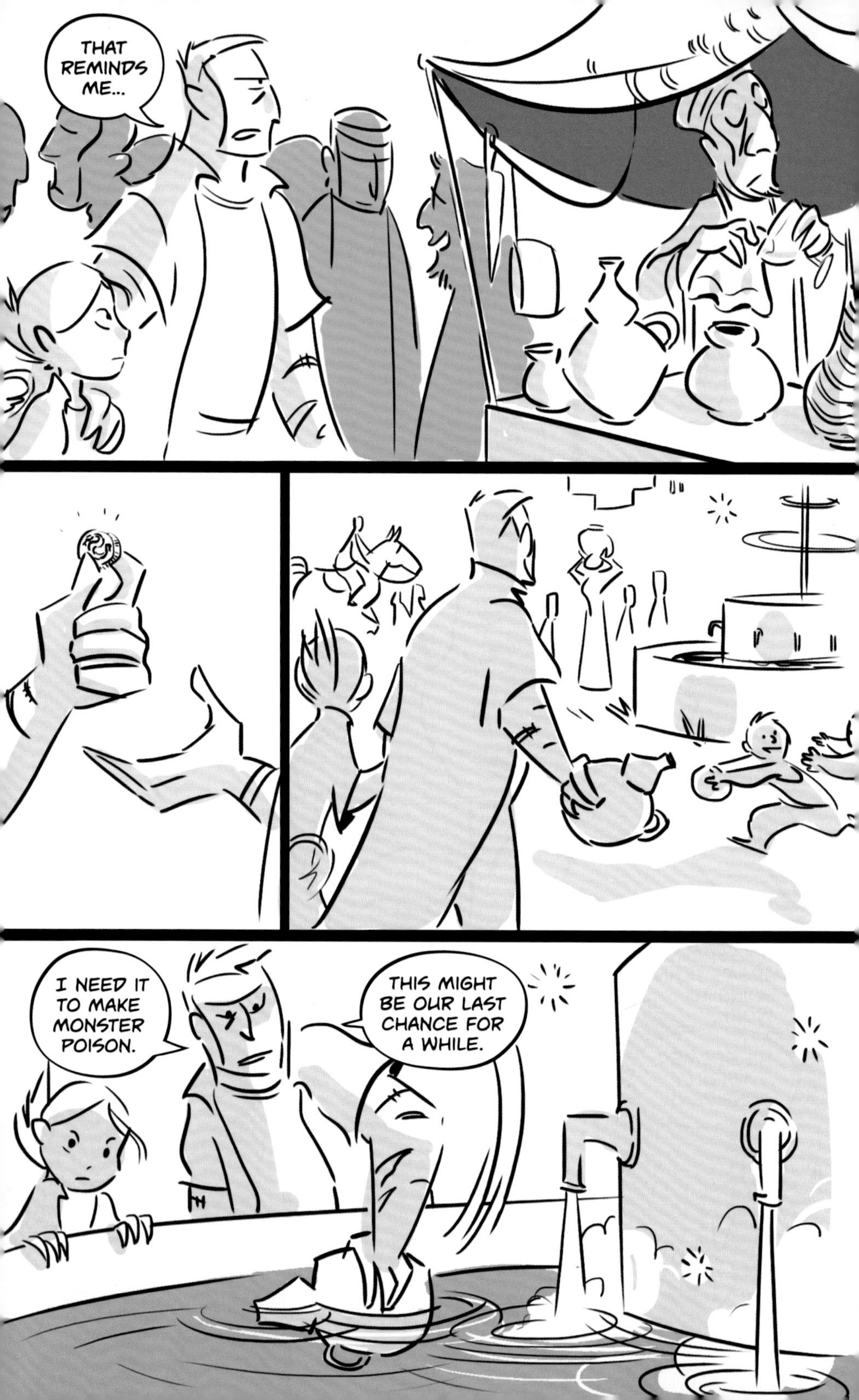
THAT REMINDS ME...
I NEED IT TO MAKE MONSTER POISON.
THIS MIGHT BE OUR LAST CHANCE FOR A WHILE.

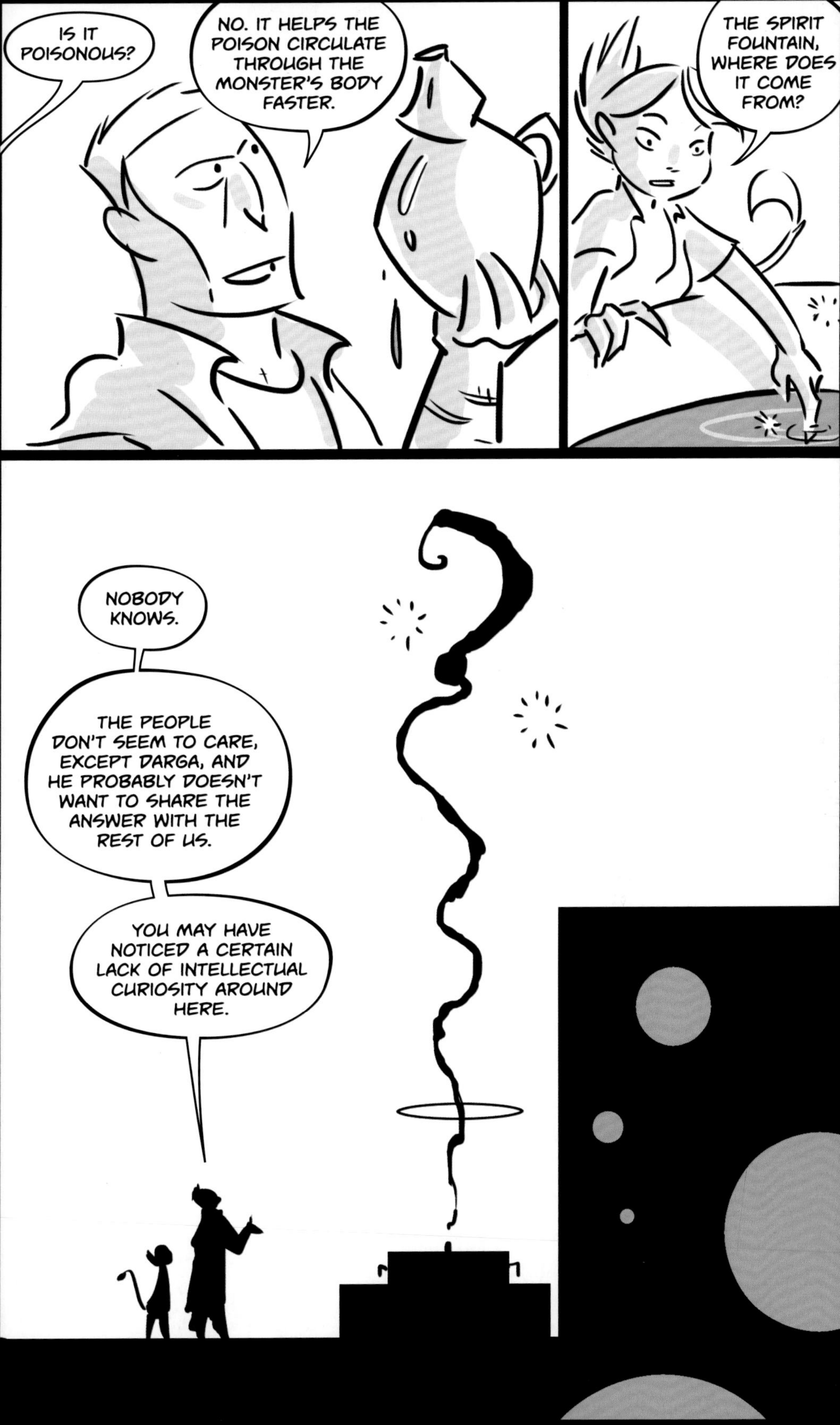
IS IT POISONOUS?
NO. IT HELPS THE POISON CIRCULATE THROUGH THE MONSTER'S BODY FASTER.
THE SPIRIT FOUNTAIN, WHERE DOES IT COME FROM?
NOBODY KNOWS.
THE PEOPLE DON'T SEEM TO CARE, EXCEPT DARGA, AND HE PROBABLY DOESN'T WANT TO SHARE THE ANSWER WITH THE REST OF US.
YOU MAY HAVE NOTICED A CERTAIN LACK OF INTELLECTUAL CURIOSITY AROUND HERE.

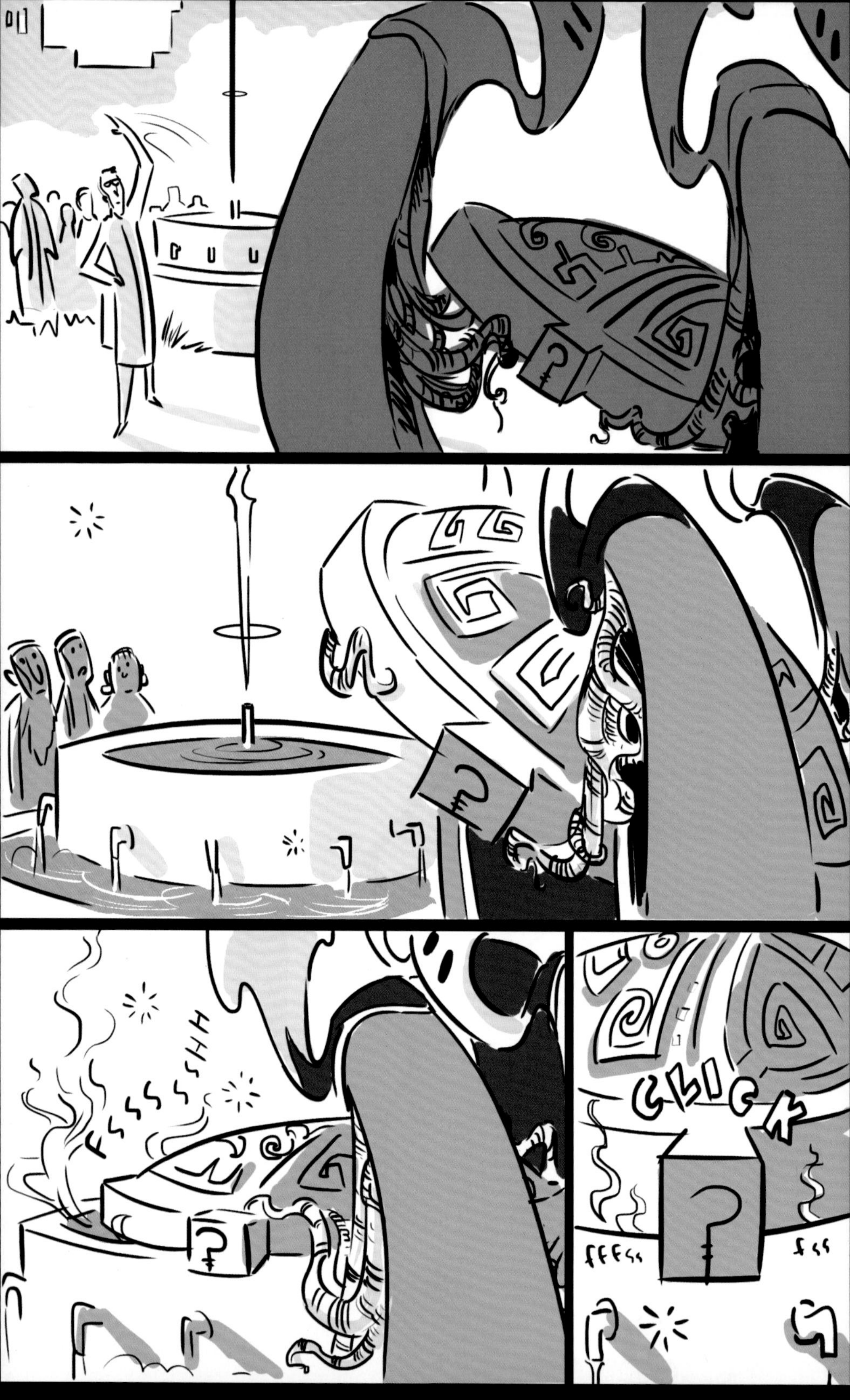
FSSSSSSHH
CLICK
FFFSS
FSS

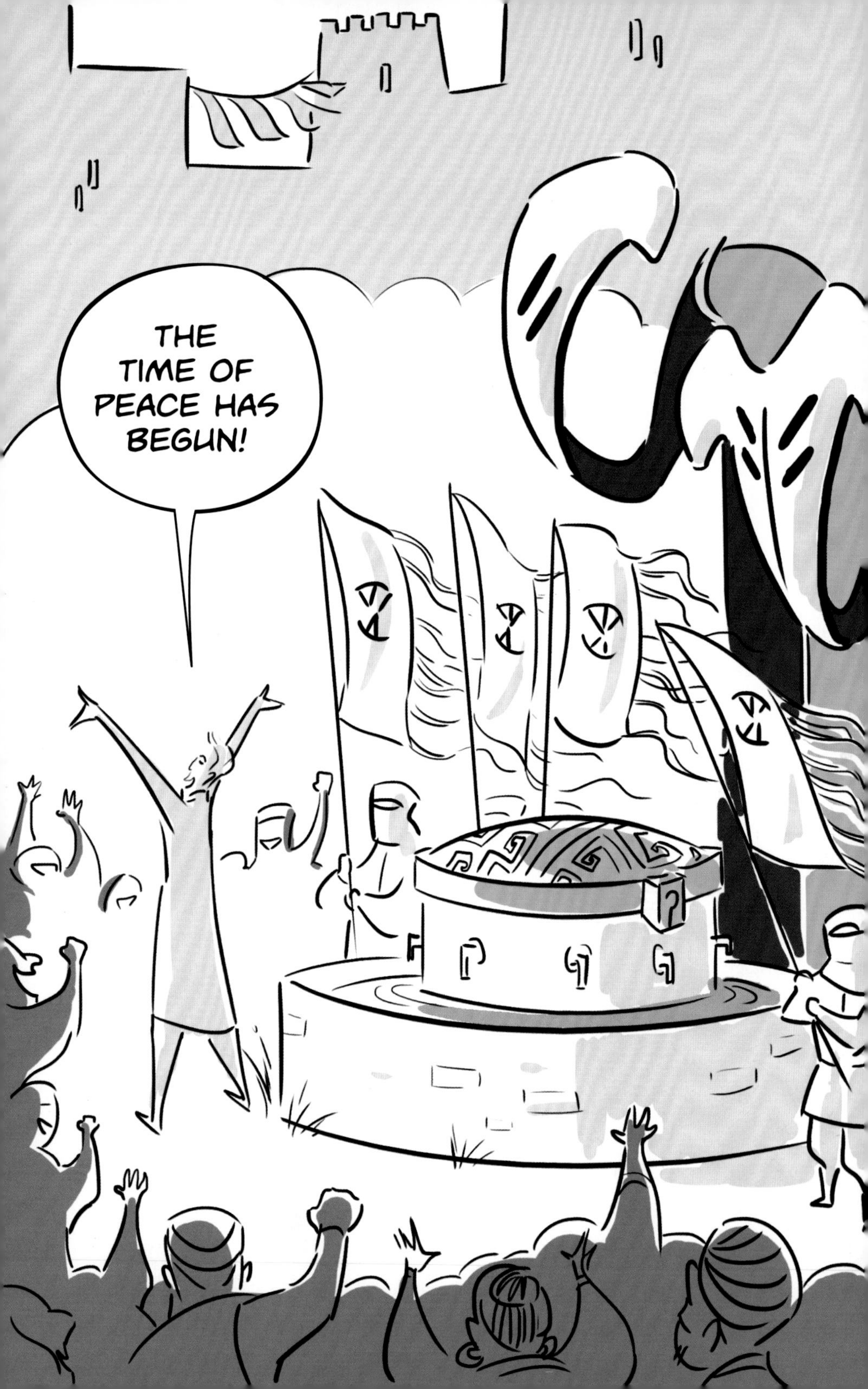
THE TIME OF PEACE HAS BEGUN!

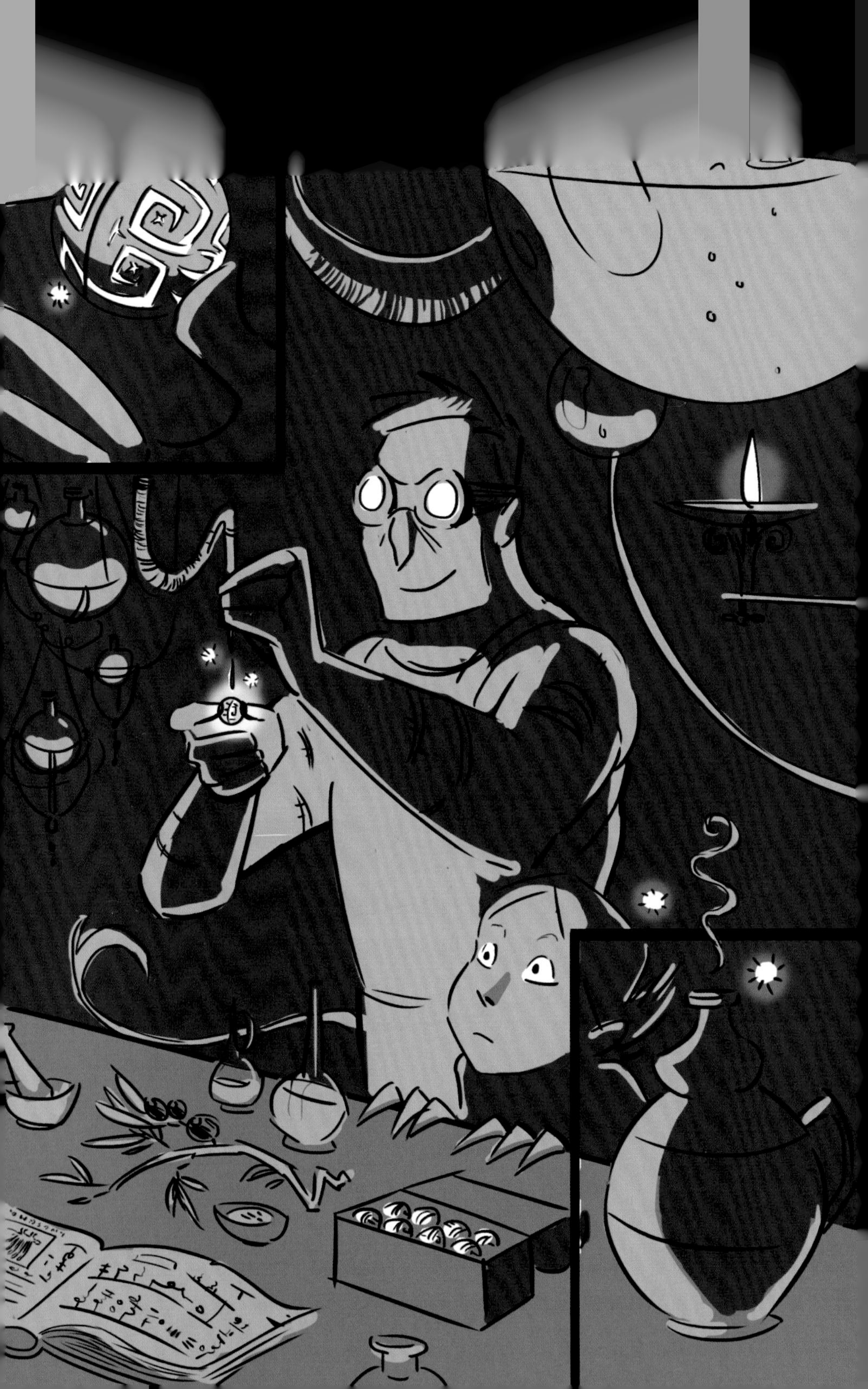

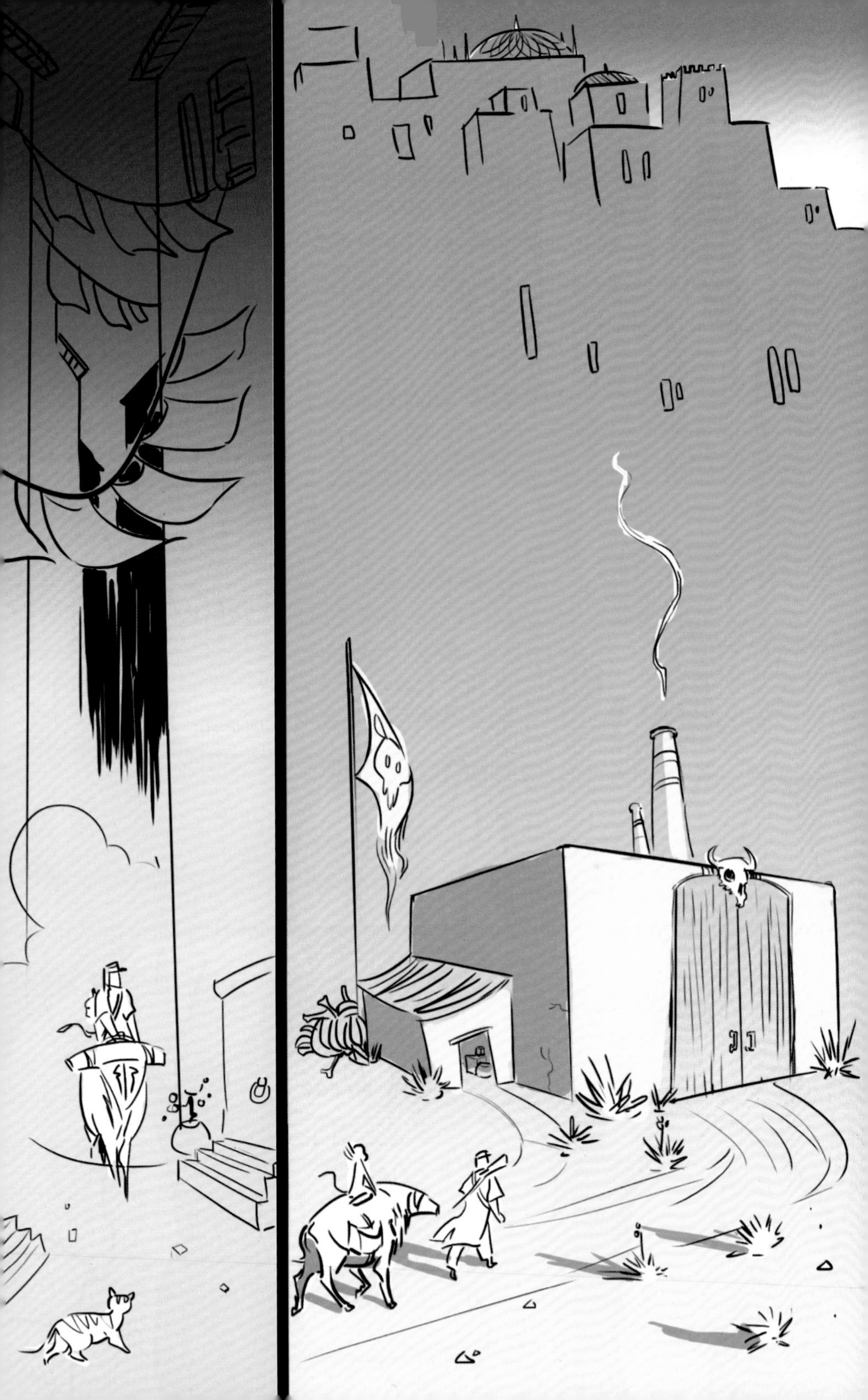

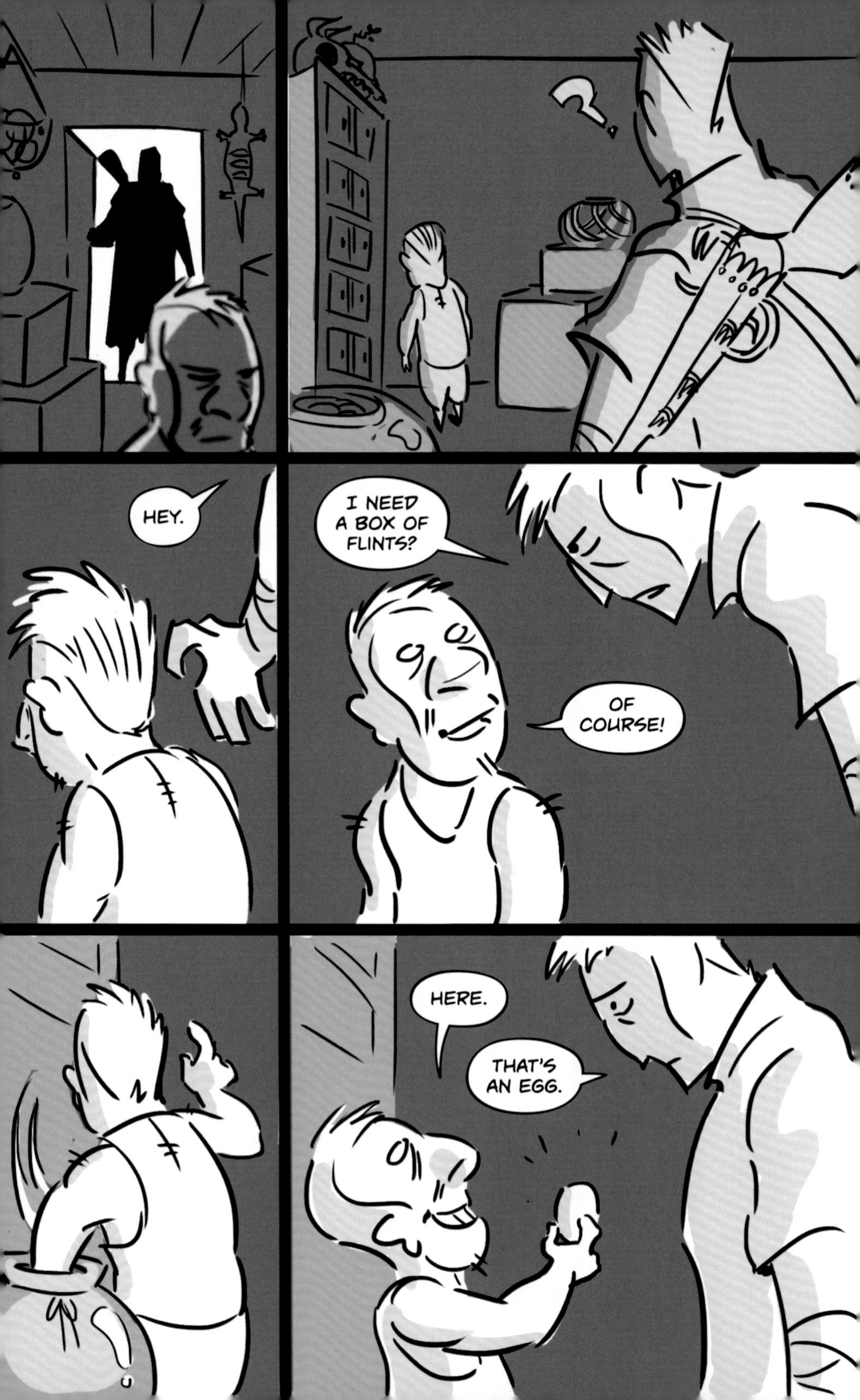
?
HEY.
I NEED A BOX OF FLINTS?
OF COURSE!
HERE.
THAT'S AN EGG.

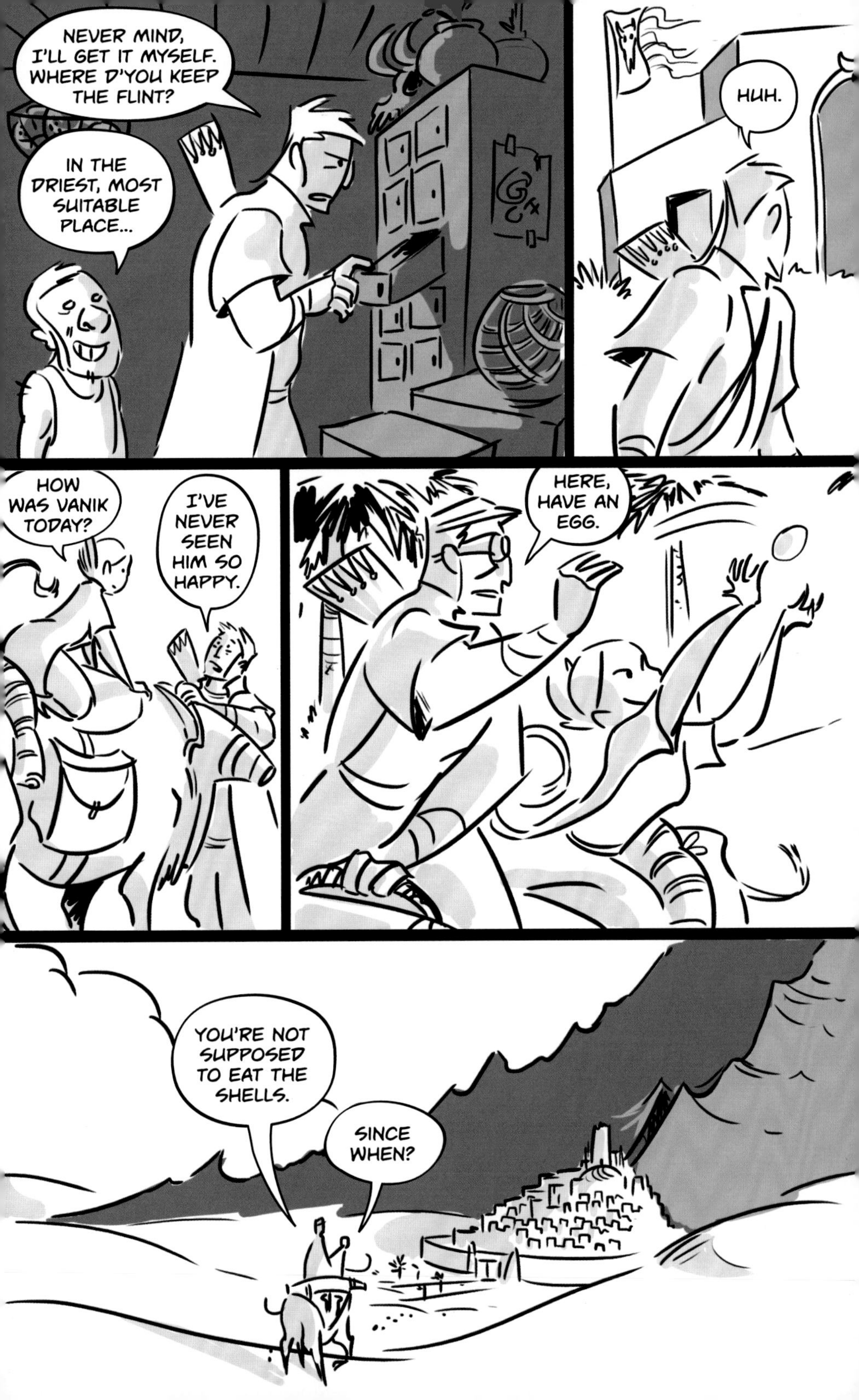
NEVER MIND, I'LL GET IT MYSELF. WHERE D'YOU KEEP THE FLINT?
IN THE DRIEST, MOST SUITABLE PLACE...
HUH.
HOW WAS VANIK TODAY?
I'VE NEVER SEEN HIM SO HAPPY.
HERE, HAVE AN EGG.
YOU'RE NOT SUPPOSED TO EAT THE SHELLS.
SINCE WHEN?

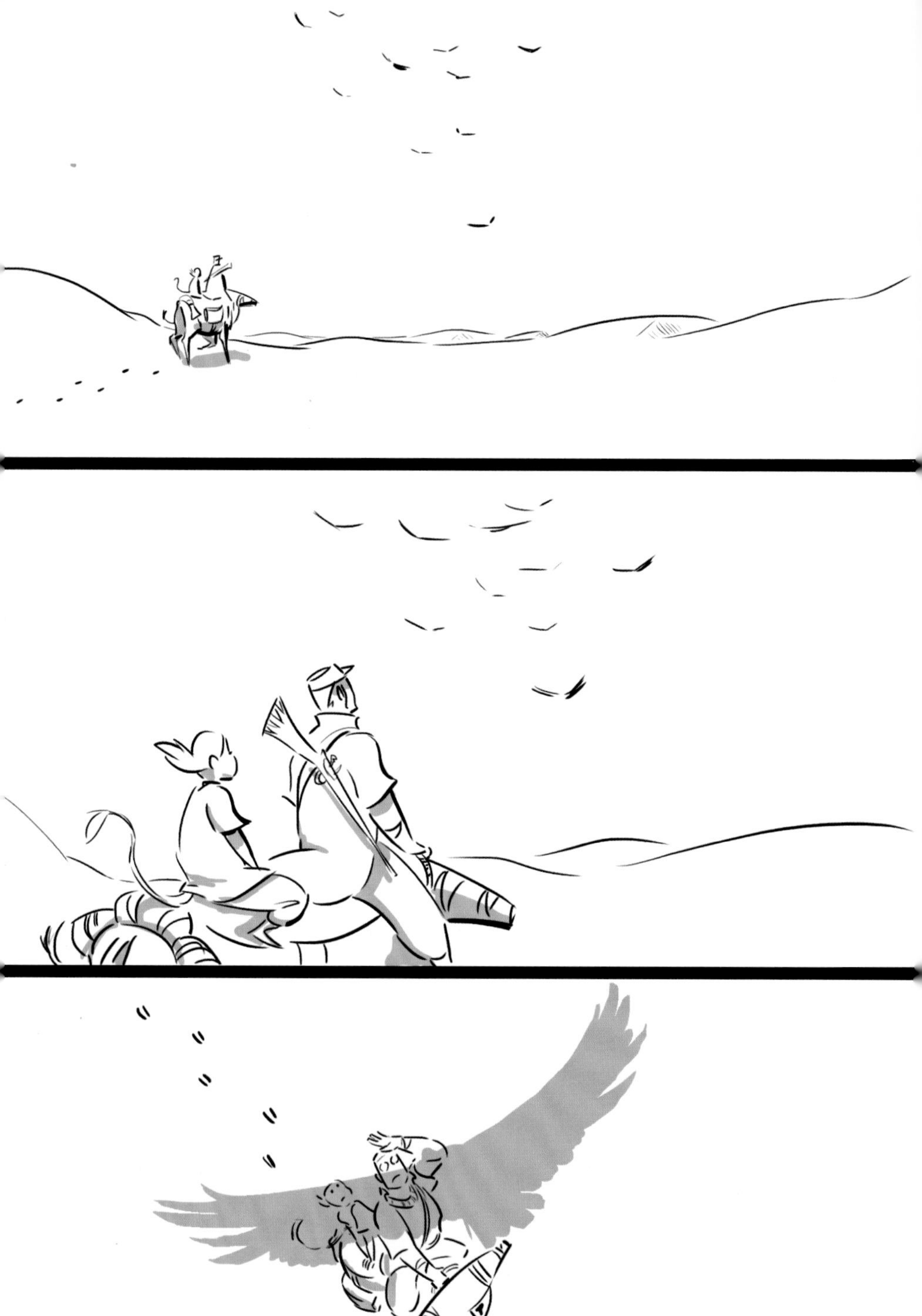

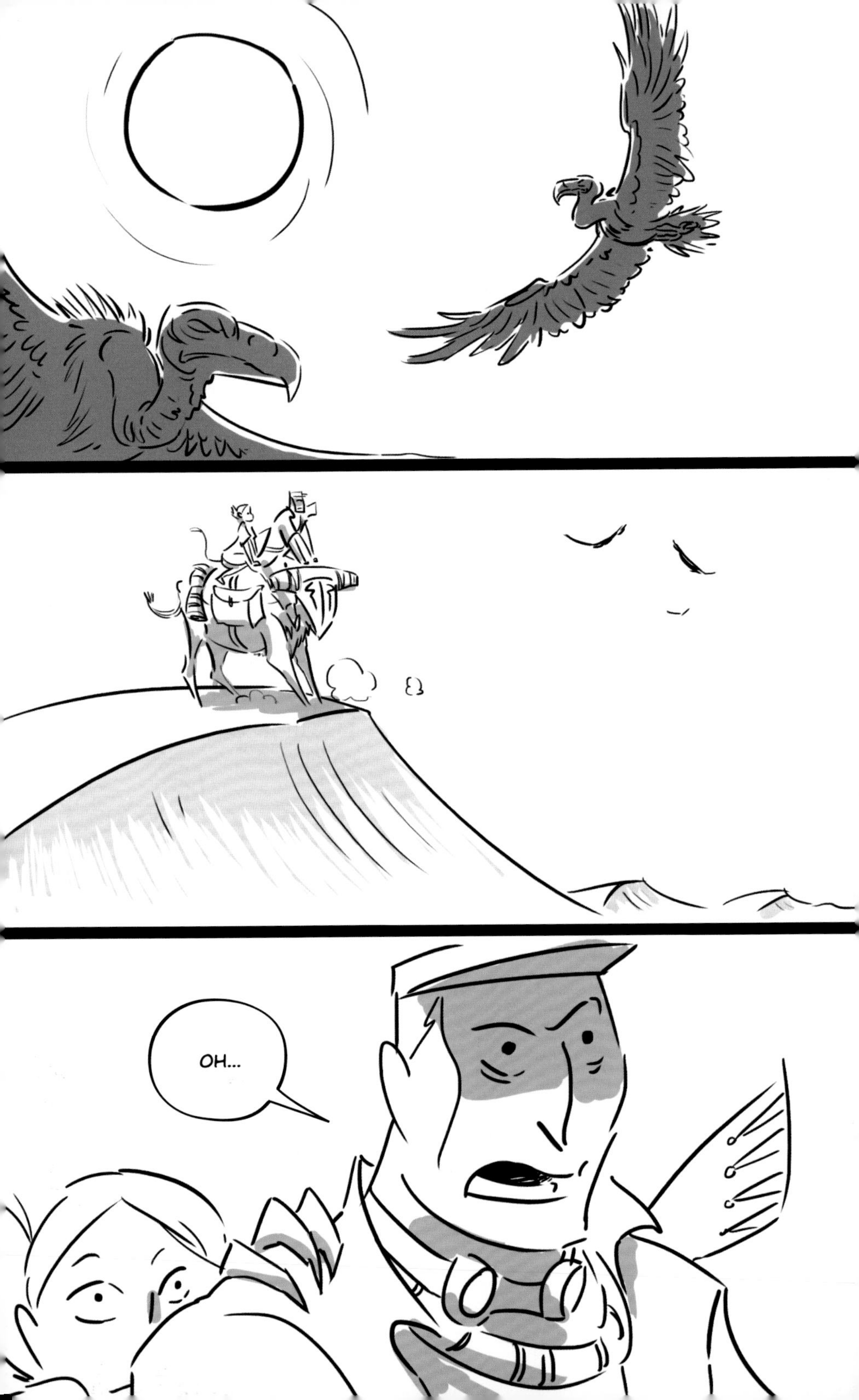
OH...

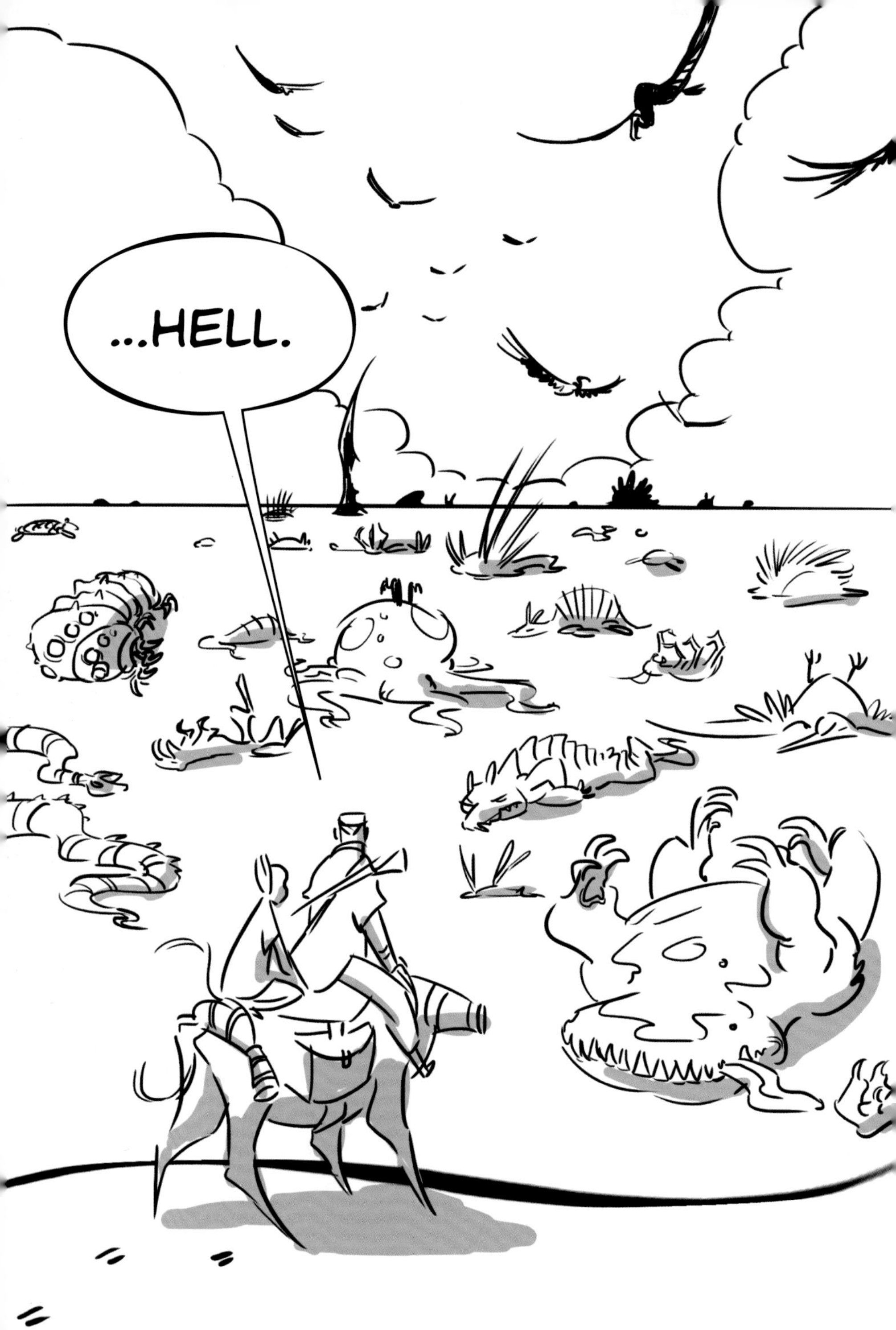
...HELL.

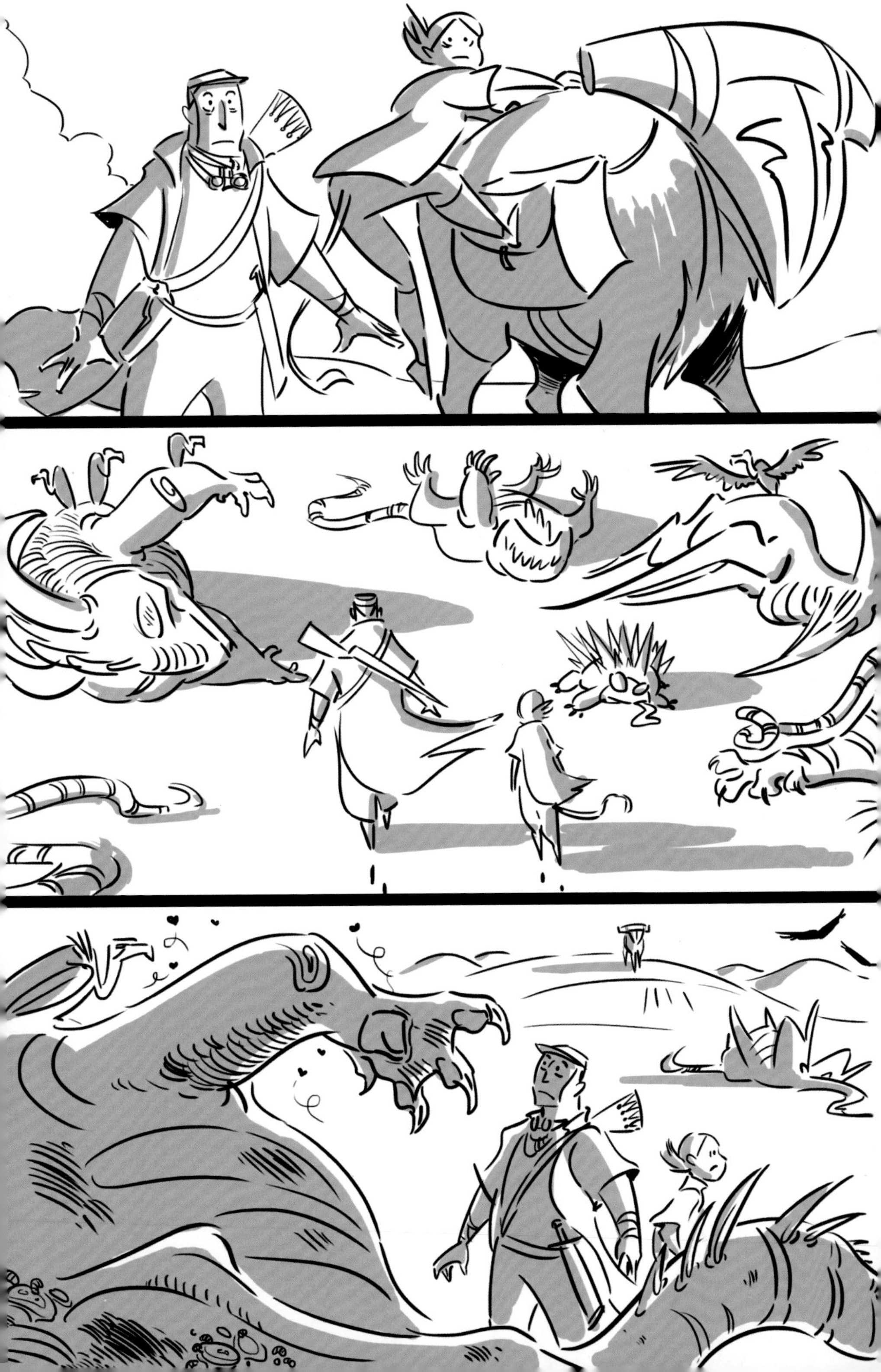

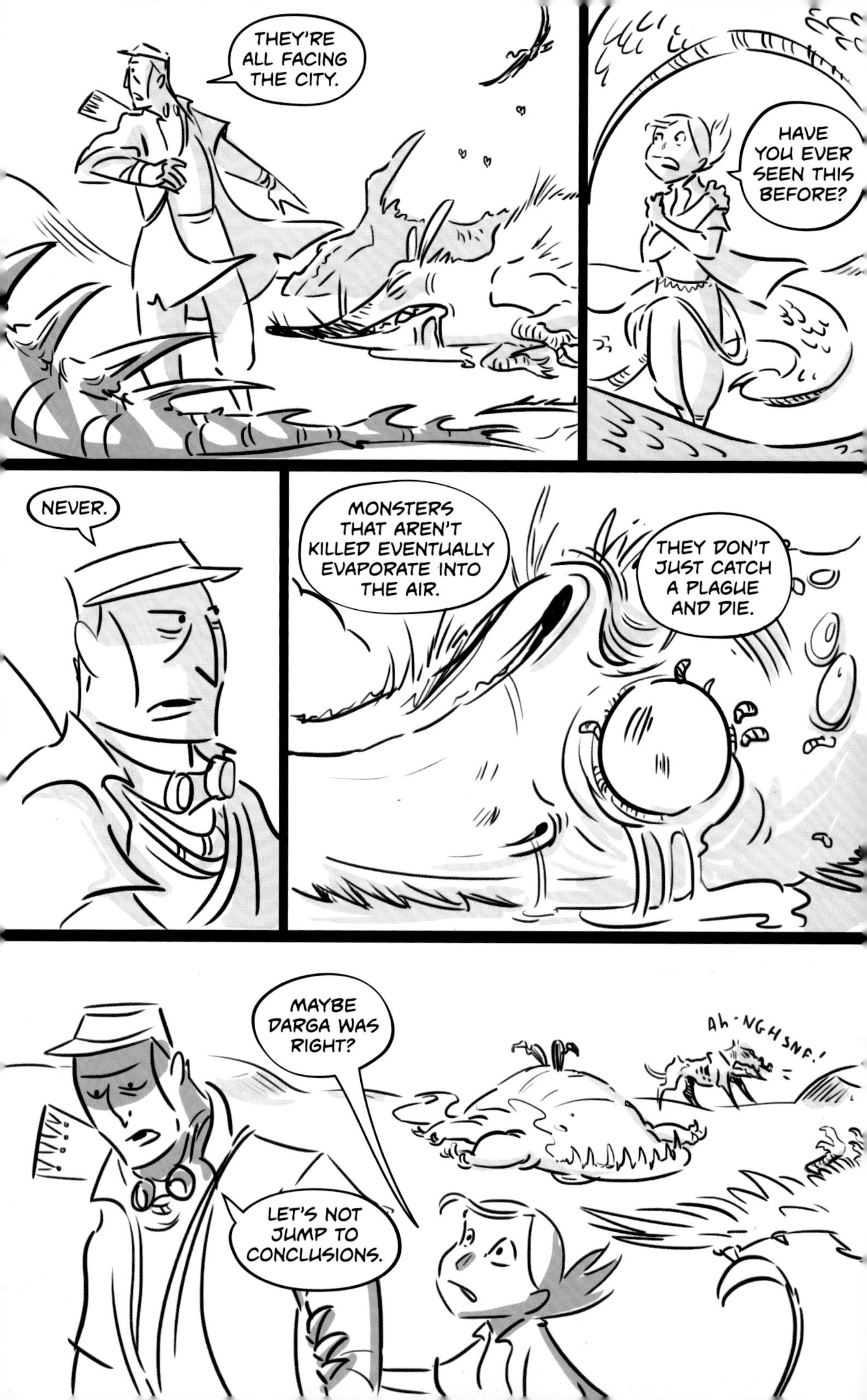
THEY'RE ALL FACING THE CITY.
HAVE YOU EVER SEEN THIS BEFORE?
NEVER.
MONSTERS THAT AREN'T KILLED EVENTUALLY EVAPORATE INTO THE AIR.
THEY DON'T JUST CATCH A PLAGUE AND DIE.
MAYBE DARGA WAS RIGHT?
AH-NGHSNF!
LET'S NOT JUMP TO CONCLUSIONS.

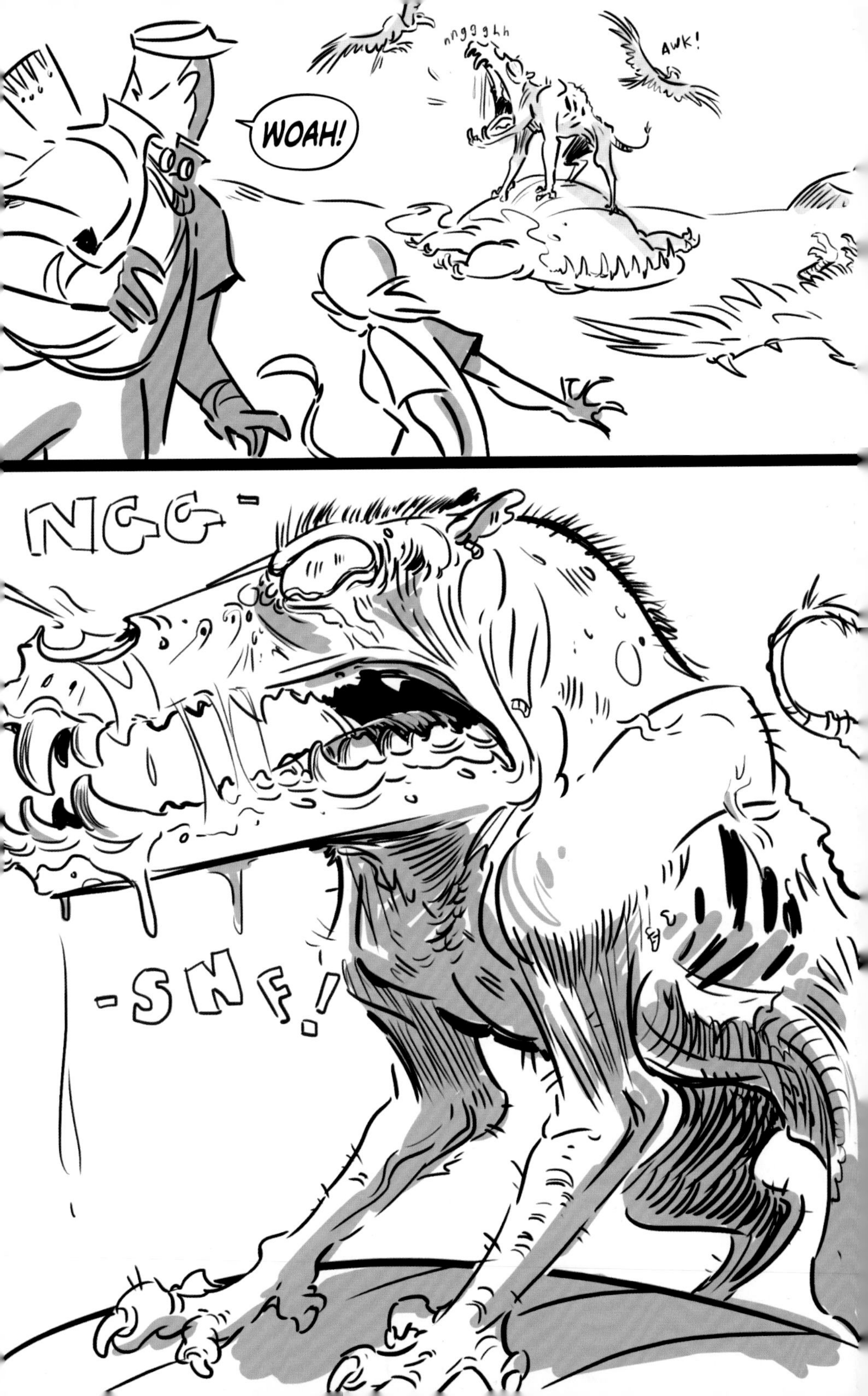
WOAH!
nngggghh
AWK!
NGG-
-SNF!

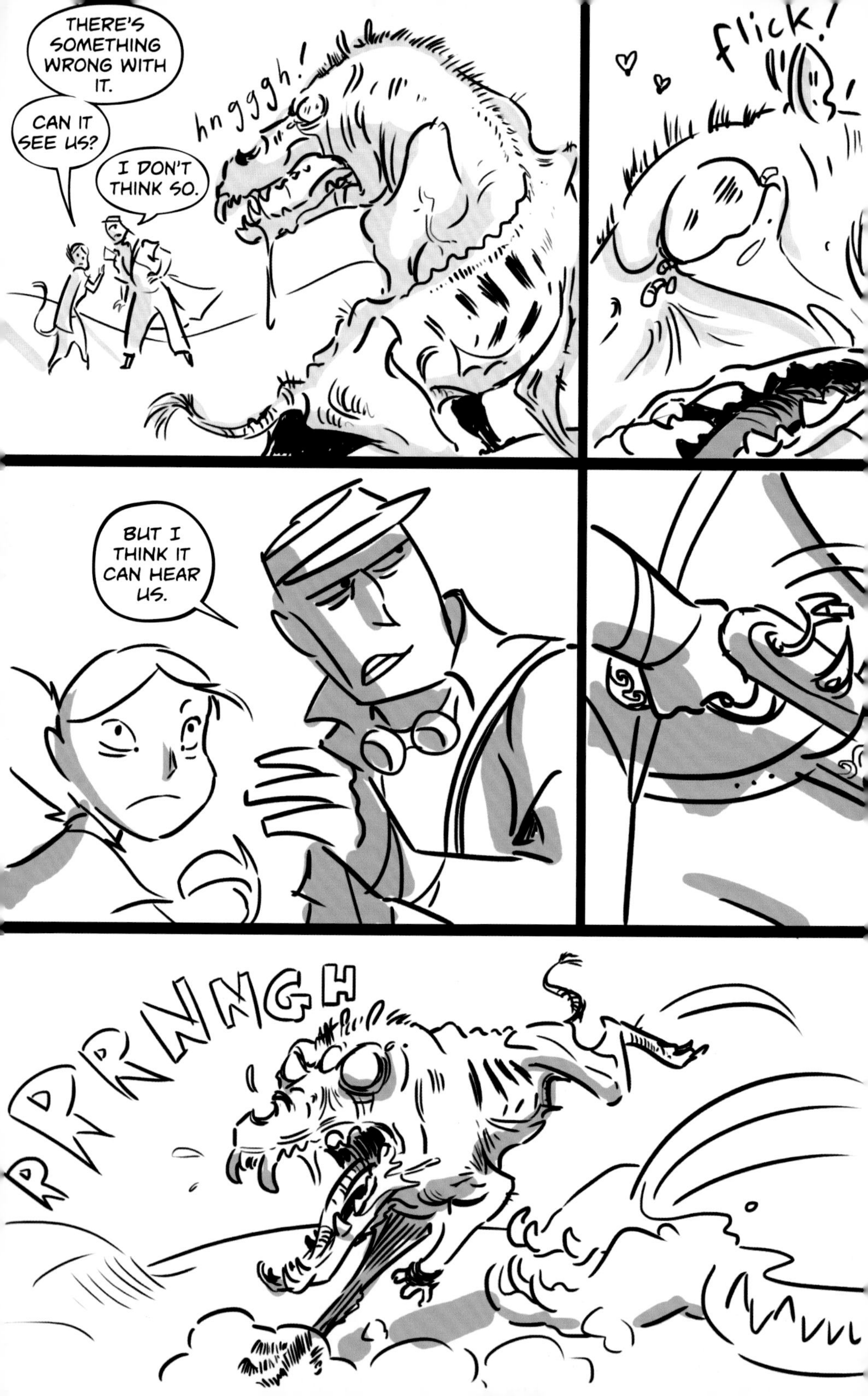
THERE'S SOMETHING WRONG WITH IT.
CAN IT SEE US?
I DON'T THINK SO.
hngggh!
flick!
BUT I THINK IT CAN HEAR US.
RRRNNGH

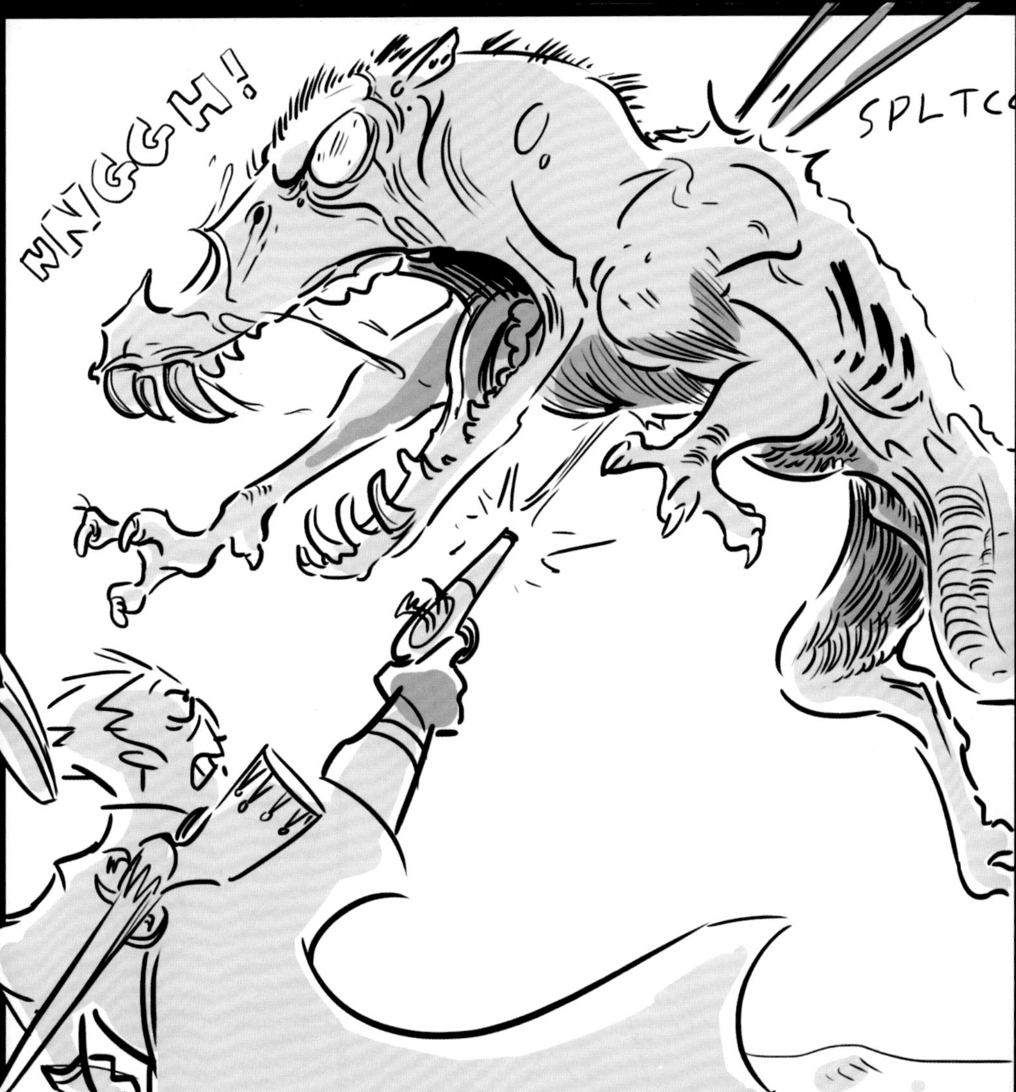
NNGGH!
SPLTCC
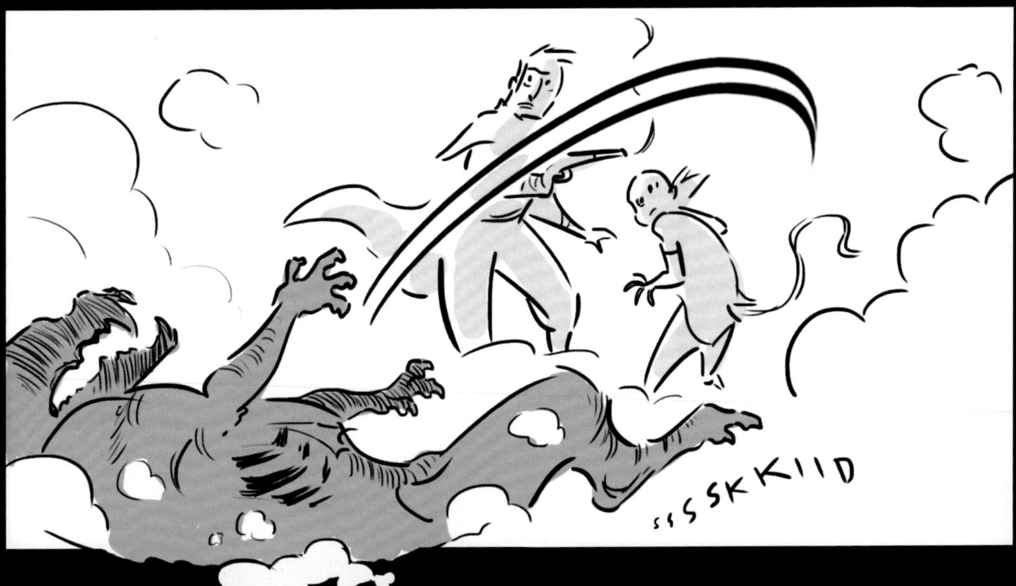
sssSKKIID

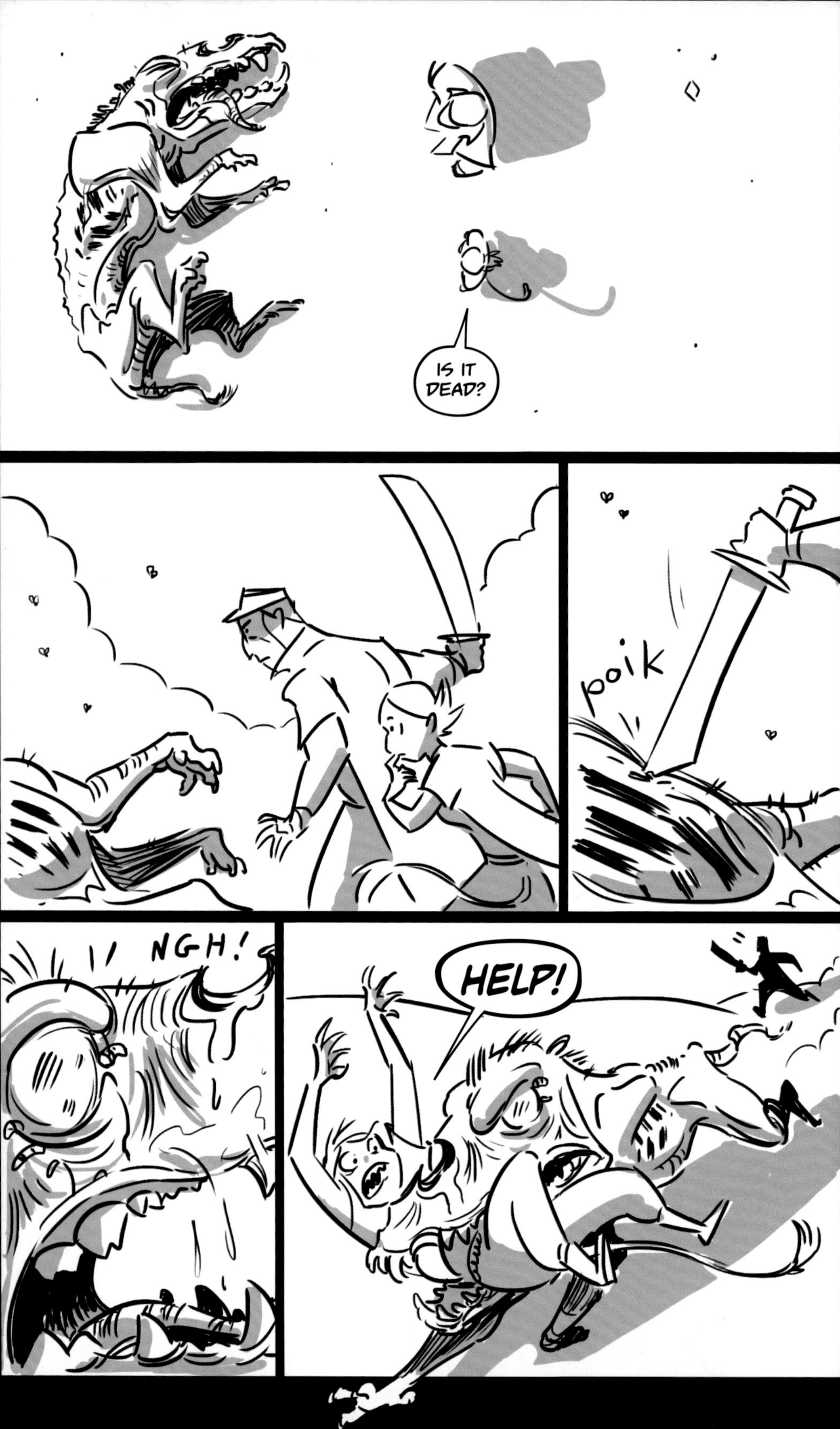
IS IT DEAD?
poik
NGH!
HELP!

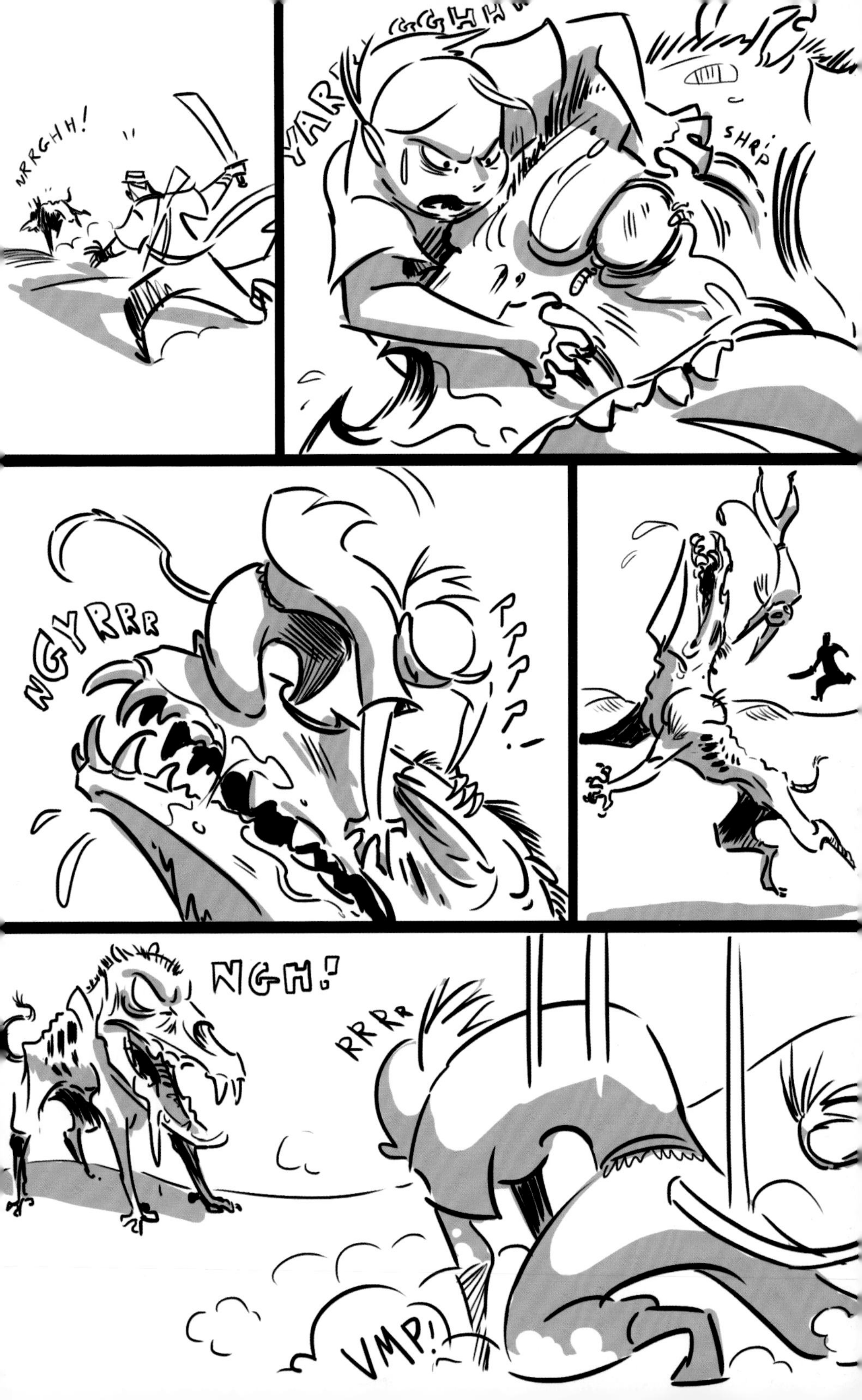
NRRGHH!
YAR!
GGHH
SHRP
NGYRRR
RRRR!
NGH!
RRRR
VMP!

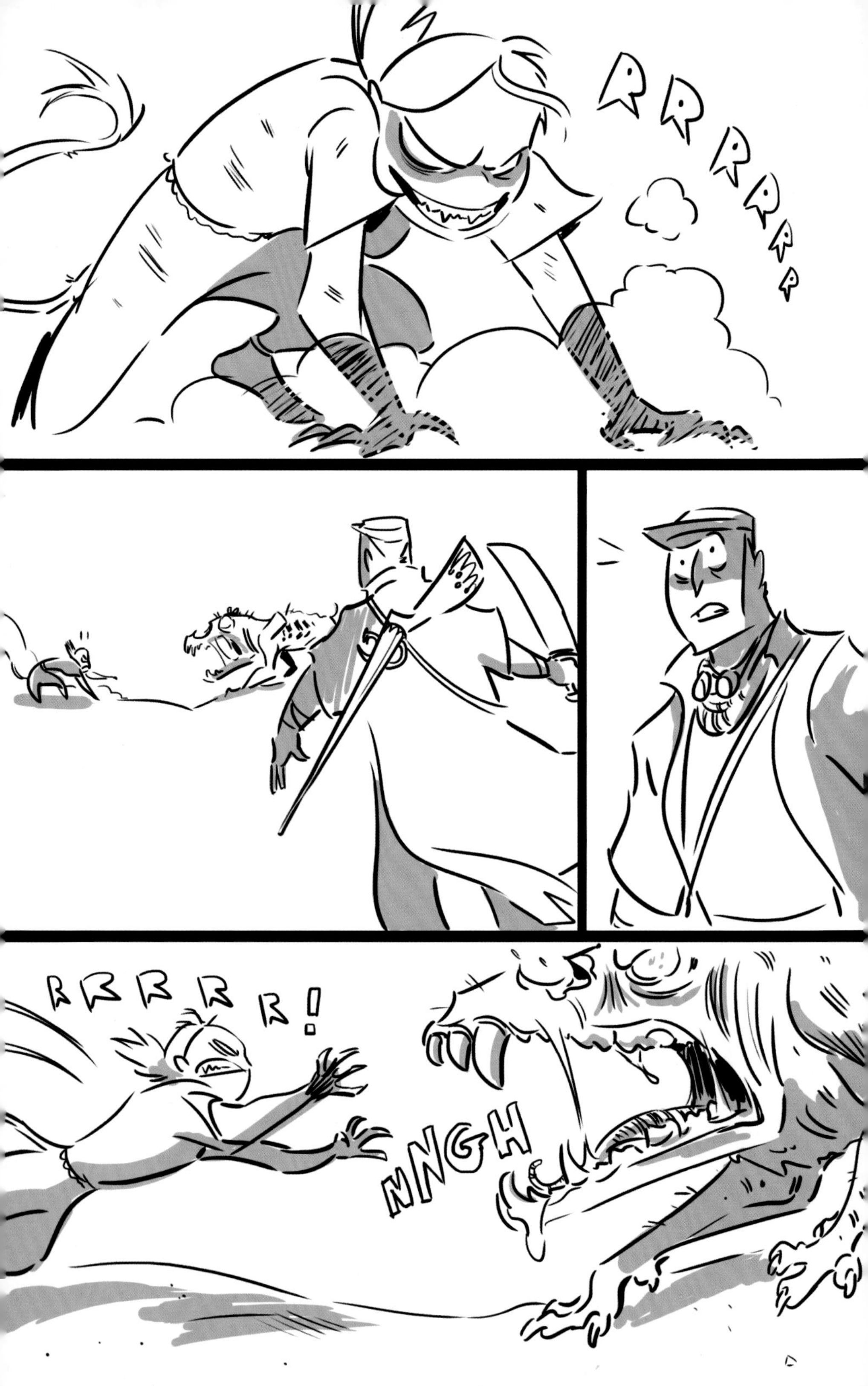

RRRRRRR
RRRRRR!
NNGH

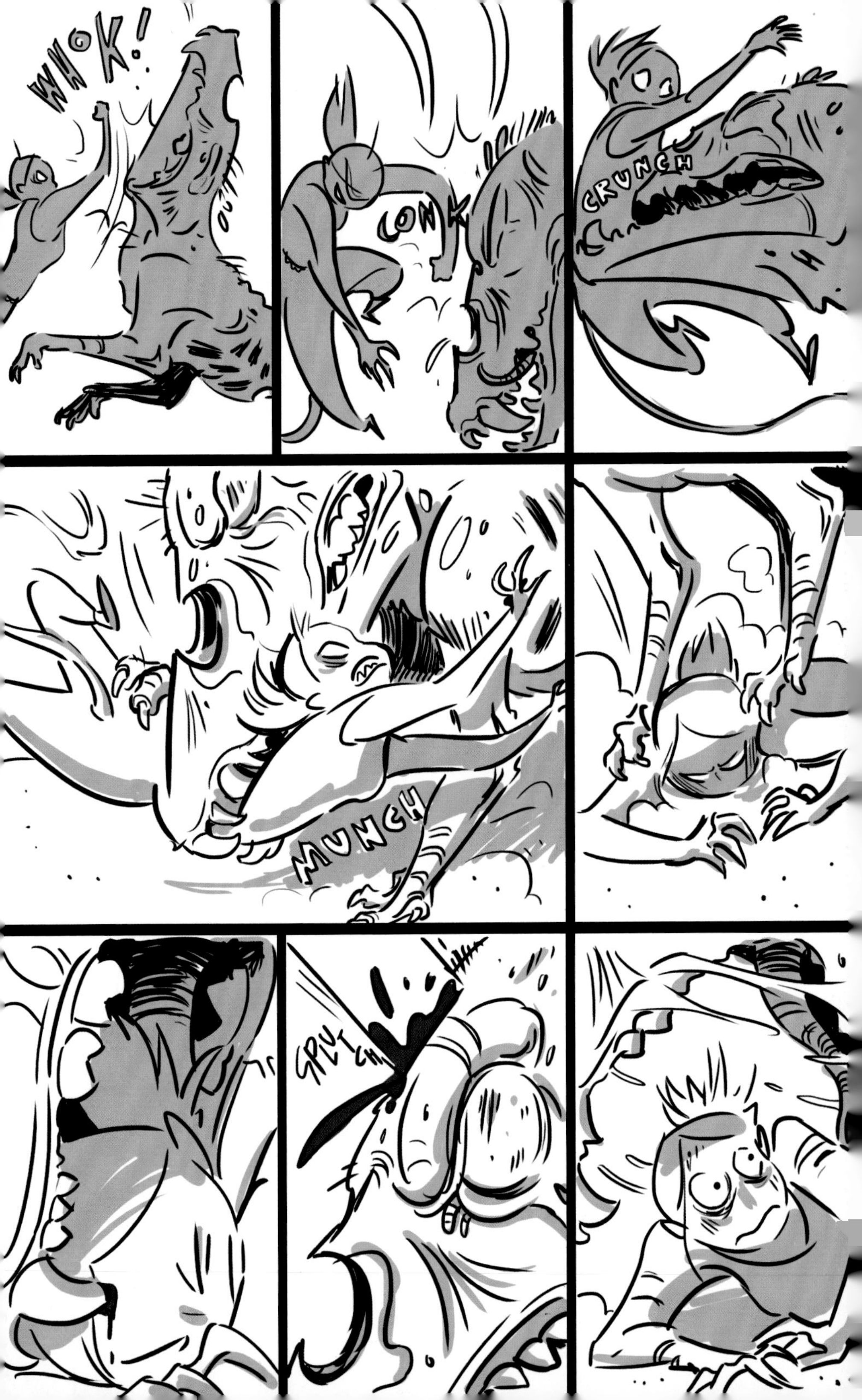
WHOK!
CONK
CRUNCH
MUNCH
SPLUTCH

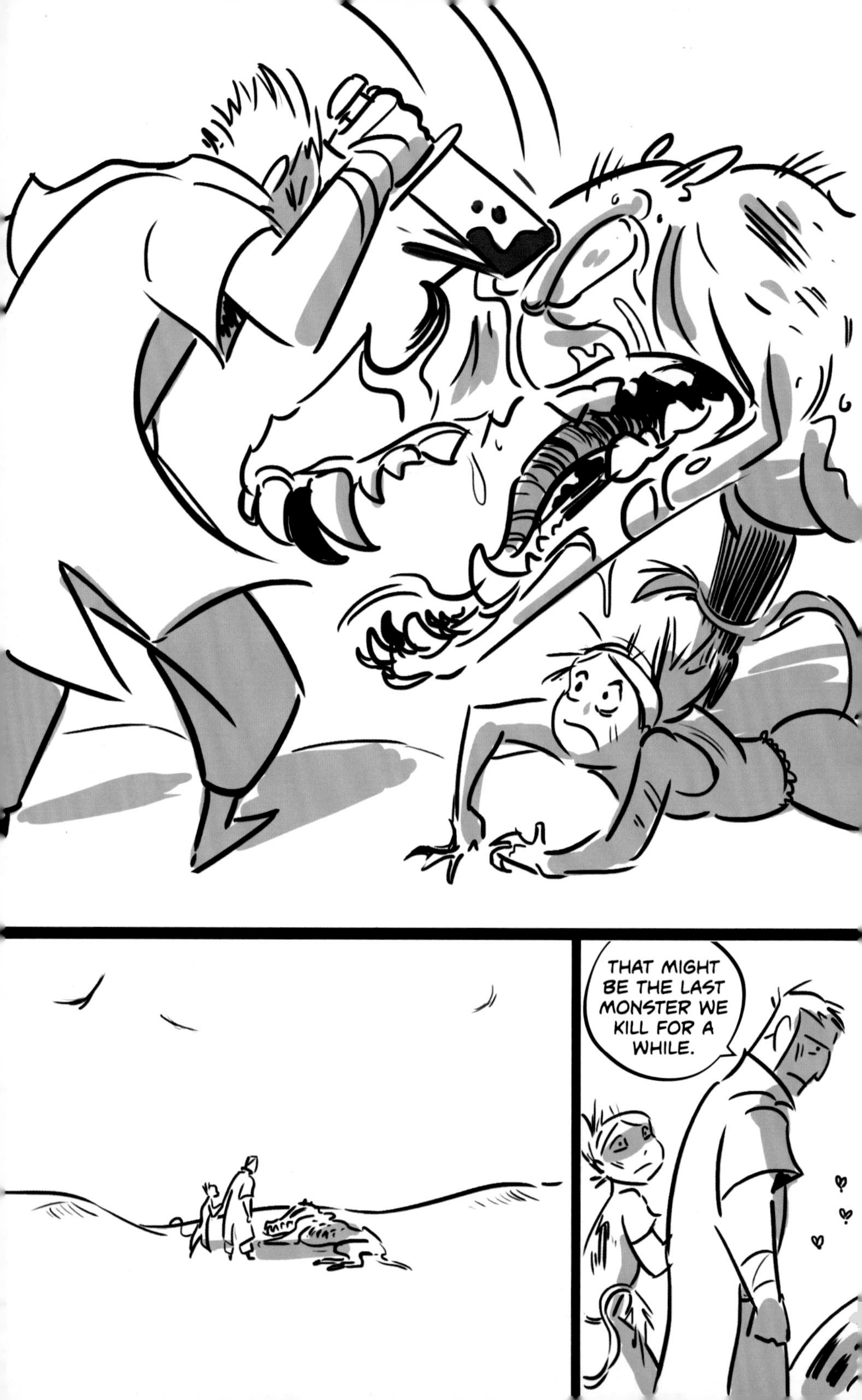
THAT MIGHT BE THE LAST MONSTER WE KILL FOR A WHILE.

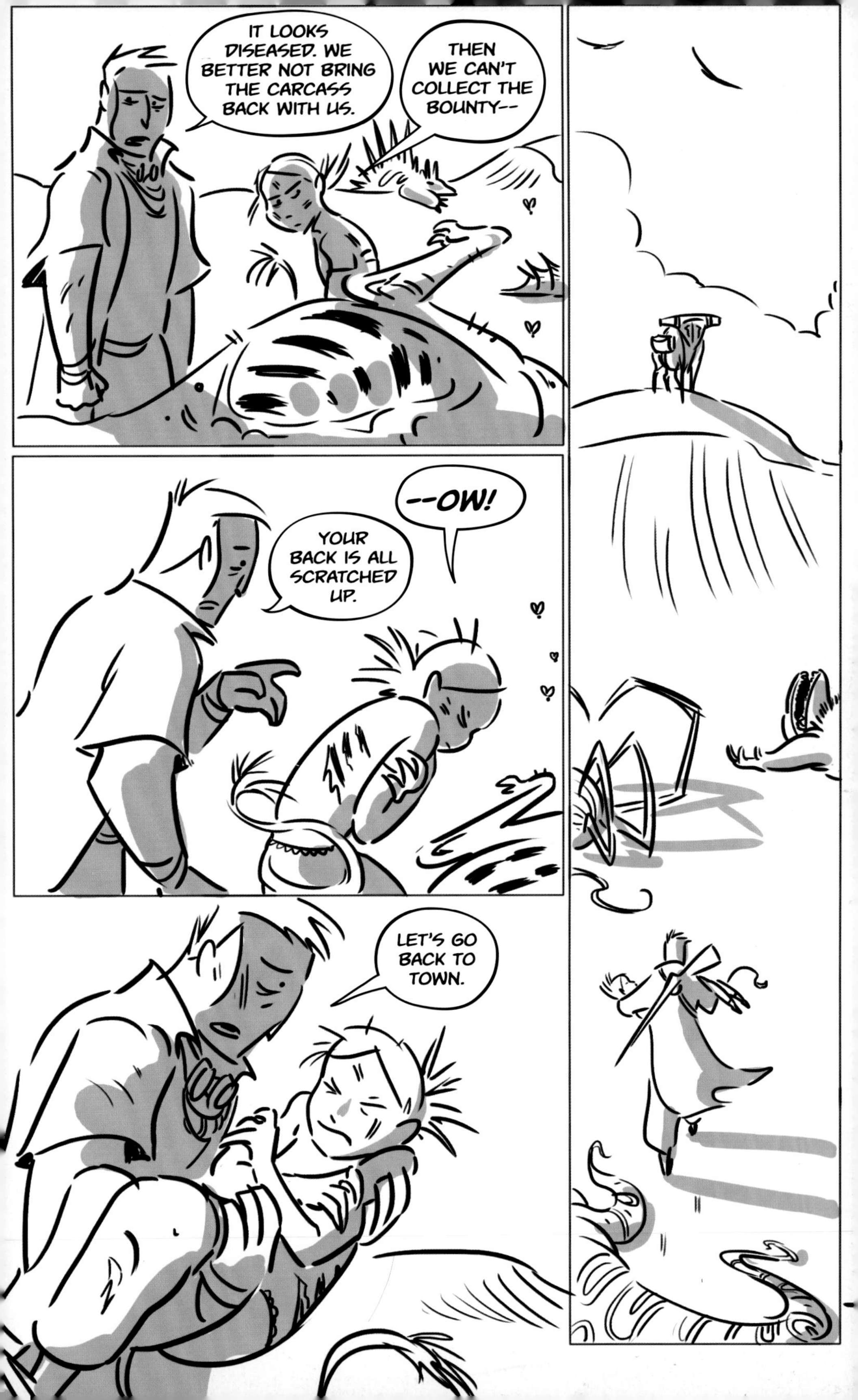
IT LOOKS DISEASED. WE BETTER NOT BRING THE CARCASS BACK WITH US.
THEN WE CAN'T COLLECT THE BOUNTY--
--OW!
YOUR BACK IS ALL SCRATCHED UP.
LET'S GO BACK TO TOWN.

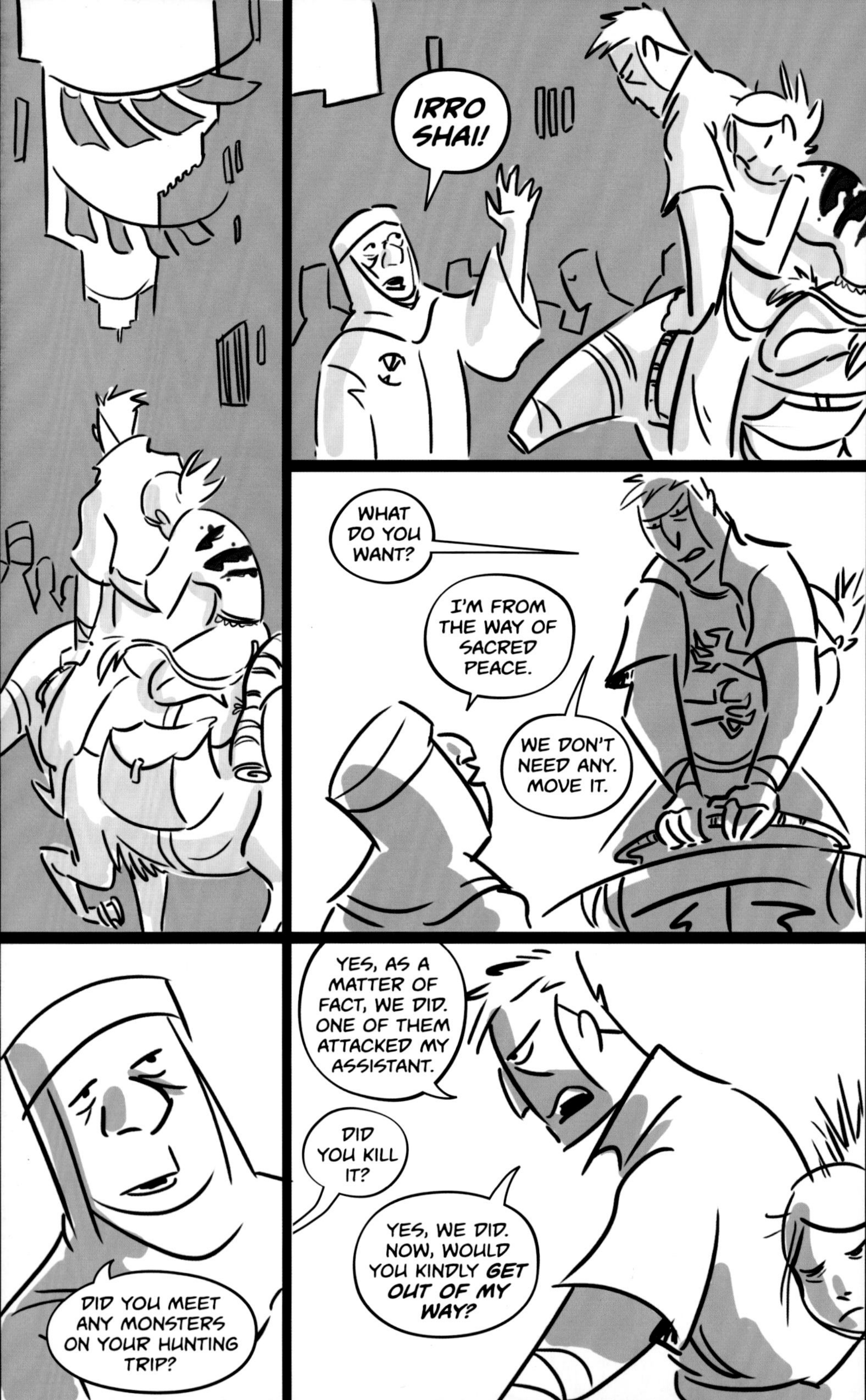
IRRO SHAI!
WHAT DO YOU WANT?
I'M FROM THE WAY OF SACRED PEACE.
WE DON'T NEED ANY. MOVE IT.
DID YOU MEET ANY MONSTERS ON YOUR HUNTING TRIP?
YES, AS A MATTER OF FACT, WE DID. ONE OF THEM ATTACKED MY ASSISTANT.
DID YOU KILL IT?
YES, WE DID. NOW, WOULD YOU KINDLY **GET OUT OF MY WAY?**

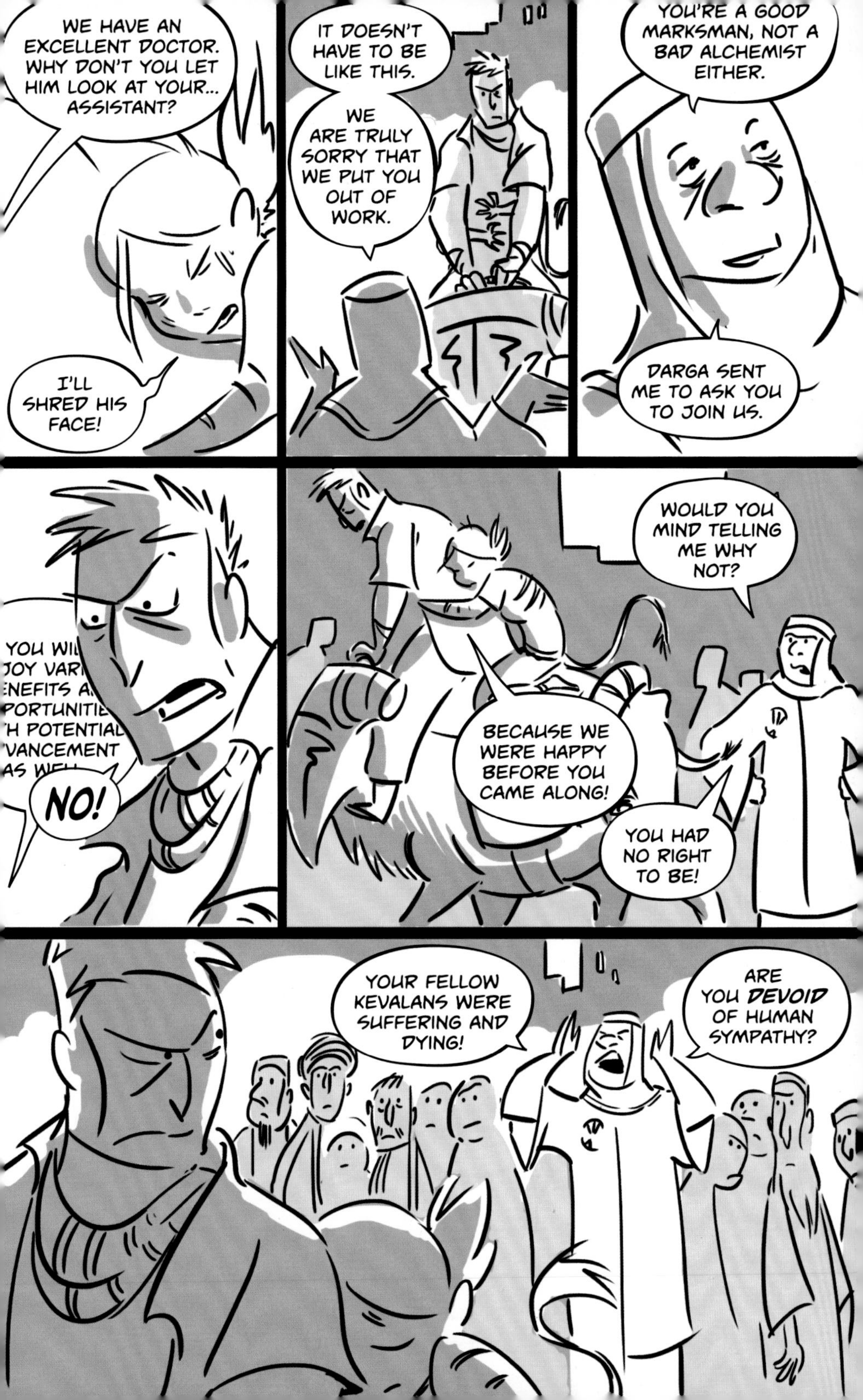
WE HAVE AN EXCELLENT DOCTOR. WHY DON'T YOU LET HIM LOOK AT YOUR... ASSISTANT?
I'LL SHRED HIS FACE!
IT DOESN'T HAVE TO BE LIKE THIS.
WE ARE TRULY SORRY THAT WE PUT YOU OUT OF WORK.
YOU'RE A GOOD MARKSMAN, NOT A BAD ALCHEMIST EITHER.
DARGA SENT ME TO ASK YOU TO JOIN US.
YOU WIL JOY VARI ENEFITS A PORTUNITIE H POTENTIAL VANCEMENT AS WE
NO!
WOULD YOU MIND TELLING ME WHY NOT?
BECAUSE WE WERE HAPPY BEFORE YOU CAME ALONG!
YOU HAD NO RIGHT TO BE!
YOUR FELLOW KEVALANS WERE SUFFERING AND DYING!
ARE YOU DEVOID OF HUMAN SYMPATHY?

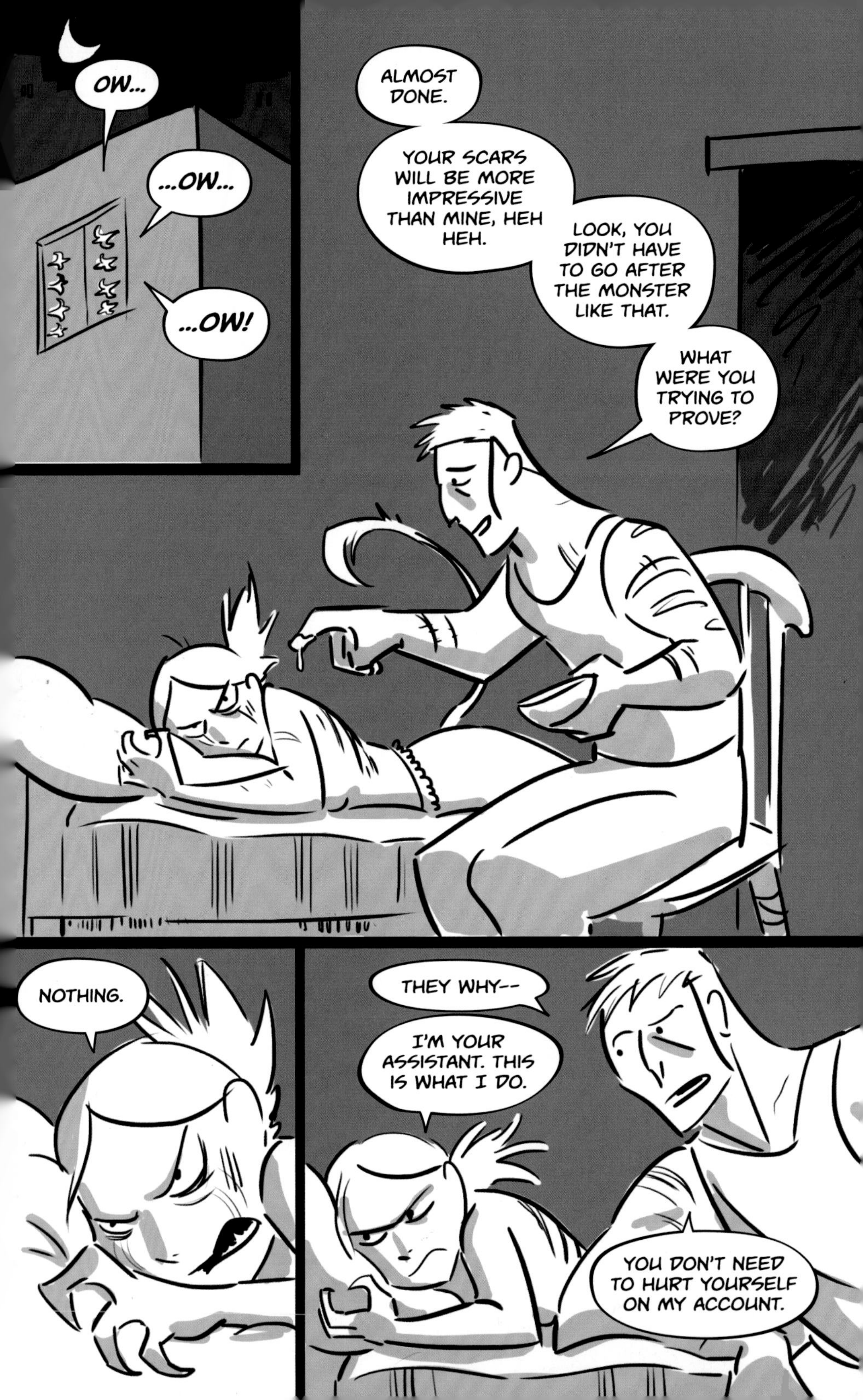
OW...
...OW...
...OW!
ALMOST DONE.
YOUR SCARS WILL BE MORE IMPRESSIVE THAN MINE, HEH HEH.
LOOK, YOU DIDN'T HAVE TO GO AFTER THE MONSTER LIKE THAT.
WHAT WERE YOU TRYING TO PROVE?
NOTHING.
THEY WHY--
I'M YOUR ASSISTANT. THIS IS WHAT I DO.
YOU DON'T NEED TO HURT YOURSELF ON MY ACCOUNT.

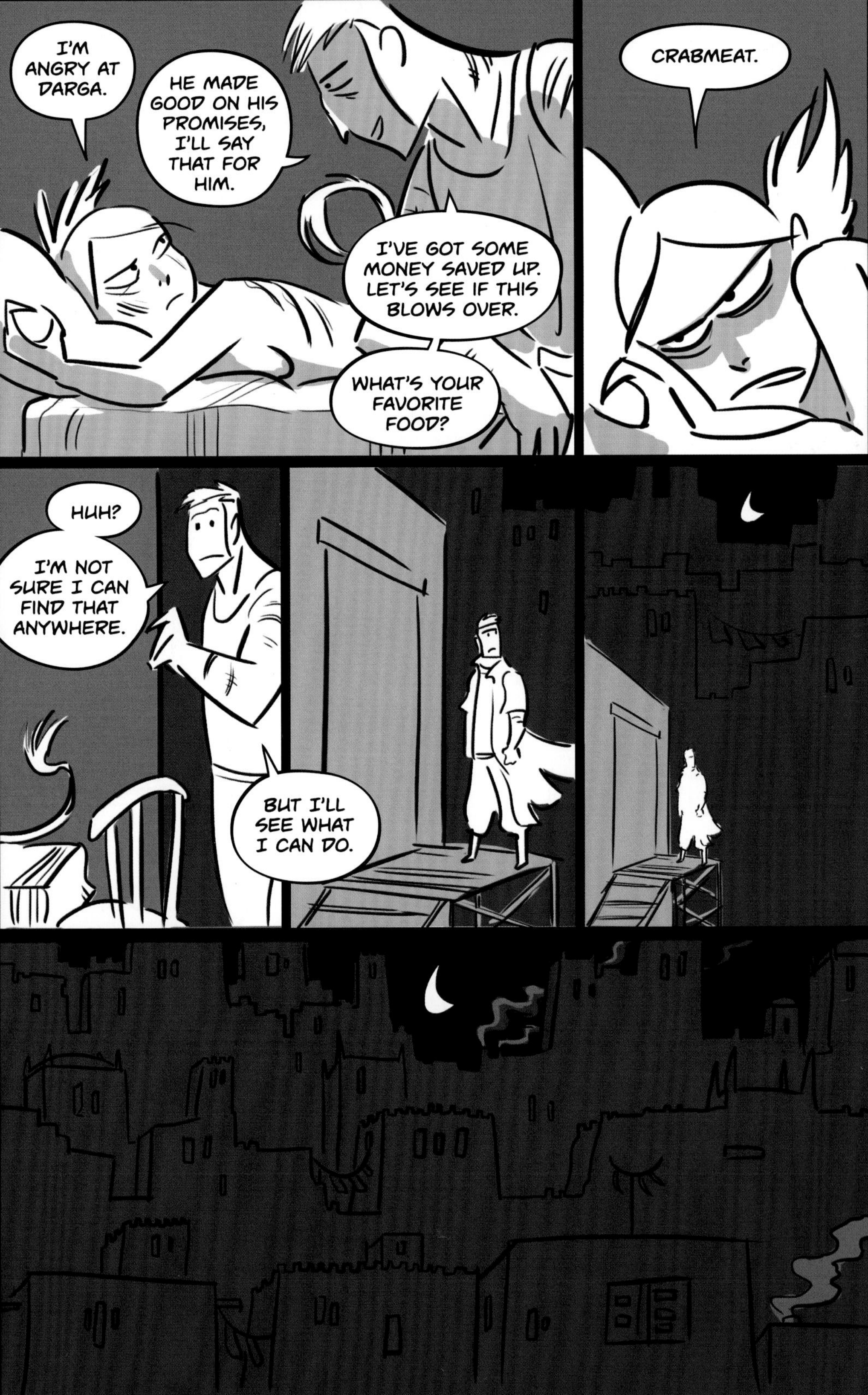
I'M ANGRY AT DARGA.
HE MADE GOOD ON HIS PROMISES, I'LL SAY THAT FOR HIM.
I'VE GOT SOME MONEY SAVED UP. LET'S SEE IF THIS BLOWS OVER.
WHAT'S YOUR FAVORITE FOOD?
CRABMEAT.
HUH?
I'M NOT SURE I CAN FIND THAT ANYWHERE.
BUT I'LL SEE WHAT I CAN DO.

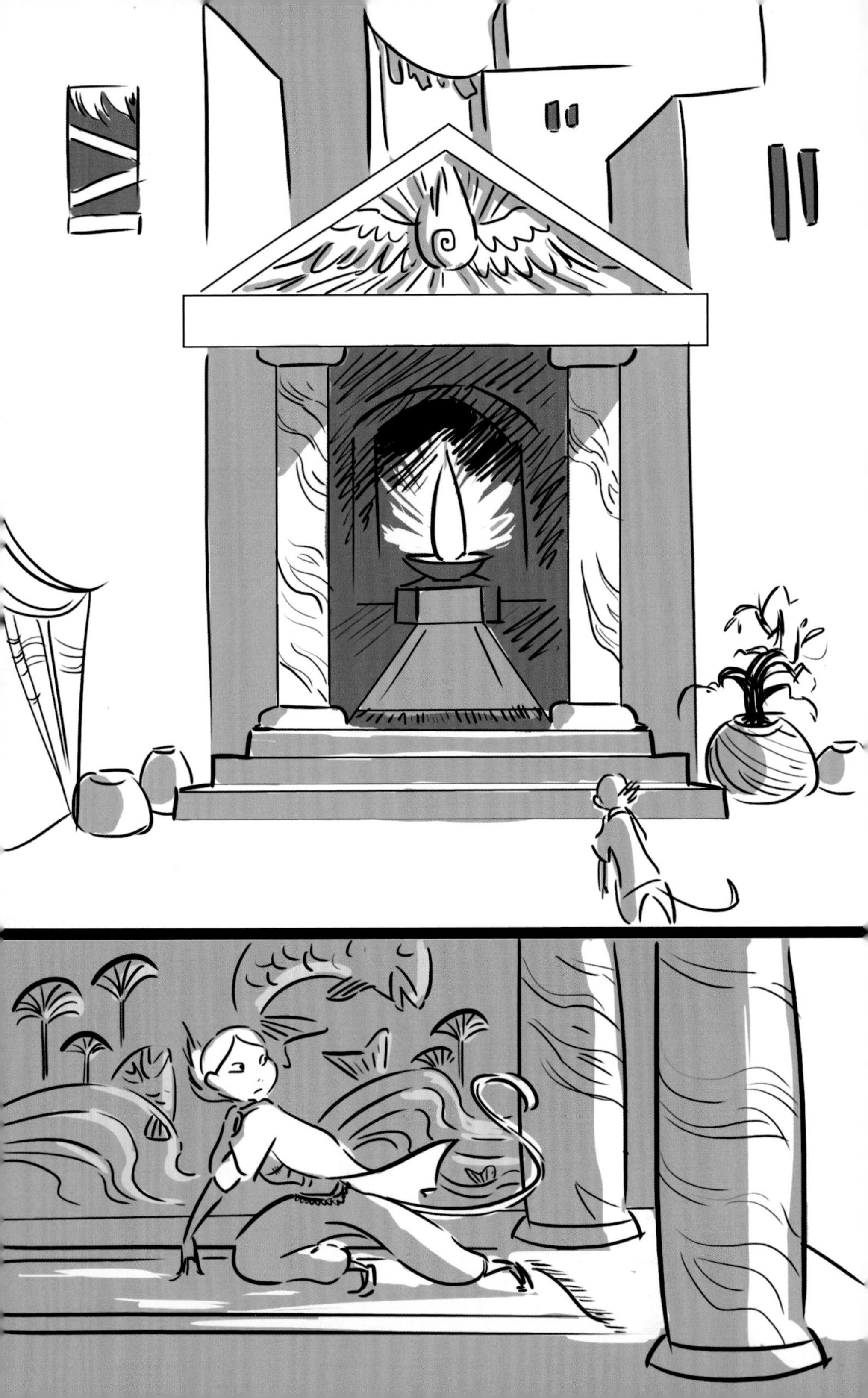

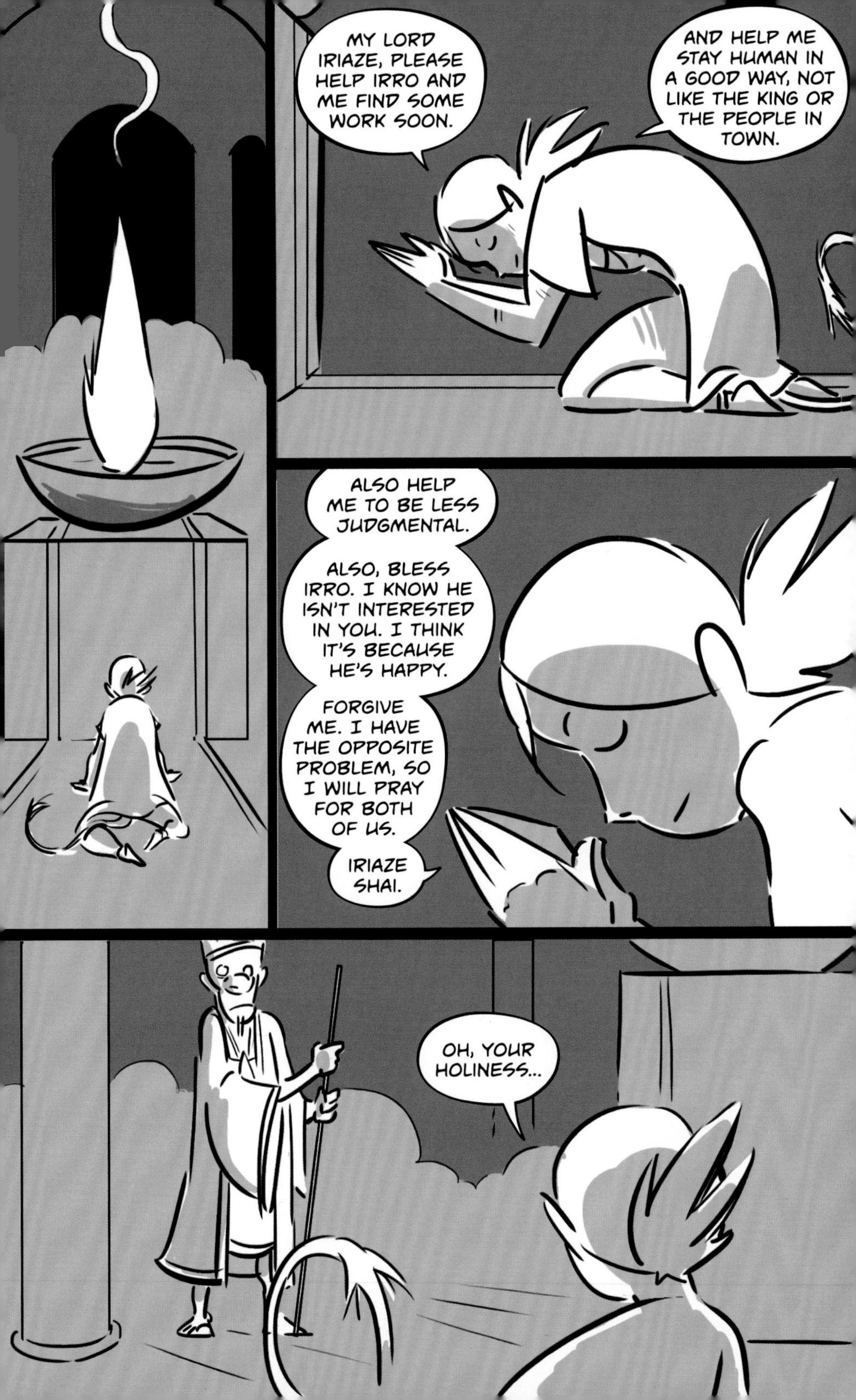
MY LORD IRIAZE, PLEASE HELP IRRO AND ME FIND SOME WORK SOON.
AND HELP ME STAY HUMAN IN A GOOD WAY, NOT LIKE THE KING OR THE PEOPLE IN TOWN.
ALSO HELP ME TO BE LESS JUDGMENTAL.
ALSO, BLESS IRRO. I KNOW HE ISN'T INTERESTED IN YOU. I THINK IT'S BECAUSE HE'S HAPPY.
FORGIVE ME. I HAVE THE OPPOSITE PROBLEM, SO I WILL PRAY FOR BOTH OF US.
IRIAZE SHAI.
OH, YOUR HOLINESS...

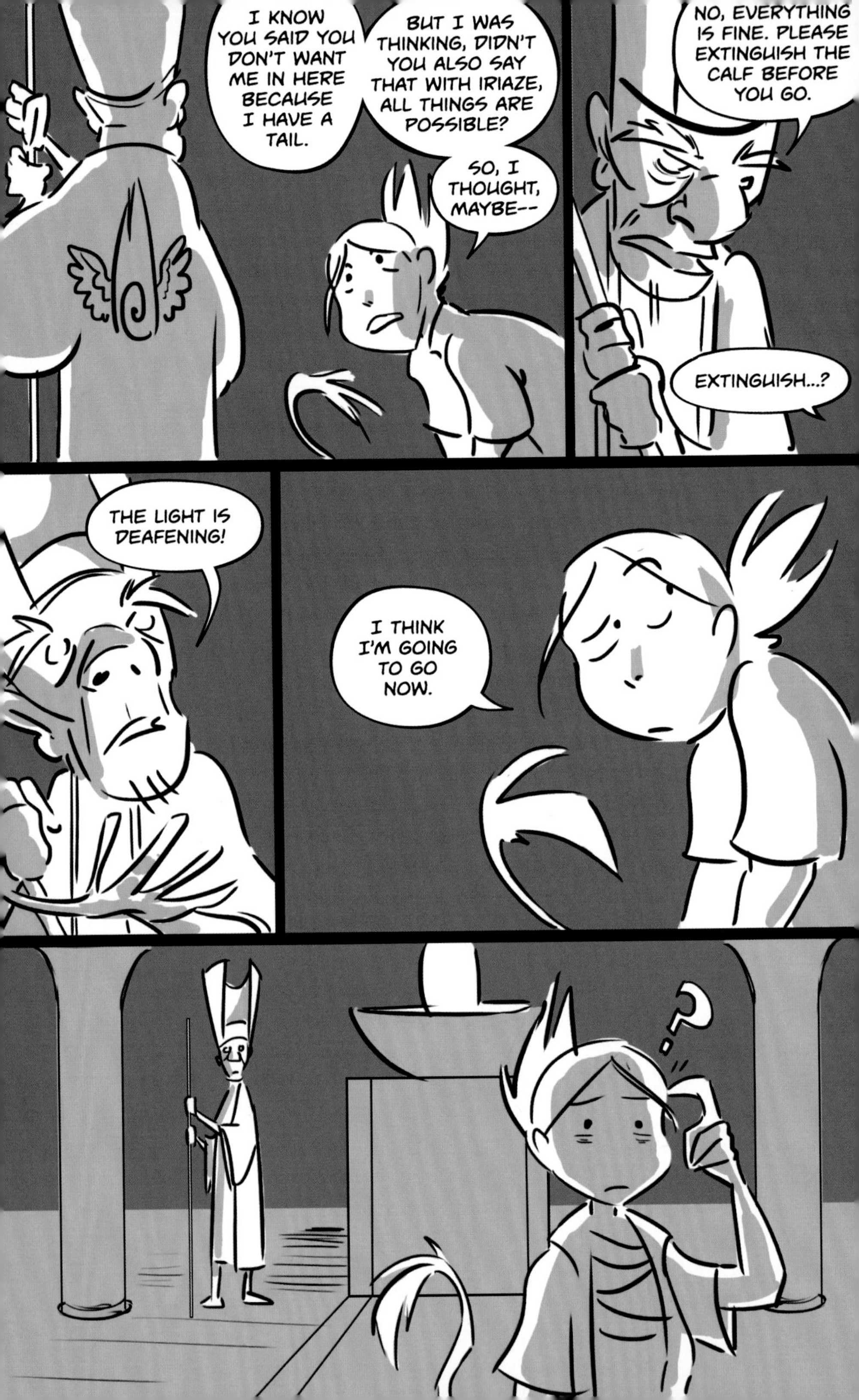
I KNOW YOU SAID YOU DON'T WANT ME IN HERE BECAUSE I HAVE A TAIL.
BUT I WAS THINKING, DIDN'T YOU ALSO SAY THAT WITH IRIAZE, ALL THINGS ARE POSSIBLE?
SO, I THOUGHT, MAYBE--
NO, EVERYTHING IS FINE. PLEASE EXTINGUISH THE CALF BEFORE YOU GO.
EXTINGUISH...?
THE LIGHT IS DEAFENING!
I THINK I'M GOING TO GO NOW.
?

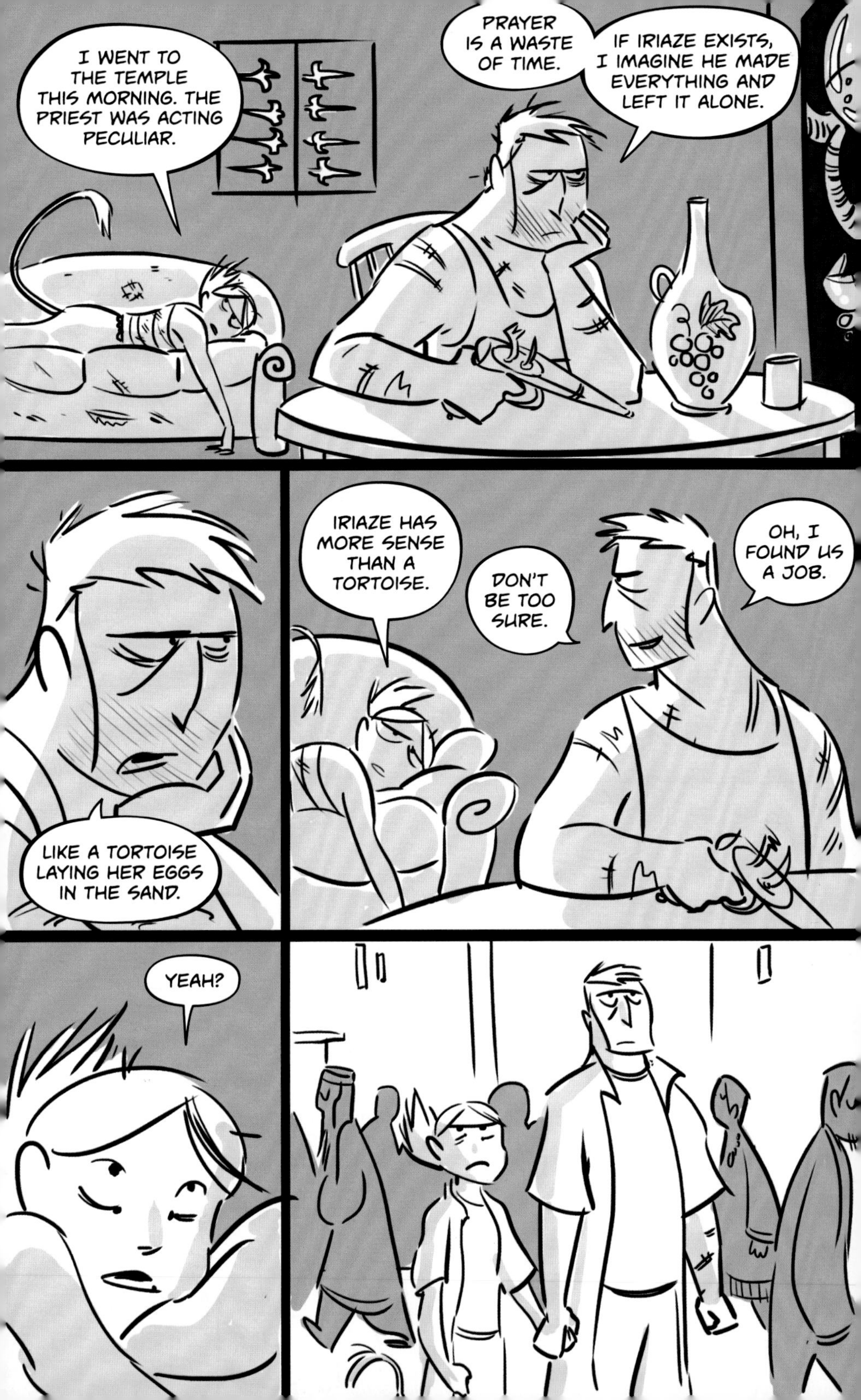
I WENT TO THE TEMPLE THIS MORNING. THE PRIEST WAS ACTING PECULIAR.
PRAYER IS A WASTE OF TIME.
IF IRIAZE EXISTS, I IMAGINE HE MADE EVERYTHING AND LEFT IT ALONE.
LIKE A TORTOISE LAYING HER EGGS IN THE SAND.
IRIAZE HAS MORE SENSE THAN A TORTOISE.
DON'T BE TOO SURE.
OH, I FOUND US A JOB.
YEAH?

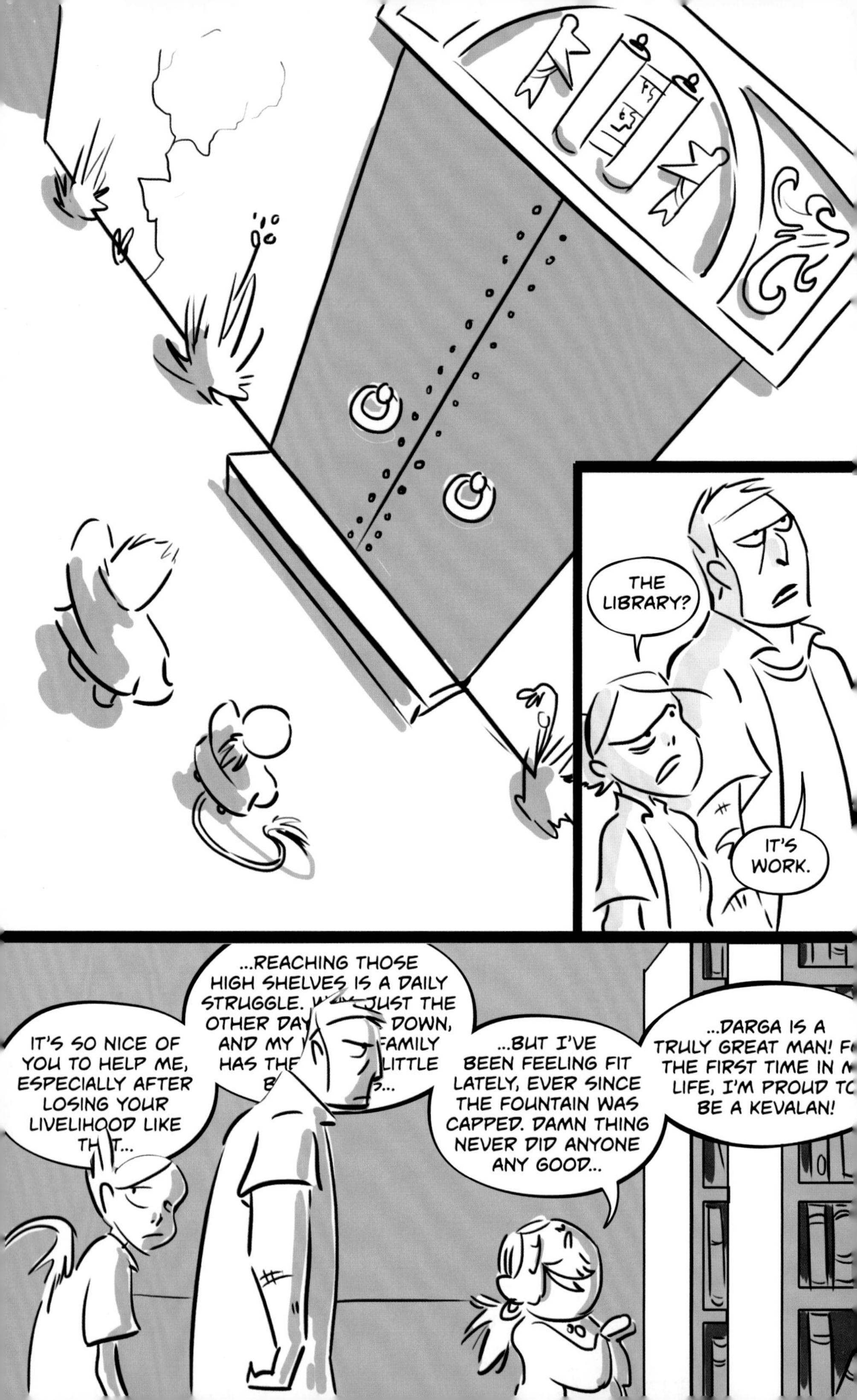
THE LIBRARY?
IT'S WORK.
IT'S SO NICE OF YOU TO HELP ME, ESPECIALLY AFTER LOSING YOUR LIVELIHOOD LIKE TH T...
...REACHING THOSE HIGH SHELVES IS A DAILY STRUGGLE. W JUST THE OTHER DAY DOWN, AND MY FAMILY HAS THE LITTLE B ...
...BUT I'VE BEEN FEELING FIT LATELY, EVER SINCE THE FOUNTAIN WAS CAPPED. DAMN THING NEVER DID ANYONE ANY GOOD...
...DARGA IS A TRULY GREAT MAN! F THE FIRST TIME IN LIFE, I'M PROUD T BE A KEVALAN!

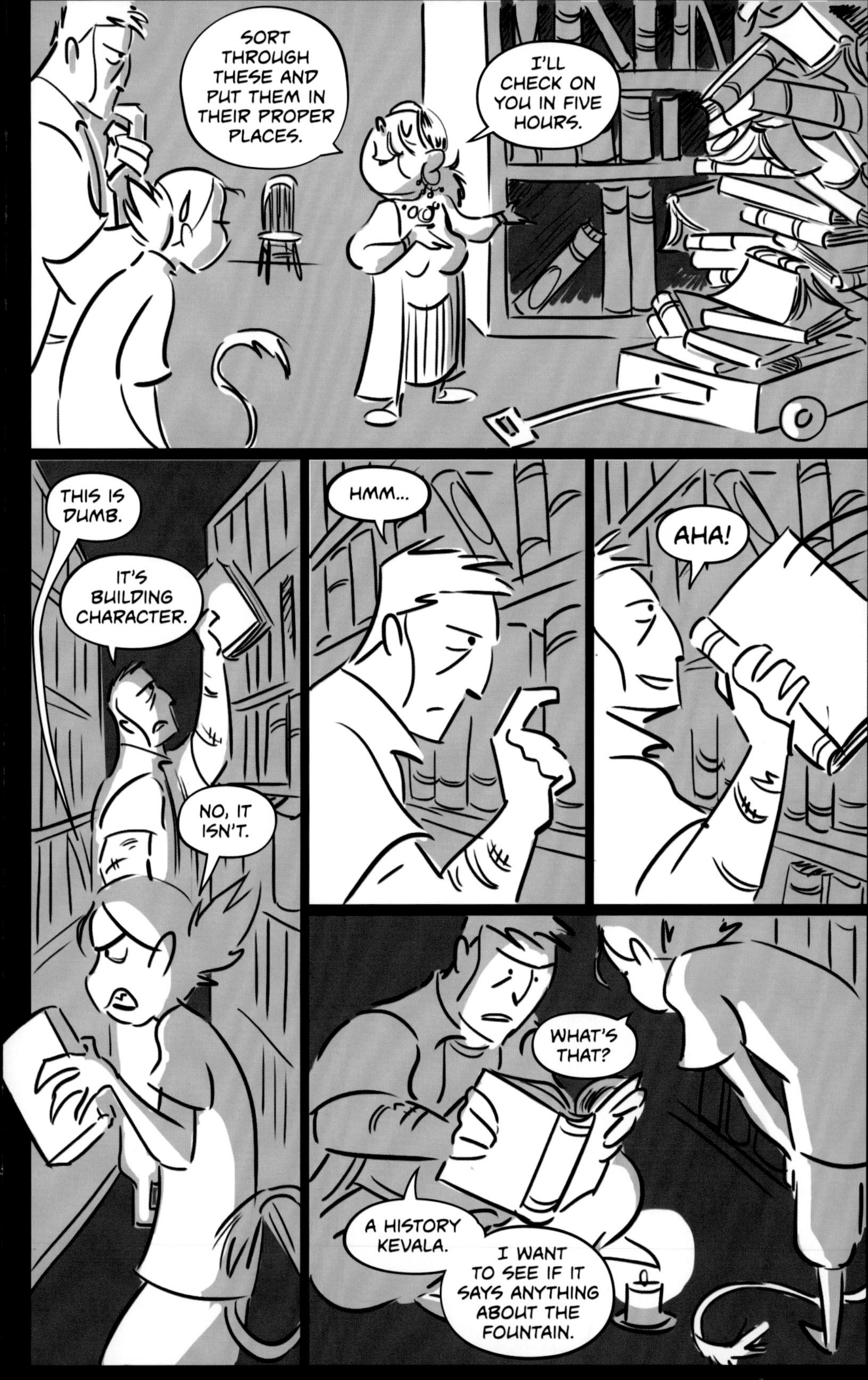
SORT THROUGH THESE AND PUT THEM IN THEIR PROPER PLACES.
I'LL CHECK ON YOU IN FIVE HOURS.
THIS IS DUMB.
IT'S BUILDING CHARACTER.
NO, IT ISN'T.
HMM...
AHA!
WHAT'S THAT?
A HISTORY KEVALA.
I WANT TO SEE IF IT SAYS ANYTHING ABOUT THE FOUNTAIN.

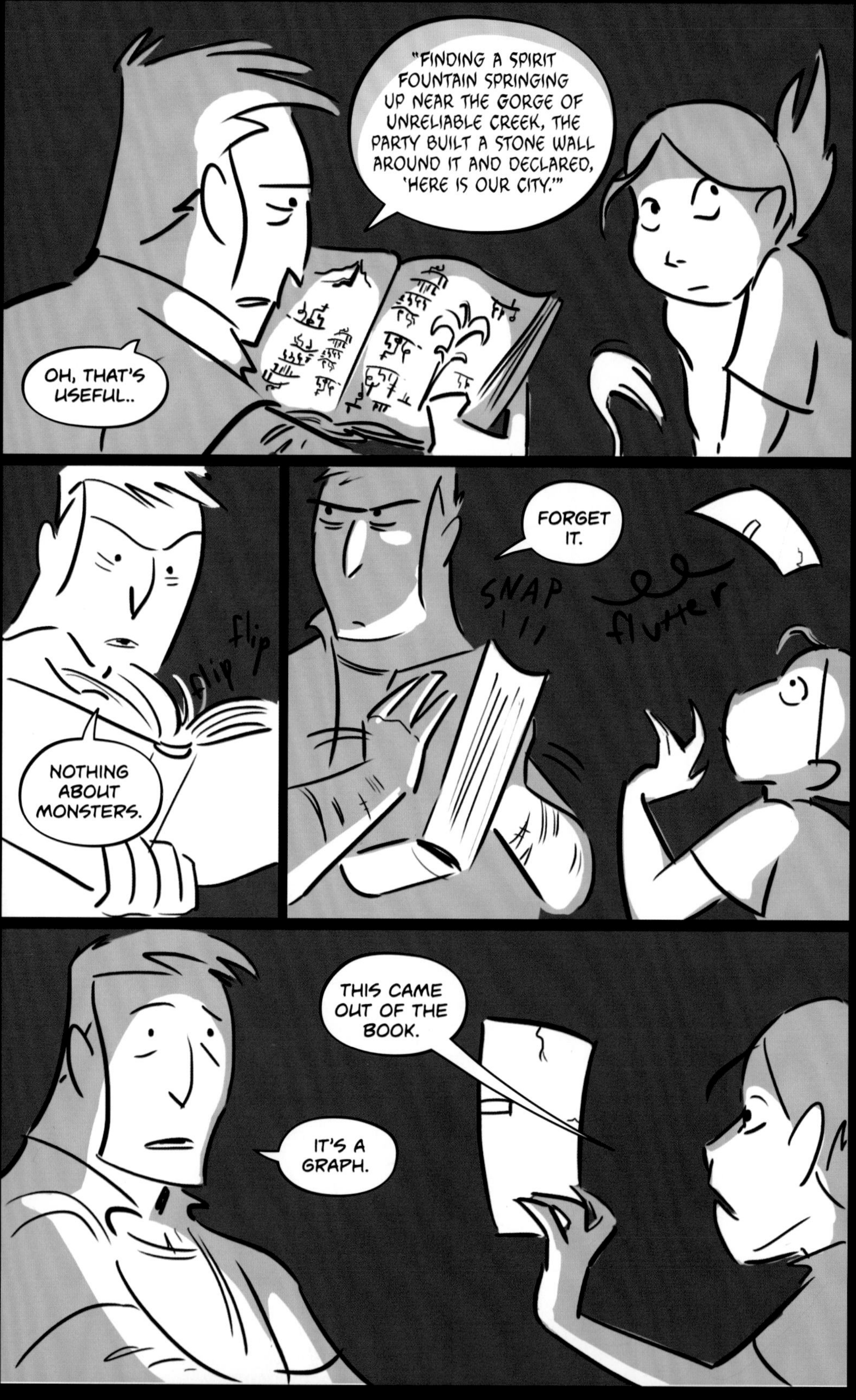
"FINDING A SPIRIT FOUNTAIN SPRINGING UP NEAR THE GORGE OF UNRELIABLE CREEK, THE PARTY BUILT A STONE WALL AROUND IT AND DECLARED, 'HERE IS OUR CITY.'"
OH, THAT'S USEFUL..
flip flip
NOTHING ABOUT MONSTERS.
FORGET IT.
SNAP
flutter
THIS CAME OUT OF THE BOOK.
IT'S A GRAPH.

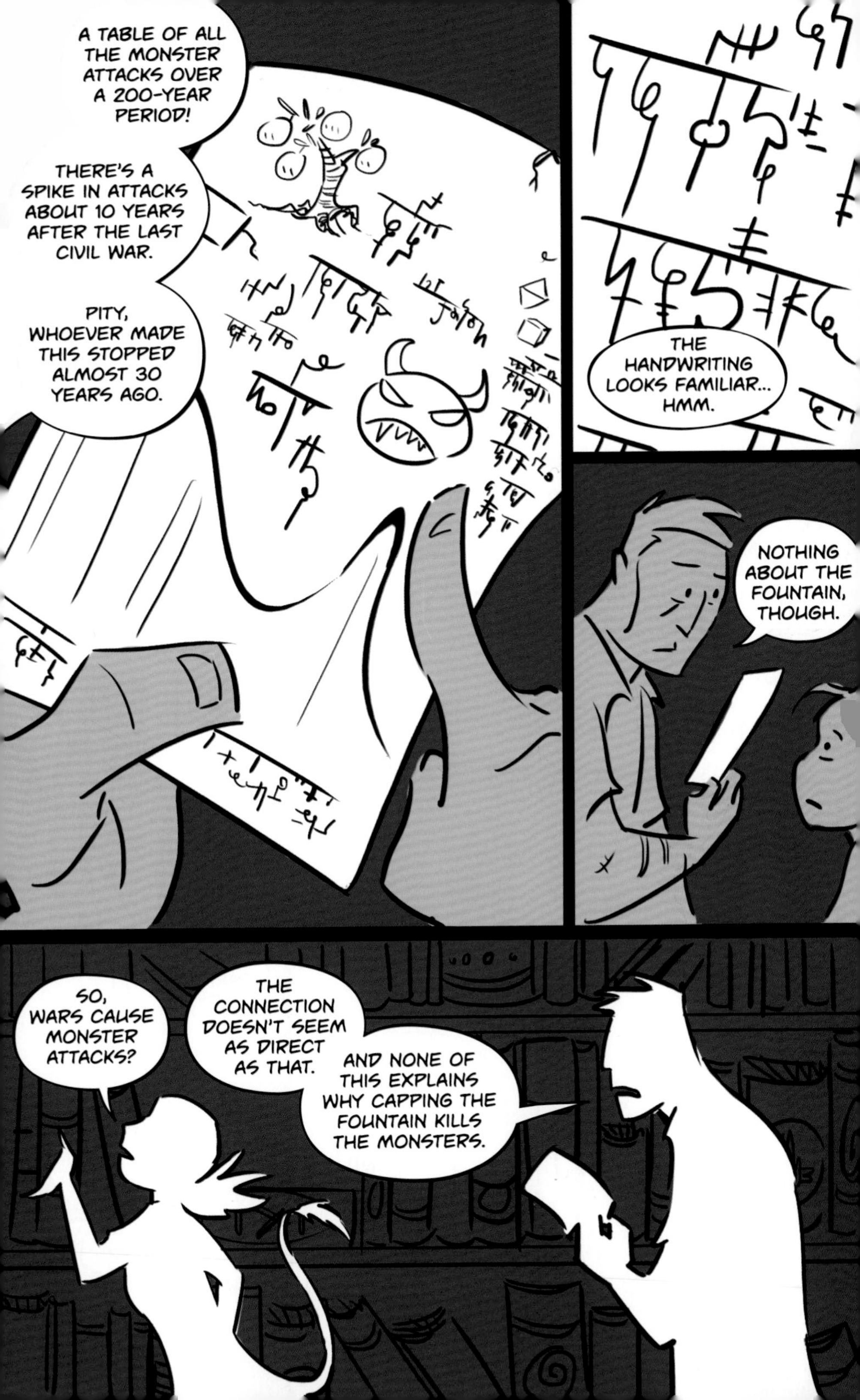
A TABLE OF ALL THE MONSTER ATTACKS OVER A 200-YEAR PERIOD!
THERE'S A SPIKE IN ATTACKS ABOUT 10 YEARS AFTER THE LAST CIVIL WAR.
PITY, WHOEVER MADE THIS STOPPED ALMOST 30 YEARS AGO.
THE HANDWRITING LOOKS FAMILIAR... HMM.
NOTHING ABOUT THE FOUNTAIN, THOUGH.
SO, WARS CAUSE MONSTER ATTACKS?
THE CONNECTION DOESN'T SEEM AS DIRECT AS THAT.
AND NONE OF THIS EXPLAINS WHY CAPPING THE FOUNTAIN KILLS THE MONSTERS.

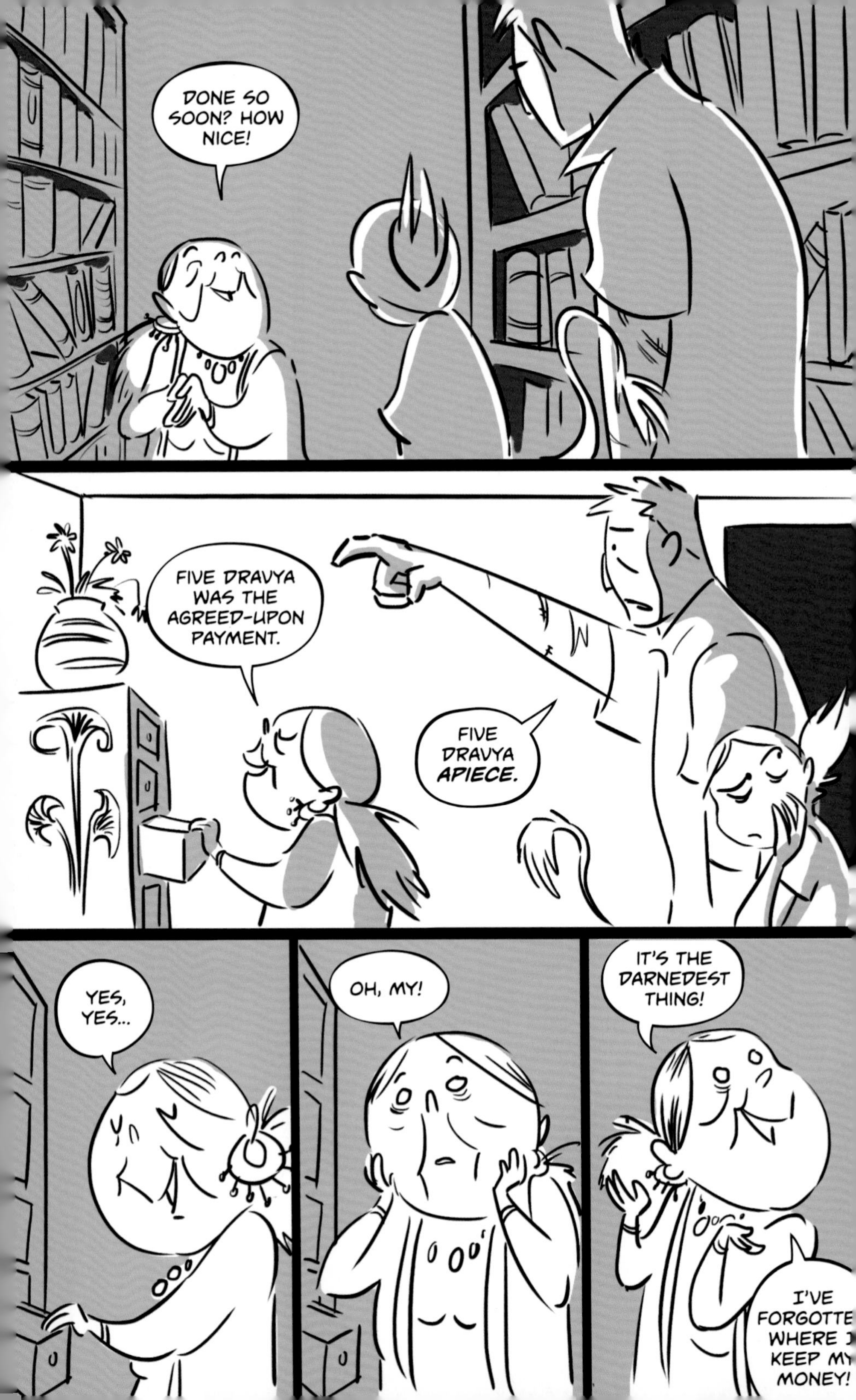
DONE SO SOON? HOW NICE!
FIVE DRAVYA WAS THE AGREED-UPON PAYMENT.
FIVE DRAVYA APIECE.
YES, YES...
OH, MY!
IT'S THE DARNEDEST THING!
I'VE FORGOTTE WHERE I KEEP MY MONEY!

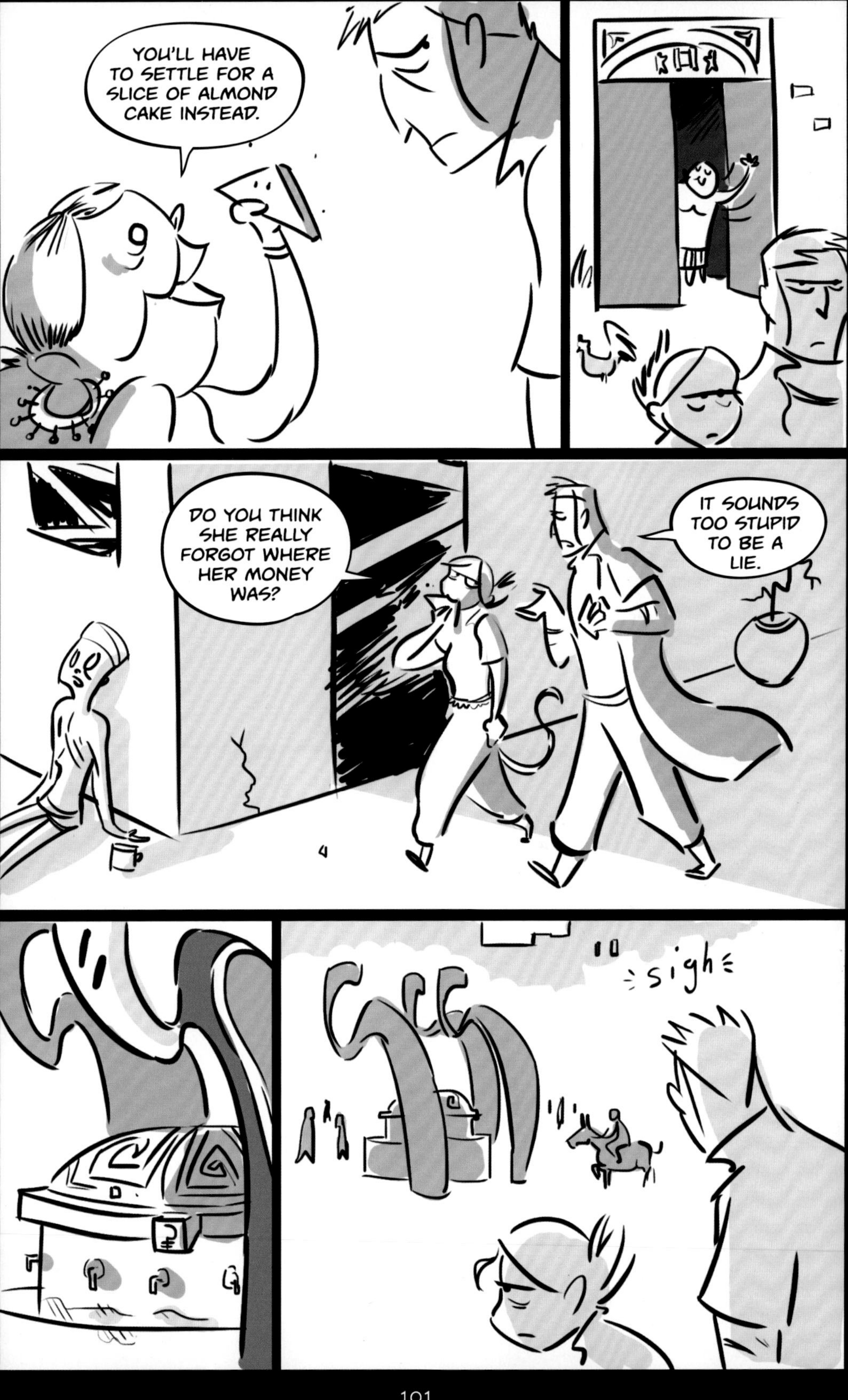
YOU'LL HAVE TO SETTLE FOR A SLICE OF ALMOND CAKE INSTEAD.
DO YOU THINK SHE REALLY FORGOT WHERE HER MONEY WAS?
IT SOUNDS TOO STUPID TO BE A LIE.
sigh

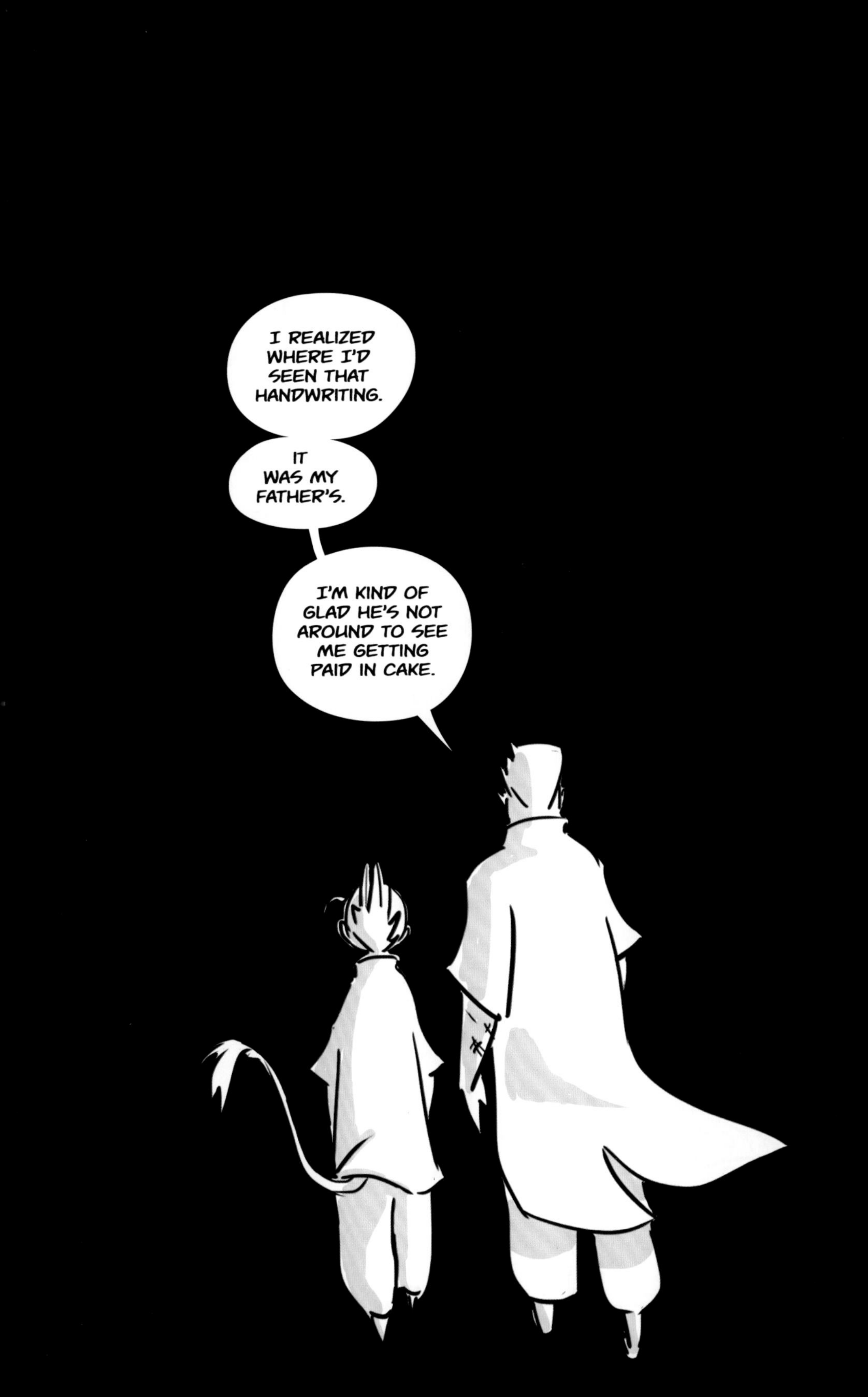
I REALIZED WHERE I'D SEEN THAT HANDWRITING.
IT WAS MY FATHER'S.
I'M KIND OF GLAD HE'S NOT AROUND TO SEE ME GETTING PAID IN CAKE.

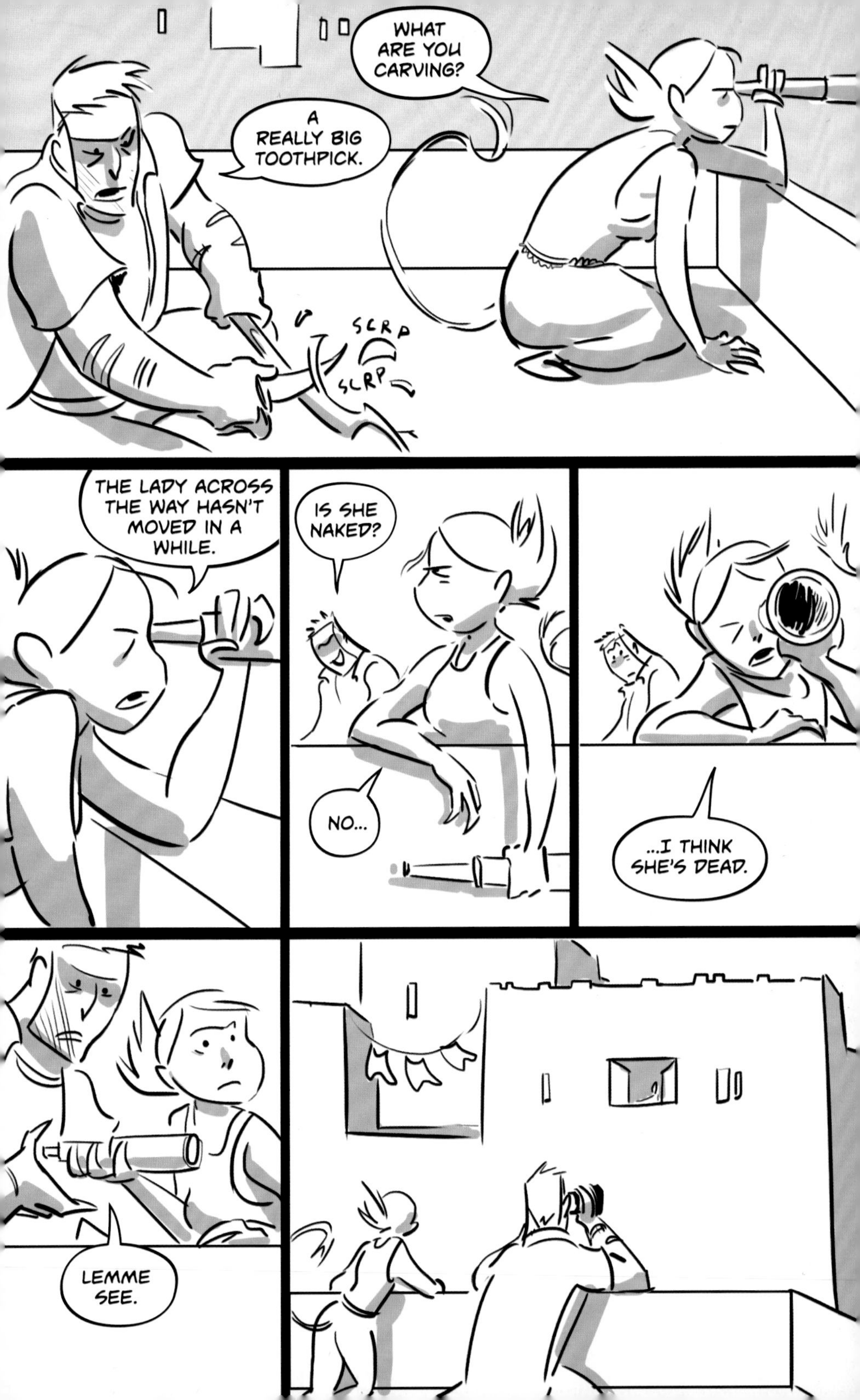
WHAT ARE YOU CARVING?
A REALLY BIG TOOTHPICK.
SCRP
SCRP
THE LADY ACROSS THE WAY HASN'T MOVED IN A WHILE.
IS SHE NAKED?
NO...
...I THINK SHE'S DEAD.
LEMME SEE.

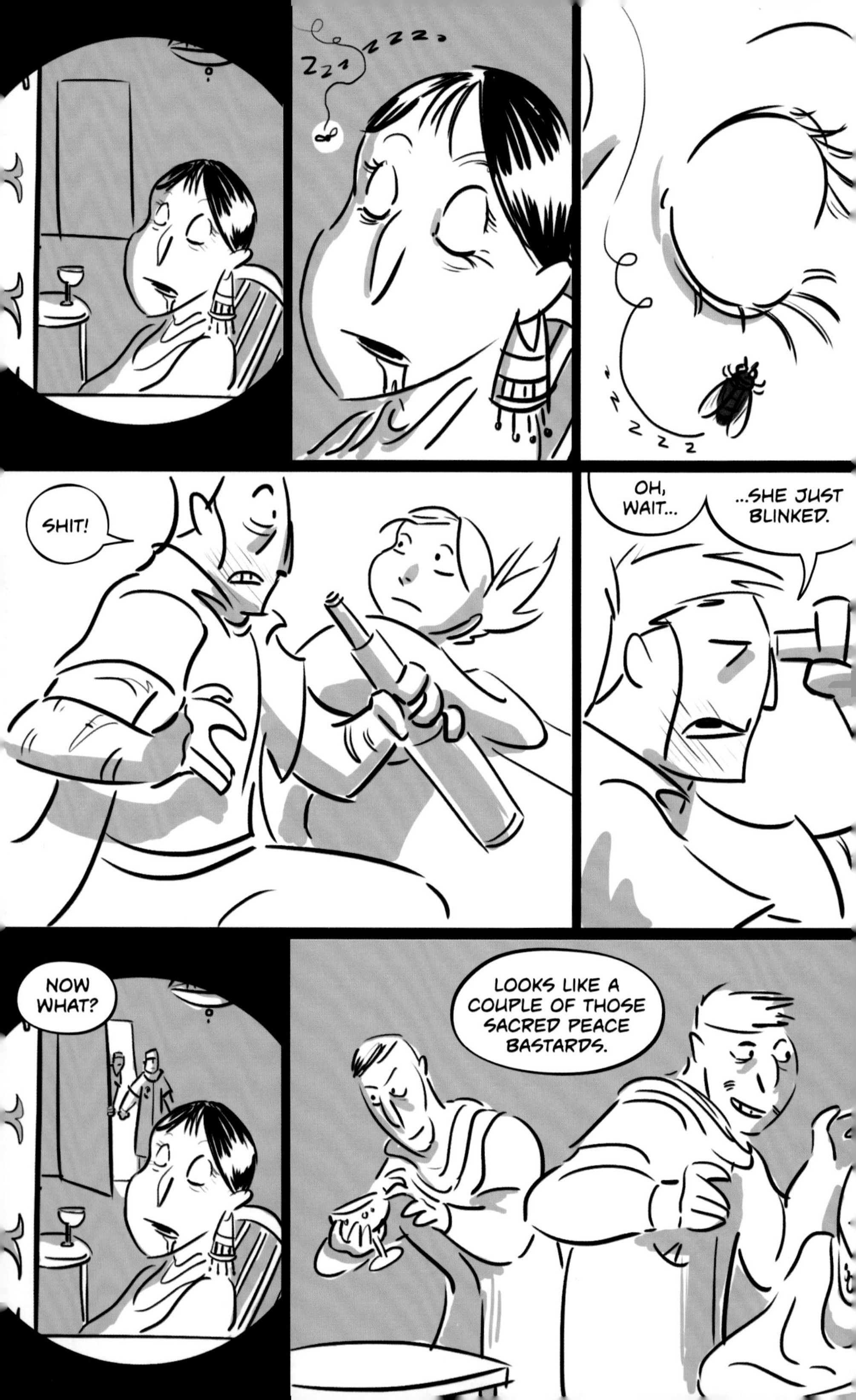
Zzz
zzzzz
SHIT!
OH, WAIT...
...SHE JUST BLINKED.
NOW WHAT?
LOOKS LIKE A COUPLE OF THOSE SACRED PEACE BASTARDS.

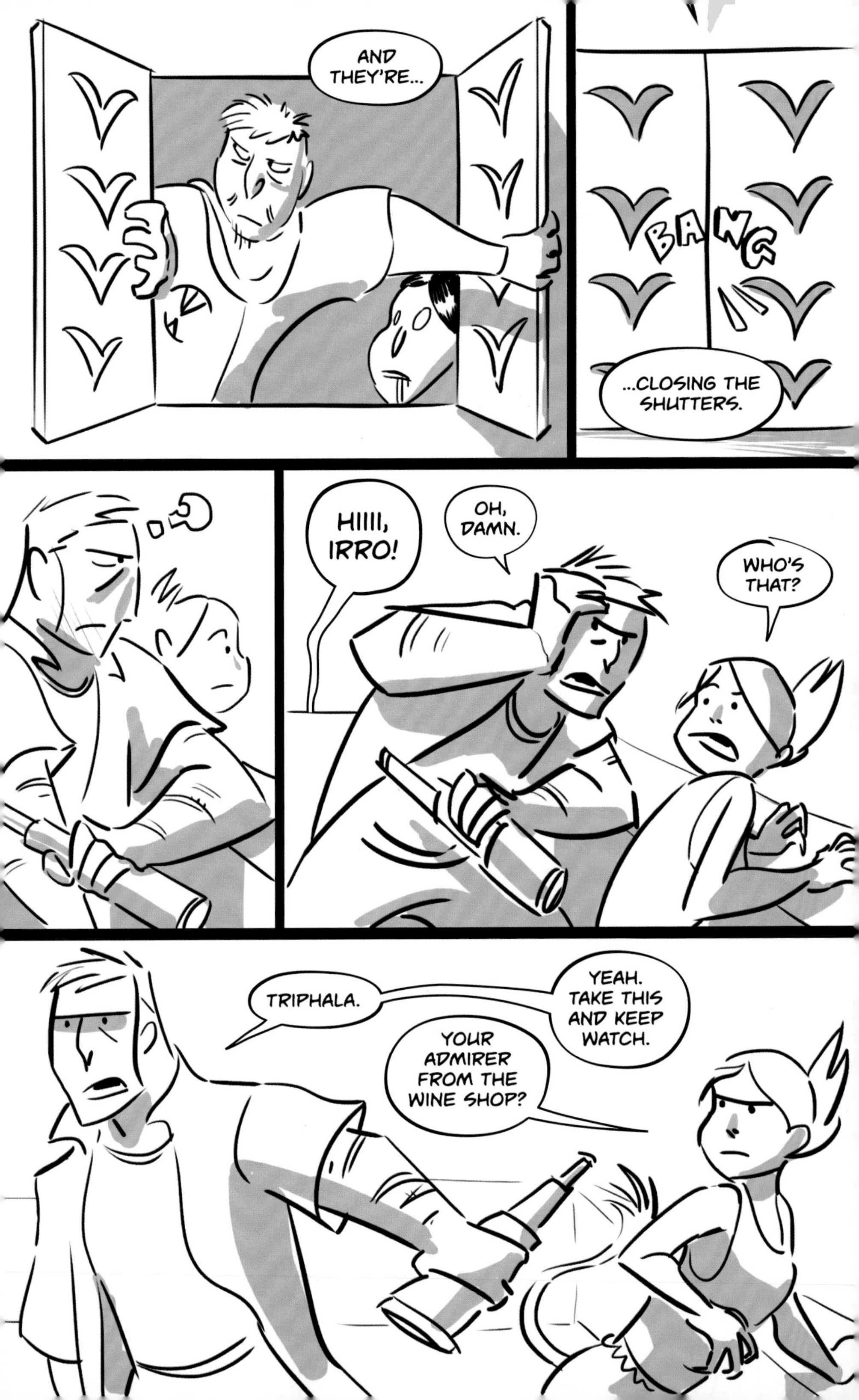
AND THEY'RE...
BANG
...CLOSING THE SHUTTERS.
HIIII, IRRO!
OH, DAMN.
WHO'S THAT?
TRIPHALA.
YOUR ADMIRER FROM THE WINE SHOP?
YEAH. TAKE THIS AND KEEP WATCH.

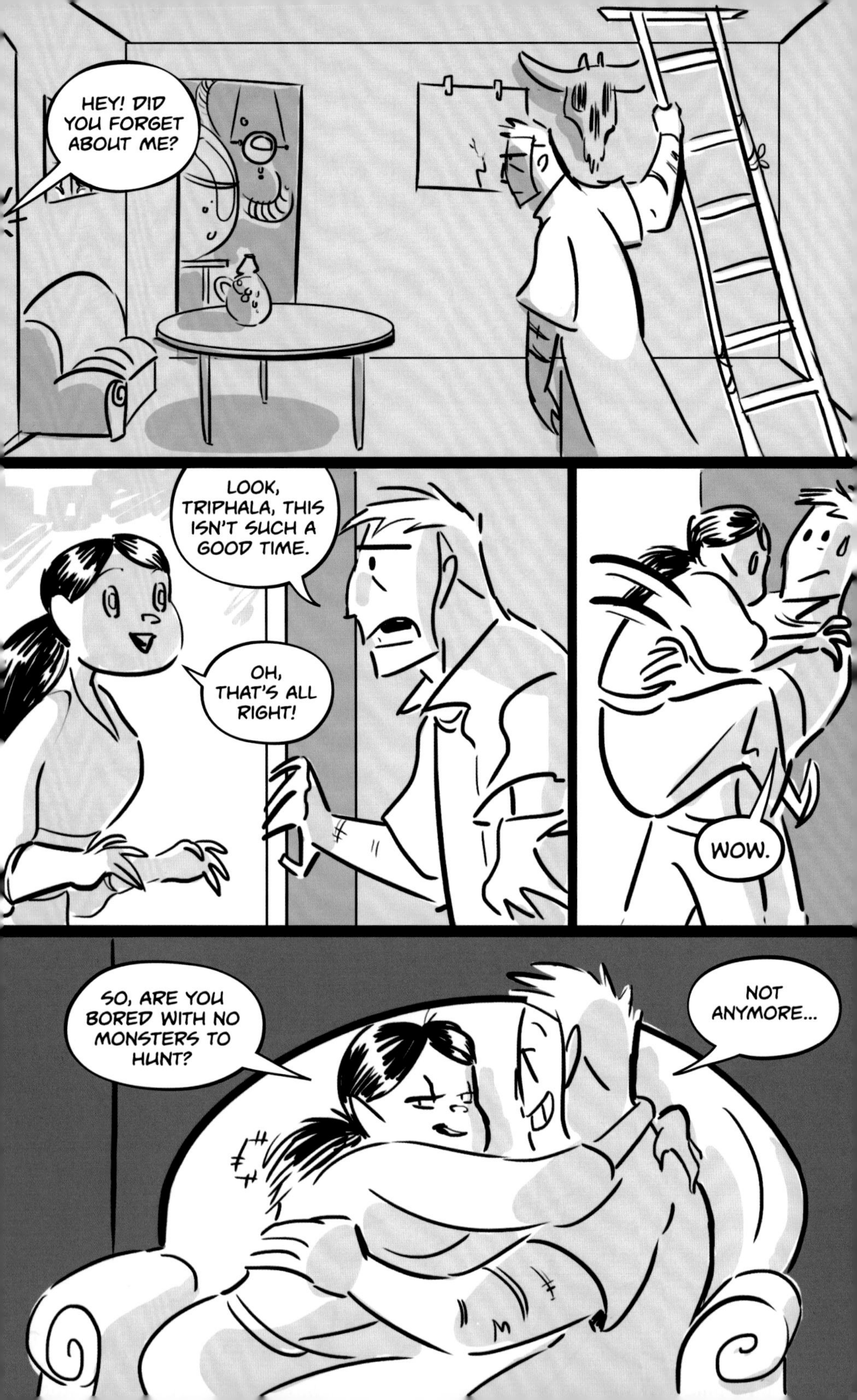
HEY! DID YOU FORGET ABOUT ME?
LOOK, TRIPHALA, THIS ISN'T SUCH A GOOD TIME.
OH, THAT'S ALL RIGHT!
WOW.
SO, ARE YOU BORED WITH NO MONSTERS TO HUNT?
NOT ANYMORE...

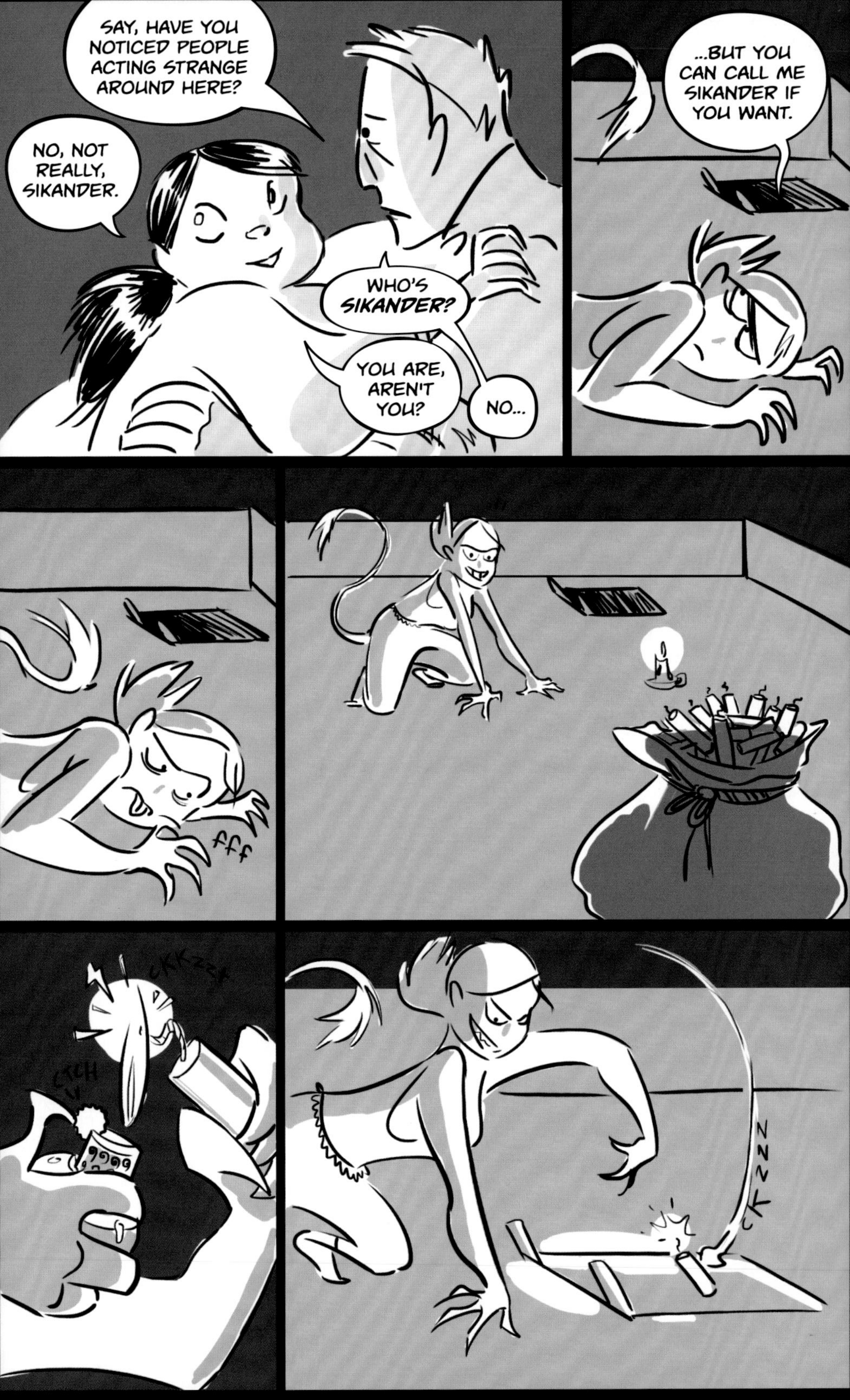
SAY, HAVE YOU NOTICED PEOPLE ACTING STRANGE AROUND HERE?
NO, NOT REALLY, SIKANDER.
WHO'S SIKANDER?
YOU ARE, AREN'T YOU?
NO...
...BUT YOU CAN CALL ME SIKANDER IF YOU WANT.
fff
CKKzzt
CTCH
NNNCK

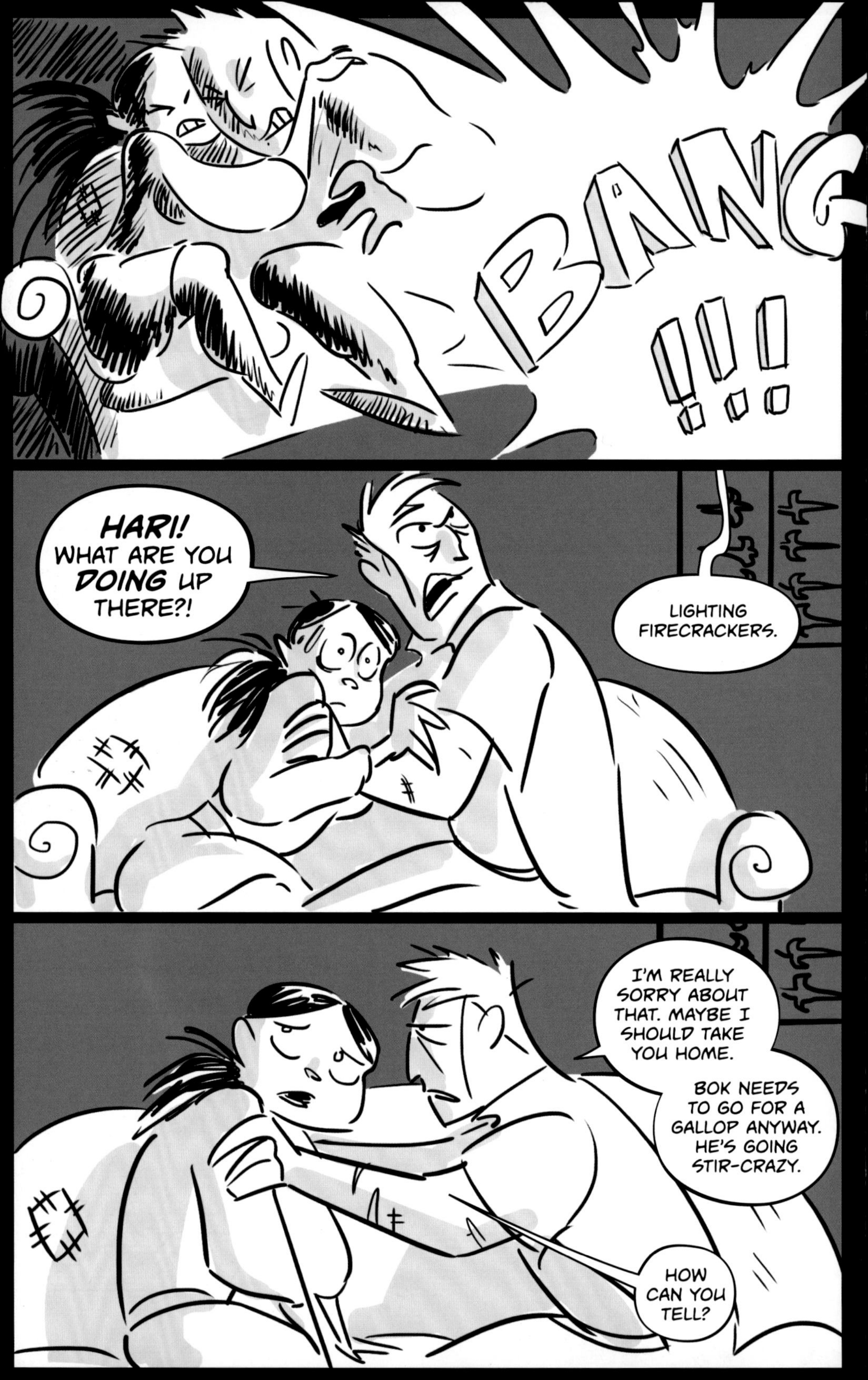
BANG!!!!
HARI! WHAT ARE YOU DOING UP THERE?!
LIGHTING FIRECRACKERS.
I'M REALLY SORRY ABOUT THAT. MAYBE I SHOULD TAKE YOU HOME.
BOK NEEDS TO GO FOR A GALLOP ANYWAY. HE'S GOING STIR-CRAZY.
HOW CAN YOU TELL?

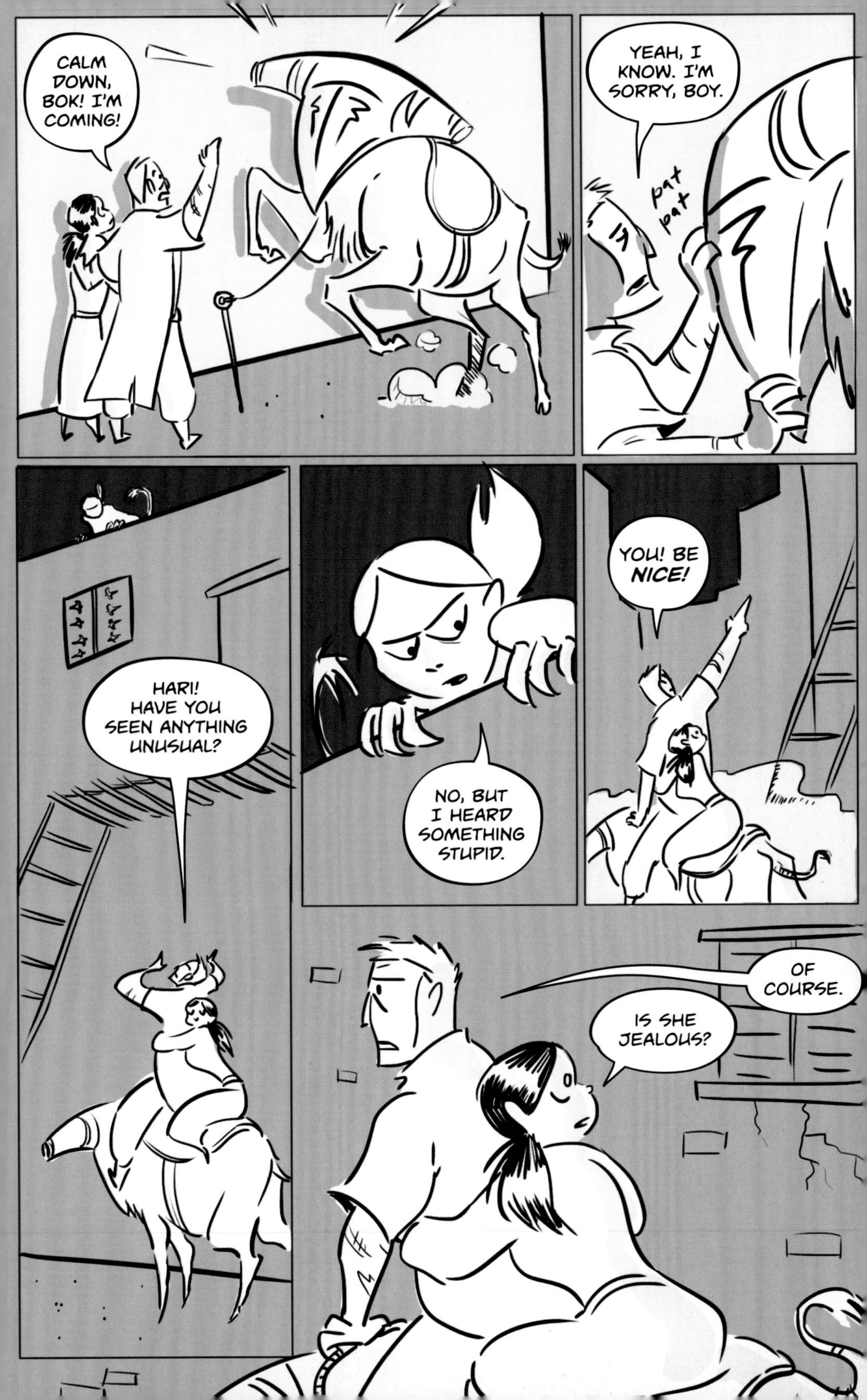
CALM DOWN, BOK! I'M COMING!
YEAH, I KNOW. I'M SORRY, BOY.
pat pat
HARI! HAVE YOU SEEN ANYTHING UNUSUAL?
NO, BUT I HEARD SOMETHING STUPID.
YOU! BE NICE!
IS SHE JEALOUS?
OF COURSE.

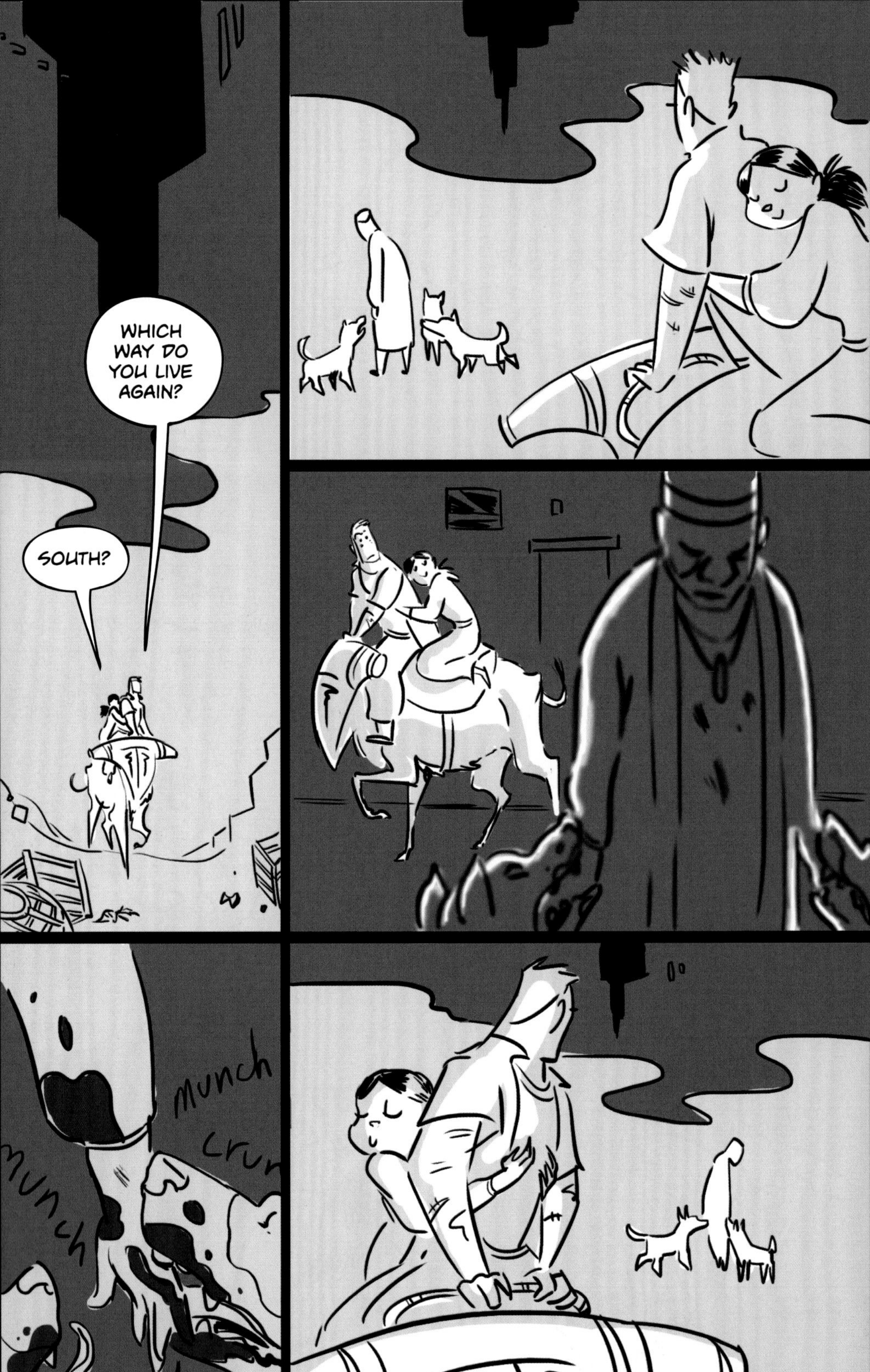
WHICH WAY DO YOU LIVE AGAIN?
SOUTH?
munch
crun
munch

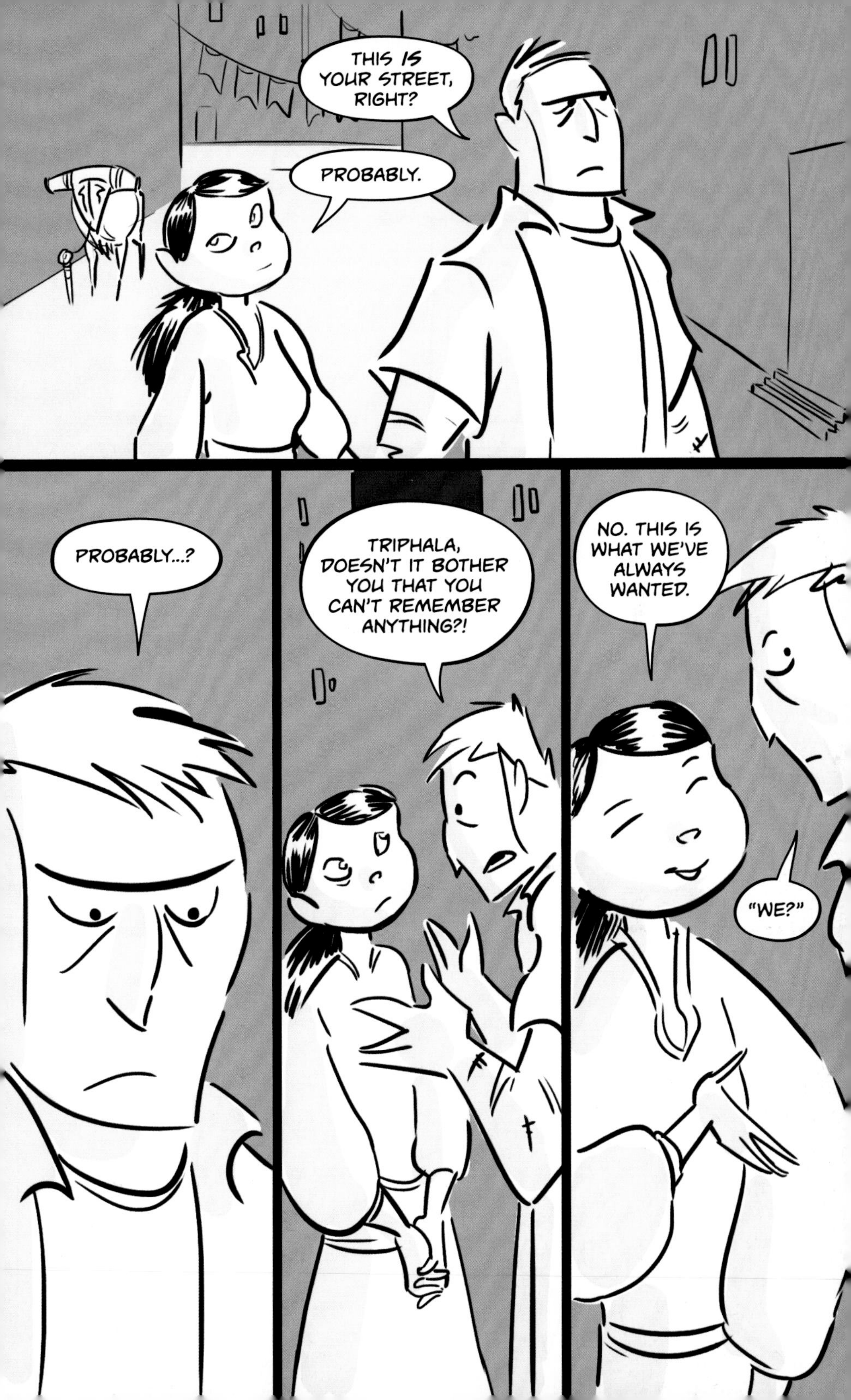
THIS IS YOUR STREET, RIGHT?
PROBABLY.
PROBABLY...?
TRIPHALA, DOESN'T IT BOTHER YOU THAT YOU CAN'T REMEMBER ANYTHING?!
NO. THIS IS WHAT WE'VE ALWAYS WANTED.
"WE?"

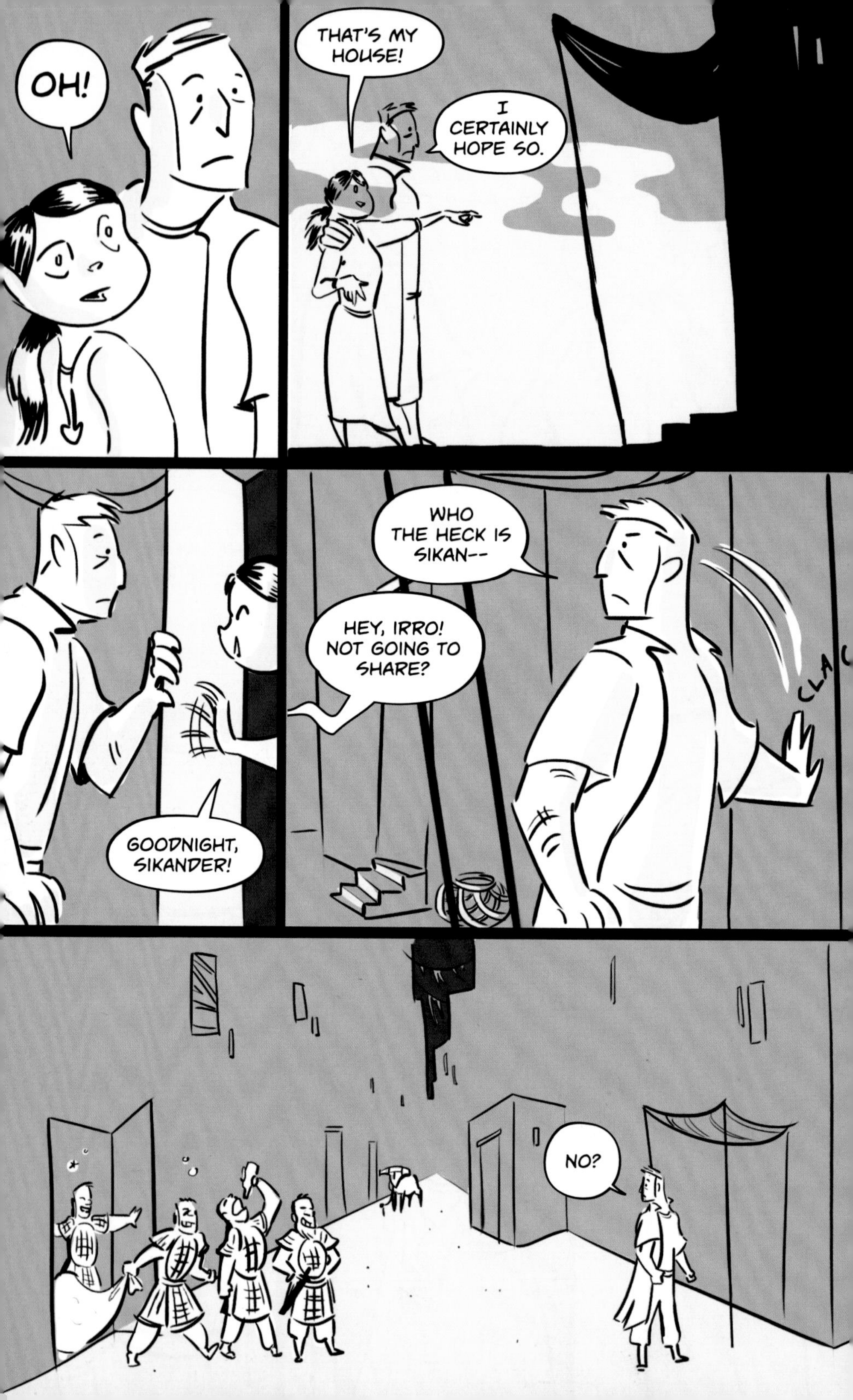
OH!
THAT'S MY HOUSE!
I CERTAINLY HOPE SO.
GOODNIGHT, SIKANDER!
WHO THE HECK IS SIKAN--
HEY, IRRO! NOT GOING TO SHARE?
CLAC
NO?

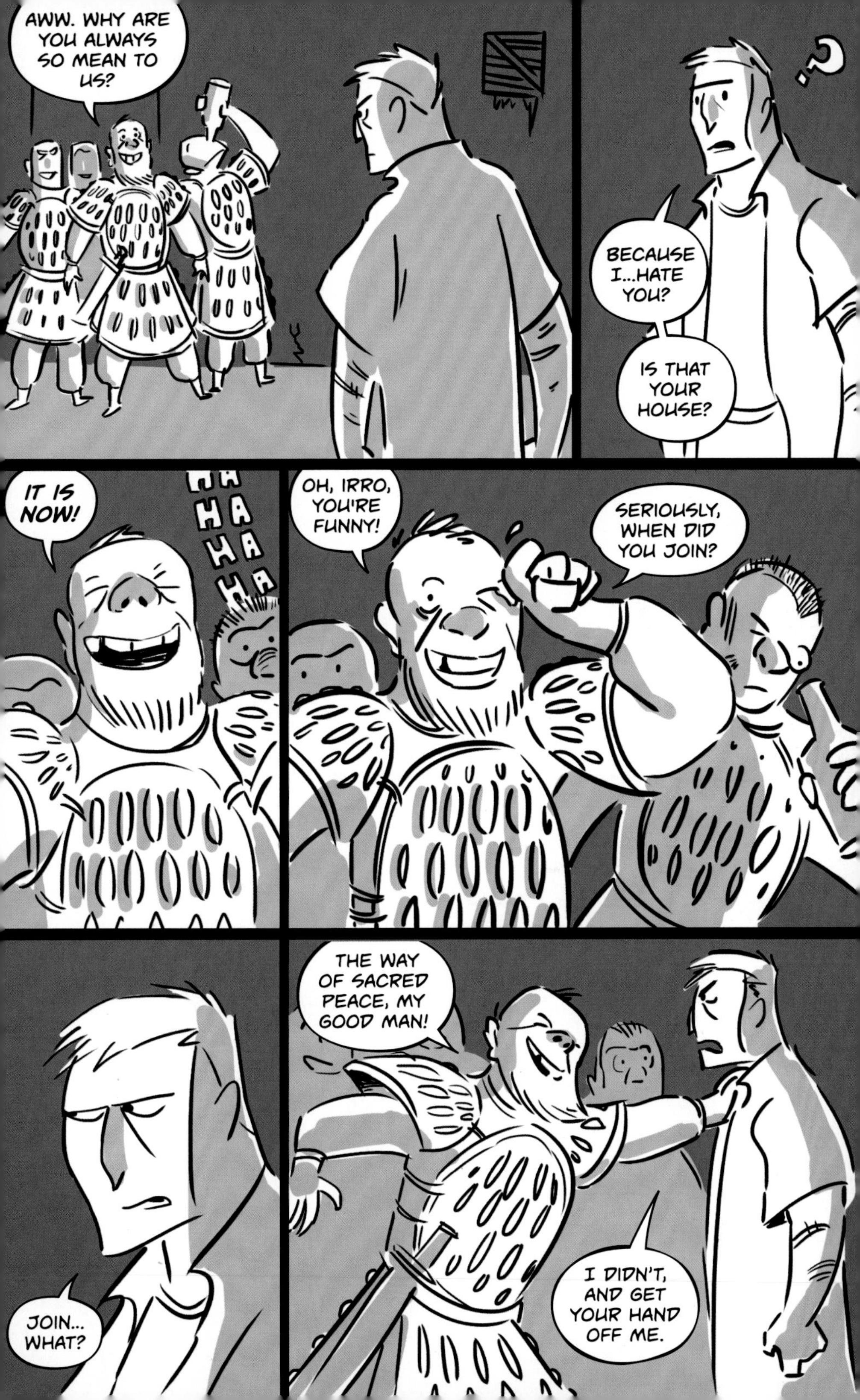
AWW. WHY ARE YOU ALWAYS SO MEAN TO US?
BECAUSE I...HATE YOU?
IS THAT YOUR HOUSE?
IT IS NOW!
HA HA HA HA HA HA HA HA
OH, IRRO, YOU'RE FUNNY!
SERIOUSLY, WHEN DID YOU JOIN?
JOIN... WHAT?
THE WAY OF SACRED PEACE, MY GOOD MAN!
I DIDN'T, AND GET YOUR HAND OFF ME.

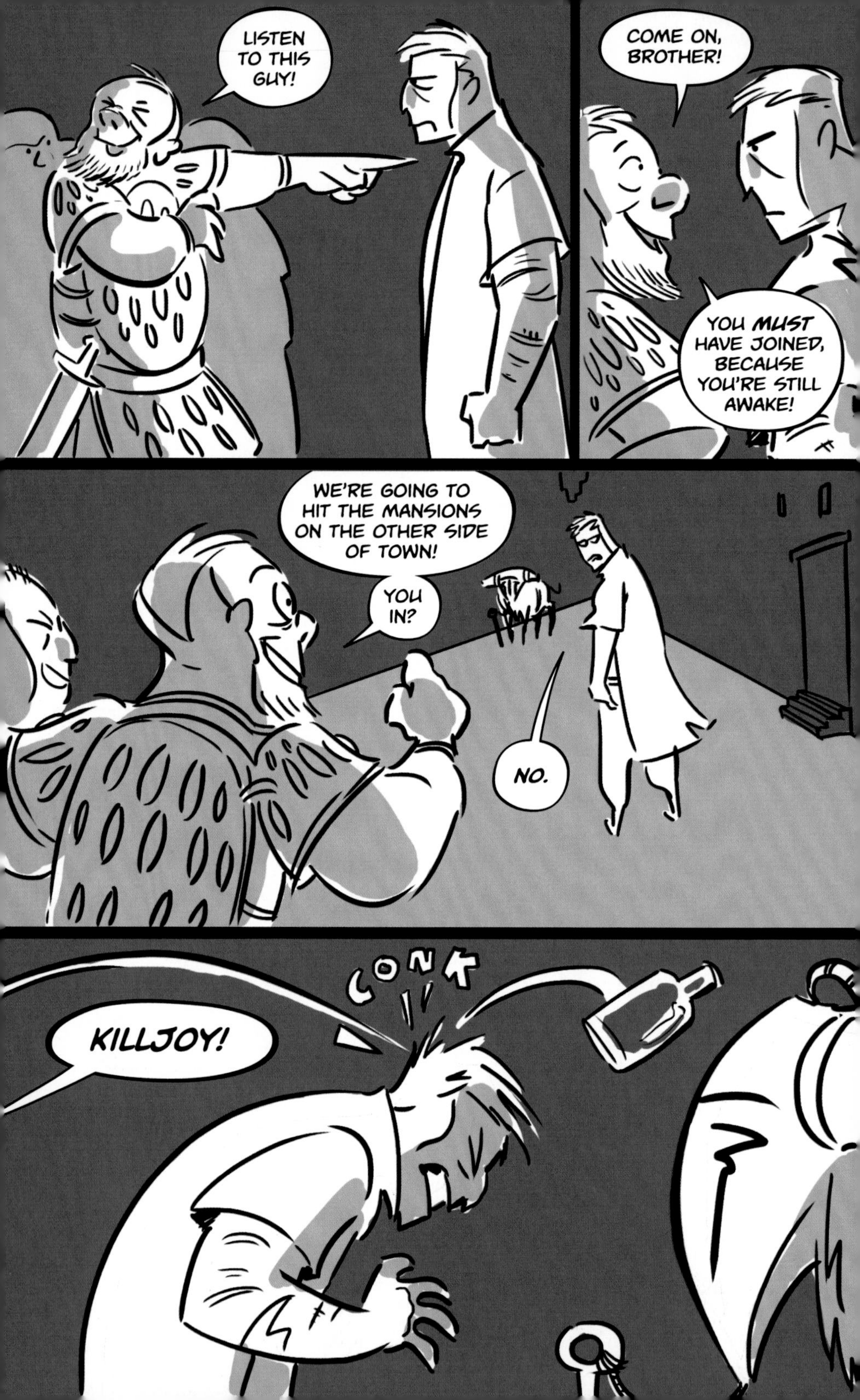
LISTEN TO THIS GUY!
COME ON, BROTHER!
YOU MUST HAVE JOINED, BECAUSE YOU'RE STILL AWAKE!
WE'RE GOING TO HIT THE MANSIONS ON THE OTHER SIDE OF TOWN!
YOU IN?
NO.
CONK
KILLJOY!

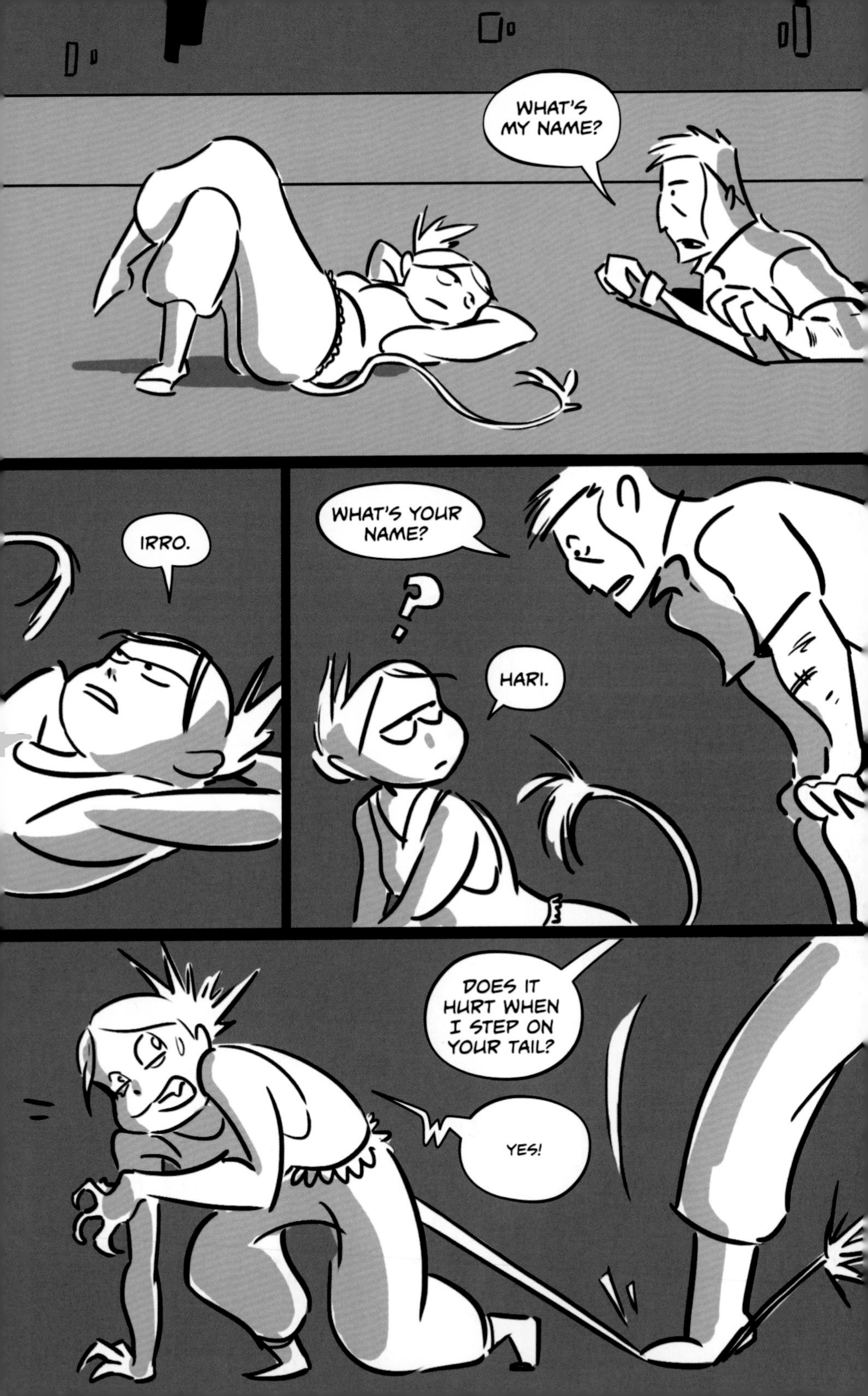
WHAT'S MY NAME?
IRRO.
WHAT'S YOUR NAME?
?
HARI.
DOES IT HURT WHEN I STEP ON YOUR TAIL?
YES!

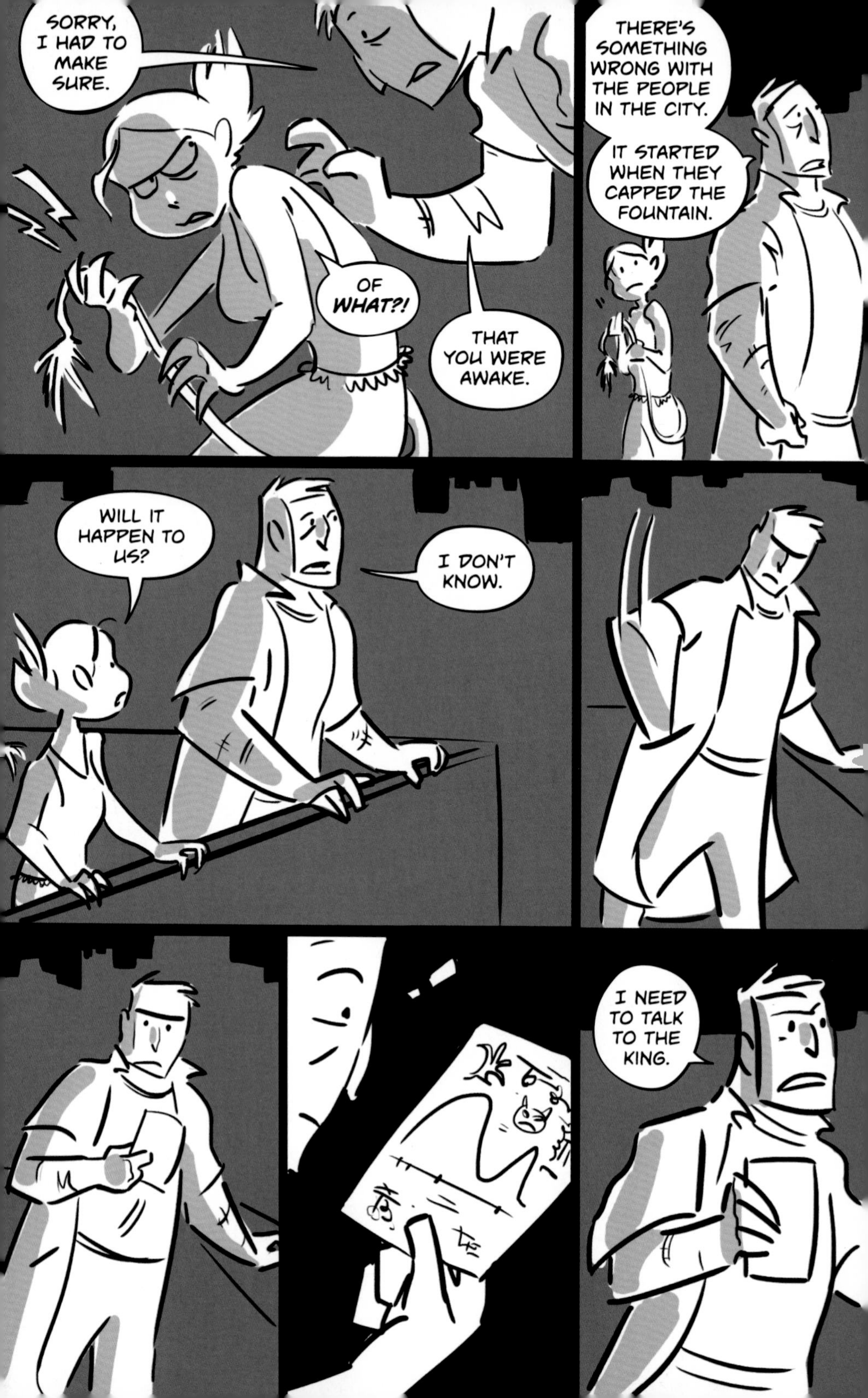
SORRY, I HAD TO MAKE SURE.
OF WHAT?!
THAT YOU WERE AWAKE.
THERE'S SOMETHING WRONG WITH THE PEOPLE IN THE CITY.
IT STARTED WHEN THEY CAPPED THE FOUNTAIN.
WILL IT HAPPEN TO US?
I DON'T KNOW.
I NEED TO TALK TO THE KING.

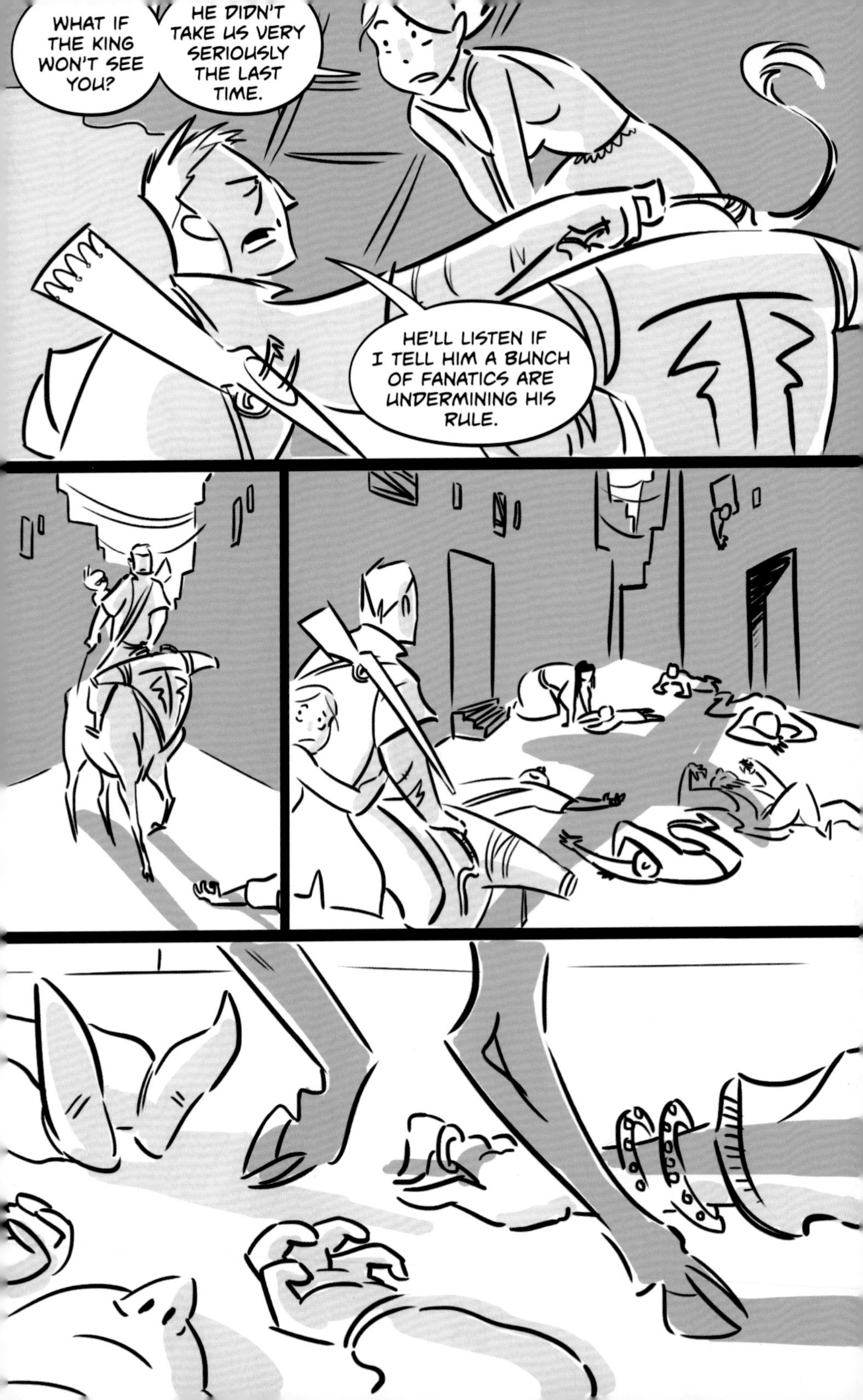
WHAT IF THE KING WON'T SEE YOU?
HE DIDN'T TAKE US VERY SERIOUSLY THE LAST TIME.
HE'LL LISTEN IF I TELL HIM A BUNCH OF FANATICS ARE UNDERMINING HIS RULE.

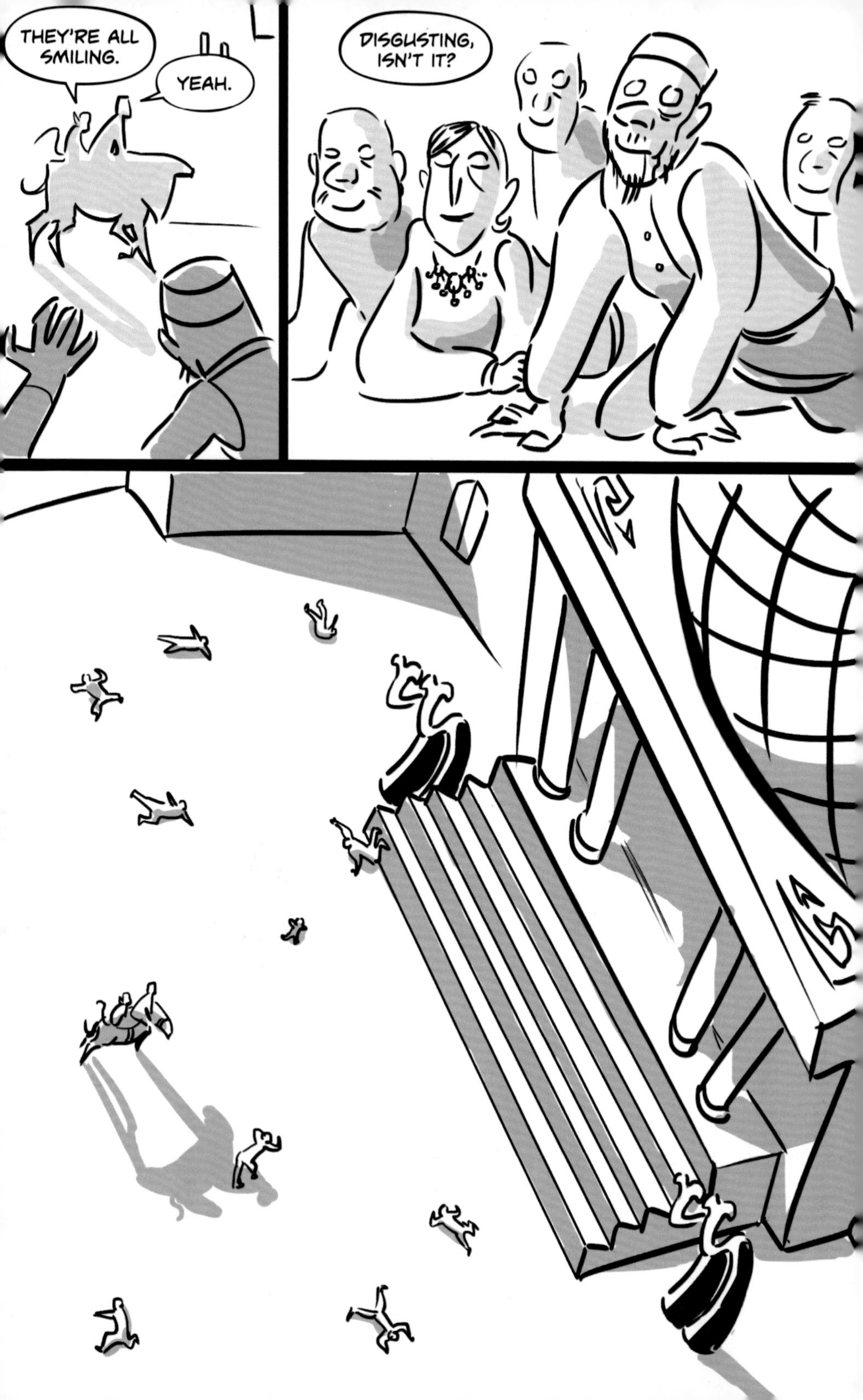
THEY'RE ALL SMILING.
YEAH.
DISGUSTING, ISN'T IT?

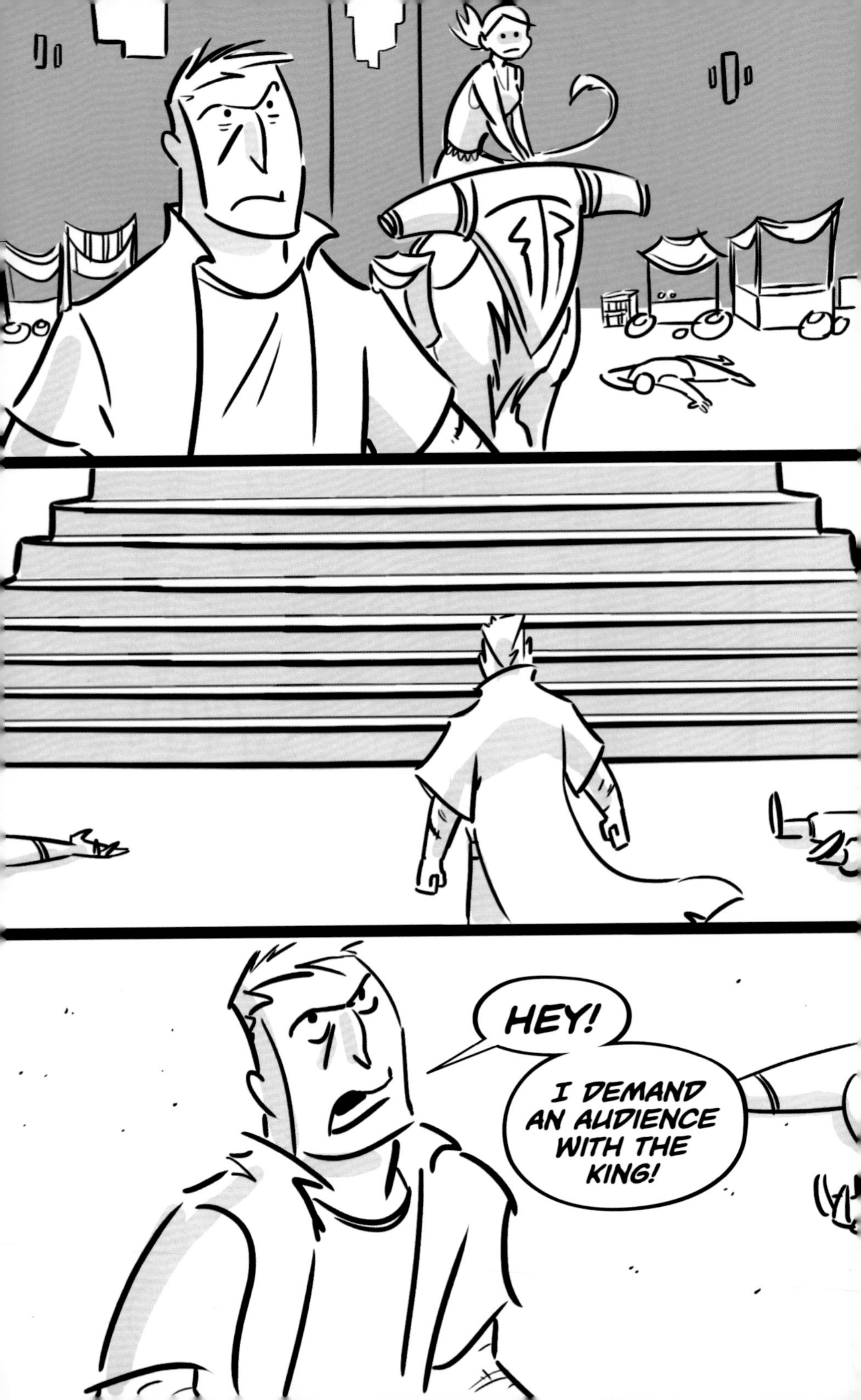
HEY!
I DEMAND AN AUDIENCE WITH THE KING!

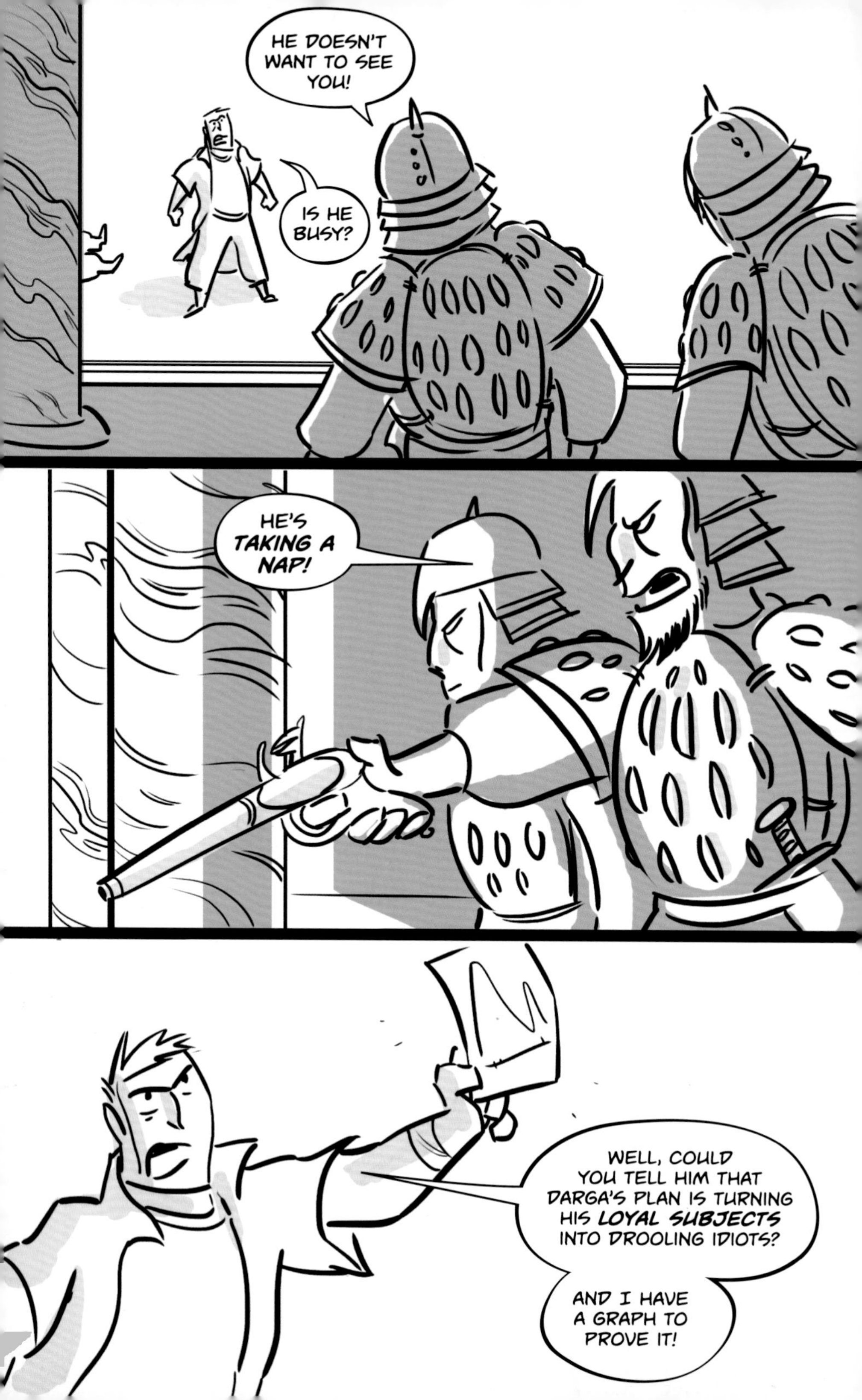
HE DOESN'T WANT TO SEE YOU!
IS HE BUSY?
HE'S *TAKING A NAP!*
WELL, COULD YOU TELL HIM THAT DARGA'S PLAN IS TURNING HIS *LOYAL SUBJECTS* INTO DROOLING IDIOTS?
AND I HAVE A GRAPH TO PROVE IT!

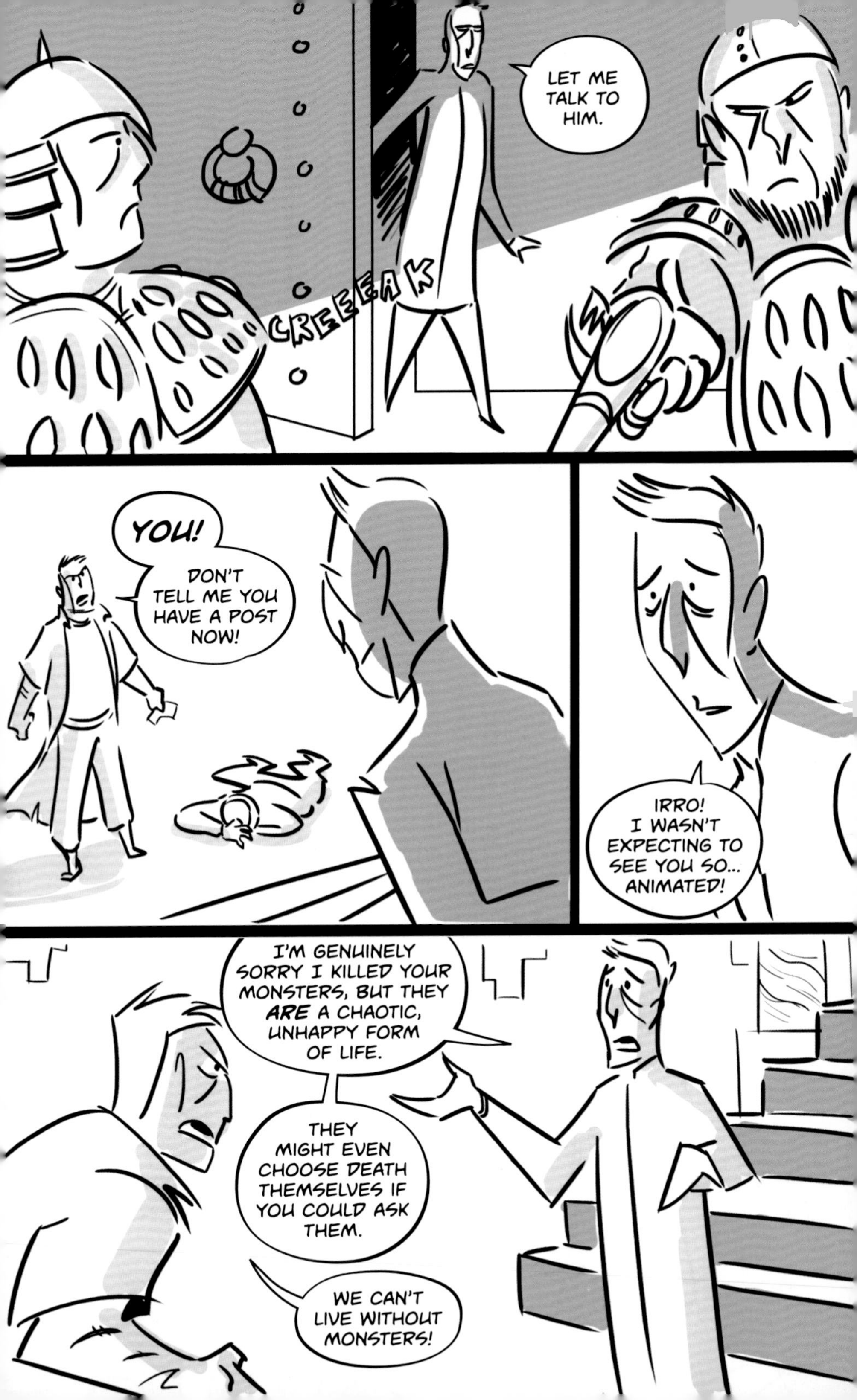
LET ME TALK TO HIM.
CREEEAK
YOU!
DON'T TELL ME YOU HAVE A POST NOW!
IRRO! I WASN'T EXPECTING TO SEE YOU SO... ANIMATED!
I'M GENUINELY SORRY I KILLED YOUR MONSTERS, BUT THEY *ARE* A CHAOTIC, UNHAPPY FORM OF LIFE.
THEY MIGHT EVEN CHOOSE DEATH THEMSELVES IF YOU COULD ASK THEM.
WE CAN'T LIVE WITHOUT MONSTERS!

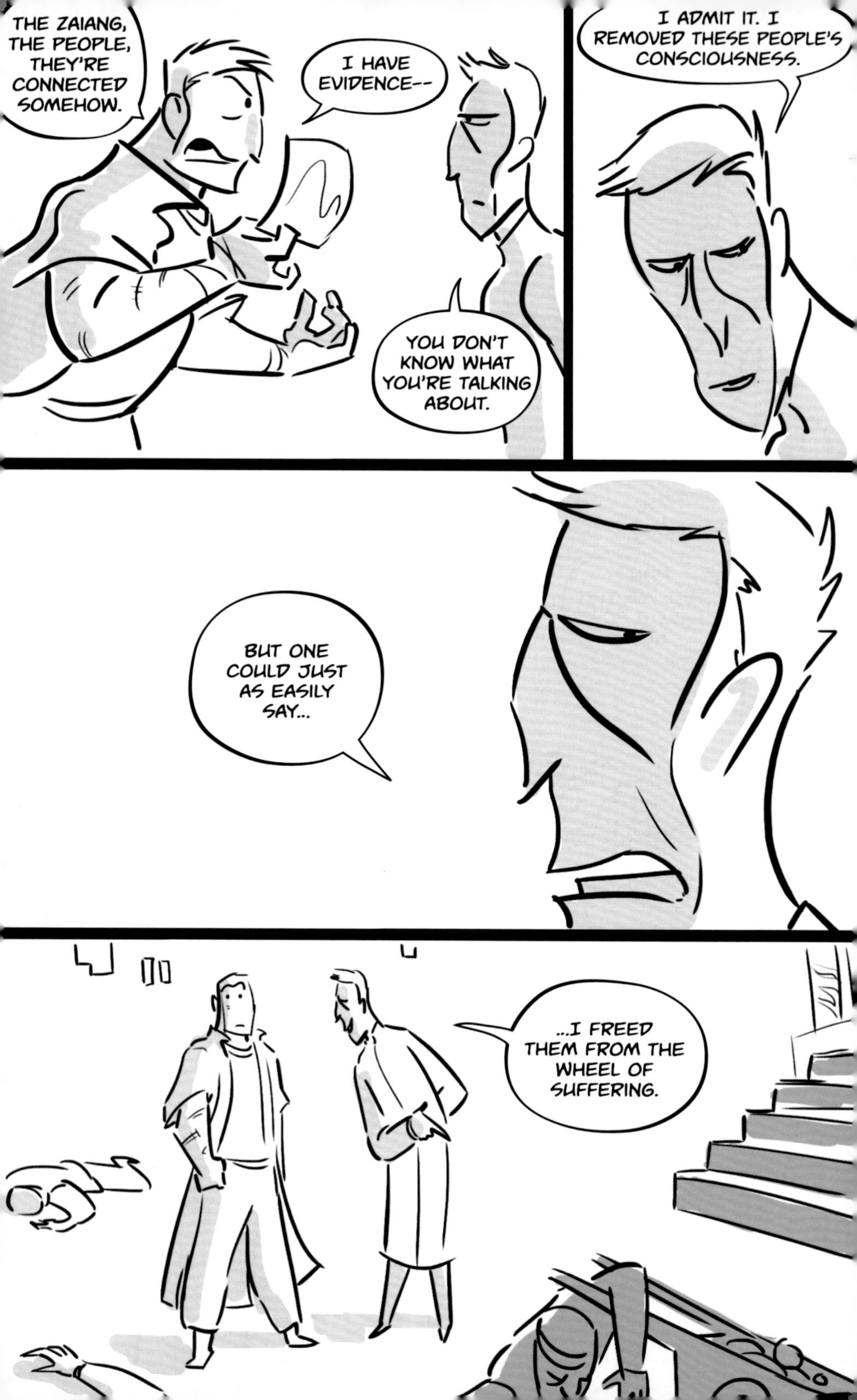
THE ZAIANG, THE PEOPLE, THEY'RE CONNECTED SOMEHOW.
I HAVE EVIDENCE--
YOU DON'T KNOW WHAT YOU'RE TALKING ABOUT.
I ADMIT IT. I REMOVED THESE PEOPLE'S CONSCIOUSNESS.
BUT ONE COULD JUST AS EASILY SAY...
...I FREED THEM FROM THE WHEEL OF SUFFERING.

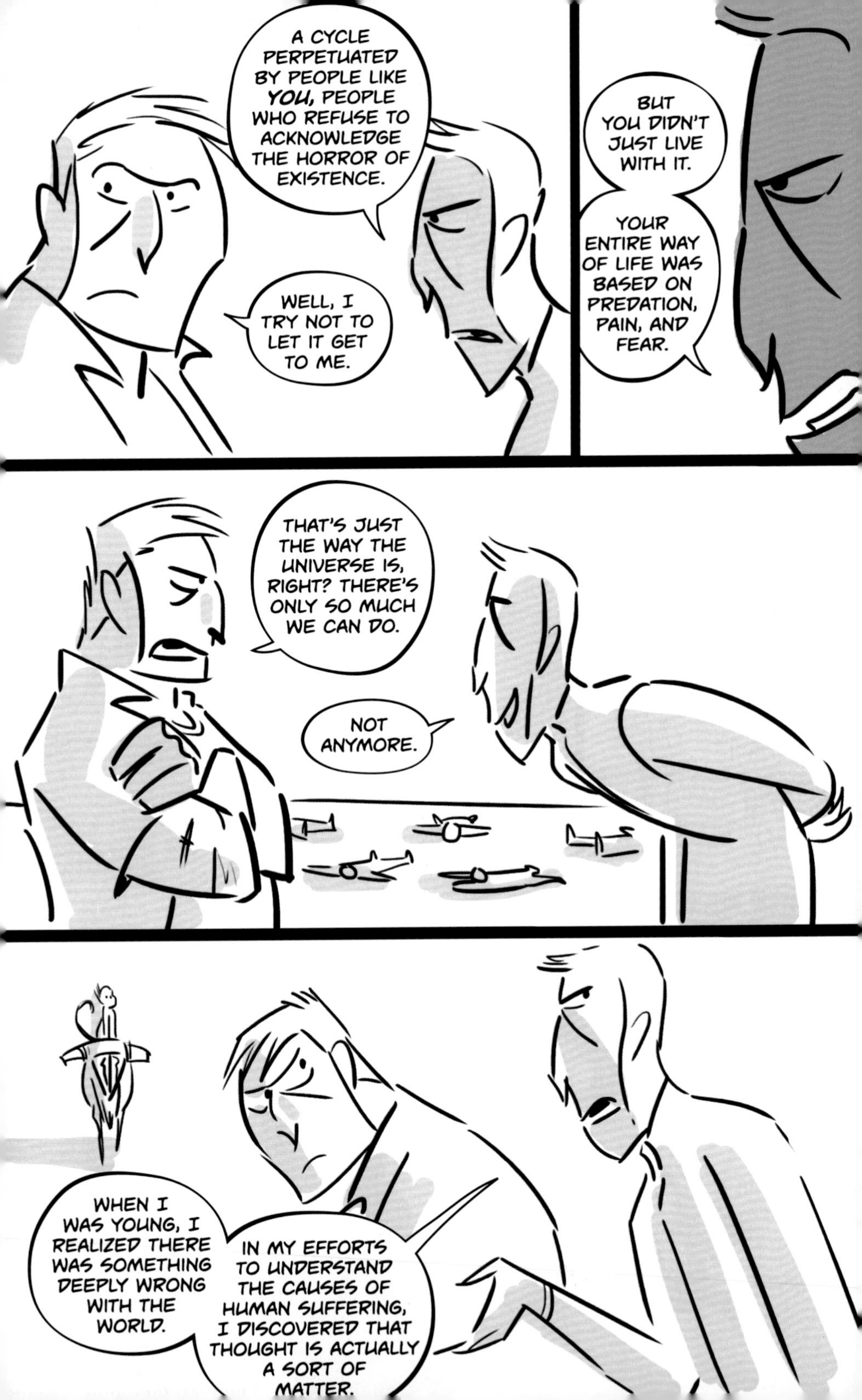
A CYCLE PERPETUATED BY PEOPLE LIKE *YOU*, PEOPLE WHO REFUSE TO ACKNOWLEDGE THE HORROR OF EXISTENCE.
WELL, I TRY NOT TO LET IT GET TO ME.
BUT YOU DIDN'T JUST LIVE WITH IT.
YOUR ENTIRE WAY OF LIFE WAS BASED ON PREDATION, PAIN, AND FEAR.
THAT'S JUST THE WAY THE UNIVERSE IS, RIGHT? THERE'S ONLY SO MUCH WE CAN DO.
NOT ANYMORE.
WHEN I WAS YOUNG, I REALIZED THERE WAS SOMETHING DEEPLY WRONG WITH THE WORLD.
IN MY EFFORTS TO UNDERSTAND THE CAUSES OF HUMAN SUFFERING, I DISCOVERED THAT THOUGHT IS ACTUALLY A SORT OF MATTER.

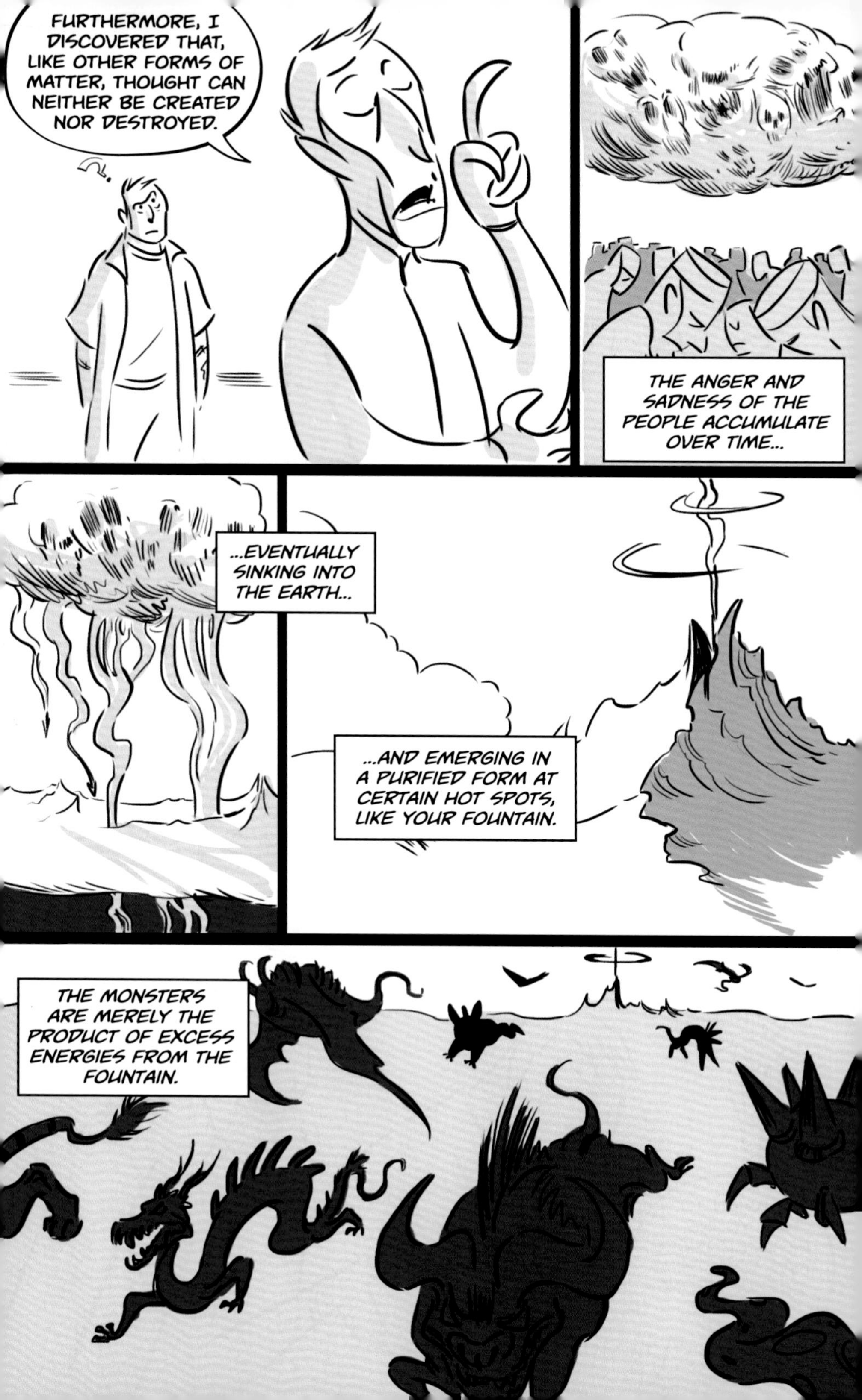
FURTHERMORE, I DISCOVERED THAT, LIKE OTHER FORMS OF MATTER, THOUGHT CAN NEITHER BE CREATED NOR DESTROYED.
THE ANGER AND SADNESS OF THE PEOPLE ACCUMULATE OVER TIME...
...EVENTUALLY SINKING INTO THE EARTH...
...AND EMERGING IN A PURIFIED FORM AT CERTAIN HOT SPOTS, LIKE YOUR FOUNTAIN.
THE MONSTERS ARE MERELY THE PRODUCT OF EXCESS ENERGIES FROM THE FOUNTAIN.

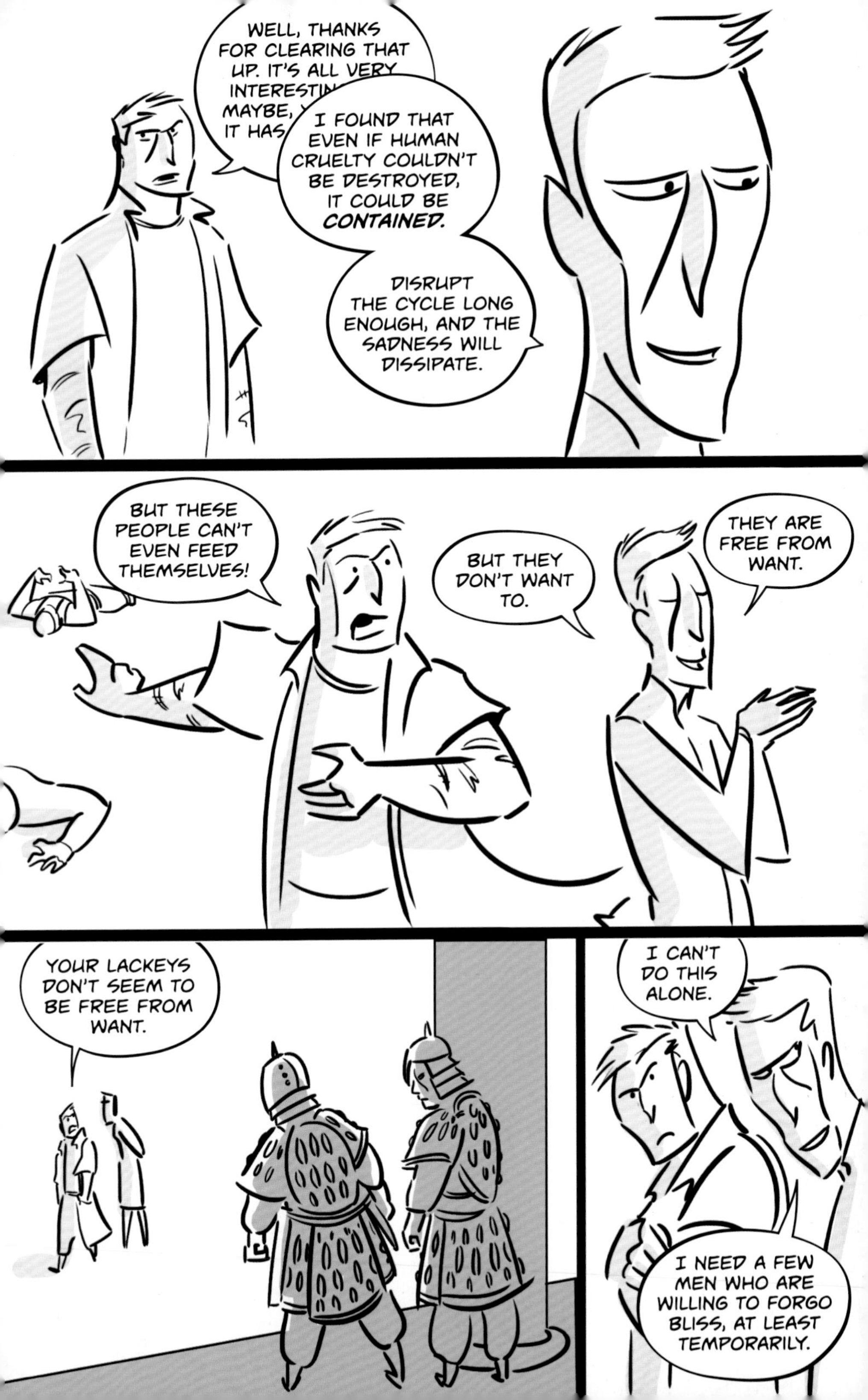
WELL, THANKS FOR CLEARING THAT UP. IT'S ALL VERY INTERESTIN
MAYBE,
IT HAS
I FOUND THAT EVEN IF HUMAN CRUELTY COULDN'T BE DESTROYED, IT COULD BE CONTAINED.
DISRUPT THE CYCLE LONG ENOUGH, AND THE SADNESS WILL DISSIPATE.
BUT THESE PEOPLE CAN'T EVEN FEED THEMSELVES!
BUT THEY DON'T WANT TO.
THEY ARE FREE FROM WANT.
YOUR LACKEYS DON'T SEEM TO BE FREE FROM WANT.
I CAN'T DO THIS ALONE.
I NEED A FEW MEN WHO ARE WILLING TO FORGO BLISS, AT LEAST TEMPORARILY.

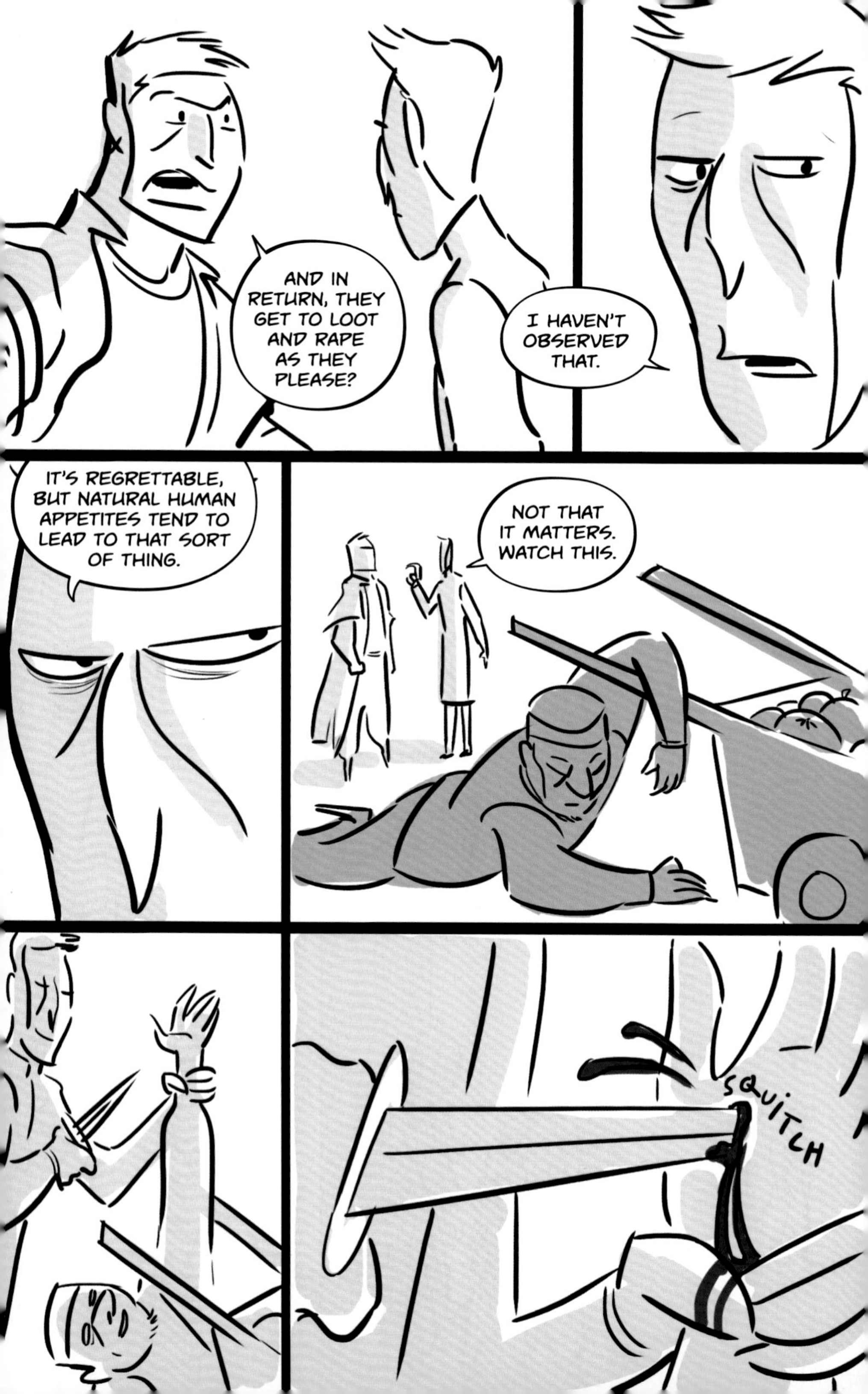
AND IN RETURN, THEY GET TO LOOT AND RAPE AS THEY PLEASE?
I HAVEN'T OBSERVED THAT.
IT'S REGRETTABLE, BUT NATURAL HUMAN APPETITES TEND TO LEAD TO THAT SORT OF THING.
NOT THAT IT MATTERS. WATCH THIS.
SQUITCH

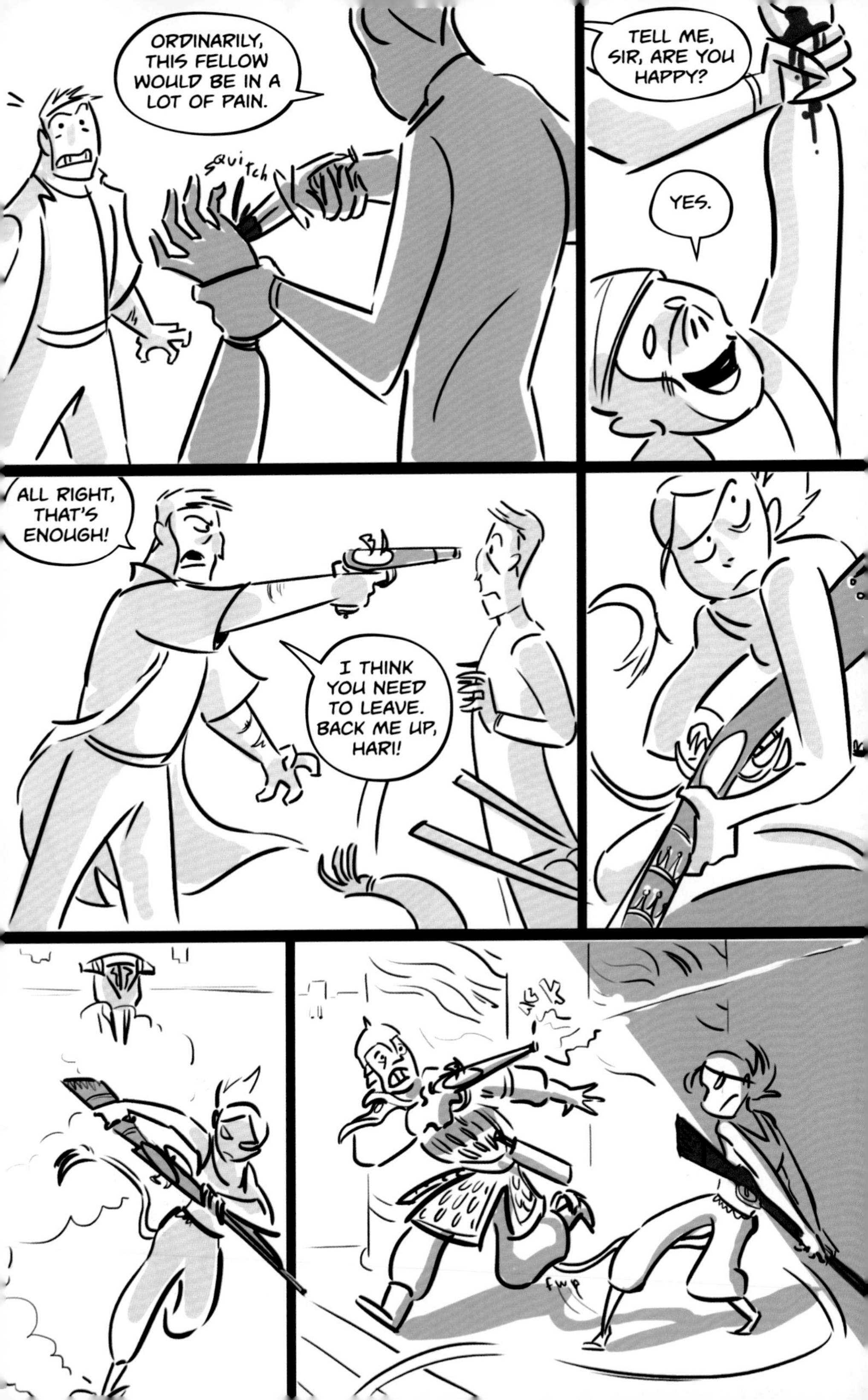
ORDINARILY, THIS FELLOW WOULD BE IN A LOT OF PAIN.
SQUITCH
TELL ME, SIR, ARE YOU HAPPY?
YES.
ALL RIGHT, THAT'S ENOUGH!
I THINK YOU NEED TO LEAVE. BACK ME UP, HARI!
FWP

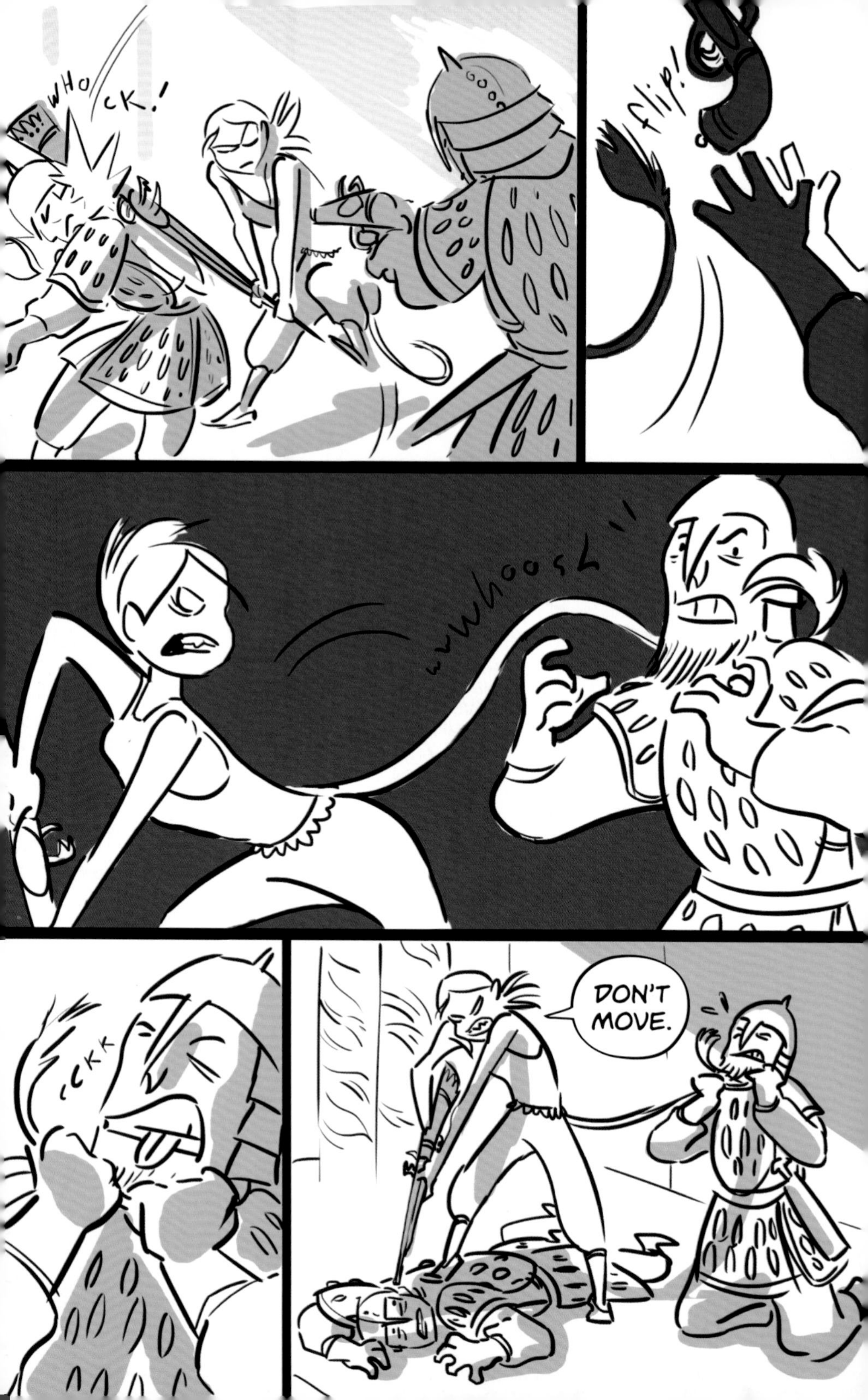
WHOCK!
flip!
wwhoosh
ckk
DON'T MOVE.

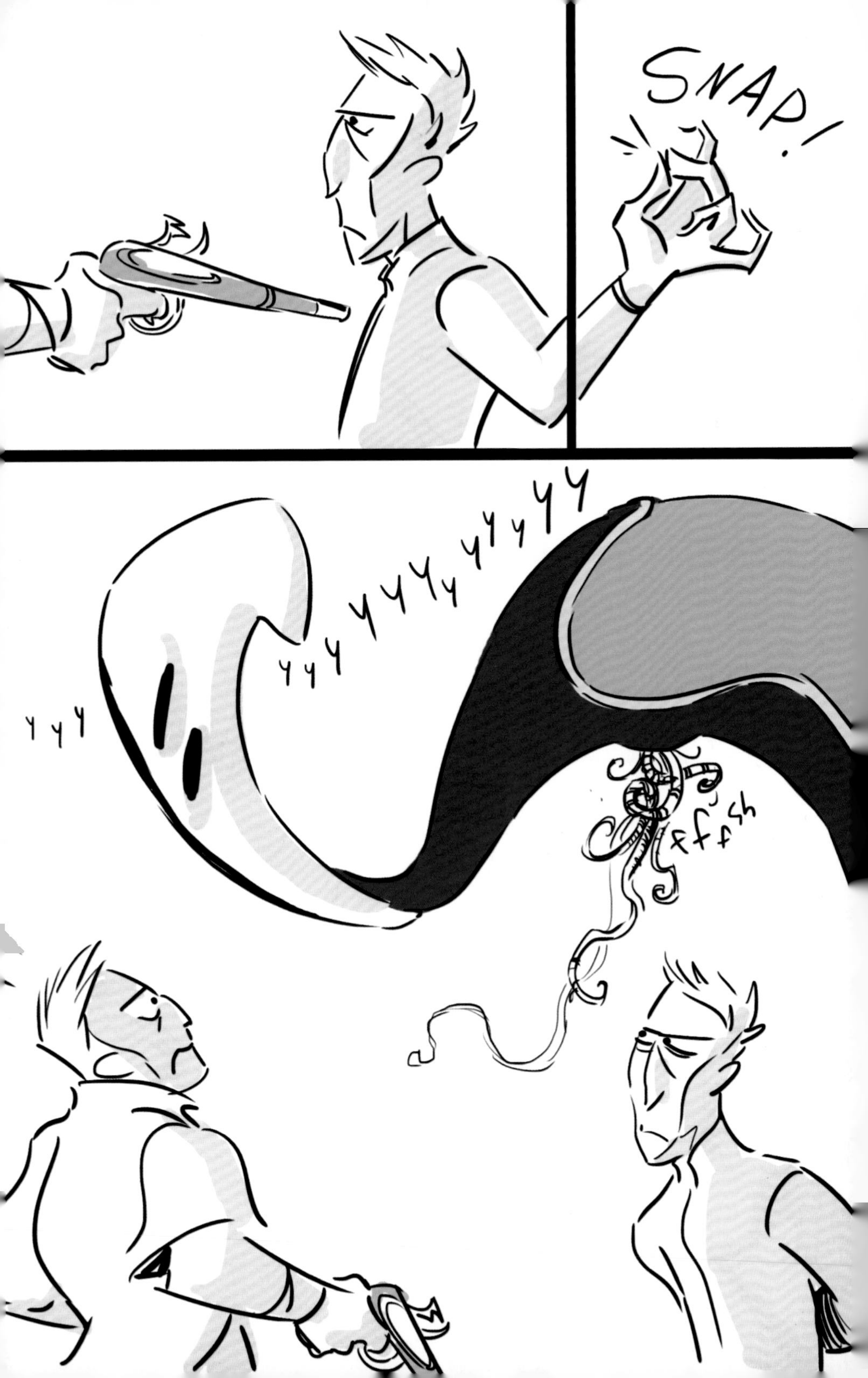
SNAP!
yyyyyyyyyyyyyyyyYY
ffssh

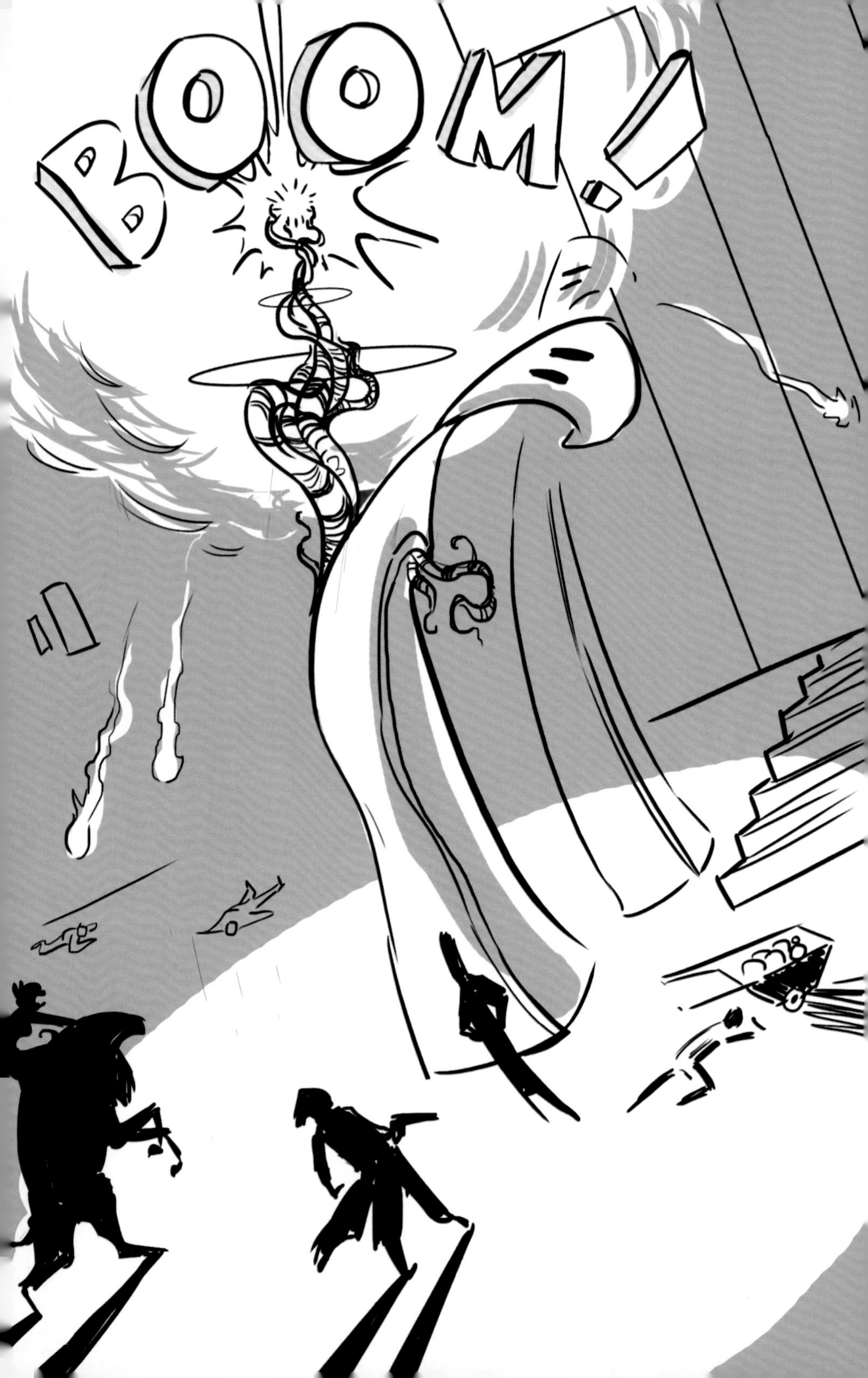
BOOM!

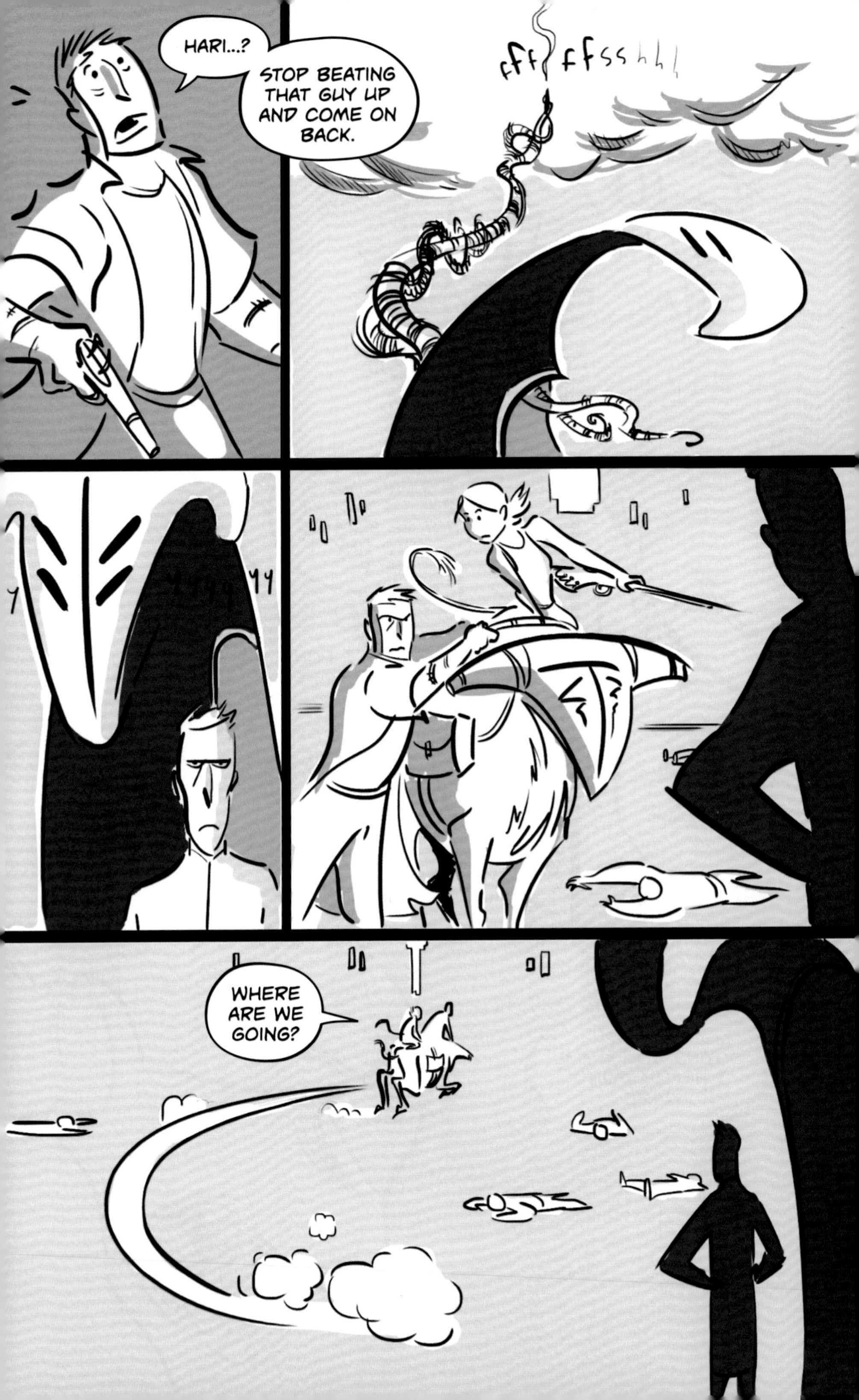
HARI...?
STOP BEATING THAT GUY UP AND COME ON BACK.
fff ffsshhh
WHERE ARE WE GOING?

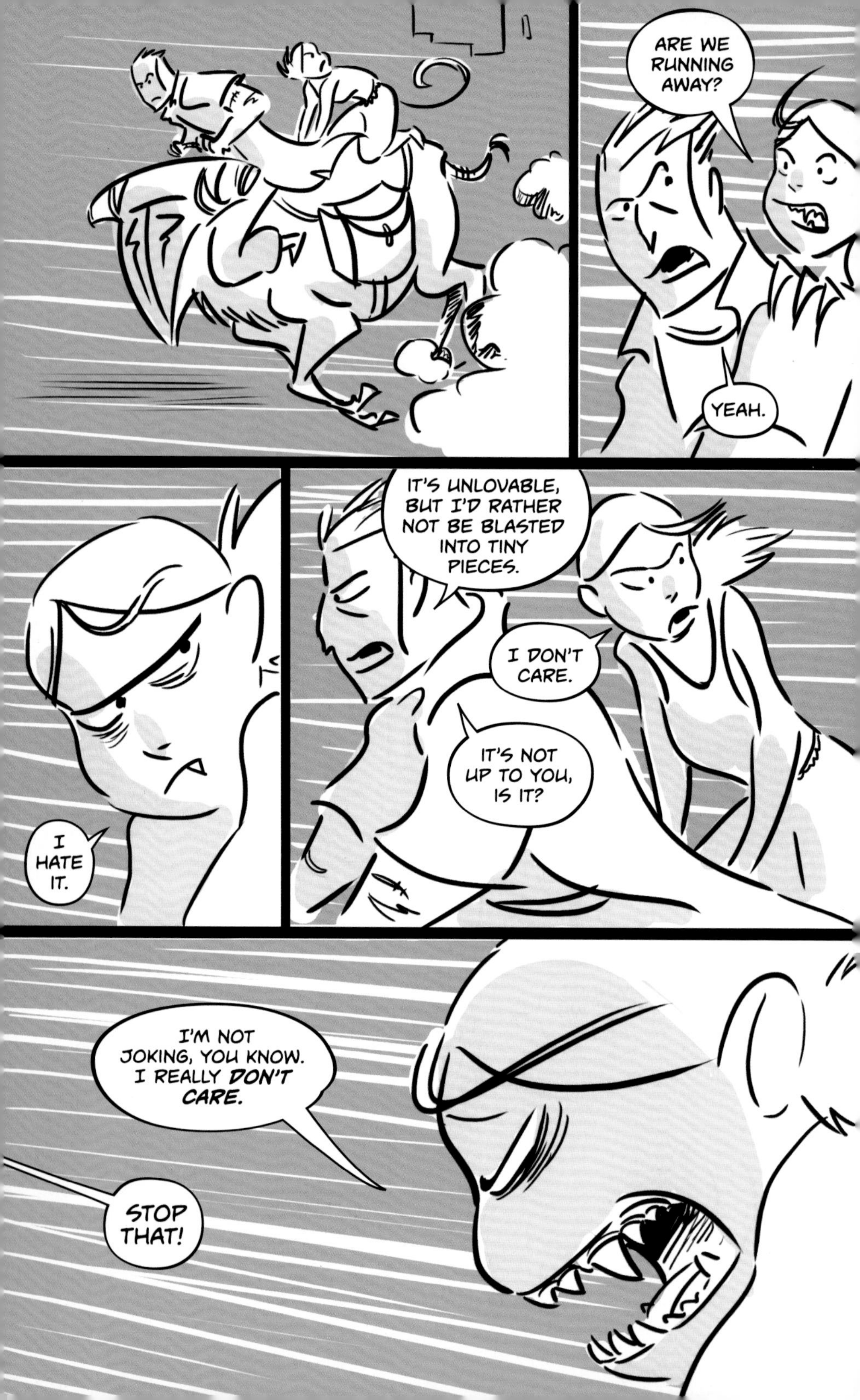
ARE WE RUNNING AWAY?
YEAH.
I HATE IT.
IT'S UNLOVABLE, BUT I'D RATHER NOT BE BLASTED INTO TINY PIECES.
I DON'T CARE.
IT'S NOT UP TO YOU, IS IT?
I'M NOT JOKING, YOU KNOW. I REALLY ***DON'T CARE.***
STOP THAT!

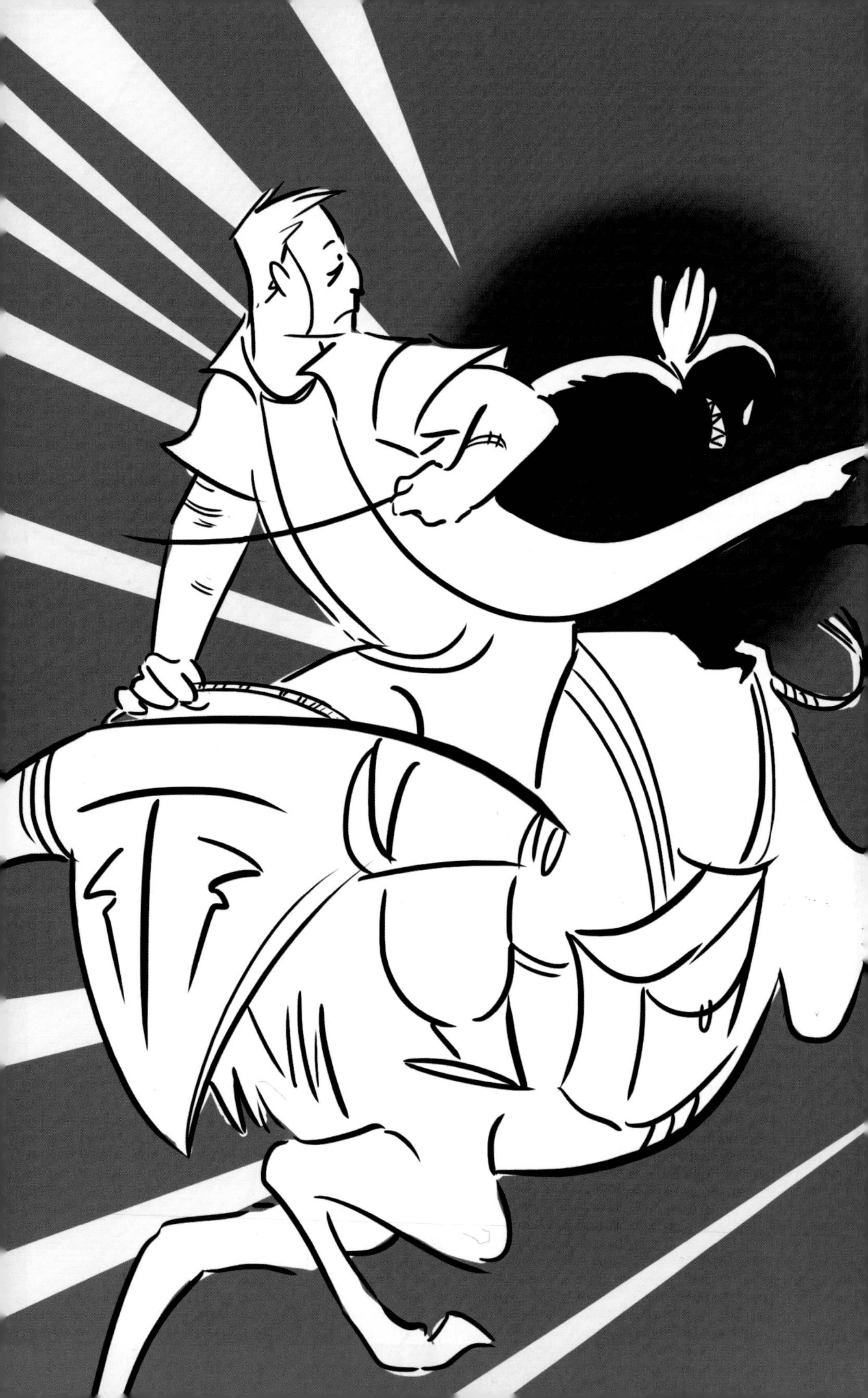

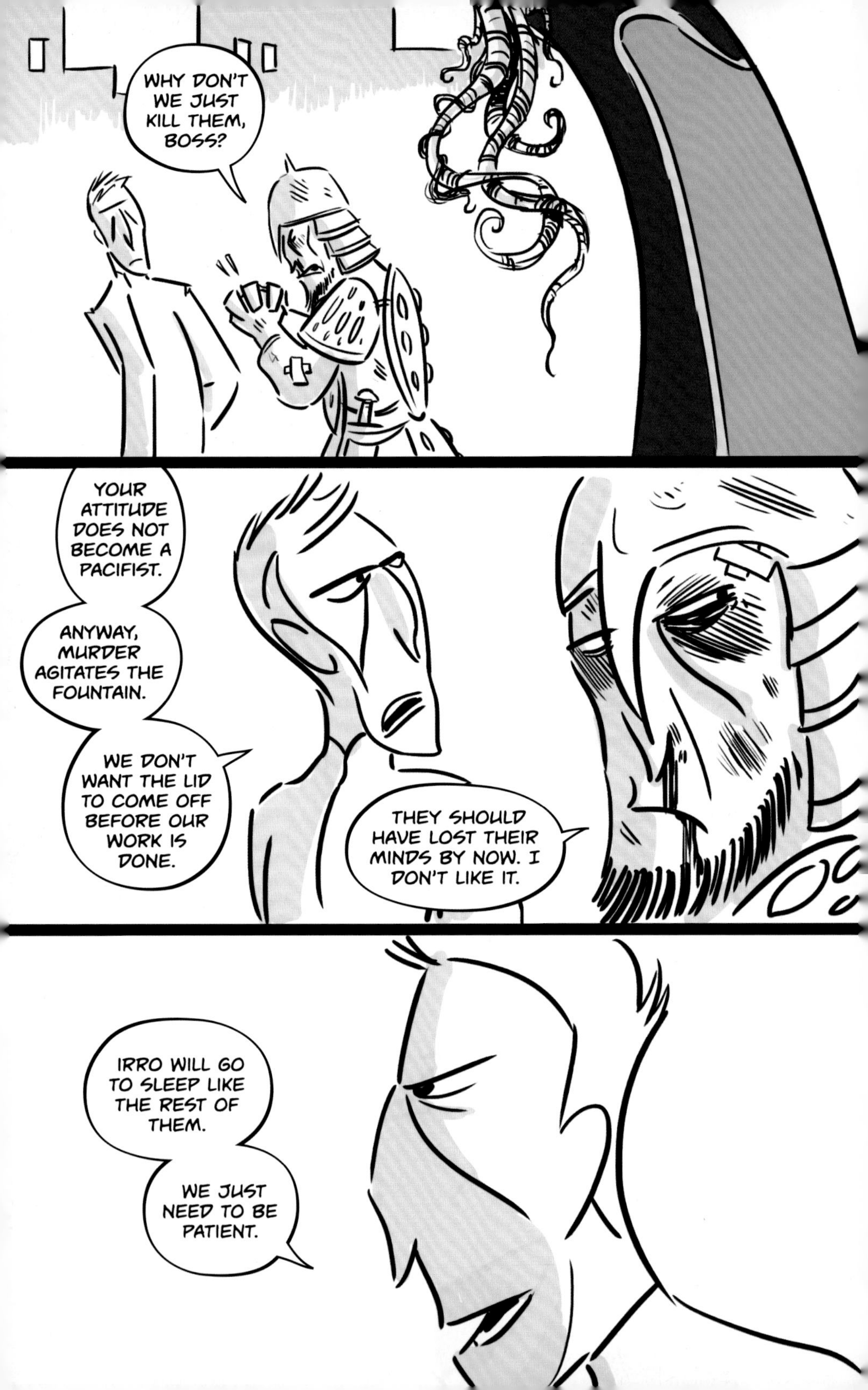
WHY DON'T WE JUST KILL THEM, BOSS?
YOUR ATTITUDE DOES NOT BECOME A PACIFIST.
ANYWAY, MURDER AGITATES THE FOUNTAIN.
WE DON'T WANT THE LID TO COME OFF BEFORE OUR WORK IS DONE.
THEY SHOULD HAVE LOST THEIR MINDS BY NOW. I DON'T LIKE IT.
IRRO WILL GO TO SLEEP LIKE THE REST OF THEM.
WE JUST NEED TO BE PATIENT.

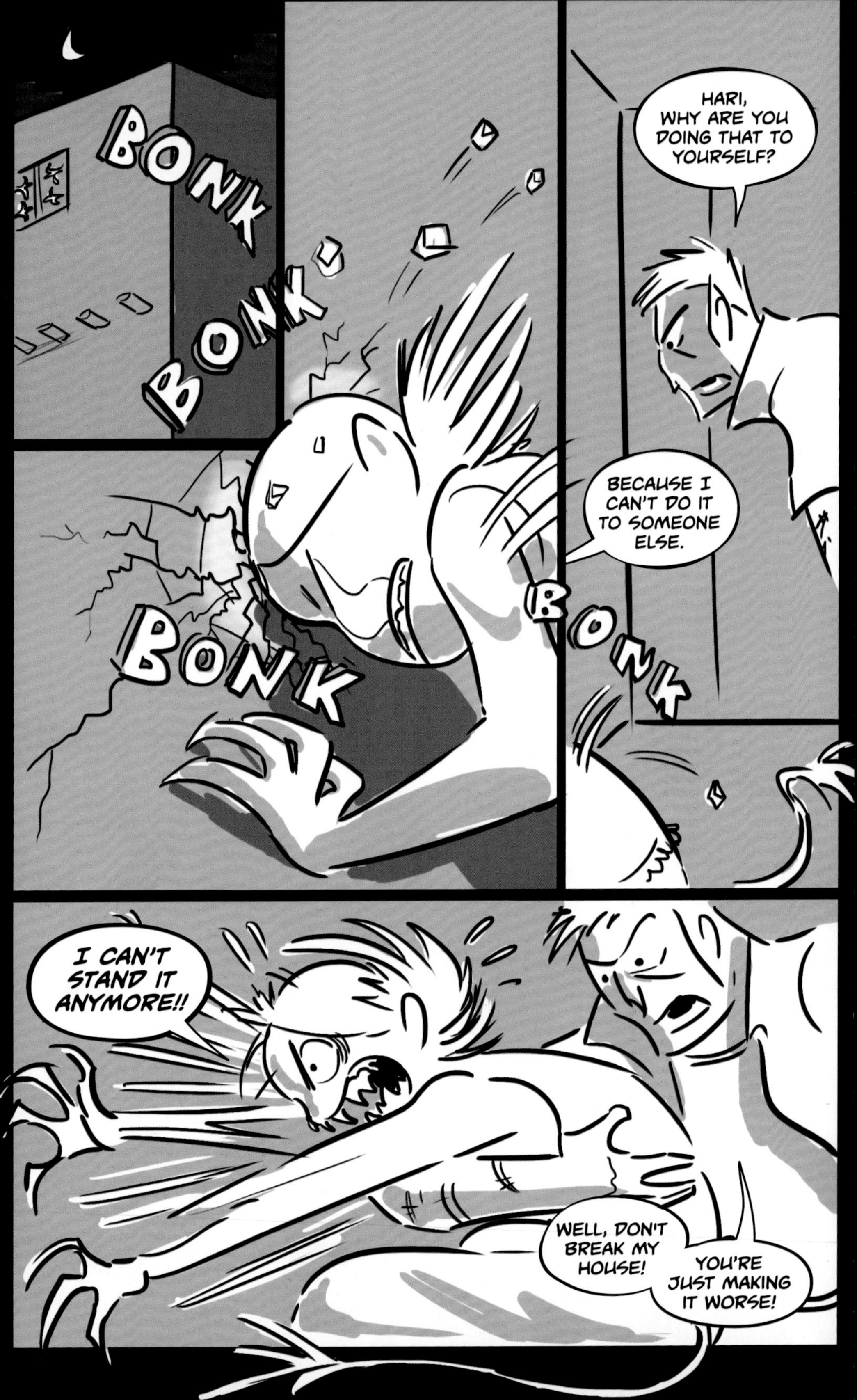
BONK
BONK
BONK
HARI, WHY ARE YOU DOING THAT TO YOURSELF?
BECAUSE I CAN'T DO IT TO SOMEONE ELSE.
BONK
BONK
I CAN'T STAND IT ANYMORE!!
WELL, DON'T BREAK MY HOUSE!
YOU'RE JUST MAKING IT WORSE!

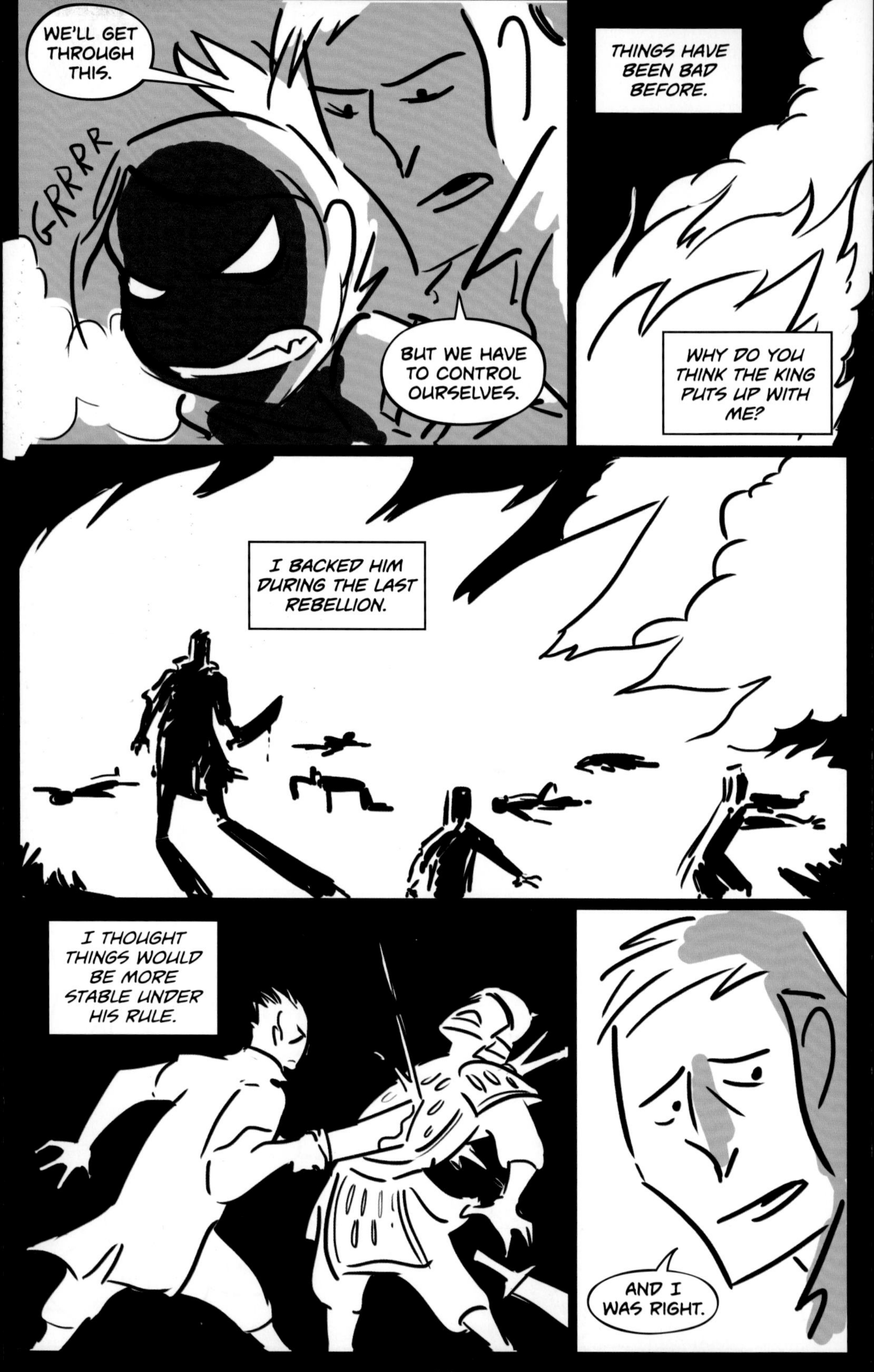
WE'LL GET THROUGH THIS.
GRRRR
BUT WE HAVE TO CONTROL OURSELVES.
THINGS HAVE BEEN BAD BEFORE.
WHY DO YOU THINK THE KING PUTS UP WITH ME?
I BACKED HIM DURING THE LAST REBELLION.
I THOUGHT THINGS WOULD BE MORE STABLE UNDER HIS RULE.
AND I WAS RIGHT.

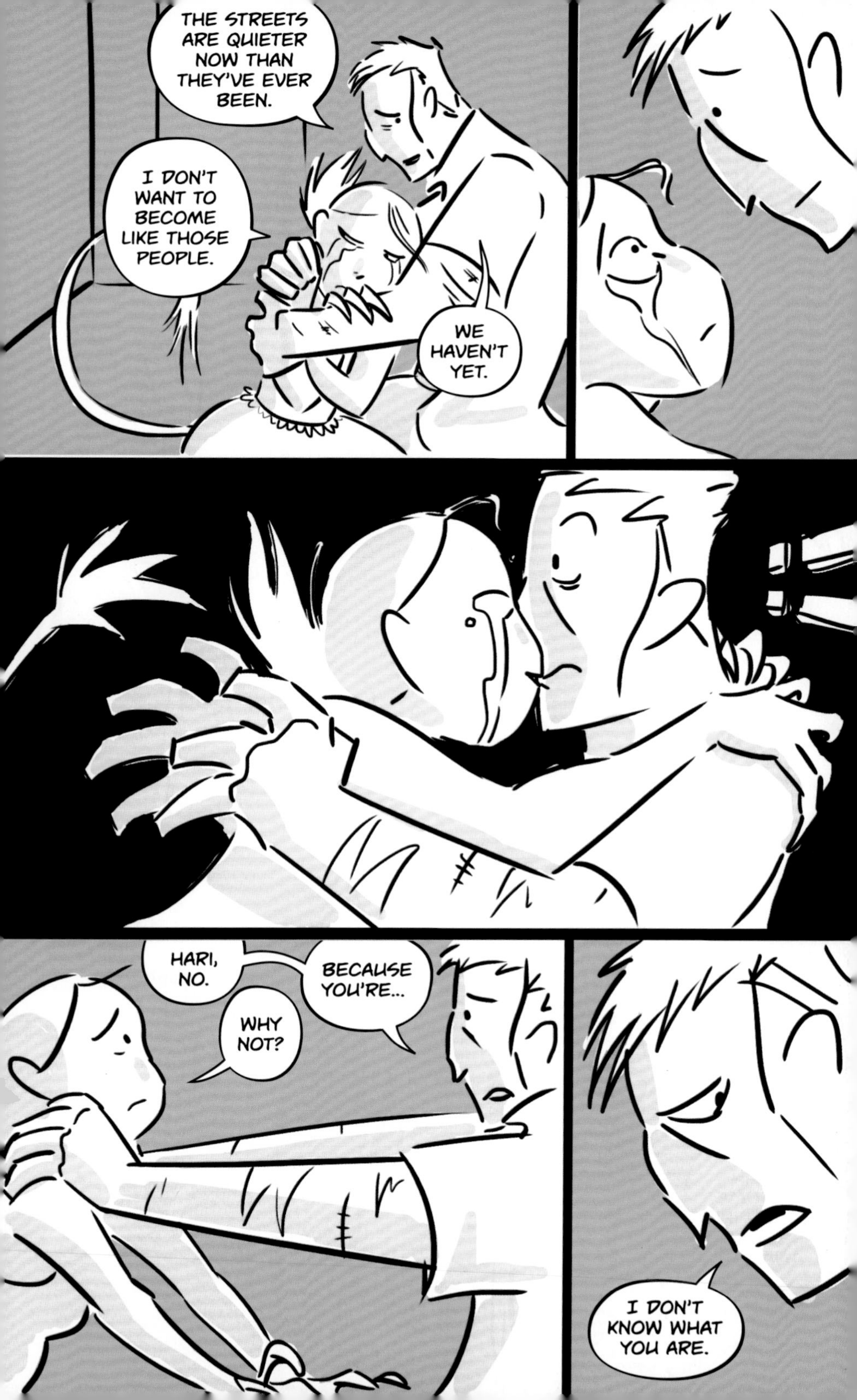
THE STREETS ARE QUIETER NOW THAN THEY'VE EVER BEEN.
I DON'T WANT TO BECOME LIKE THOSE PEOPLE.
WE HAVEN'T YET.
HARI, NO.
WHY NOT?
BECAUSE YOU'RE...
I DON'T KNOW WHAT YOU ARE.

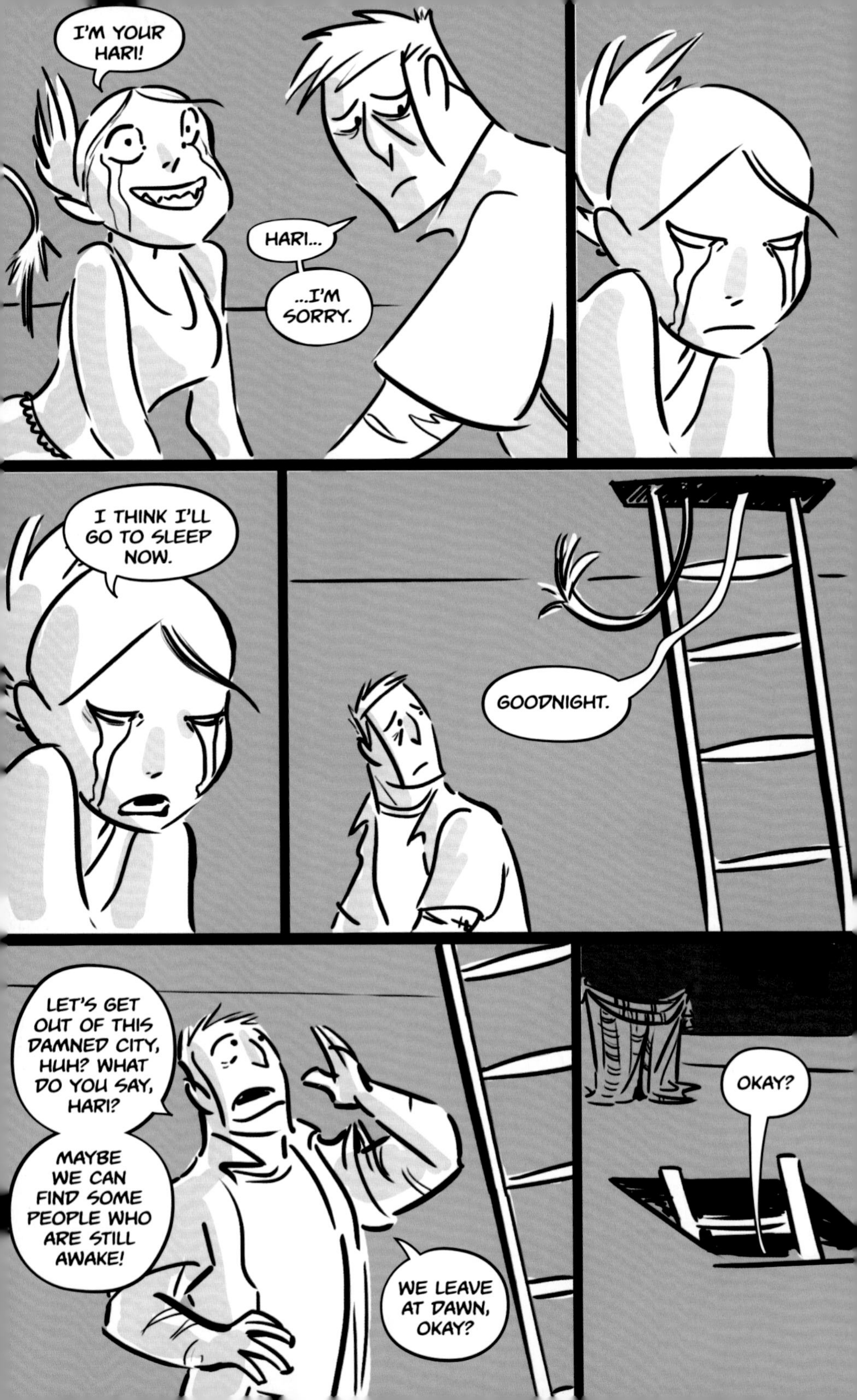
I'M YOUR HARI!
HARI...
...I'M SORRY.
I THINK I'LL GO TO SLEEP NOW.
GOODNIGHT.
LET'S GET OUT OF THIS DAMNED CITY, HUH? WHAT DO YOU SAY, HARI?
MAYBE WE CAN FIND SOME PEOPLE WHO ARE STILL AWAKE!
WE LEAVE AT DAWN, OKAY?
OKAY?

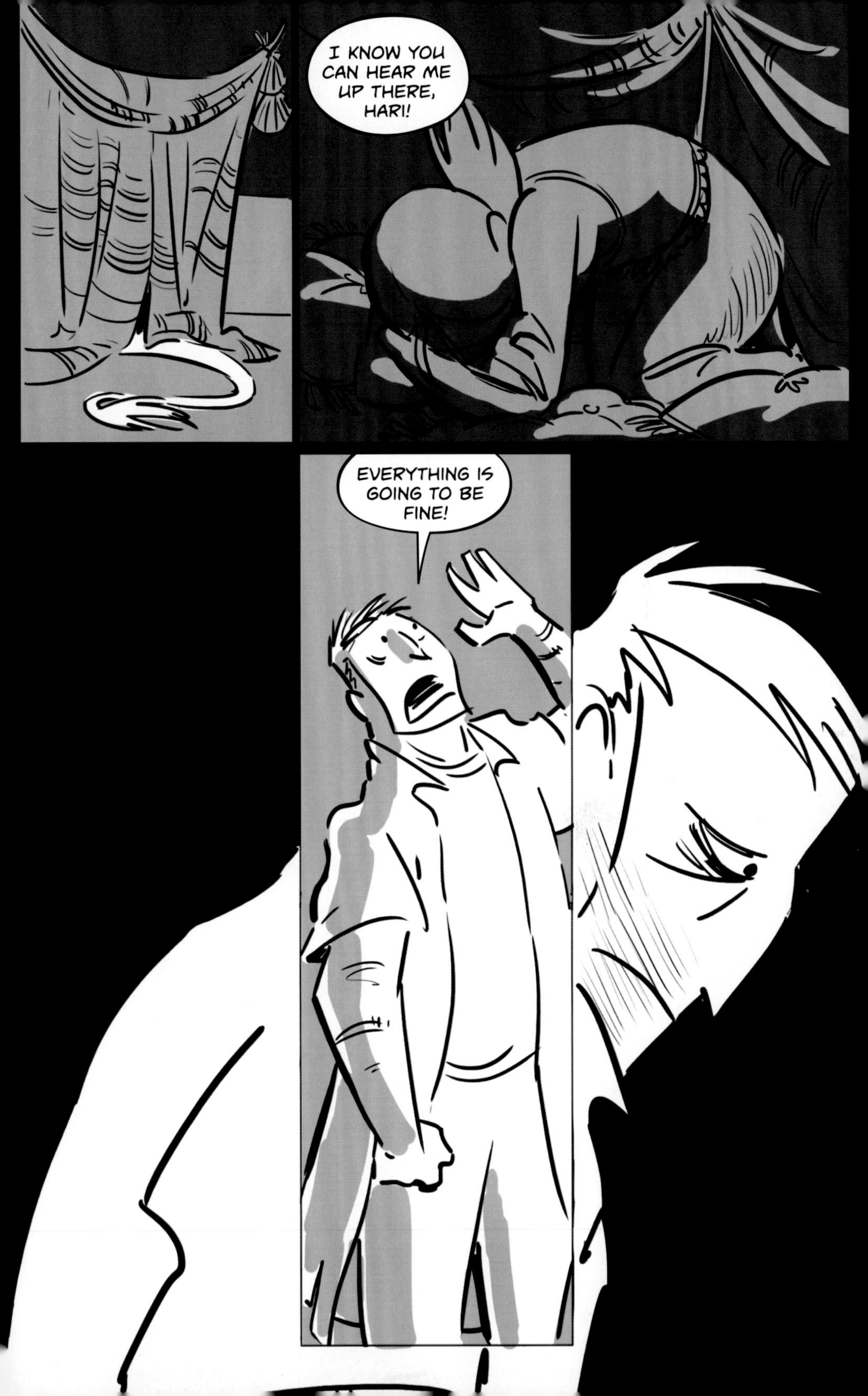
I KNOW YOU CAN HEAR ME UP THERE, HARI!
EVERYTHING IS GOING TO BE FINE!

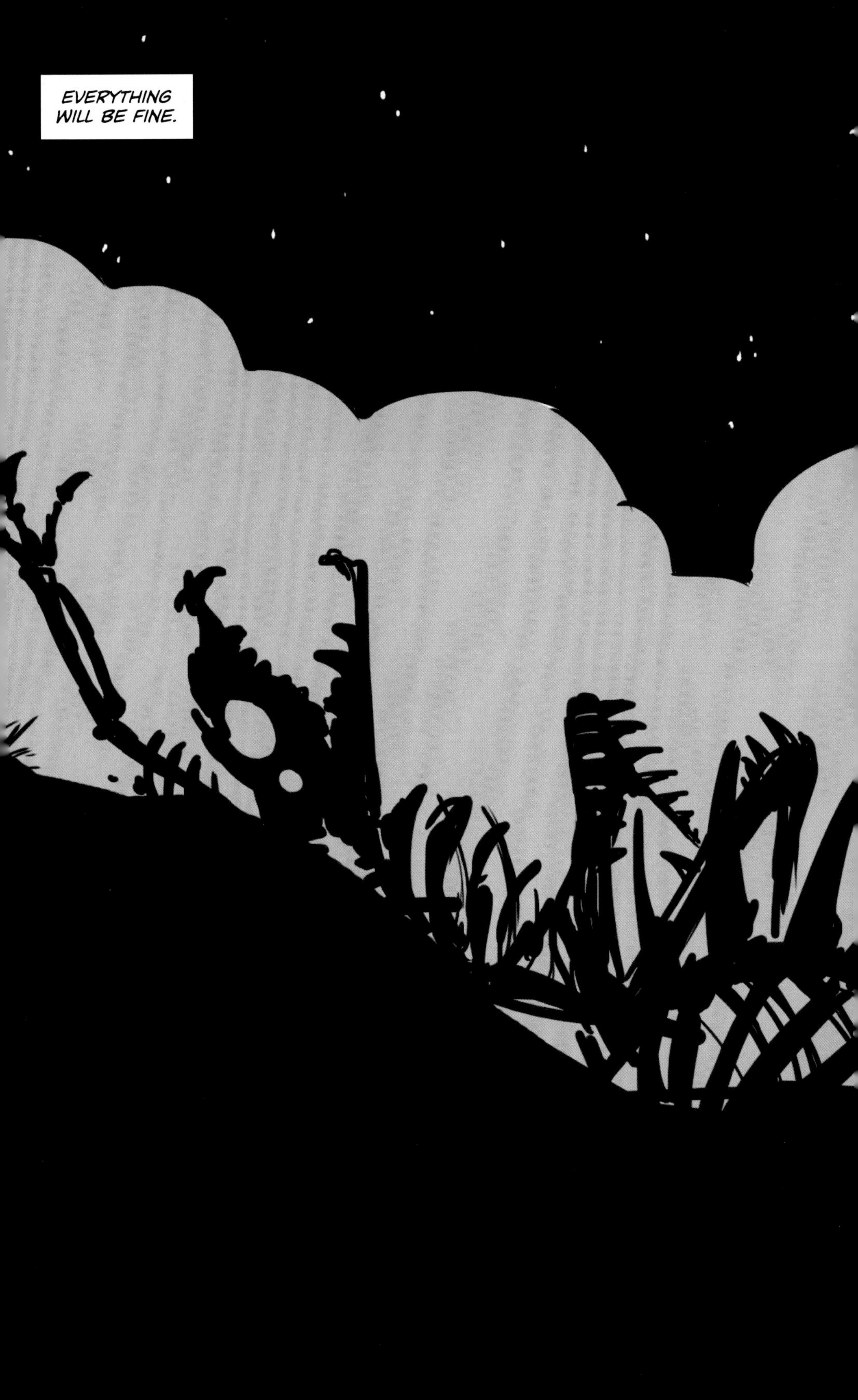
EVERYTHING WILL BE FINE.

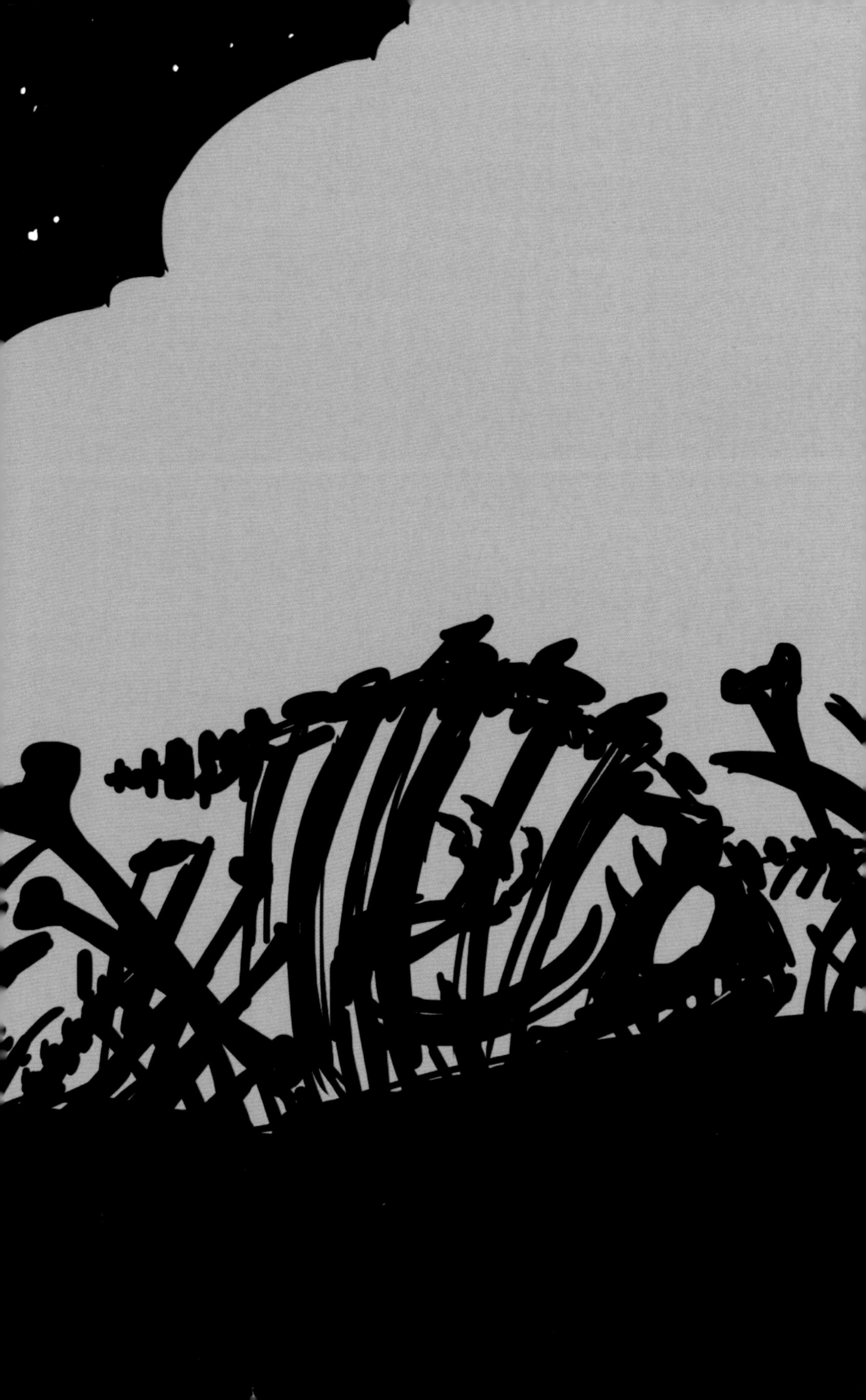

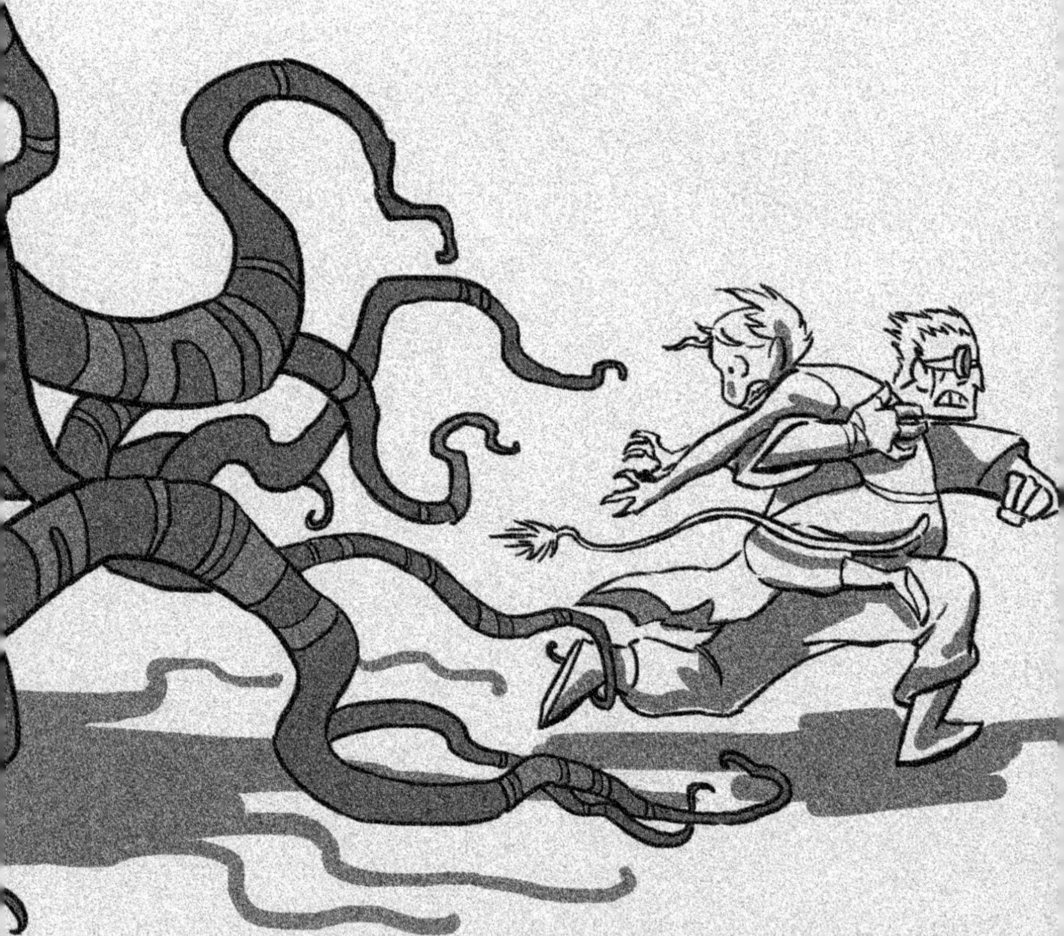

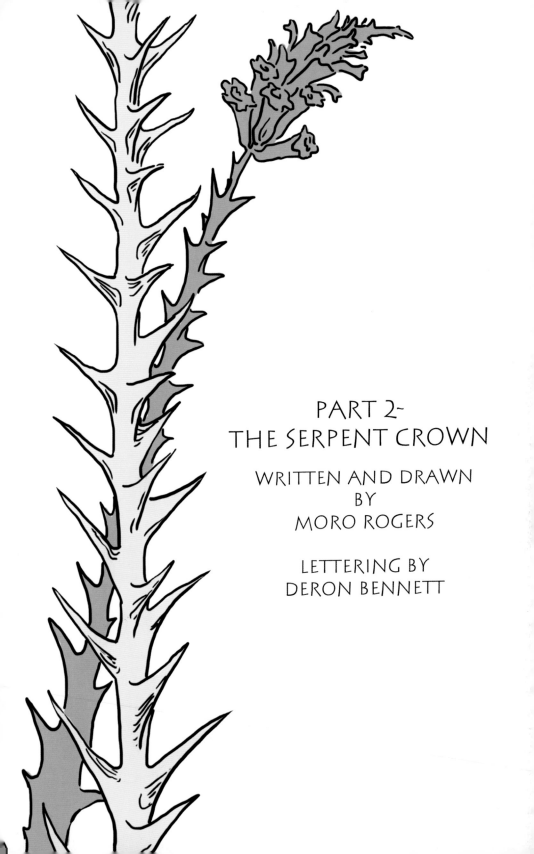

PART 2 -
THE SERPENT CROWN

WRITTEN AND DRAWN
BY
MORO ROGERS

LETTERING BY
DERON BENNETT

FOR MY MOTHER,
WHO TOLD ME ABOUT
THE FORMS.

TWO
YEARS
AGO...

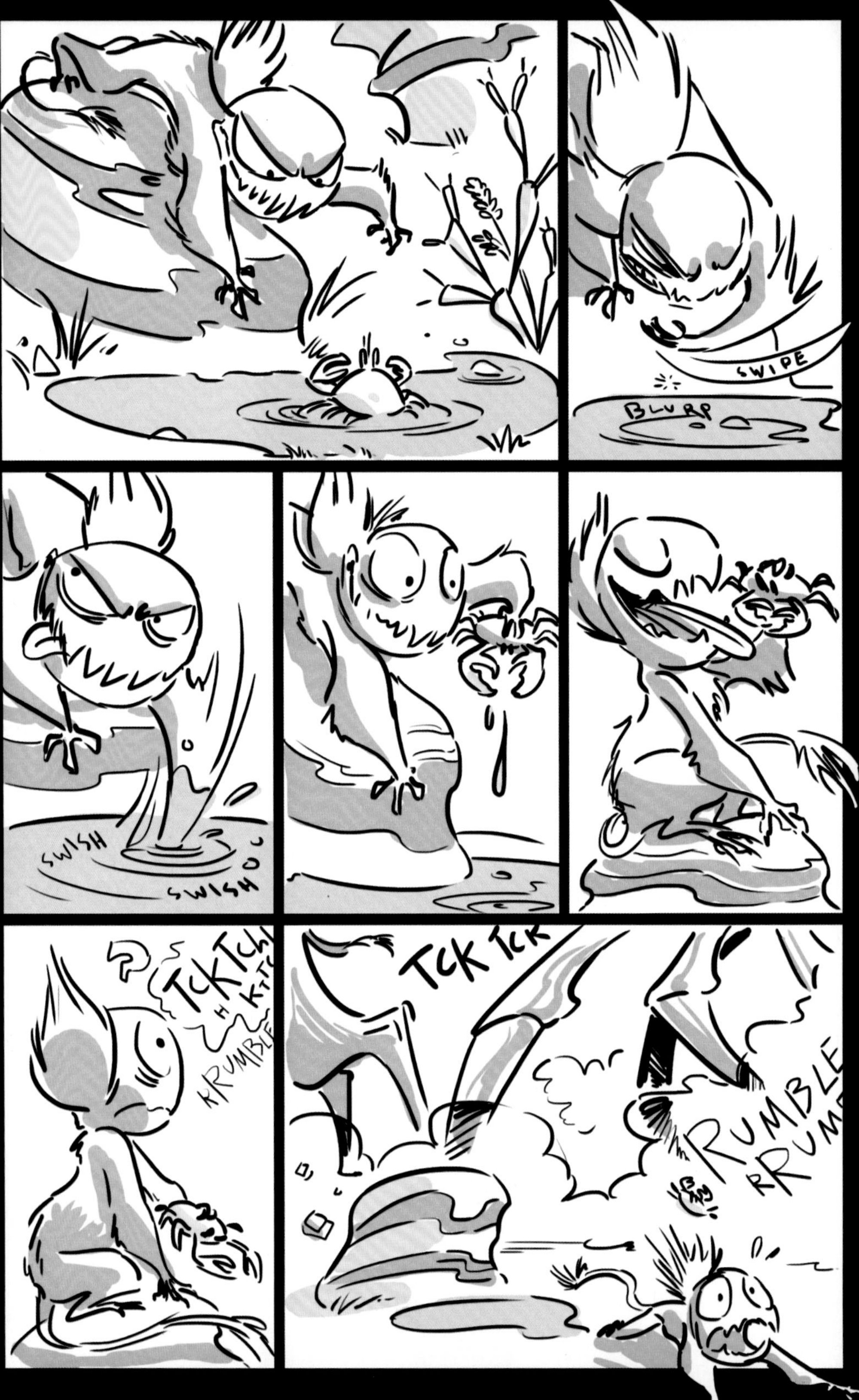
SWIPE
BLURP
SWISH
SWISH
?
TCKTCH
RUMBLE
TCK TCK
RUMBLE

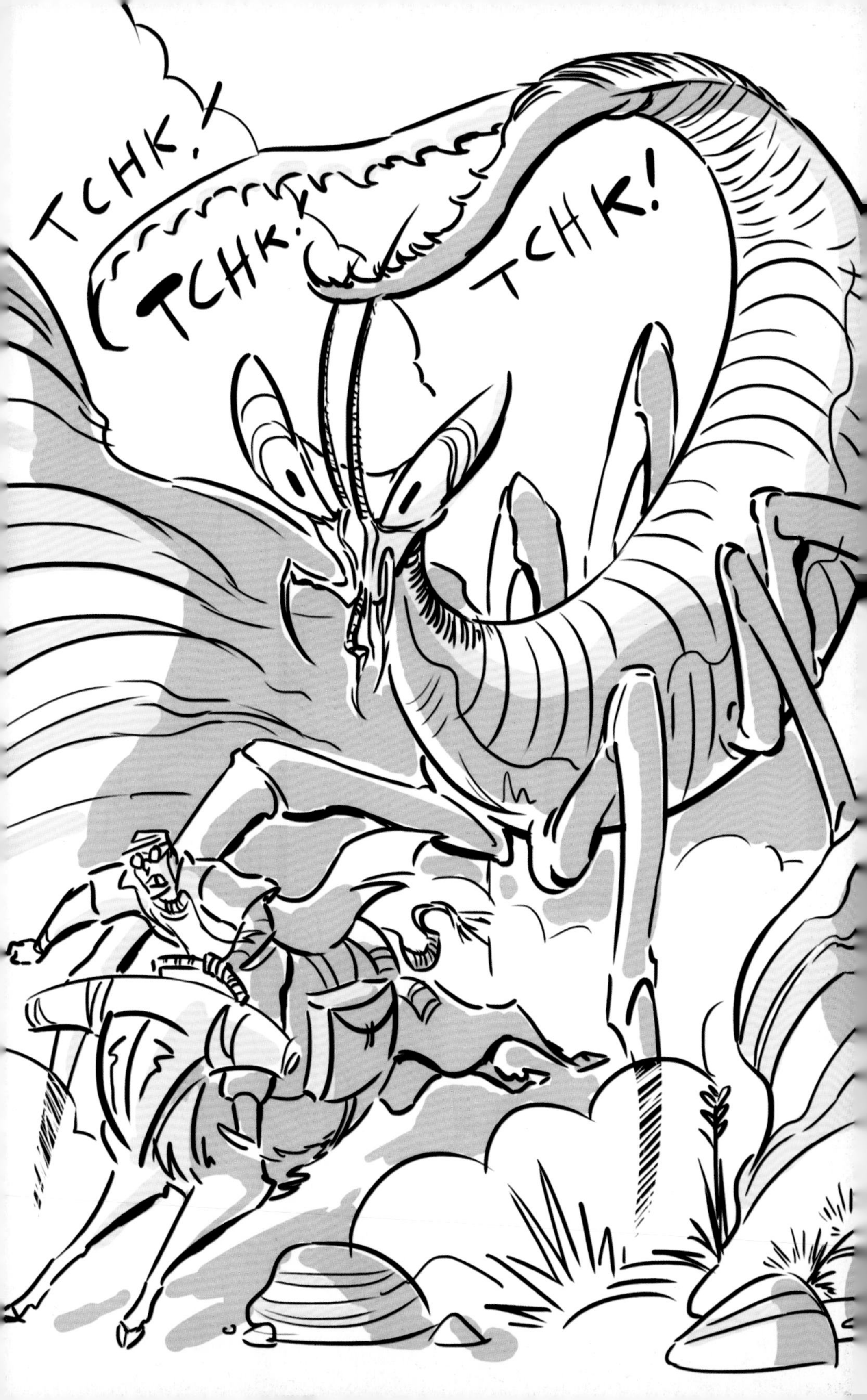
TCHK!
TCHK!
TCHK!

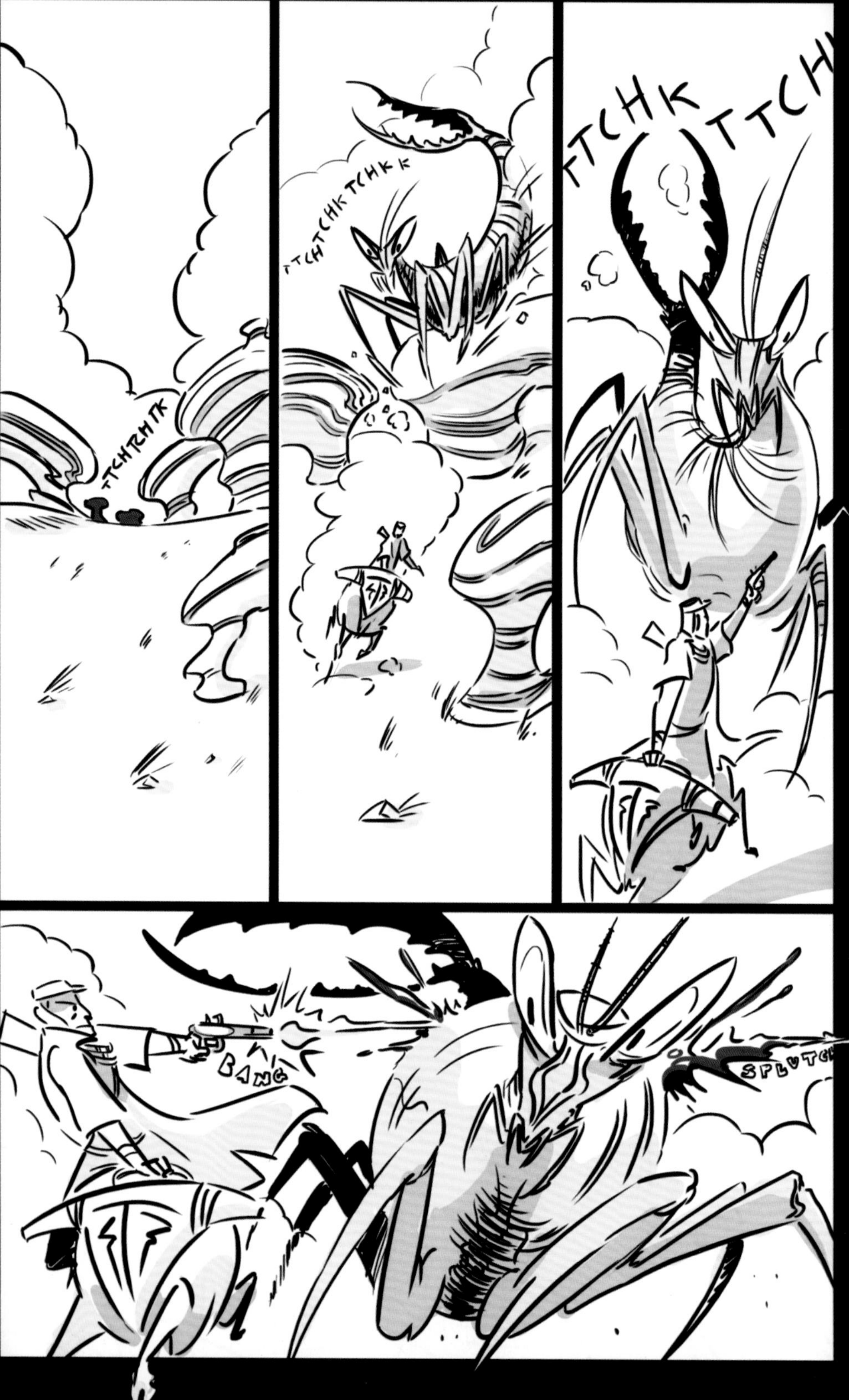
TTCHTCHTK
TTCHTCHKTCHKK
TTCHK TTCH
BANG
SPLUTCH

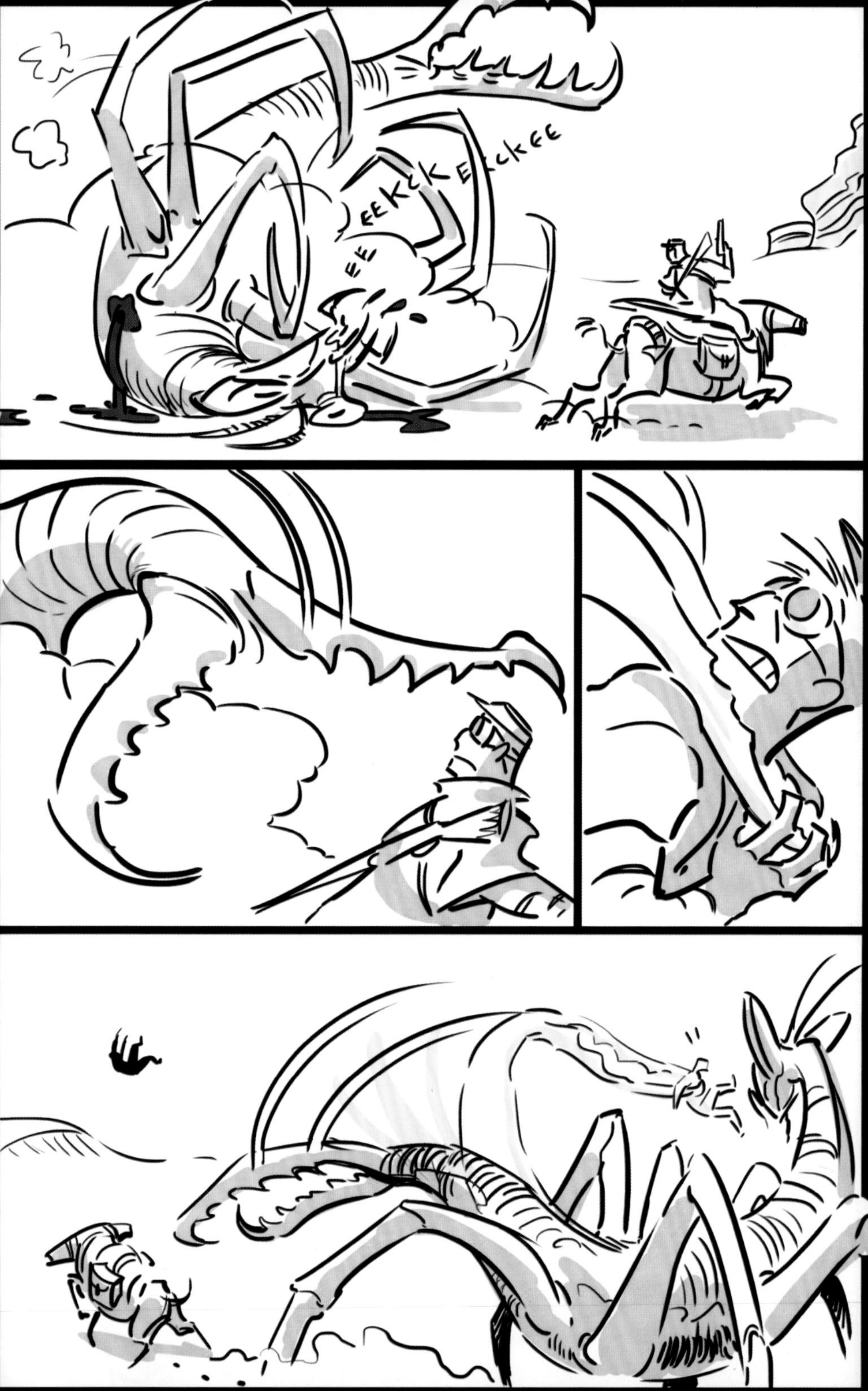
EEEEKcKKEckEE

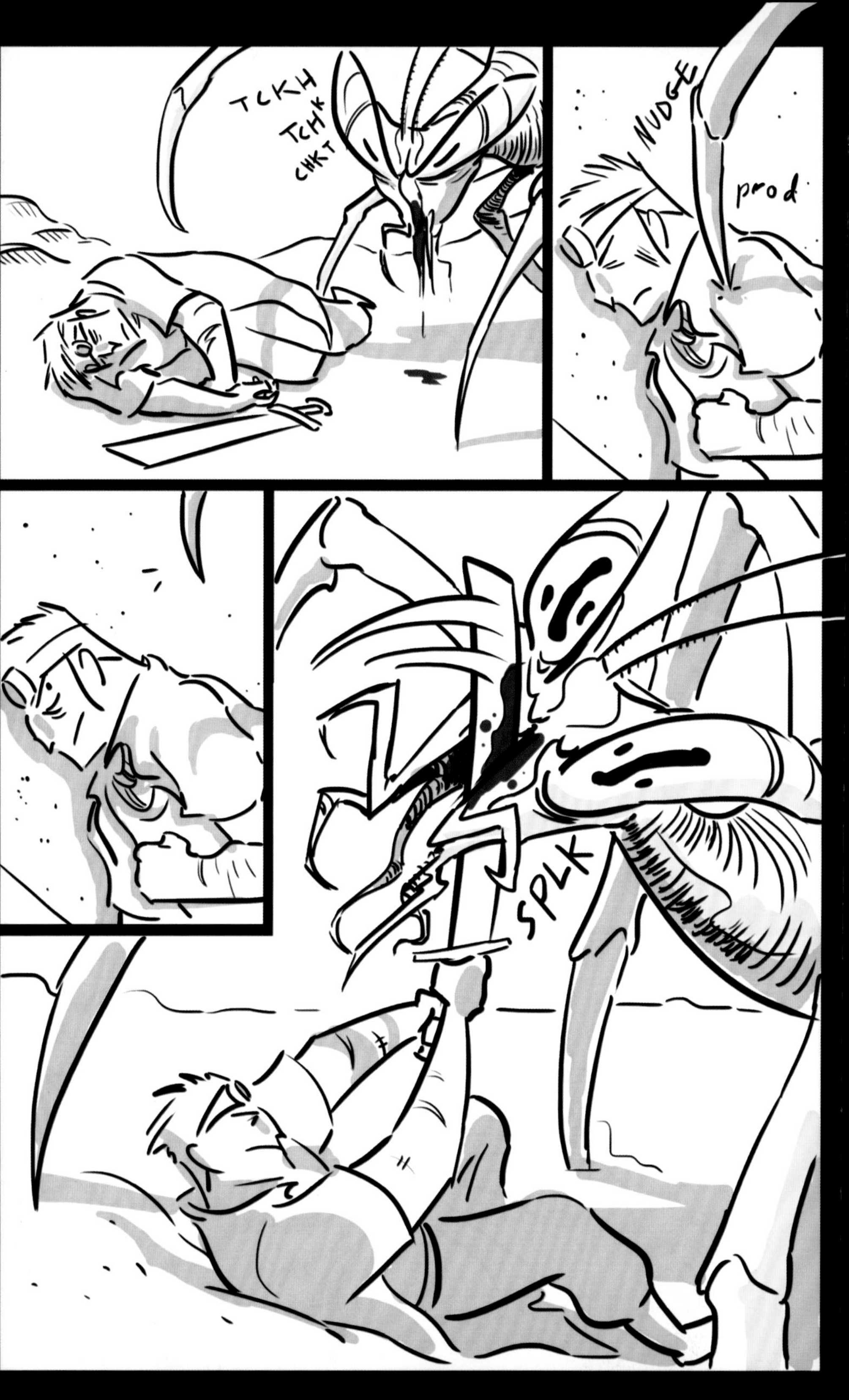
TCKH
TCHK
CHKT
NUDGE
prod
SPLK

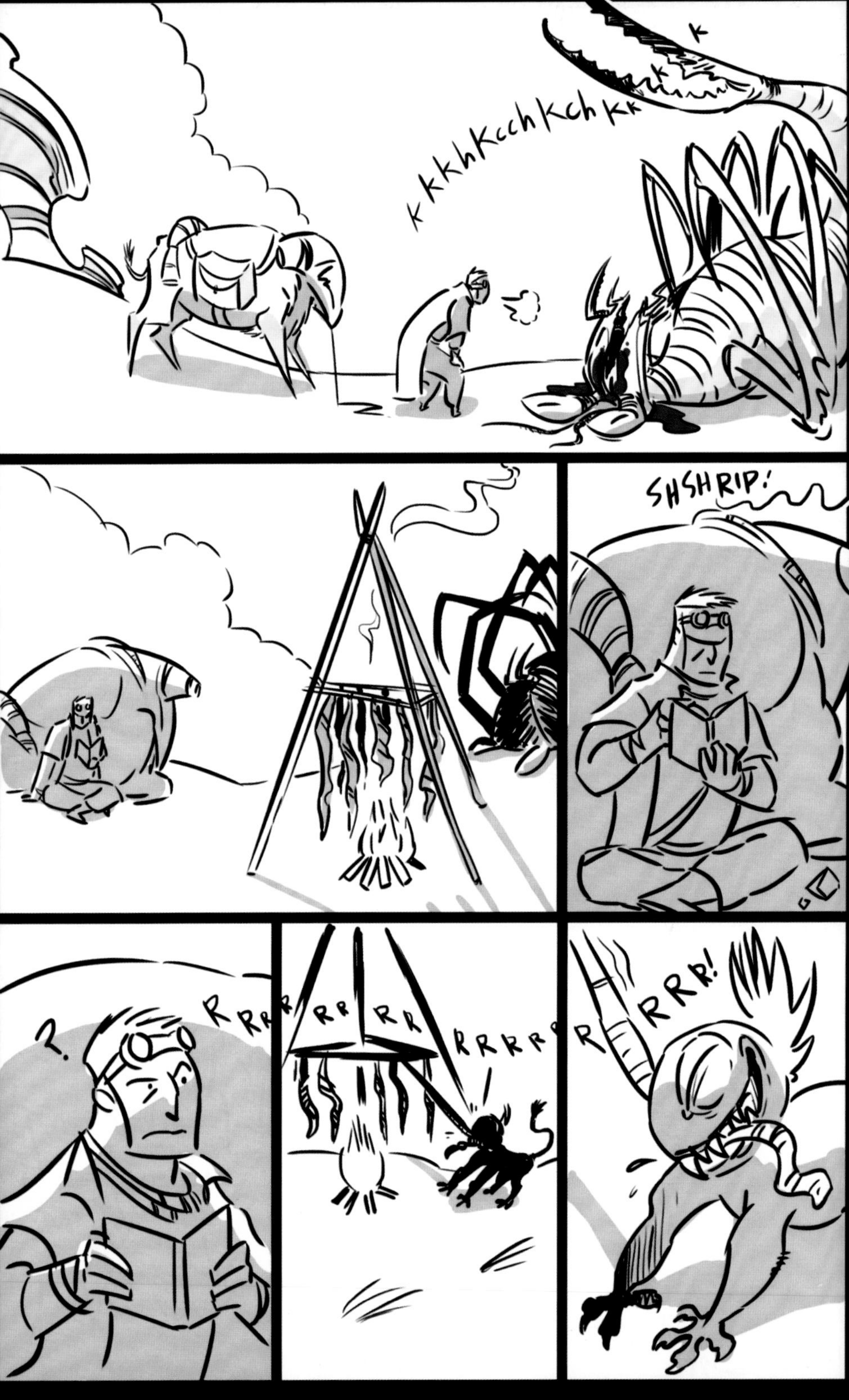
KKKhKcchKchKK K K K
SHSHRIP!
?
RRRR
RR RR
RRRRRR
RRR!

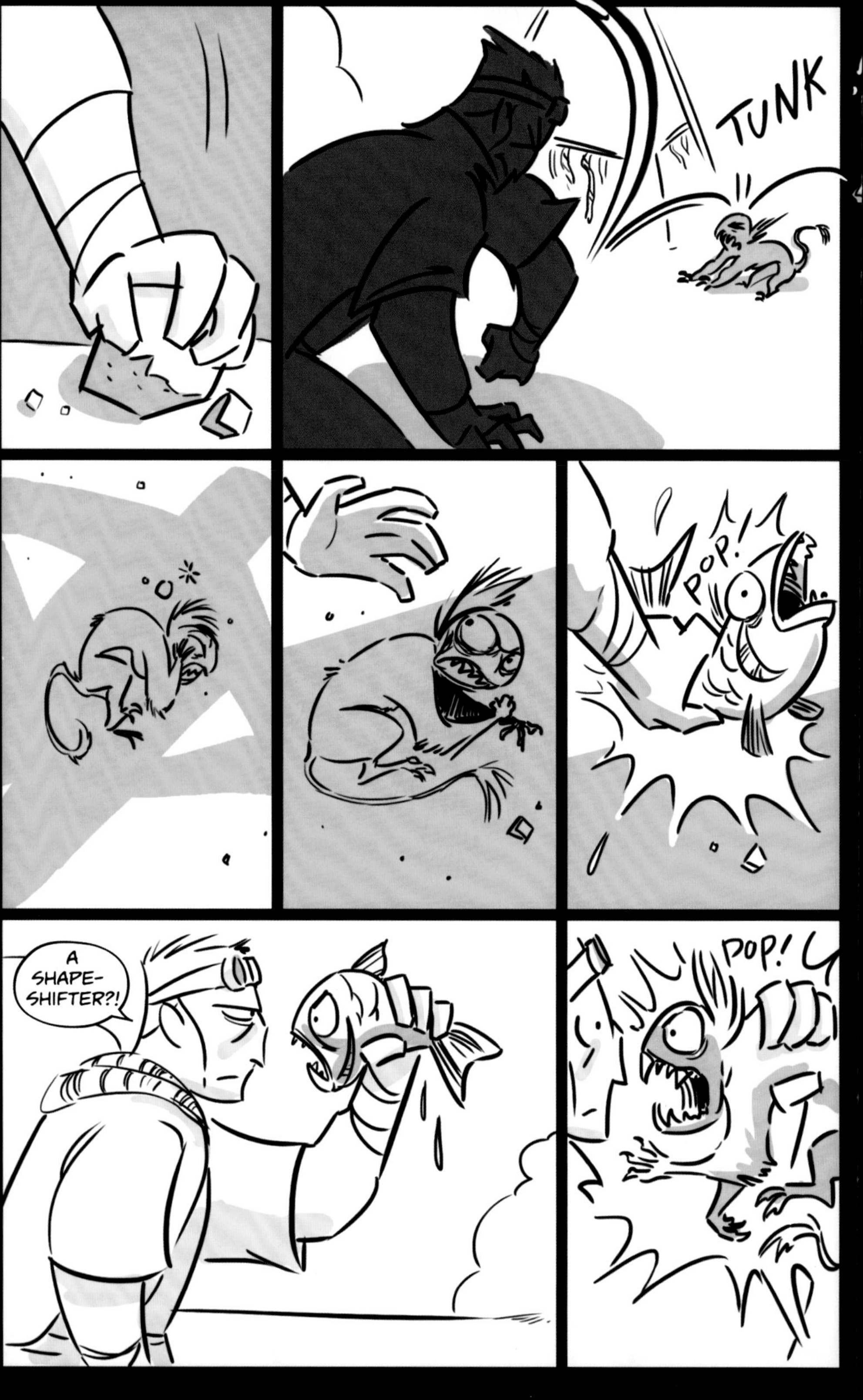
TUNK
POP!
A SHAPE-SHIFTER?!
POP!

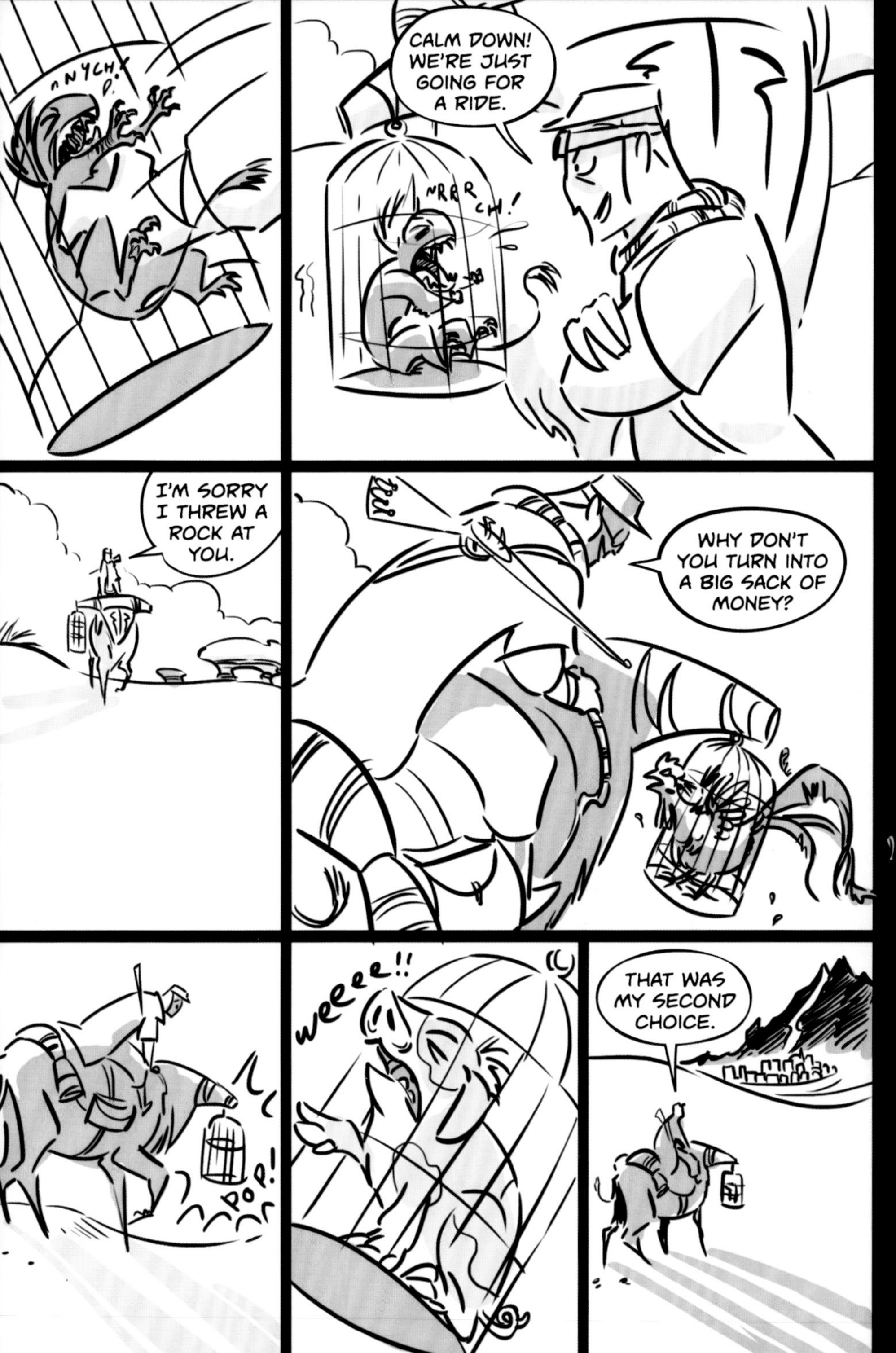
CALM DOWN! WE'RE JUST GOING FOR A RIDE.
I'M SORRY I THREW A ROCK AT YOU.
WHY DON'T YOU TURN INTO A BIG SACK OF MONEY?
POP!
weeee!!
THAT WAS MY SECOND CHOICE.

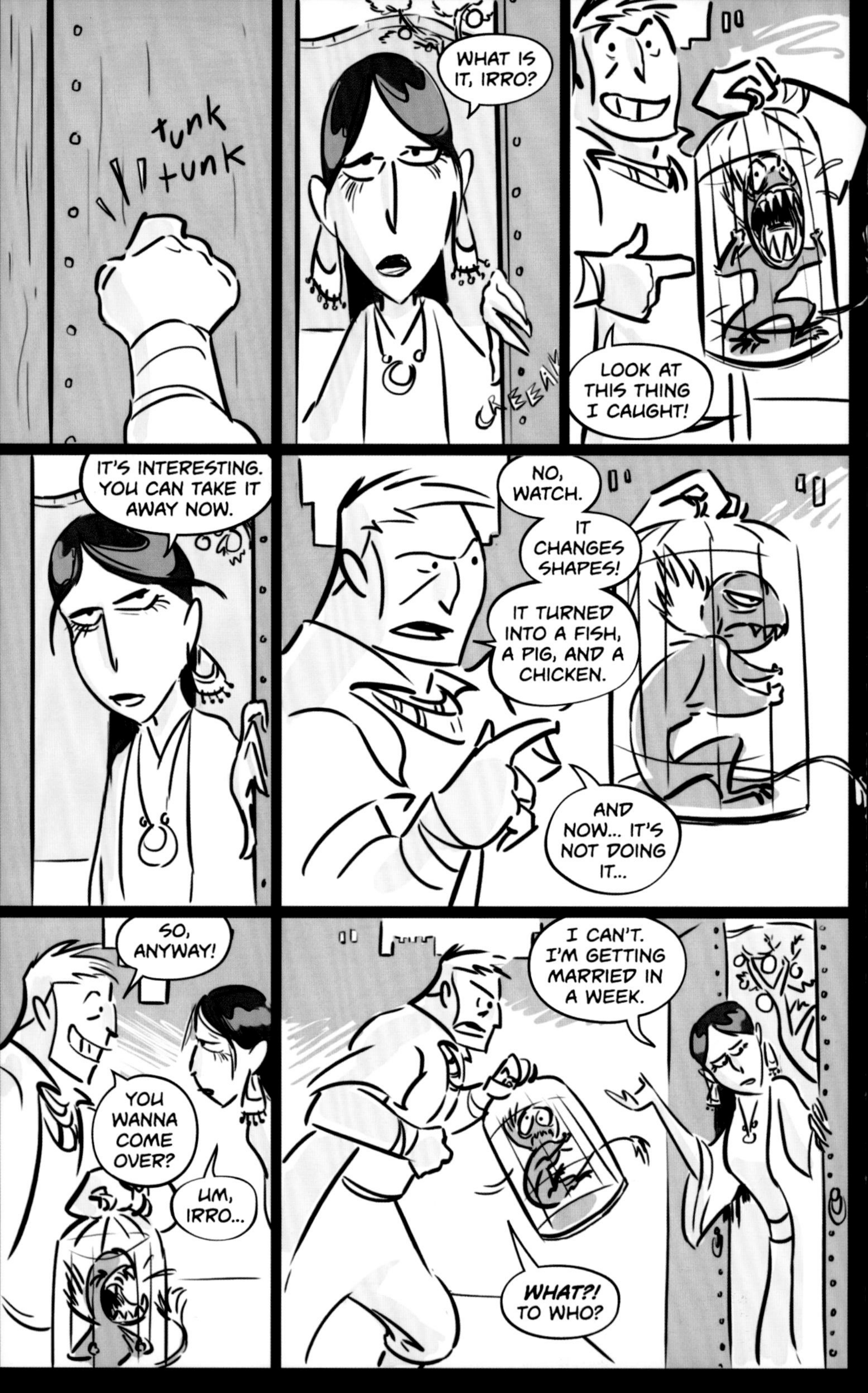
tunk
tunk
WHAT IS IT, IRRO?
CREEAK
LOOK AT THIS THING I CAUGHT!
IT'S INTERESTING. YOU CAN TAKE IT AWAY NOW.
NO, WATCH.
IT CHANGES SHAPES!
IT TURNED INTO A FISH, A PIG, AND A CHICKEN.
AND NOW... IT'S NOT DOING IT...
SO, ANYWAY!
YOU WANNA COME OVER?
UM, IRRO...
I CAN'T. I'M GETTING MARRIED IN A WEEK.
WHAT?! TO WHO?

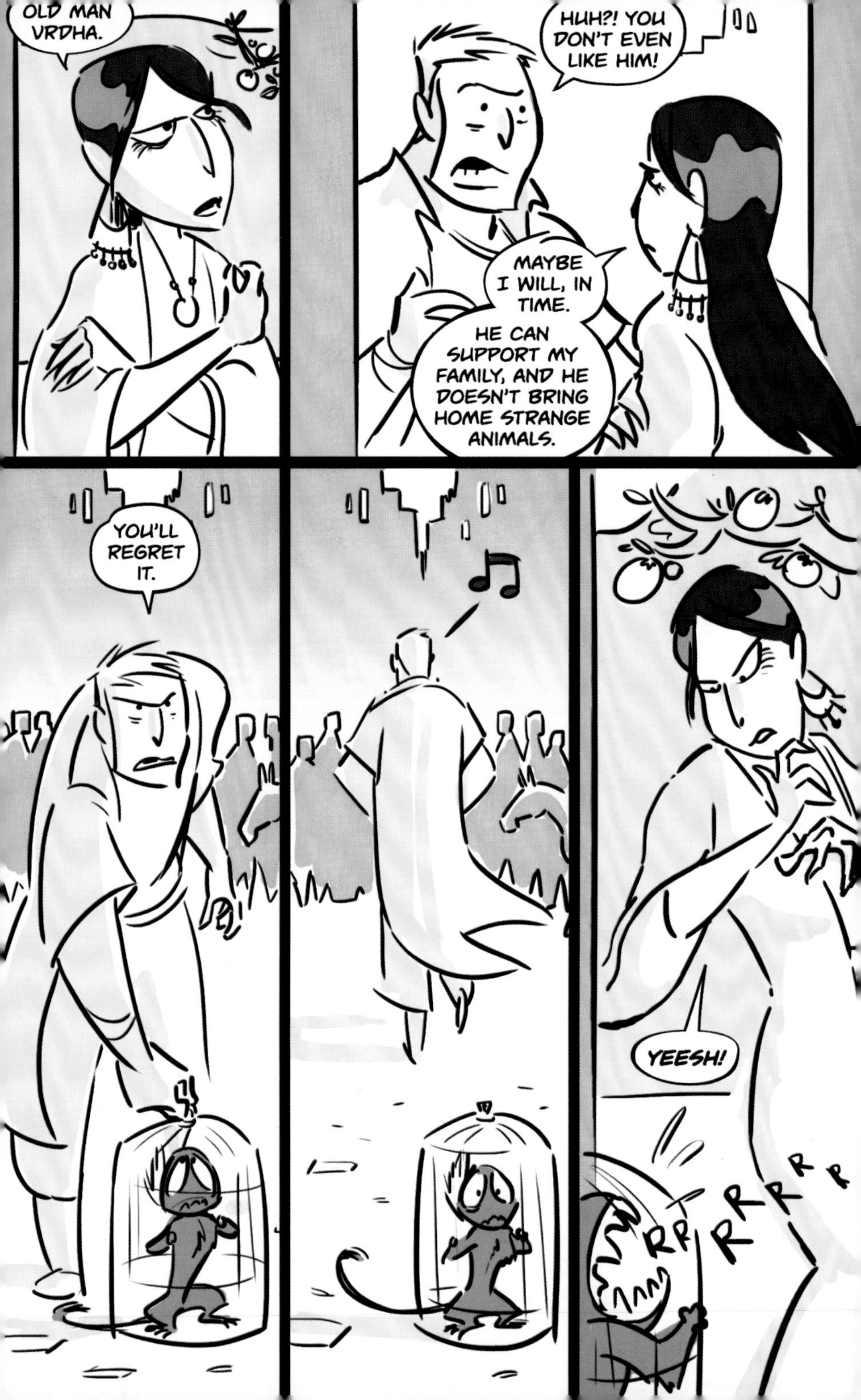
OLD MAN VRDHA.
HUH?! YOU DON'T EVEN LIKE HIM!
MAYBE I WILL, IN TIME.
HE CAN SUPPORT MY FAMILY, AND HE DOESN'T BRING HOME STRANGE ANIMALS.
YOU'LL REGRET IT.
YEESH!
RRRRRRR

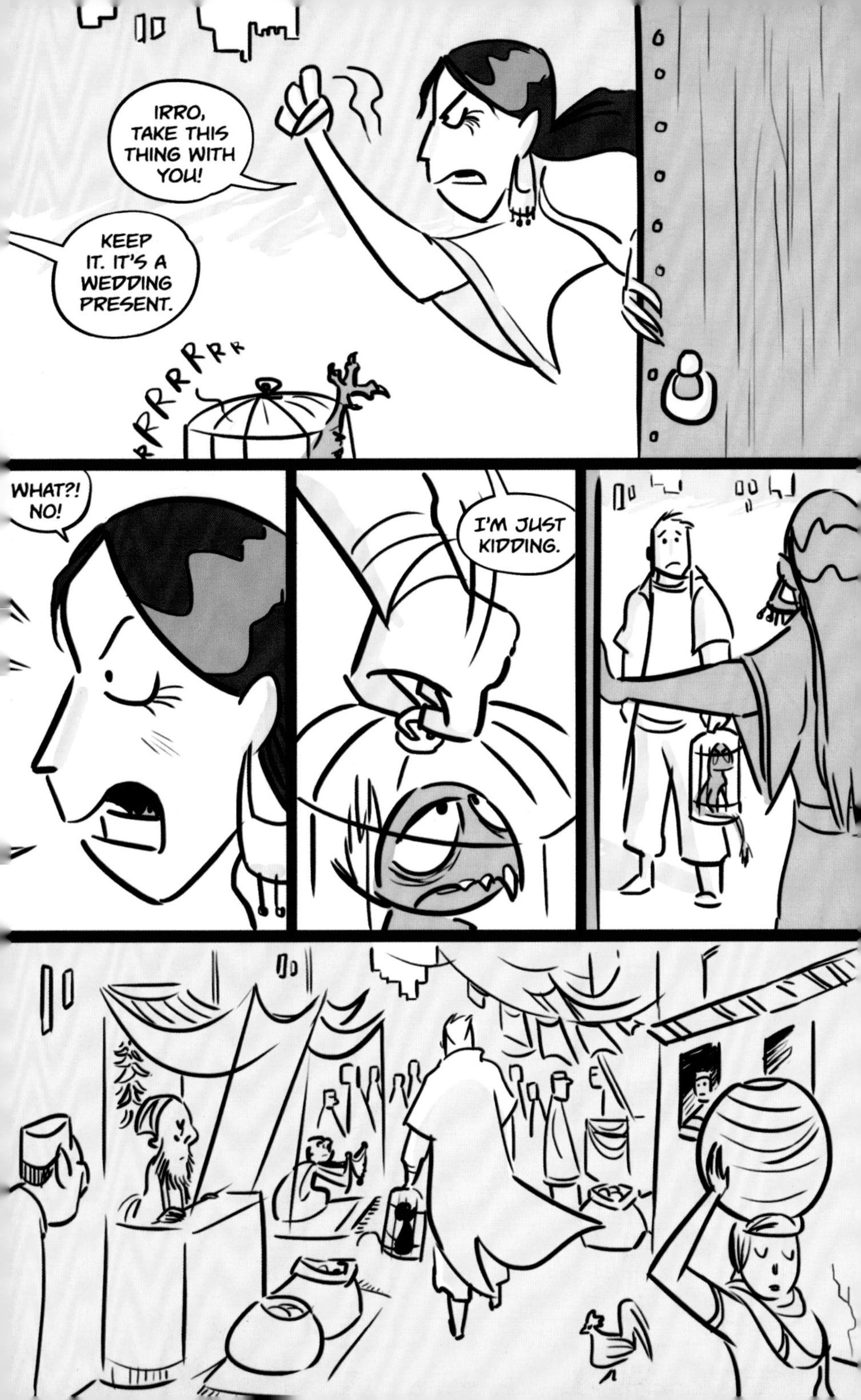
IRRO, TAKE THIS THING WITH YOU!
KEEP IT. IT'S A WEDDING PRESENT.
RRRRRRRR
WHAT?! NO!
I'M JUST KIDDING.

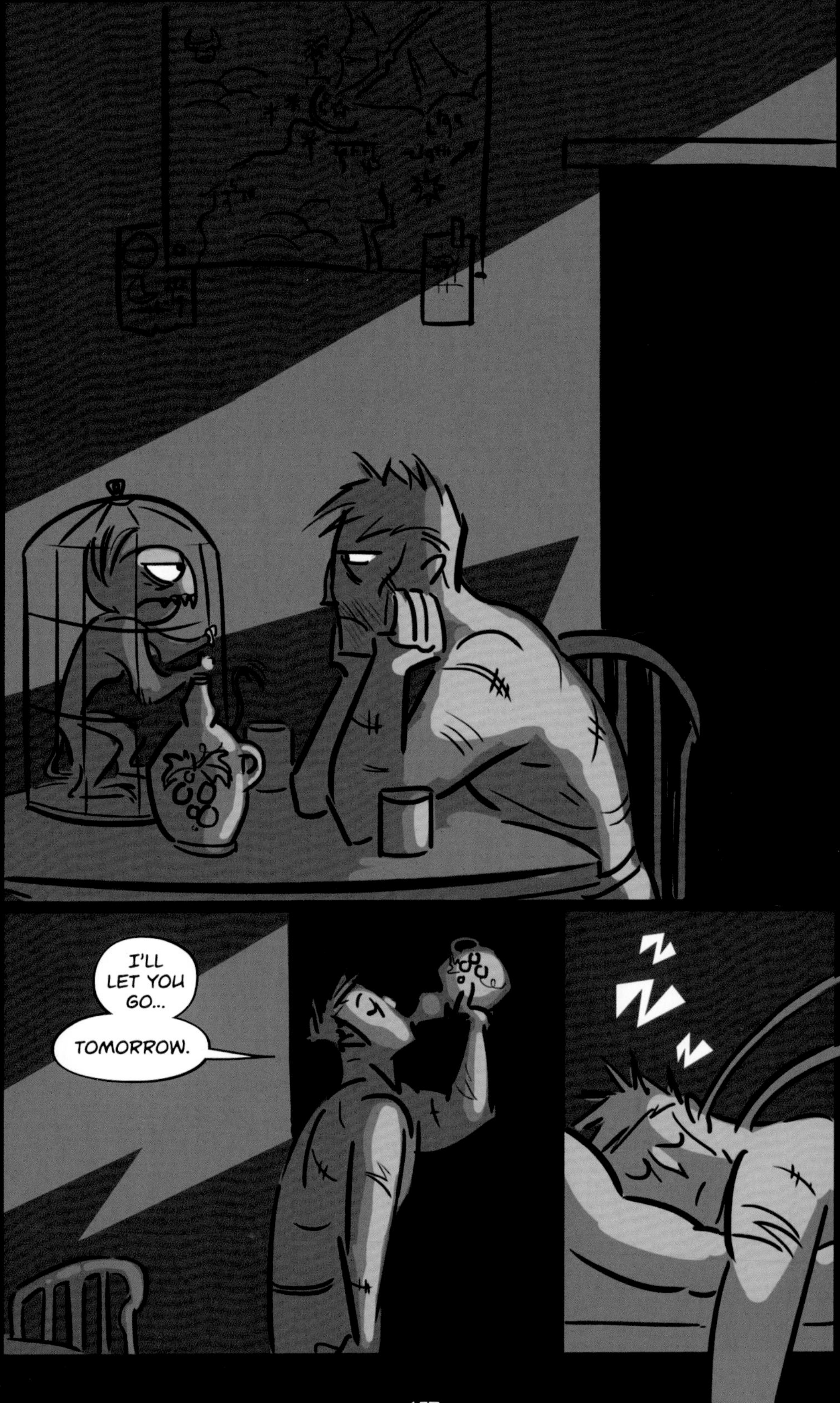
I'LL LET YOU GO...
TOMORROW.
Z Z Z

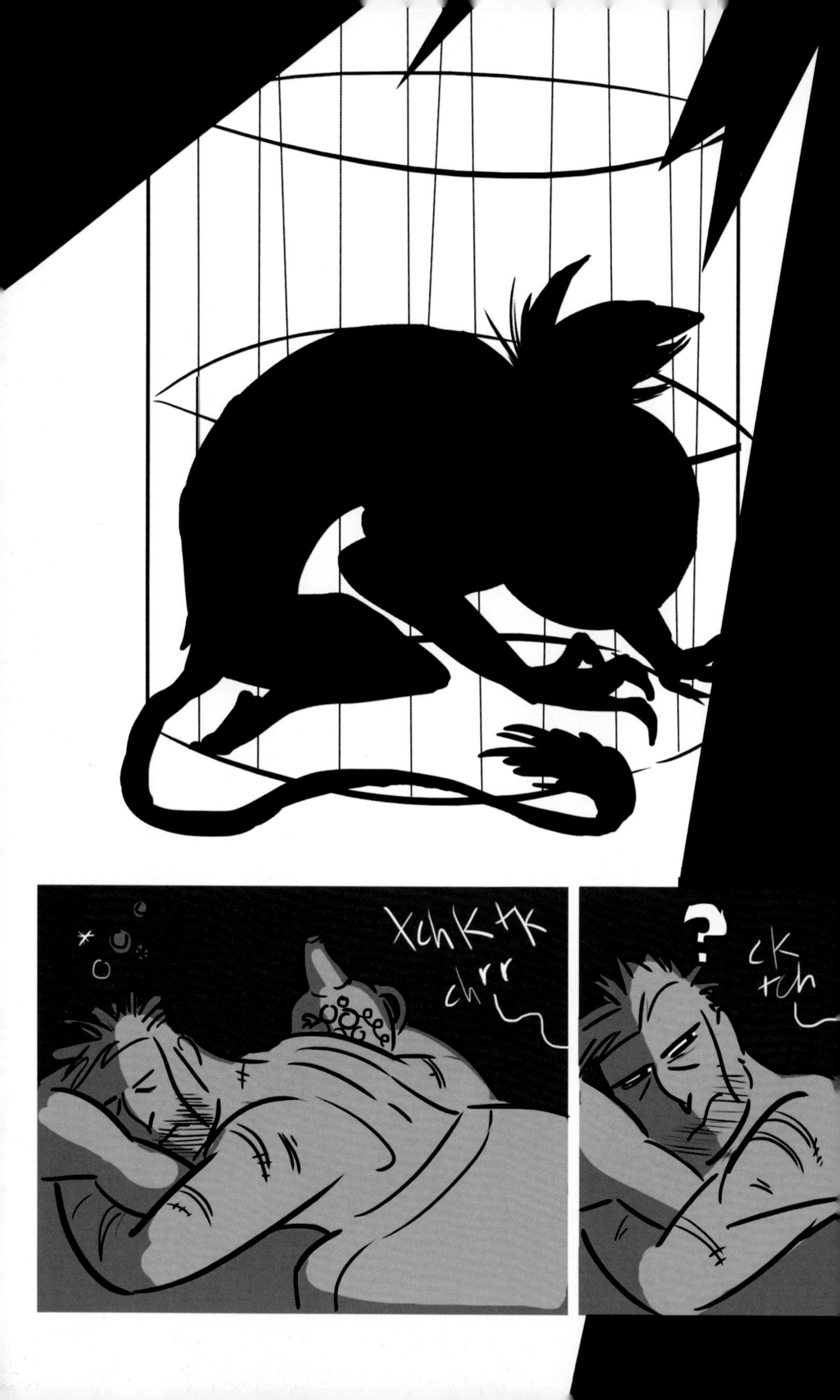
XchKtK
chrr
?
cK
tch

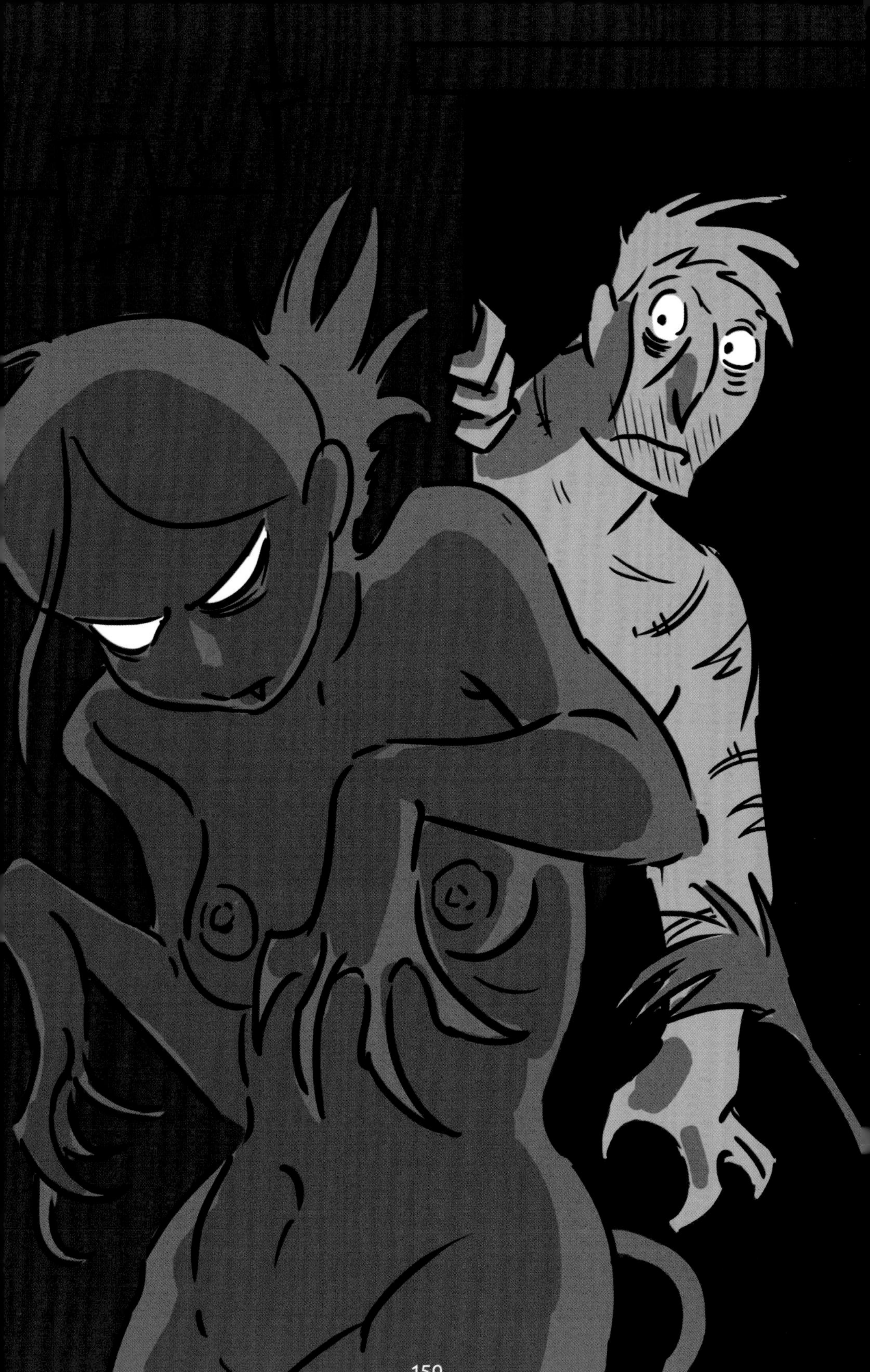

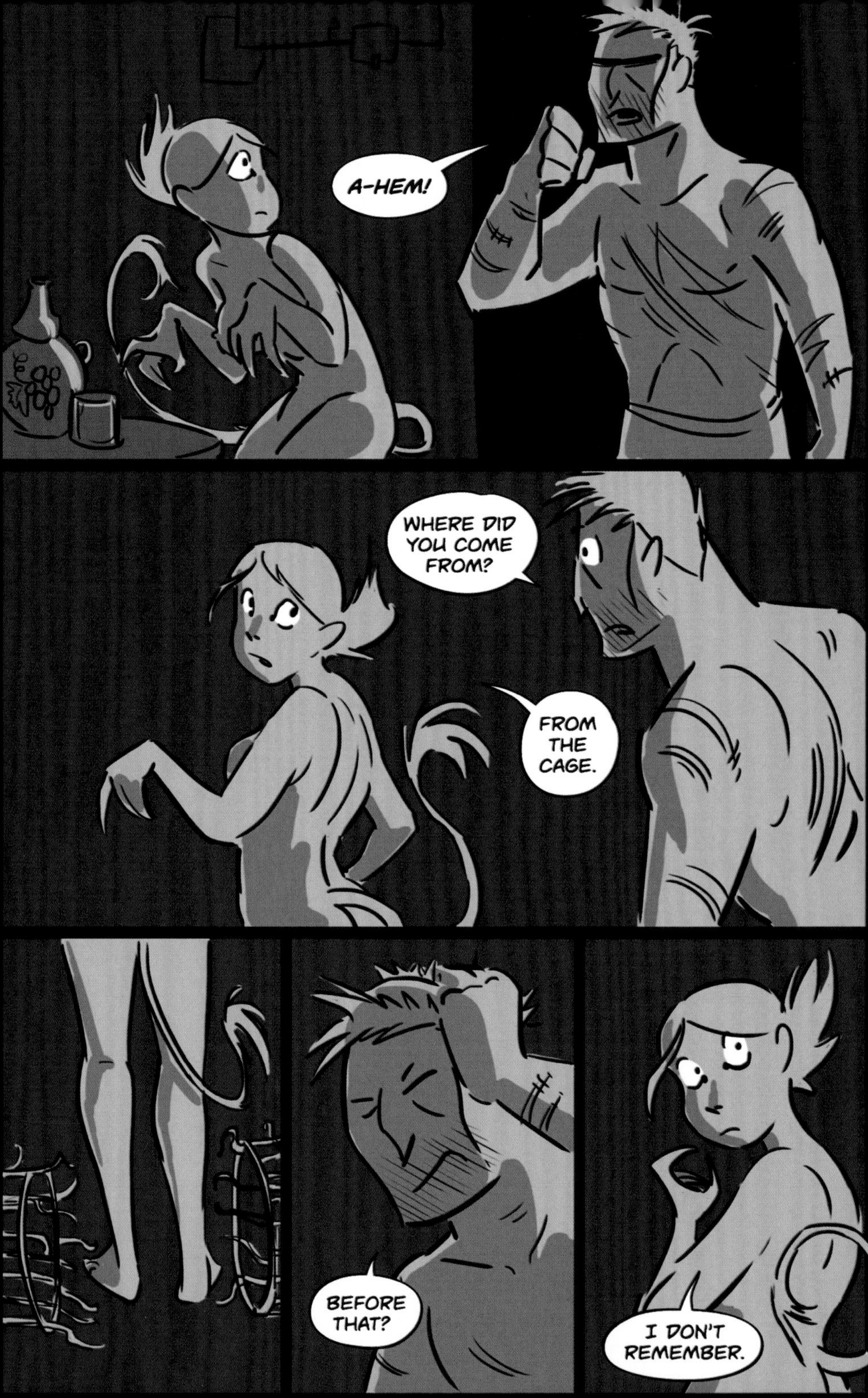
A-HEM!
WHERE DID YOU COME FROM?
FROM THE CAGE.
BEFORE THAT?
I DON'T REMEMBER.

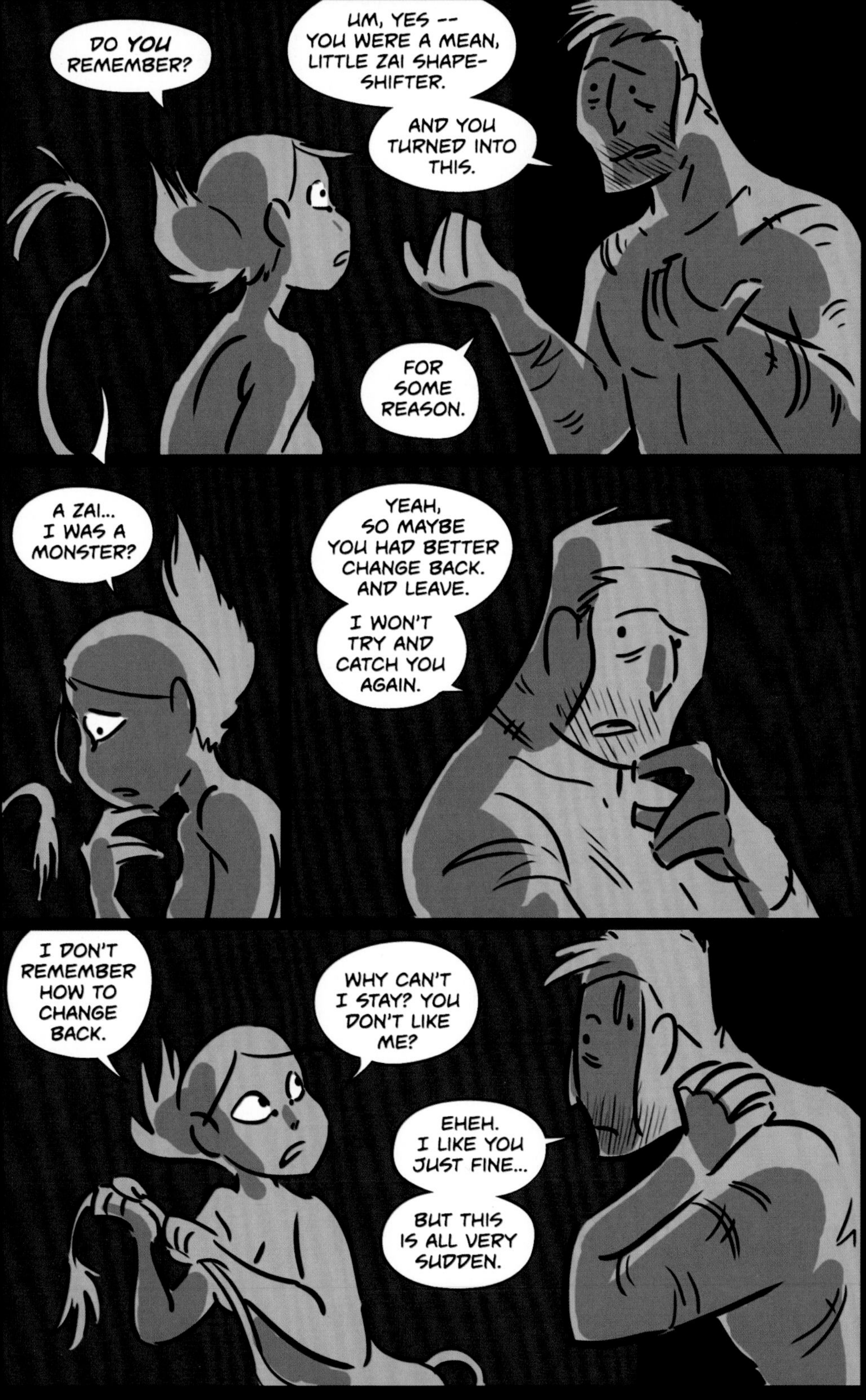
DO YOU REMEMBER?
UM, YES -- YOU WERE A MEAN, LITTLE ZAI SHAPE-SHIFTER.
AND YOU TURNED INTO THIS.
FOR SOME REASON.
A ZAI... I WAS A MONSTER?
YEAH, SO MAYBE YOU HAD BETTER CHANGE BACK. AND LEAVE.
I WON'T TRY AND CATCH YOU AGAIN.
I DON'T REMEMBER HOW TO CHANGE BACK.
WHY CAN'T I STAY? YOU DON'T LIKE ME?
EHEH. I LIKE YOU JUST FINE...
BUT THIS IS ALL VERY SUDDEN.

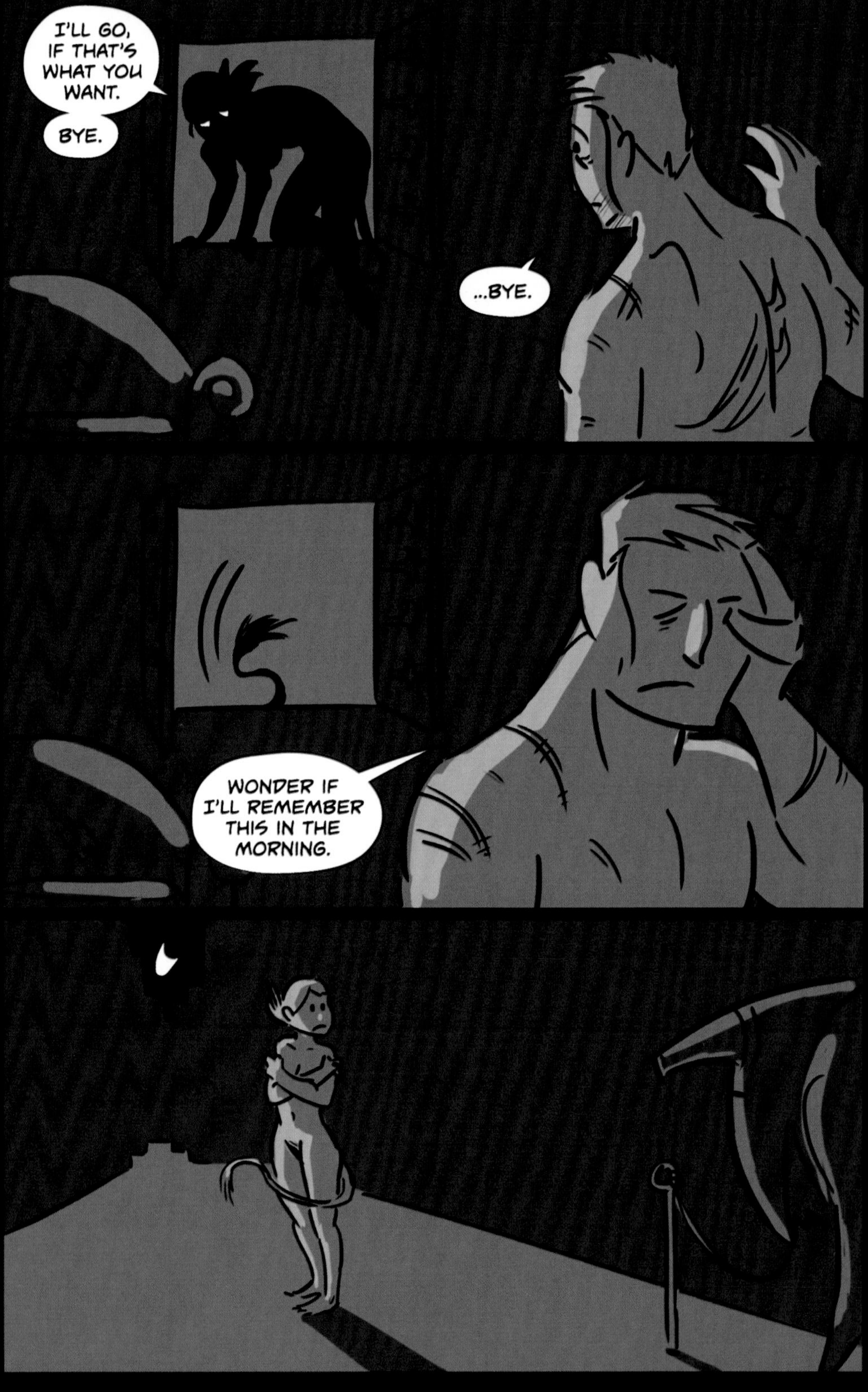
I'LL GO, IF THAT'S WHAT YOU WANT.
BYE.
...BYE.
WONDER IF I'LL REMEMBER THIS IN THE MORNING.

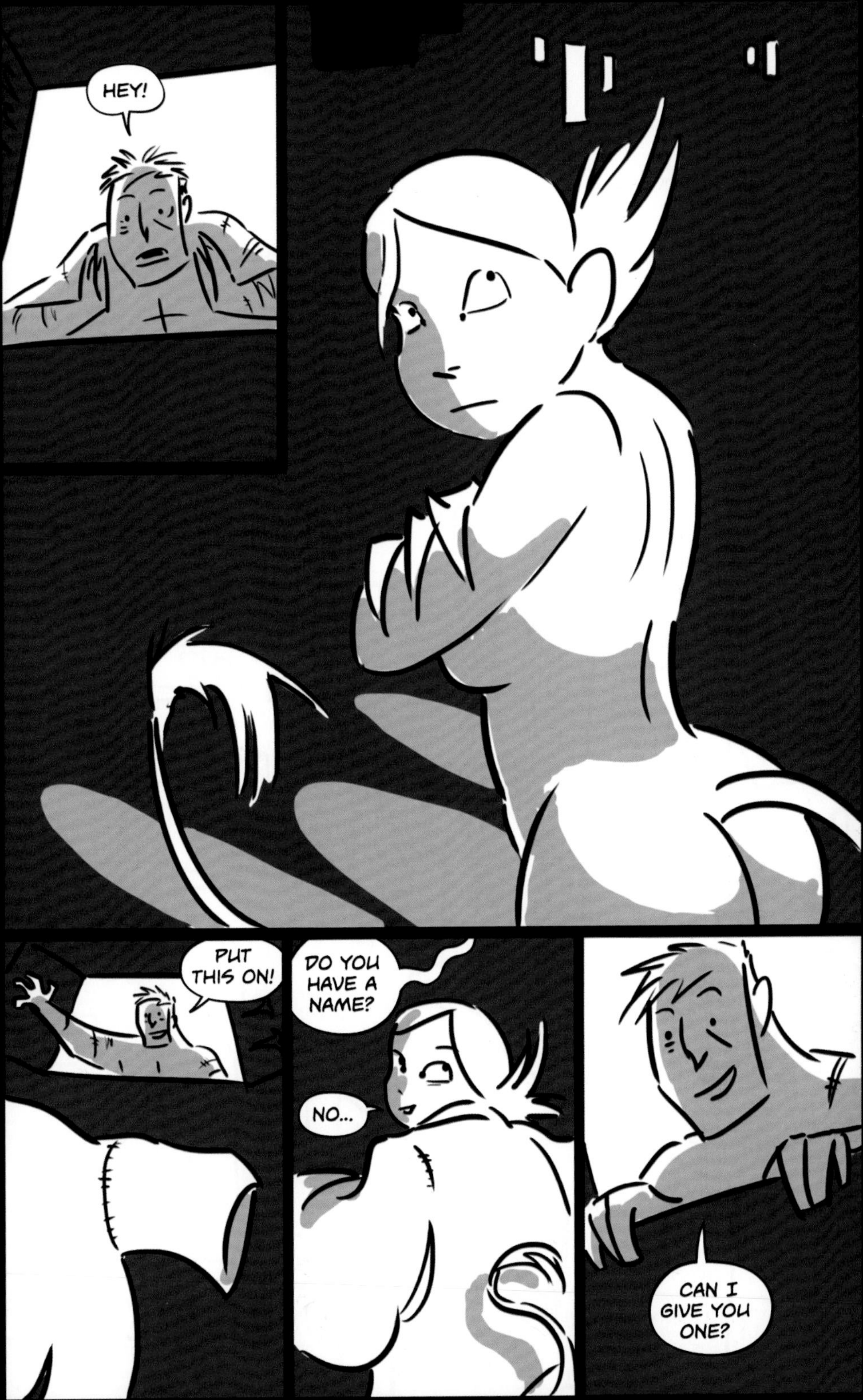
HEY!
PUT THIS ON!
DO YOU HAVE A NAME?
NO...
CAN I GIVE YOU ONE?

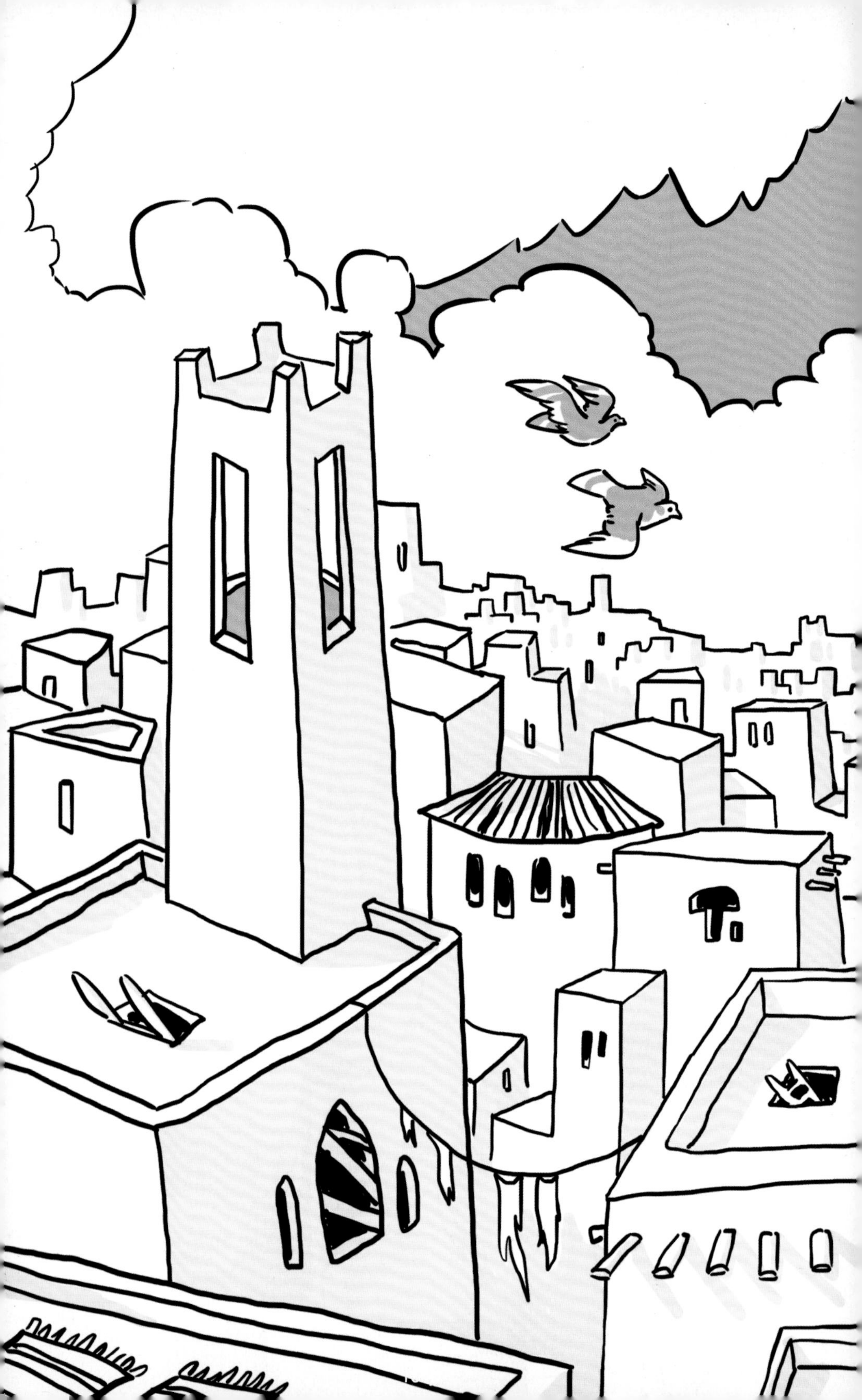

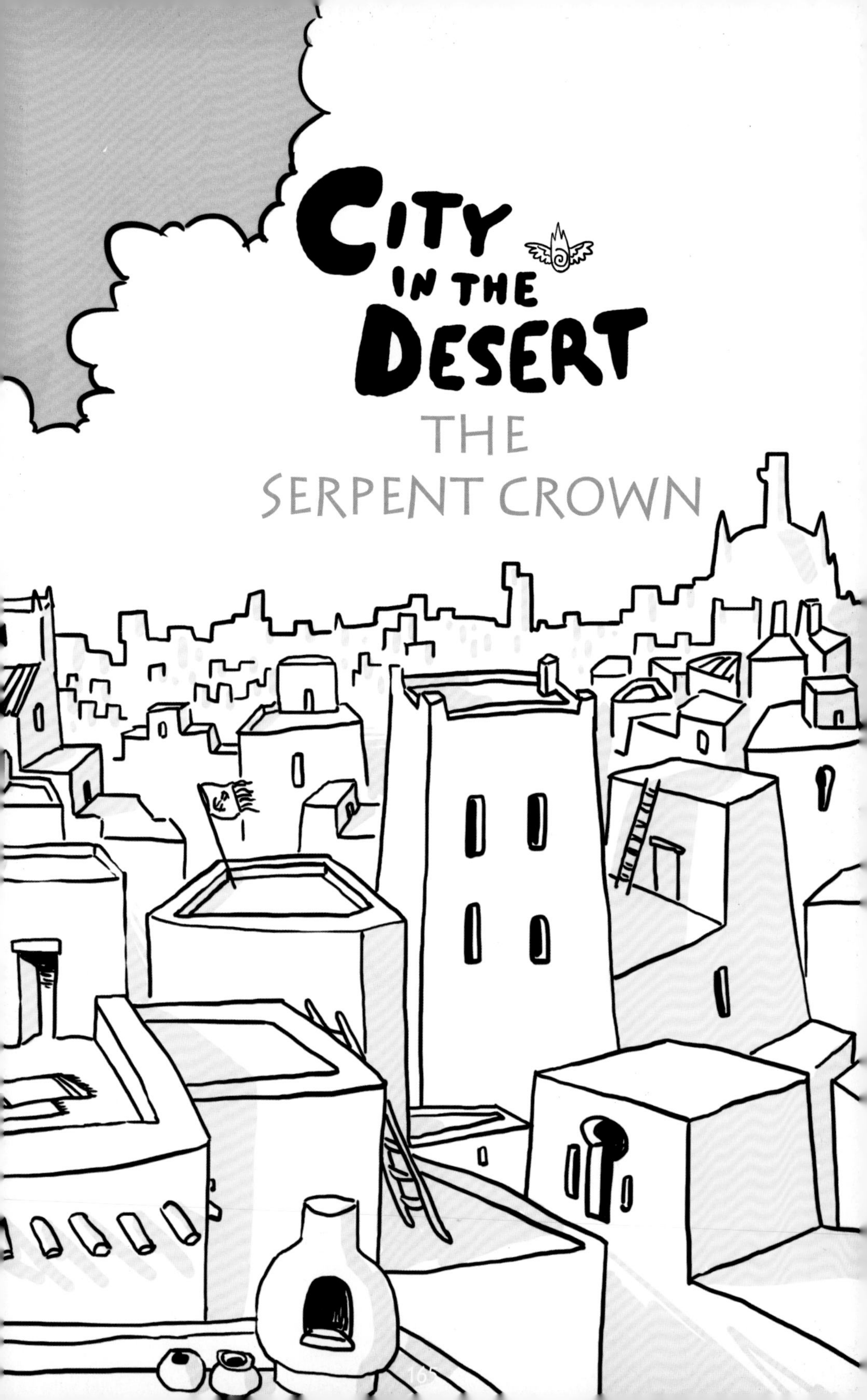
CITY IN THE DESERT
THE SERPENT CROWN

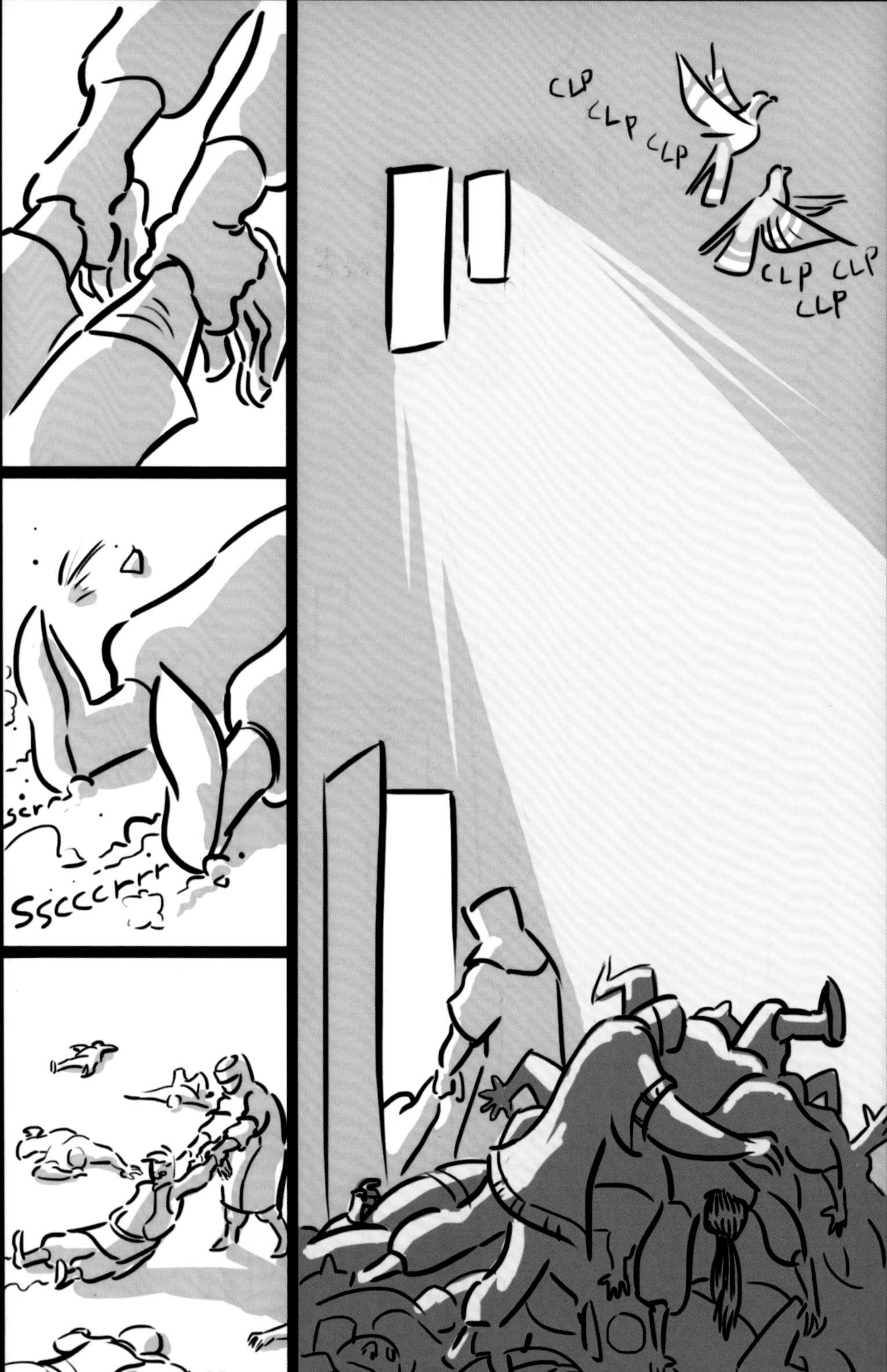
scrr
Ssccrrr
CLP CLP CLP
CLP CLP
CLP

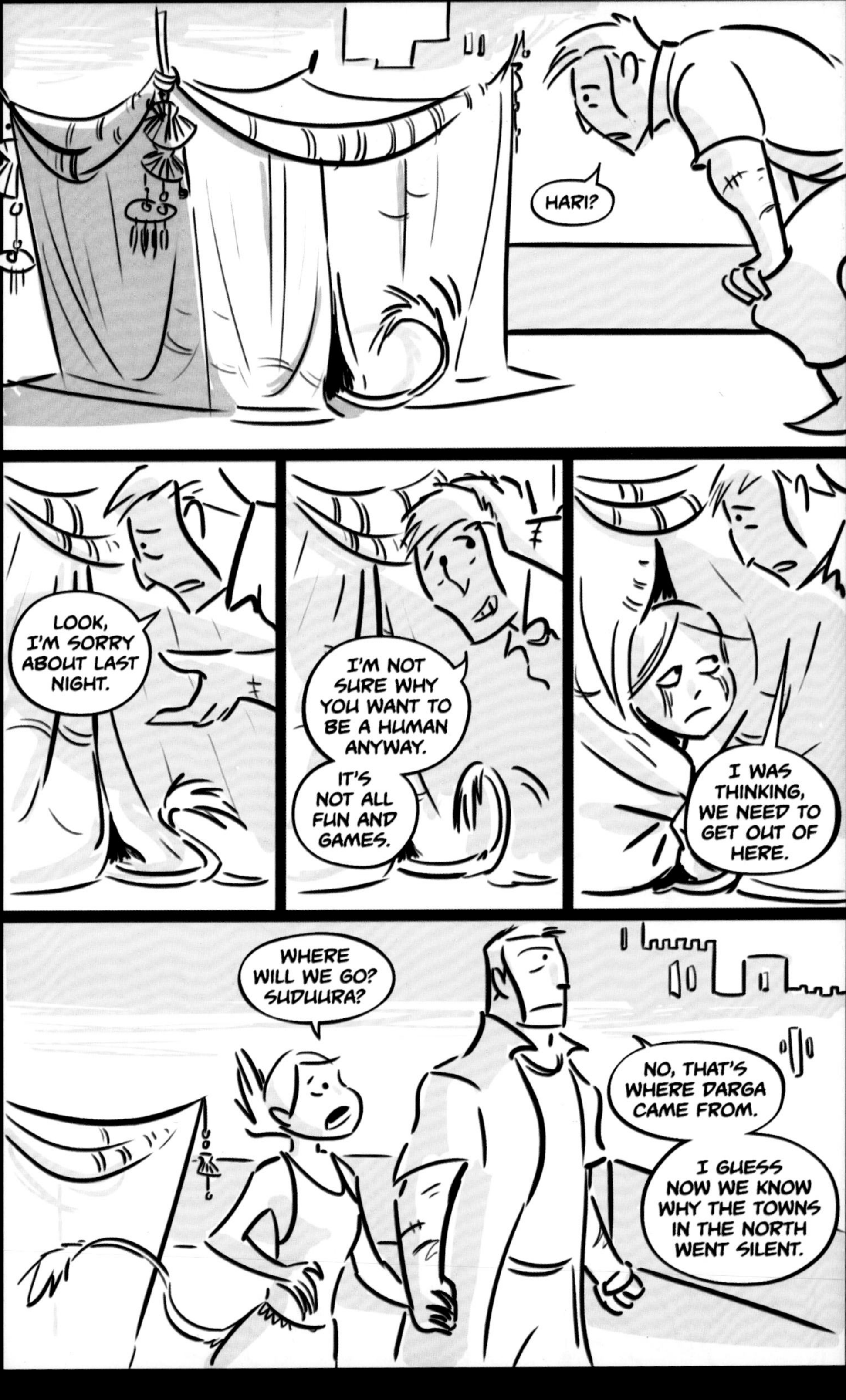
HARI?
LOOK, I'M SORRY ABOUT LAST NIGHT.
I'M NOT SURE WHY YOU WANT TO BE A HUMAN ANYWAY.
IT'S NOT ALL FUN AND GAMES.
I WAS THINKING, WE NEED TO GET OUT OF HERE.
WHERE WILL WE GO? SUDUURA?
NO, THAT'S WHERE DARGA CAME FROM.
I GUESS NOW WE KNOW WHY THE TOWNS IN THE NORTH WENT SILENT.

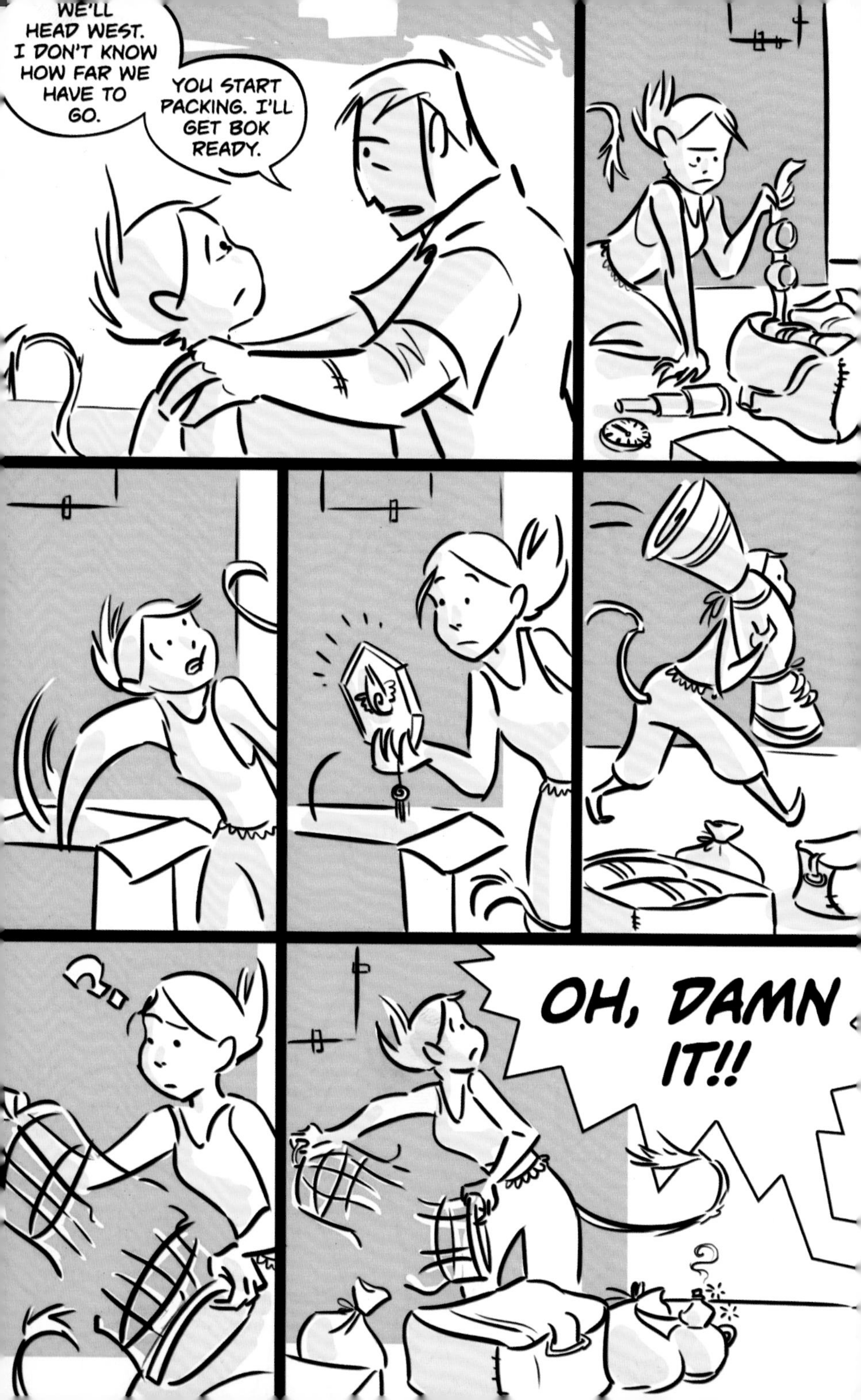
WE'LL HEAD WEST. I DON'T KNOW HOW FAR WE HAVE TO GO.
YOU START PACKING. I'LL GET BOK READY.
OH, DAMN IT!!

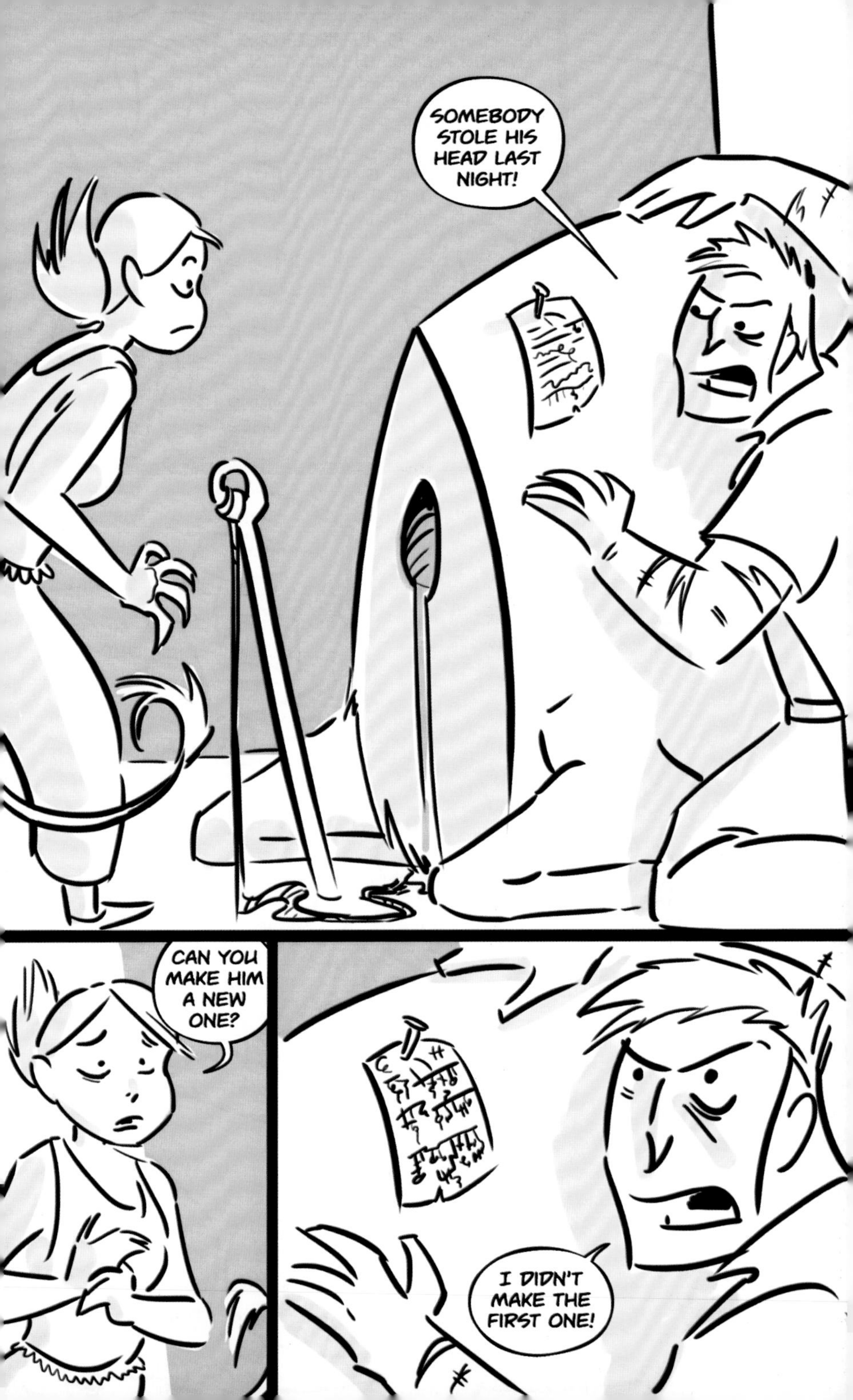
SOMEBODY STOLE HIS HEAD LAST NIGHT!
CAN YOU MAKE HIM A NEW ONE?
I DIDN'T MAKE THE FIRST ONE!

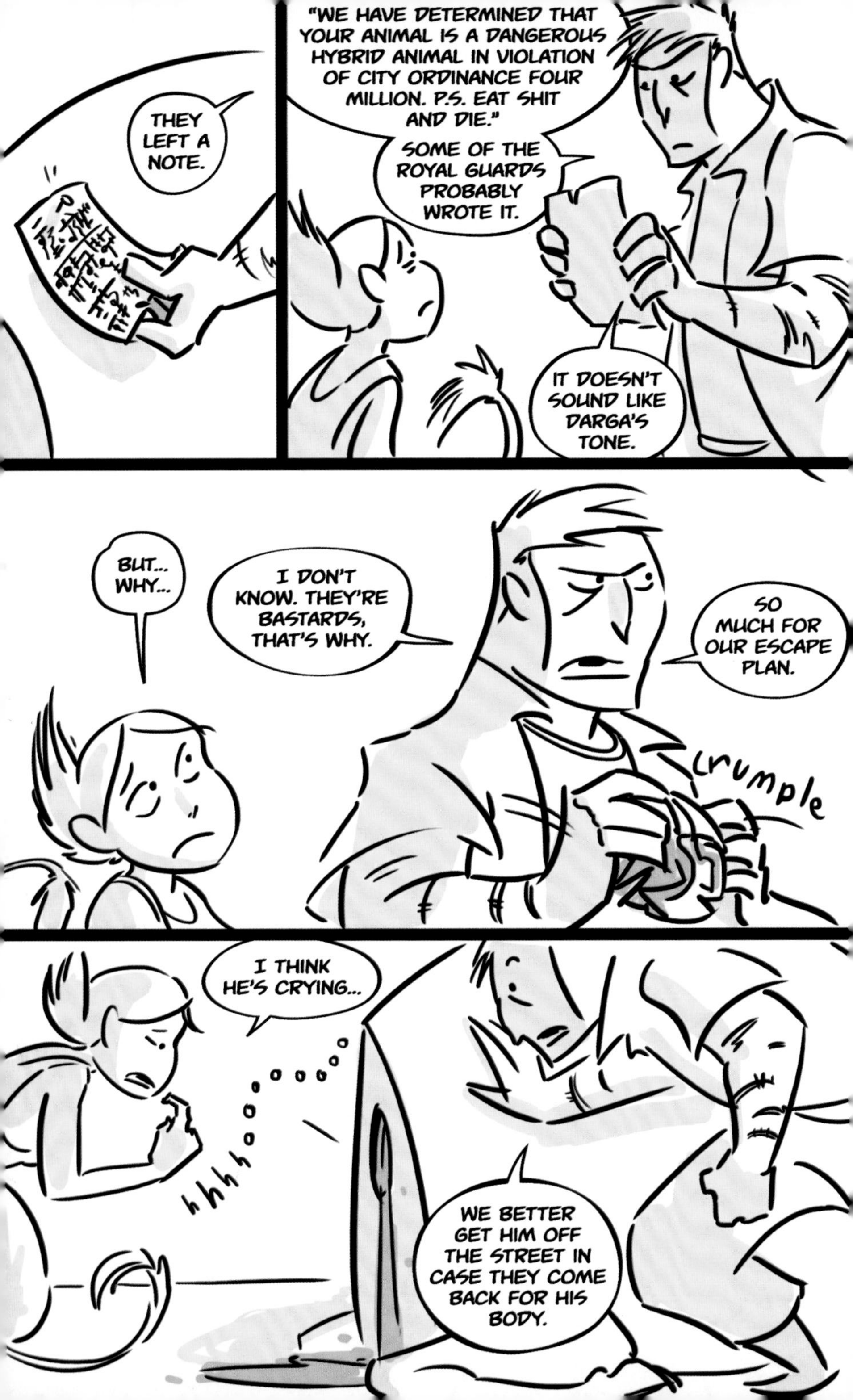
THEY LEFT A NOTE.
"WE HAVE DETERMINED THAT YOUR ANIMAL IS A DANGEROUS HYBRID ANIMAL IN VIOLATION OF CITY ORDINANCE FOUR MILLION. P.S. EAT SHIT AND DIE."
SOME OF THE ROYAL GUARDS PROBABLY WROTE IT.
IT DOESN'T SOUND LIKE DARGA'S TONE.
BUT... WHY...
I DON'T KNOW. THEY'RE BASTARDS, THAT'S WHY.
SO MUCH FOR OUR ESCAPE PLAN.
crumple
I THINK HE'S CRYING...
hhhhooooooo
WE BETTER GET HIM OFF THE STREET IN CASE THEY COME BACK FOR HIS BODY.

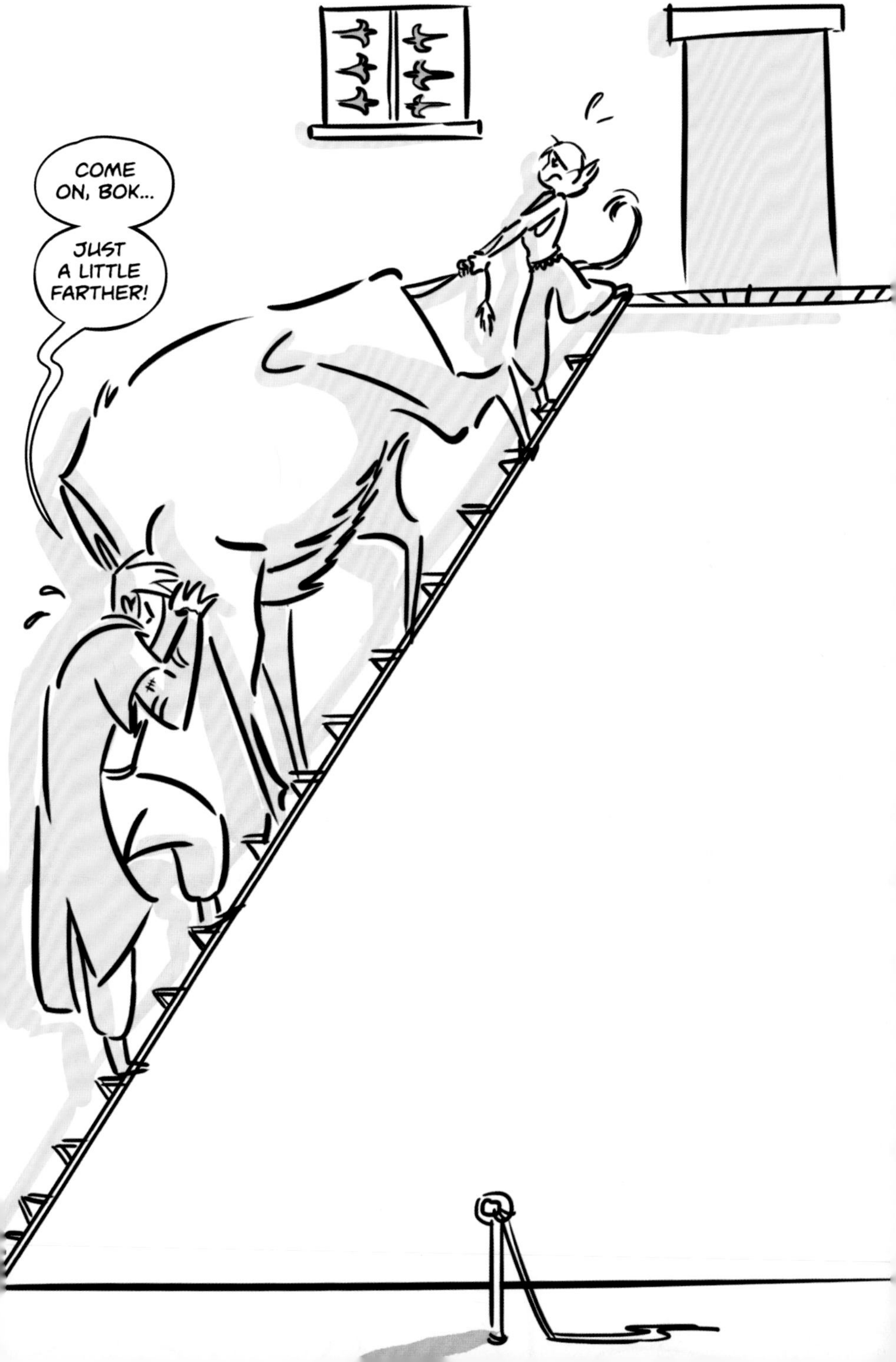
COME ON, BOK...
JUST A LITTLE FARTHER!

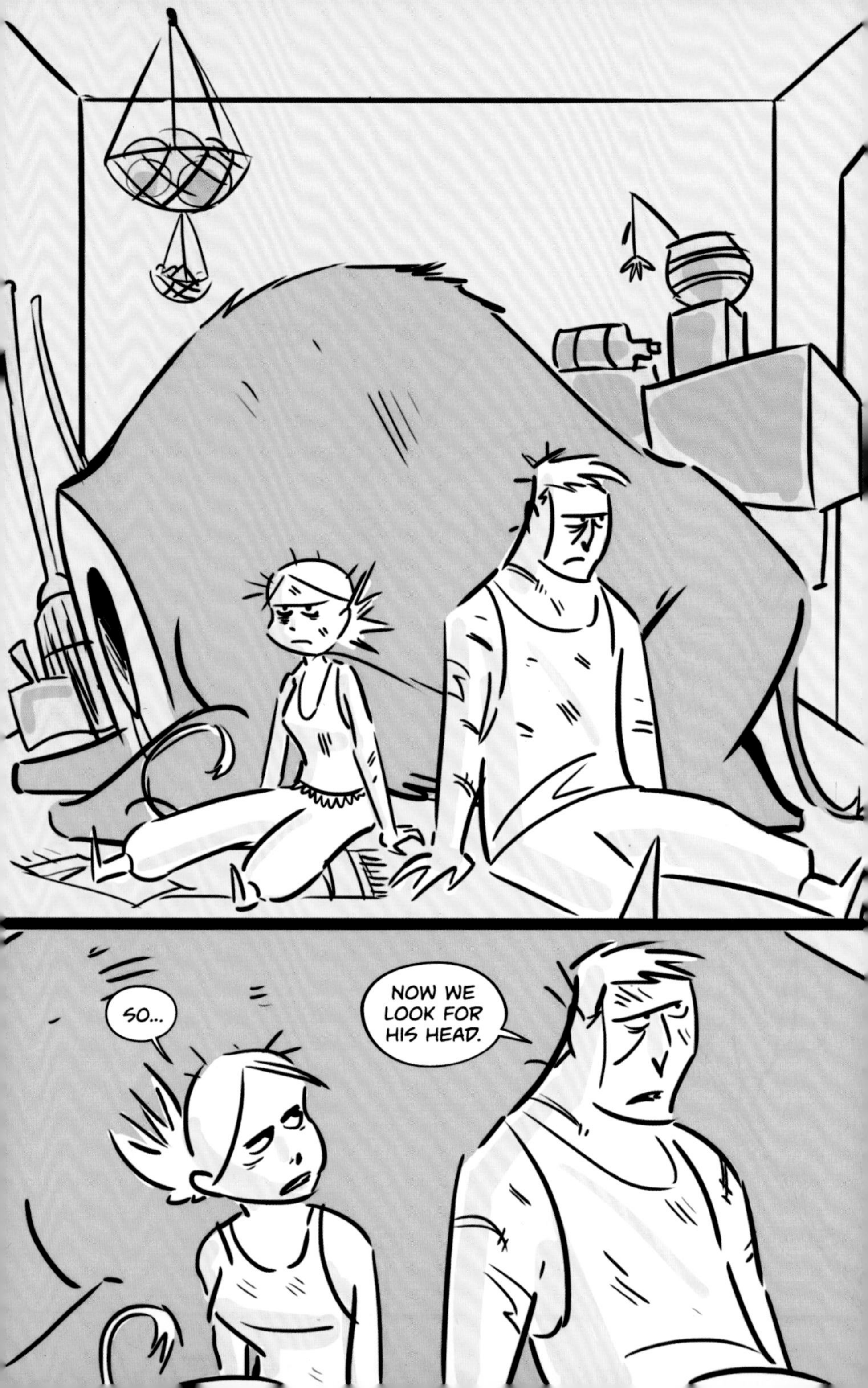
SO...
NOW WE LOOK FOR HIS HEAD.

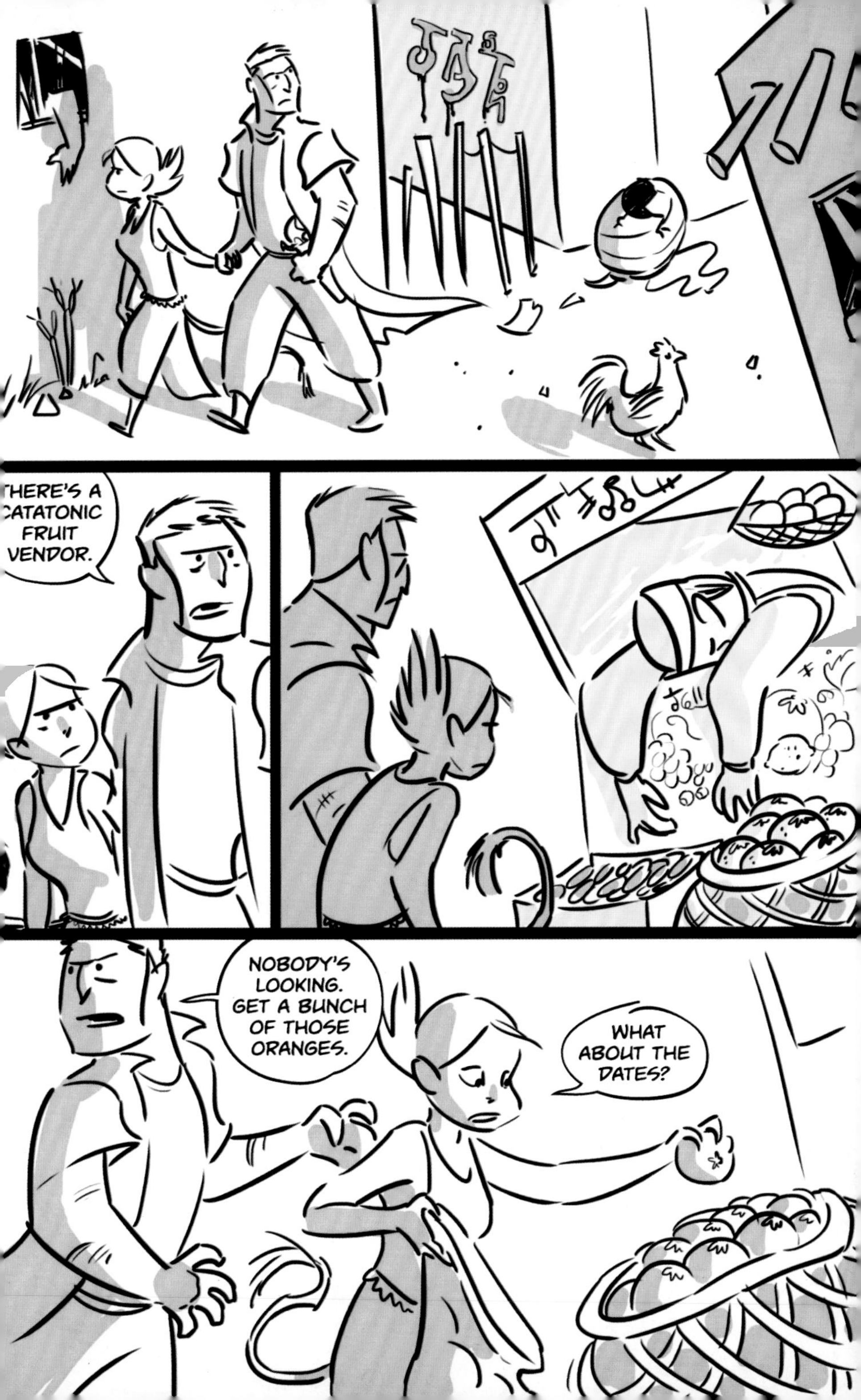
THERE'S A CATATONIC FRUIT VENDOR.
NOBODY'S LOOKING. GET A BUNCH OF THOSE ORANGES.
WHAT ABOUT THE DATES?

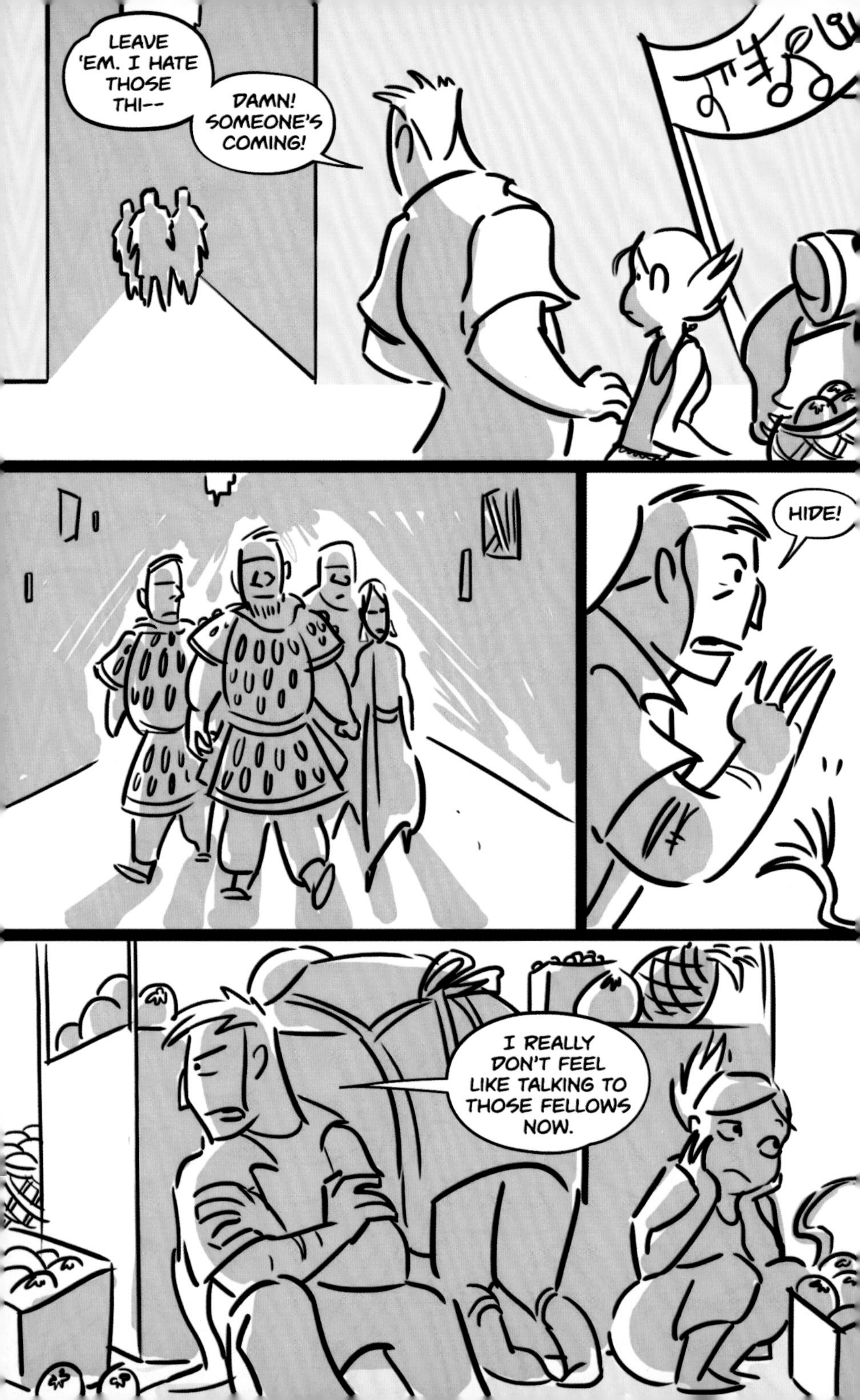

LEAVE 'EM. I HATE THOSE THI--
DAMN! SOMEONE'S COMING!
HIDE!
I REALLY DON'T FEEL LIKE TALKING TO THOSE FELLOWS NOW.

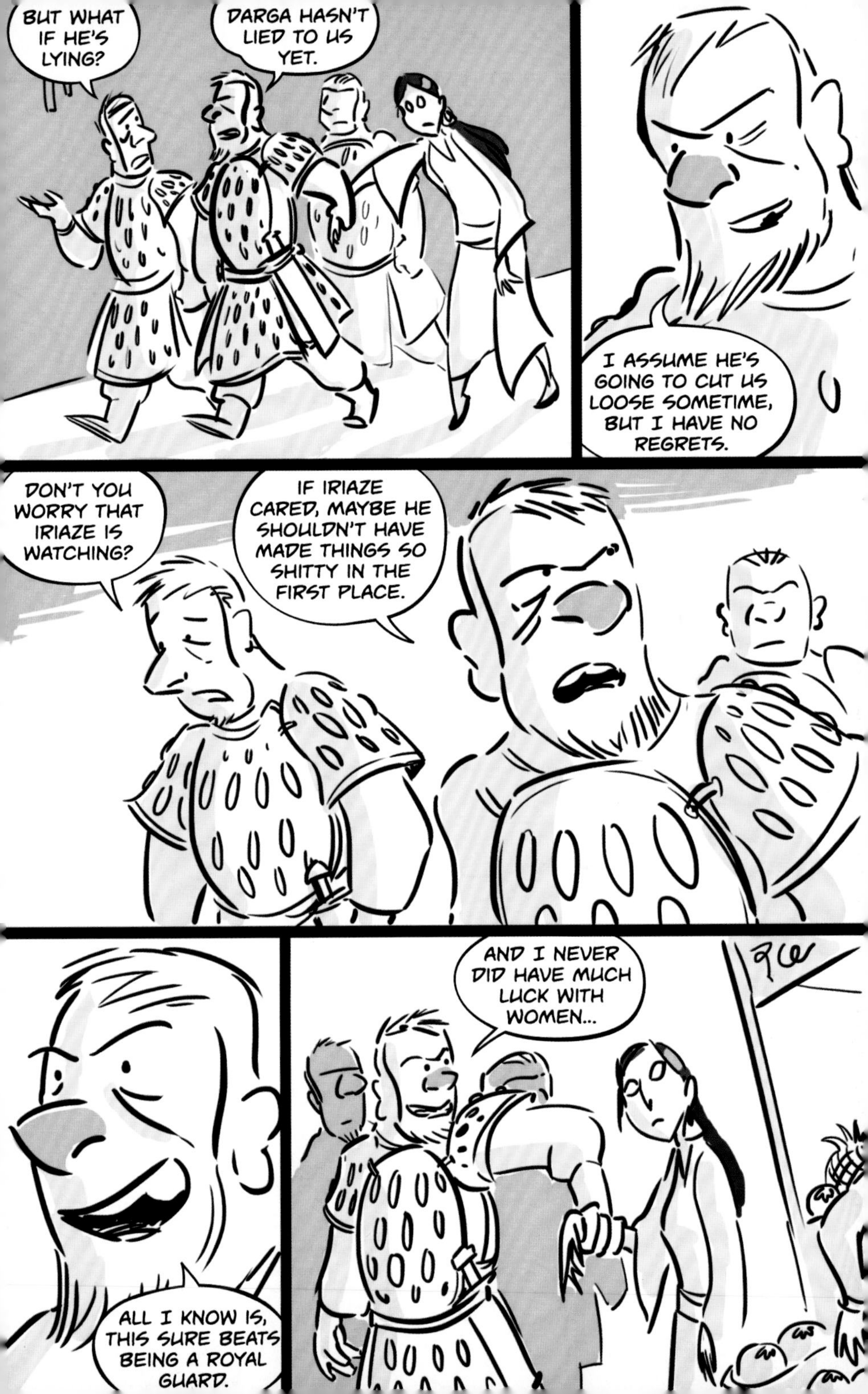
BUT WHAT IF HE'S LYING?
DARGA HASN'T LIED TO US YET.
I ASSUME HE'S GOING TO CUT US LOOSE SOMETIME, BUT I HAVE NO REGRETS.
DON'T YOU WORRY THAT IRIAZE IS WATCHING?
IF IRIAZE CARED, MAYBE HE SHOULDN'T HAVE MADE THINGS SO SHITTY IN THE FIRST PLACE.
ALL I KNOW IS, THIS SURE BEATS BEING A ROYAL GUARD.
AND I NEVER DID HAVE MUCH LUCK WITH WOMEN...

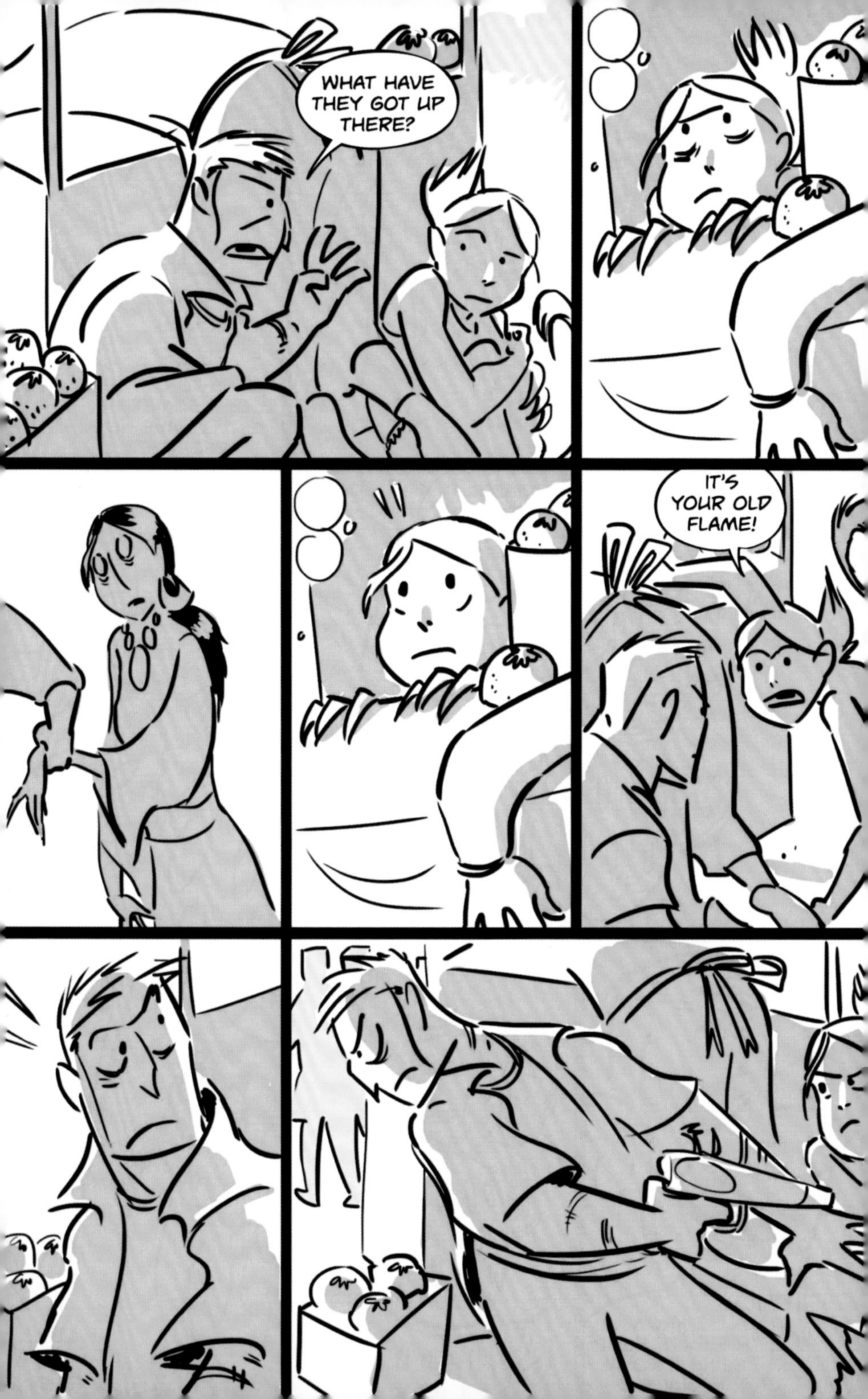
WHAT HAVE THEY GOT UP THERE?
IT'S YOUR OLD FLAME!

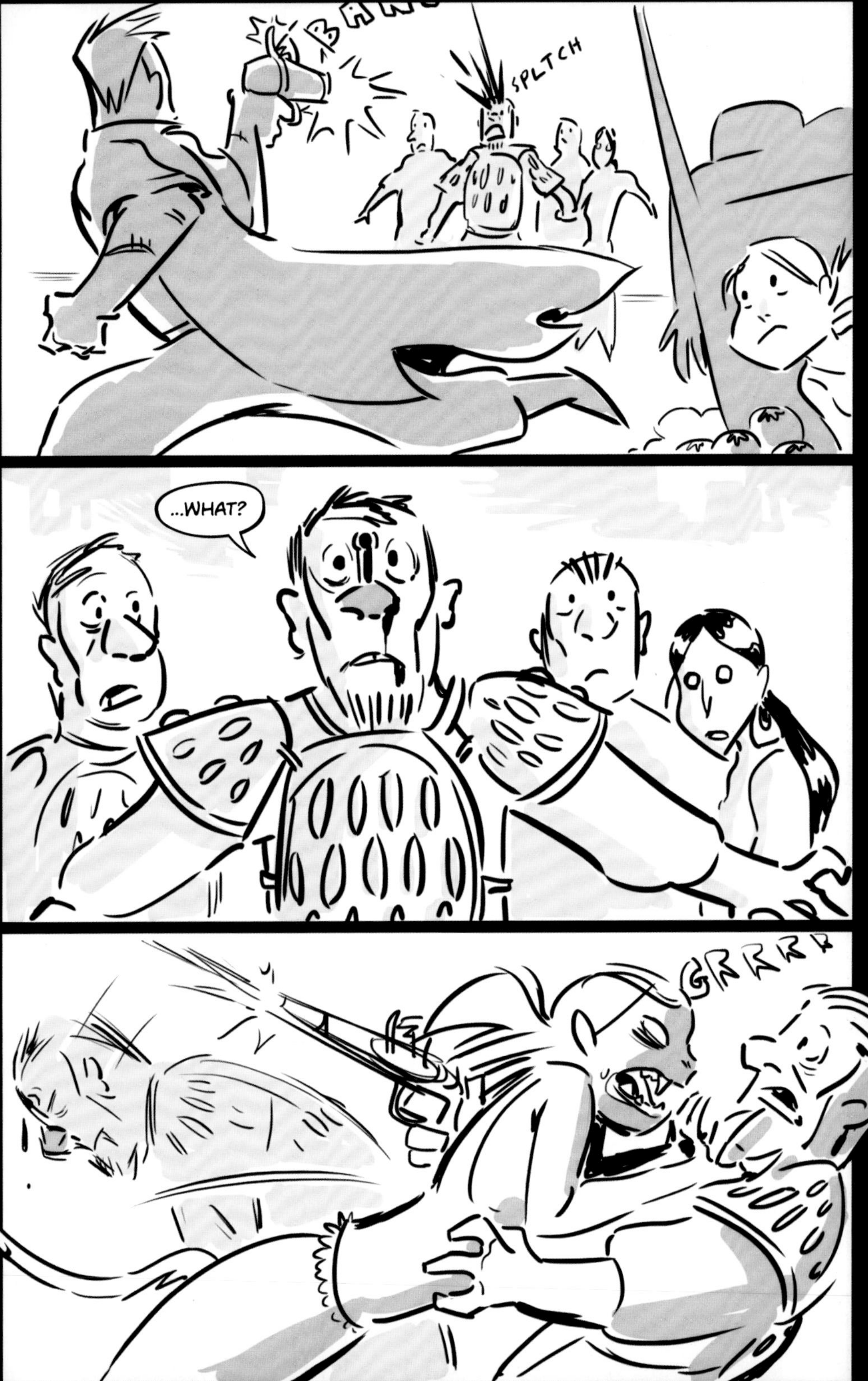
BANG
SPLTCH
...WHAT?
GRRRR

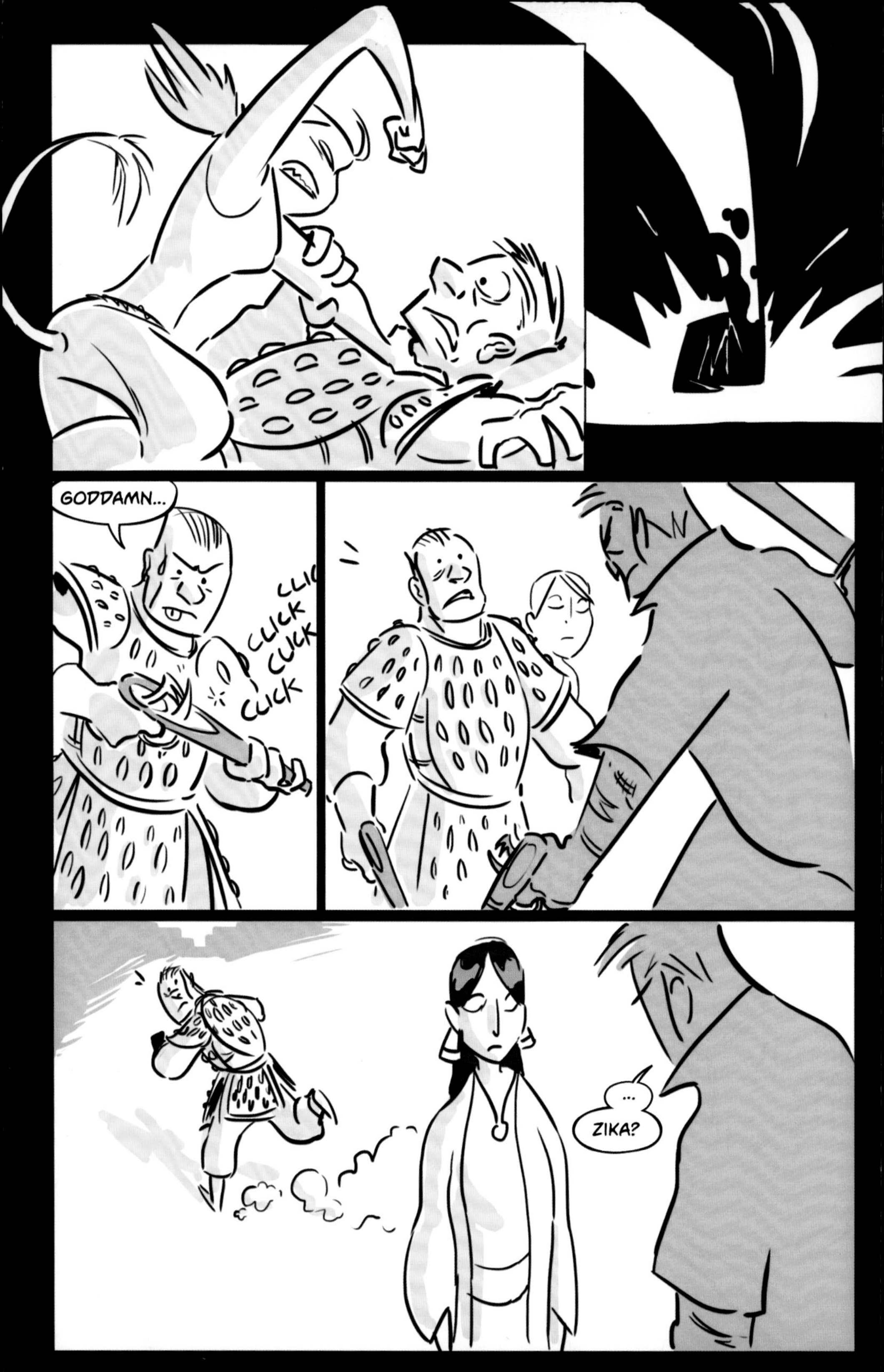
GODDAMN...
CLIC
CLICK
CLICK
CLICK
...
ZIKA?

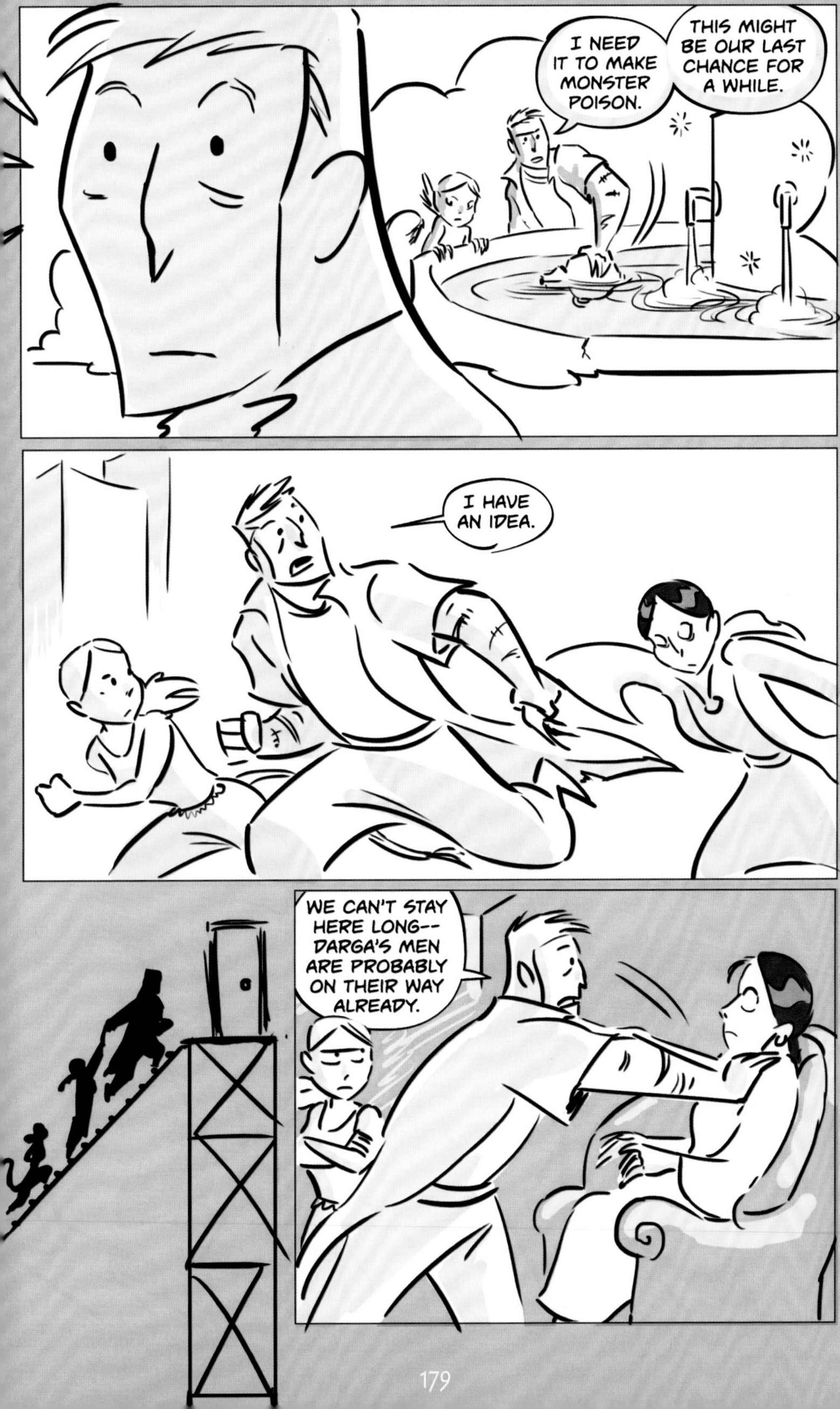
I NEED IT TO MAKE MONSTER POISON.
THIS MIGHT BE OUR LAST CHANCE FOR A WHILE.
I HAVE AN IDEA.
WE CAN'T STAY HERE LONG-- DARGA'S MEN ARE PROBABLY ON THEIR WAY ALREADY.

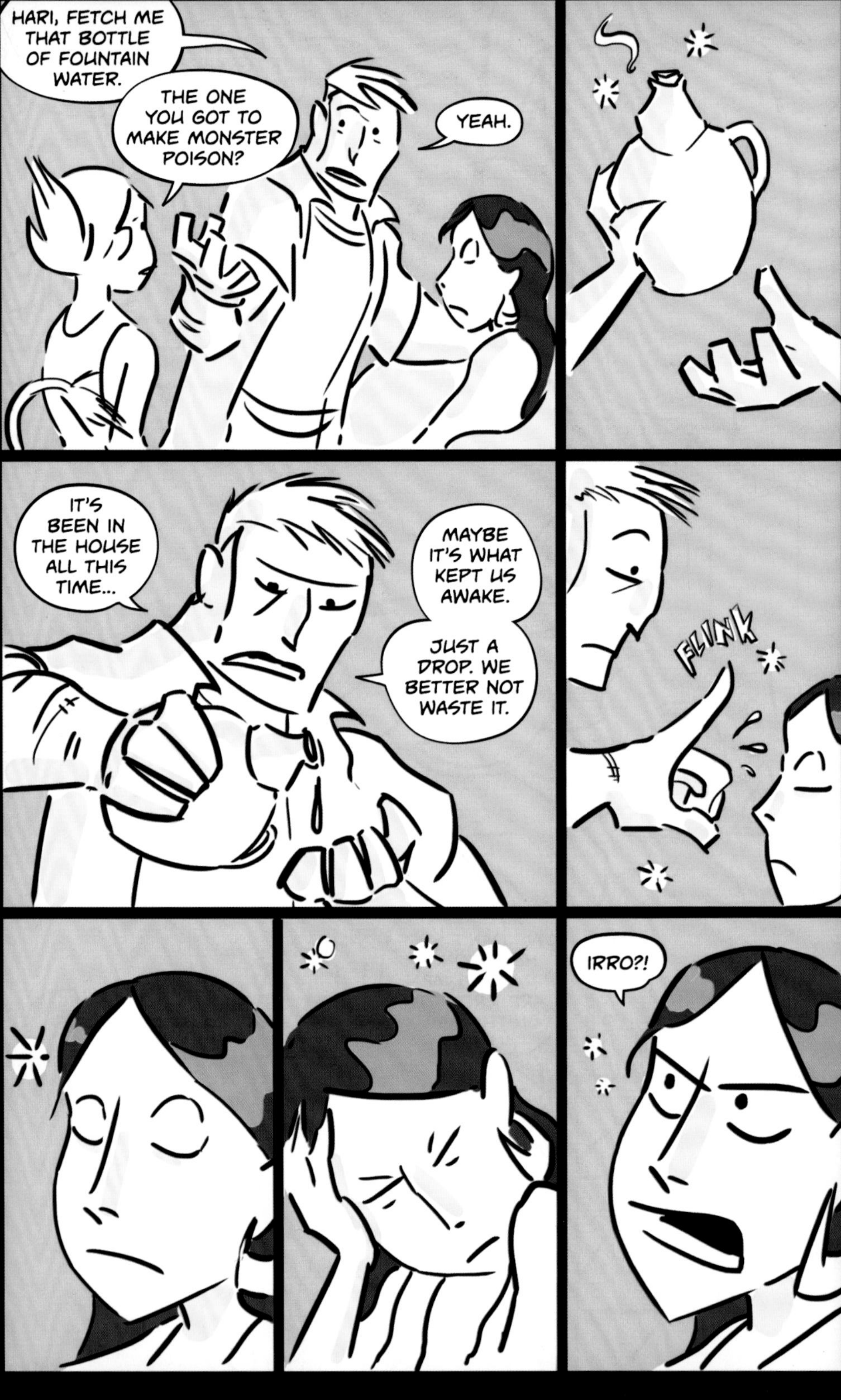
HARI, FETCH ME THAT BOTTLE OF FOUNTAIN WATER.
THE ONE YOU GOT TO MAKE MONSTER POISON?
YEAH.
IT'S BEEN IN THE HOUSE ALL THIS TIME...
MAYBE IT'S WHAT KEPT US AWAKE.
JUST A DROP. WE BETTER NOT WASTE IT.
FLINK
IRRO?!

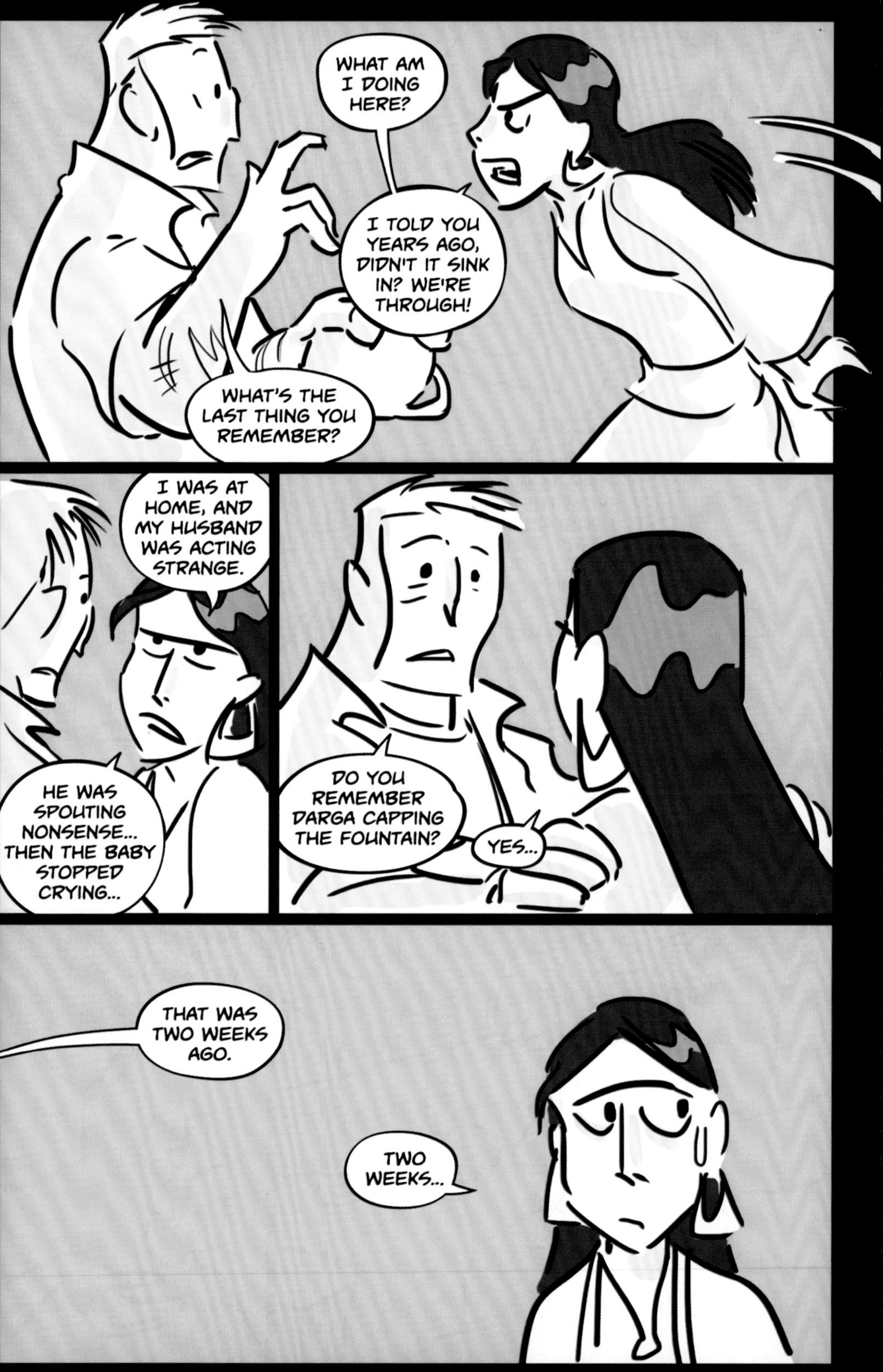
WHAT AM I DOING HERE?
I TOLD YOU YEARS AGO, DIDN'T IT SINK IN? WE'RE THROUGH!
WHAT'S THE LAST THING YOU REMEMBER?
I WAS AT HOME, AND MY HUSBAND WAS ACTING STRANGE.
HE WAS SPOUTING NONSENSE... THEN THE BABY STOPPED CRYING...
DO YOU REMEMBER DARGA CAPPING THE FOUNTAIN?
YES...
THAT WAS TWO WEEKS AGO.
TWO WEEKS...

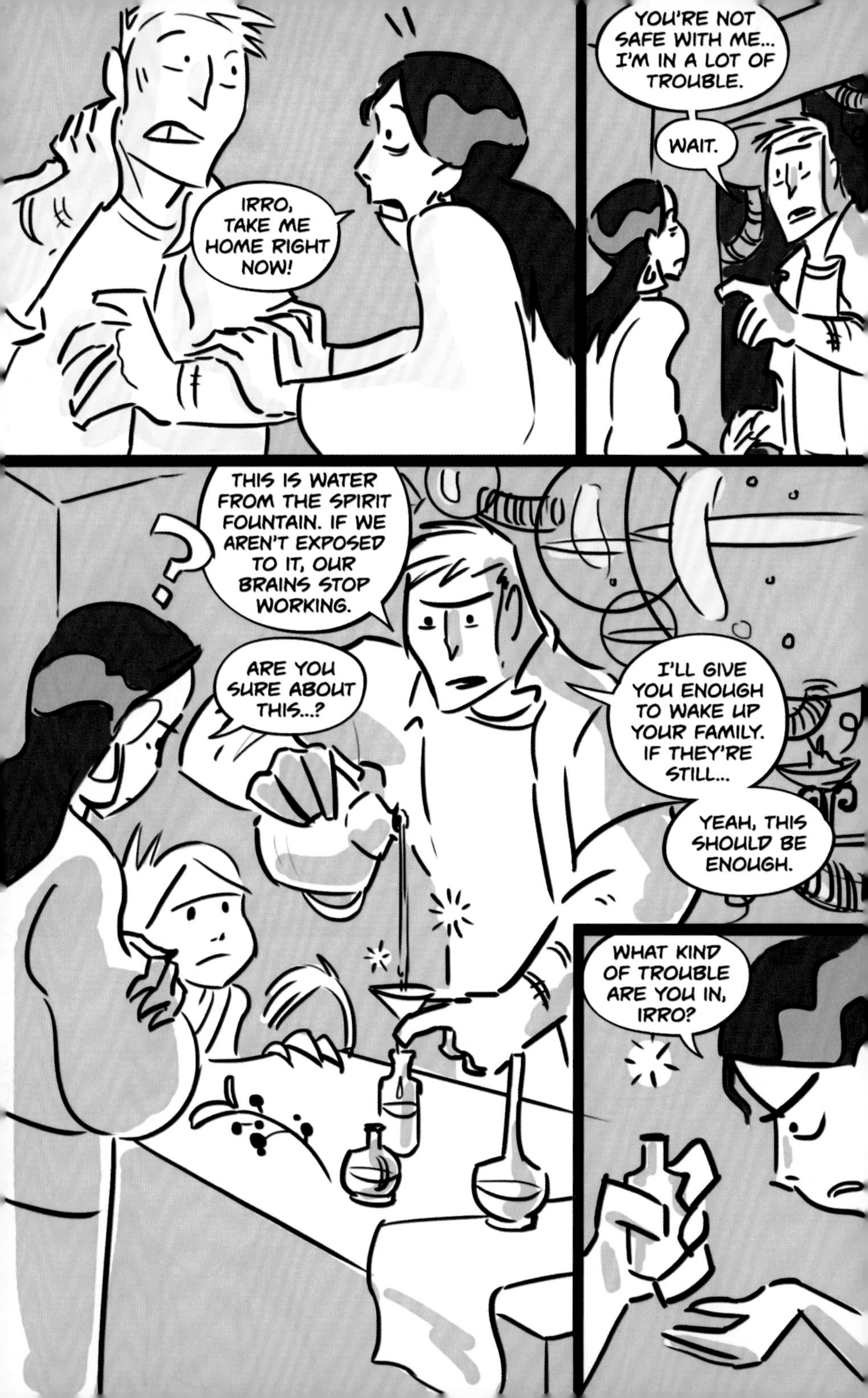
IRRO, TAKE ME HOME RIGHT NOW!
YOU'RE NOT SAFE WITH ME... I'M IN A LOT OF TROUBLE.
WAIT.
THIS IS WATER FROM THE SPIRIT FOUNTAIN. IF WE AREN'T EXPOSED TO IT, OUR BRAINS STOP WORKING.
ARE YOU SURE ABOUT THIS...?
I'LL GIVE YOU ENOUGH TO WAKE UP YOUR FAMILY. IF THEY'RE STILL...
YEAH, THIS SHOULD BE ENOUGH.
WHAT KIND OF TROUBLE ARE YOU IN, IRRO?

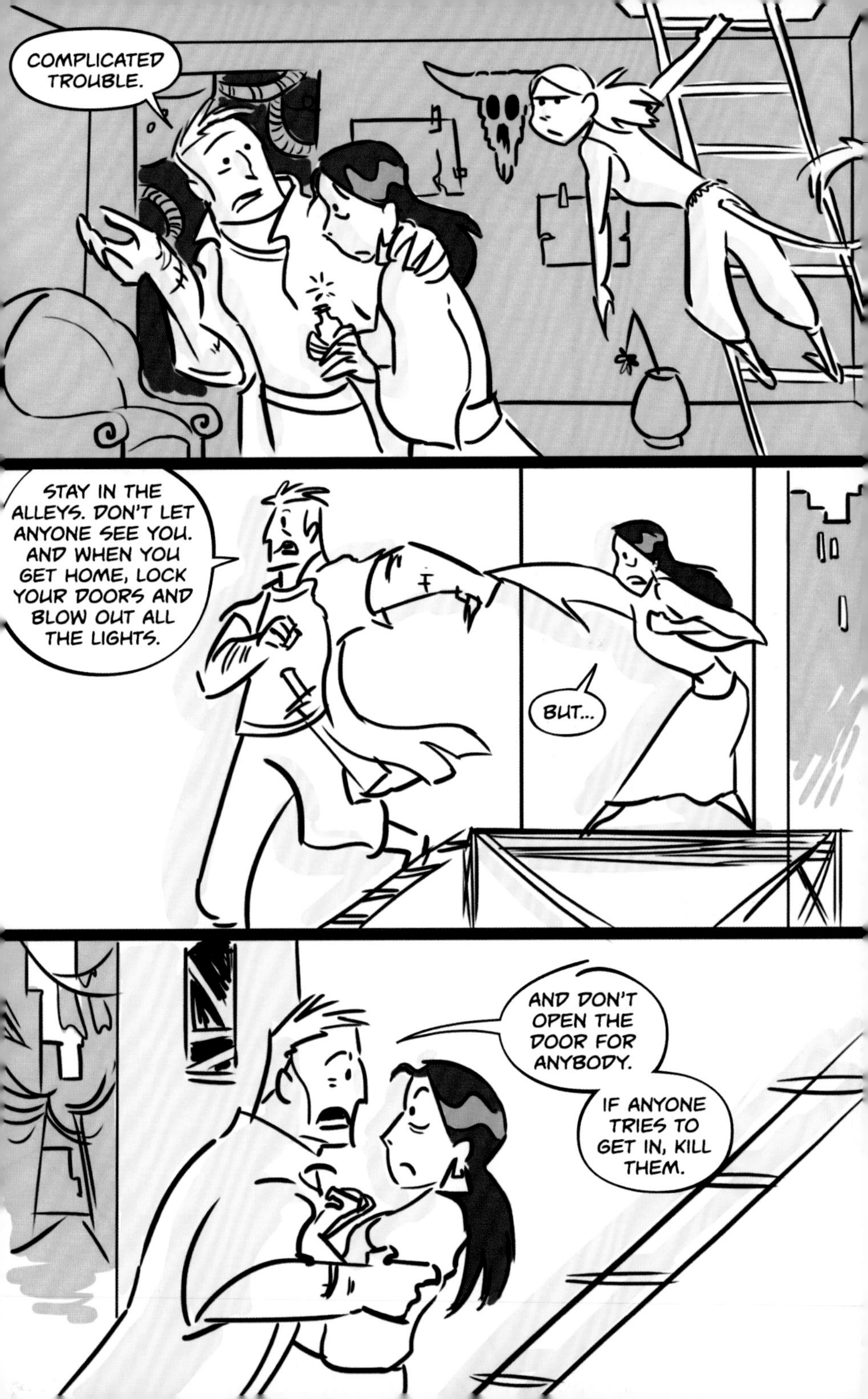
COMPLICATED TROUBLE.
STAY IN THE ALLEYS. DON'T LET ANYONE SEE YOU. AND WHEN YOU GET HOME, LOCK YOUR DOORS AND BLOW OUT ALL THE LIGHTS.
BUT...
AND DON'T OPEN THE DOOR FOR ANYBODY.
IF ANYONE TRIES TO GET IN, KILL THEM.

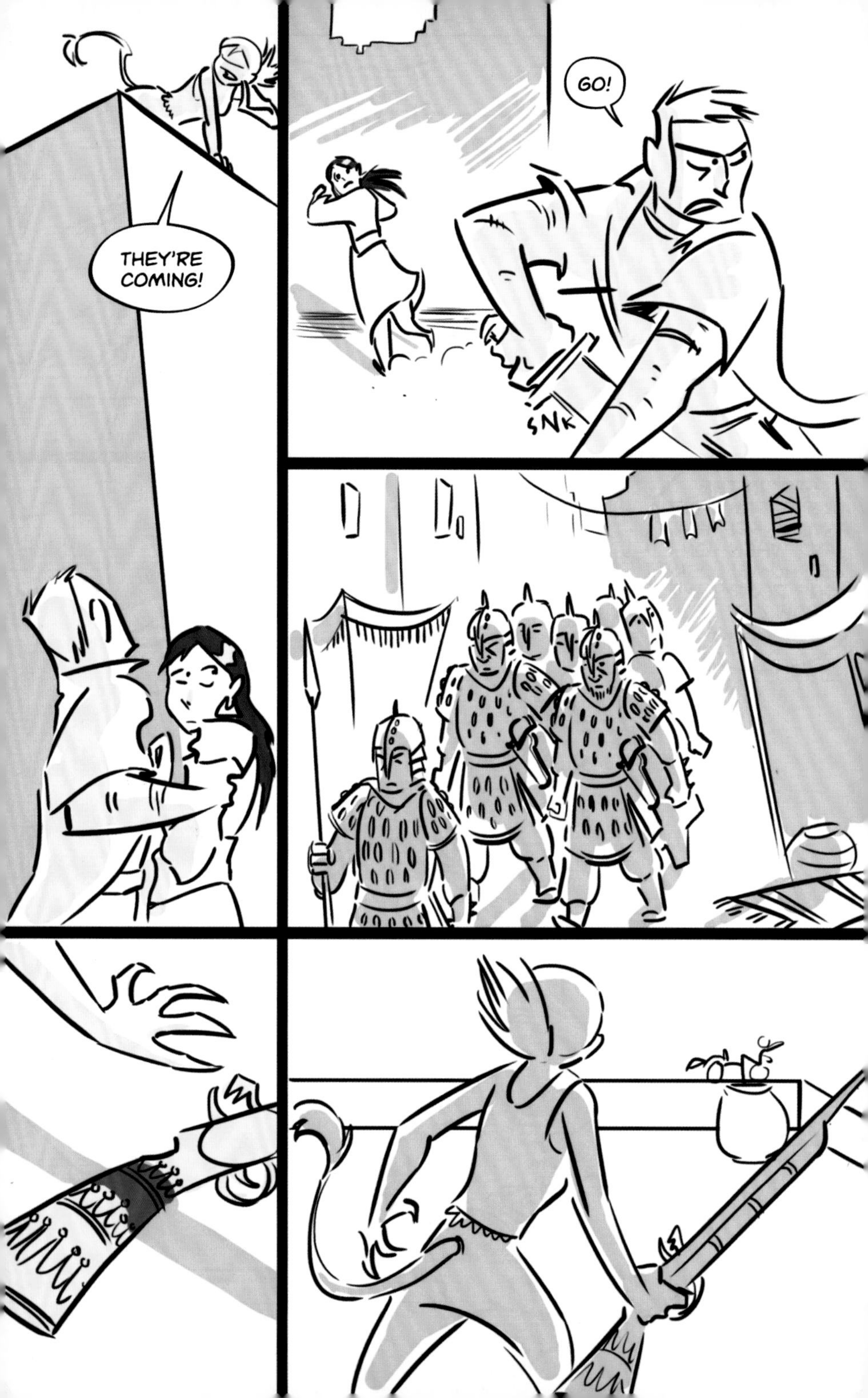
THEY'RE COMING!
GO!
SNK

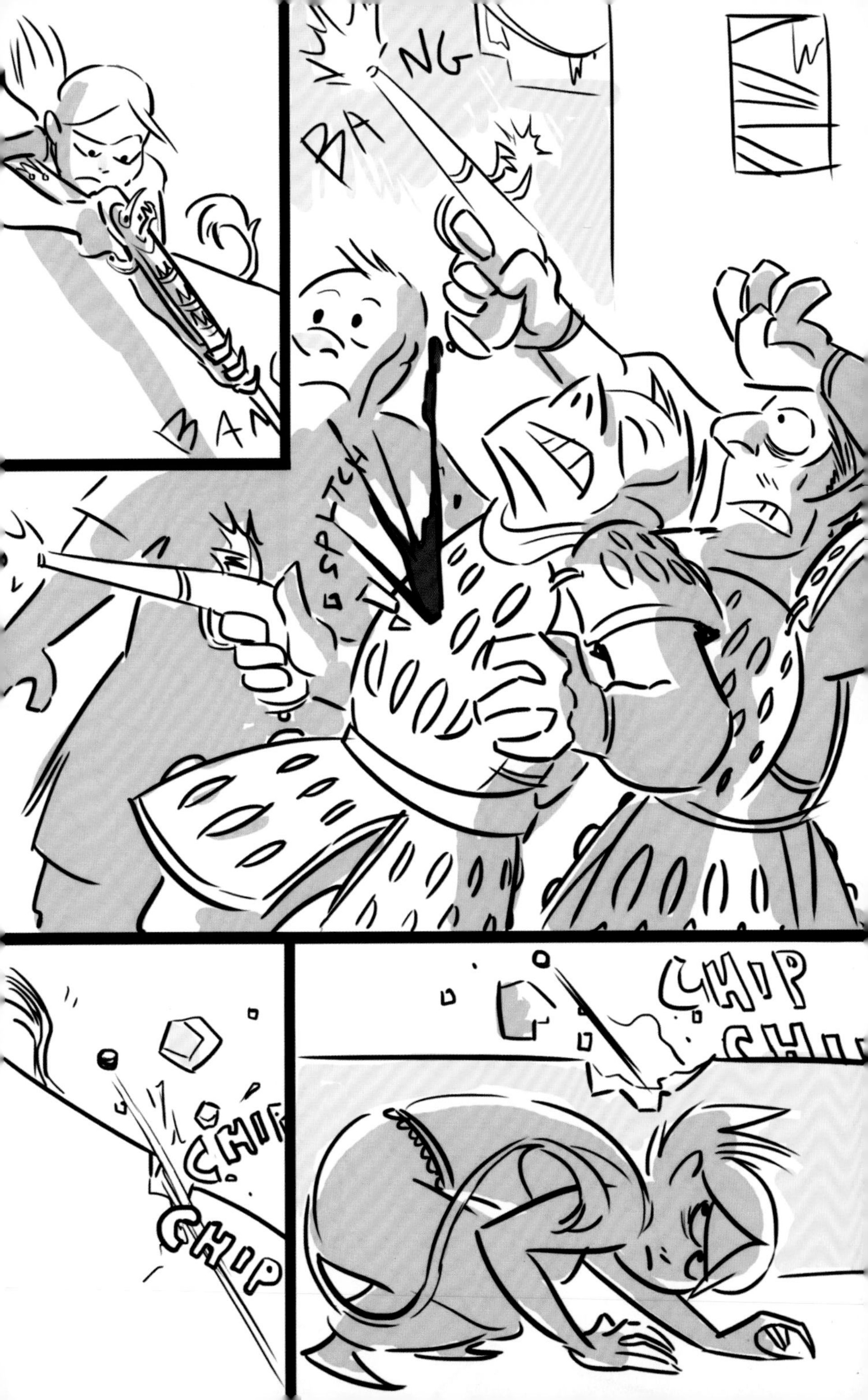
BANG
CHIP
CHIP

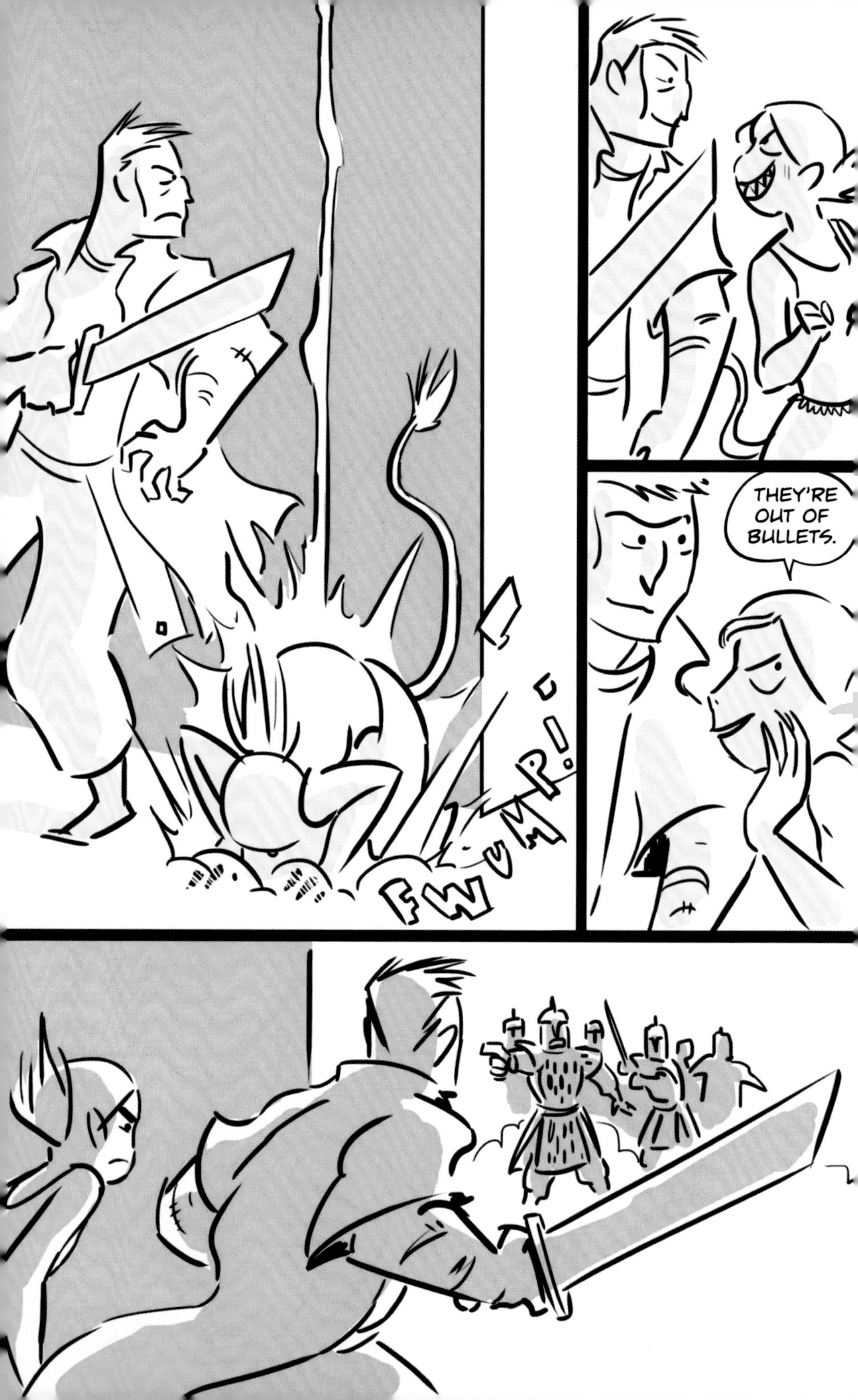
FWUMP!
THEY'RE OUT OF BULLETS.

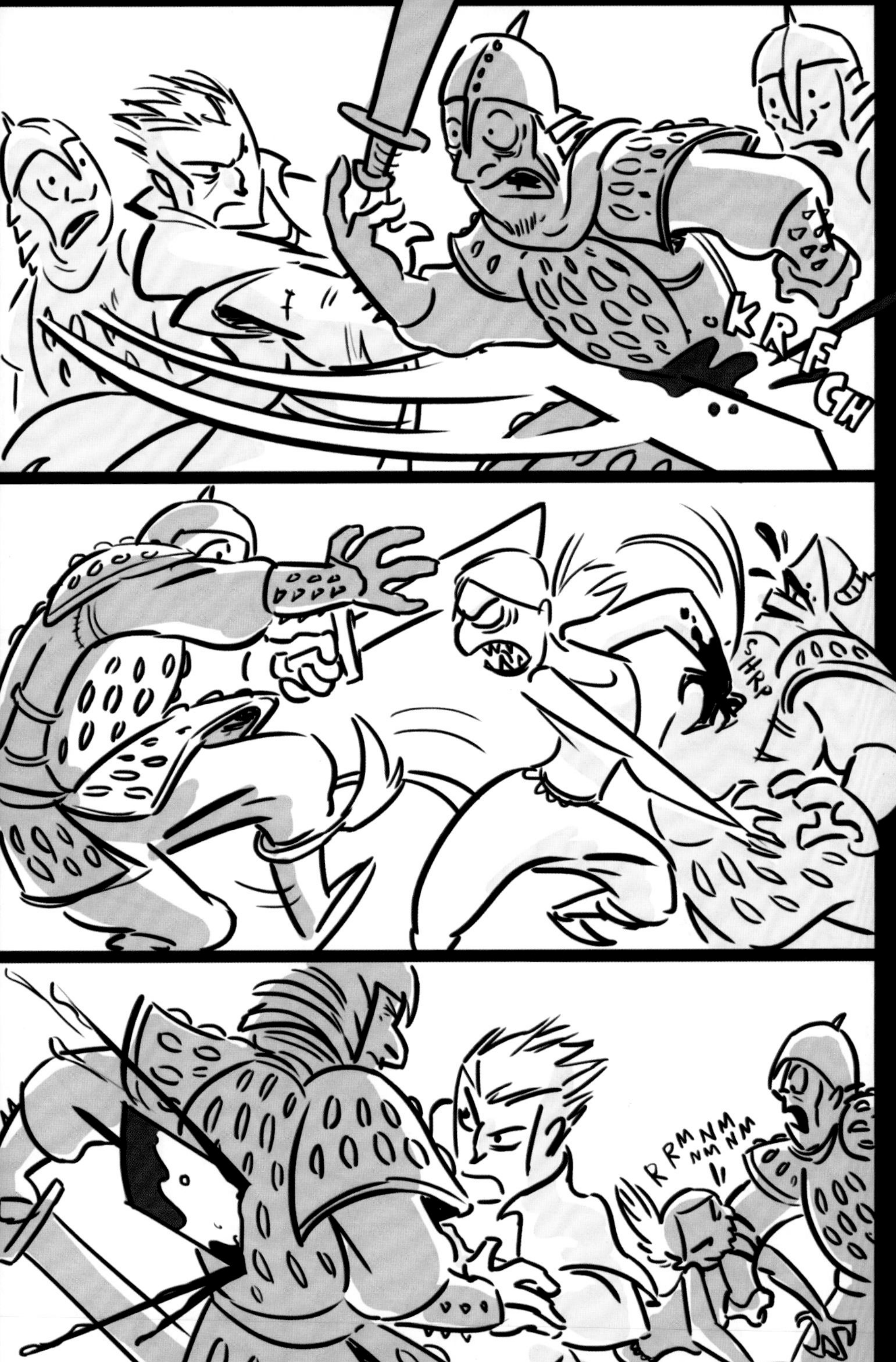
KRRECH
SHRP
RRMNM NM NM

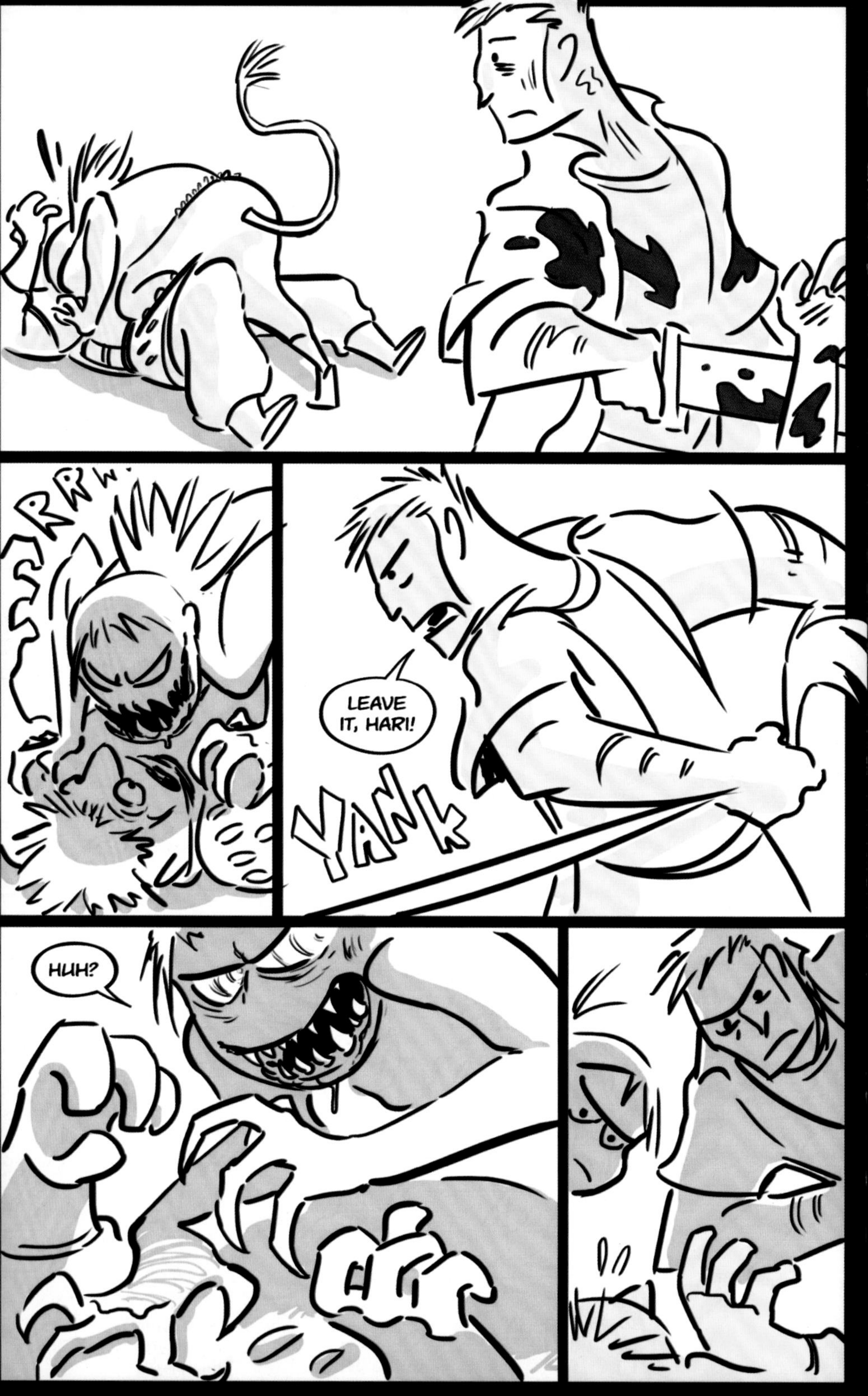
RRRW
LEAVE IT, HARI!
YANK
HUH?

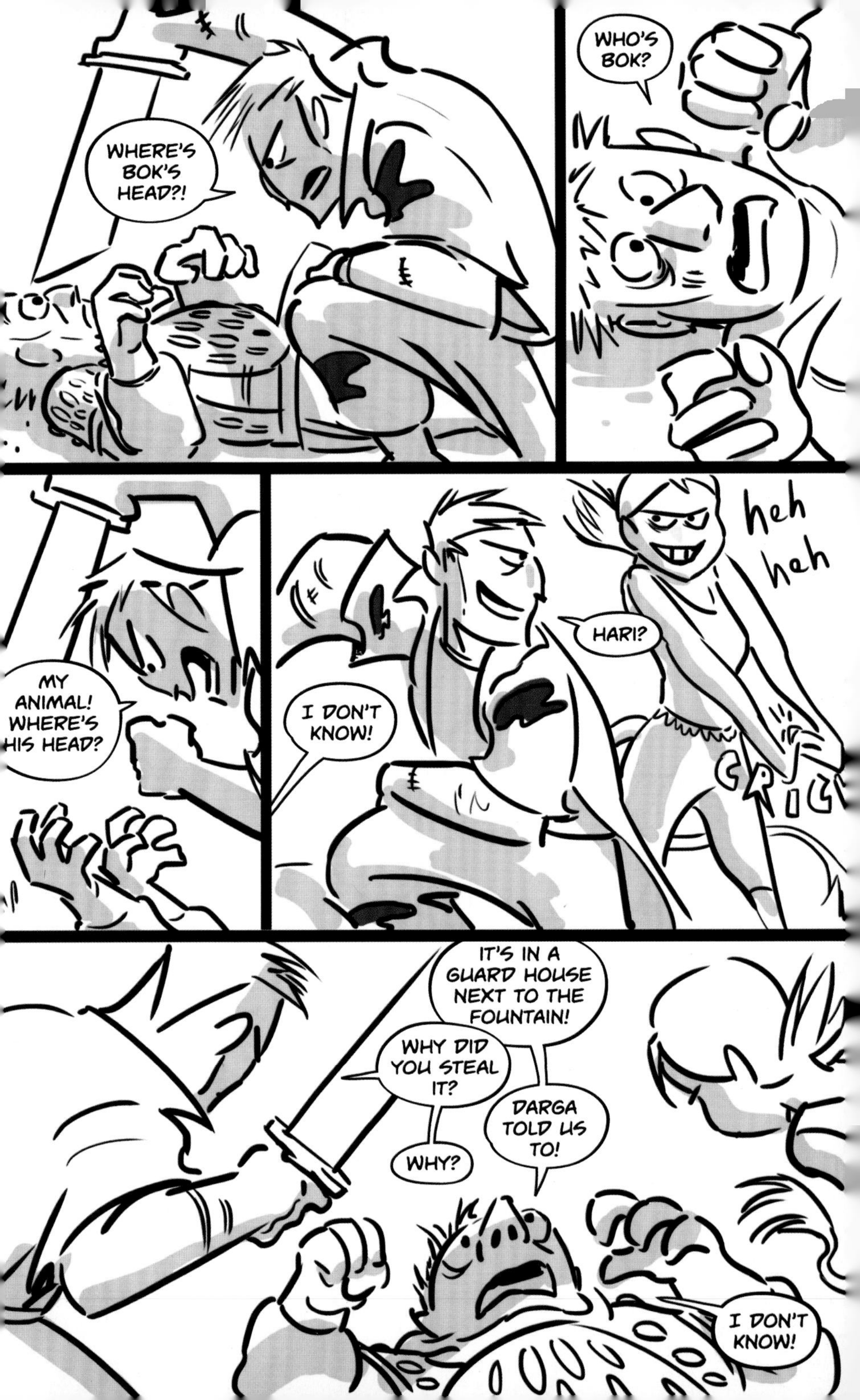
WHERE'S BOK'S HEAD?!
WHO'S BOK?
MY ANIMAL! WHERE'S HIS HEAD?
I DON'T KNOW!
HARI?
heh heh
CRIC
IT'S IN A GUARD HOUSE NEXT TO THE FOUNTAIN!
WHY DID YOU STEAL IT?
WHY?
DARGA TOLD US TO!
I DON'T KNOW!

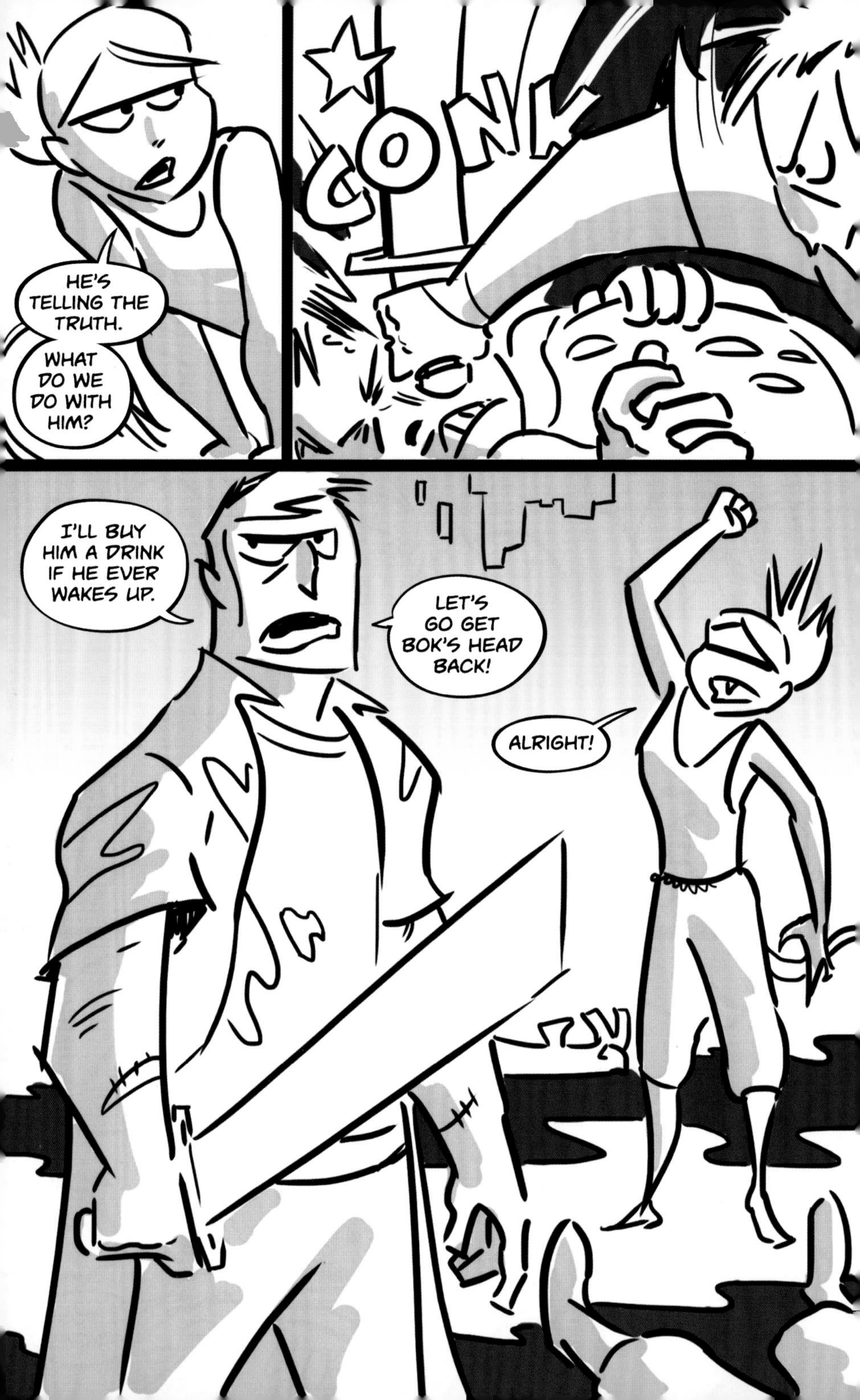
HE'S TELLING THE TRUTH.
WHAT DO WE DO WITH HIM?
CONK
I'LL BUY HIM A DRINK IF HE EVER WAKES UP.
LET'S GO GET BOK'S HEAD BACK!
ALRIGHT!

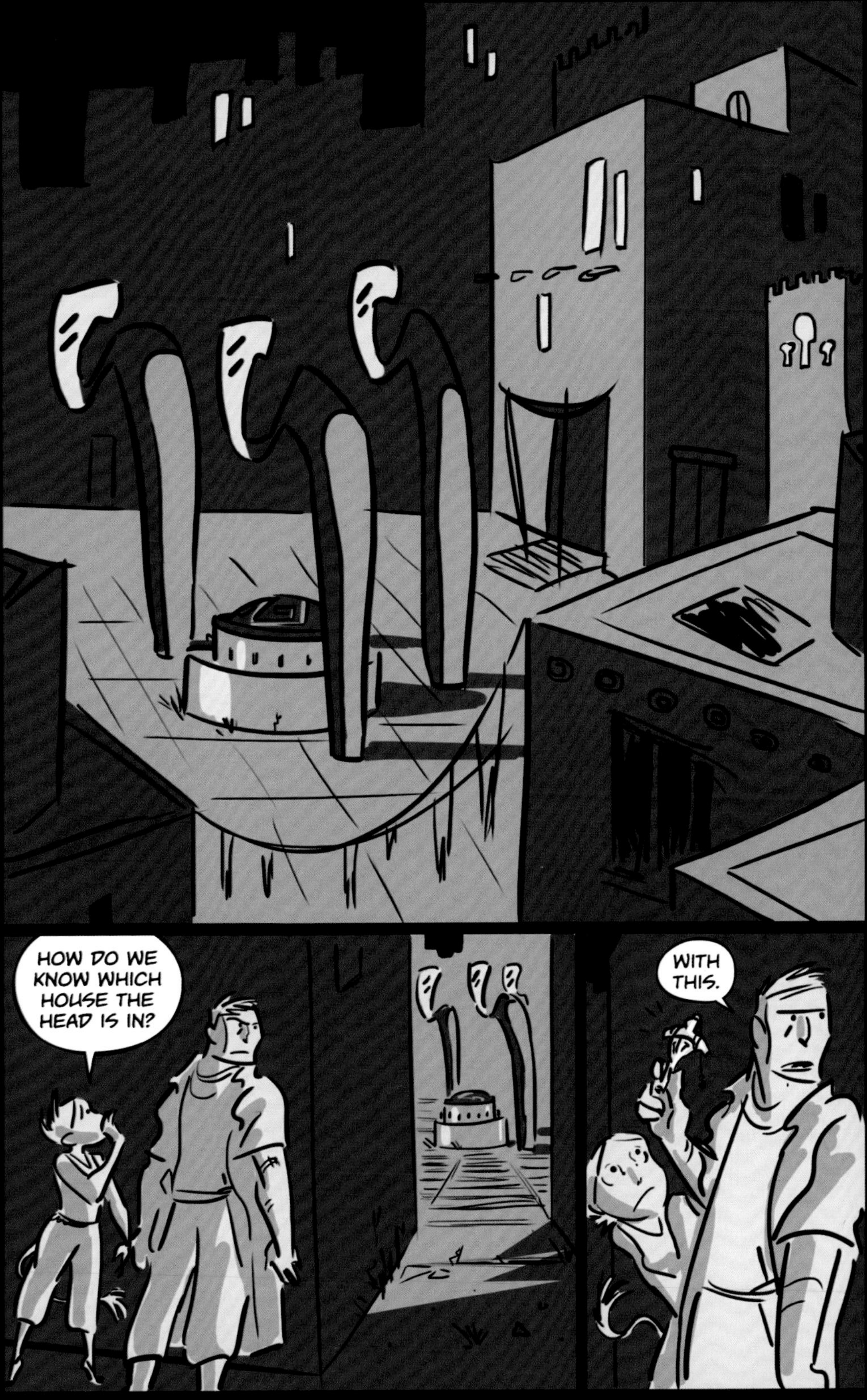
HOW DO WE KNOW WHICH HOUSE THE HEAD IS IN?
WITH THIS.

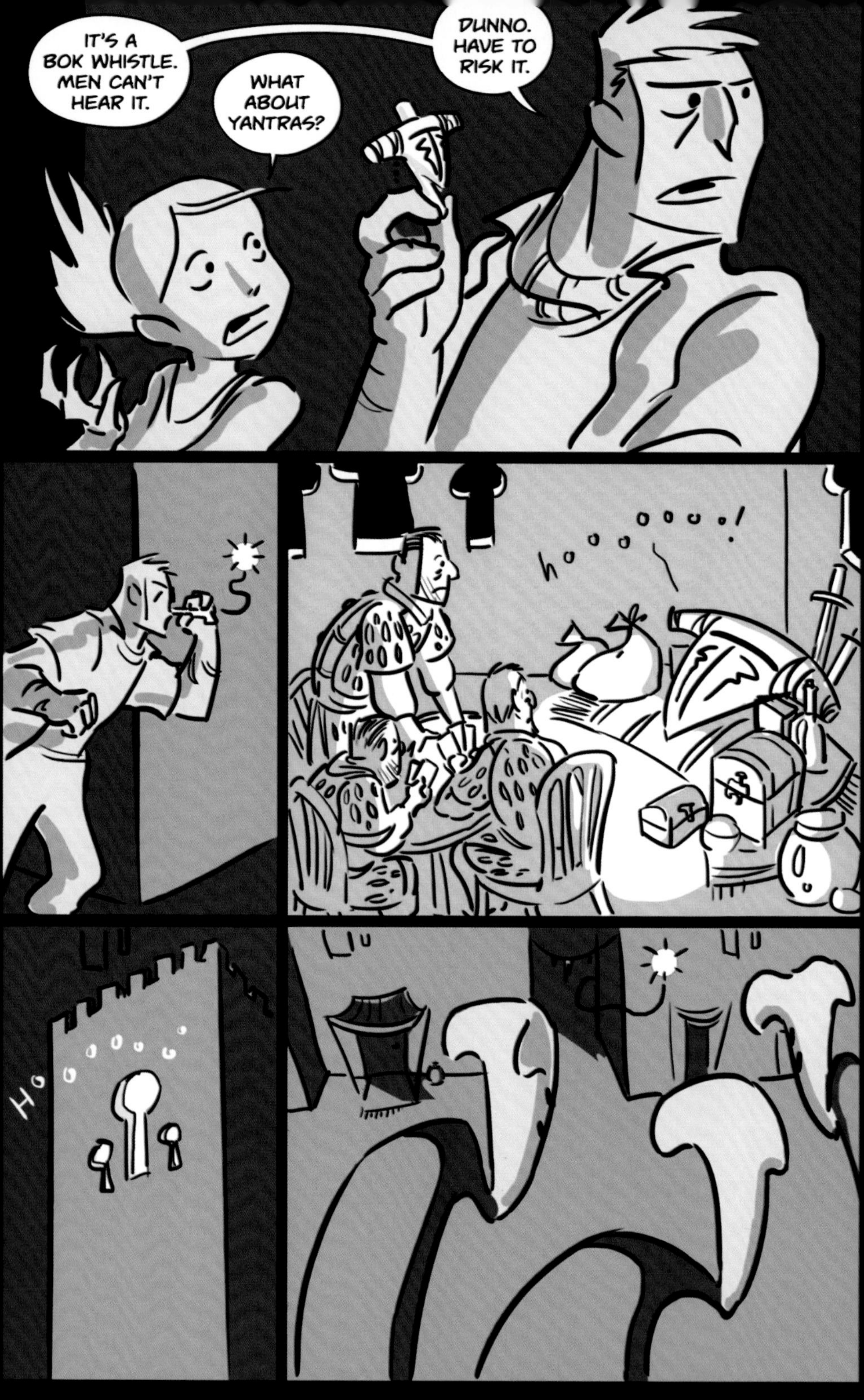
IT'S A BOK WHISTLE. MEN CAN'T HEAR IT.
WHAT ABOUT YANTRAS?
DUNNO. HAVE TO RISK IT.
hooooooo!
Hoooooooo

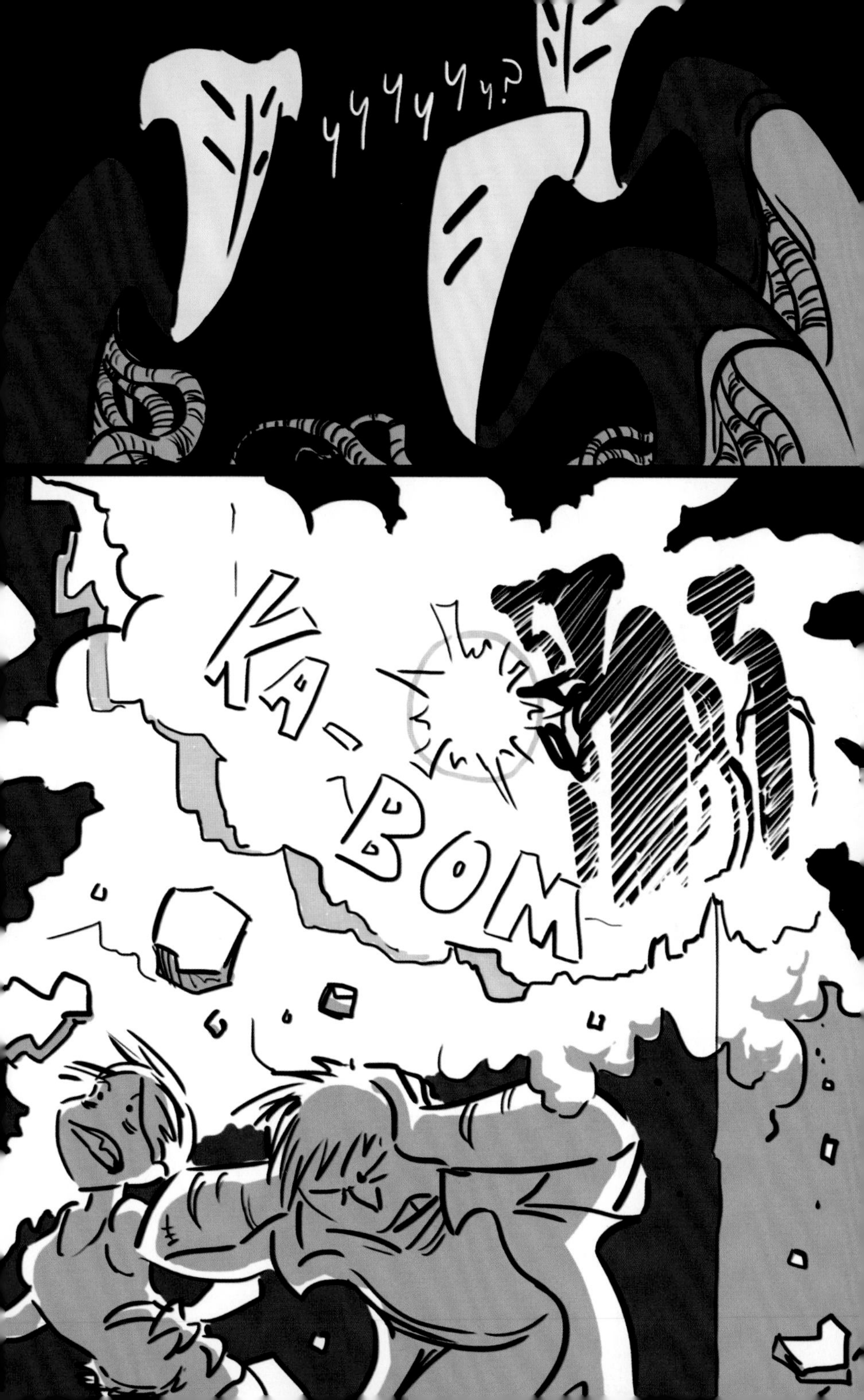
yyyyyy?
KA-BOM

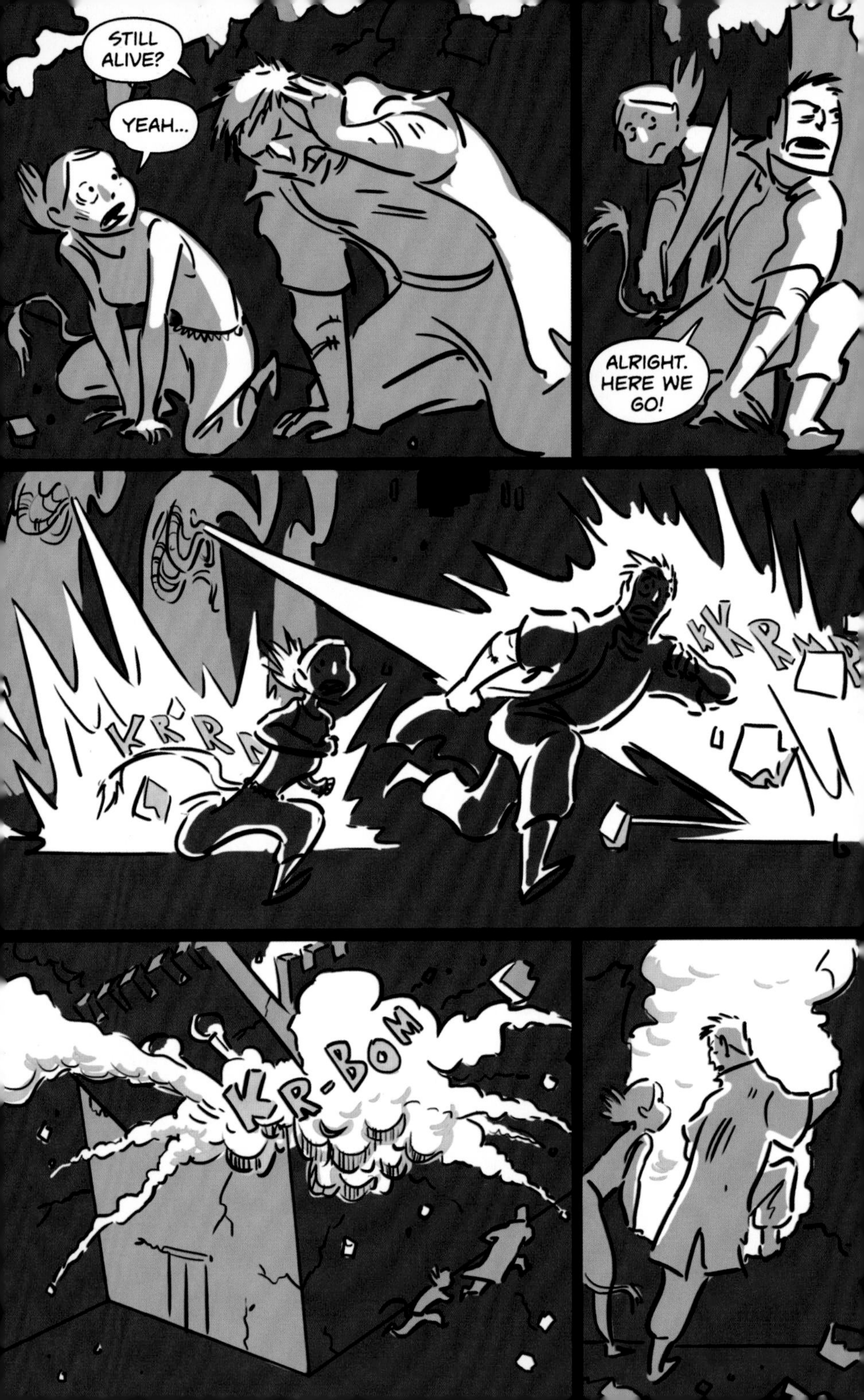
STILL ALIVE?
YEAH...
ALRIGHT. HERE WE GO!
KR'RA
KRUMP
KR-BOM

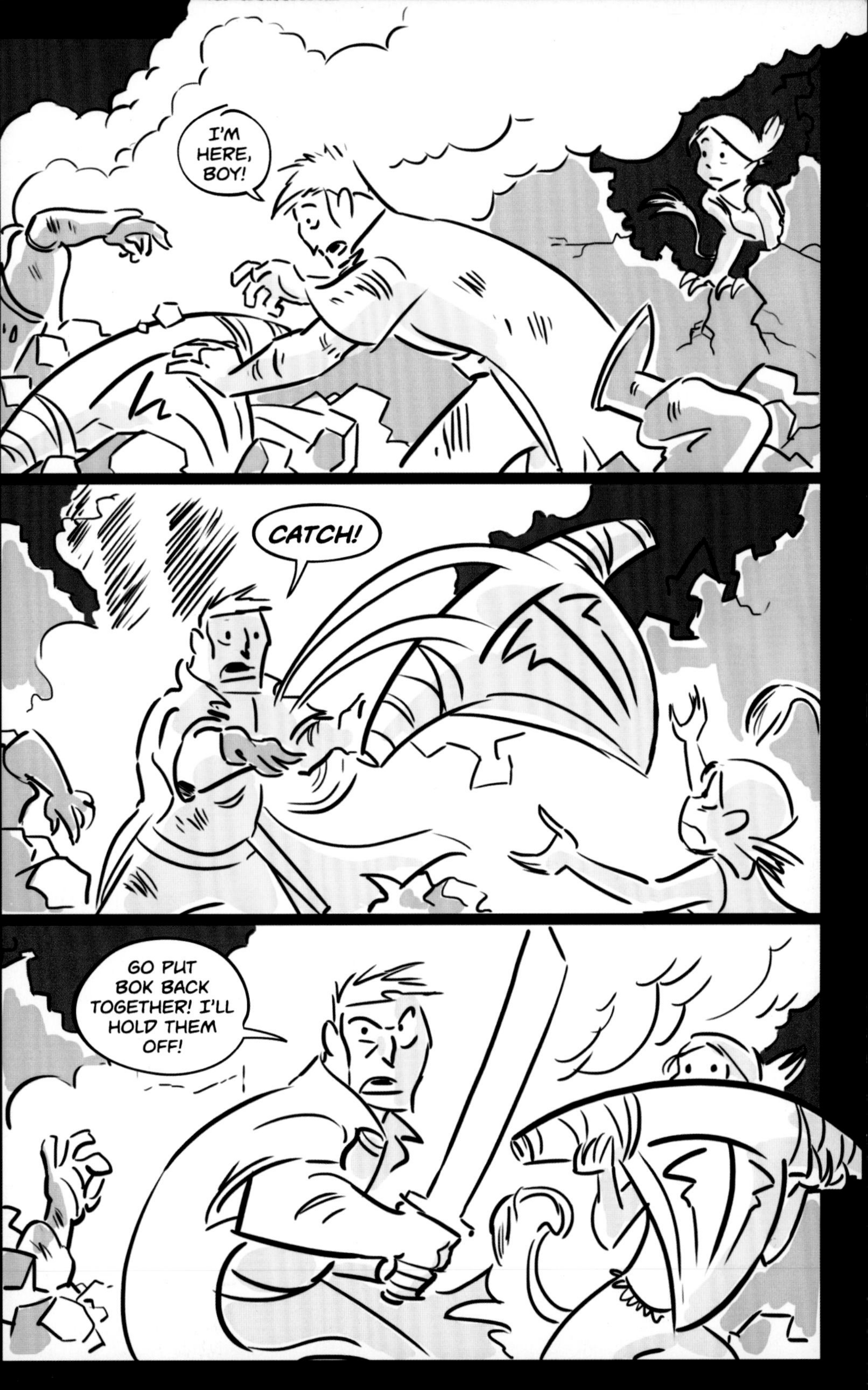
I'M HERE, BOY!
CATCH!
GO PUT BOK BACK TOGETHER! I'LL HOLD THEM OFF!

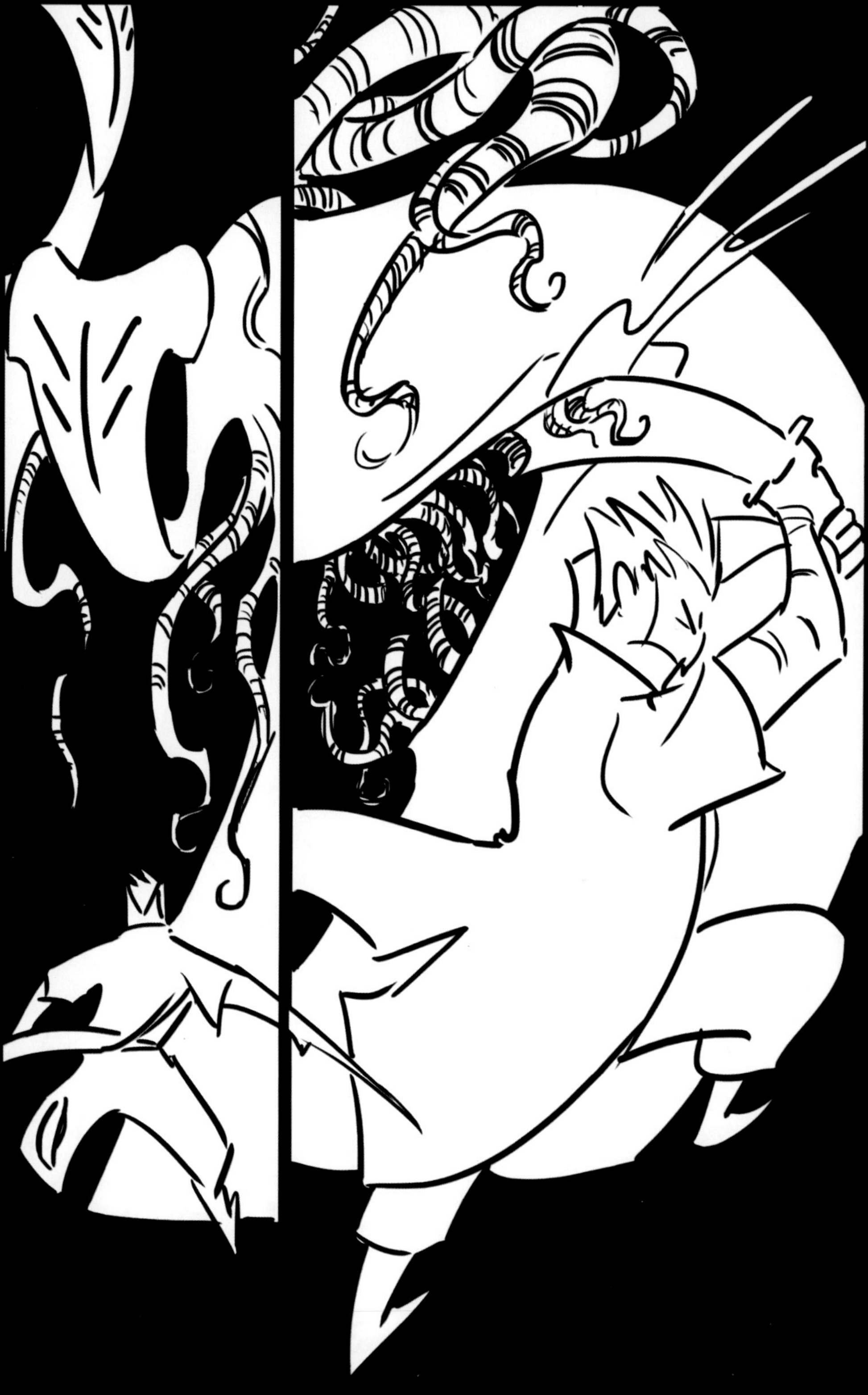

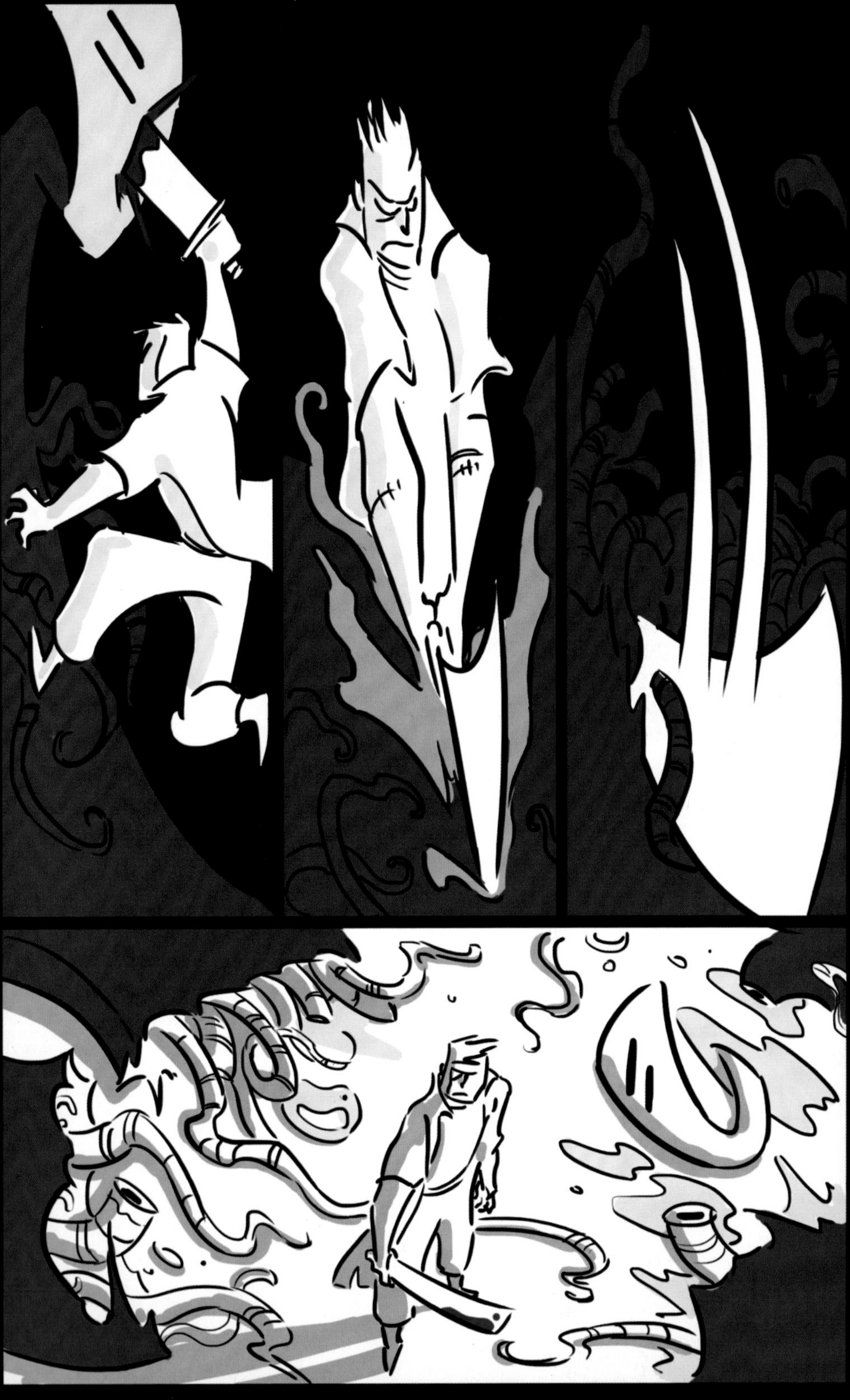

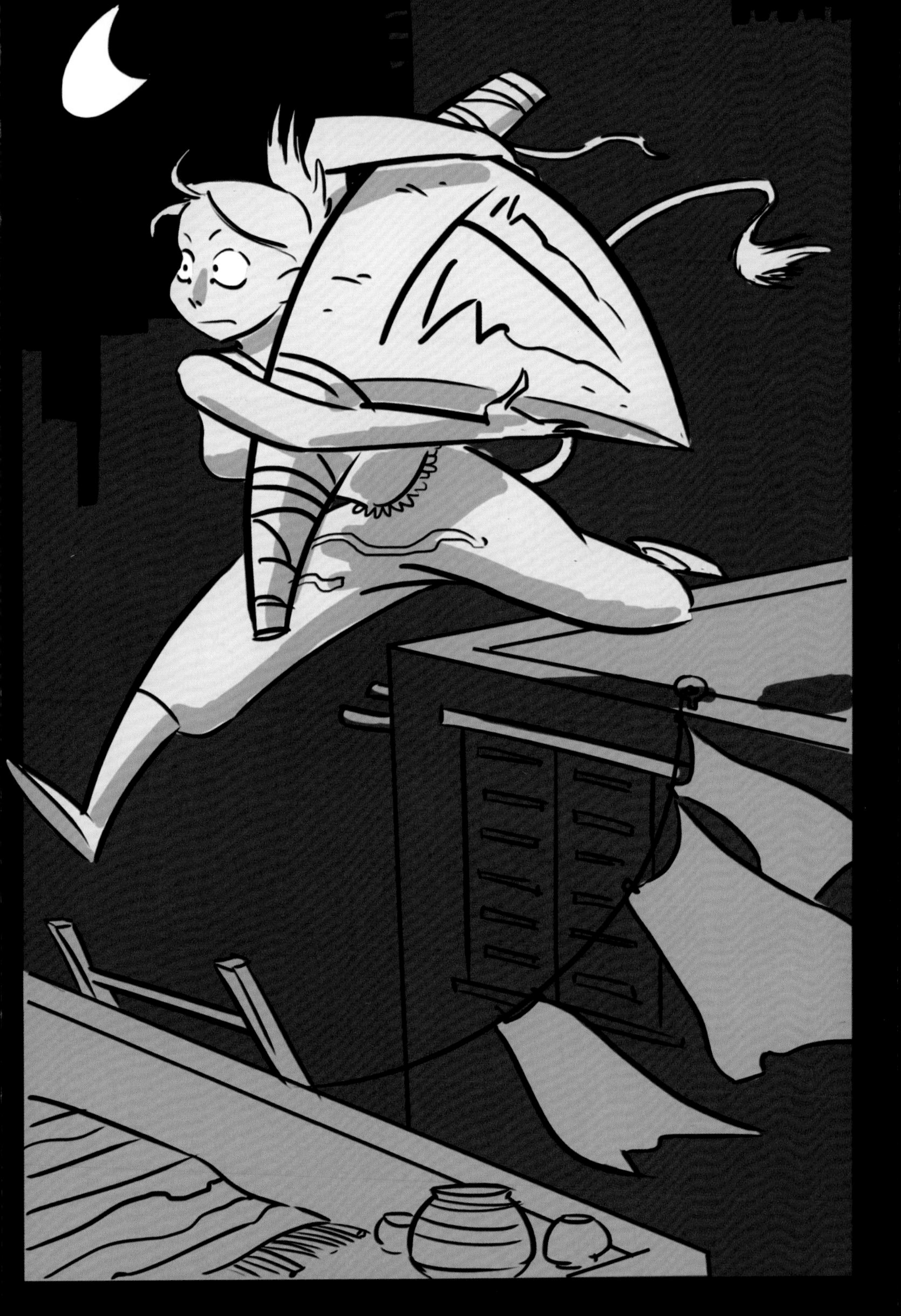

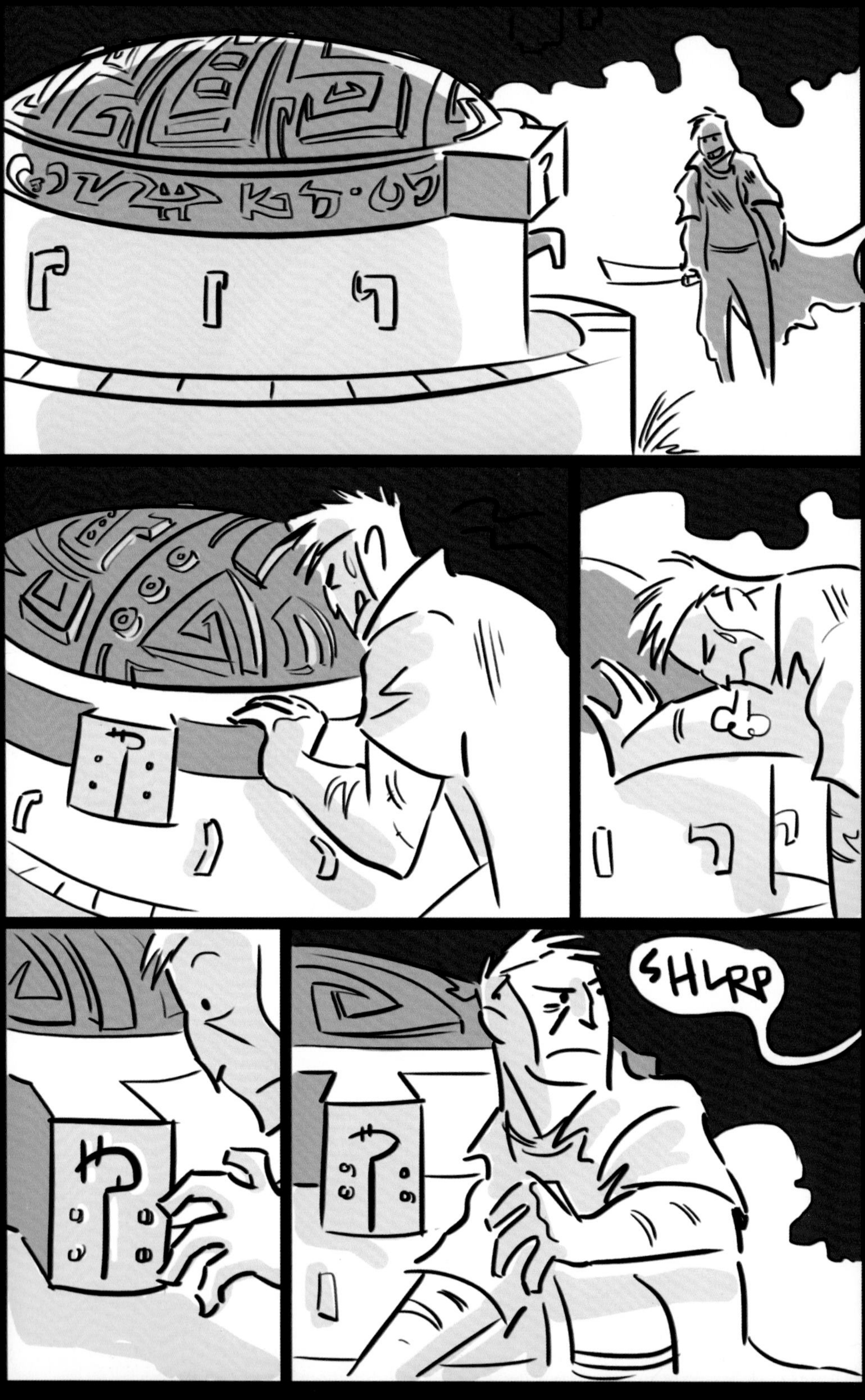
SHLRP

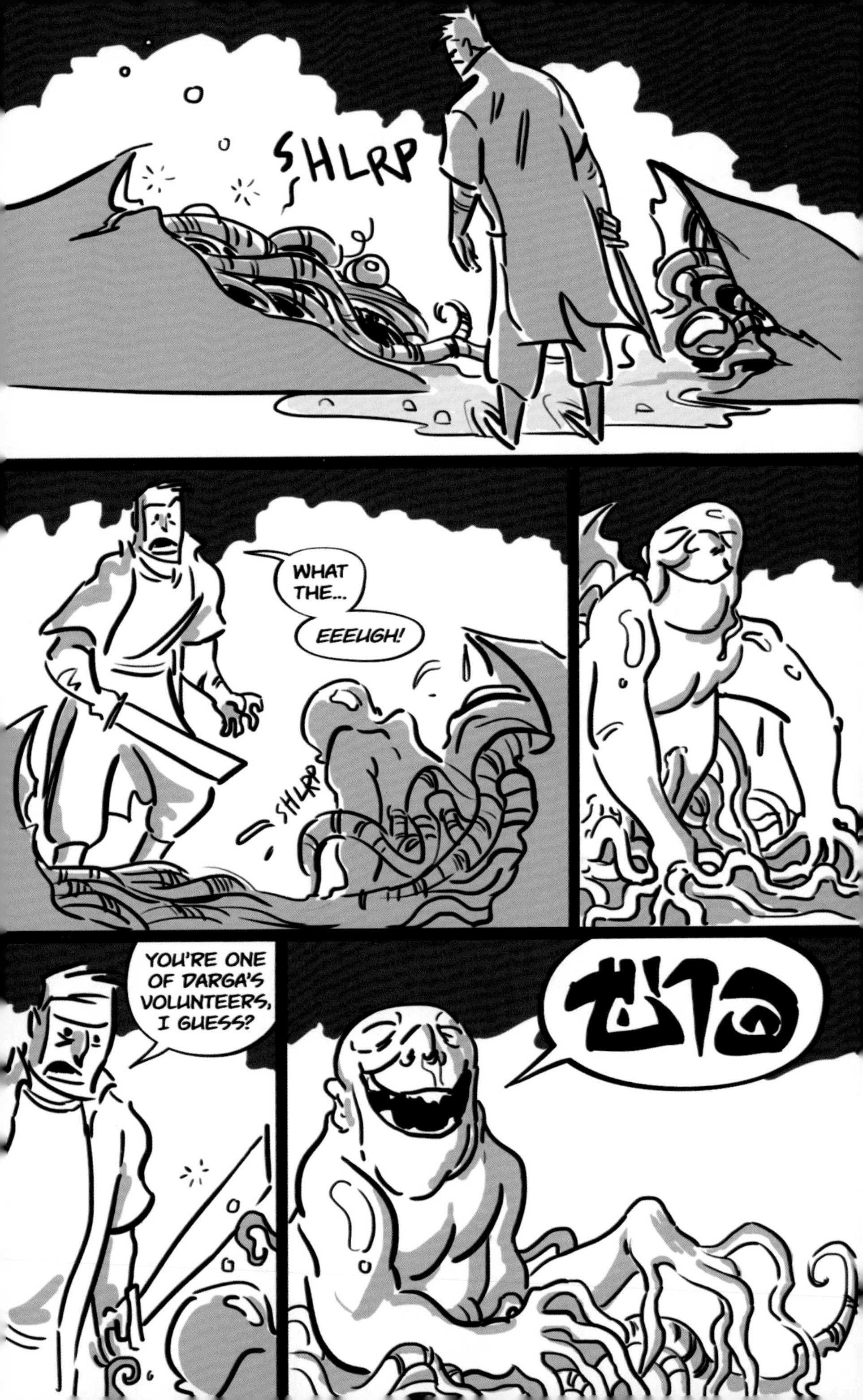
SHLRP
WHAT THE...
EEEUGH!
SHLRP
YOU'RE ONE OF DARGA'S VOLUNTEERS, I GUESS?

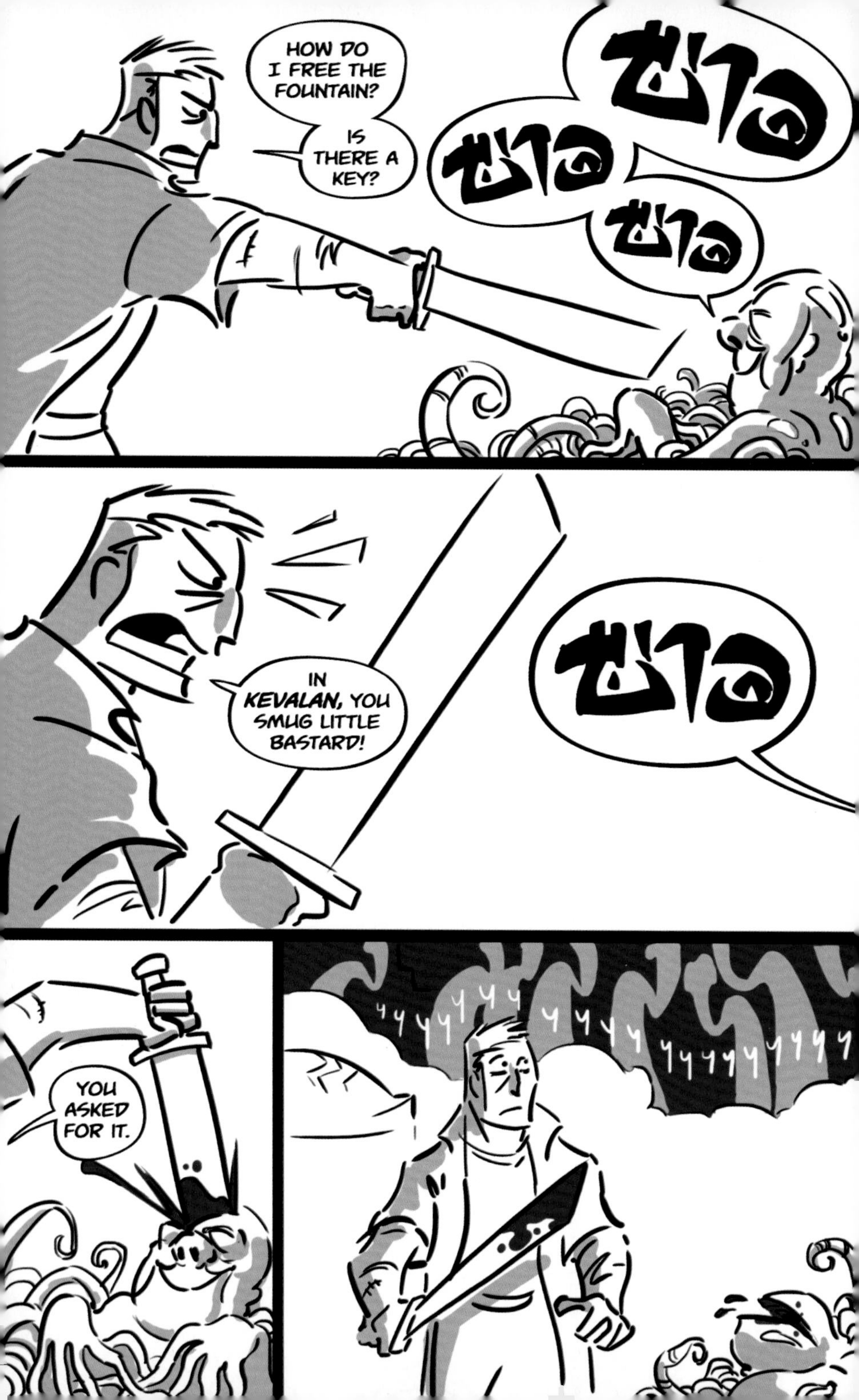
HOW DO I FREE THE FOUNTAIN?
IS THERE A KEY?
IN KEVALAN, YOU SMUG LITTLE BASTARD!
YOU ASKED FOR IT.

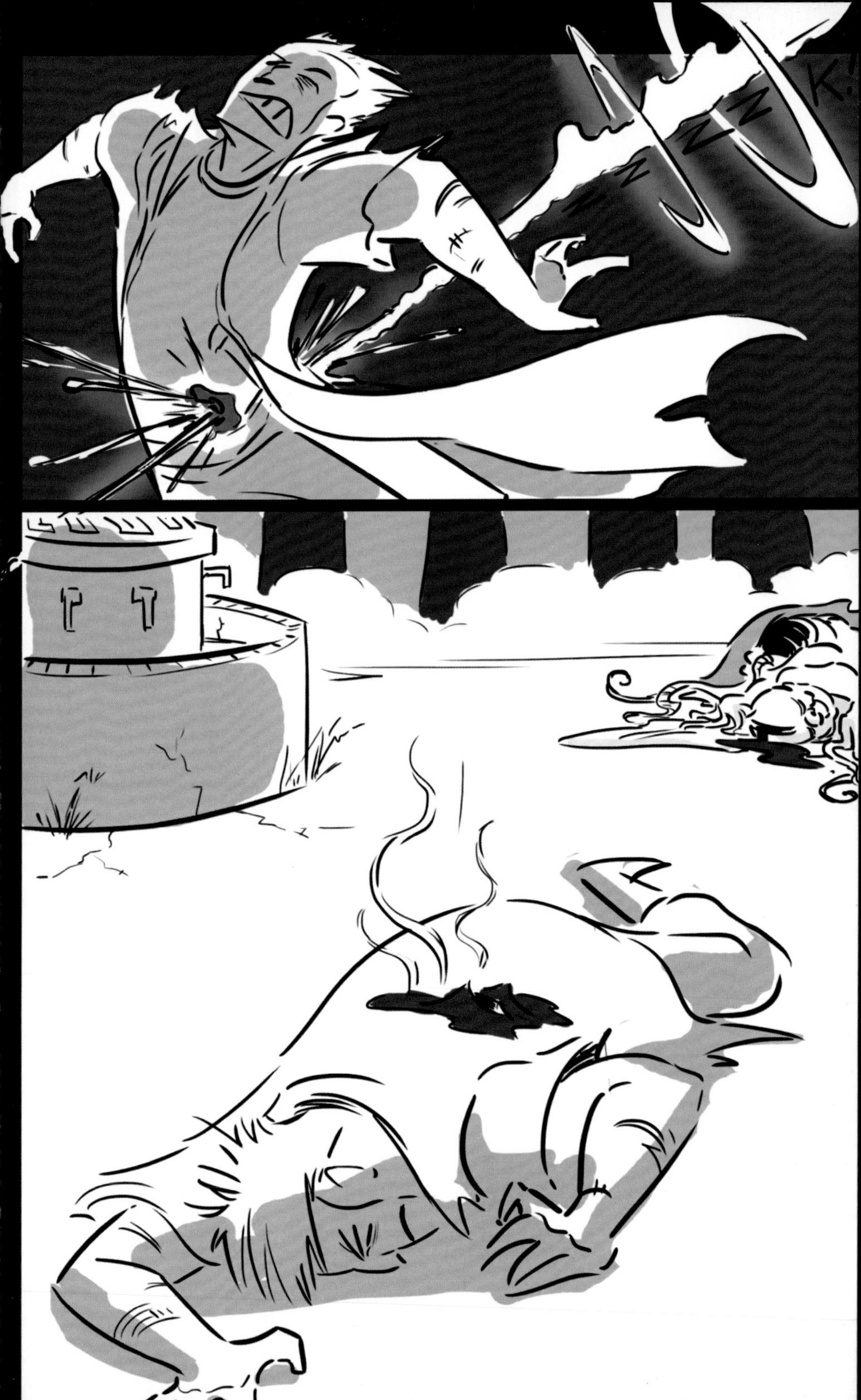
ZZZK!

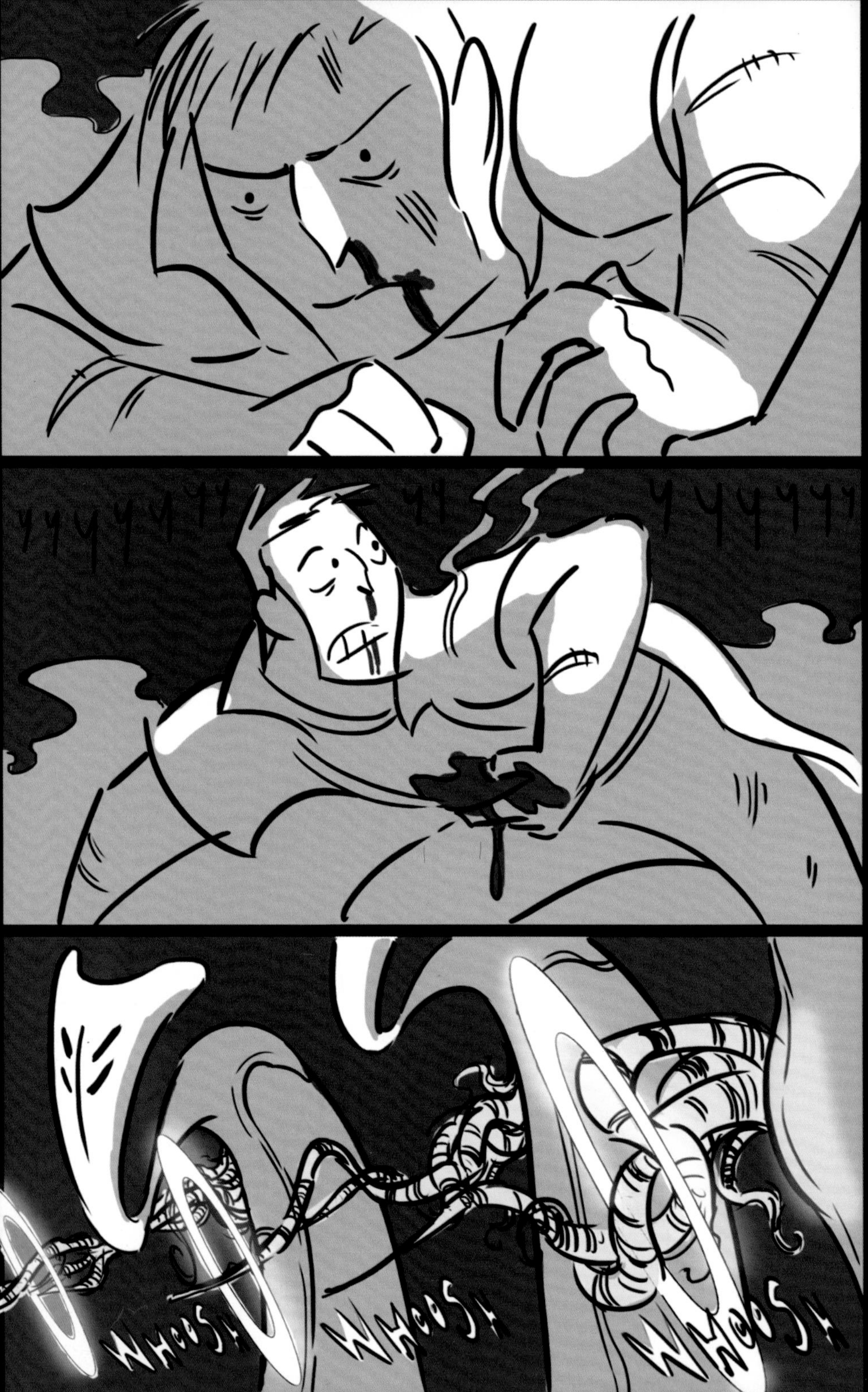
WHOOSH
WHOOSH
WHOOSH

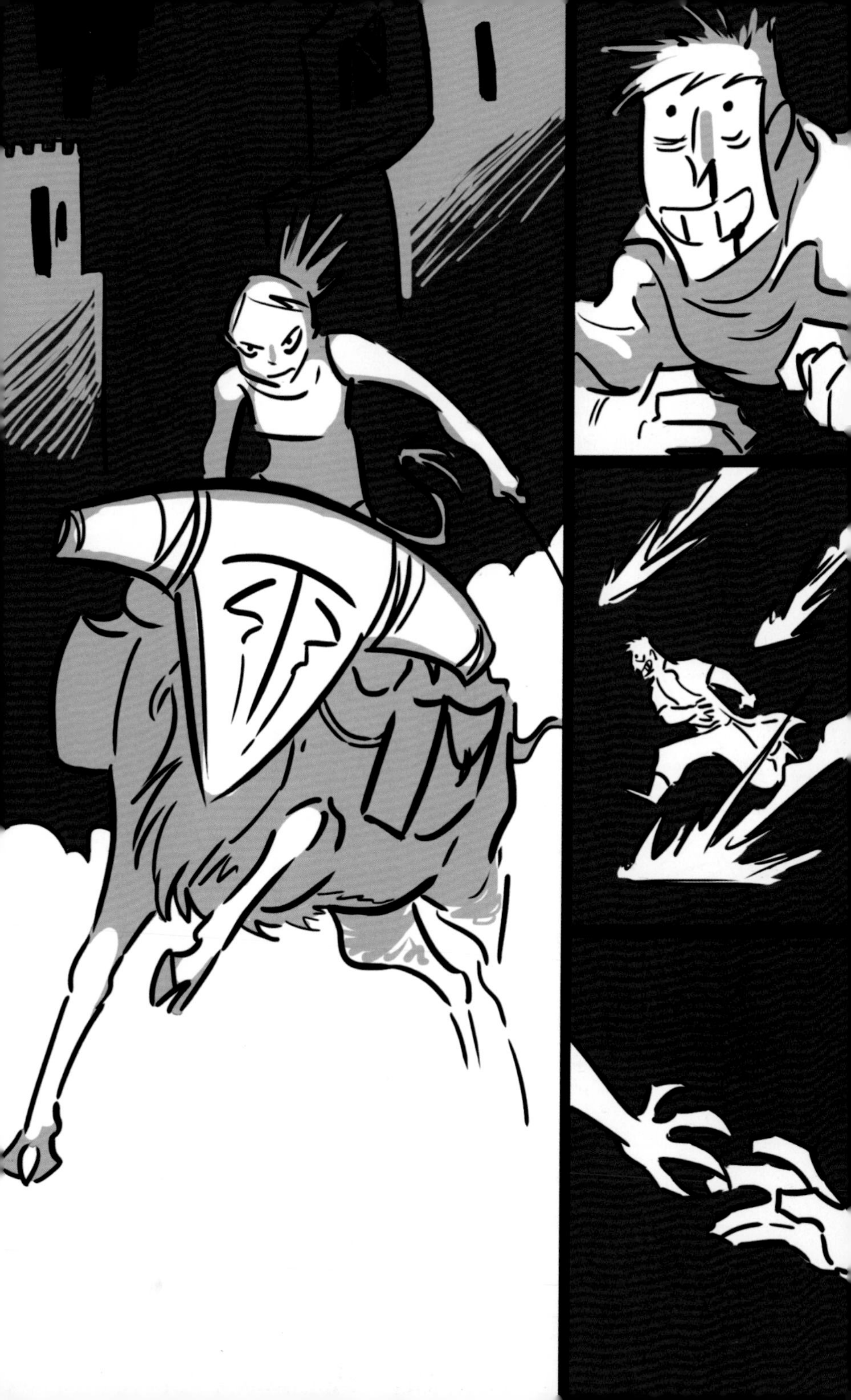

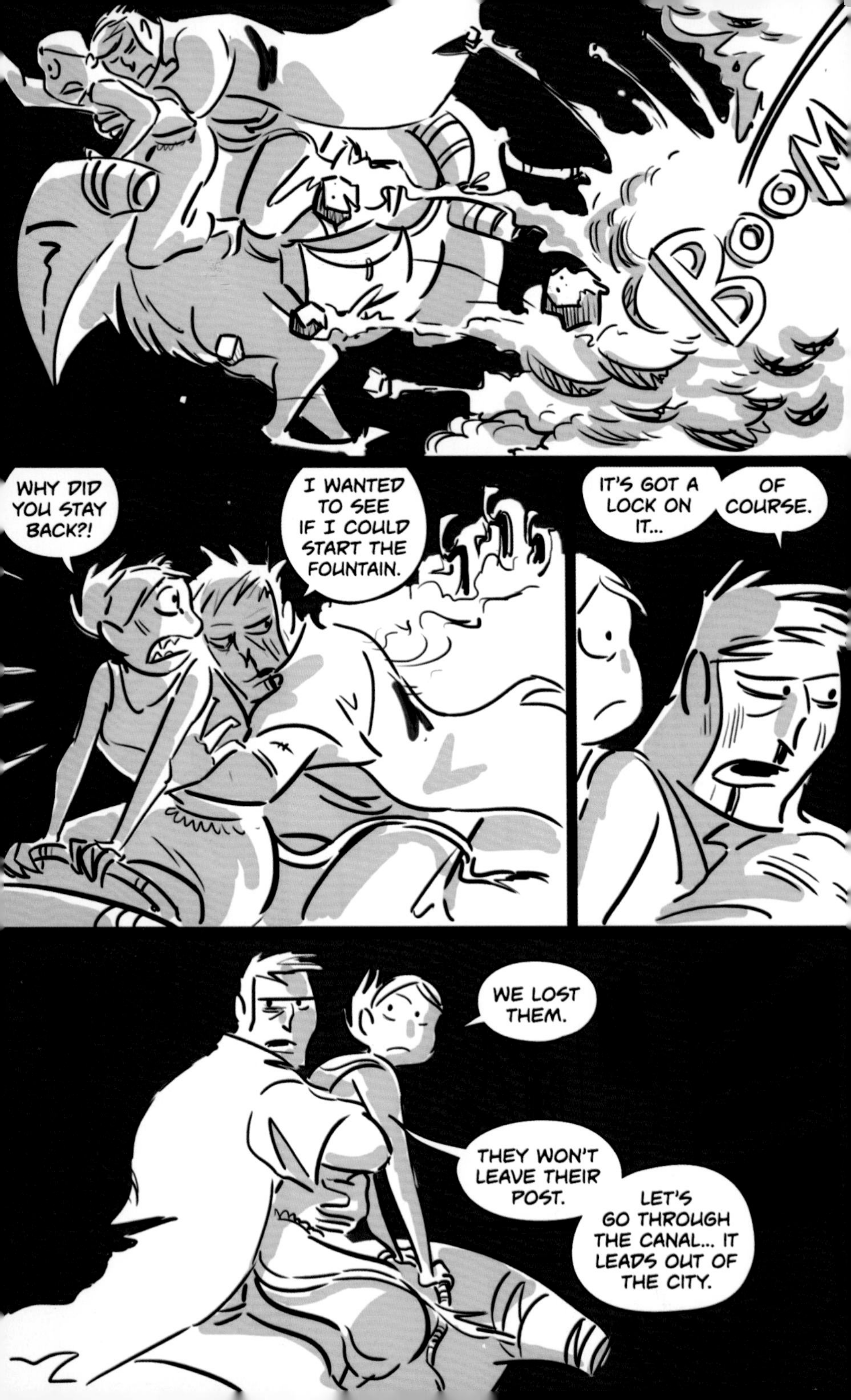
BOOM
WHY DID YOU STAY BACK?!
I WANTED TO SEE IF I COULD START THE FOUNTAIN.
IT'S GOT A LOCK ON IT...
OF COURSE.
WE LOST THEM.
THEY WON'T LEAVE THEIR POST.
LET'S GO THROUGH THE CANAL... IT LEADS OUT OF THE CITY.

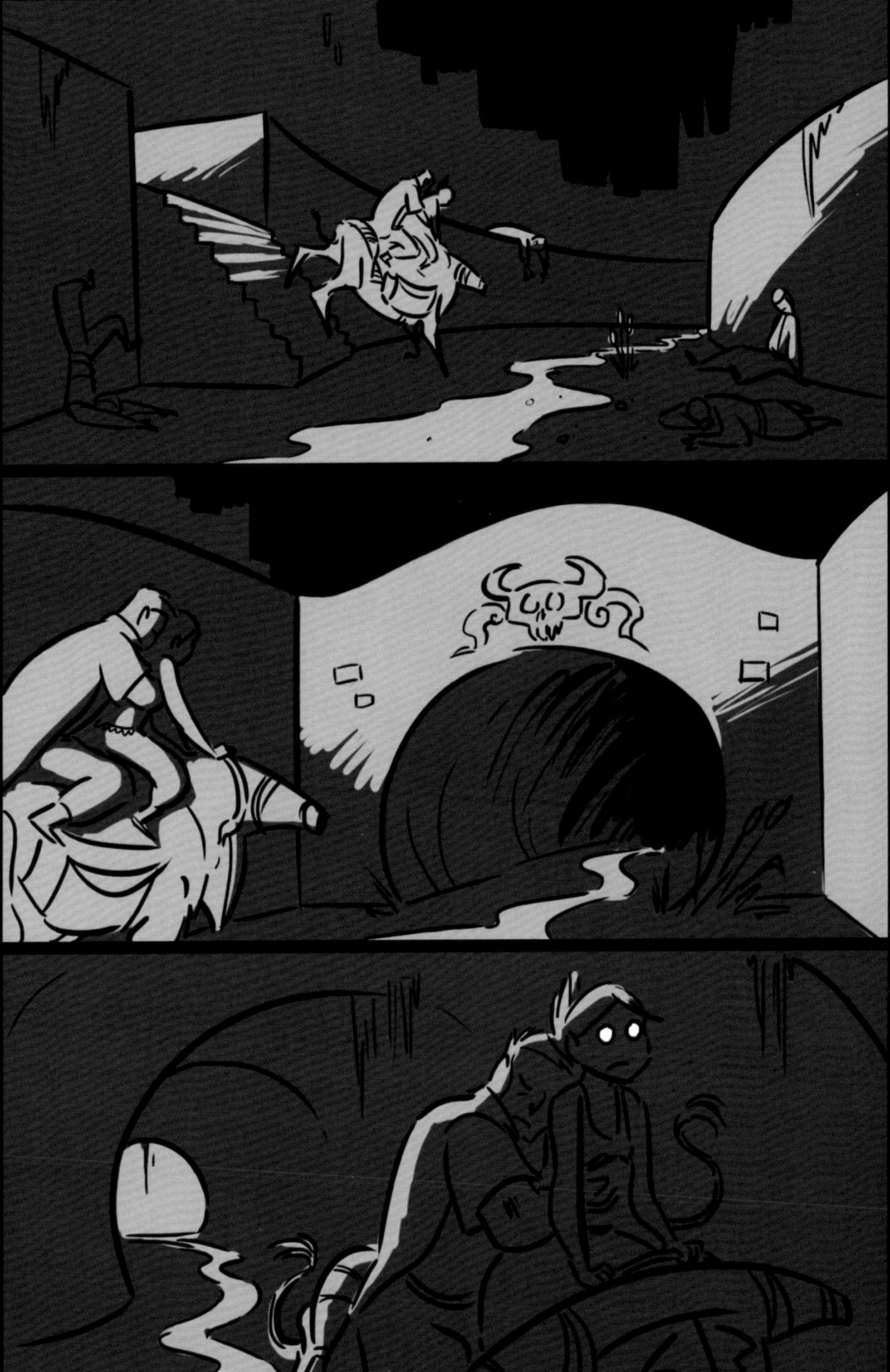

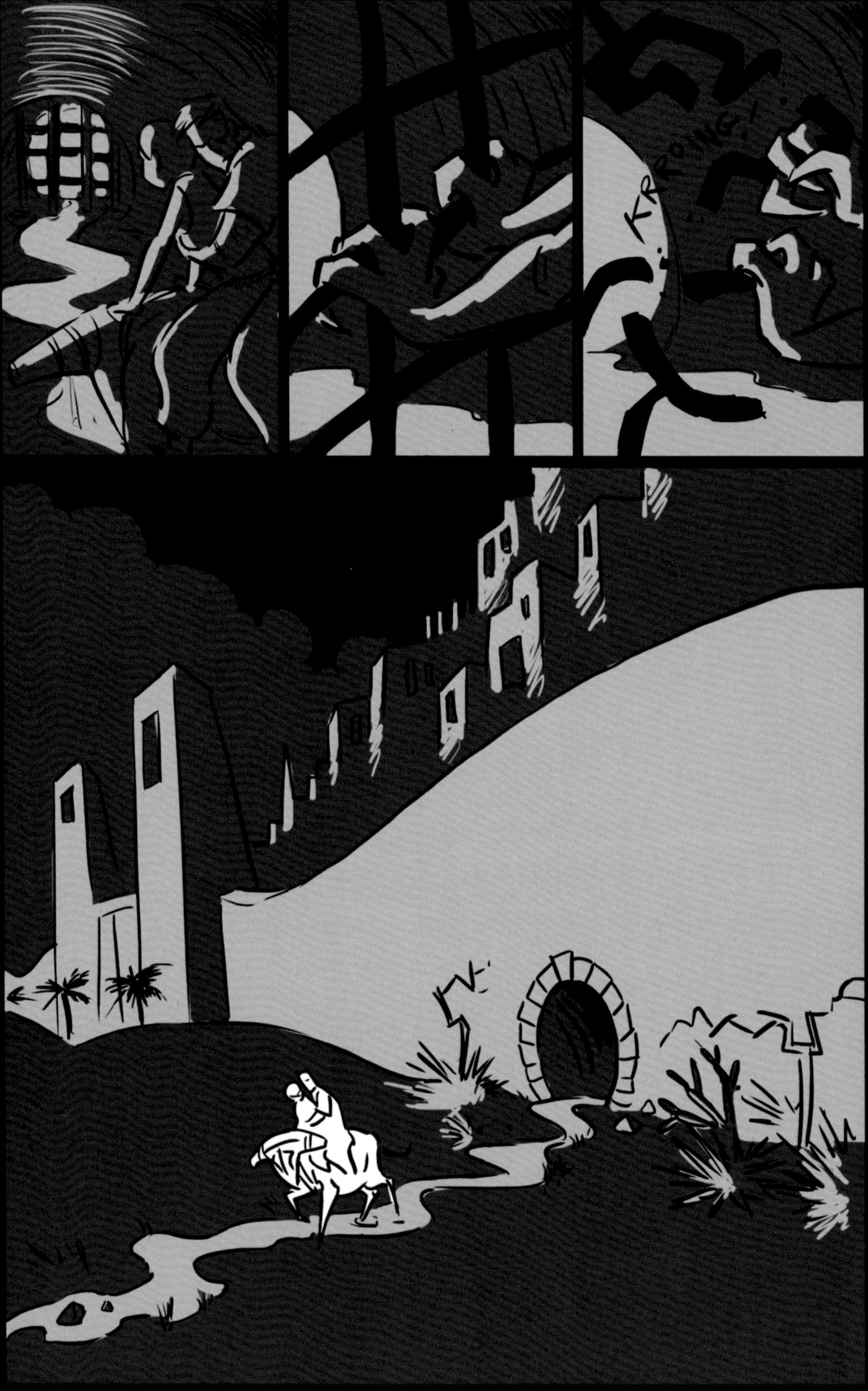
KRROING!

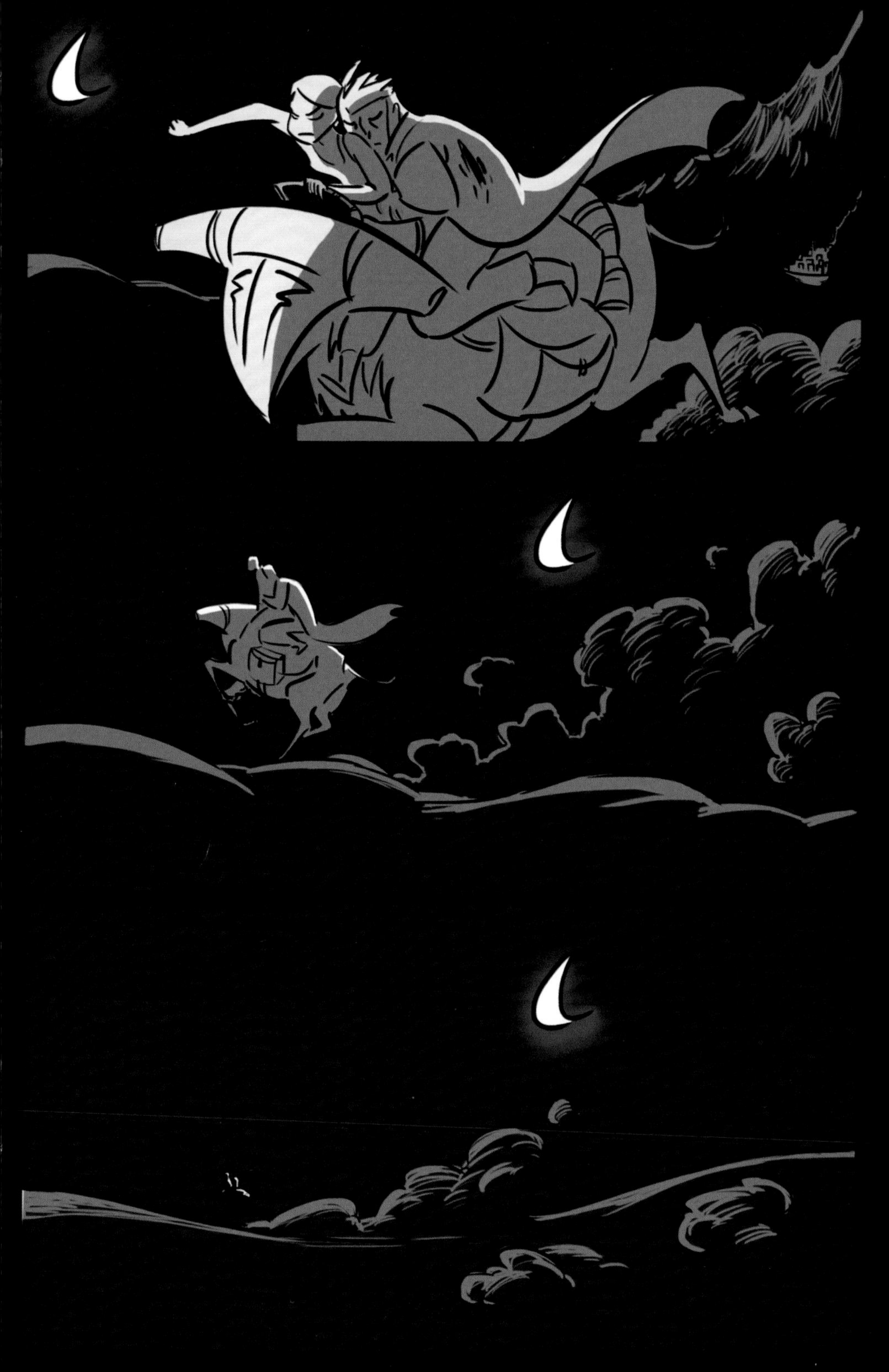

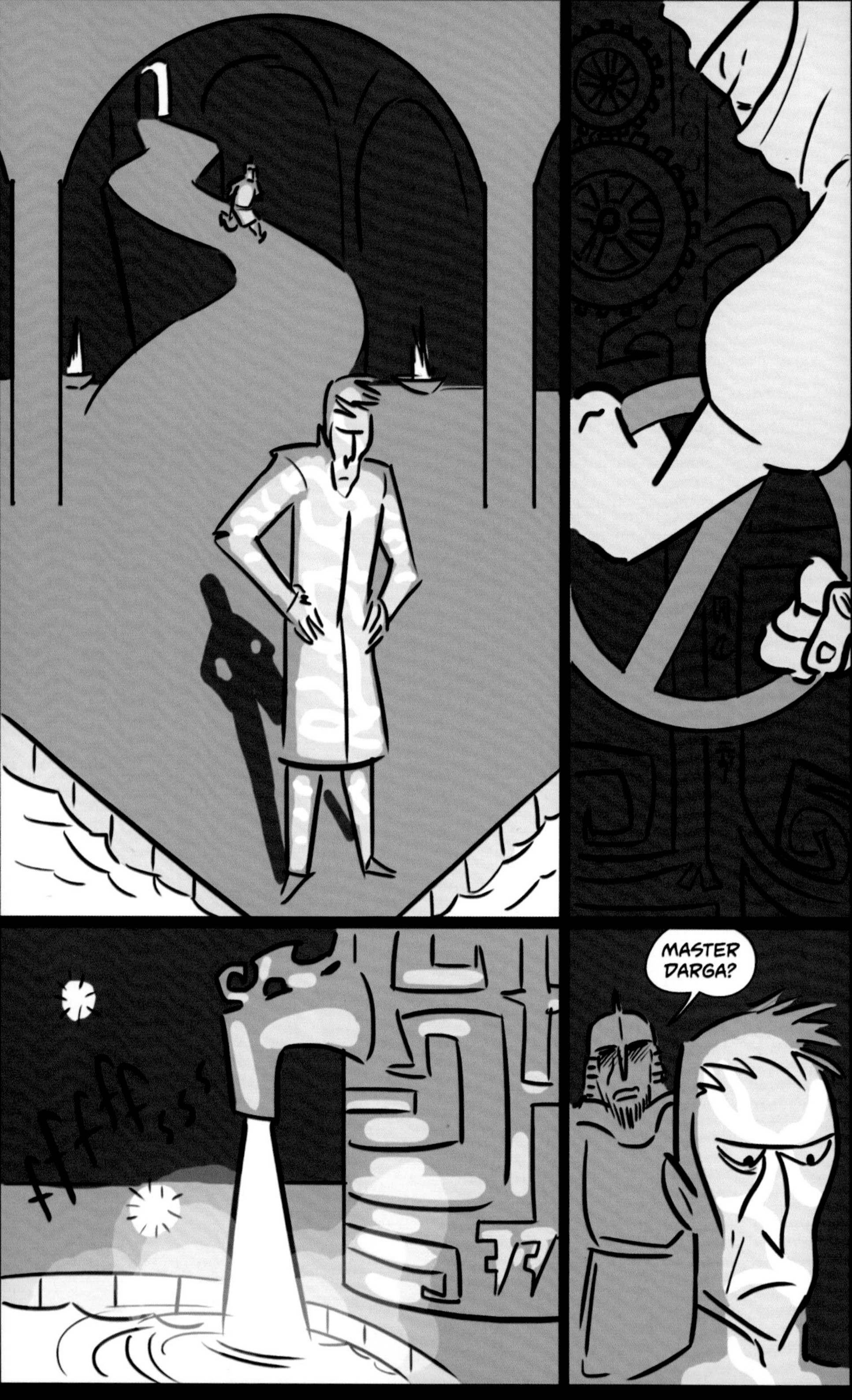
ffffsss
MASTER DARGA?

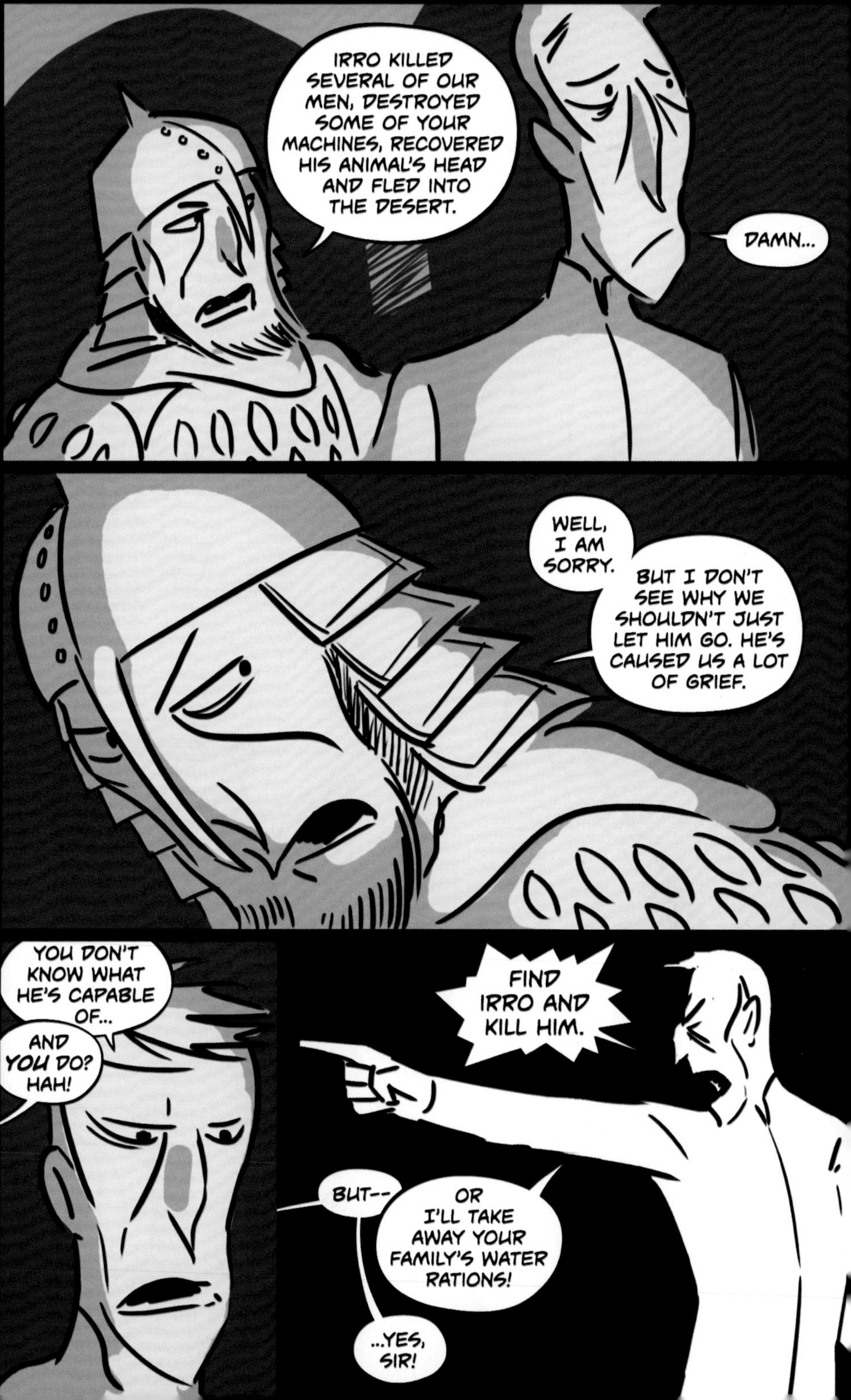
IRRO KILLED SEVERAL OF OUR MEN, DESTROYED SOME OF YOUR MACHINES, RECOVERED HIS ANIMAL'S HEAD AND FLED INTO THE DESERT.
DAMN...
WELL, I AM SORRY.
BUT I DON'T SEE WHY WE SHOULDN'T JUST LET HIM GO. HE'S CAUSED US A LOT OF GRIEF.
YOU DON'T KNOW WHAT HE'S CAPABLE OF...
AND YOU DO? HAH!
FIND IRRO AND KILL HIM.
BUT--
OR I'LL TAKE AWAY YOUR FAMILY'S WATER RATIONS!
...YES, SIR!

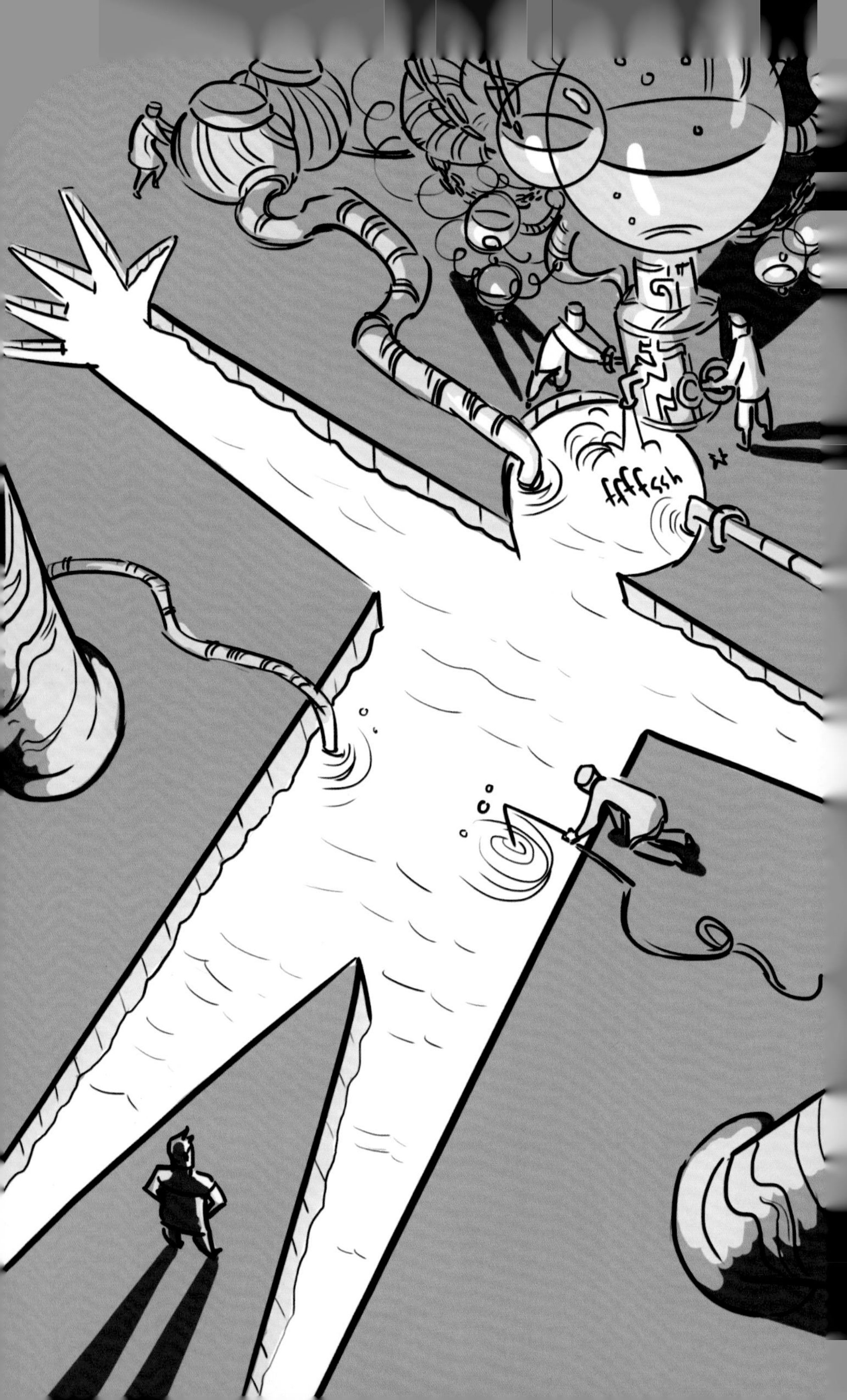
fffssh

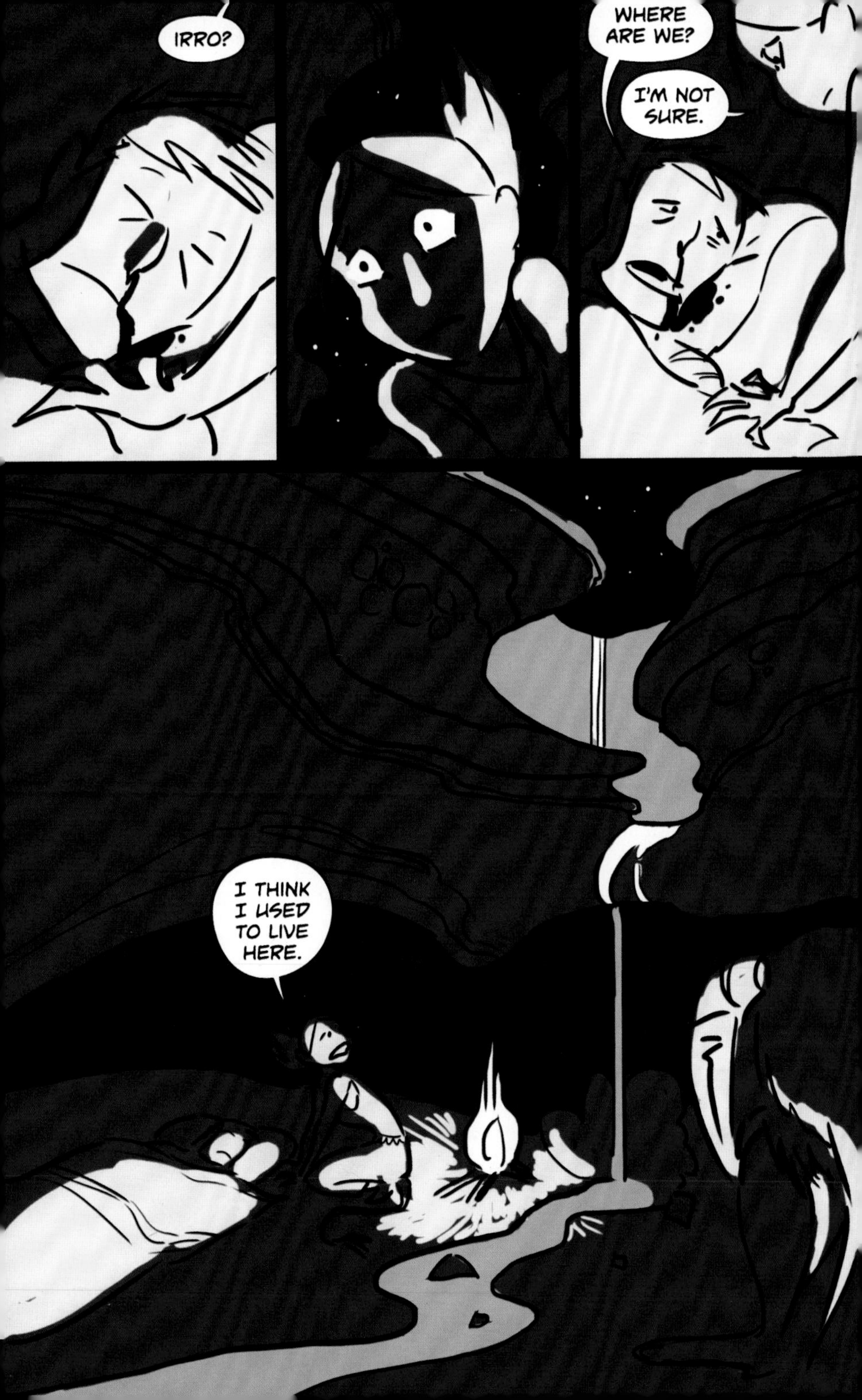
IRRO?
WHERE ARE WE?
I'M NOT SURE.
I THINK I USED TO LIVE HERE.

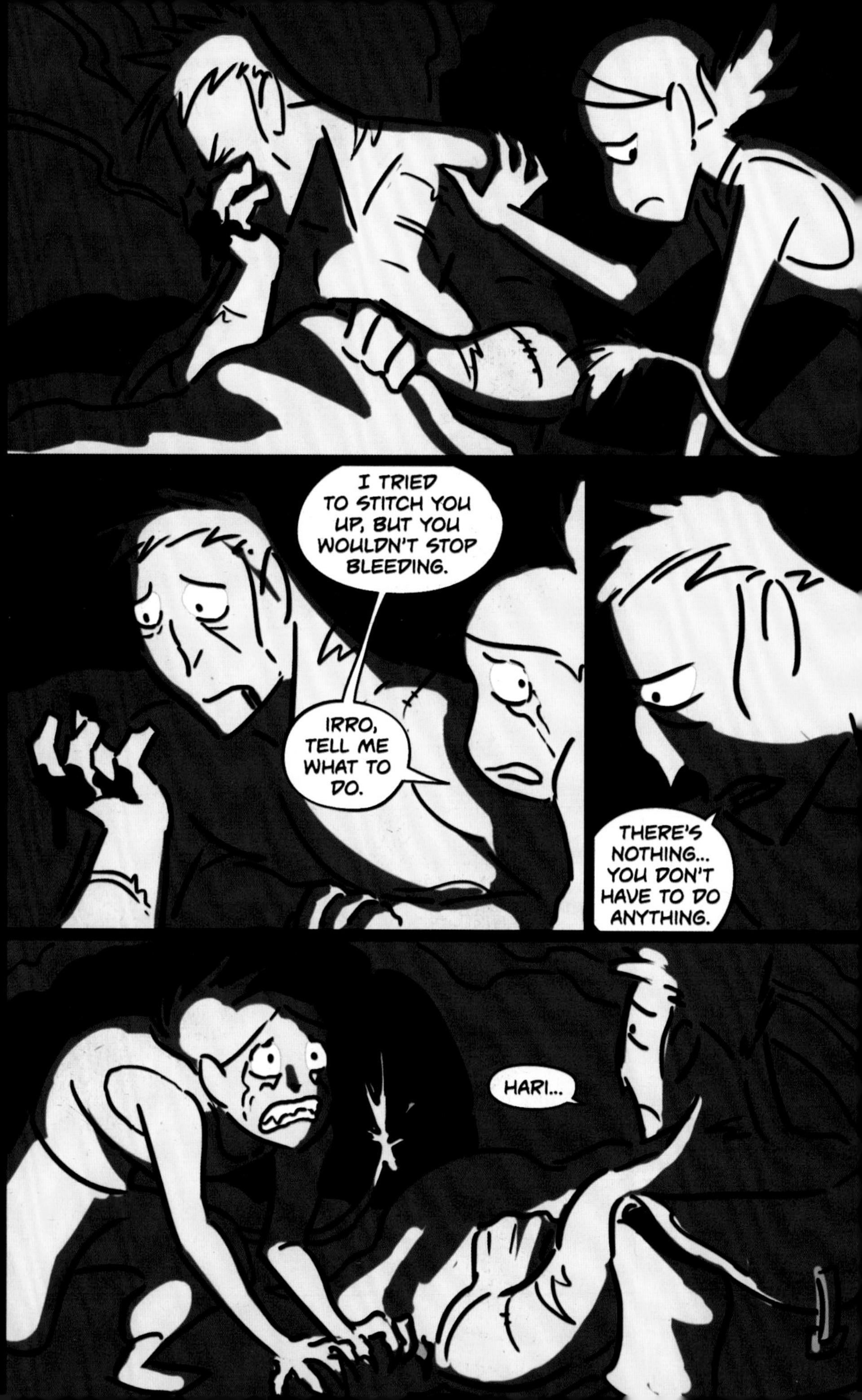
I TRIED TO STITCH YOU UP, BUT YOU WOULDN'T STOP BLEEDING.
IRRO, TELL ME WHAT TO DO.
THERE'S NOTHING... YOU DON'T HAVE TO DO ANYTHING.
HARI...

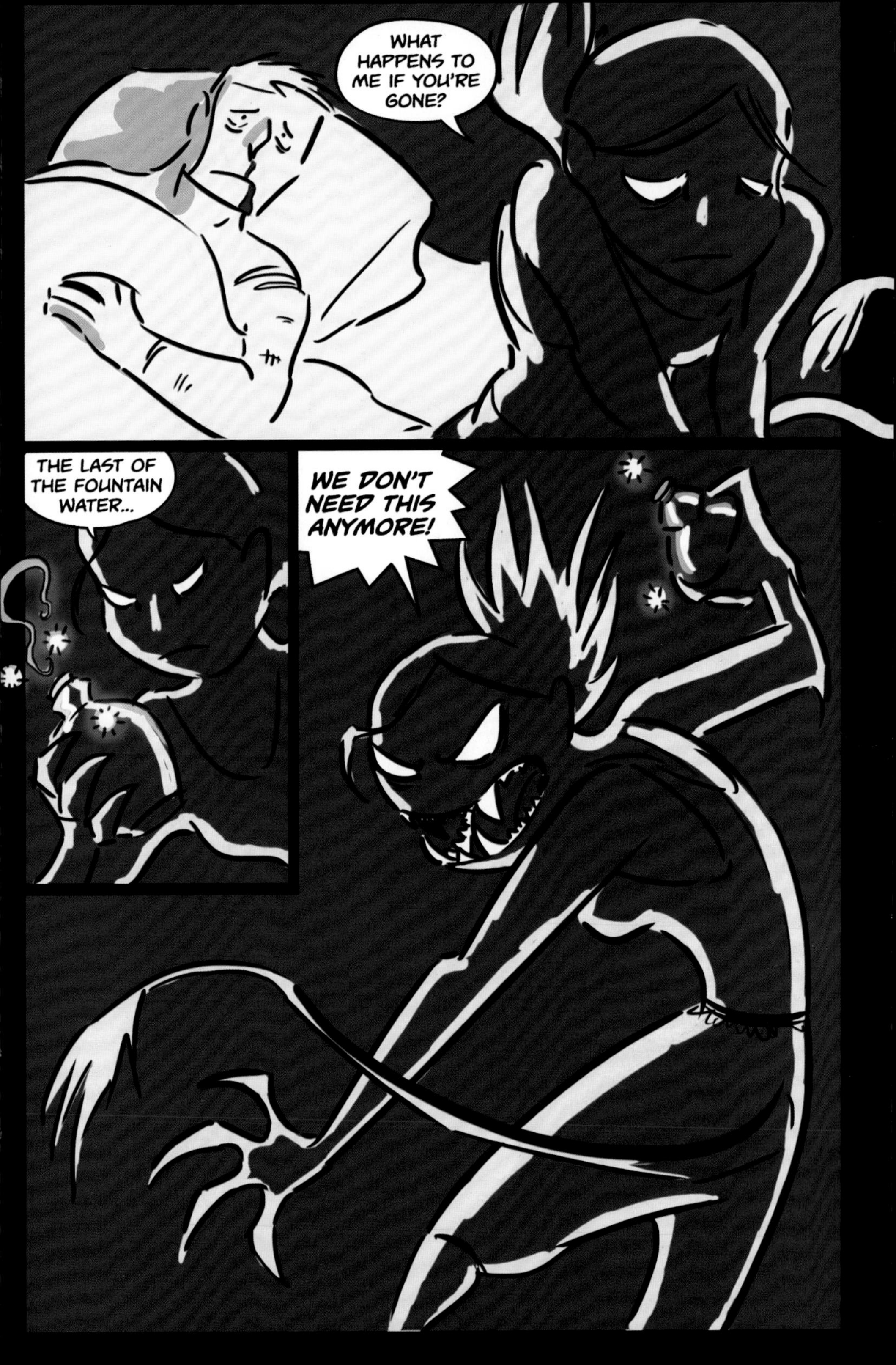
WHAT HAPPENS TO ME IF YOU'RE GONE?
THE LAST OF THE FOUNTAIN WATER...
WE DON'T NEED THIS ANYMORE!

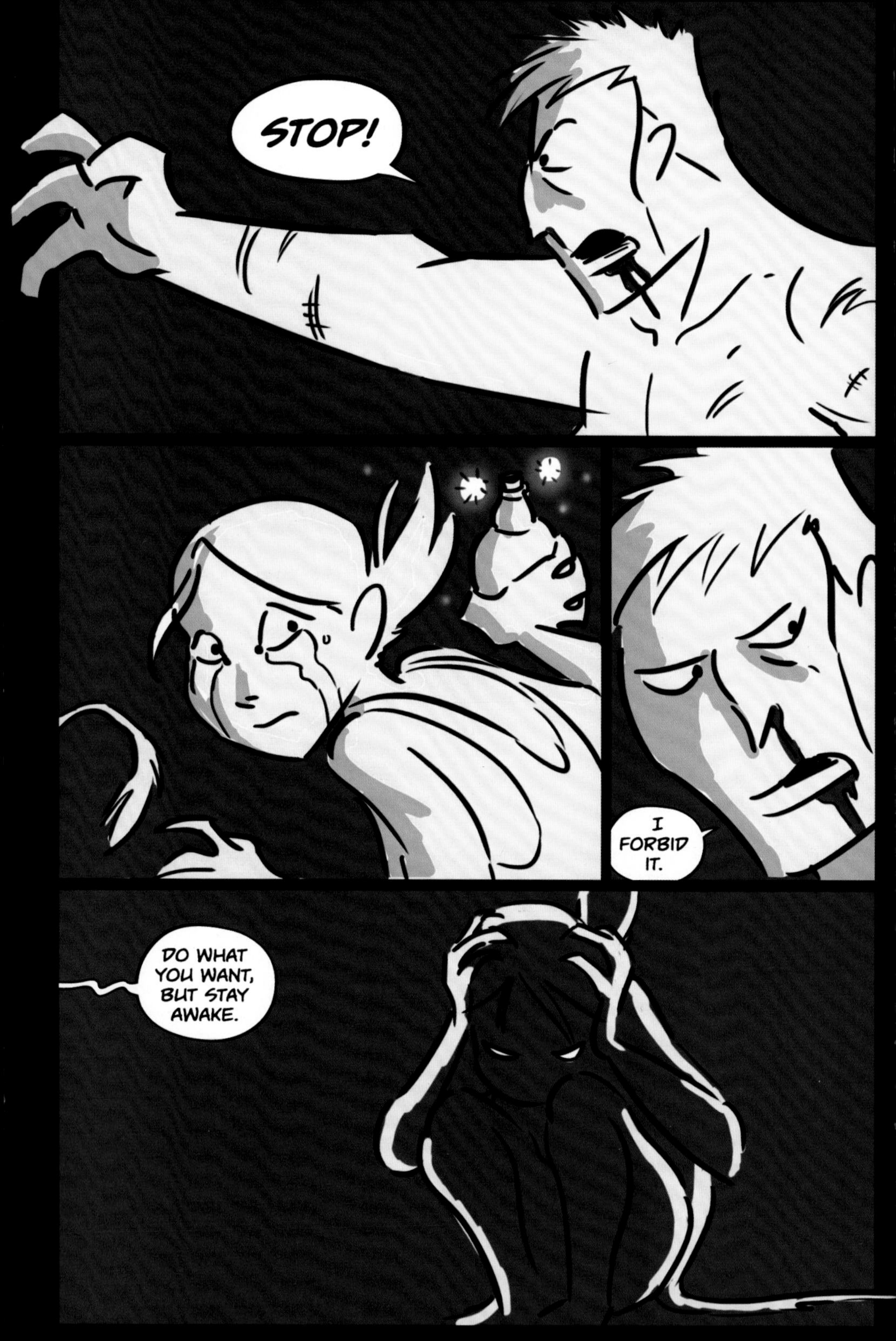
STOP!
I FORBID IT.
DO WHAT YOU WANT, BUT STAY AWAKE.

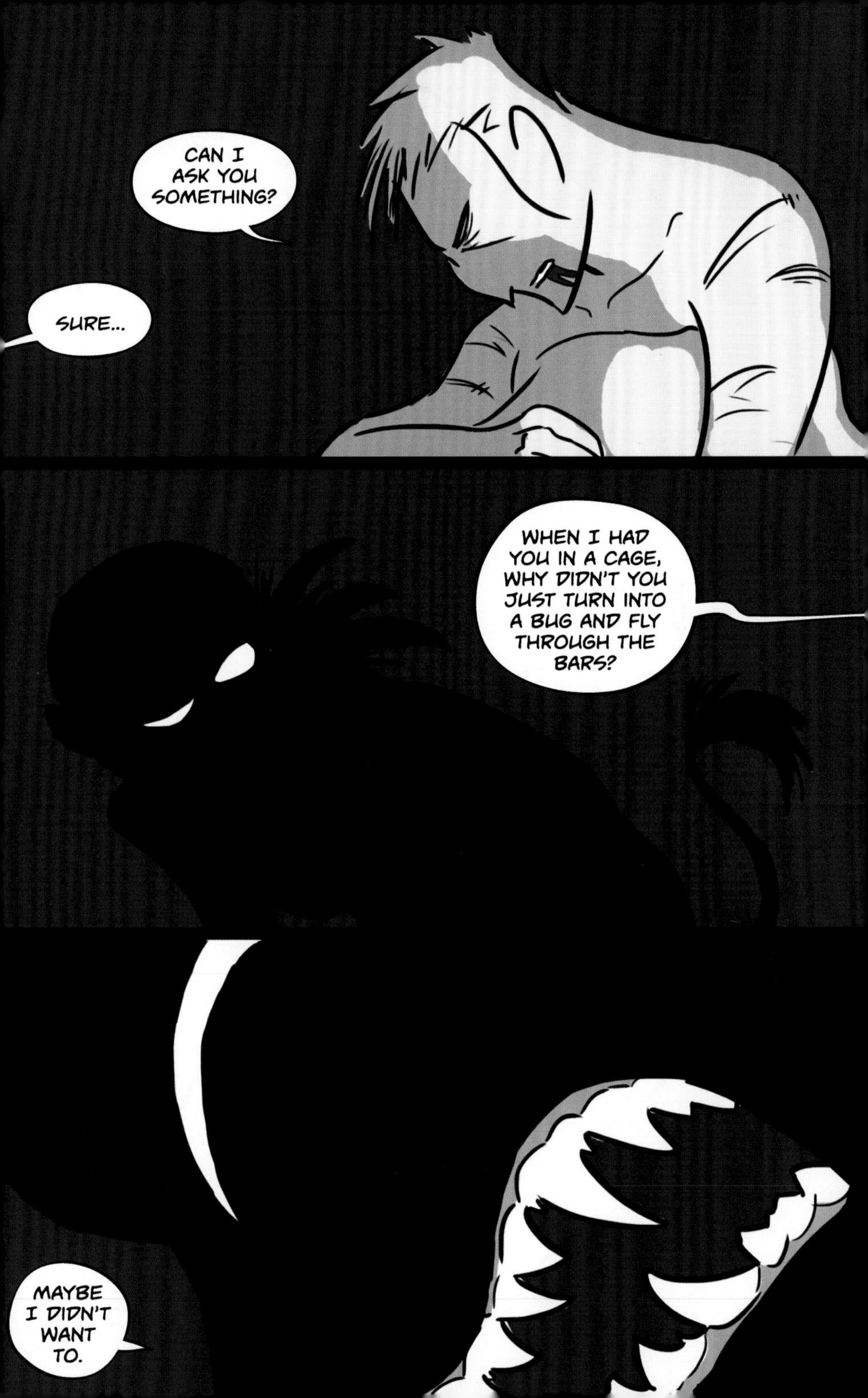
CAN I ASK YOU SOMETHING?
SURE...
WHEN I HAD YOU IN A CAGE, WHY DIDN'T YOU JUST TURN INTO A BUG AND FLY THROUGH THE BARS?
MAYBE I DIDN'T WANT TO.

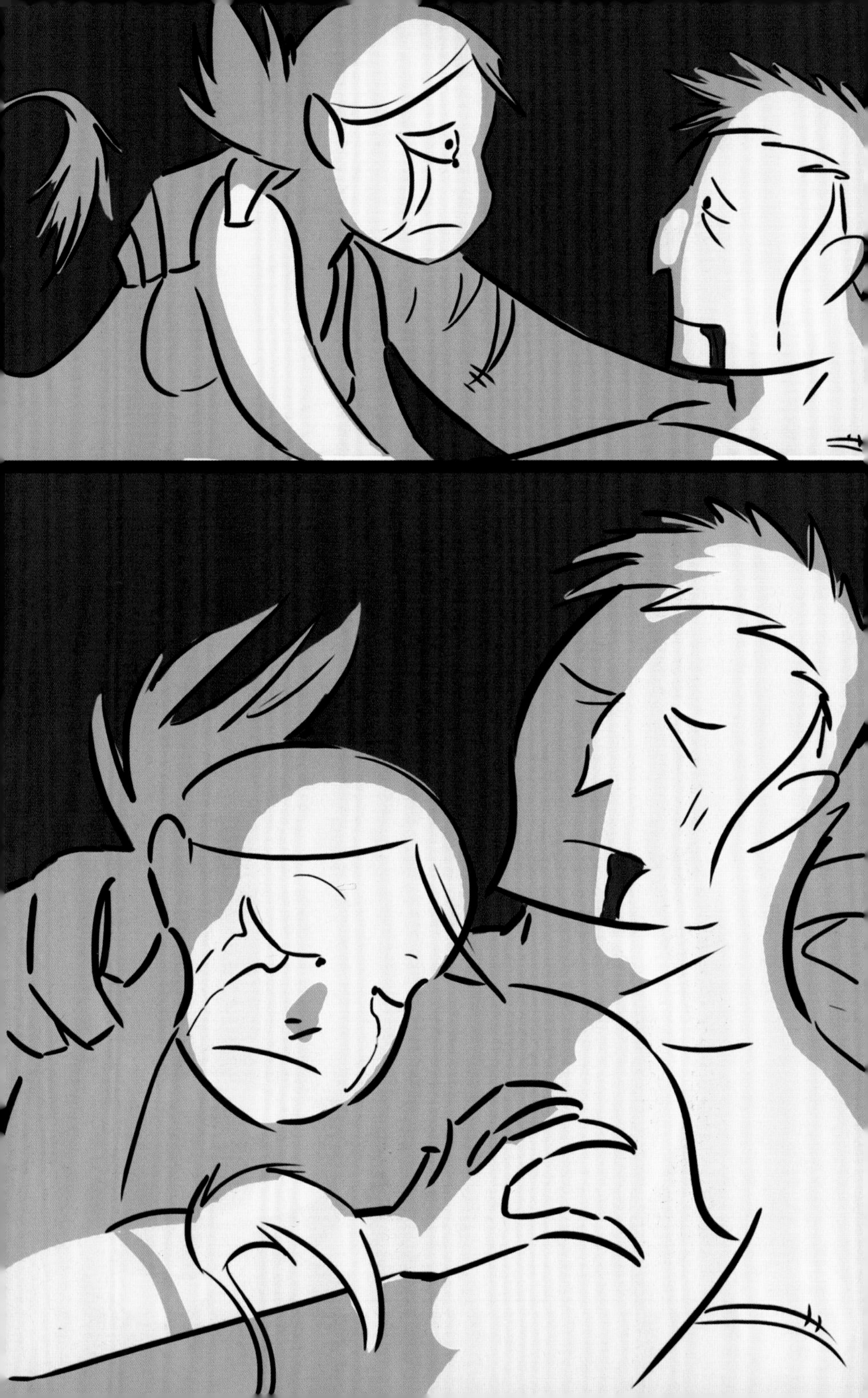

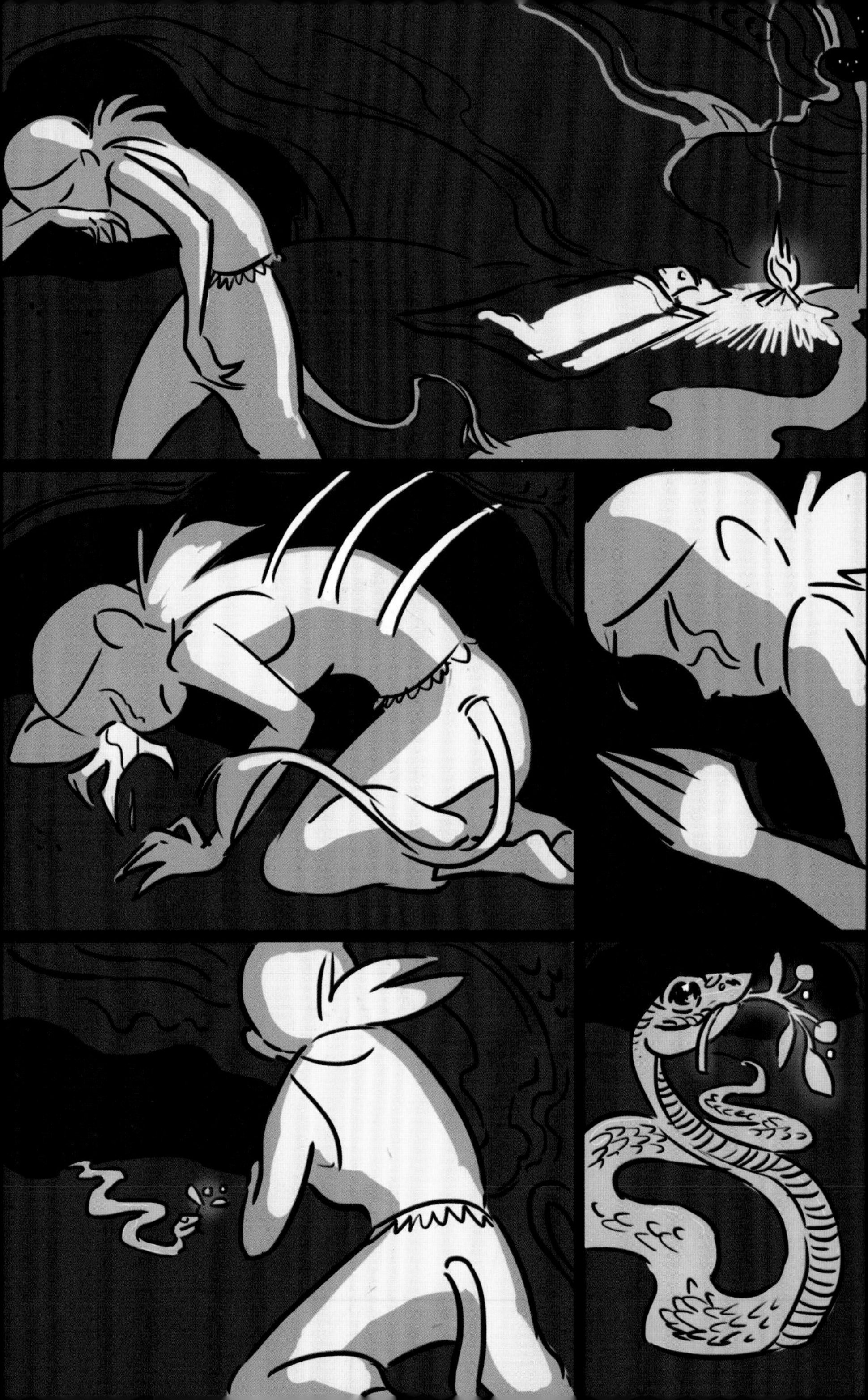

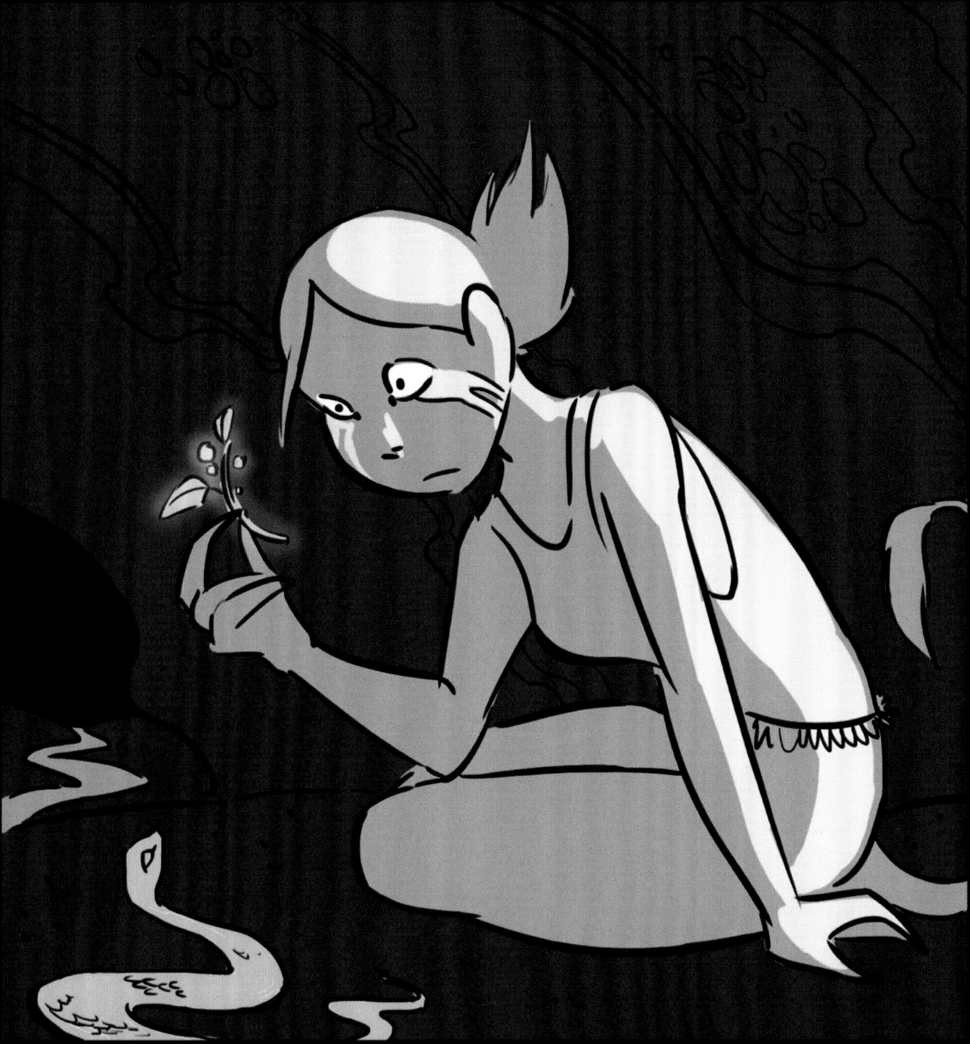

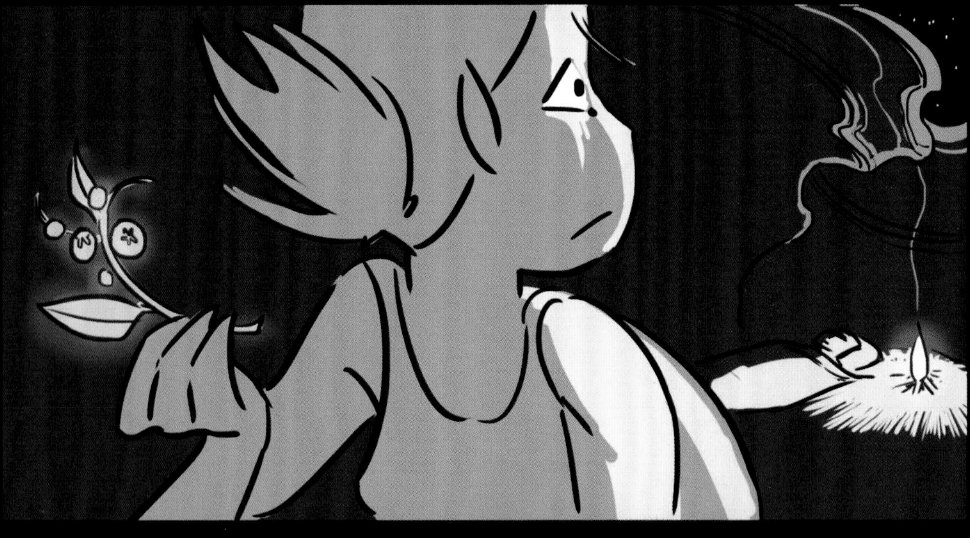

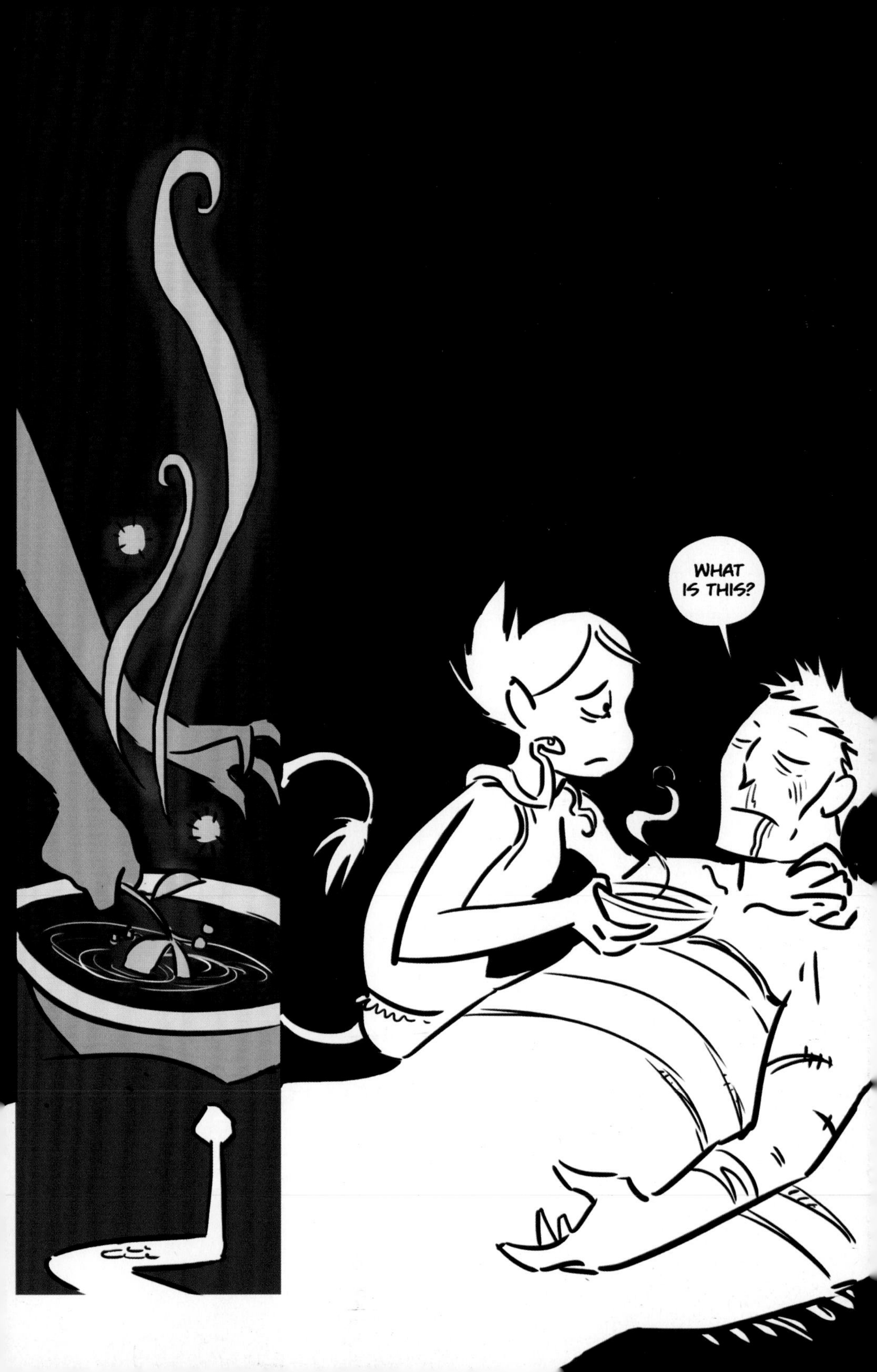
WHAT IS THIS?

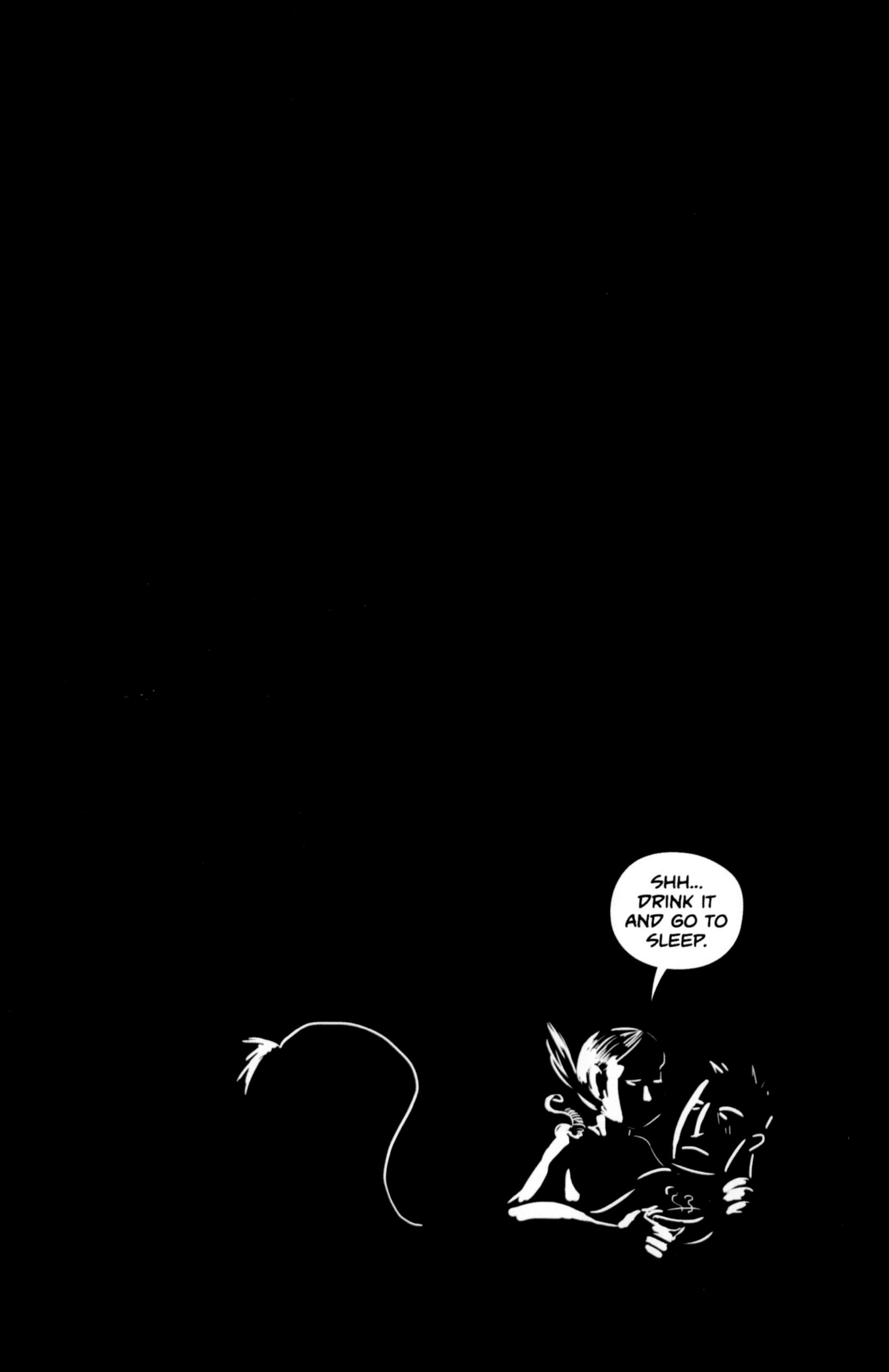
SHH... DRINK IT AND GO TO SLEEP.

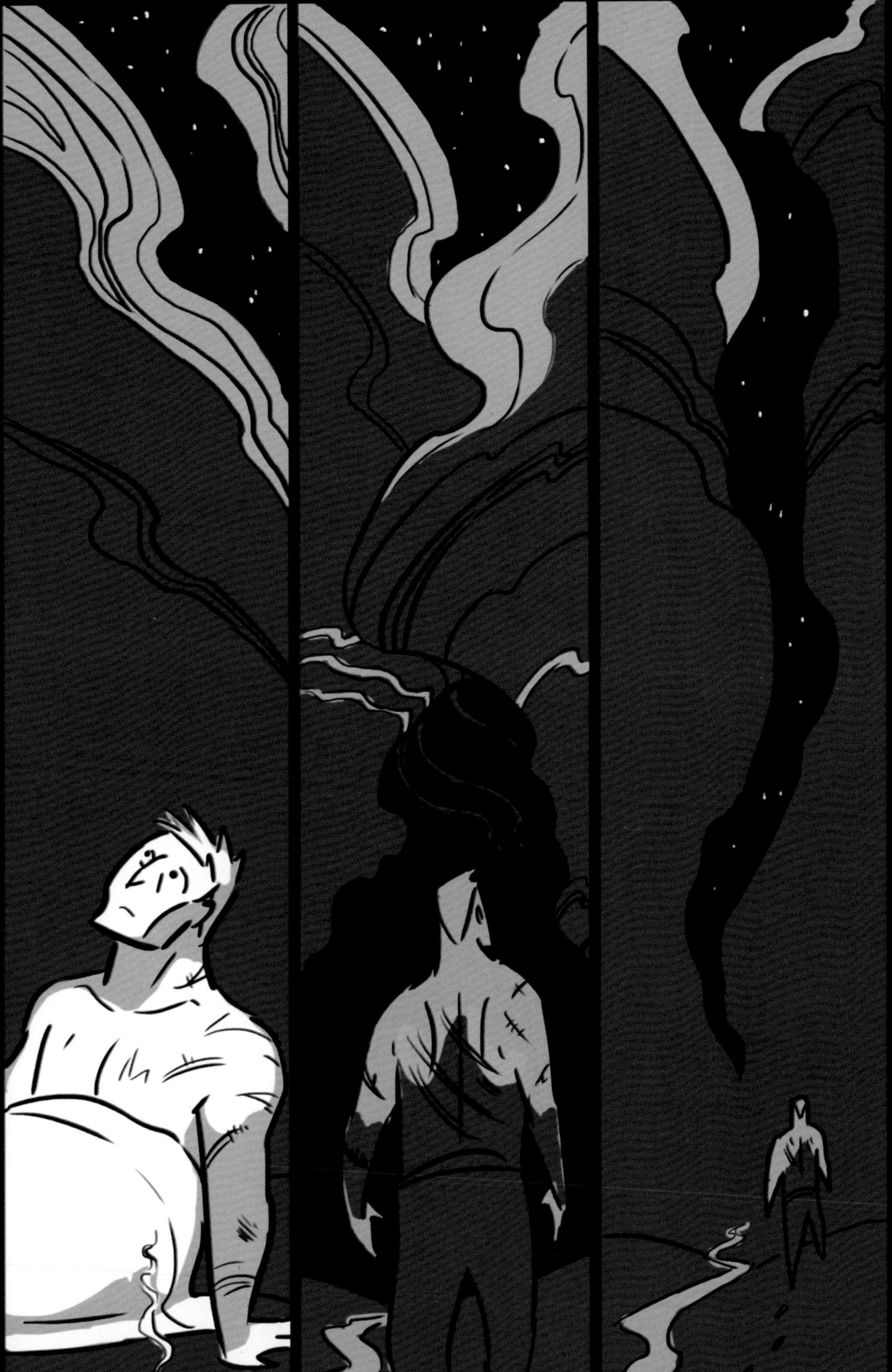

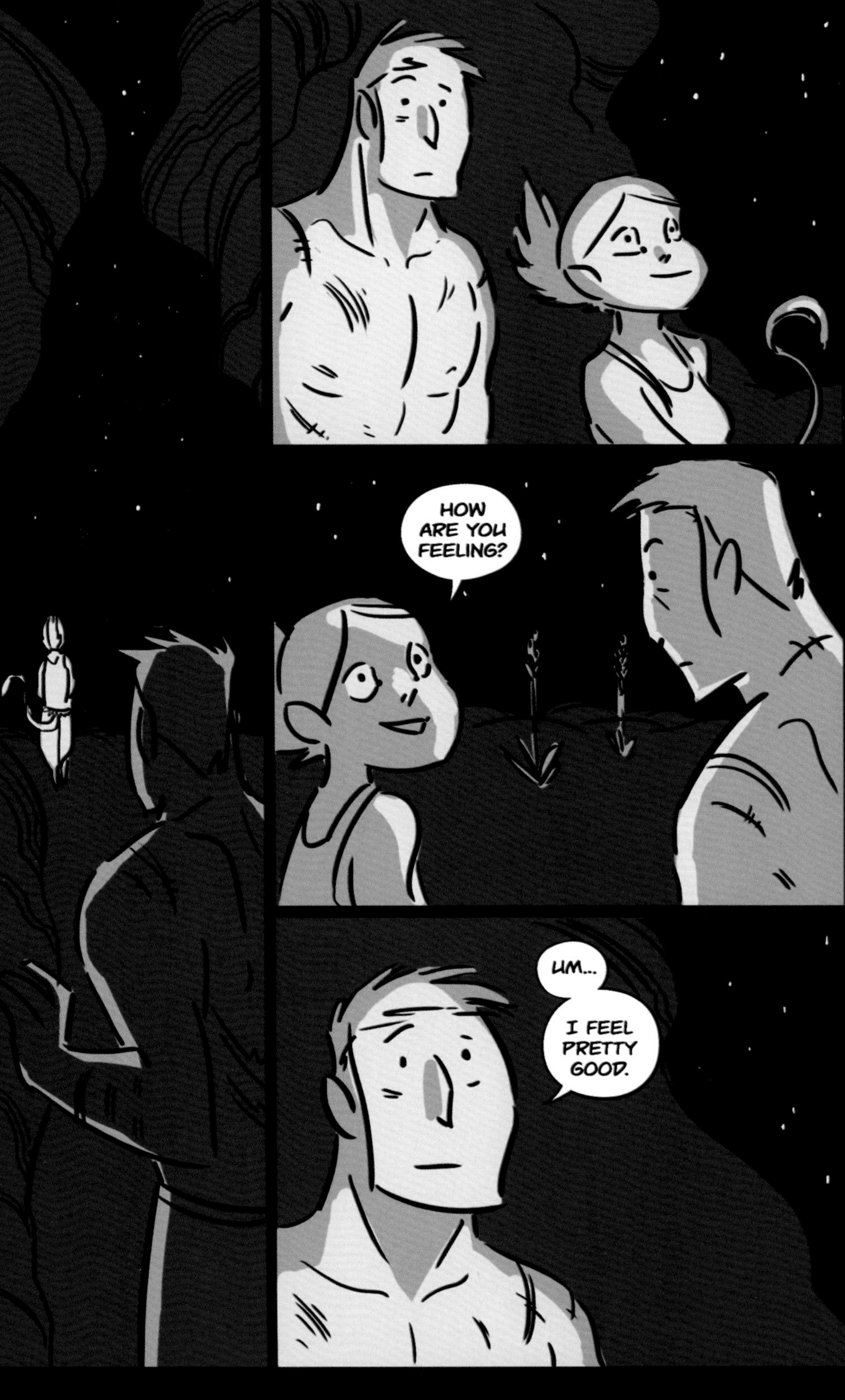
HOW ARE YOU FEELING?
UM...
I FEEL PRETTY GOOD.

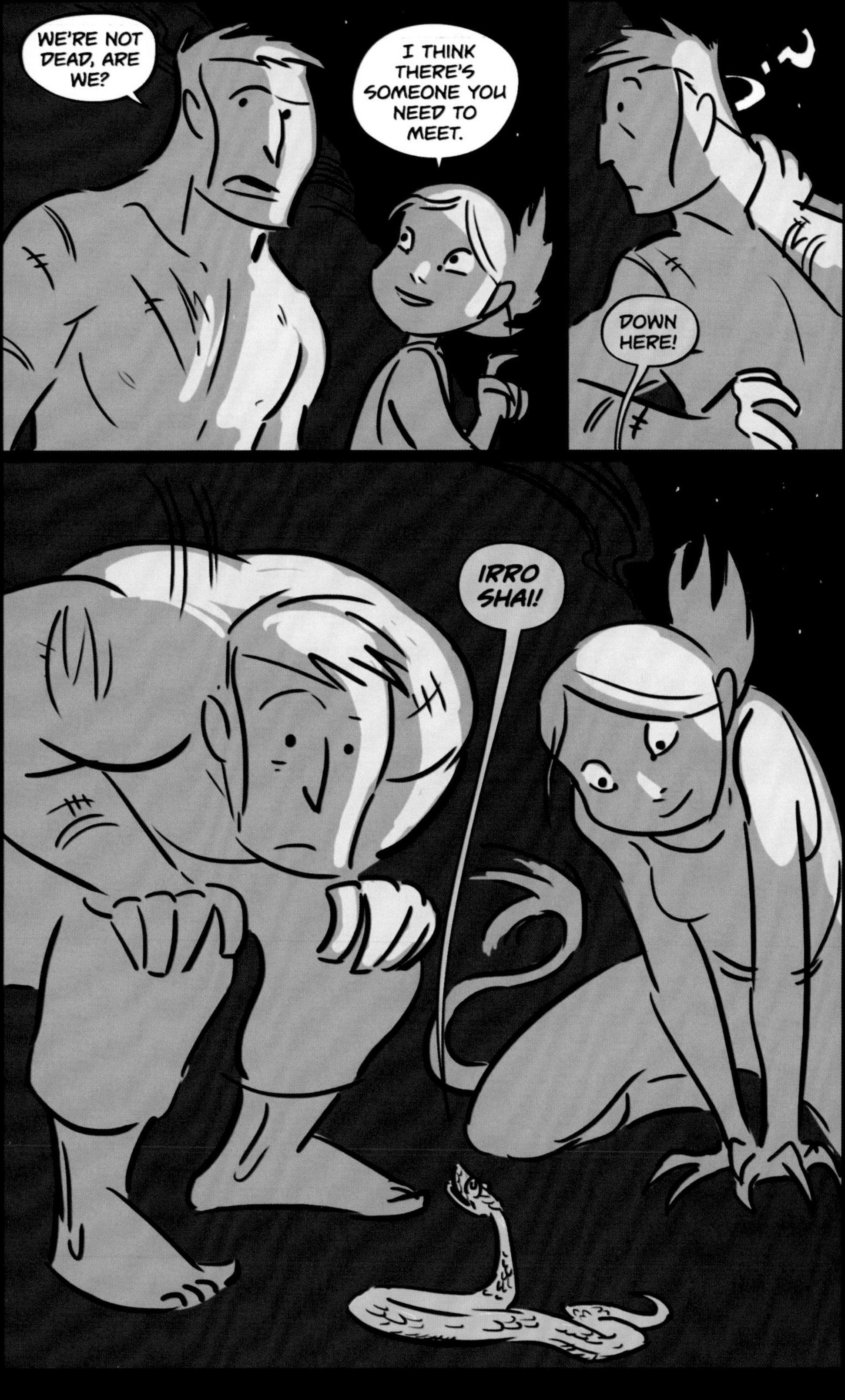
WE'RE NOT DEAD, ARE WE?
I THINK THERE'S SOMEONE YOU NEED TO MEET.
DOWN HERE!
IRRO SHAI!

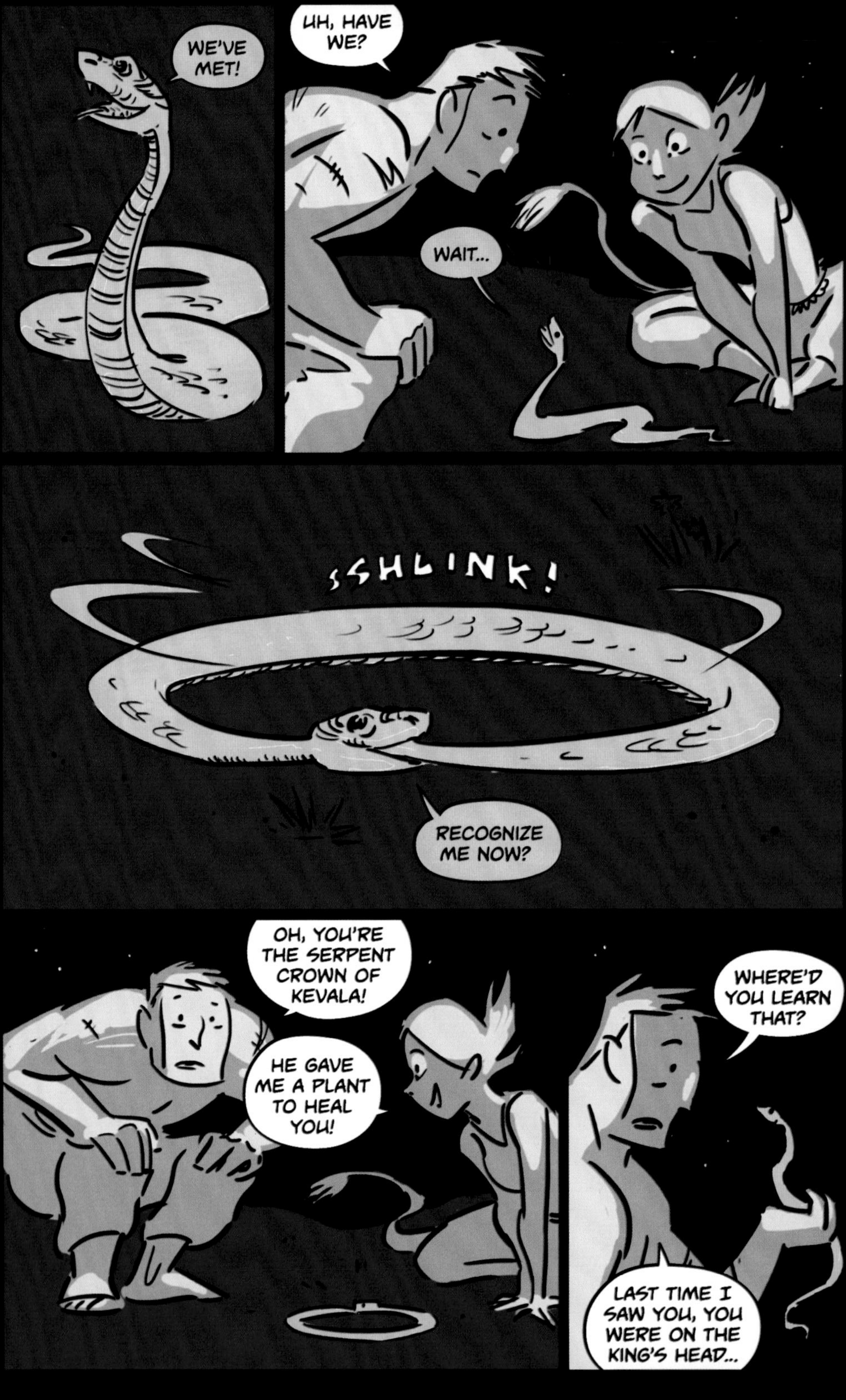
WE'VE MET!
UH, HAVE WE?
WAIT...
SHLINK!
RECOGNIZE ME NOW?
OH, YOU'RE THE SERPENT CROWN OF KEVALA!
HE GAVE ME A PLANT TO HEAL YOU!
WHERE'D YOU LEARN THAT?
LAST TIME I SAW YOU, YOU WERE ON THE KING'S HEAD...

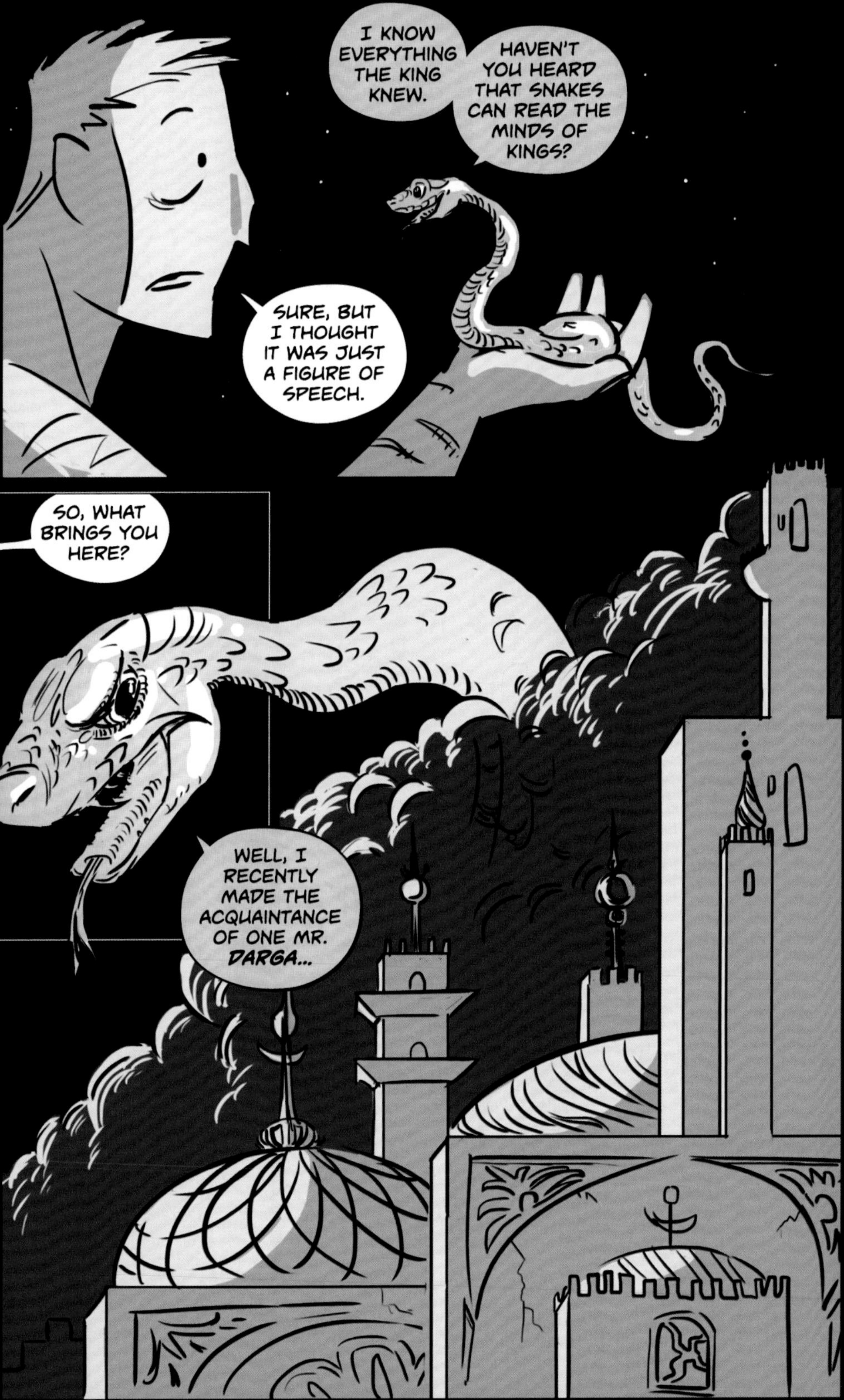
I KNOW EVERYTHING THE KING KNEW.
HAVEN'T YOU HEARD THAT SNAKES CAN READ THE MINDS OF KINGS?
SURE, BUT I THOUGHT IT WAS JUST A FIGURE OF SPEECH.
SO, WHAT BRINGS YOU HERE?
WELL, I RECENTLY MADE THE ACQUAINTANCE OF ONE MR. DARGA...

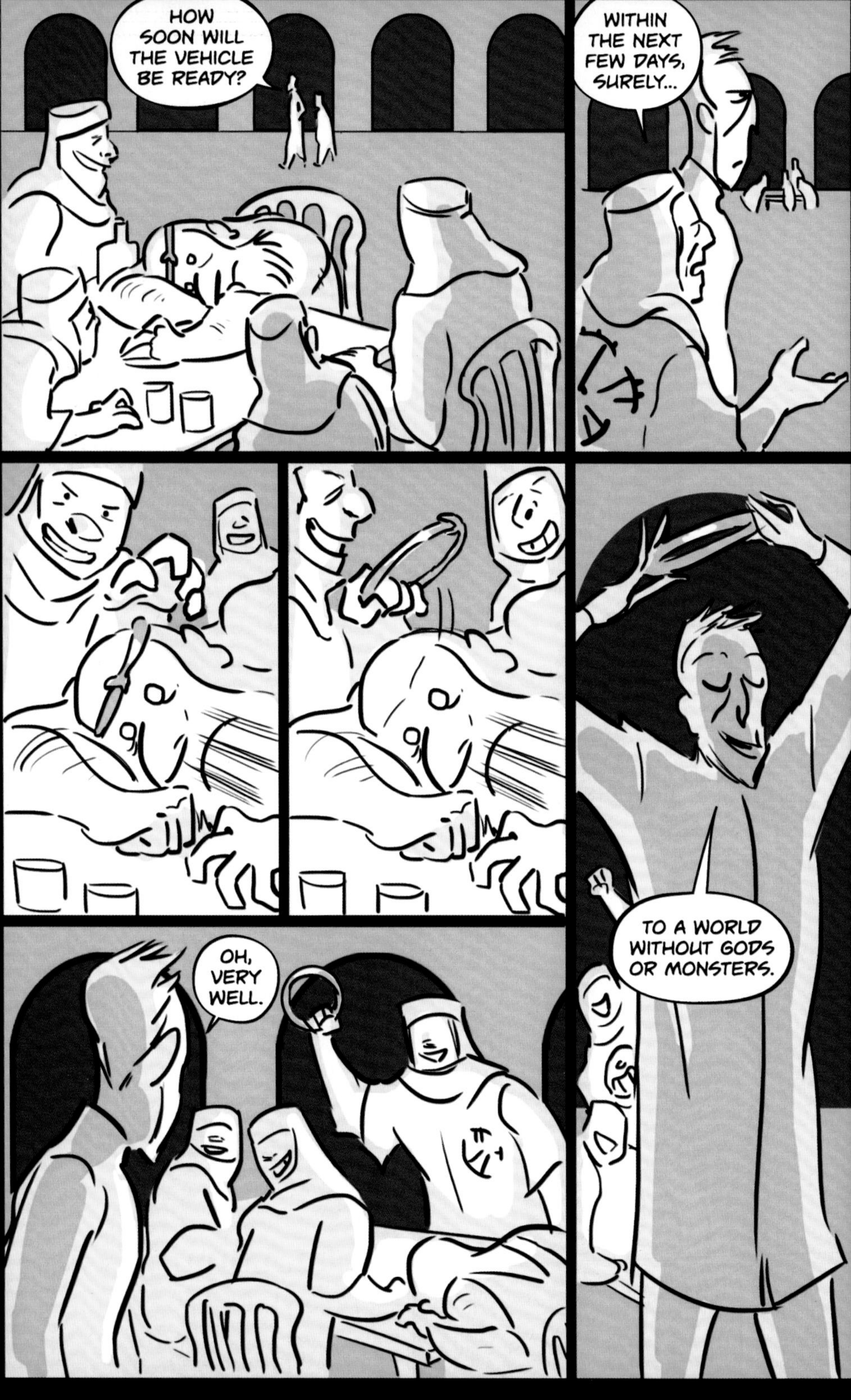
HOW SOON WILL THE VEHICLE BE READY?
WITHIN THE NEXT FEW DAYS, SURELY...
OH, VERY WELL.
TO A WORLD WITHOUT GODS OR MONSTERS.

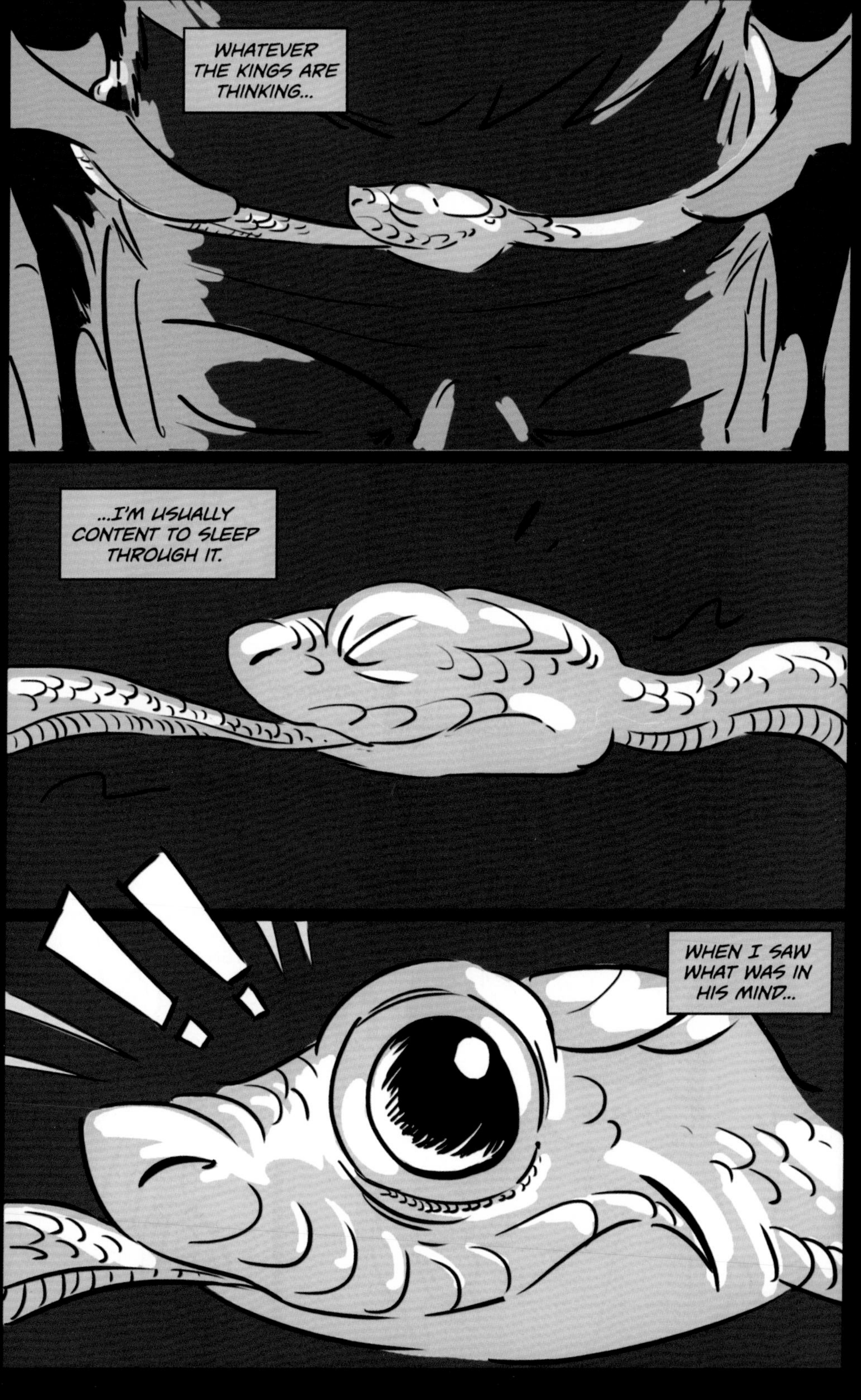
WHATEVER THE KINGS ARE THINKING...
...I'M USUALLY CONTENT TO SLEEP THROUGH IT.
WHEN I SAW WHAT WAS IN HIS MIND...

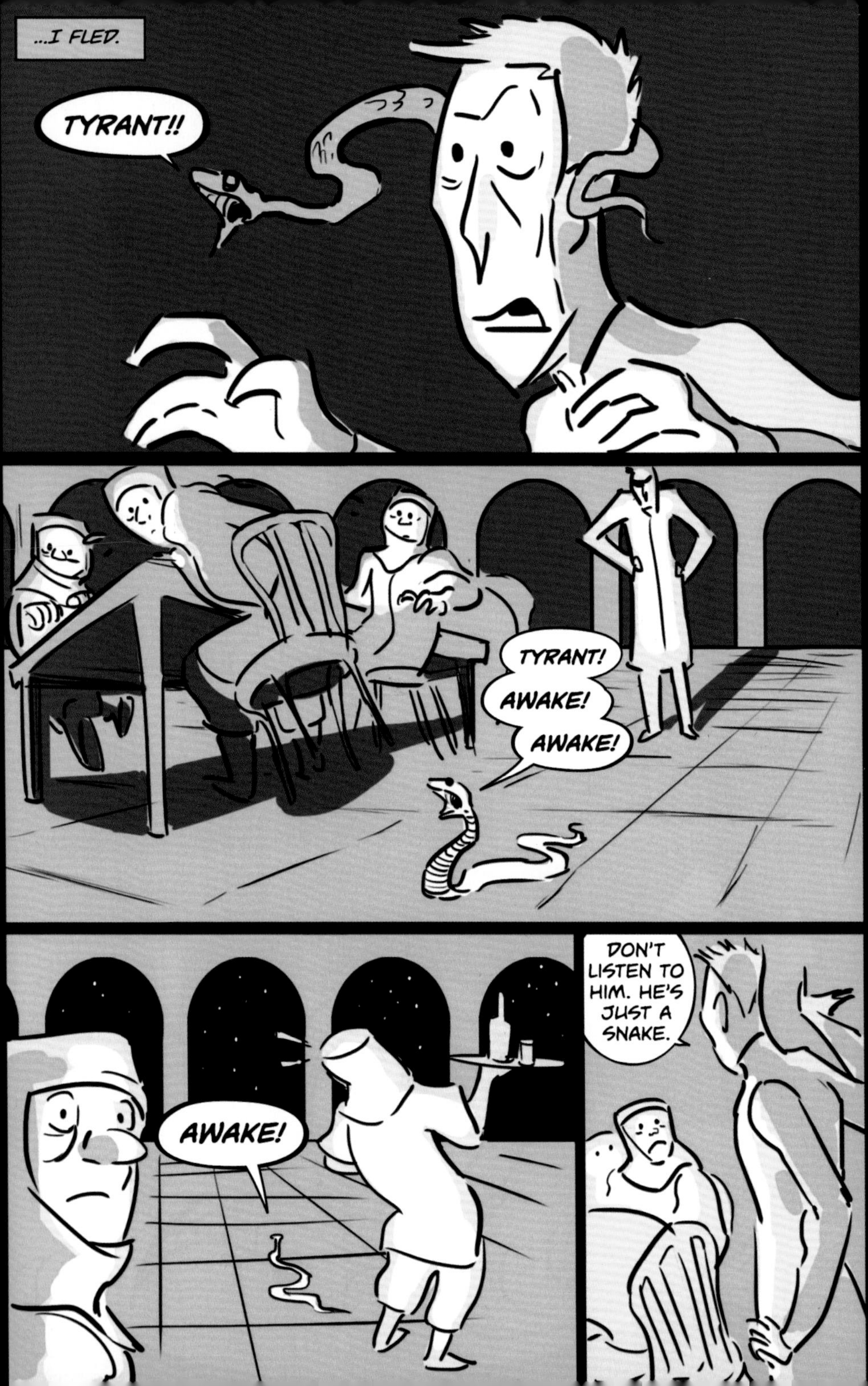
...I FLED.
TYRANT!!
TYRANT!
AWAKE!
AWAKE!
AWAKE!
DON'T LISTEN TO HIM. HE'S JUST A SNAKE.

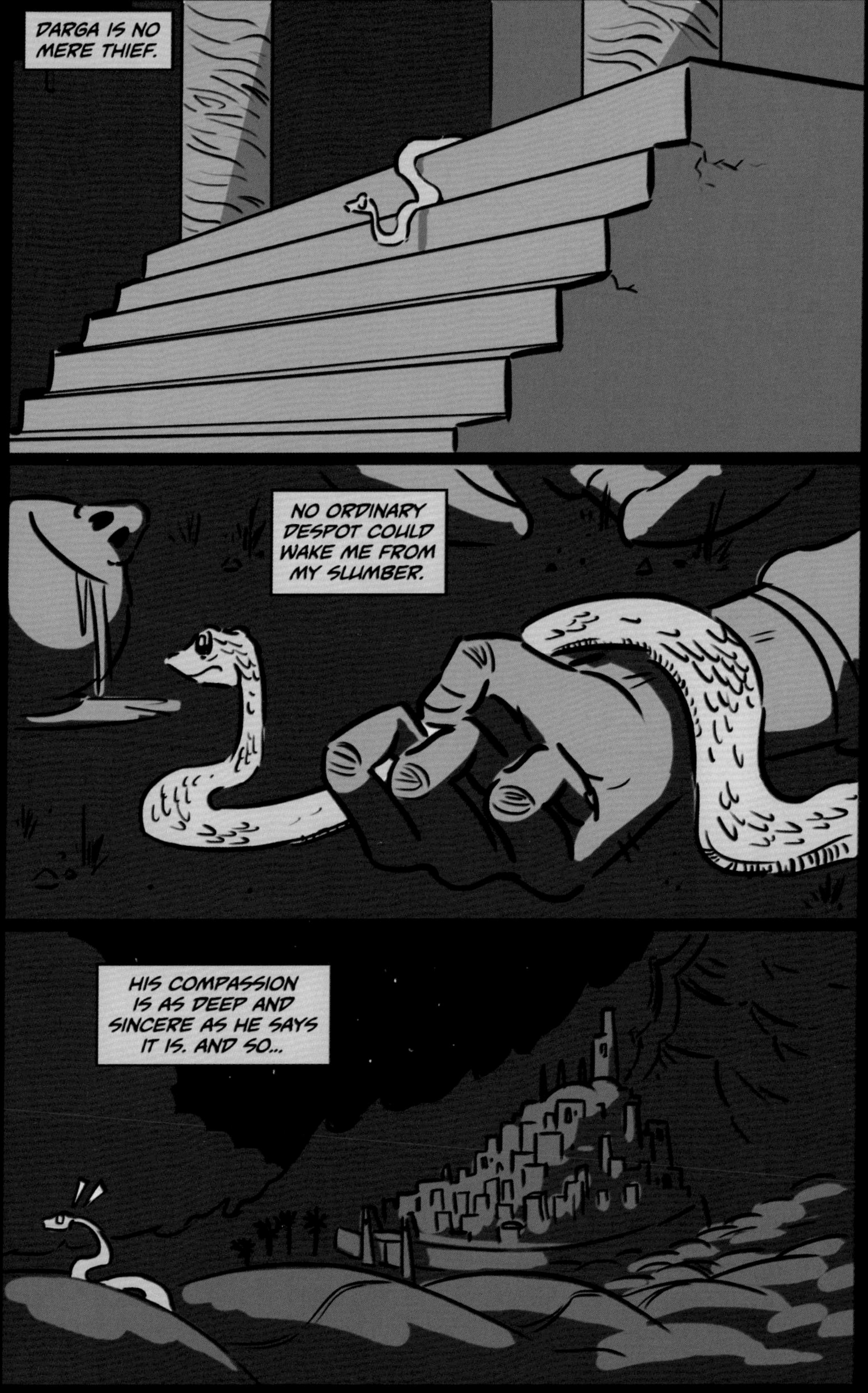
DARGA IS NO MERE THIEF.
NO ORDINARY DESPOT COULD WAKE ME FROM MY SLUMBER.
HIS COMPASSION IS AS DEEP AND SINCERE AS HE SAYS IT IS. AND SO...

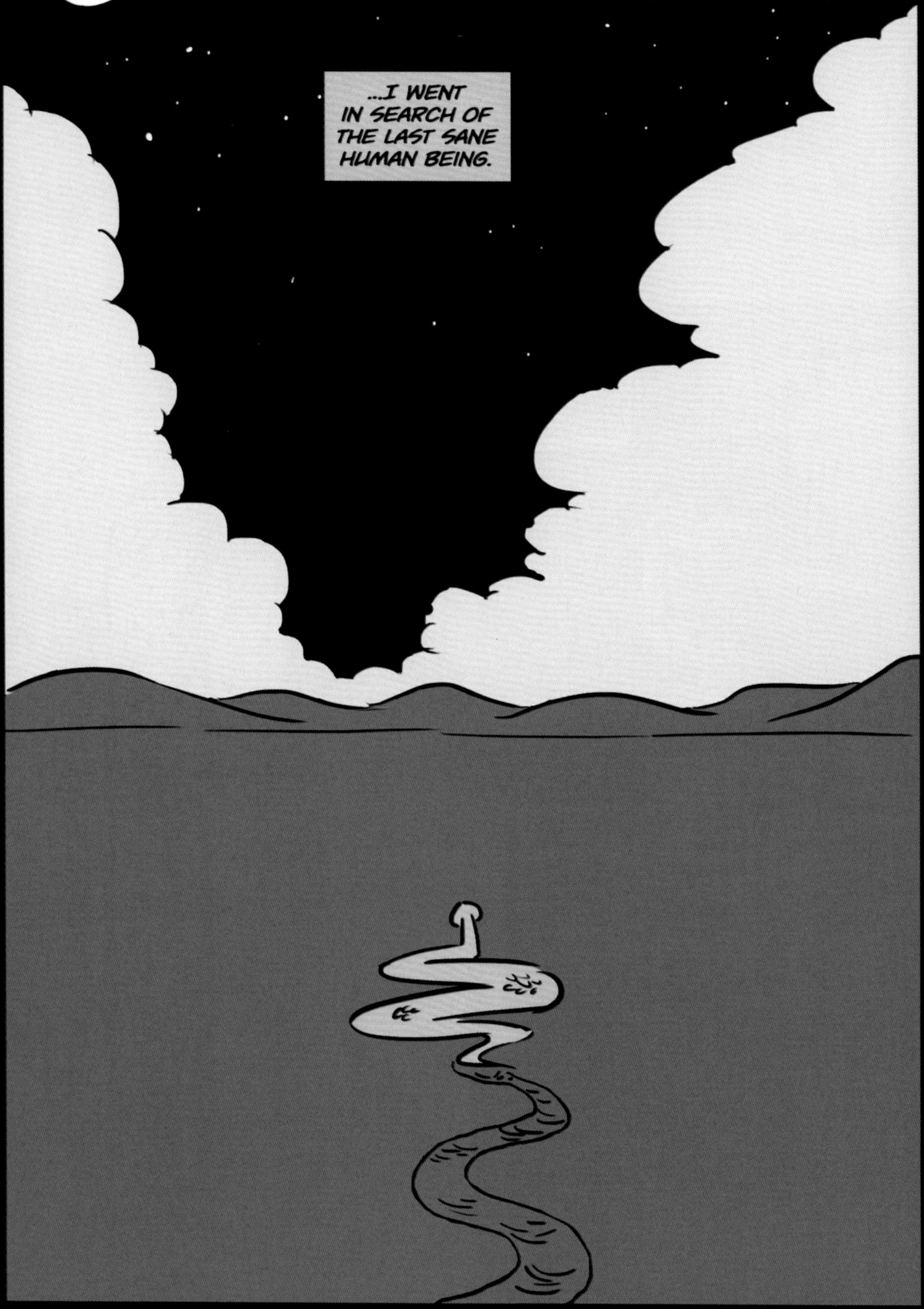
...I WENT IN SEARCH OF THE LAST SANE HUMAN BEING.

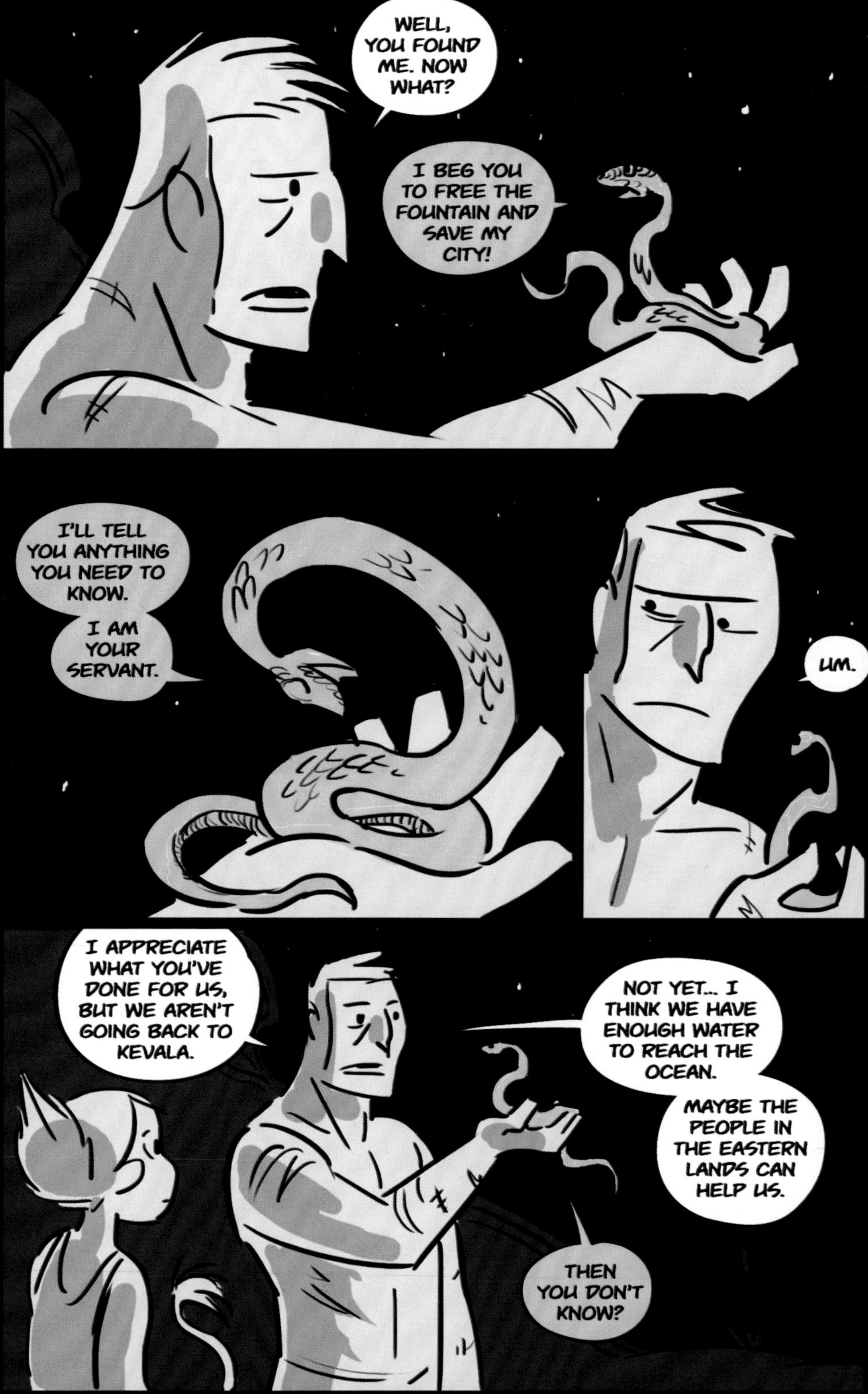
WELL, YOU FOUND ME. NOW WHAT?
I BEG YOU TO FREE THE FOUNTAIN AND SAVE MY CITY!
I'LL TELL YOU ANYTHING YOU NEED TO KNOW.
I AM YOUR SERVANT.
UM.
I APPRECIATE WHAT YOU'VE DONE FOR US, BUT WE AREN'T GOING BACK TO KEVALA.
NOT YET... I THINK WE HAVE ENOUGH WATER TO REACH THE OCEAN.
MAYBE THE PEOPLE IN THE EASTERN LANDS CAN HELP US.
THEN YOU DON'T KNOW?

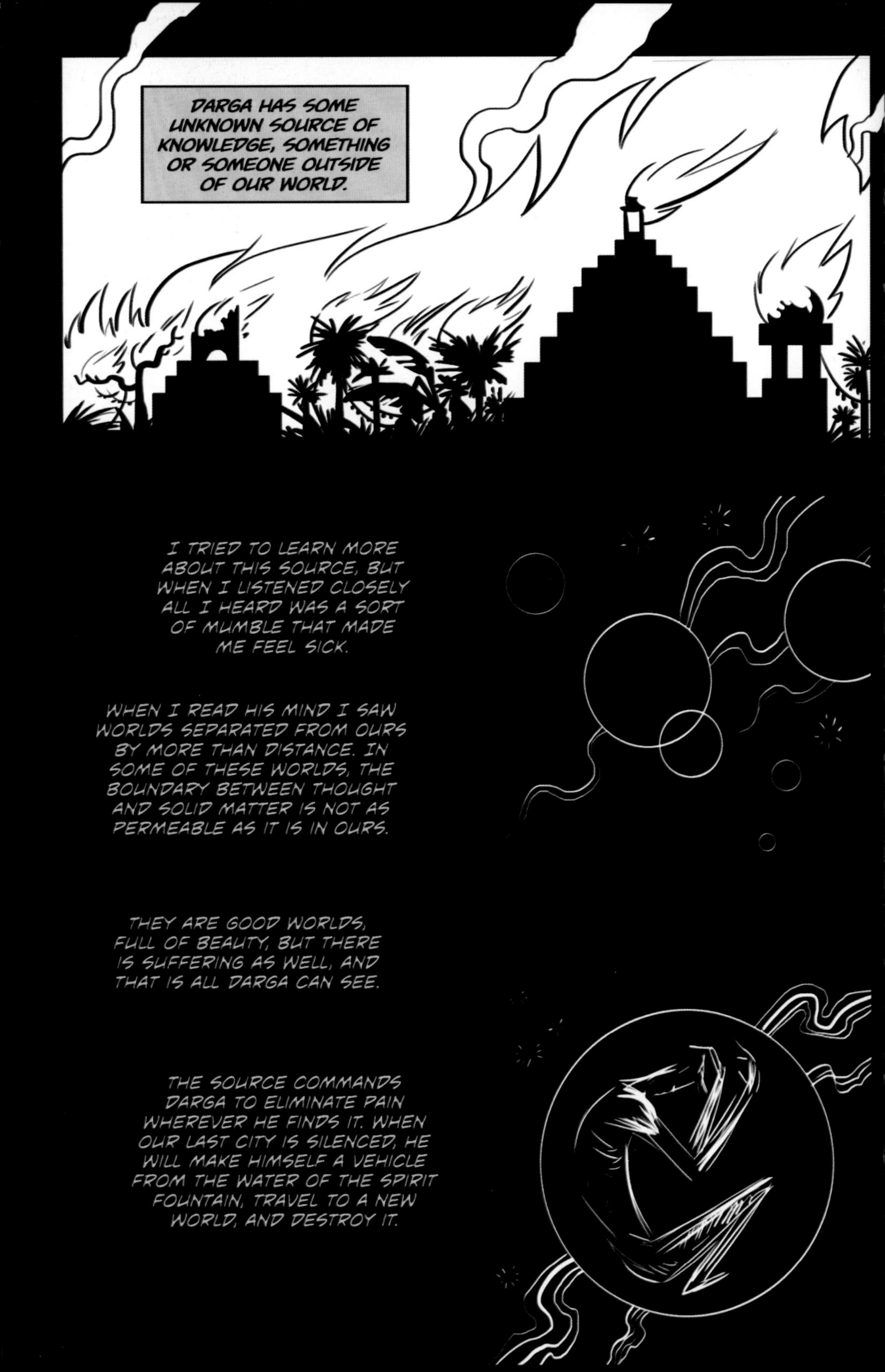
DARGA HAS SOME UNKNOWN SOURCE OF KNOWLEDGE, SOMETHING OR SOMEONE OUTSIDE OF OUR WORLD.
I TRIED TO LEARN MORE ABOUT THIS SOURCE, BUT WHEN I LISTENED CLOSELY ALL I HEARD WAS A SORT OF MUMBLE THAT MADE ME FEEL SICK.
WHEN I READ HIS MIND I SAW WORLDS SEPARATED FROM OURS BY MORE THAN DISTANCE. IN SOME OF THESE WORLDS, THE BOUNDARY BETWEEN THOUGHT AND SOLID MATTER IS NOT AS PERMEABLE AS IT IS IN OURS.
THEY ARE GOOD WORLDS, FULL OF BEAUTY, BUT THERE IS SUFFERING AS WELL, AND THAT IS ALL DARGA CAN SEE.
THE SOURCE COMMANDS DARGA TO ELIMINATE PAIN WHEREVER HE FINDS IT. WHEN OUR LAST CITY IS SILENCED, HE WILL MAKE HIMSELF A VEHICLE FROM THE WATER OF THE SPIRIT FOUNTAIN, TRAVEL TO A NEW WORLD, AND DESTROY IT.

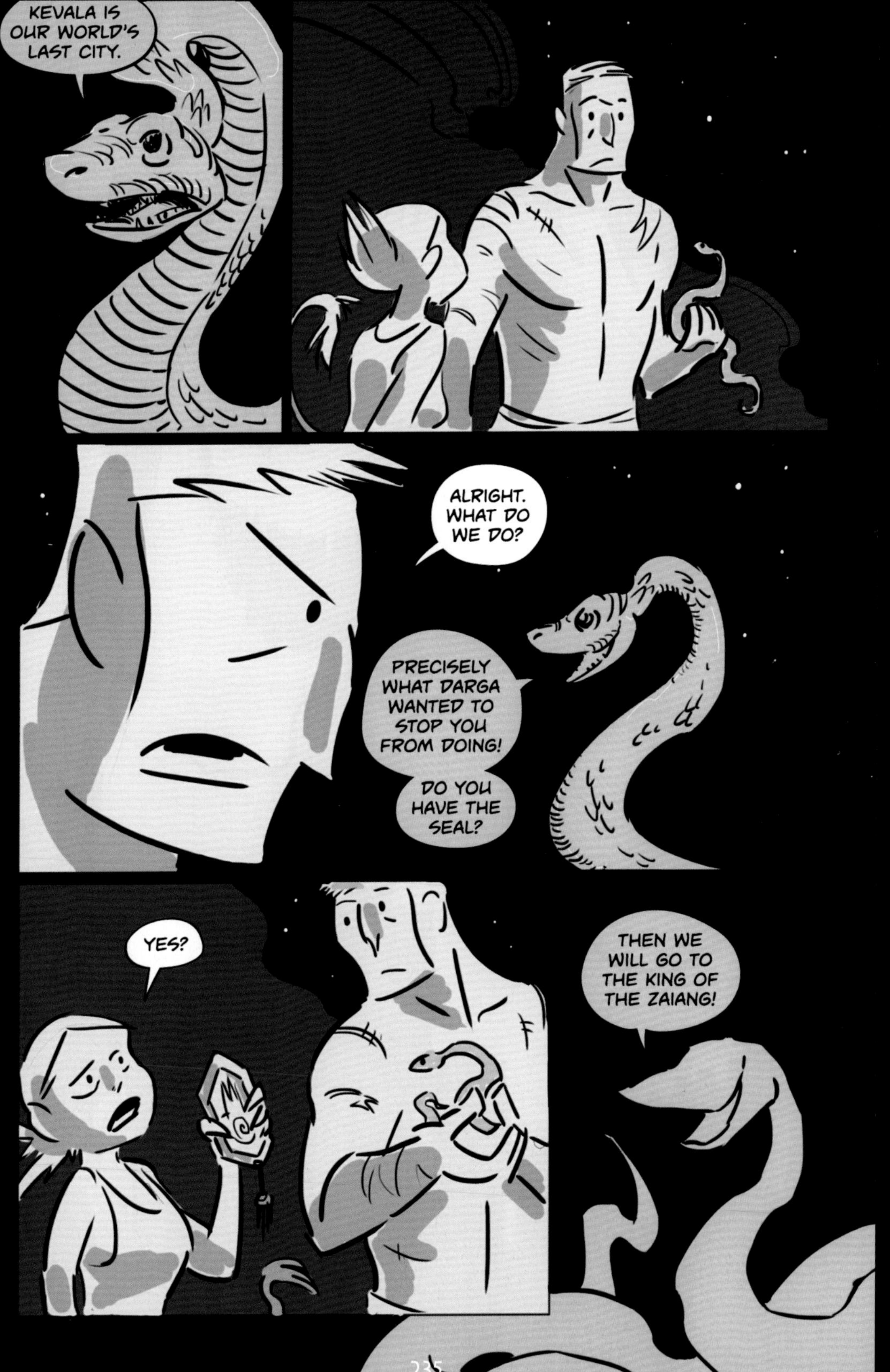
KEVALA IS OUR WORLD'S LAST CITY.
ALRIGHT. WHAT DO WE DO?
PRECISELY WHAT DARGA WANTED TO STOP YOU FROM DOING!
DO YOU HAVE THE SEAL?
YES?
THEN WE WILL GO TO THE KING OF THE ZAIANG!

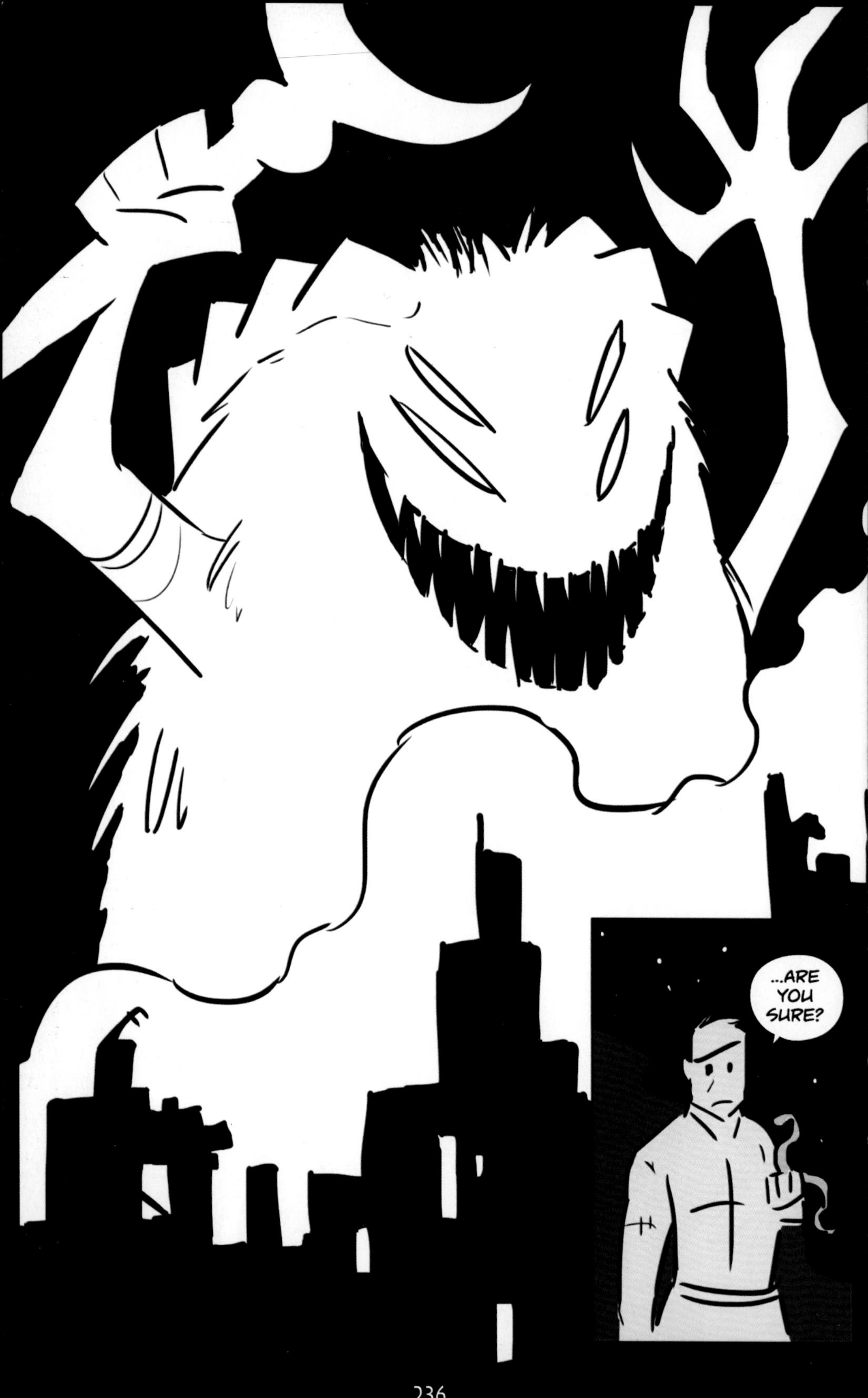
...ARE YOU SURE?

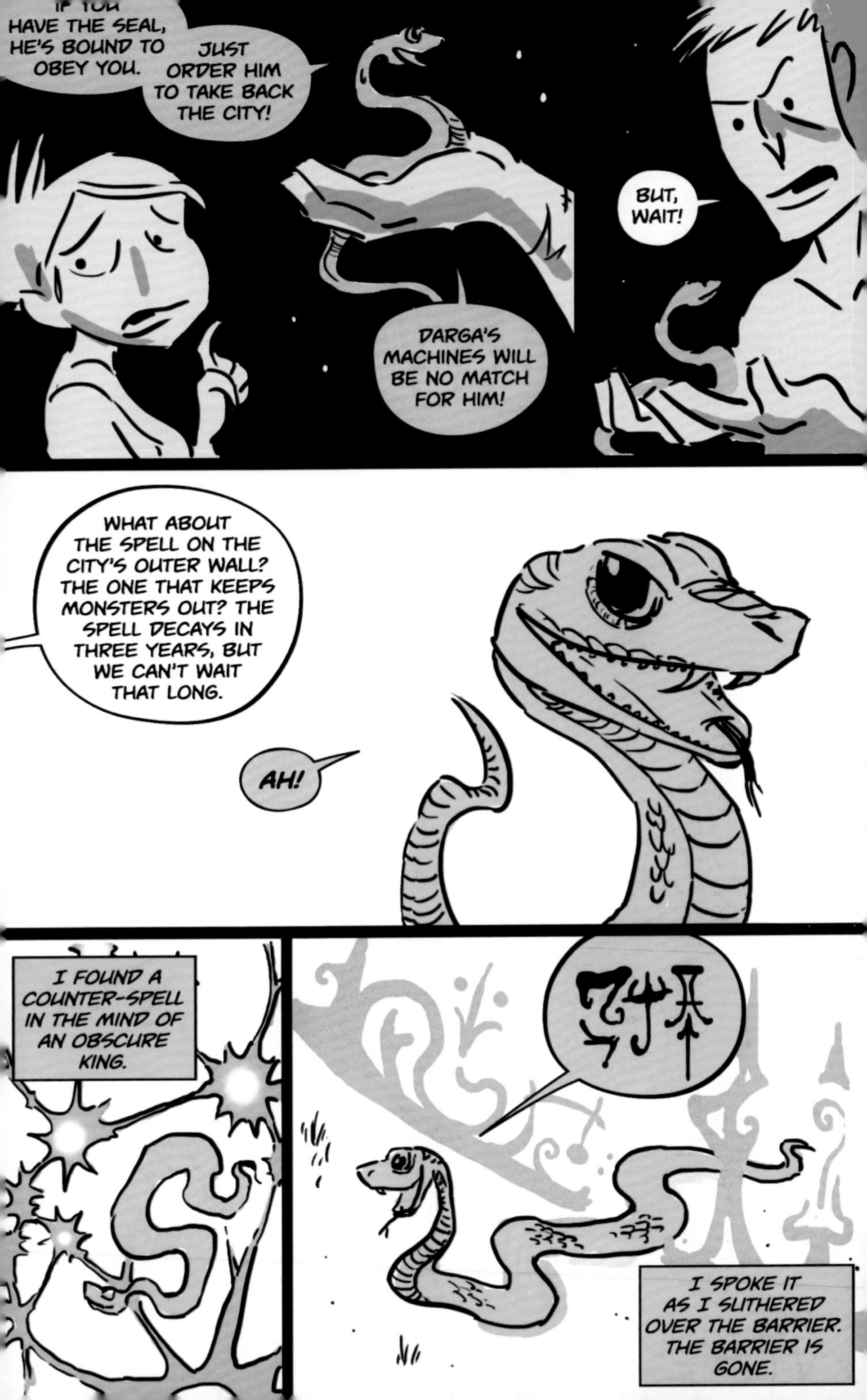
HAVE THE SEAL, HE'S BOUND TO OBEY YOU.
JUST ORDER HIM TO TAKE BACK THE CITY!
DARGA'S MACHINES WILL BE NO MATCH FOR HIM!
BUT, WAIT!
WHAT ABOUT THE SPELL ON THE CITY'S OUTER WALL? THE ONE THAT KEEPS MONSTERS OUT? THE SPELL DECAYS IN THREE YEARS, BUT WE CAN'T WAIT THAT LONG.
AH!
I FOUND A COUNTER-SPELL IN THE MIND OF AN OBSCURE KING.
I SPOKE IT AS I SLITHERED OVER THE BARRIER. THE BARRIER IS GONE.

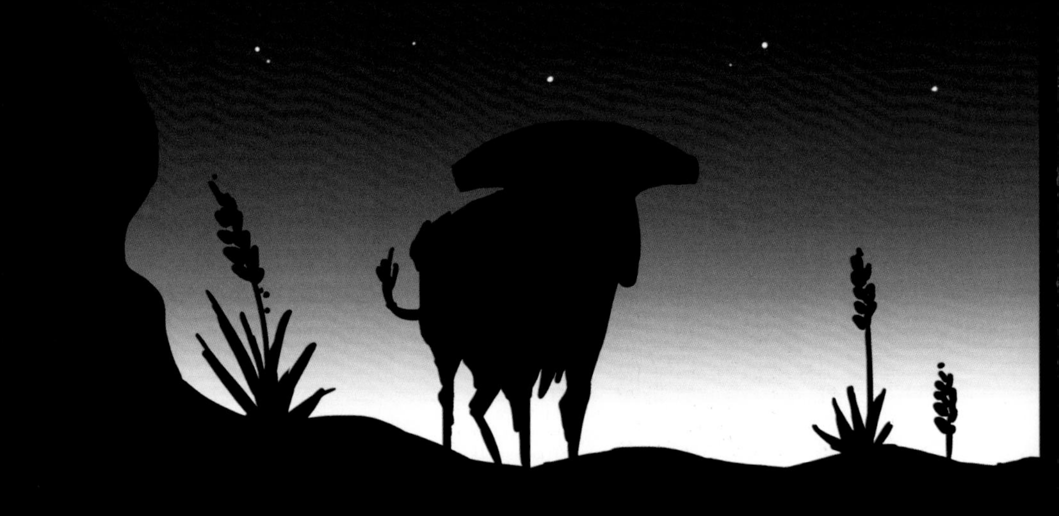

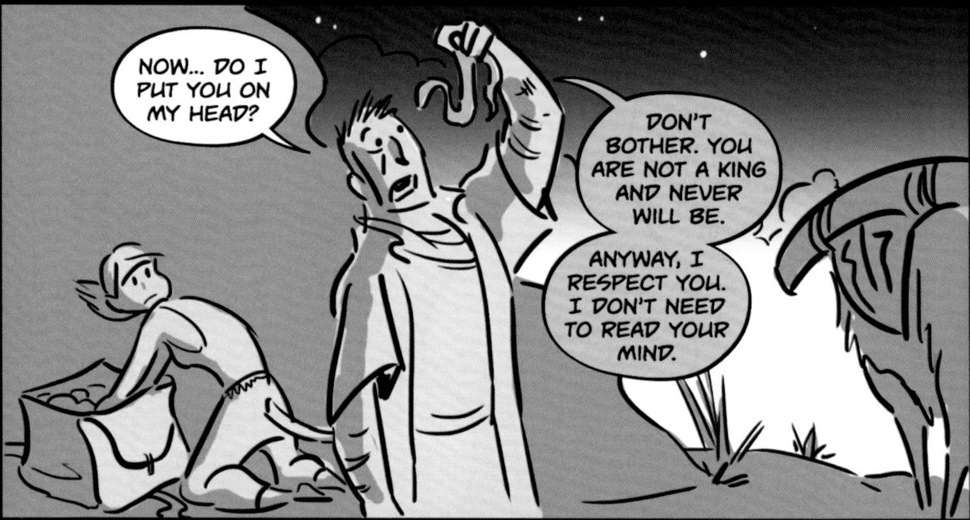
NOW... DO I PUT YOU ON MY HEAD?
DON'T BOTHER. YOU ARE NOT A KING AND NEVER WILL BE.
ANYWAY, I RESPECT YOU. I DON'T NEED TO READ YOUR MIND.

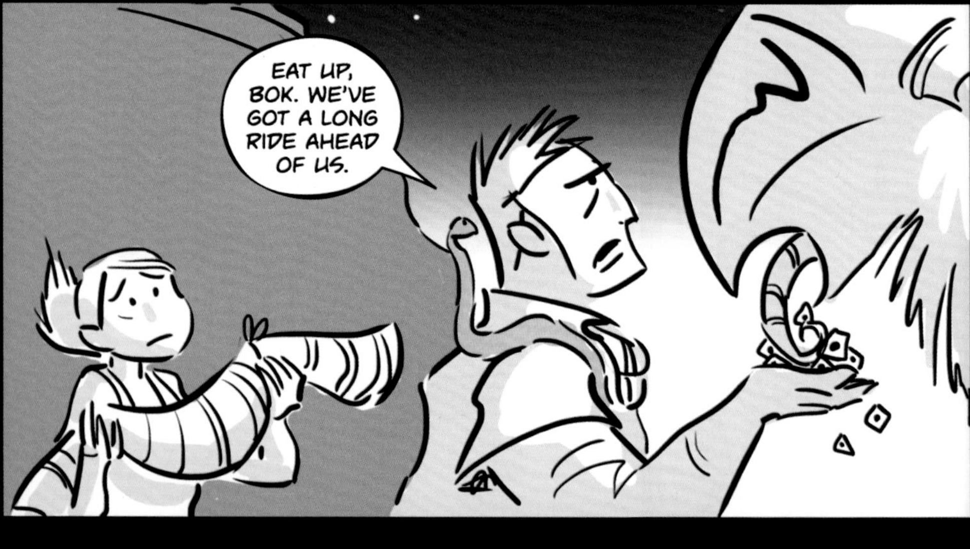
EAT UP, BOK. WE'VE GOT A LONG RIDE AHEAD OF US.

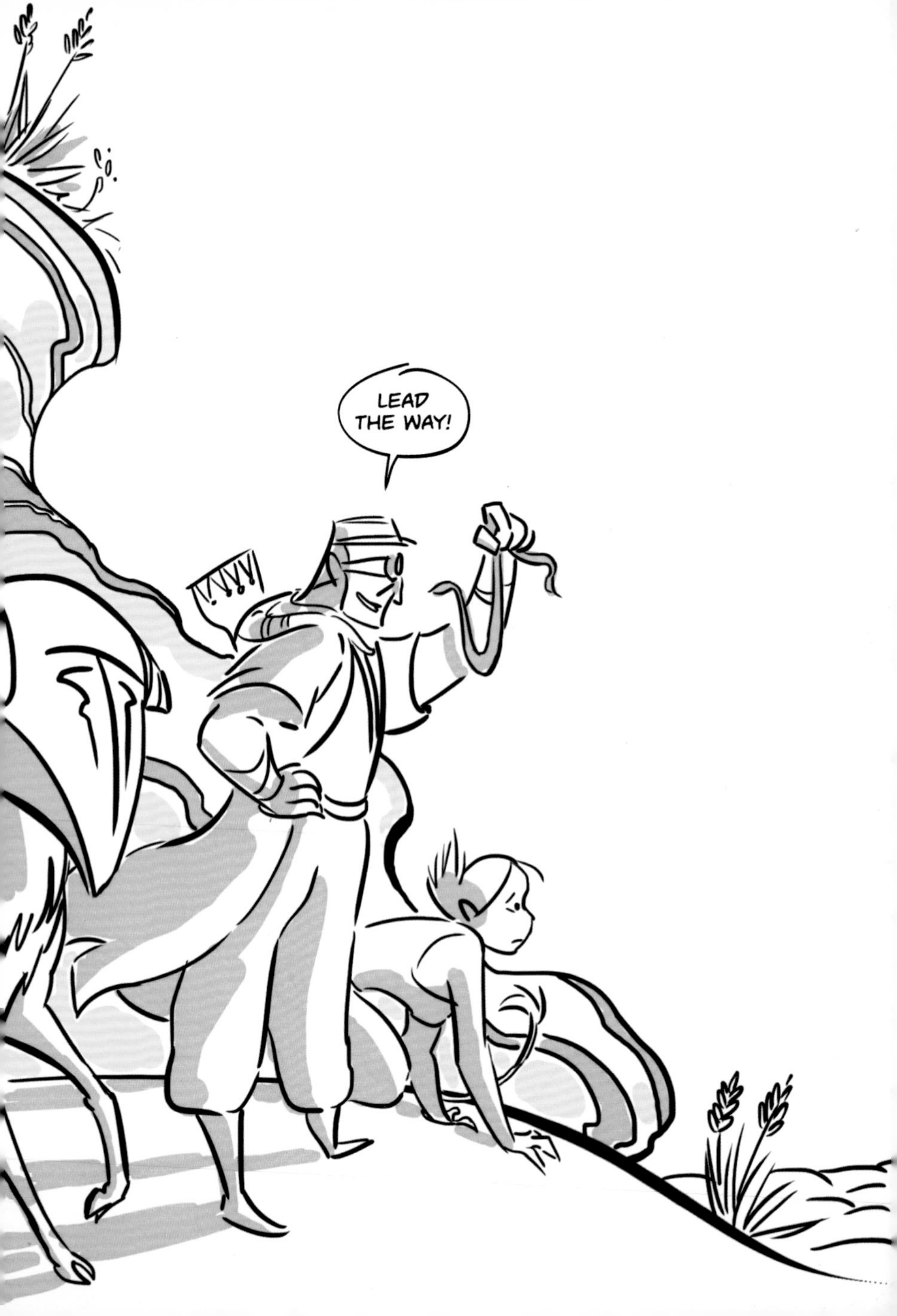
LEAD
THE WAY!

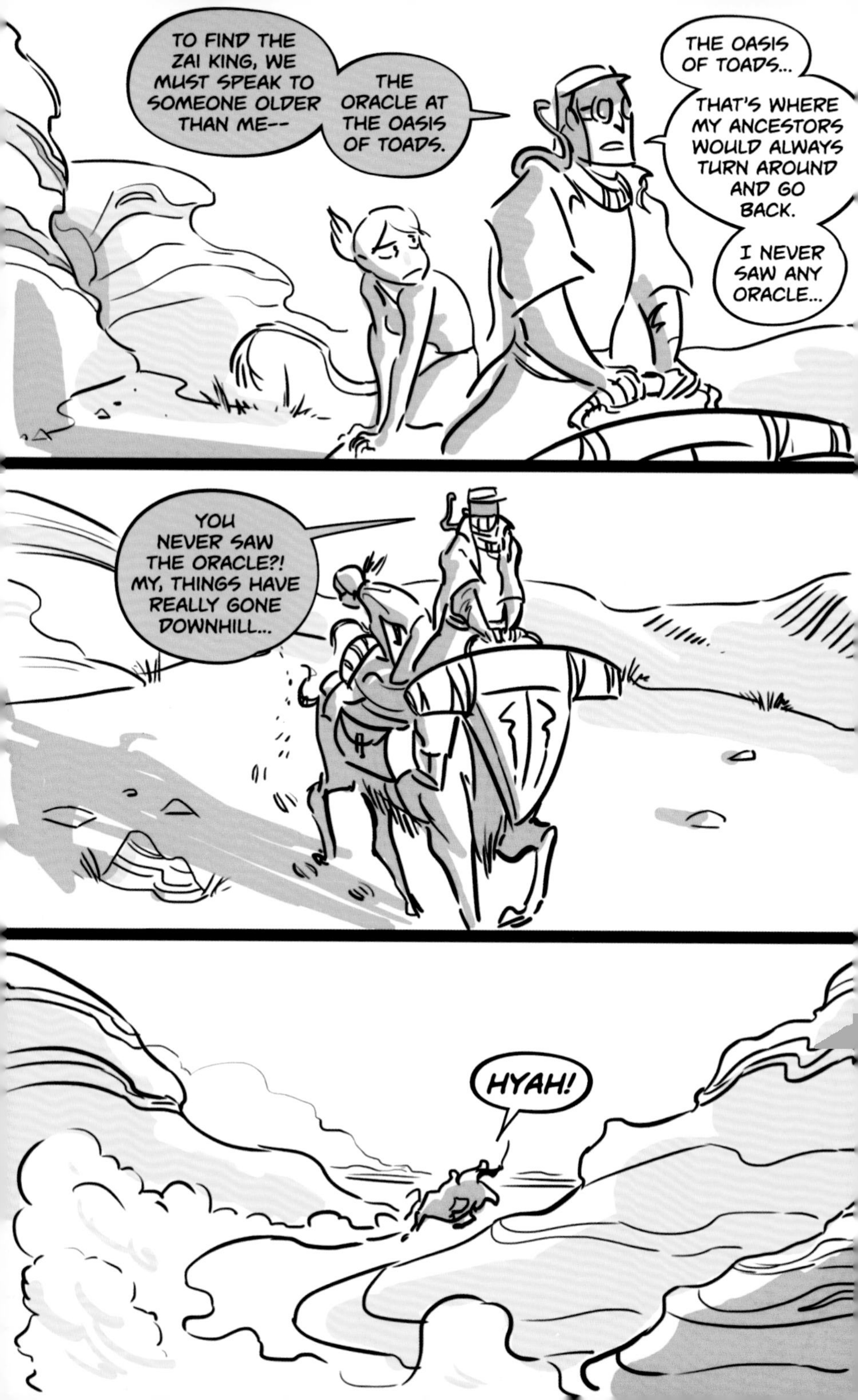
TO FIND THE ZAI KING, WE MUST SPEAK TO SOMEONE OLDER THAN ME--
THE ORACLE AT THE OASIS OF TOADS.
THE OASIS OF TOADS...
THAT'S WHERE MY ANCESTORS WOULD ALWAYS TURN AROUND AND GO BACK.
I NEVER SAW ANY ORACLE...
YOU NEVER SAW THE ORACLE?! MY, THINGS HAVE REALLY GONE DOWNHILL...
HYAH!

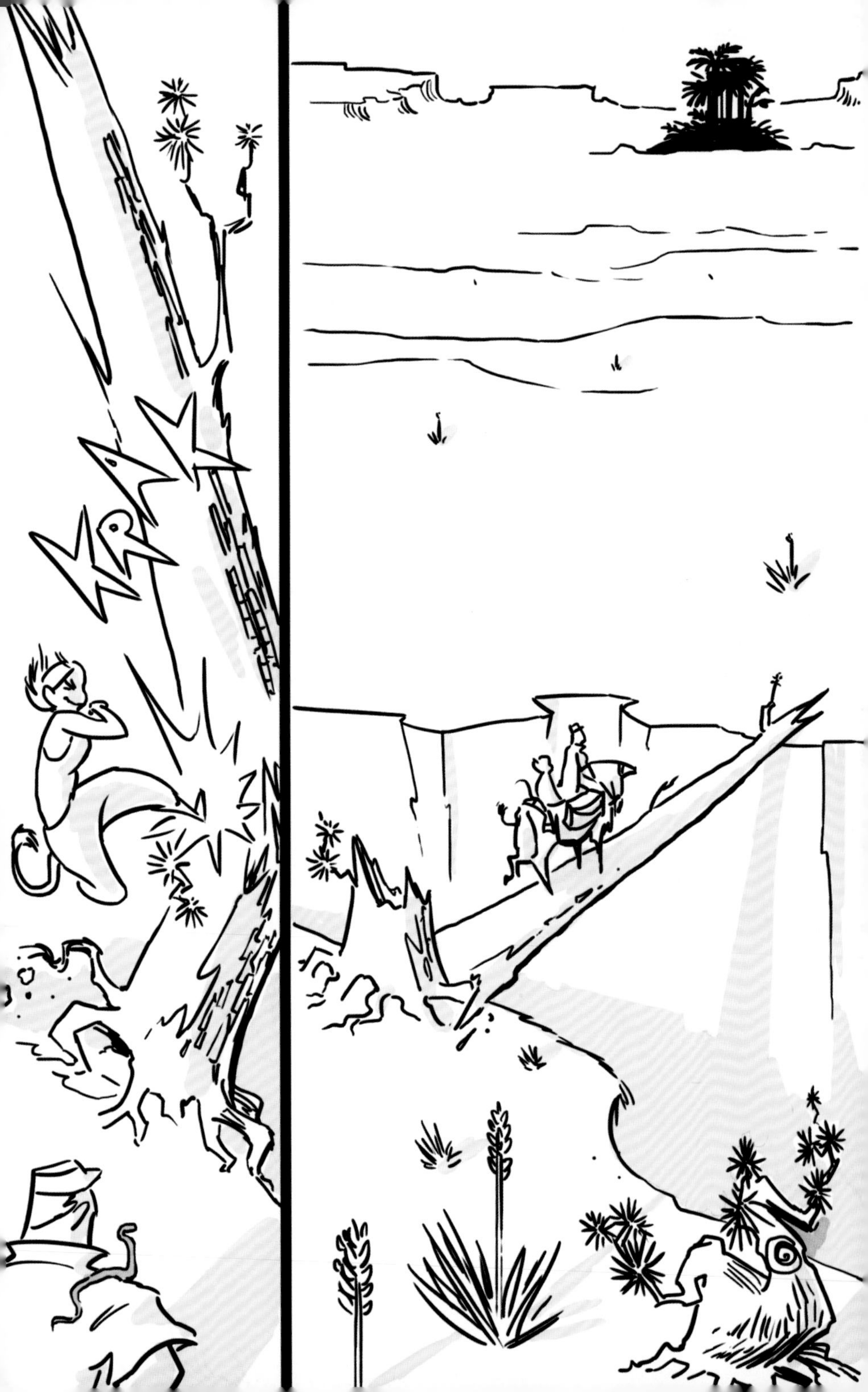
KRAK

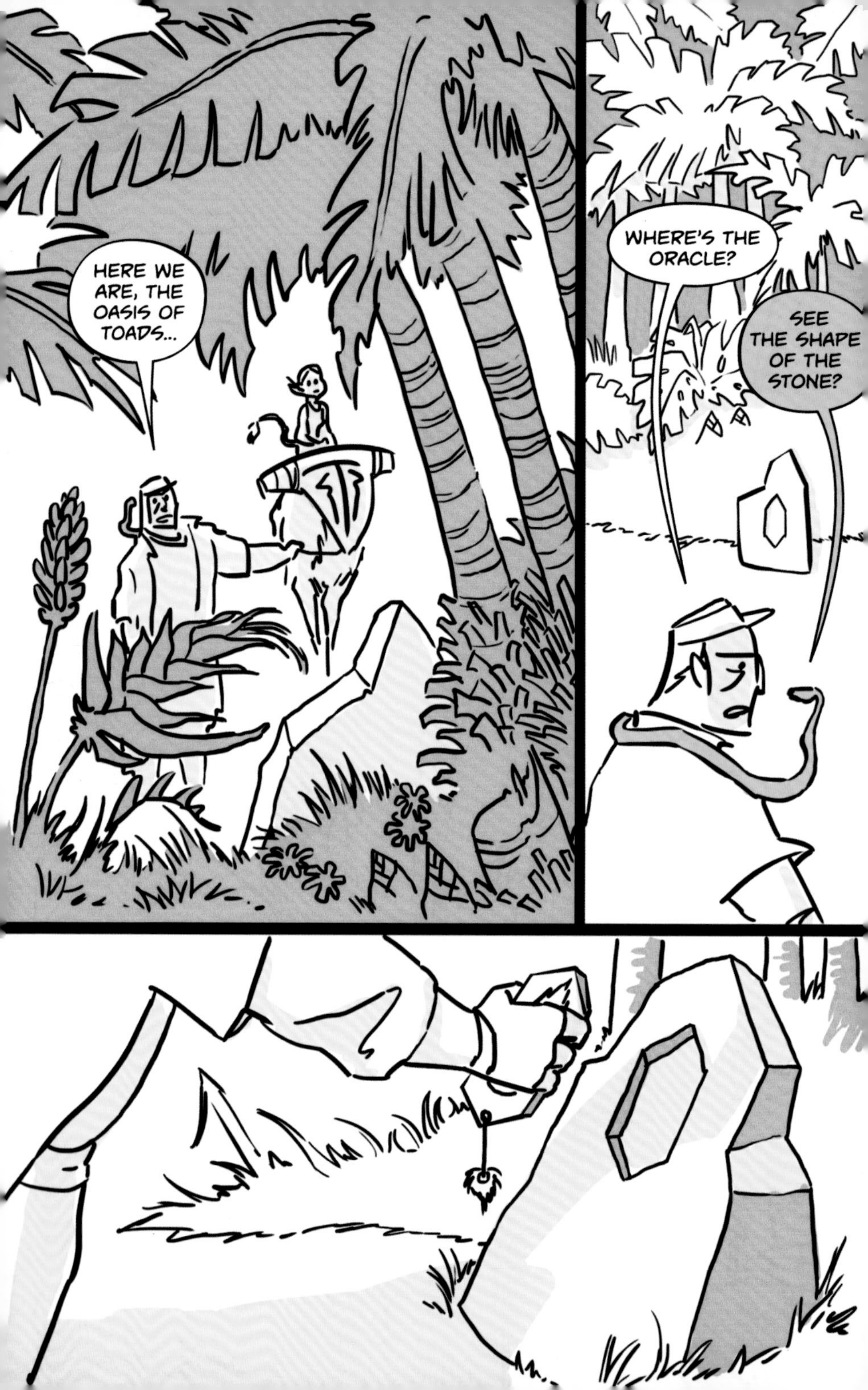
HERE WE ARE, THE OASIS OF TOADS...
WHERE'S THE ORACLE?
SEE THE SHAPE OF THE STONE?

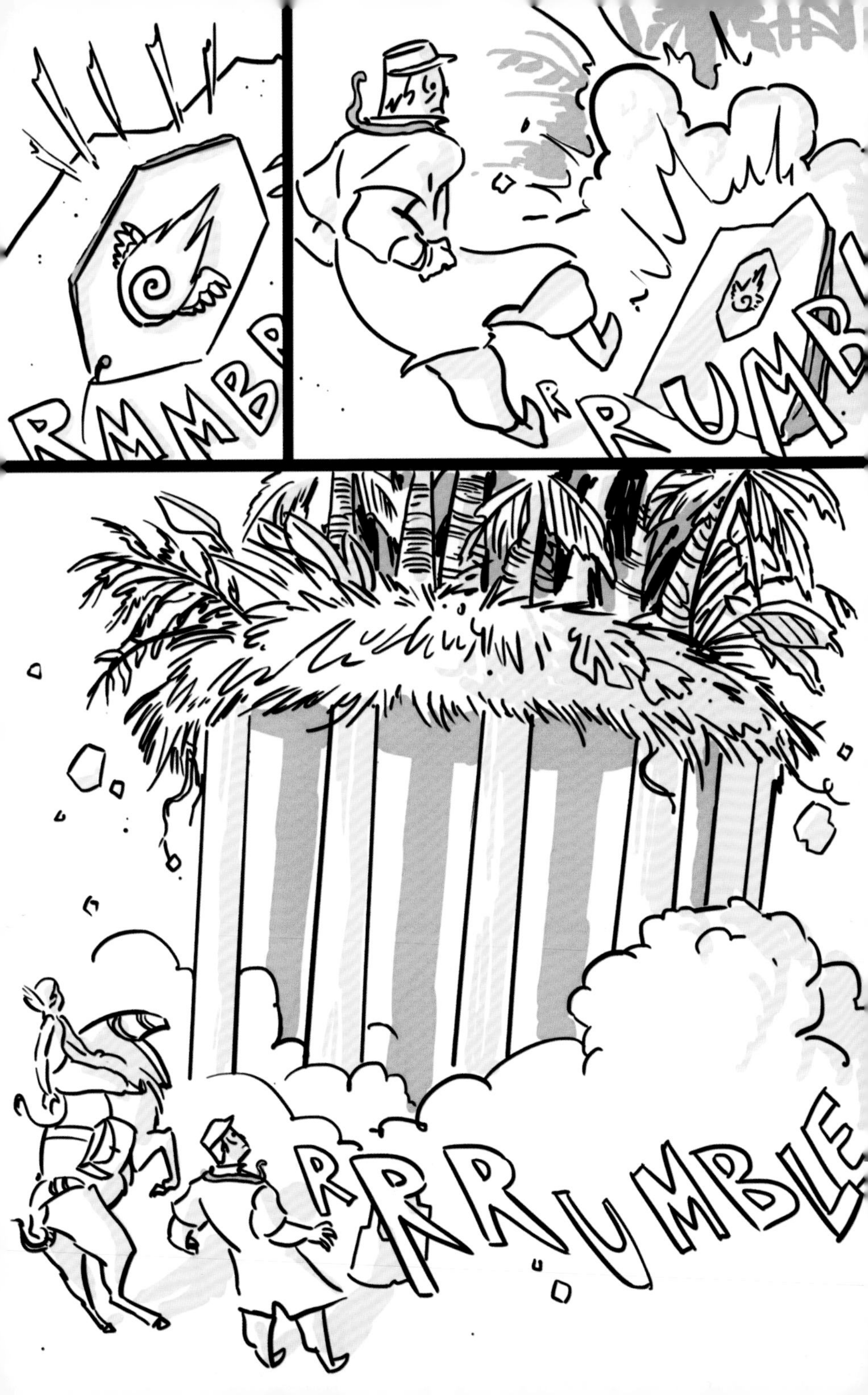
RMMB
RRUMB
RRRUMBLE

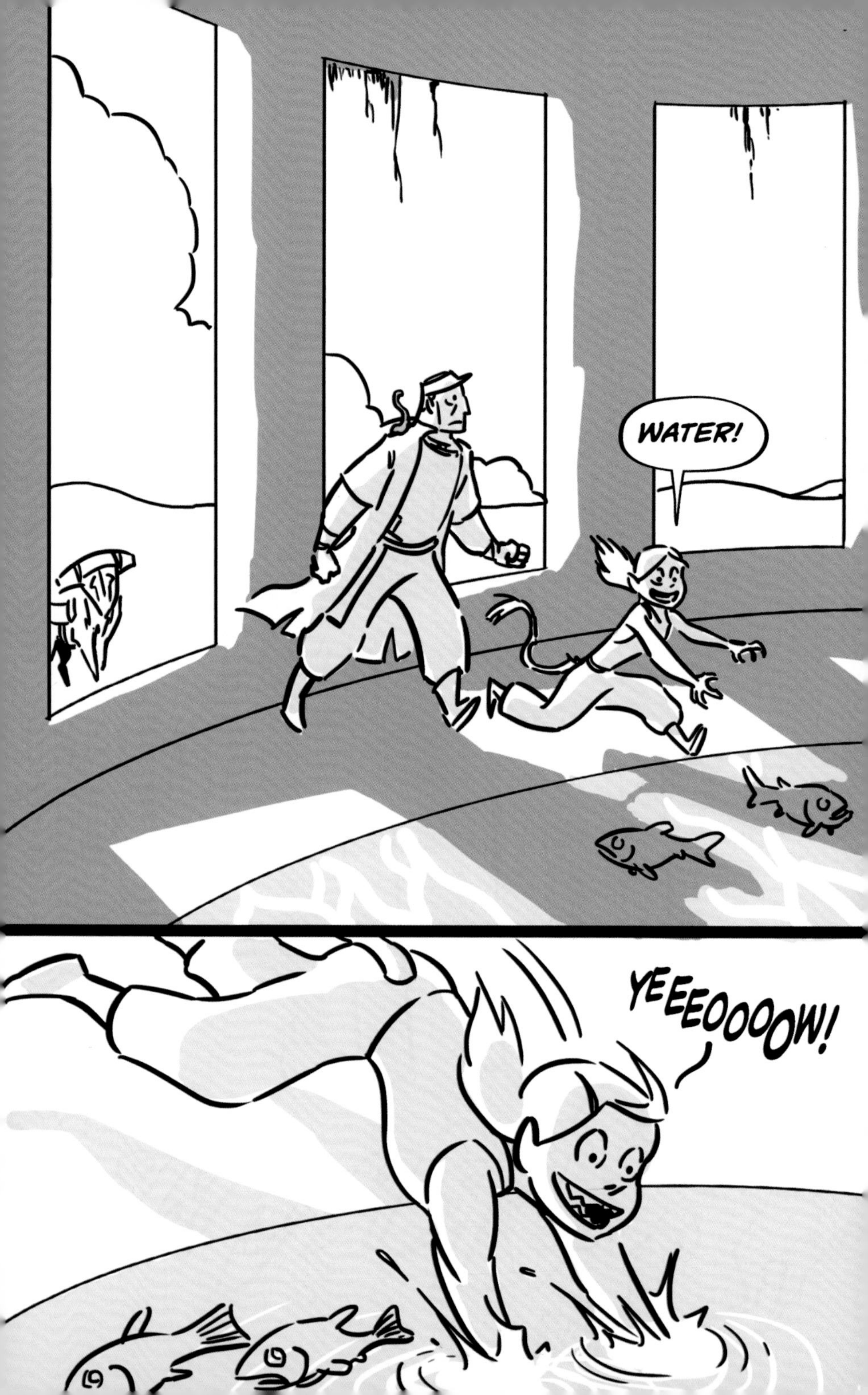
WATER!
YEEEOOOOW!

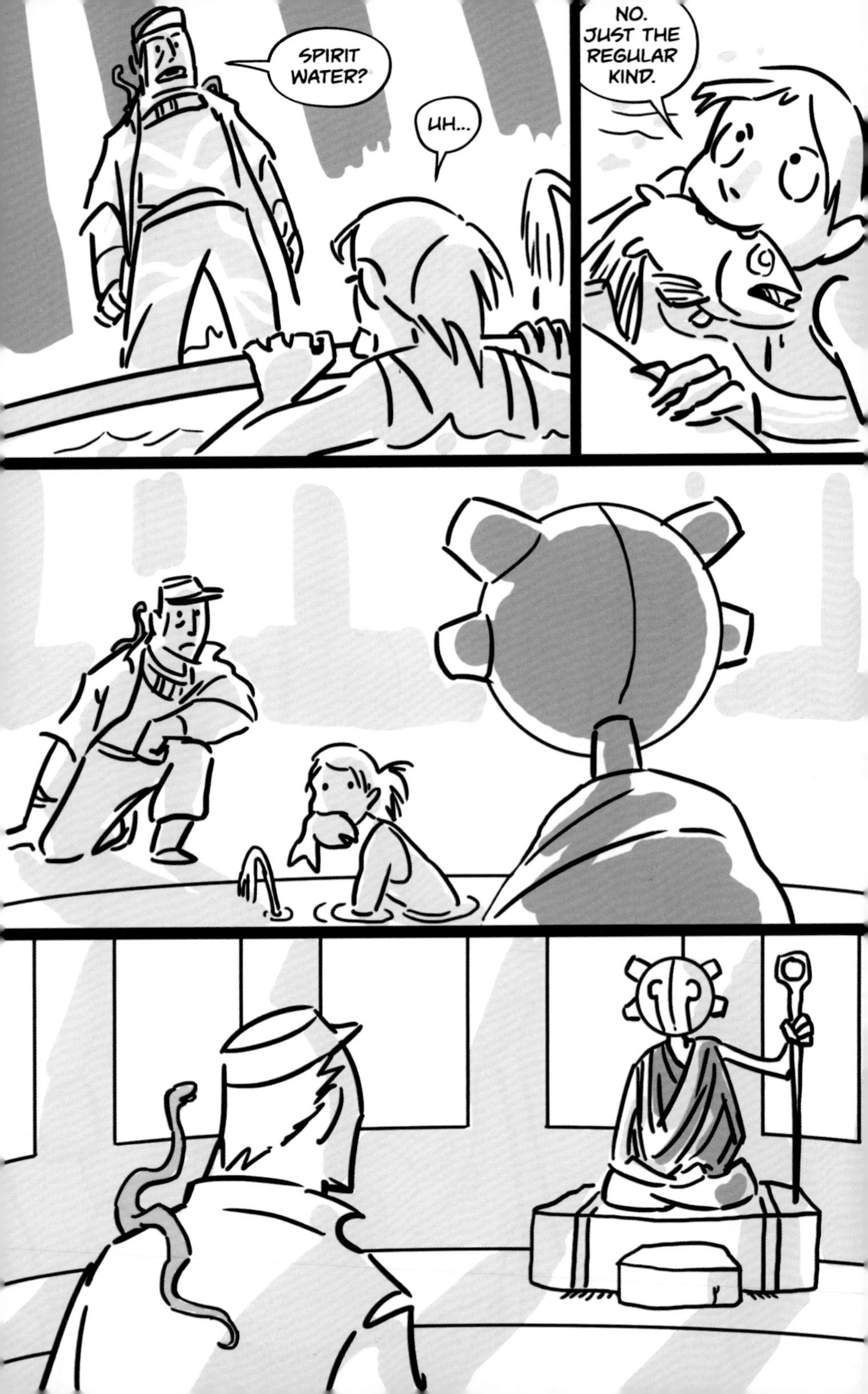
SPIRIT WATER?
UH...
NO. JUST THE REGULAR KIND.

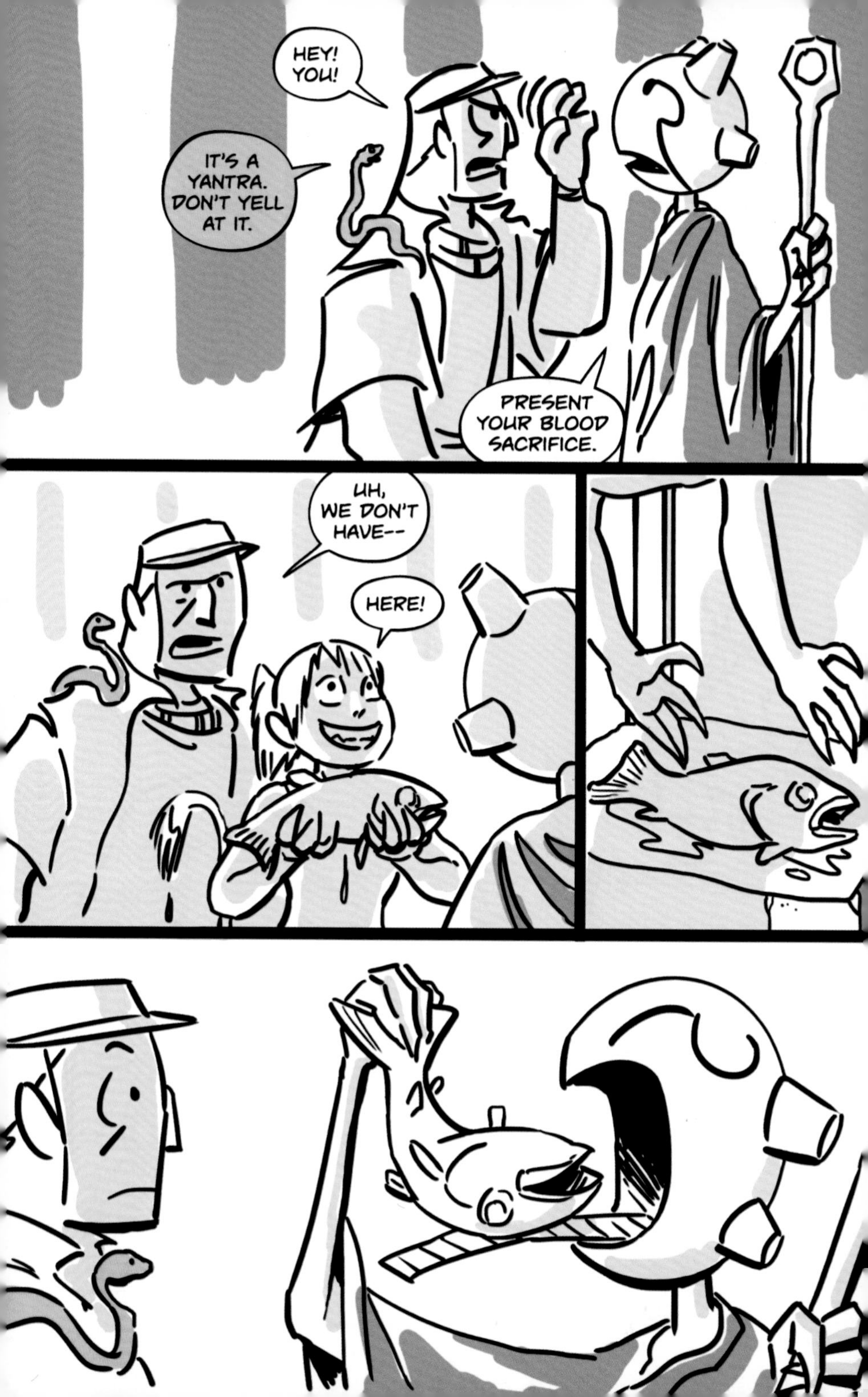
HEY! YOU!
IT'S A YANTRA. DON'T YELL AT IT.
PRESENT YOUR BLOOD SACRIFICE.
UH, WE DON'T HAVE--
HERE!

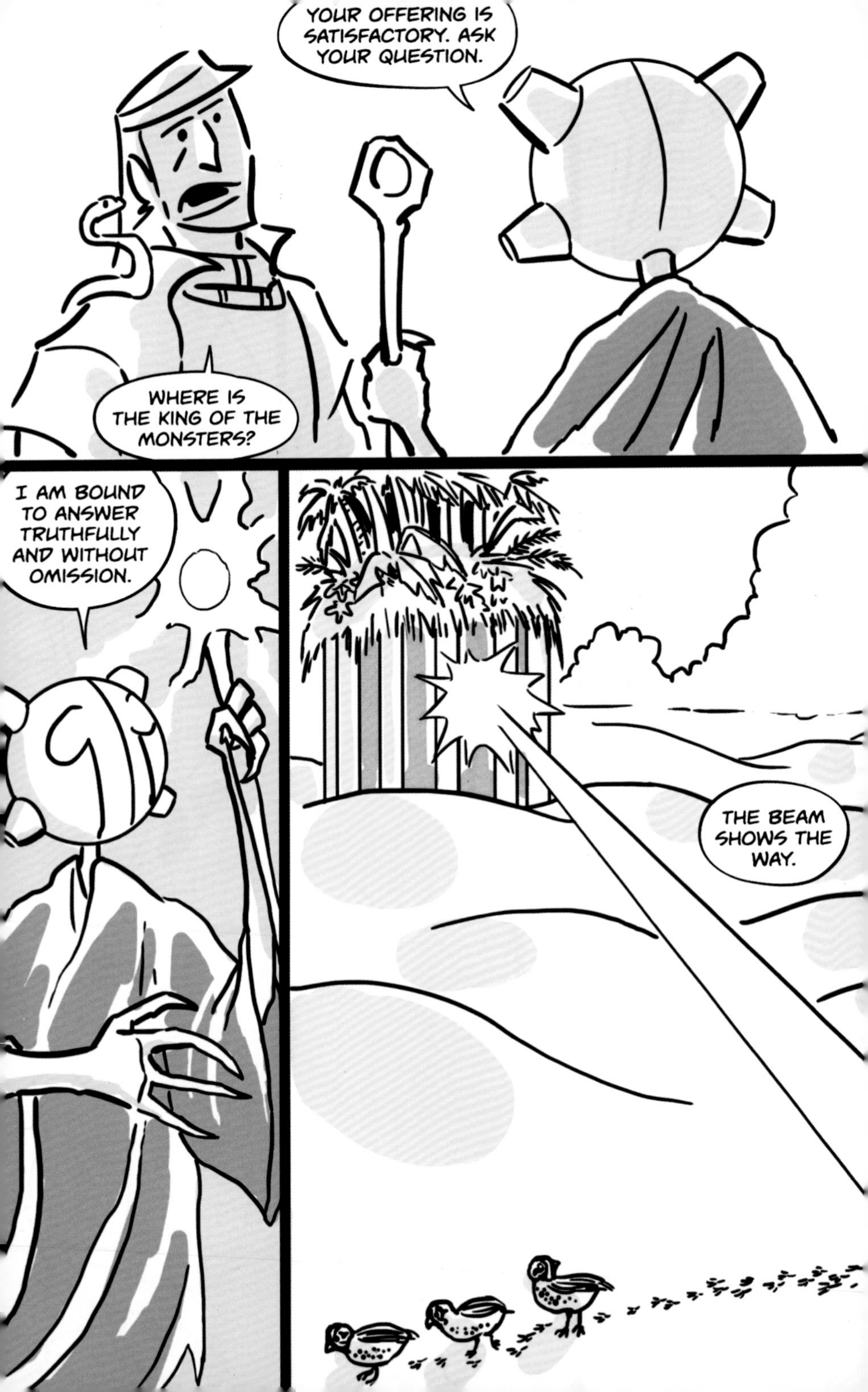
YOUR OFFERING IS SATISFACTORY. ASK YOUR QUESTION.
WHERE IS THE KING OF THE MONSTERS?
I AM BOUND TO ANSWER TRUTHFULLY AND WITHOUT OMISSION.
THE BEAM SHOWS THE WAY.

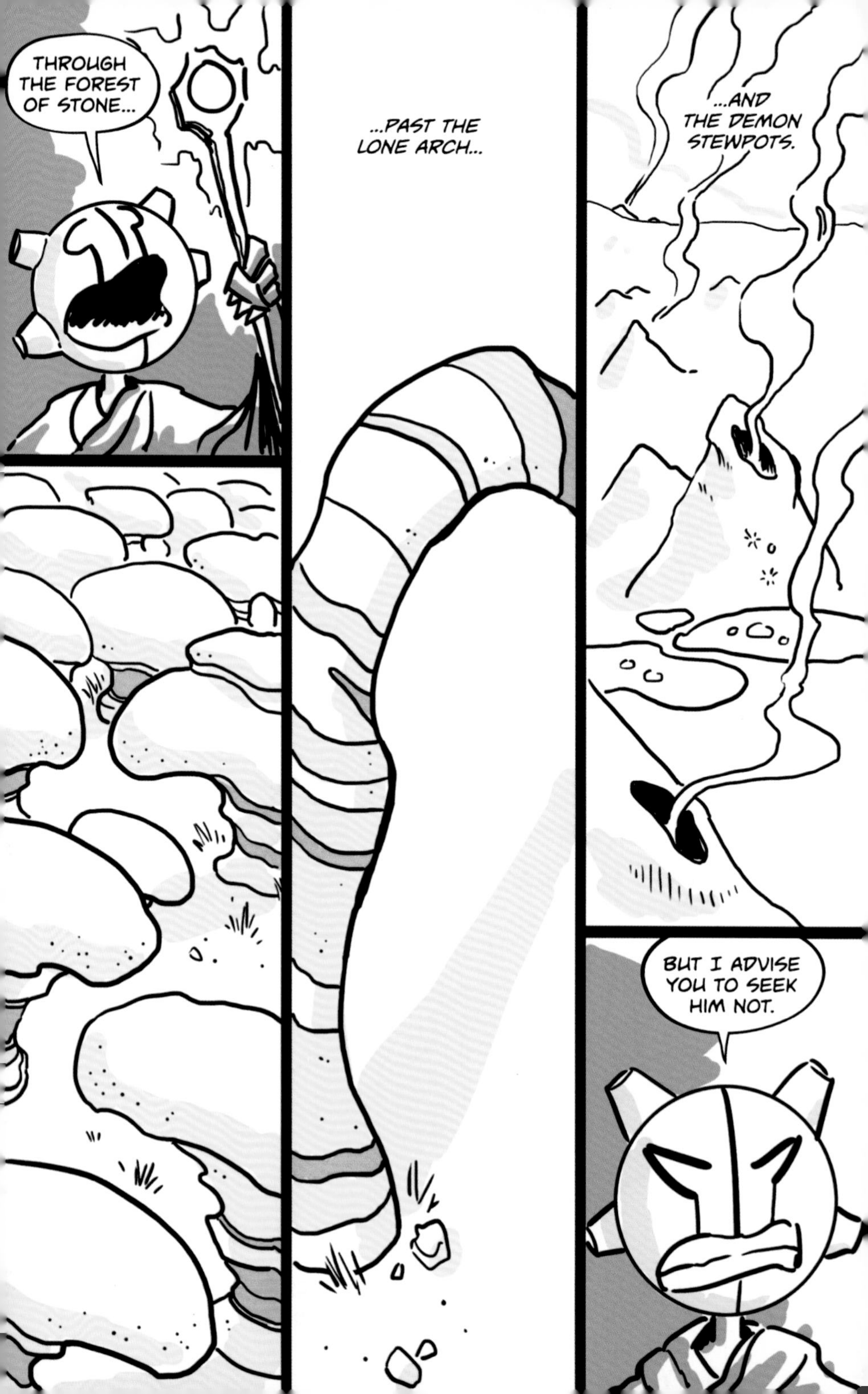
THROUGH THE FOREST OF STONE...
...PAST THE LONE ARCH...
...AND THE DEMON STEWPOTS.
BUT I ADVISE YOU TO SEEK HIM NOT.

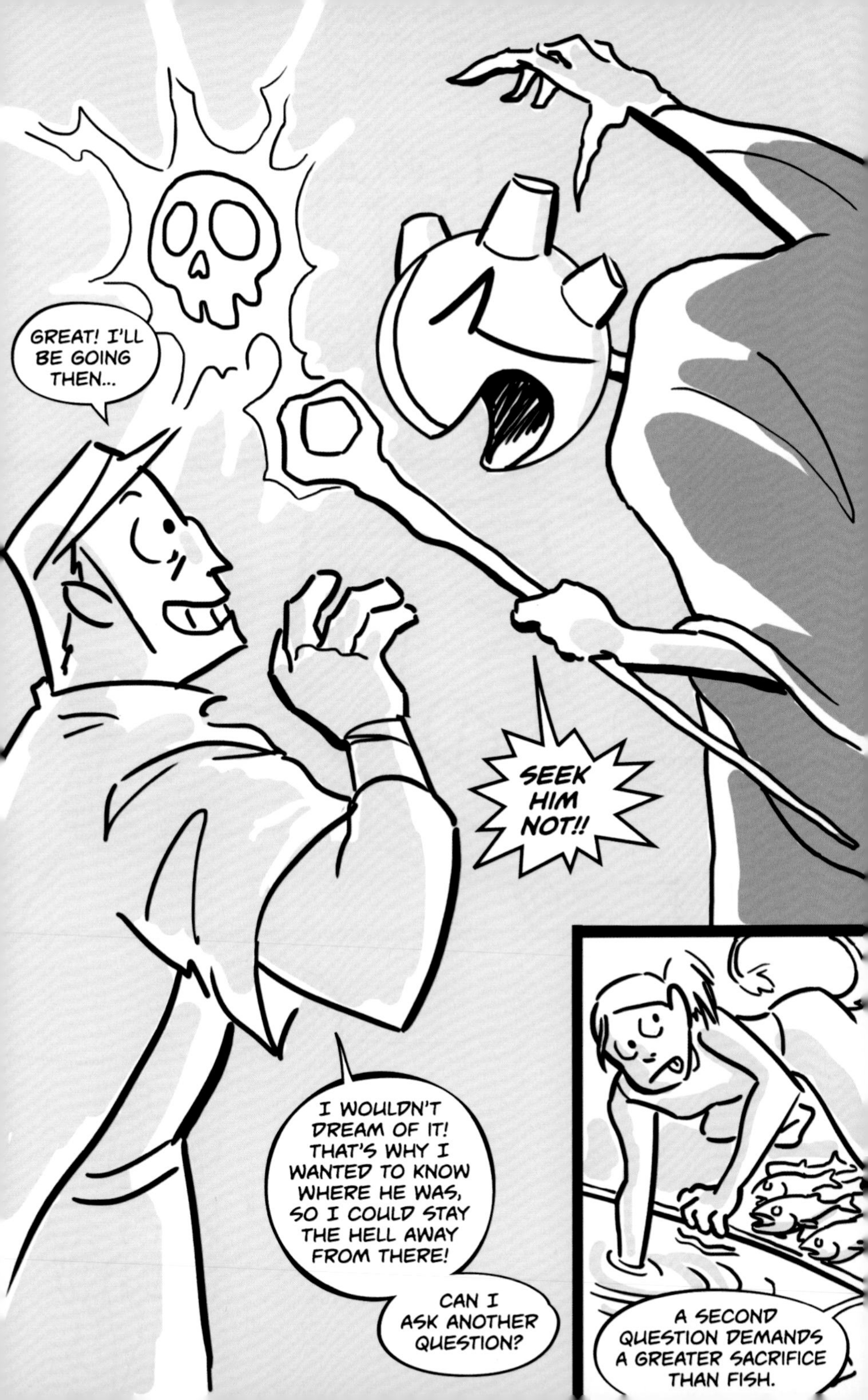
GREAT! I'LL BE GOING THEN...
SEEK HIM NOT!!
I WOULDN'T DREAM OF IT! THAT'S WHY I WANTED TO KNOW WHERE HE WAS, SO I COULD STAY THE HELL AWAY FROM THERE!
CAN I ASK ANOTHER QUESTION?
A SECOND QUESTION DEMANDS A GREATER SACRIFICE THAN FISH.

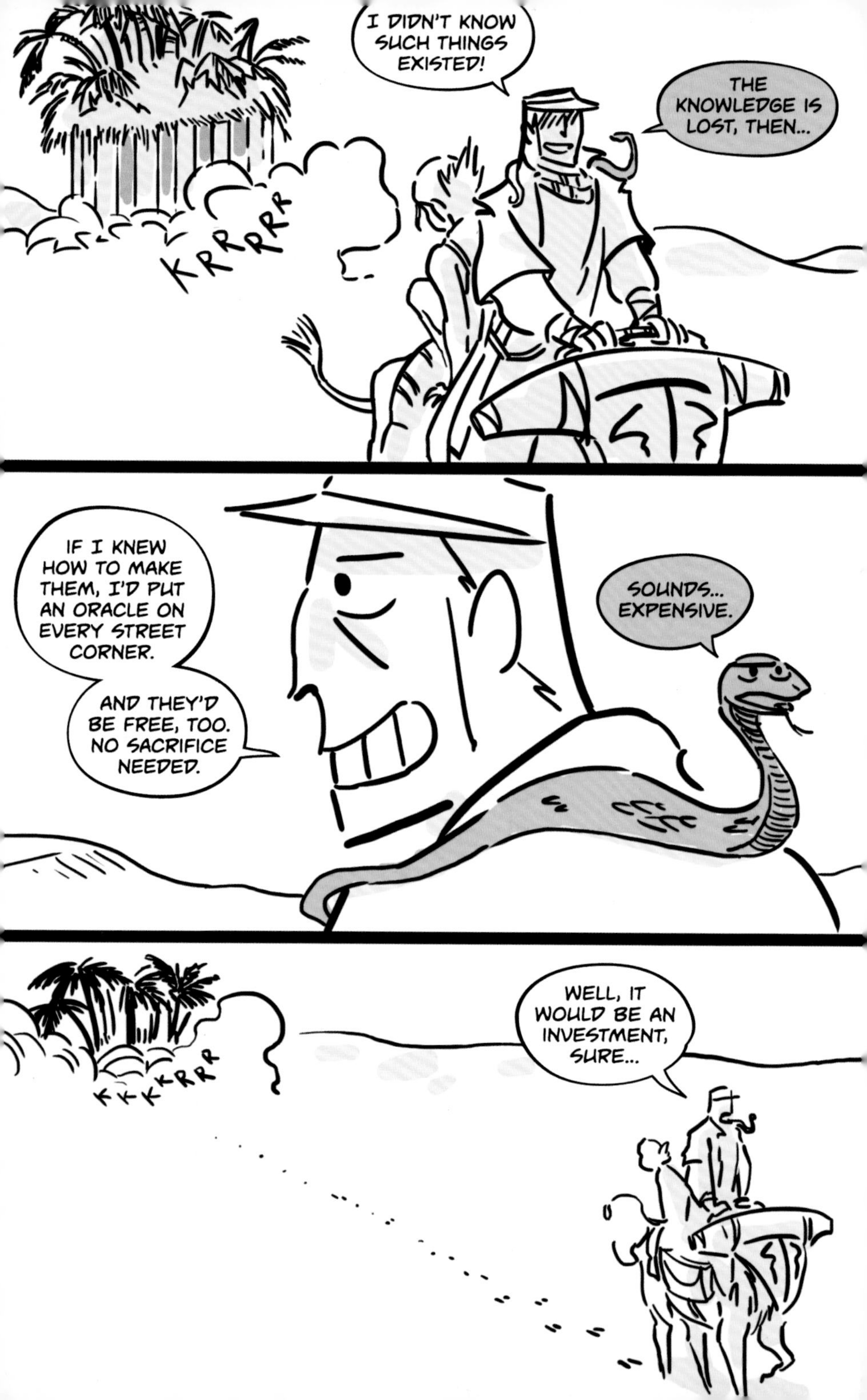
I DIDN'T KNOW SUCH THINGS EXISTED!
THE KNOWLEDGE IS LOST, THEN...
KRRRRR
IF I KNEW HOW TO MAKE THEM, I'D PUT AN ORACLE ON EVERY STREET CORNER.
AND THEY'D BE FREE, TOO. NO SACRIFICE NEEDED.
SOUNDS... EXPENSIVE.
KKKKRRR
WELL, IT WOULD BE AN INVESTMENT, SURE...

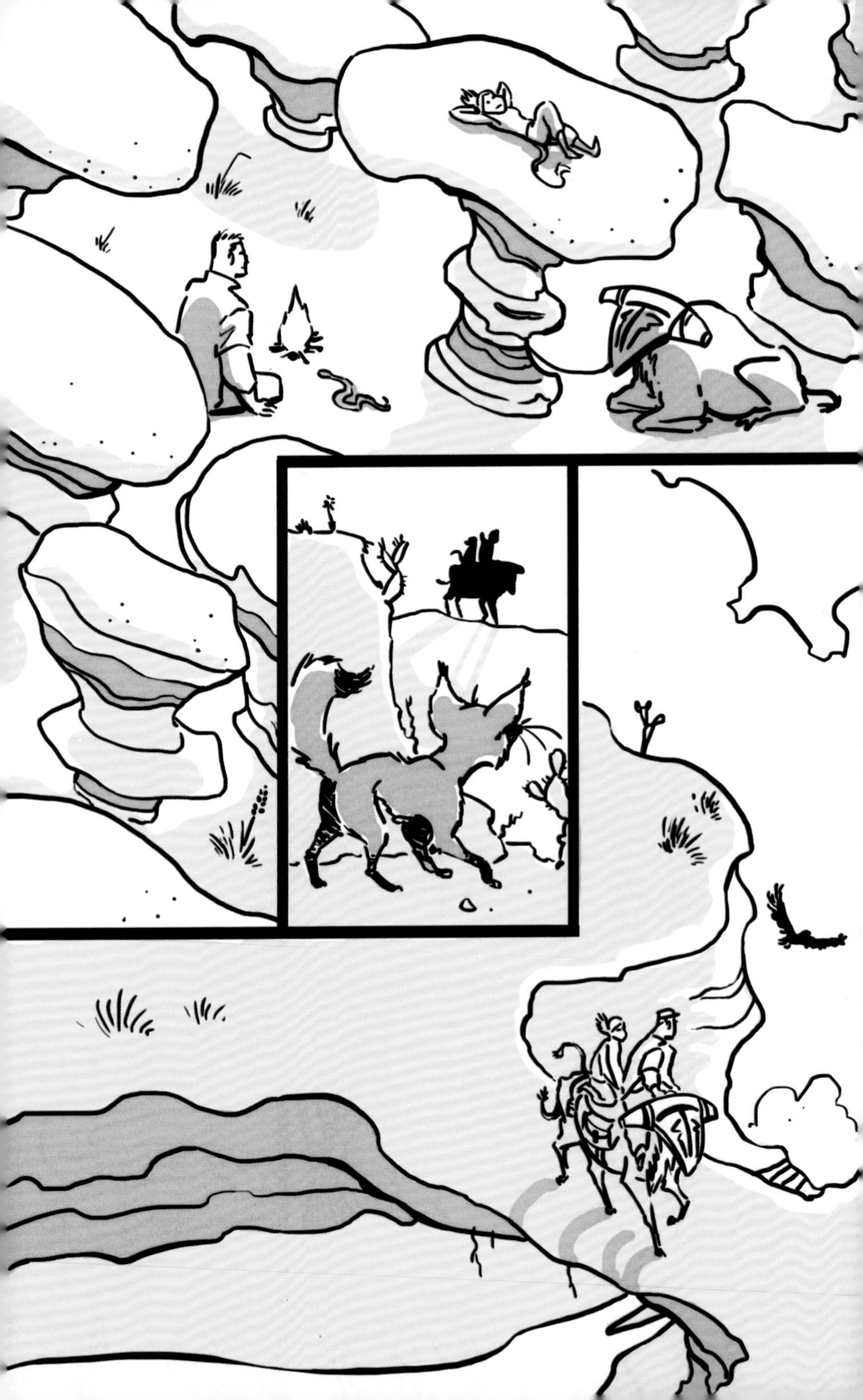

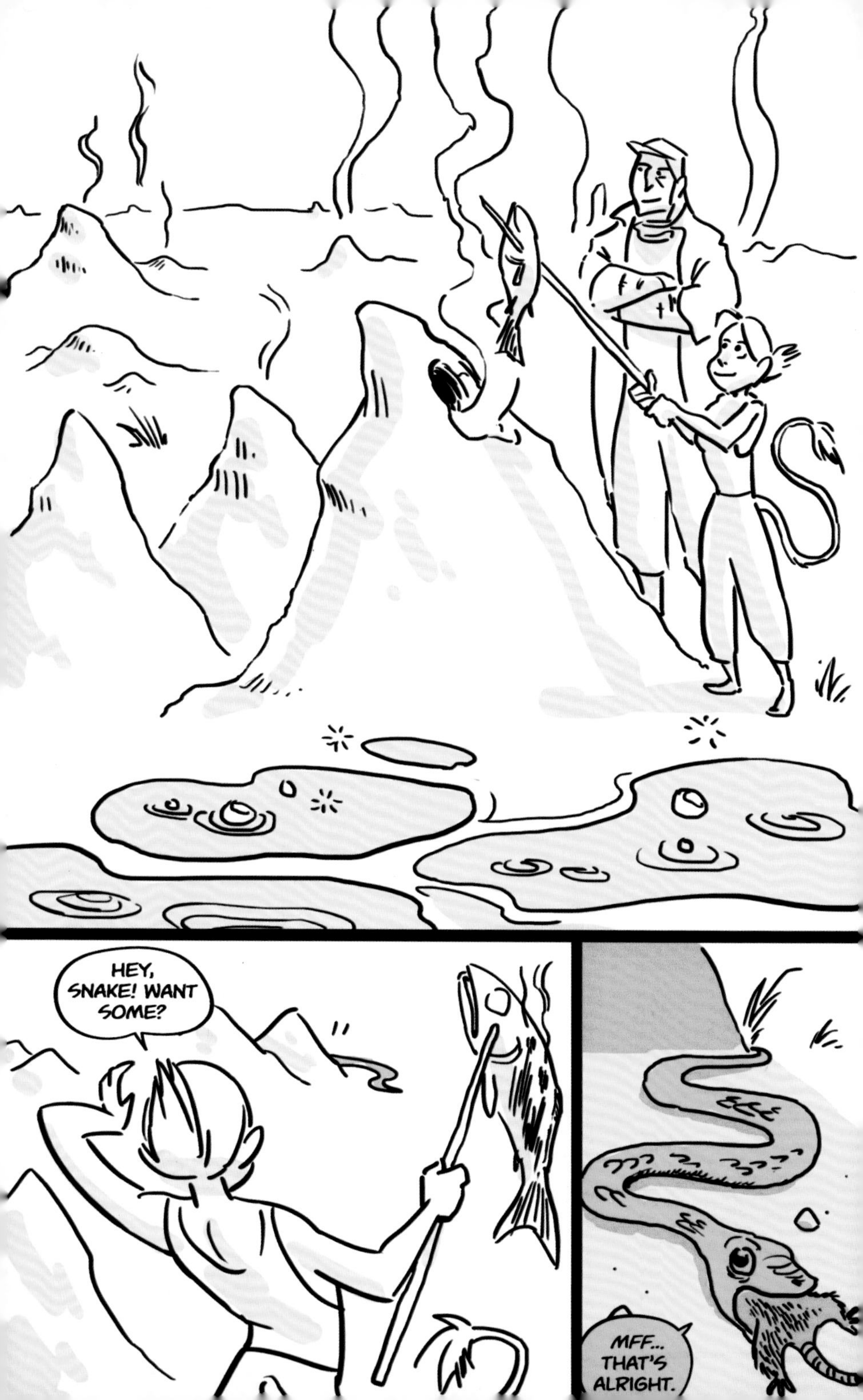
HEY, SNAKE! WANT SOME?
MFF... THAT'S ALRIGHT.

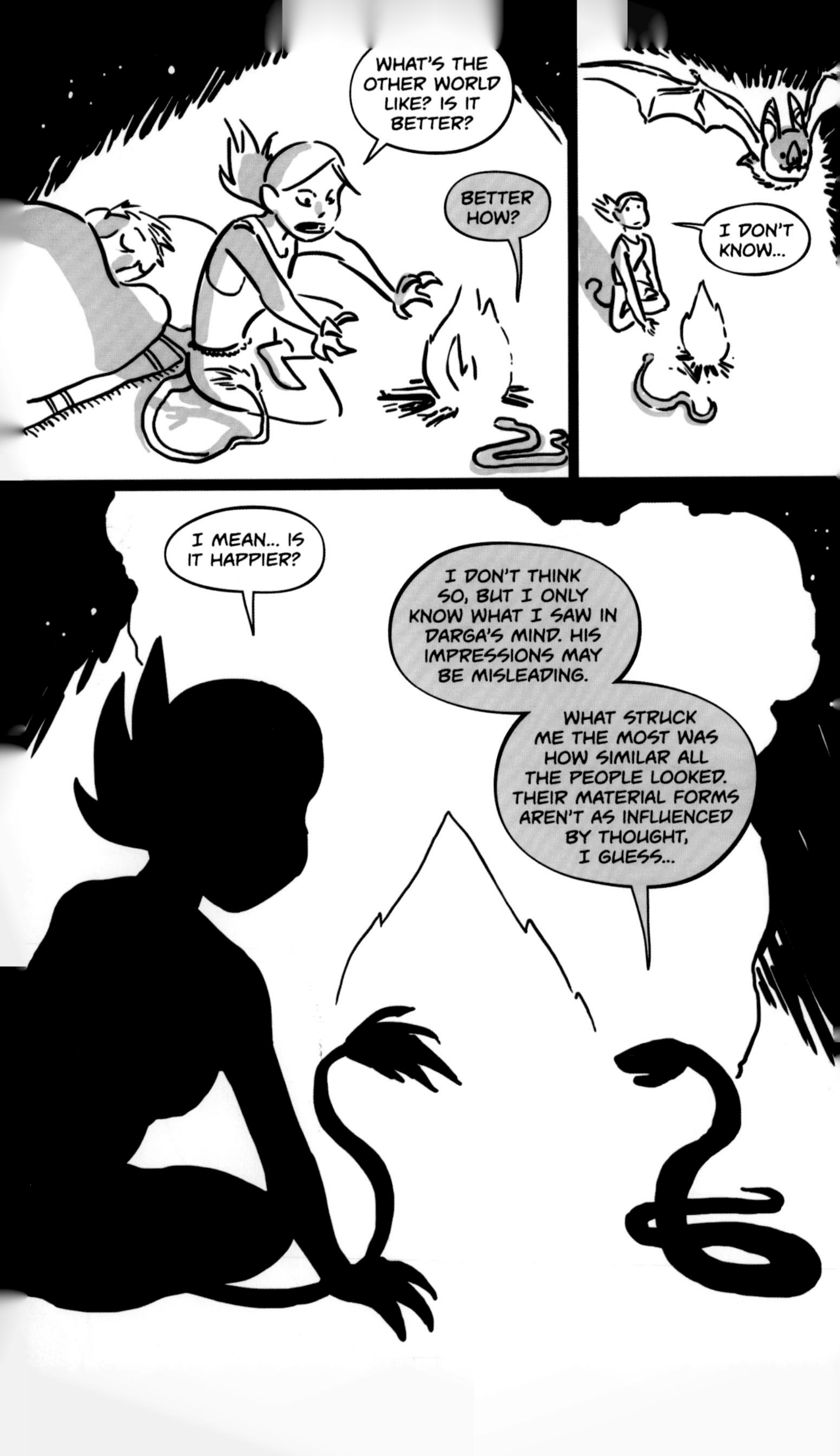
WHAT'S THE OTHER WORLD LIKE? IS IT BETTER?
BETTER HOW?
I DON'T KNOW...
I MEAN... IS IT HAPPIER?
I DON'T THINK SO, BUT I ONLY KNOW WHAT I SAW IN DARGA'S MIND. HIS IMPRESSIONS MAY BE MISLEADING.
WHAT STRUCK ME THE MOST WAS HOW SIMILAR ALL THE PEOPLE LOOKED. THEIR MATERIAL FORMS AREN'T AS INFLUENCED BY THOUGHT, I GUESS...

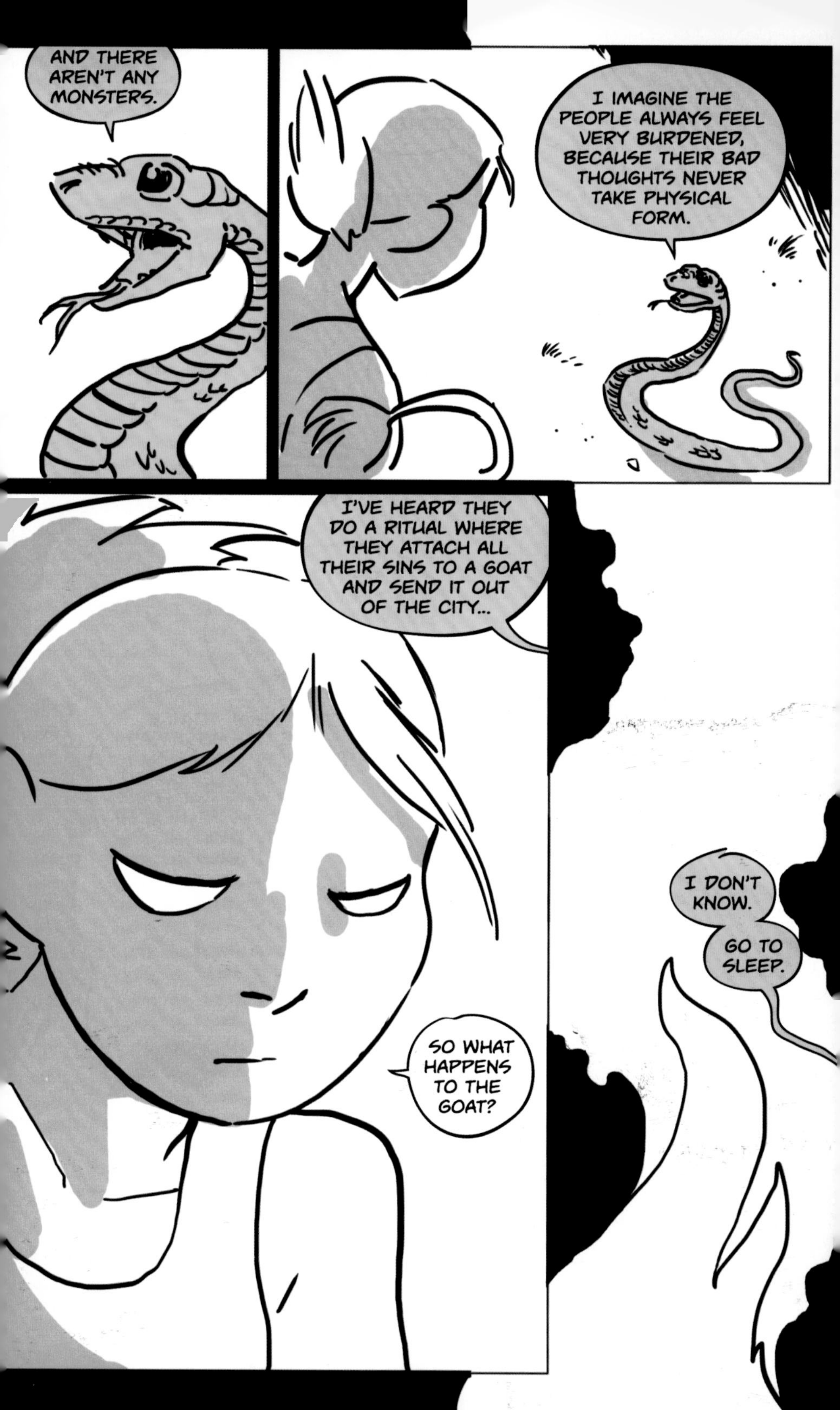
AND THERE AREN'T ANY MONSTERS.
I IMAGINE THE PEOPLE ALWAYS FEEL VERY BURDENED, BECAUSE THEIR BAD THOUGHTS NEVER TAKE PHYSICAL FORM.
I'VE HEARD THEY DO A RITUAL WHERE THEY ATTACH ALL THEIR SINS TO A GOAT AND SEND IT OUT OF THE CITY...
SO WHAT HAPPENS TO THE GOAT?
I DON'T KNOW.
GO TO SLEEP.

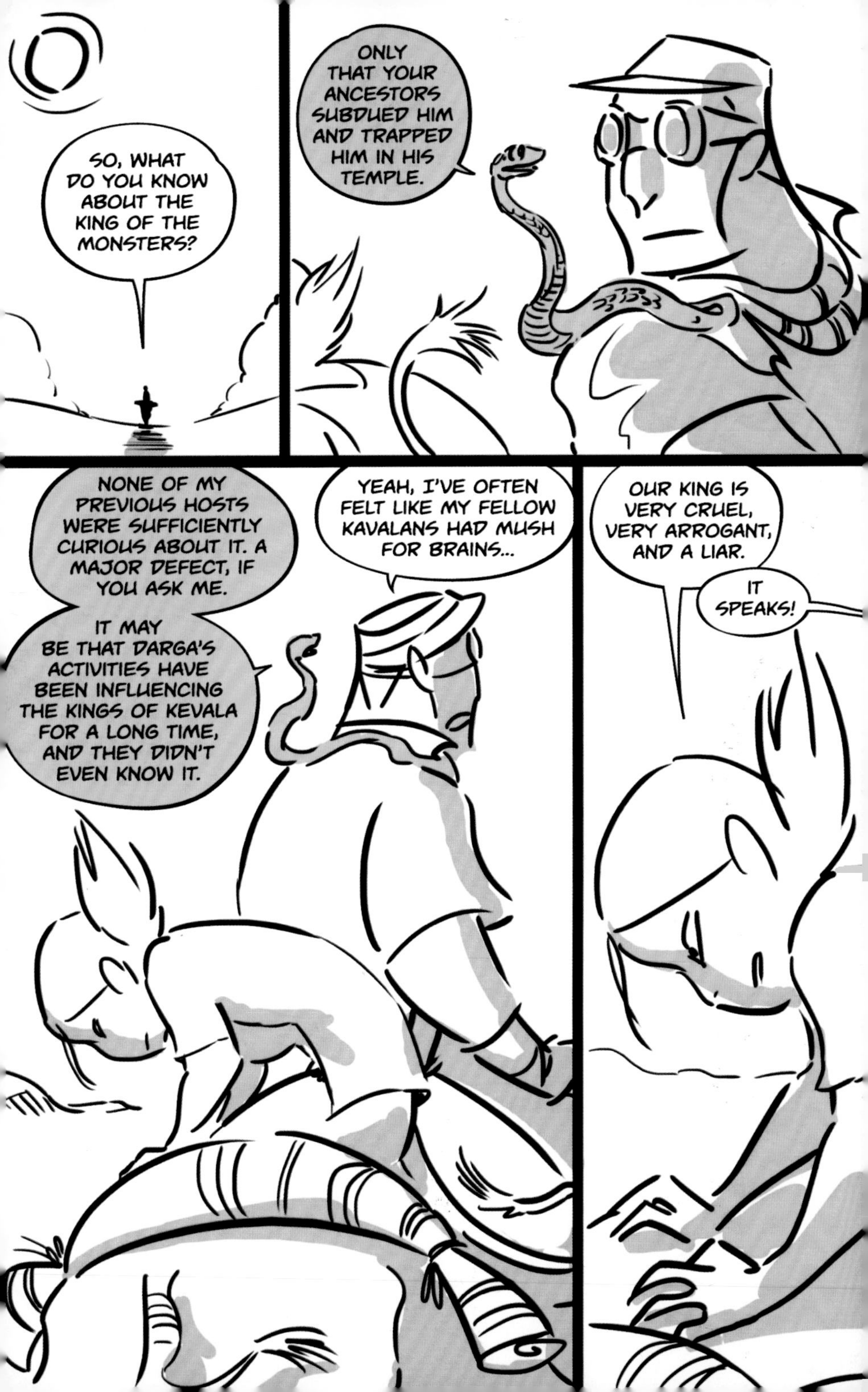
SO, WHAT DO YOU KNOW ABOUT THE KING OF THE MONSTERS?
ONLY THAT YOUR ANCESTORS SUBDUED HIM AND TRAPPED HIM IN HIS TEMPLE.
NONE OF MY PREVIOUS HOSTS WERE SUFFICIENTLY CURIOUS ABOUT IT. A MAJOR DEFECT, IF YOU ASK ME.
IT MAY BE THAT DARGA'S ACTIVITIES HAVE BEEN INFLUENCING THE KINGS OF KEVALA FOR A LONG TIME, AND THEY DIDN'T EVEN KNOW IT.
YEAH, I'VE OFTEN FELT LIKE MY FELLOW KAVALANS HAD MUSH FOR BRAINS...
OUR KING IS VERY CRUEL, VERY ARROGANT, AND A LIAR.
IT SPEAKS!

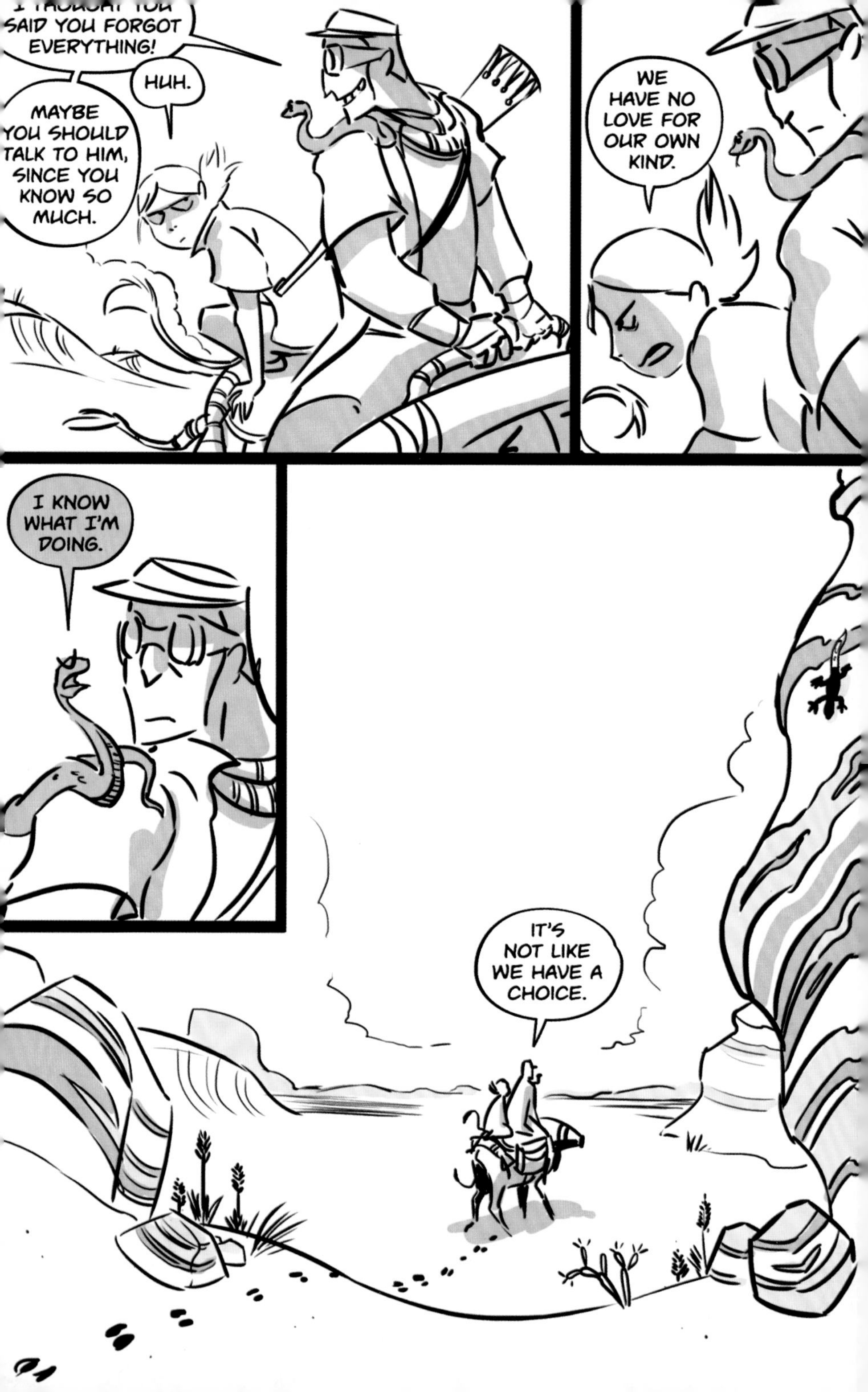
SAID YOU FORGOT EVERYTHING!
HUH.
MAYBE YOU SHOULD TALK TO HIM, SINCE YOU KNOW SO MUCH.
WE HAVE NO LOVE FOR OUR OWN KIND.
I KNOW WHAT I'M DOING.
IT'S NOT LIKE WE HAVE A CHOICE.

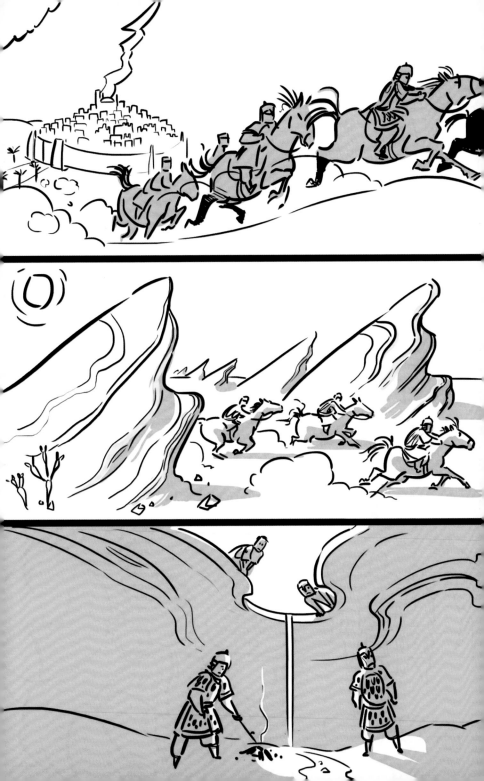

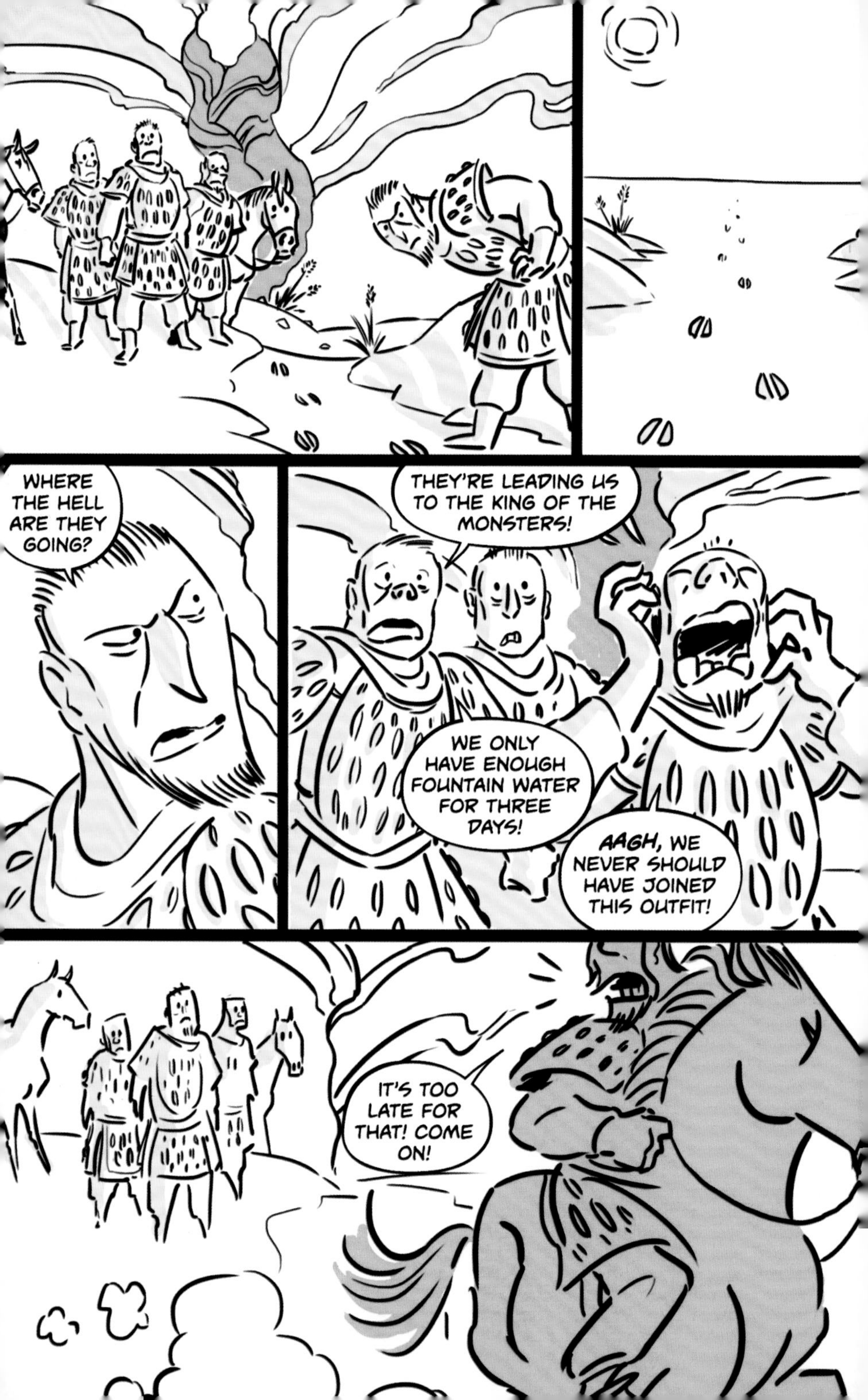
WHERE THE HELL ARE THEY GOING?
THEY'RE LEADING US TO THE KING OF THE MONSTERS!
WE ONLY HAVE ENOUGH FOUNTAIN WATER FOR THREE DAYS!
AAGH, WE NEVER SHOULD HAVE JOINED THIS OUTFIT!
IT'S TOO LATE FOR THAT! COME ON!

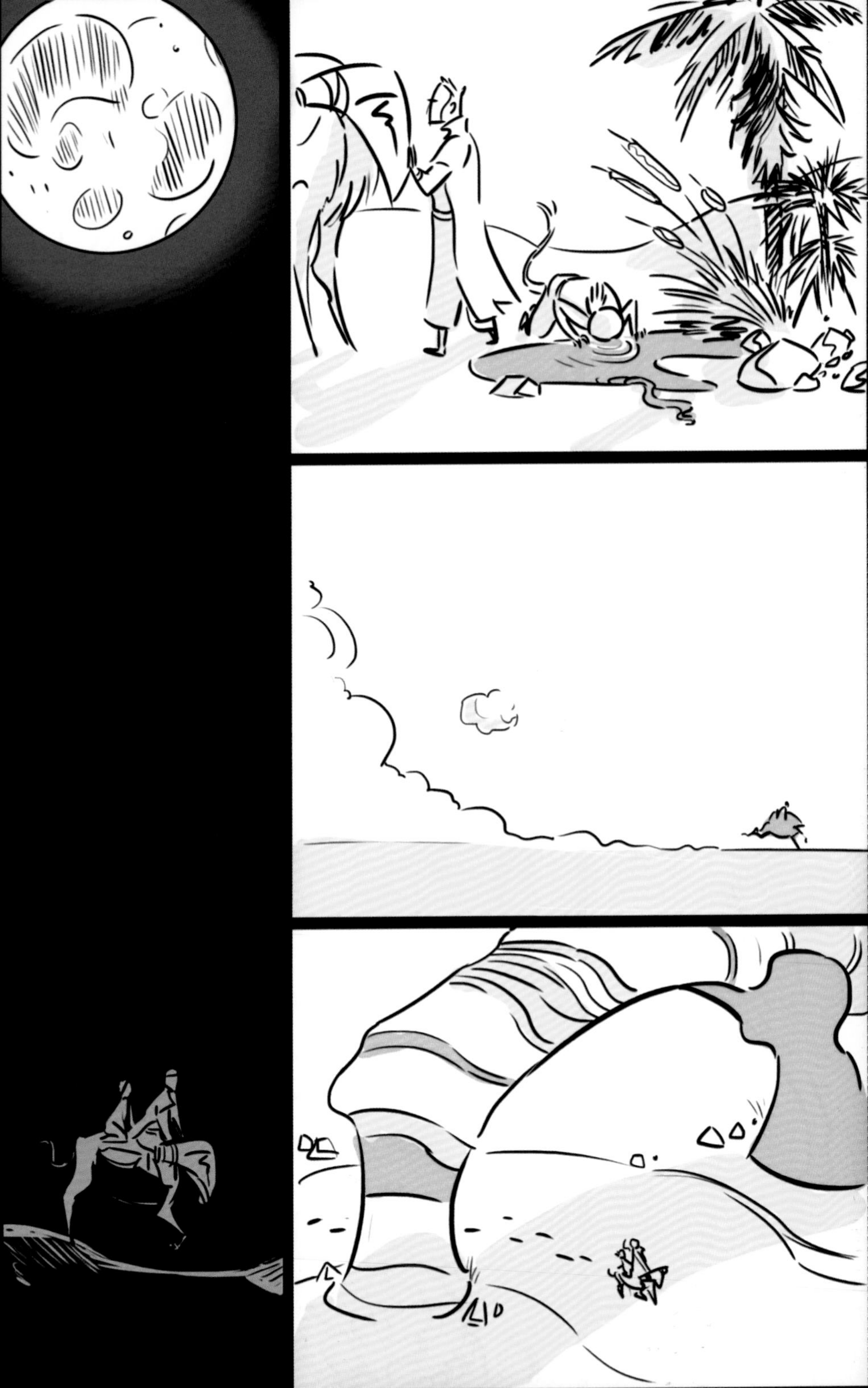

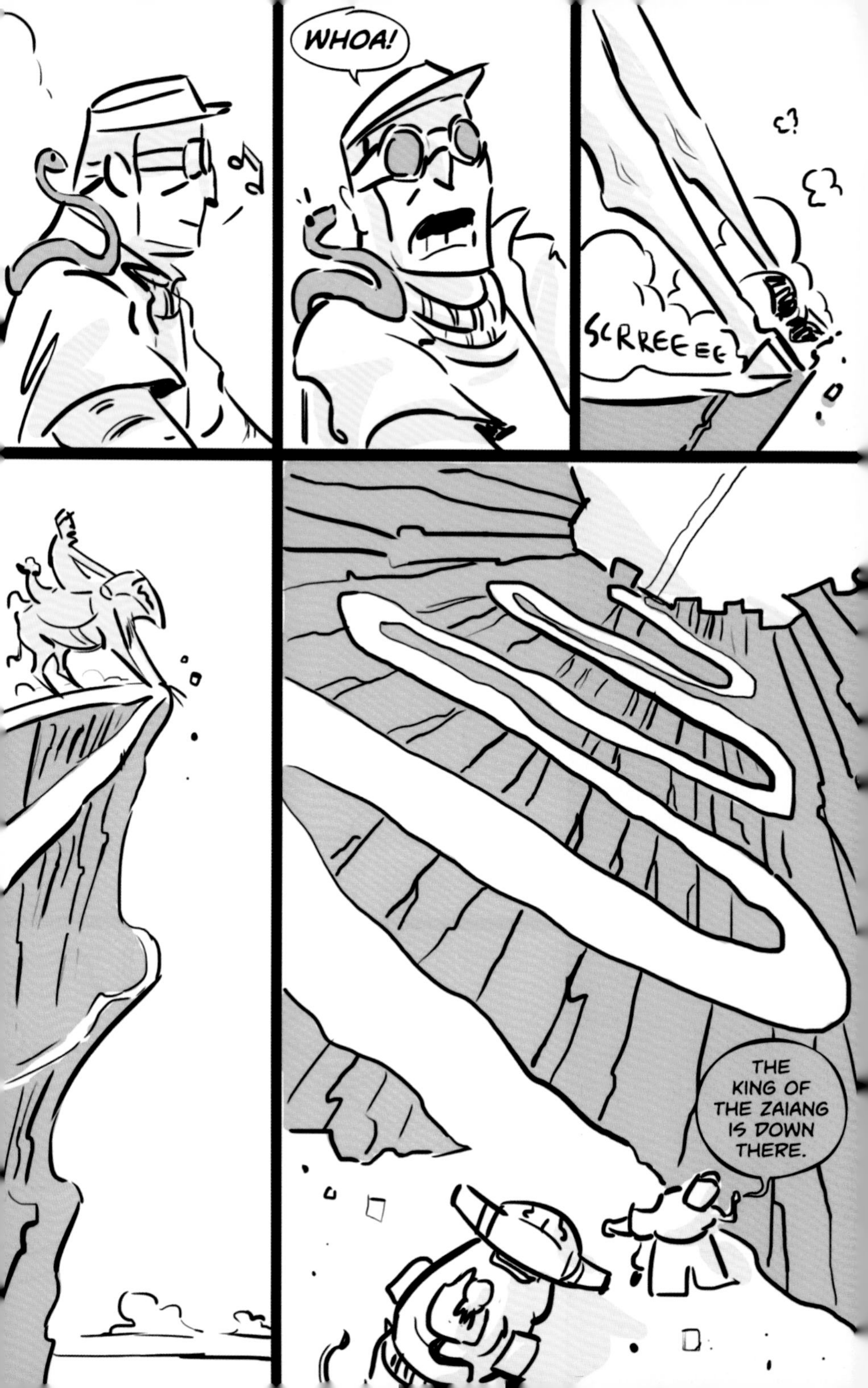
WHOA!
SCRREEEEE
THE KING OF THE ZAIANG IS DOWN THERE.

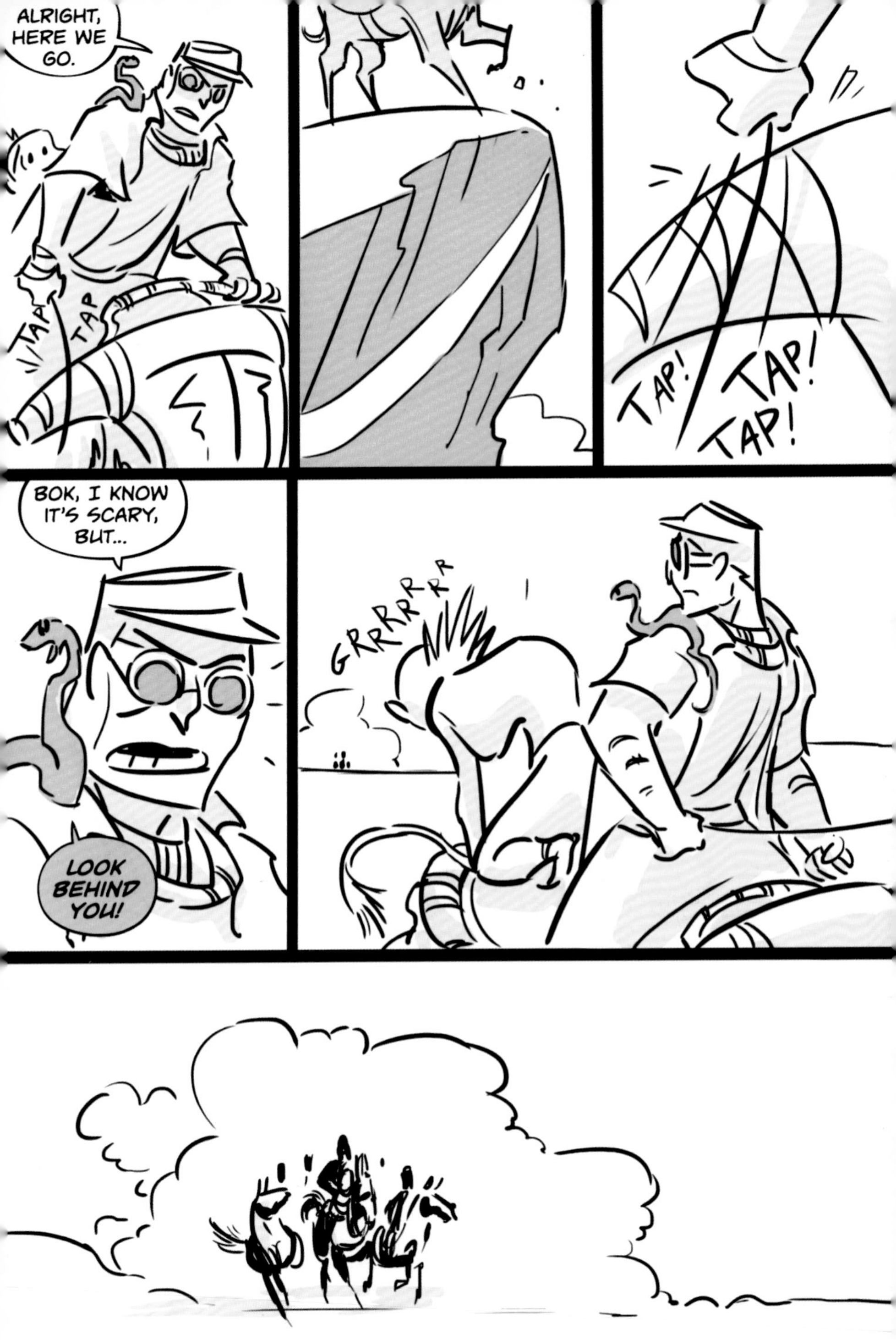
ALRIGHT, HERE WE GO.
TAP TAP
TAP! TAP! TAP!
BOK, I KNOW IT'S SCARY, BUT...
LOOK BEHIND YOU!
GRRRRRRR

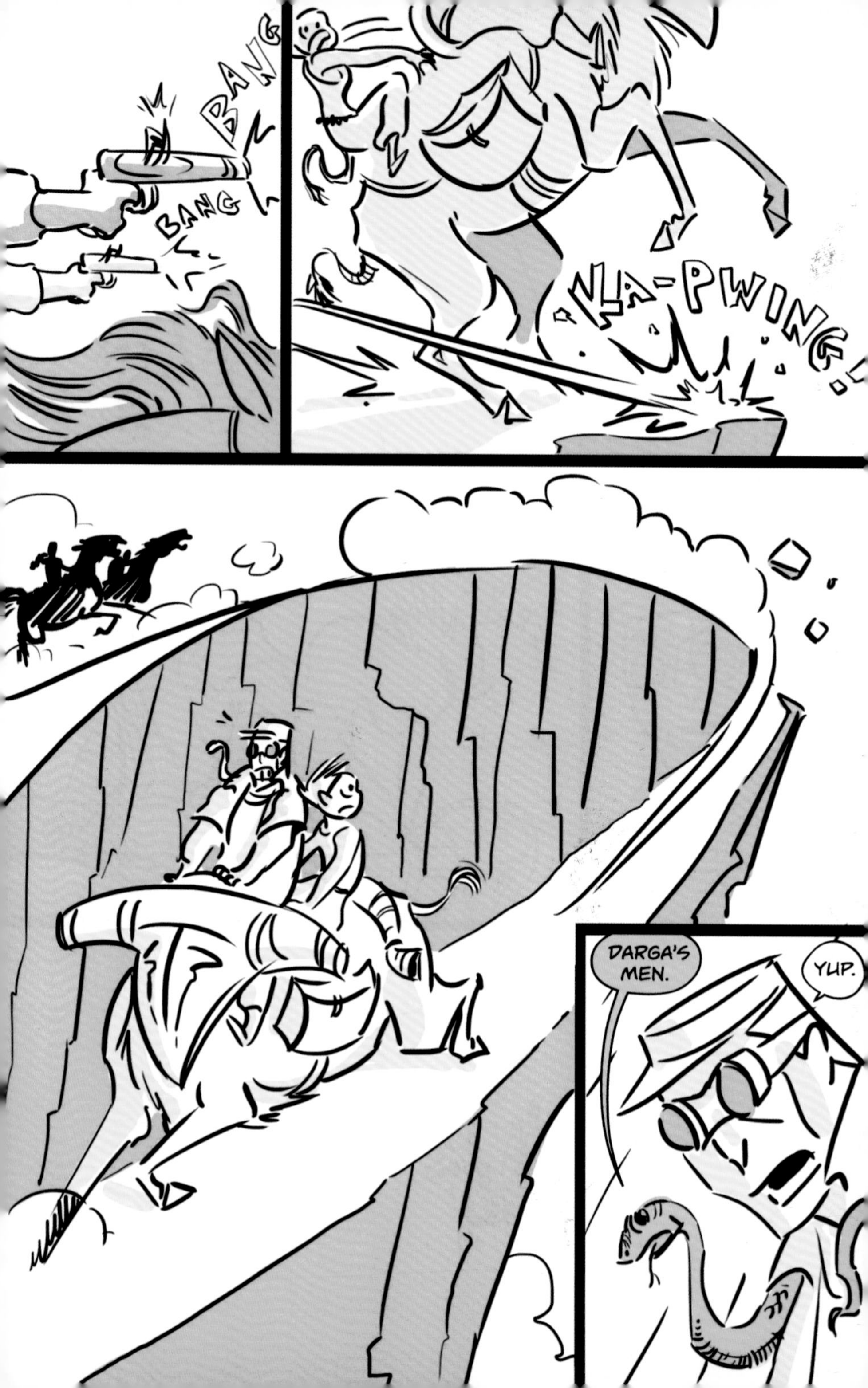
BANG
BANG
KLA-PWING!
DARGA'S MEN.
YUP.

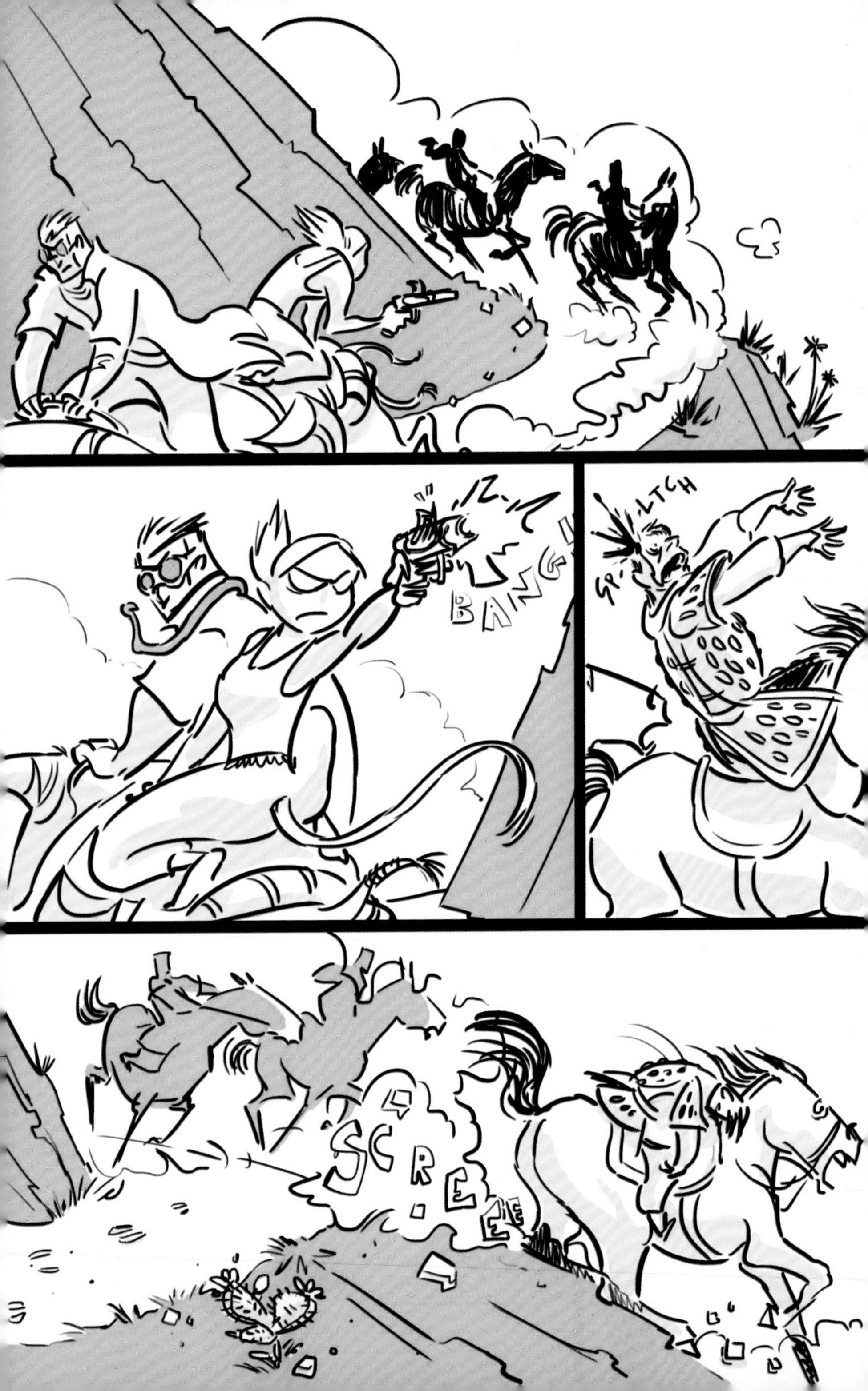
BANG!
SP-LTCH
SCREEEE

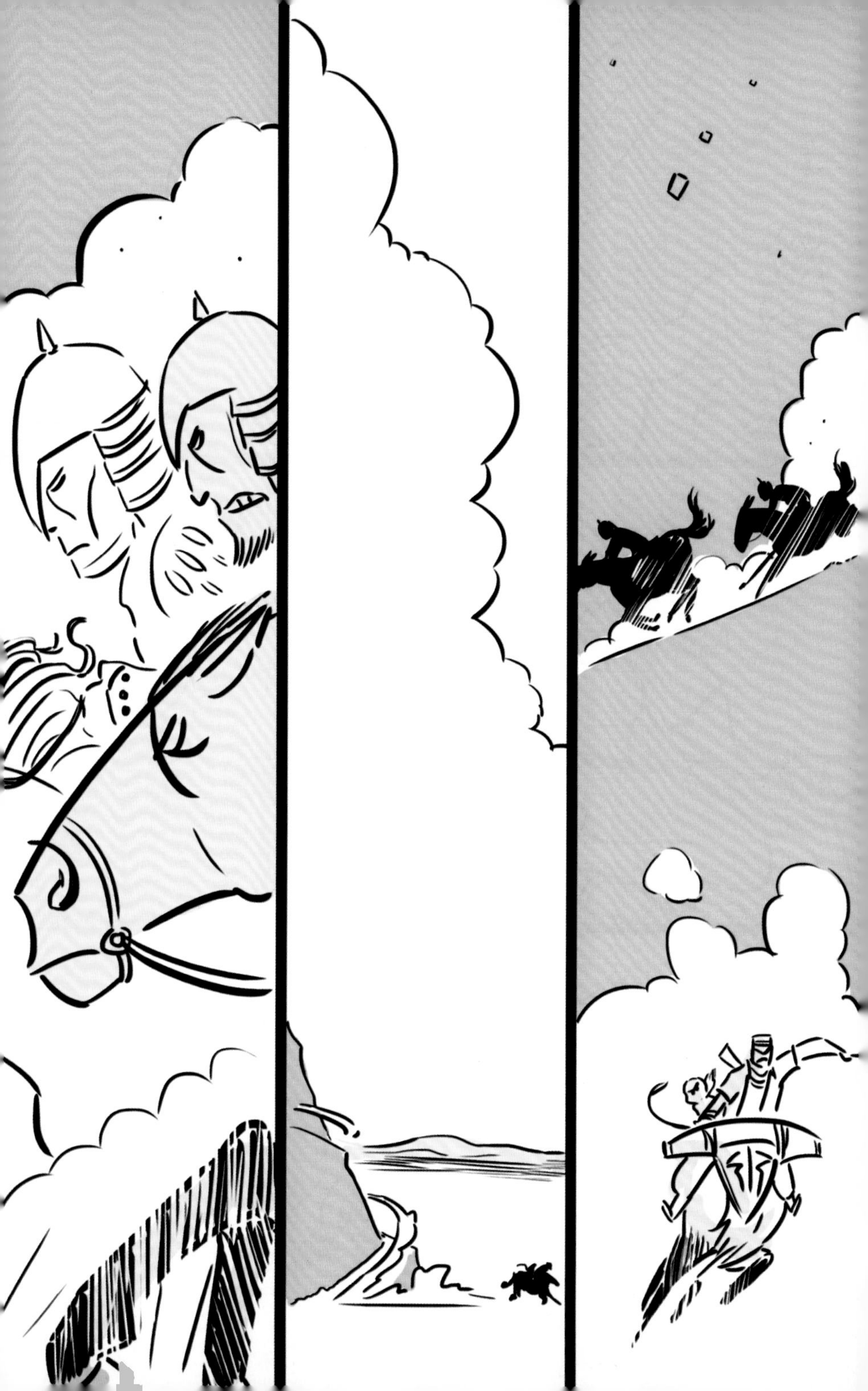

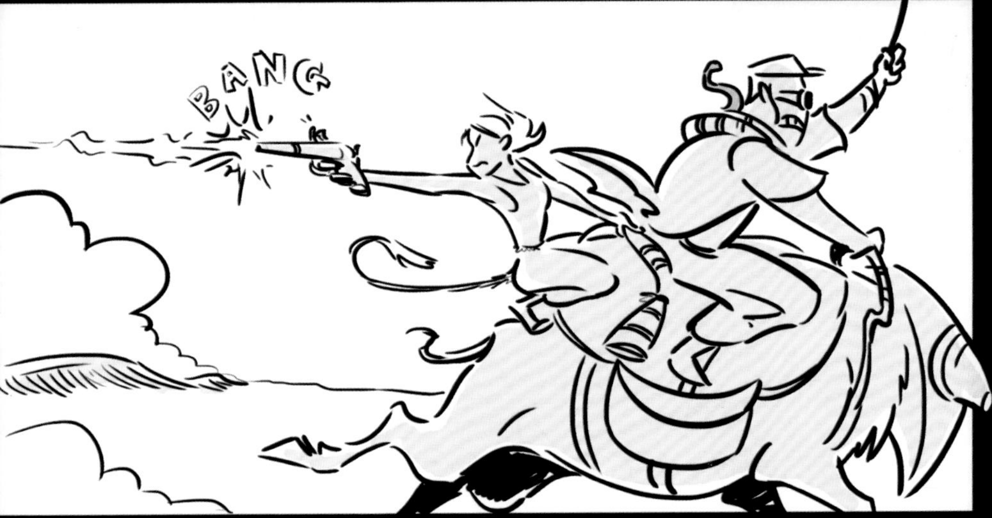
BANG
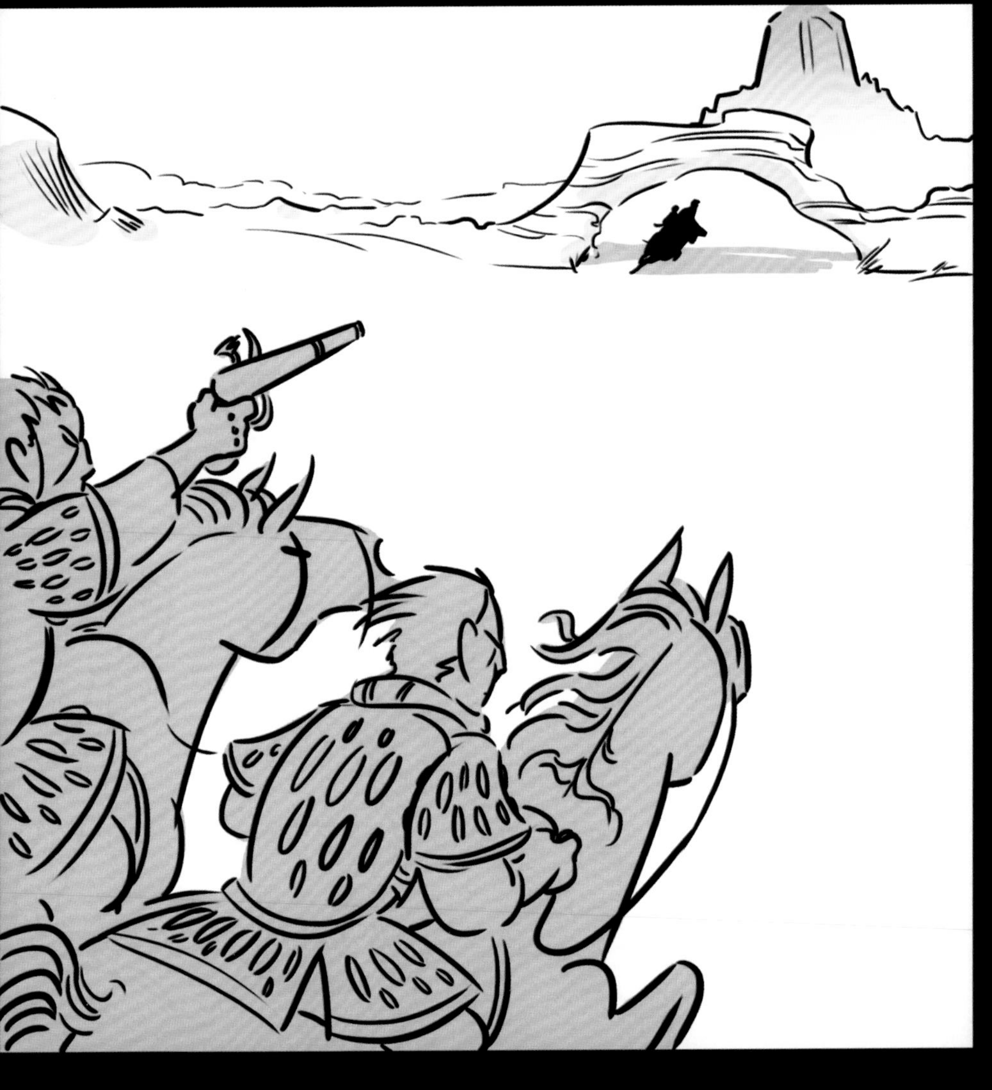

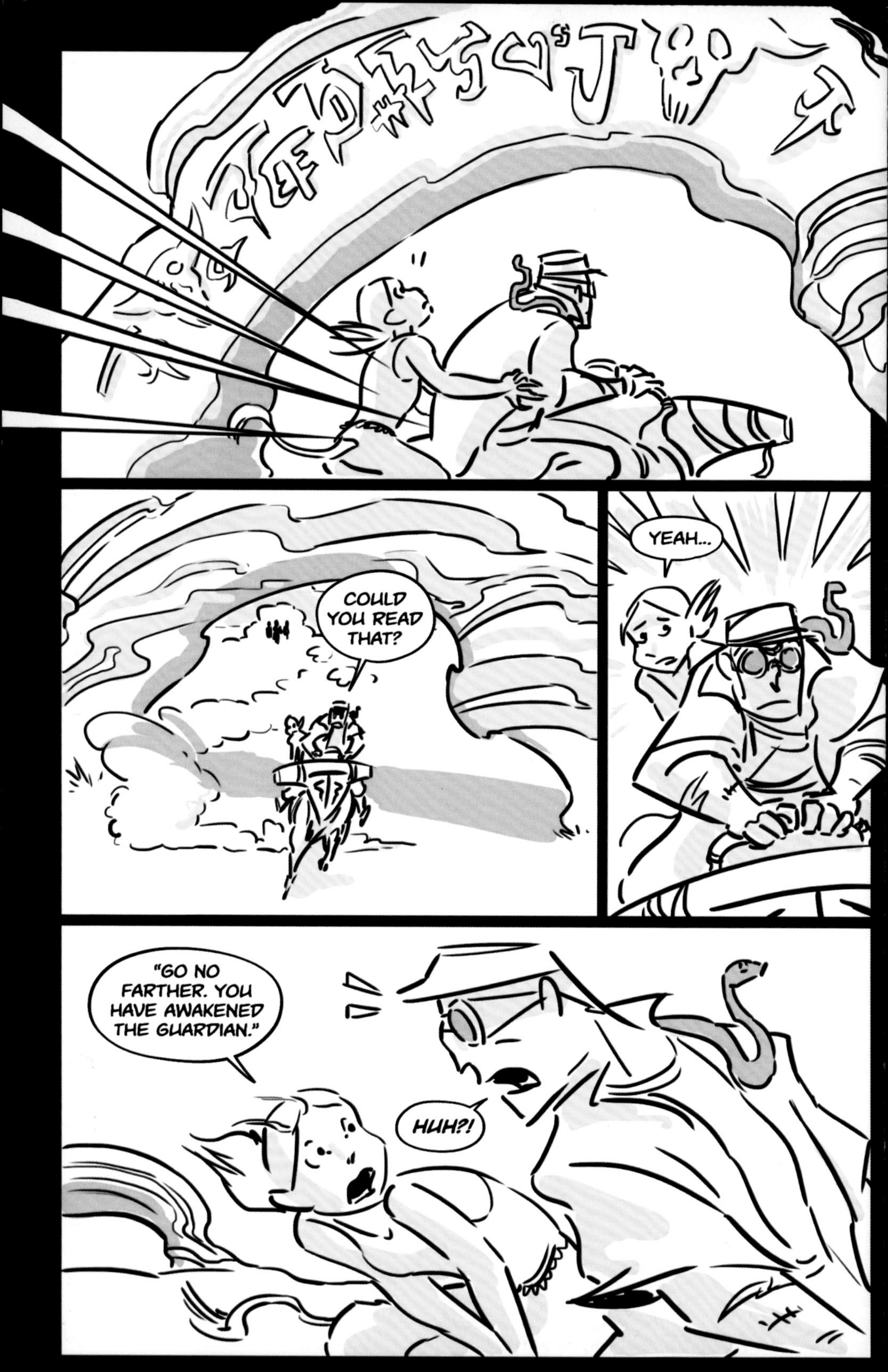
COULD YOU READ THAT?
YEAH...
"GO NO FARTHER. YOU HAVE AWAKENED THE GUARDIAN."
HUH?!

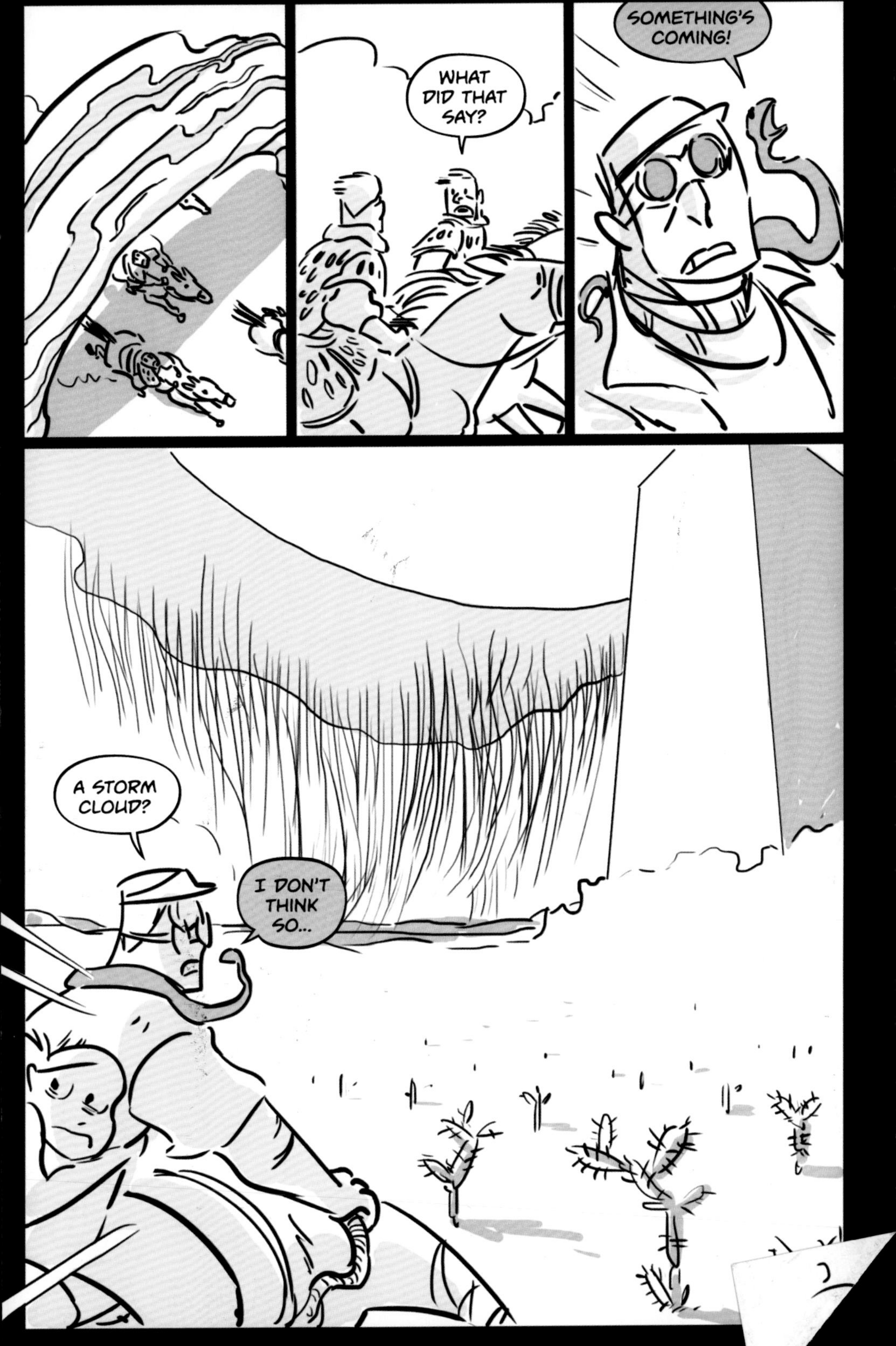
WHAT DID THAT SAY?
SOMETHING'S COMING!
A STORM CLOUD?
I DON'T THINK SO...

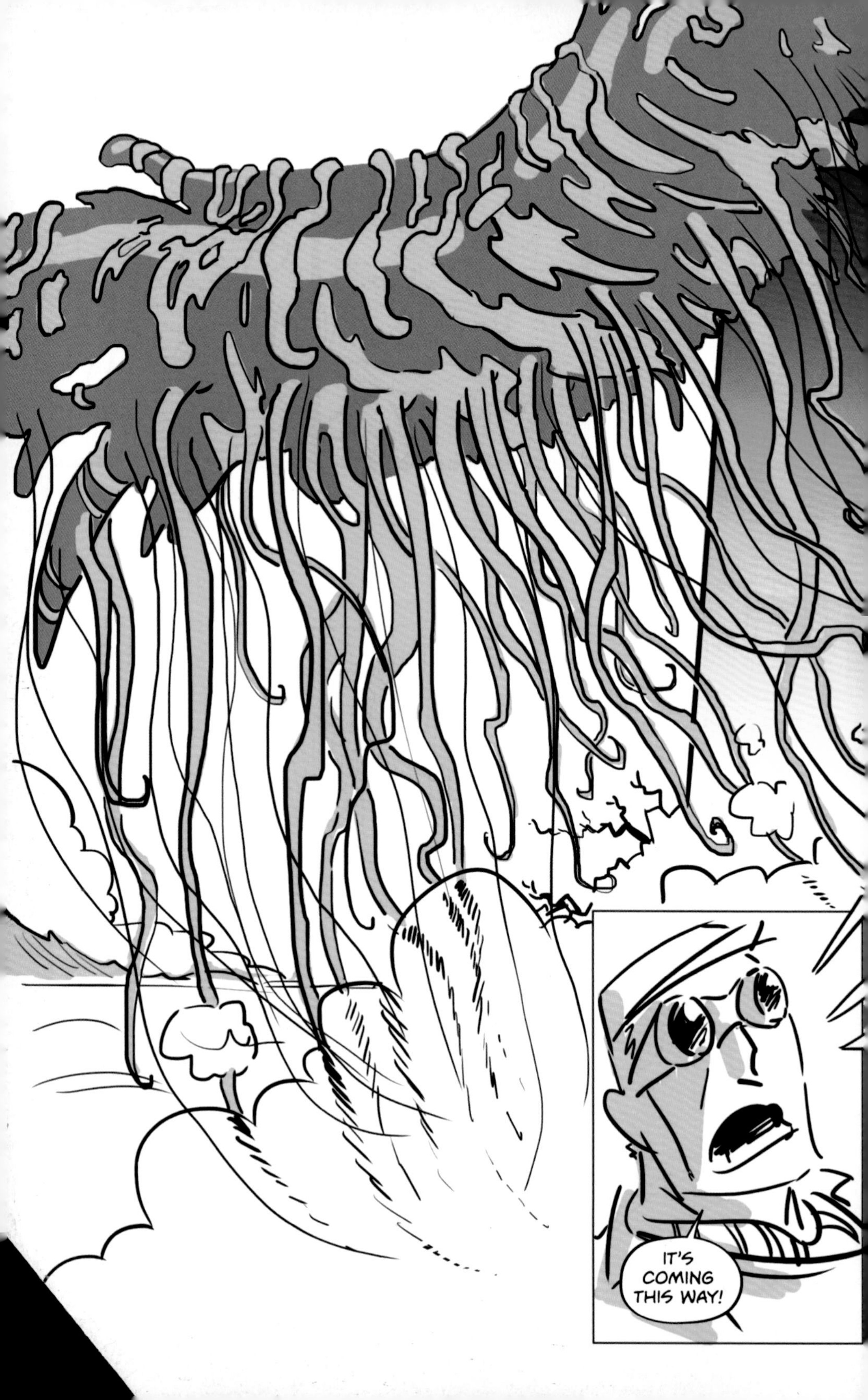
IT'S
COMING
THIS WAY!

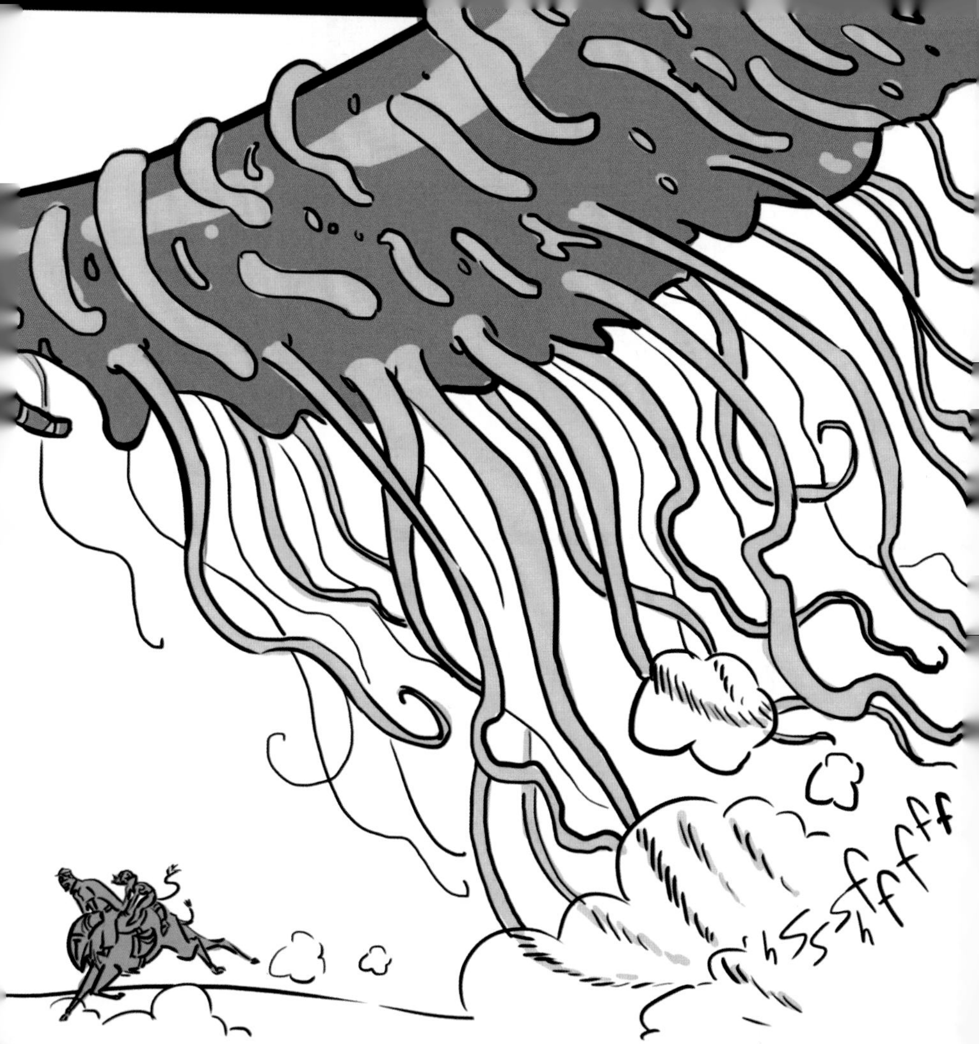
hSSShfffff

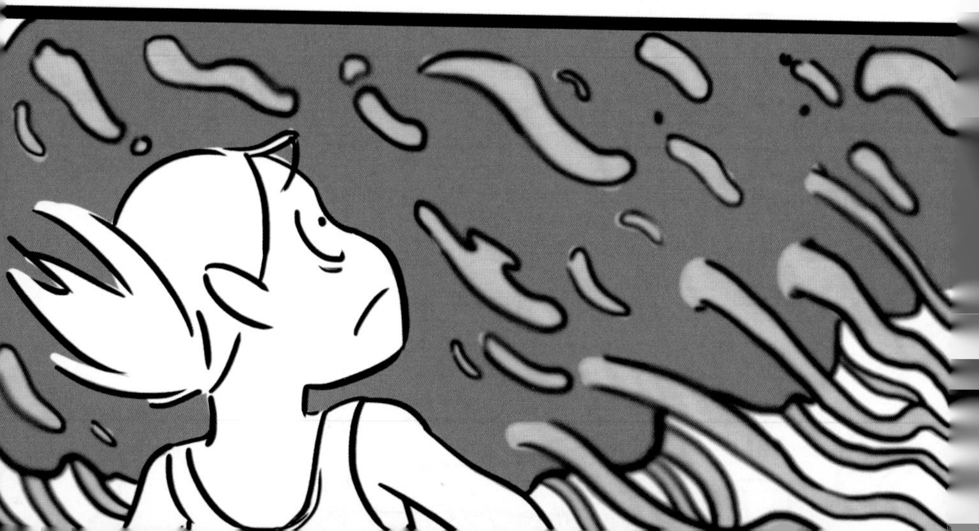

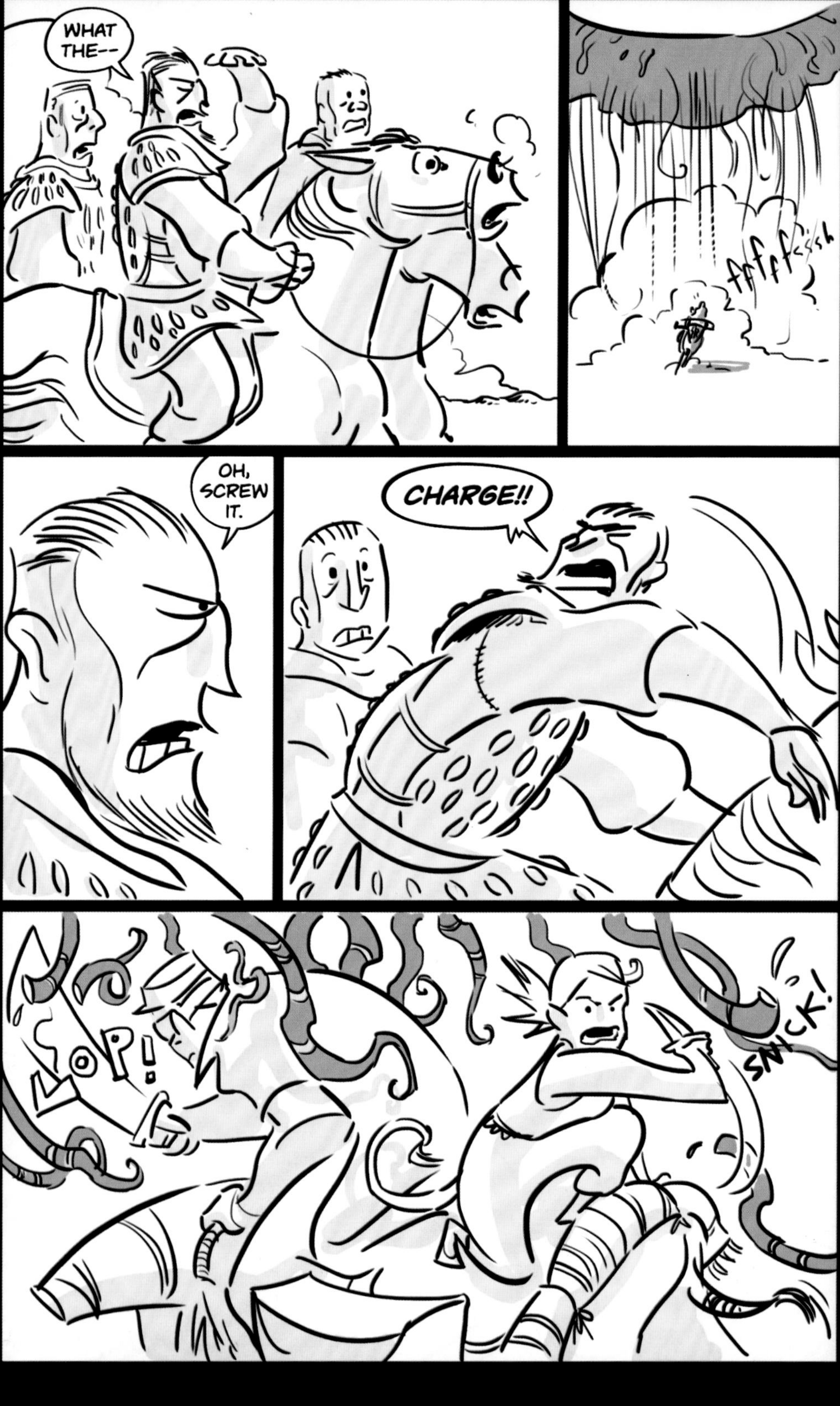
WHAT THE--
fffffcssh
OH, SCREW IT.
CHARGE!!
VOOP!
SNICK!

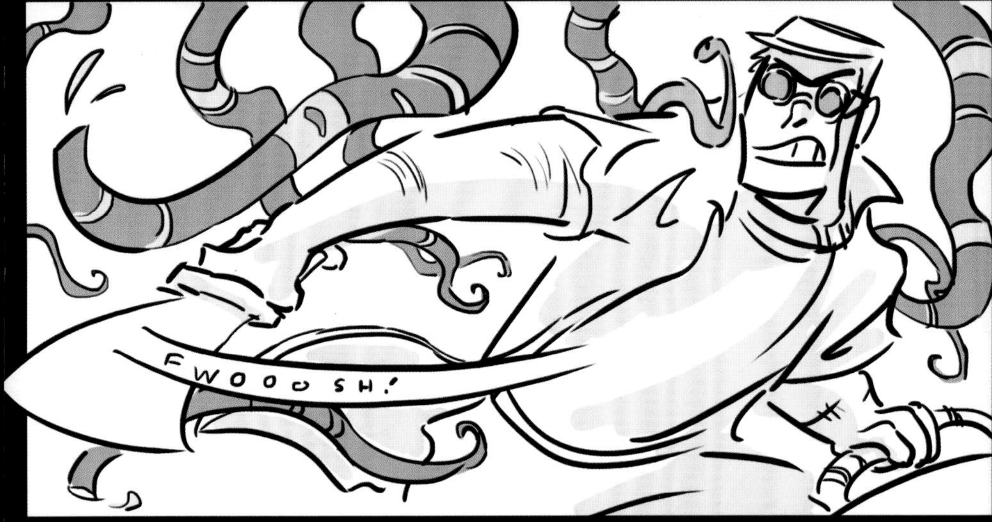
FWOOOSH!

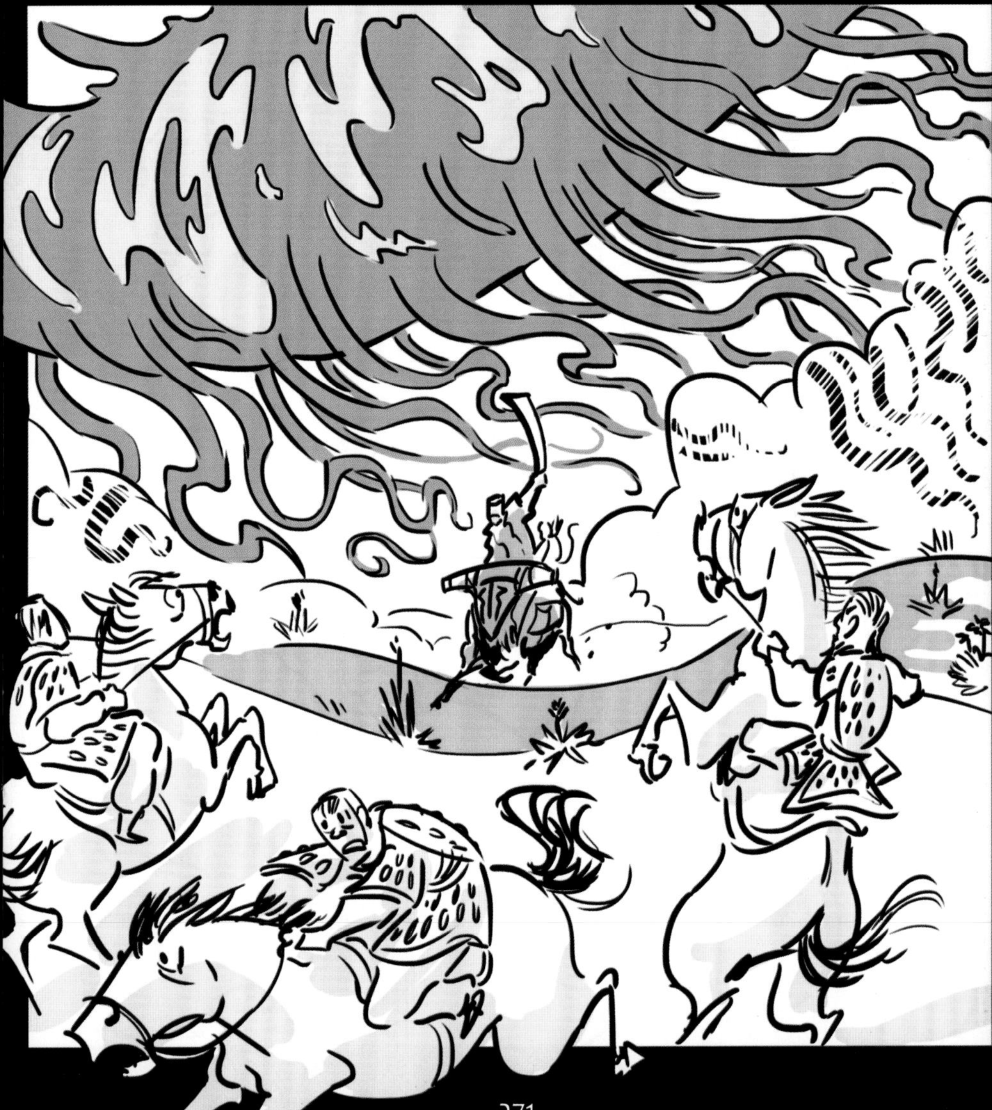

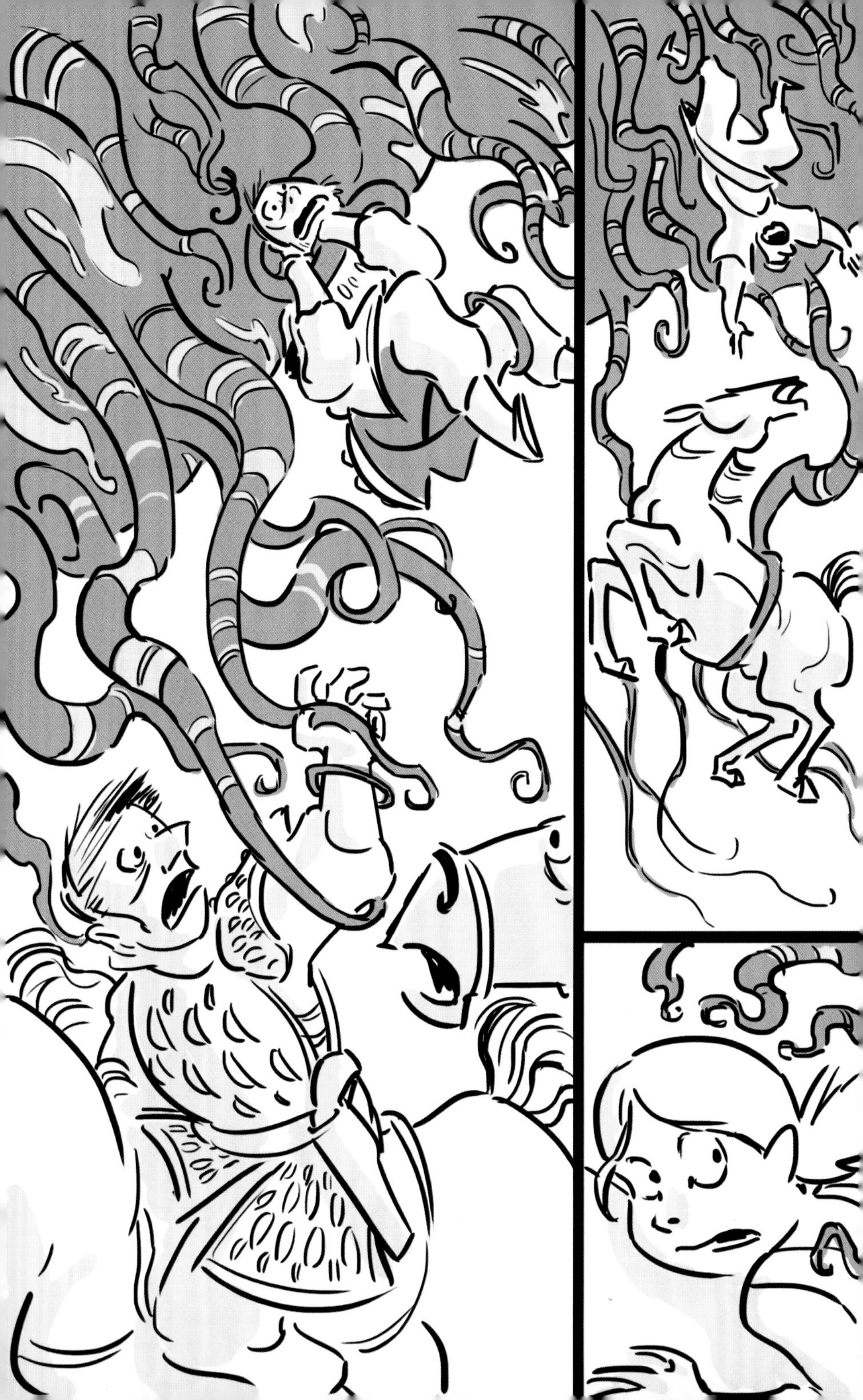

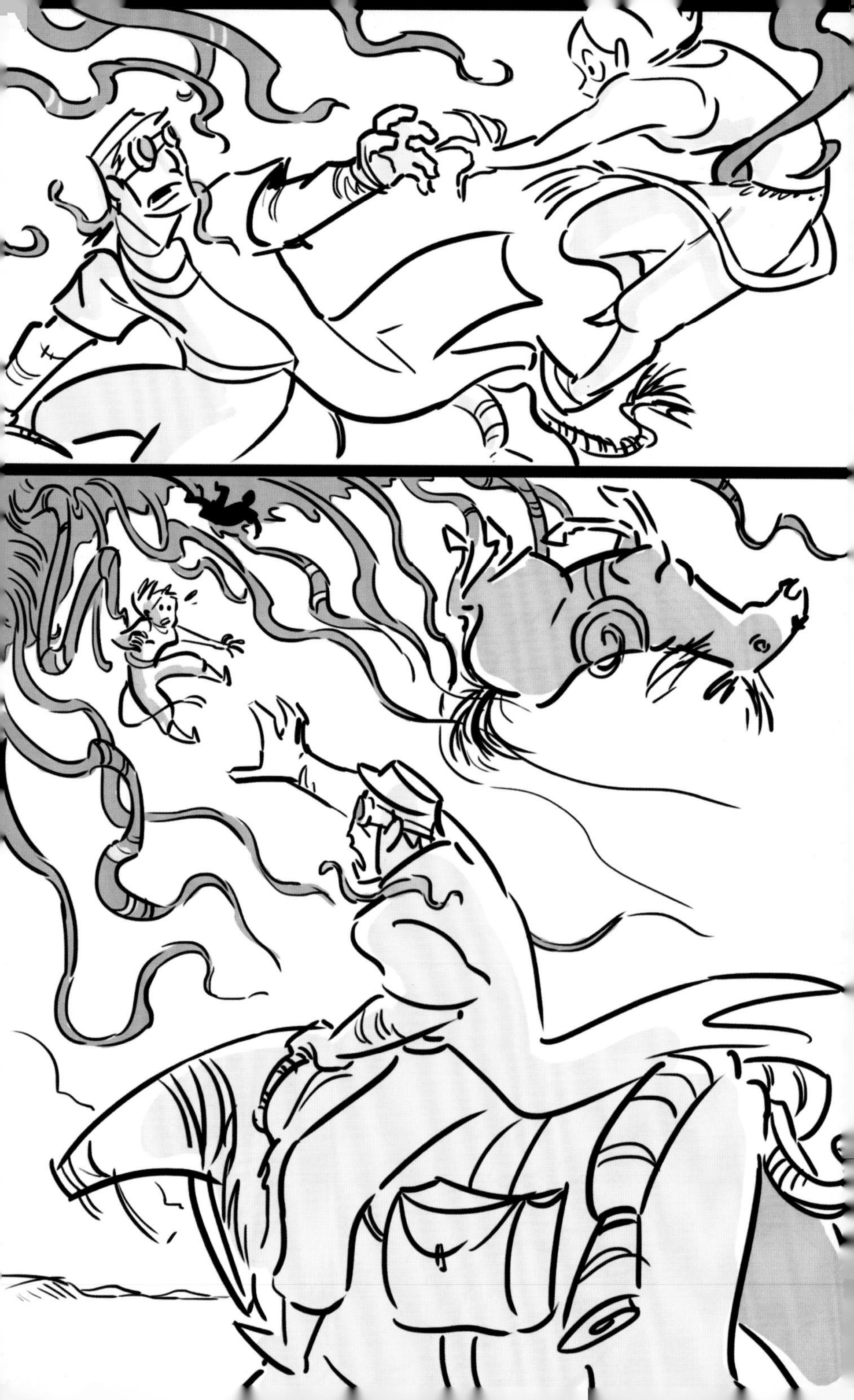

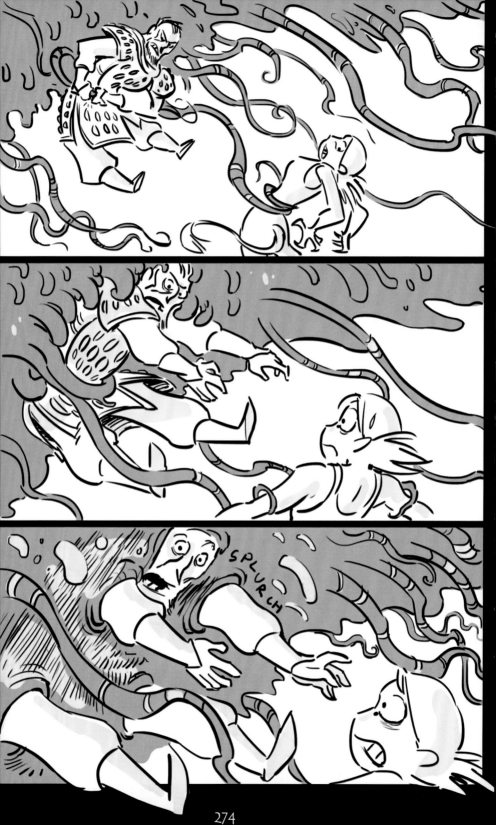

SPLURCH

274

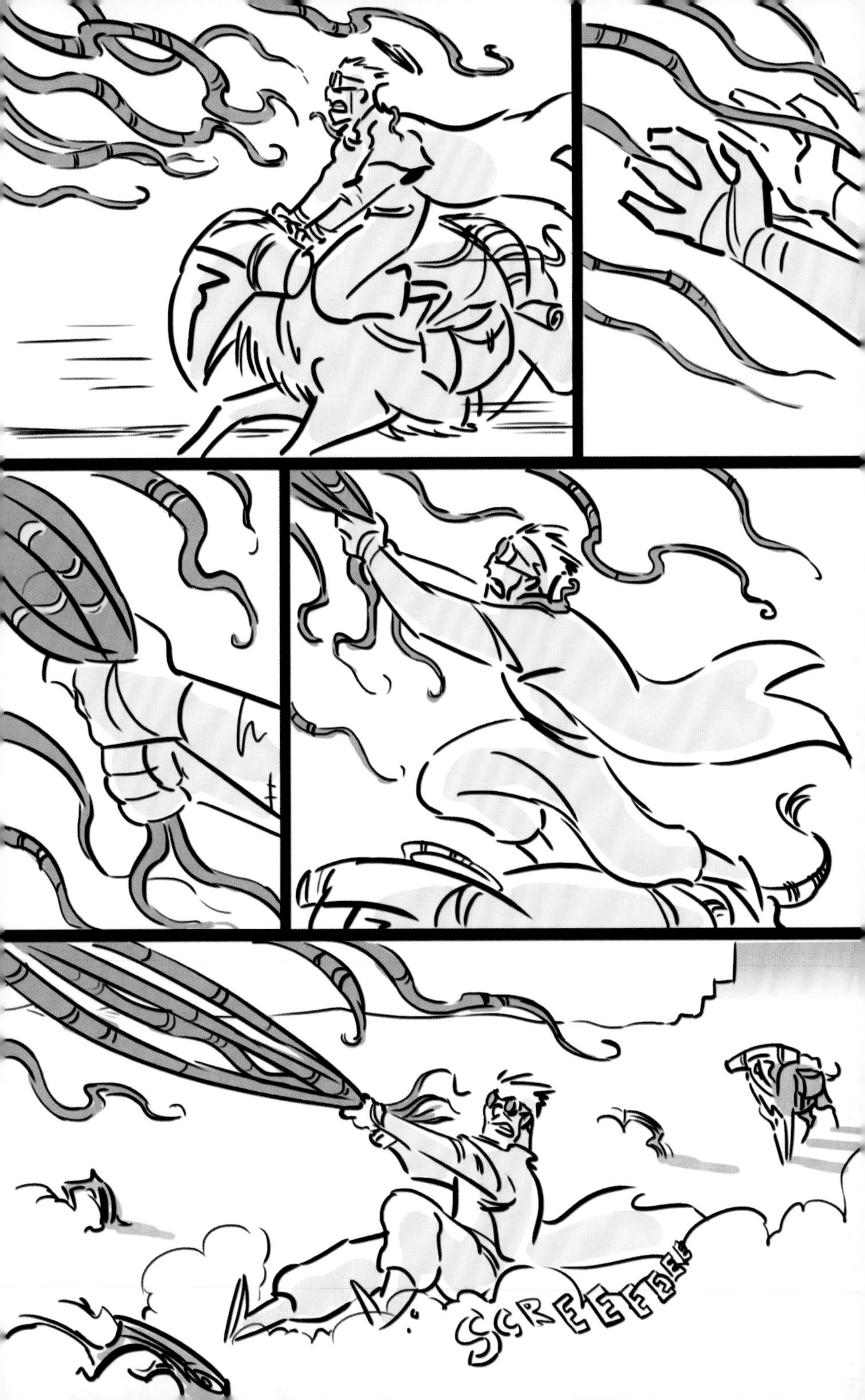
SCREEEEEE

FFSSSHH

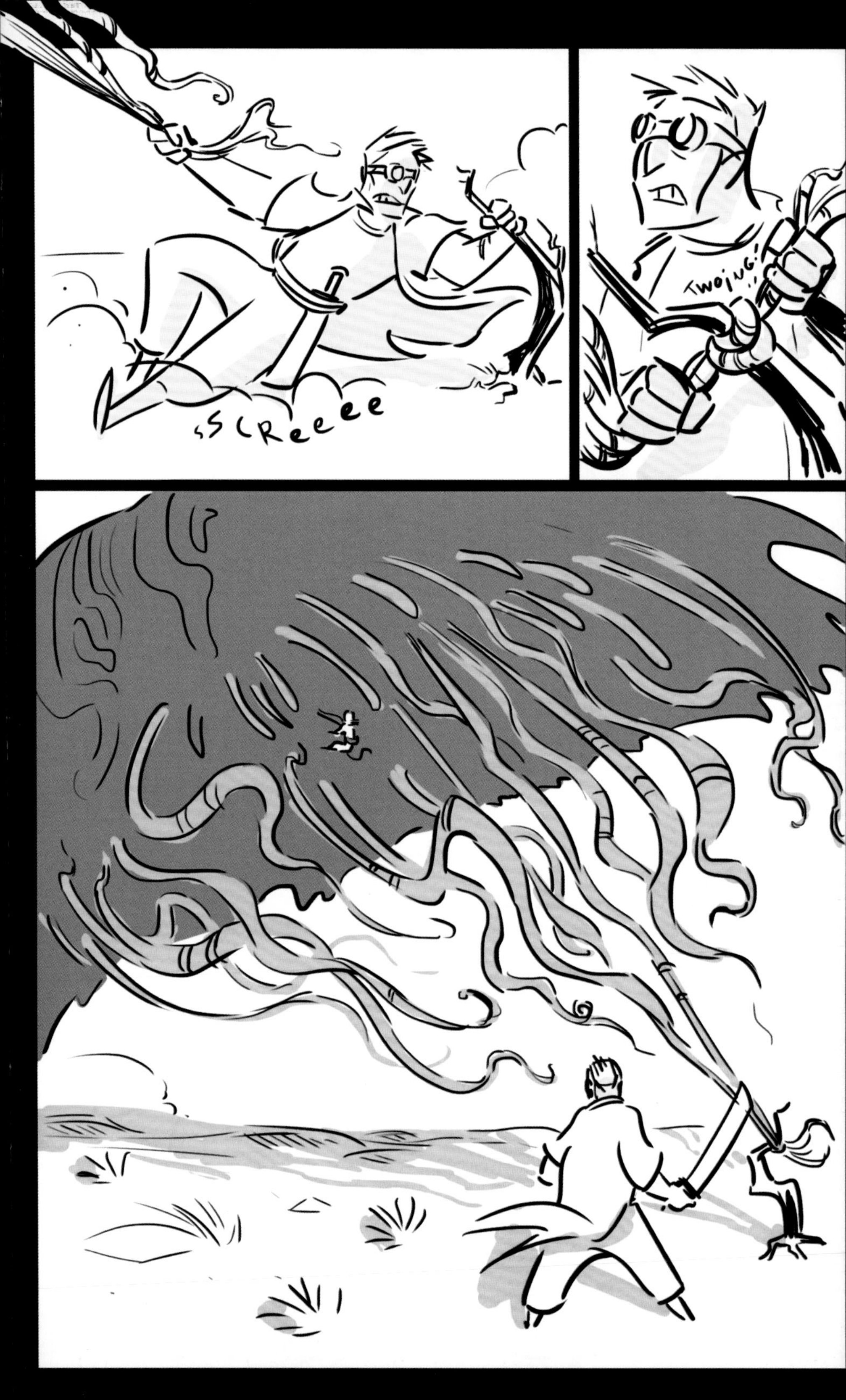
sSCReeee
TWOING!

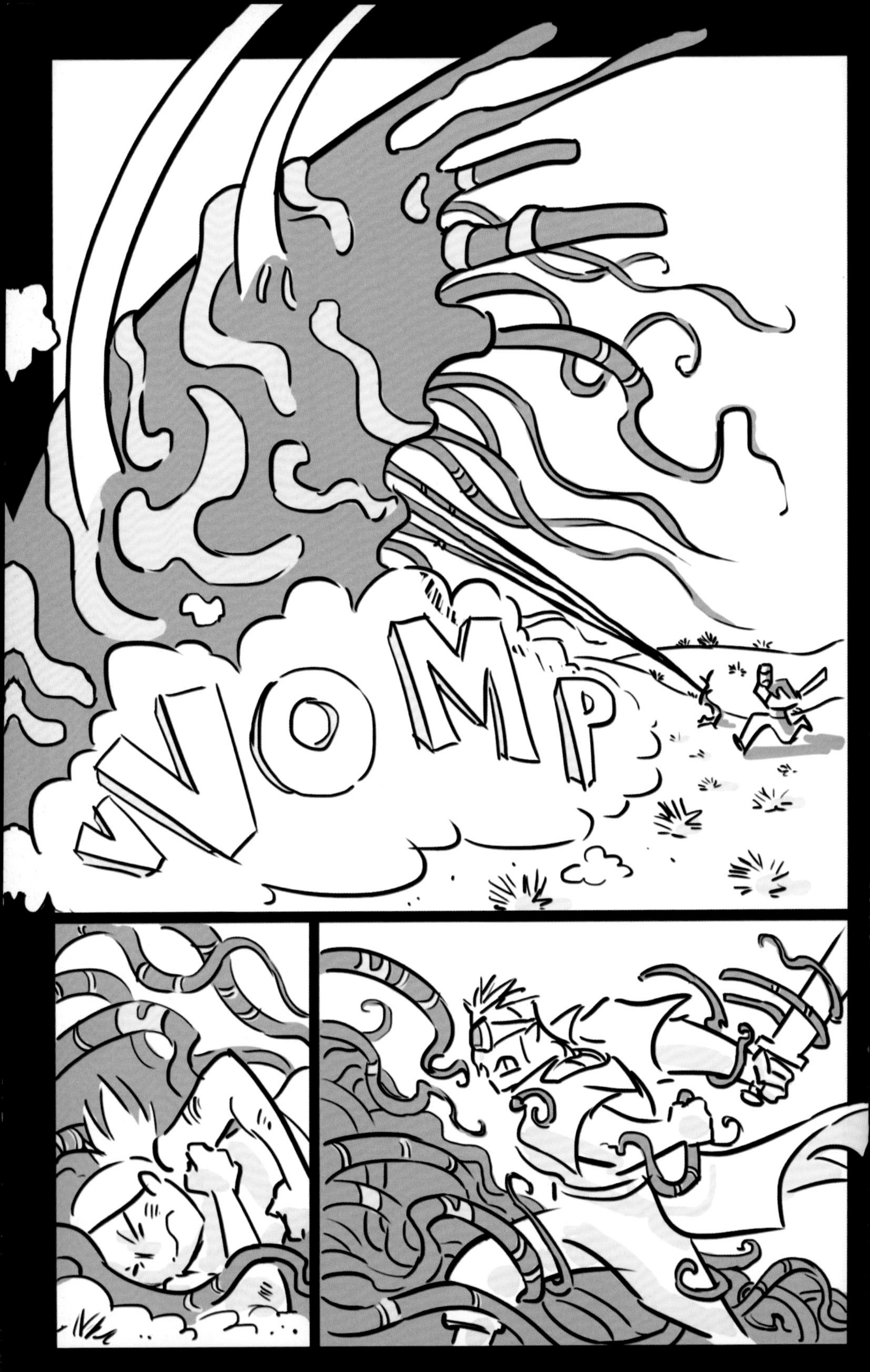
VVOMP

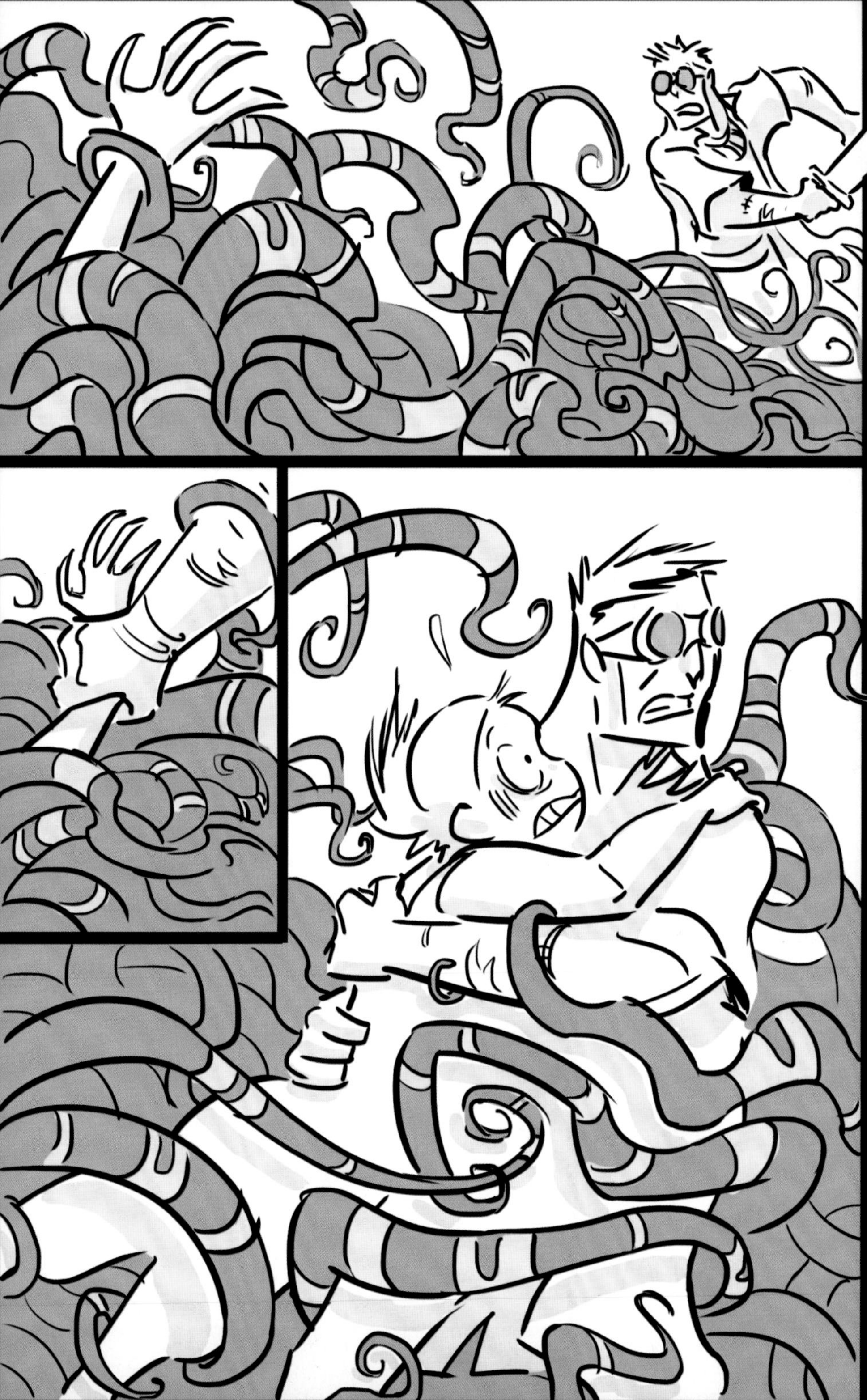

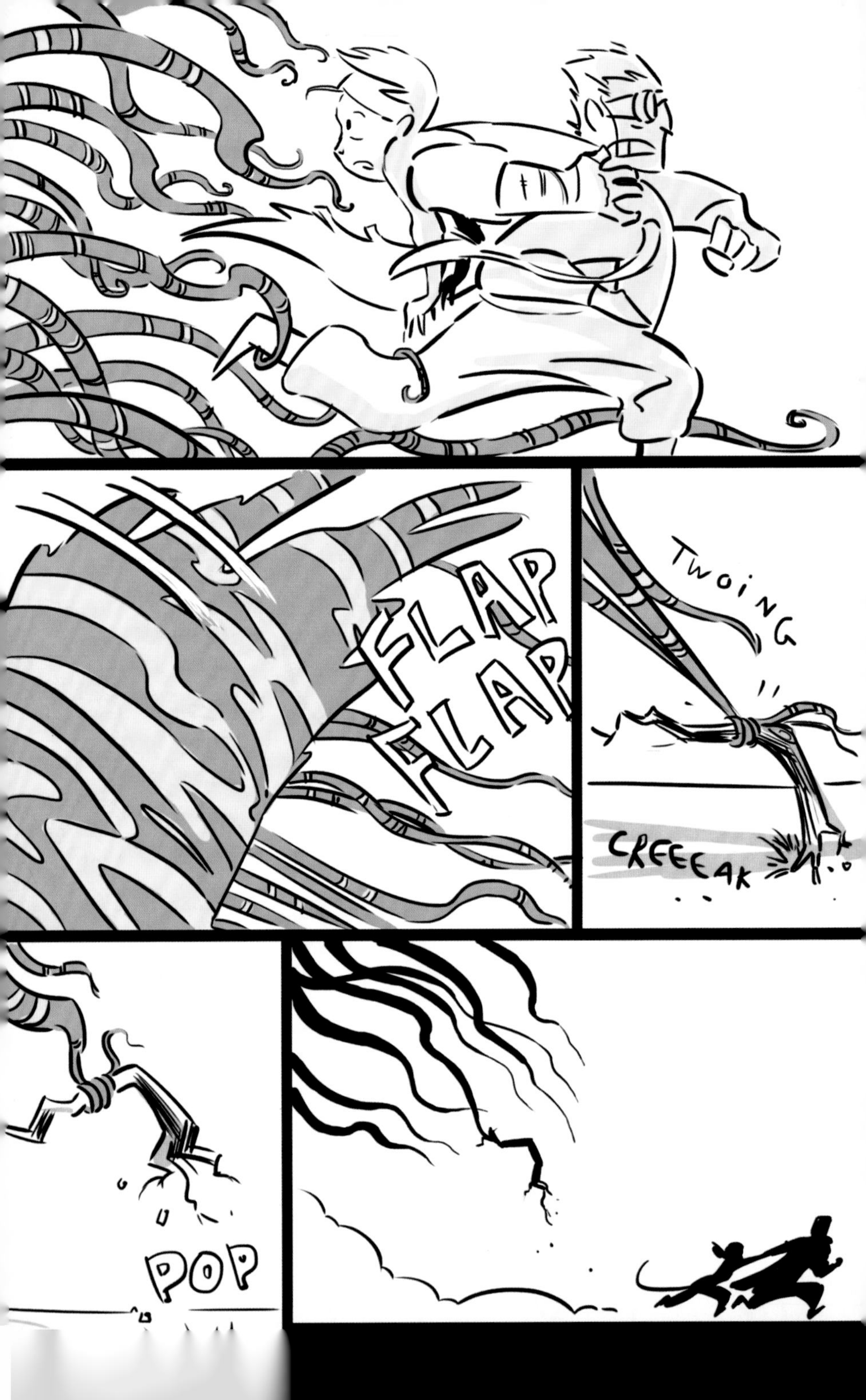

FLAP
FLAP
TWOING
CREEEAK
POP

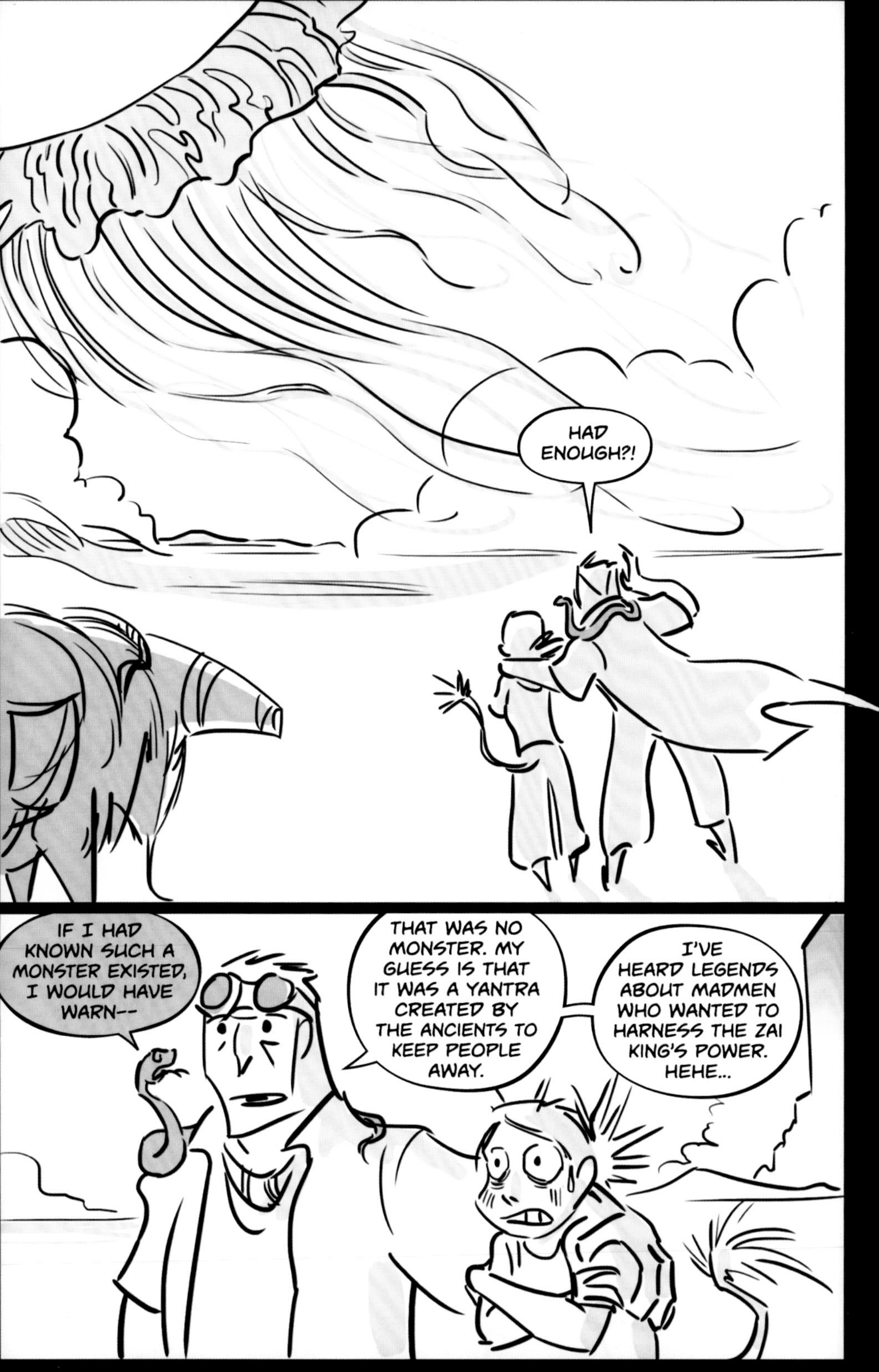
HAD ENOUGH?!
IF I HAD KNOWN SUCH A MONSTER EXISTED, I WOULD HAVE WARN--
THAT WAS NO MONSTER. MY GUESS IS THAT IT WAS A YANTRA CREATED BY THE ANCIENTS TO KEEP PEOPLE AWAY.
I'VE HEARD LEGENDS ABOUT MADMEN WHO WANTED TO HARNESS THE ZAI KING'S POWER. HEHE...

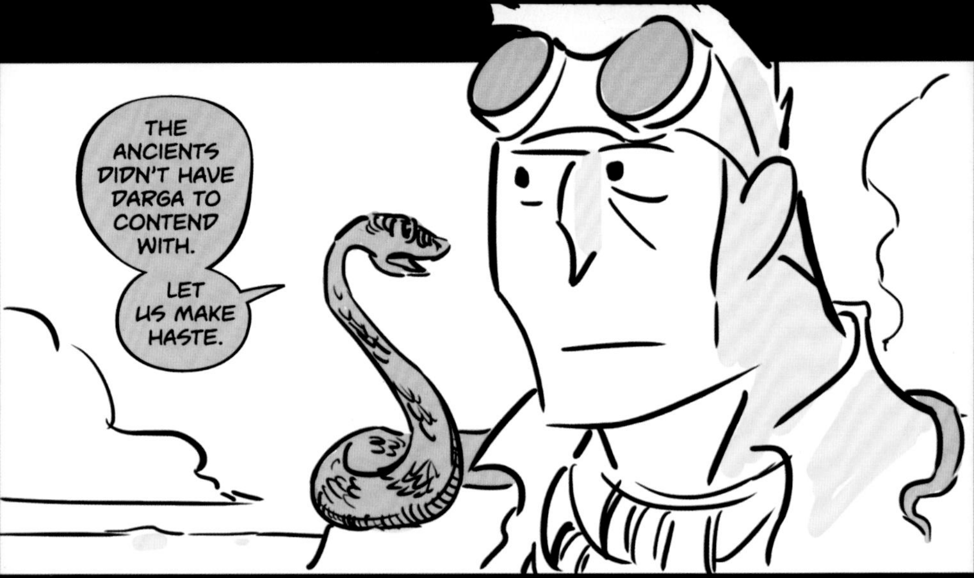
THE ANCIENTS DIDN'T HAVE DARGA TO CONTEND WITH.
LET US MAKE HASTE.

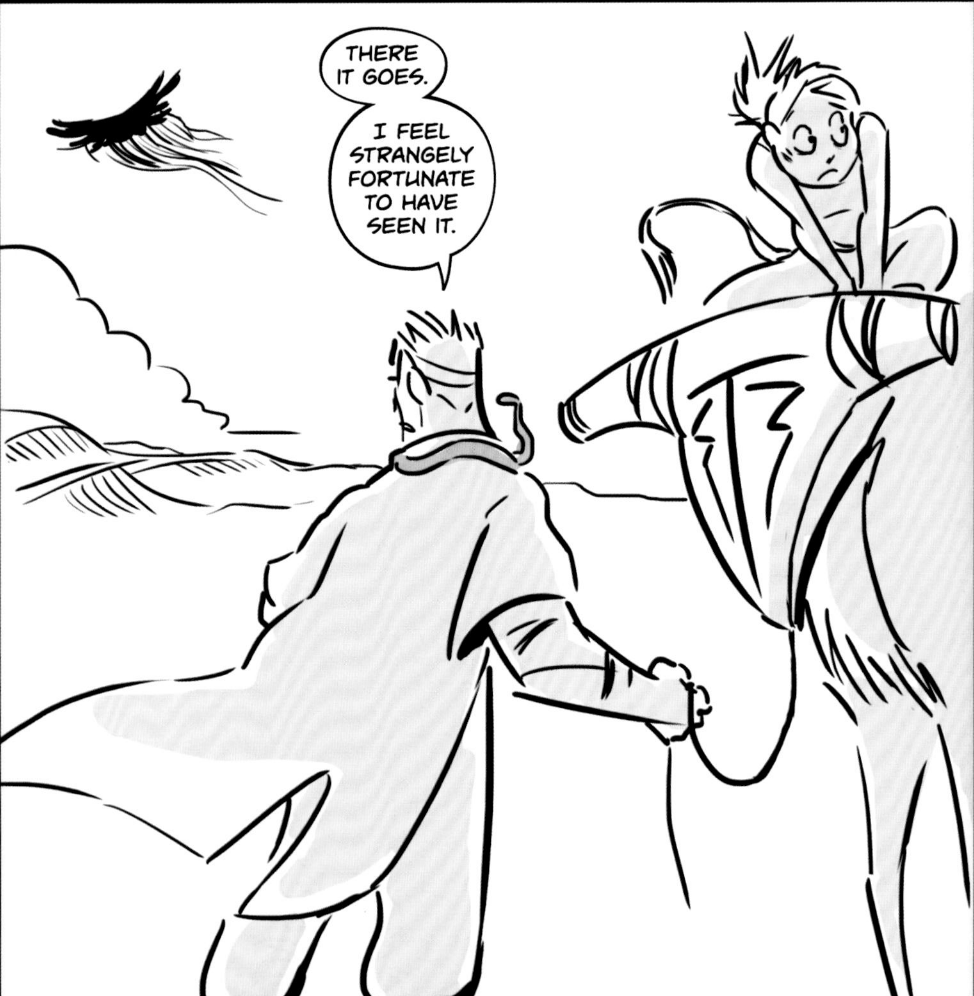
THERE IT GOES.
I FEEL STRANGELY FORTUNATE TO HAVE SEEN IT.

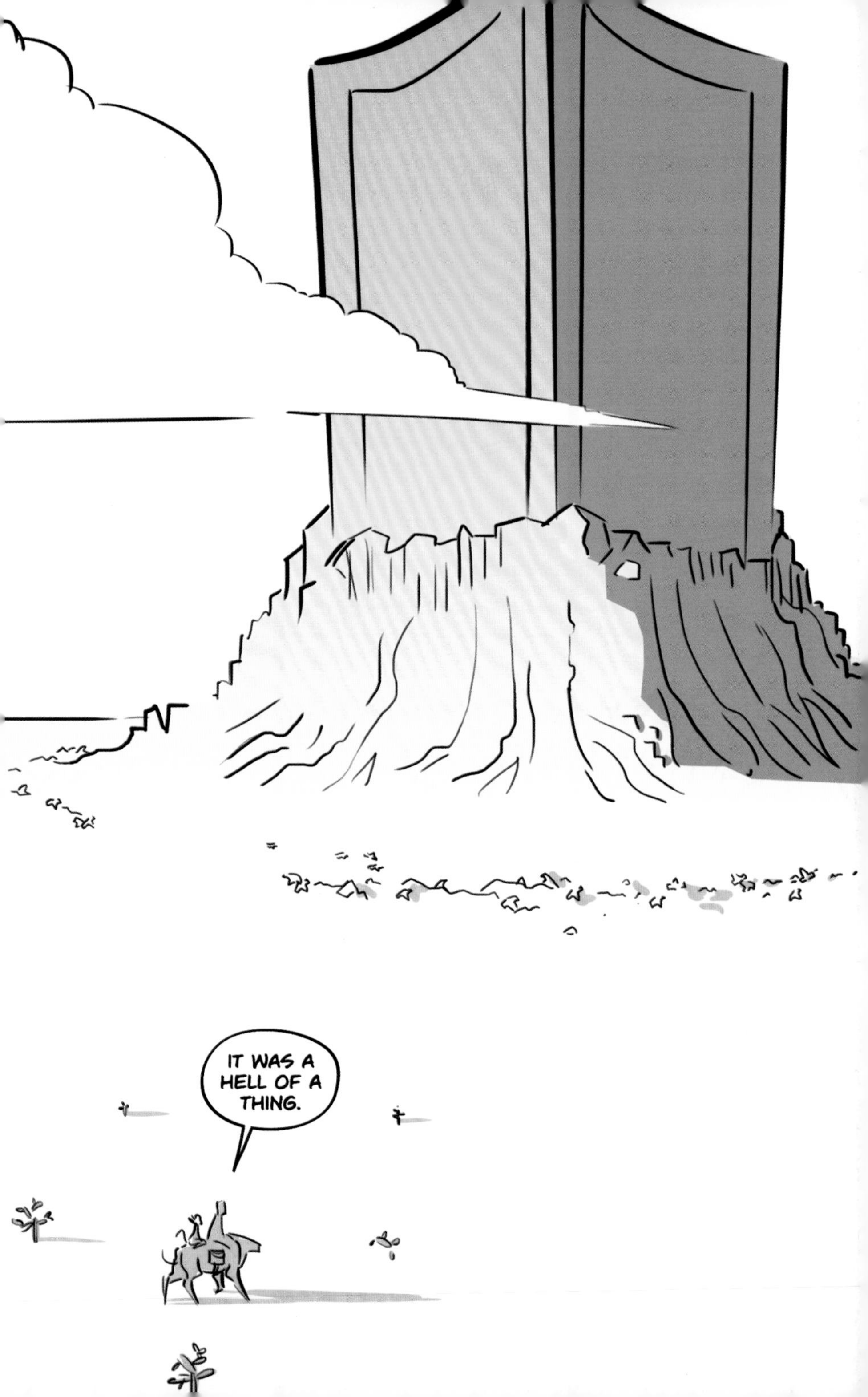
IT WAS A HELL OF A THING.

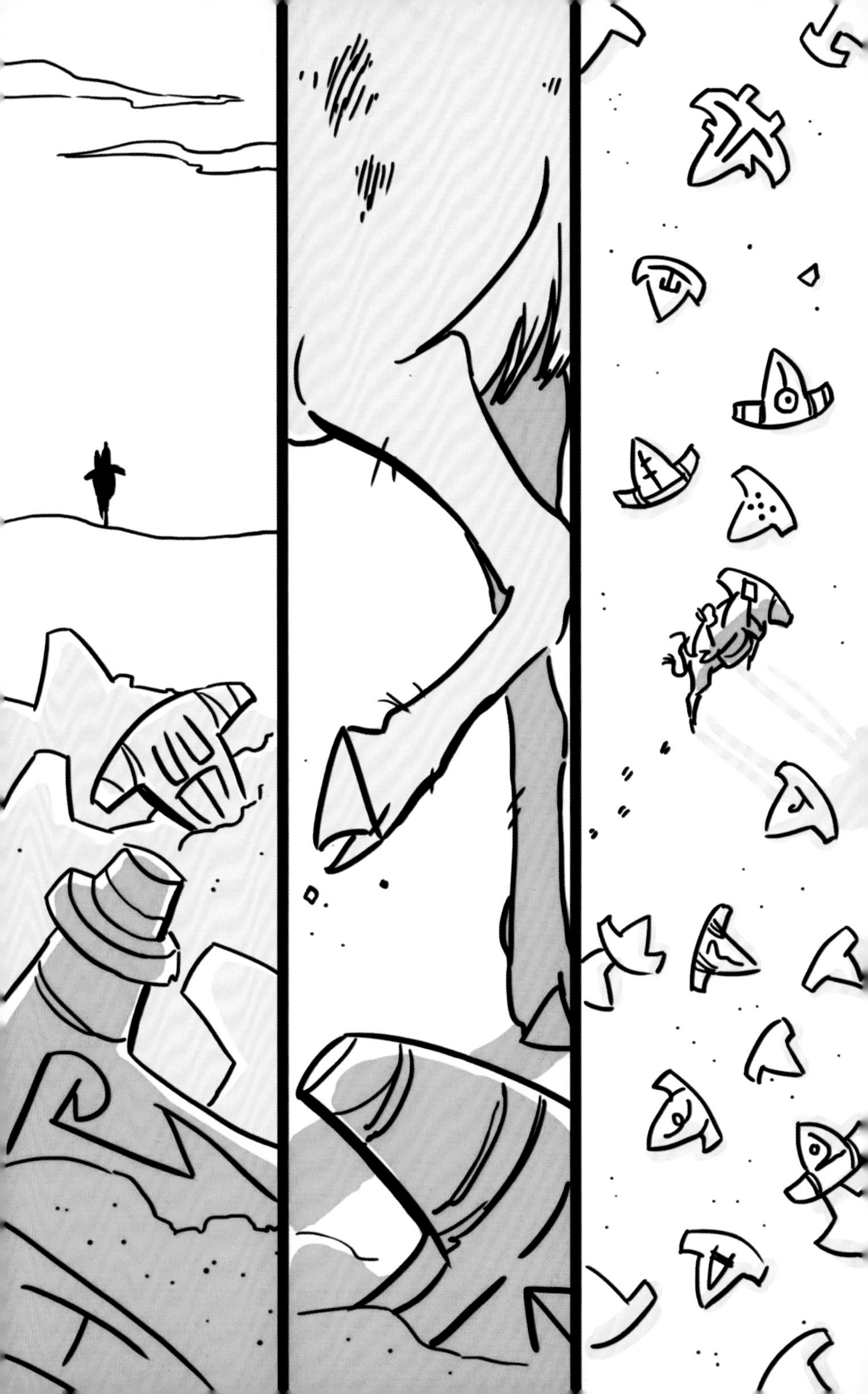

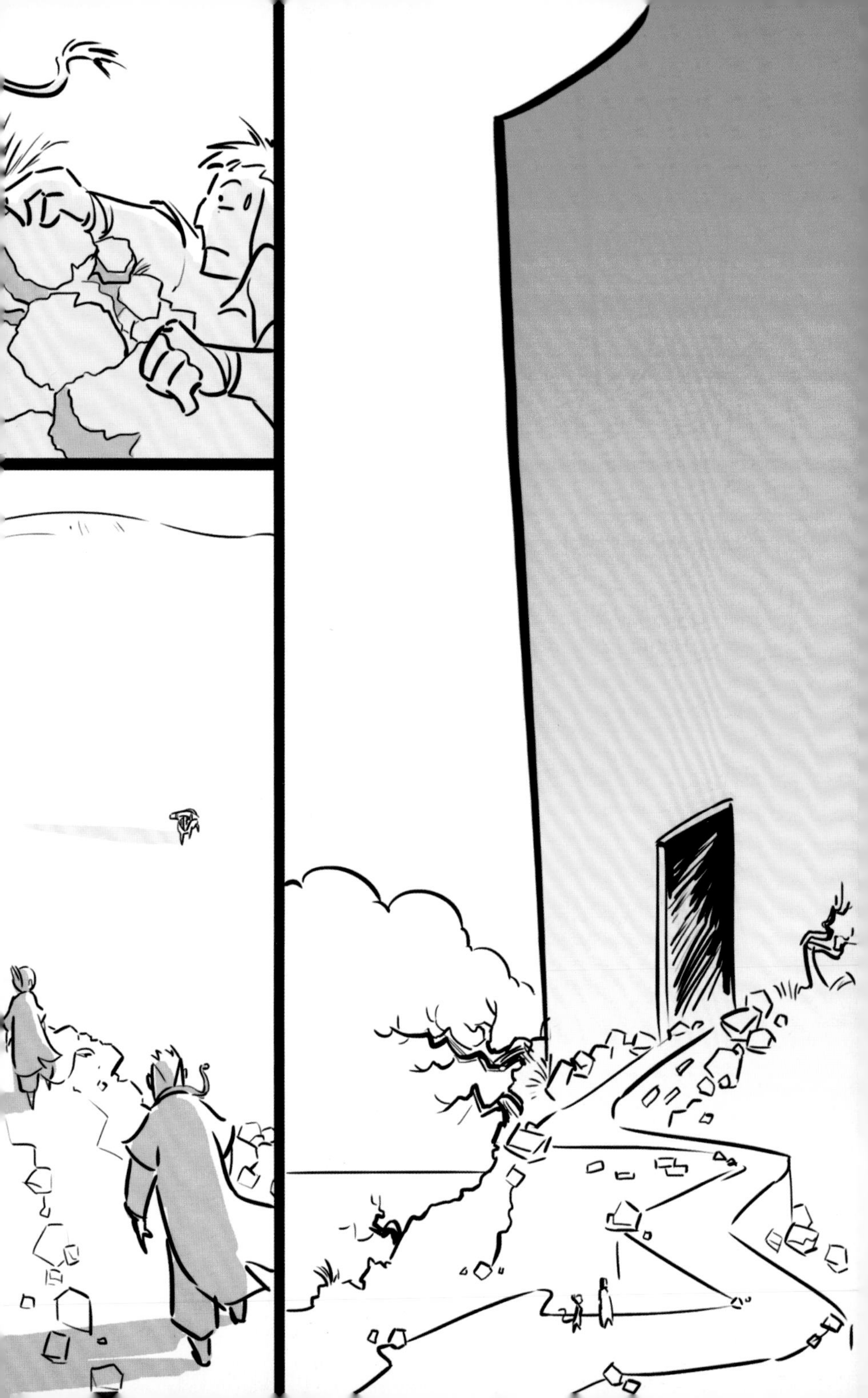

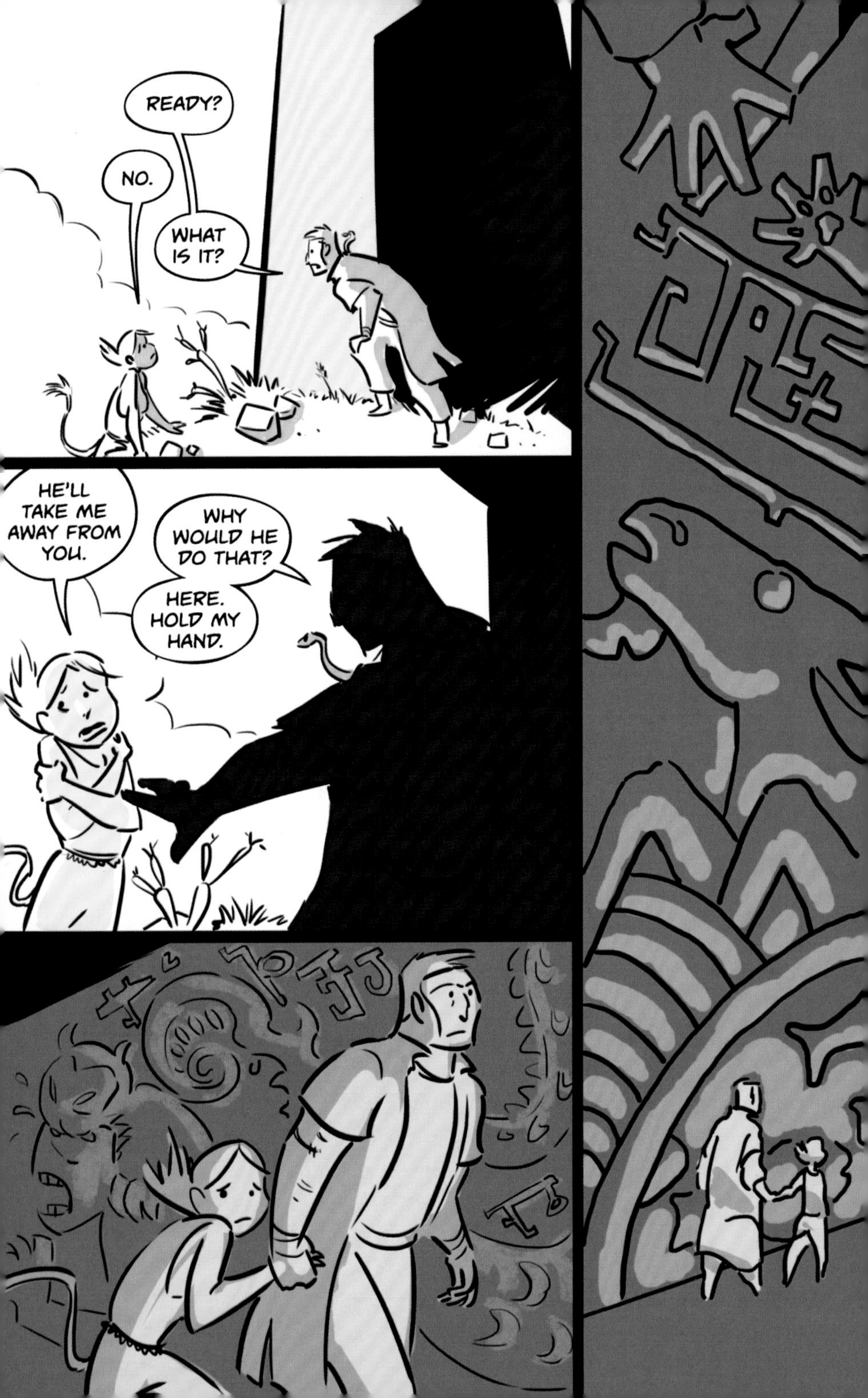
READY?
NO.
WHAT IS IT?
HE'LL TAKE ME AWAY FROM YOU.
WHY WOULD HE DO THAT?
HERE. HOLD MY HAND.

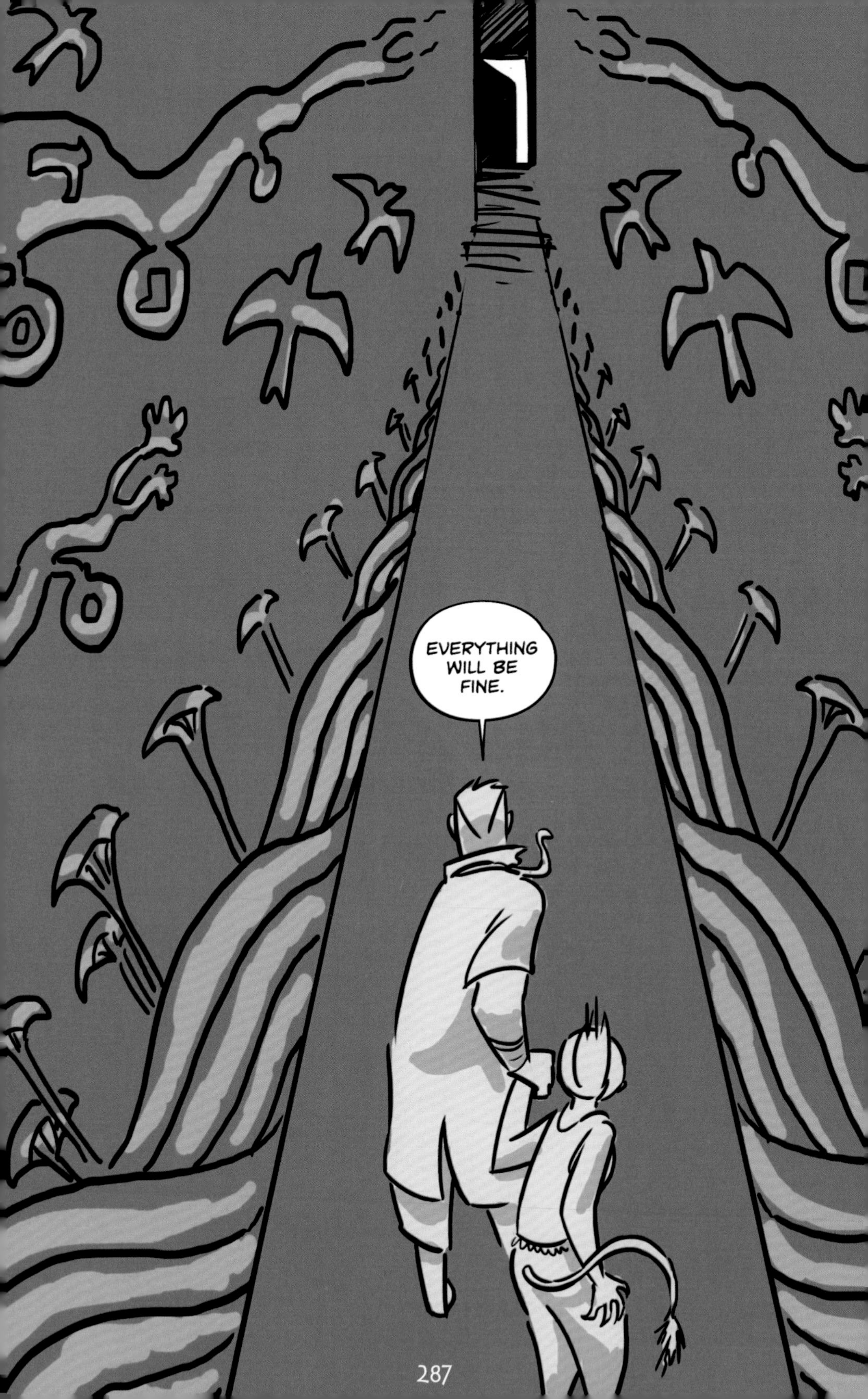
EVERYTHING WILL BE FINE.

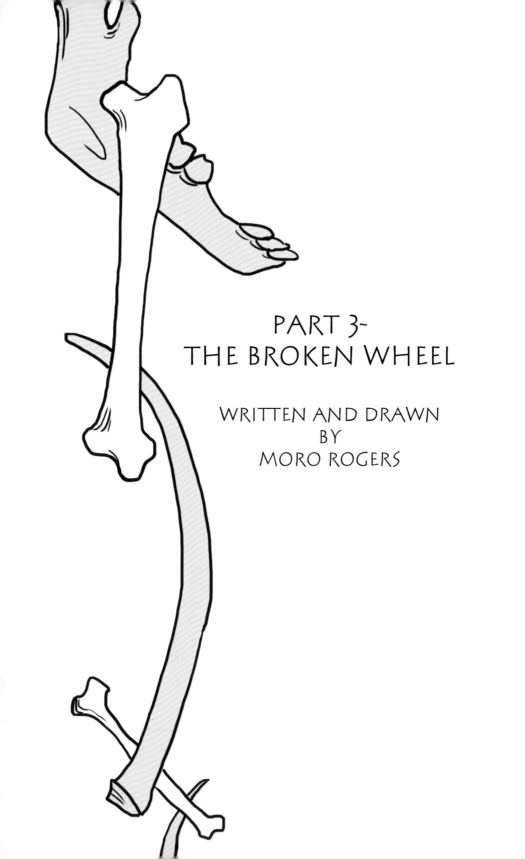

PART 3~
THE BROKEN WHEEL

WRITTEN AND DRAWN
BY
MORO ROGERS

FOR JASON

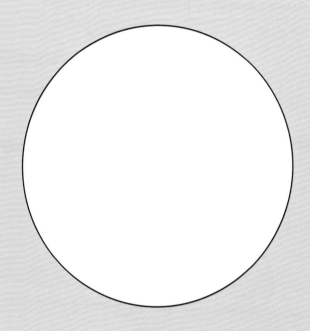

IN THE BEGINNING
WAS THE ONE.

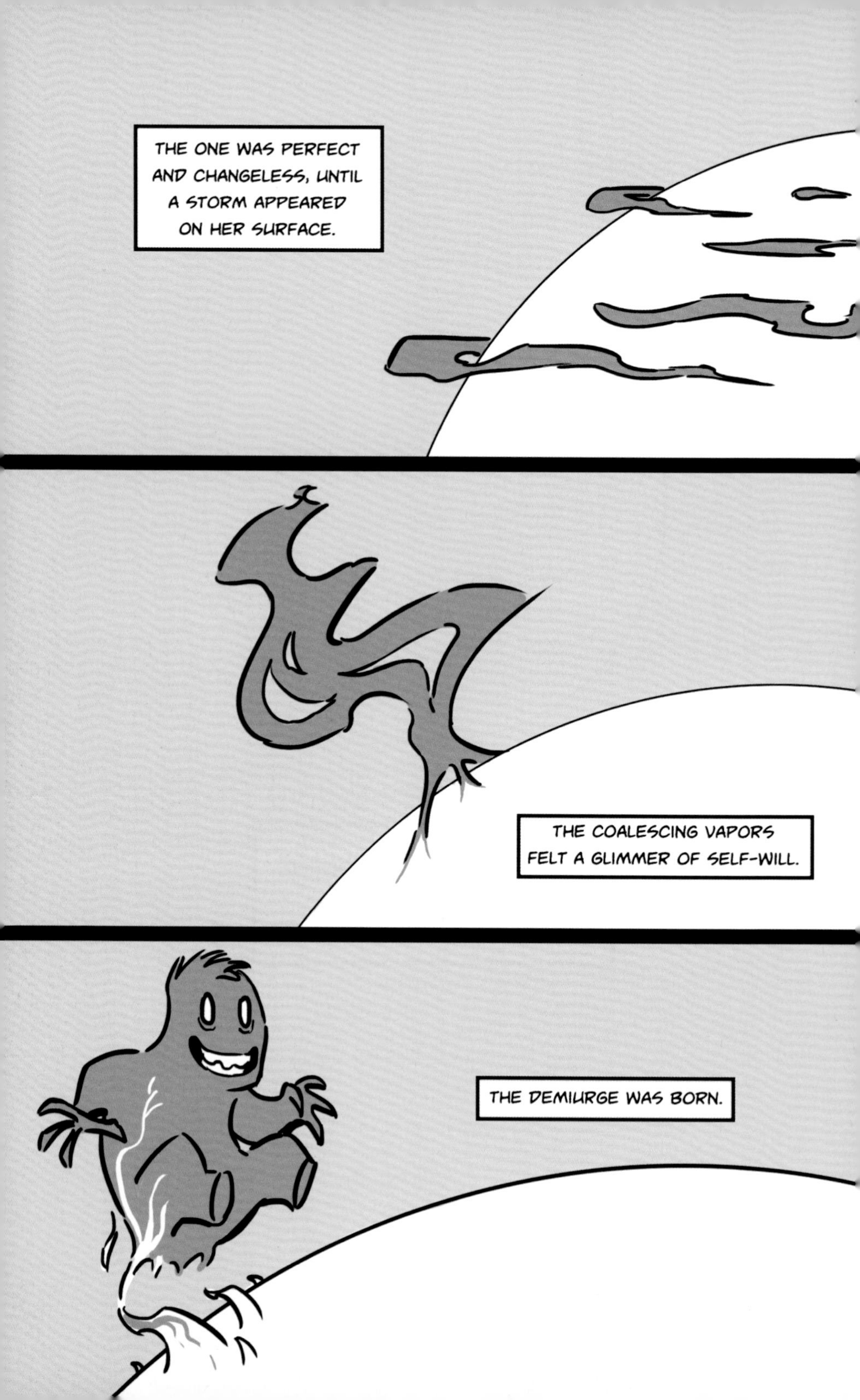
THE ONE WAS PERFECT AND CHANGELESS, UNTIL A STORM APPEARED ON HER SURFACE.
THE COALESCING VAPORS FELT A GLIMMER OF SELF-WILL.
THE DEMIURGE WAS BORN.

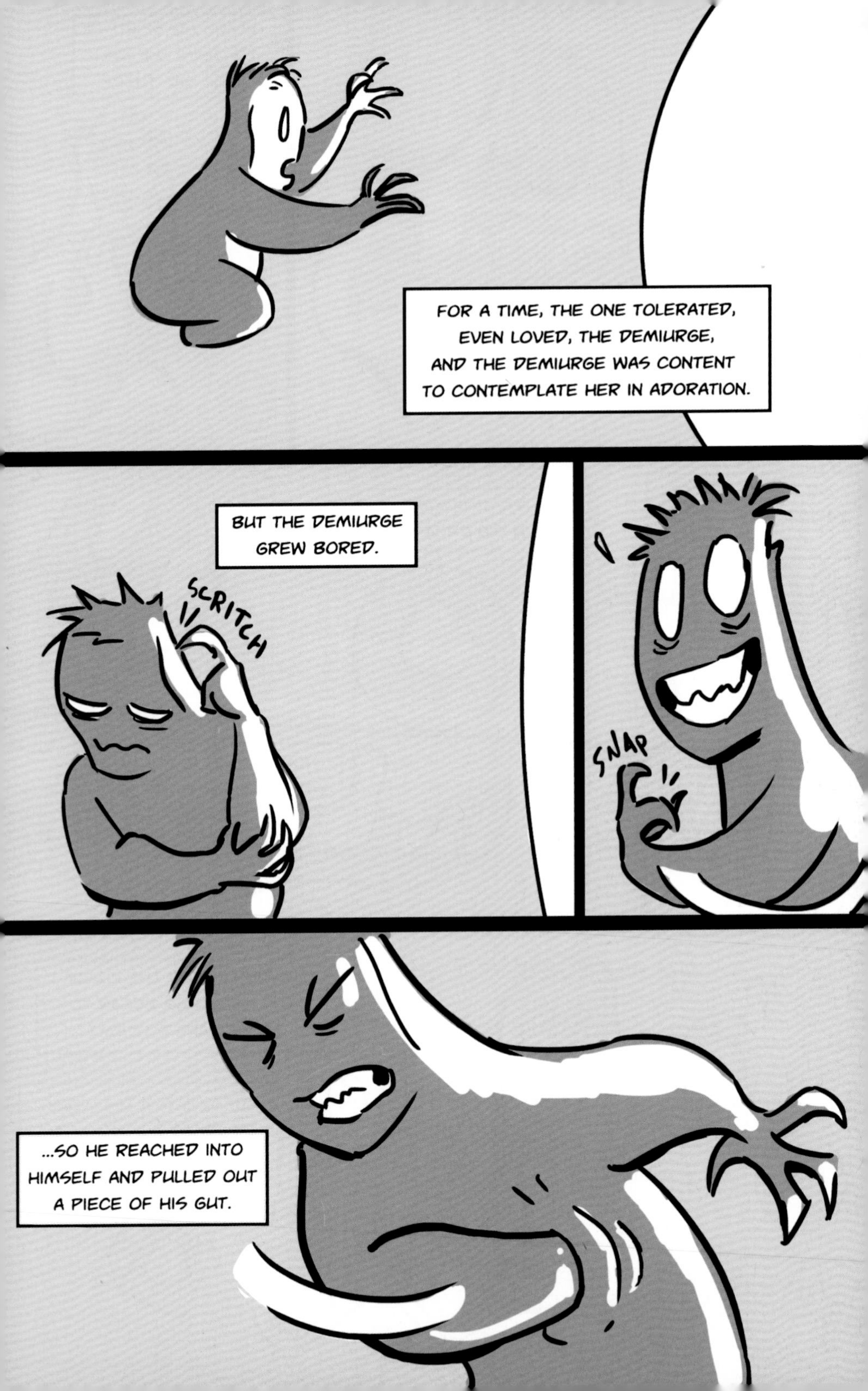
FOR A TIME, THE ONE TOLERATED, EVEN LOVED, THE DEMIURGE, AND THE DEMIURGE WAS CONTENT TO CONTEMPLATE HER IN ADORATION.
BUT THE DEMIURGE GREW BORED.
SCRITCH
SNAP
...SO HE REACHED INTO HIMSELF AND PULLED OUT A PIECE OF HIS GUT.

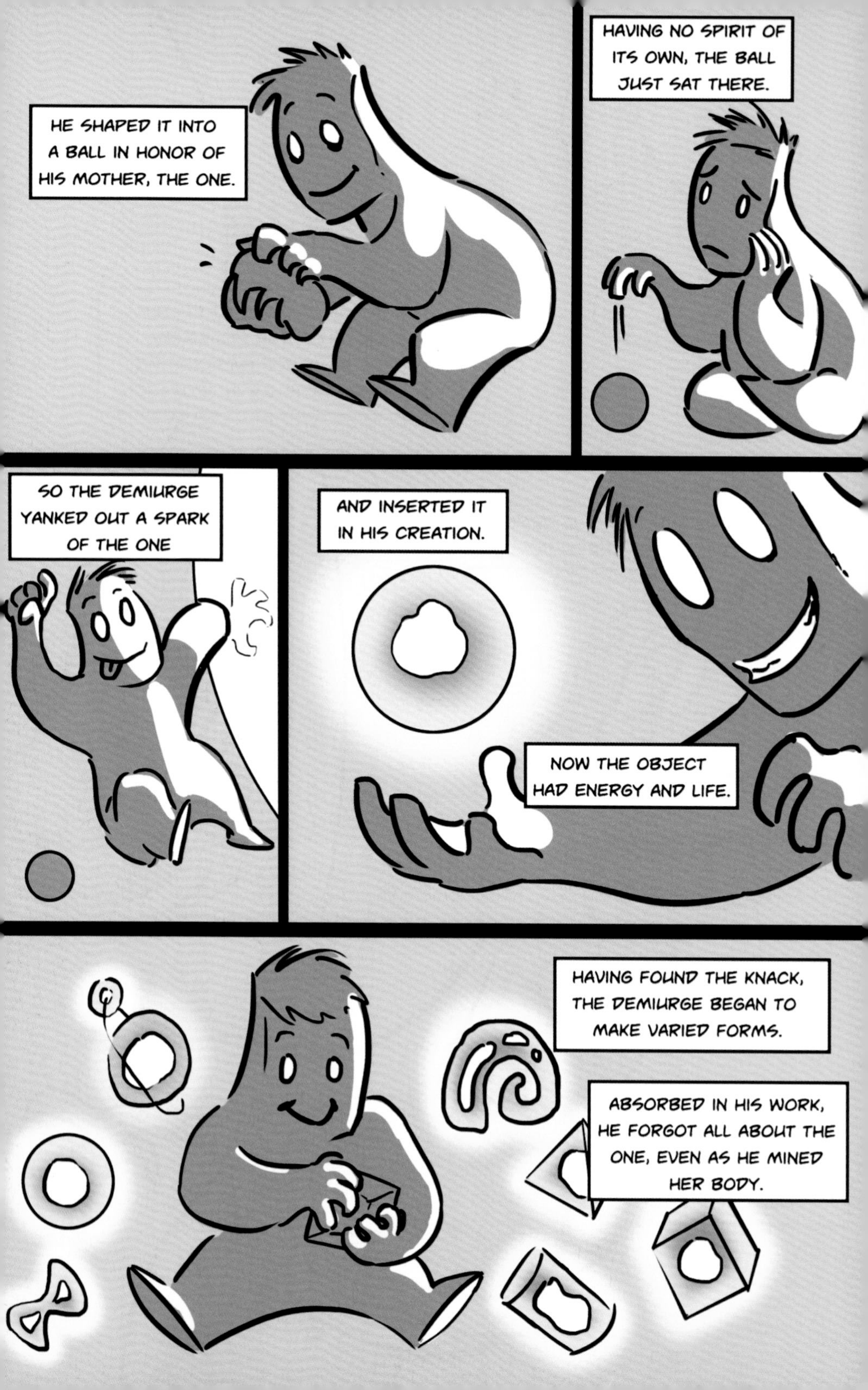
HE SHAPED IT INTO A BALL IN HONOR OF HIS MOTHER, THE ONE.
HAVING NO SPIRIT OF ITS OWN, THE BALL JUST SAT THERE.
SO THE DEMIURGE YANKED OUT A SPARK OF THE ONE
AND INSERTED IT IN HIS CREATION.
NOW THE OBJECT HAD ENERGY AND LIFE.
HAVING FOUND THE KNACK, THE DEMIURGE BEGAN TO MAKE VARIED FORMS.
ABSORBED IN HIS WORK, HE FORGOT ALL ABOUT THE ONE, EVEN AS HE MINED HER BODY.

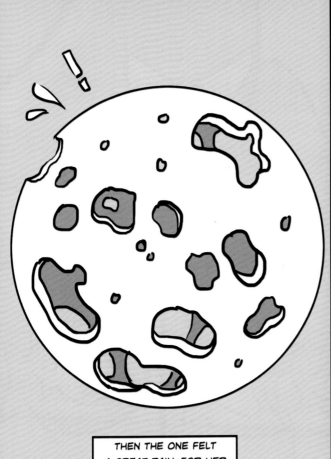

THEN THE ONE FELT A GREAT PAIN, FOR HER PERFECTION HAD BEEN COMPROMISED.

SOMETHING HAD TO BE DONE.

SHE EMANATED A BEING OF PURE SPIRIT.

...AND SENT HIM TO SMASH THE DEMIURGE'S TOYS SO THAT HER SPARKS MIGHT RETURN TO HER BODY.

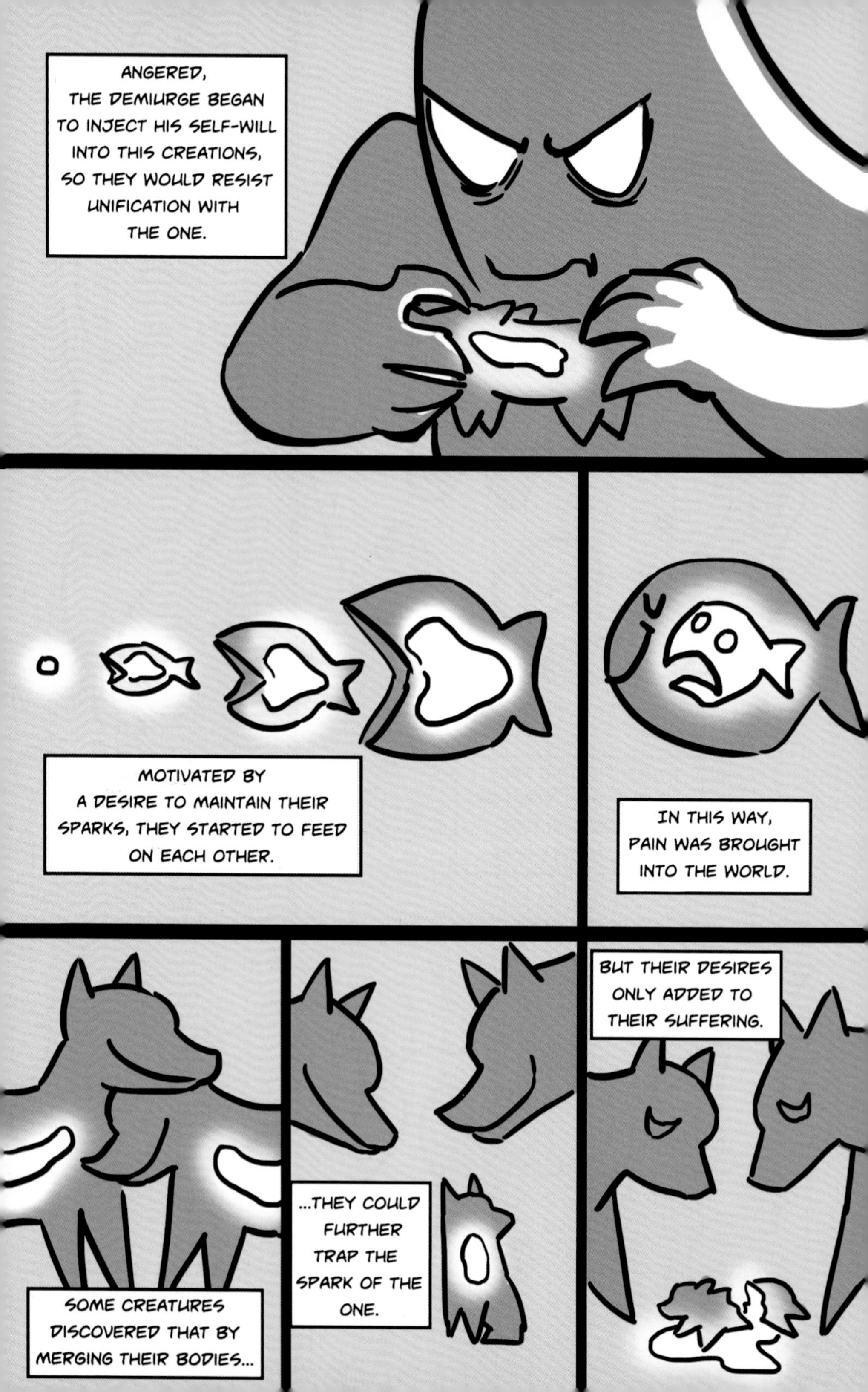
ANGERED, THE DEMIURGE BEGAN TO INJECT HIS SELF-WILL INTO THIS CREATIONS, SO THEY WOULD RESIST UNIFICATION WITH THE ONE.
MOTIVATED BY A DESIRE TO MAINTAIN THEIR SPARKS, THEY STARTED TO FEED ON EACH OTHER.
IN THIS WAY, PAIN WAS BROUGHT INTO THE WORLD.
SOME CREATURES DISCOVERED THAT BY MERGING THEIR BODIES...
...THEY COULD FURTHER TRAP THE SPARK OF THE ONE.
BUT THEIR DESIRES ONLY ADDED TO THEIR SUFFERING.

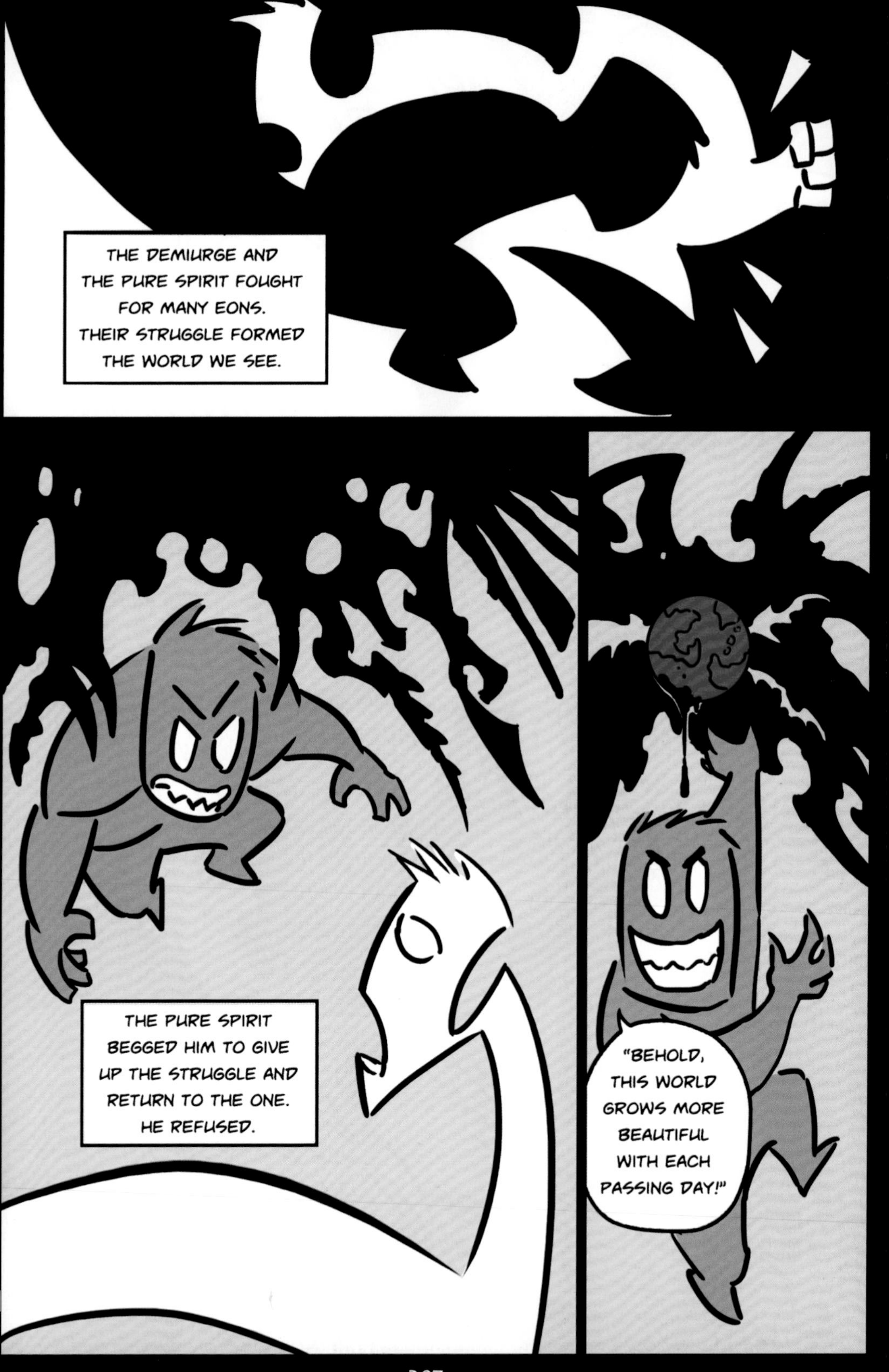
THE DEMIURGE AND THE PURE SPIRIT FOUGHT FOR MANY EONS. THEIR STRUGGLE FORMED THE WORLD WE SEE.
THE PURE SPIRIT BEGGED HIM TO GIVE UP THE STRUGGLE AND RETURN TO THE ONE. HE REFUSED.
"BEHOLD, THIS WORLD GROWS MORE BEAUTIFUL WITH EACH PASSING DAY!"

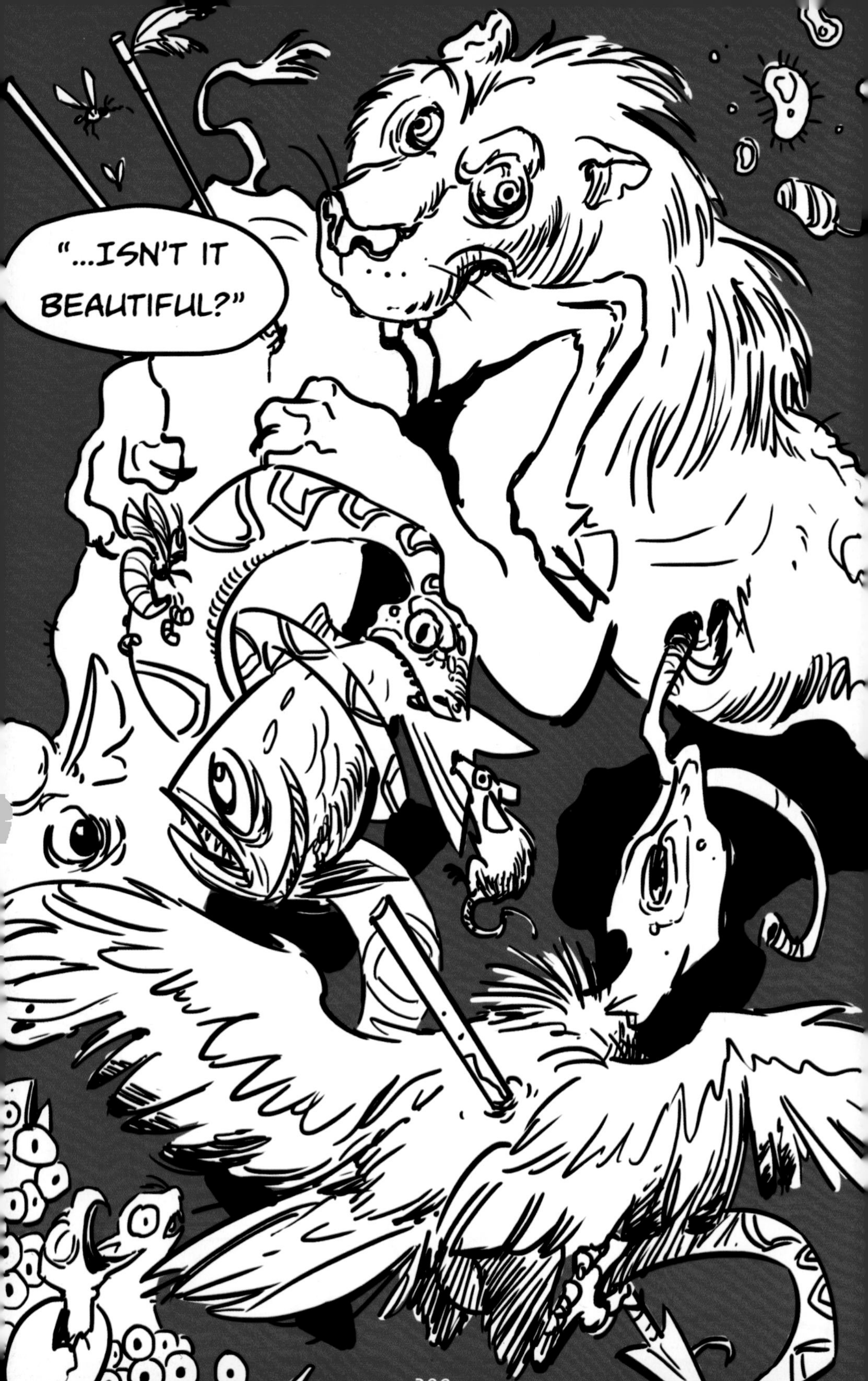
"...ISN'T IT BEAUTIFUL?"

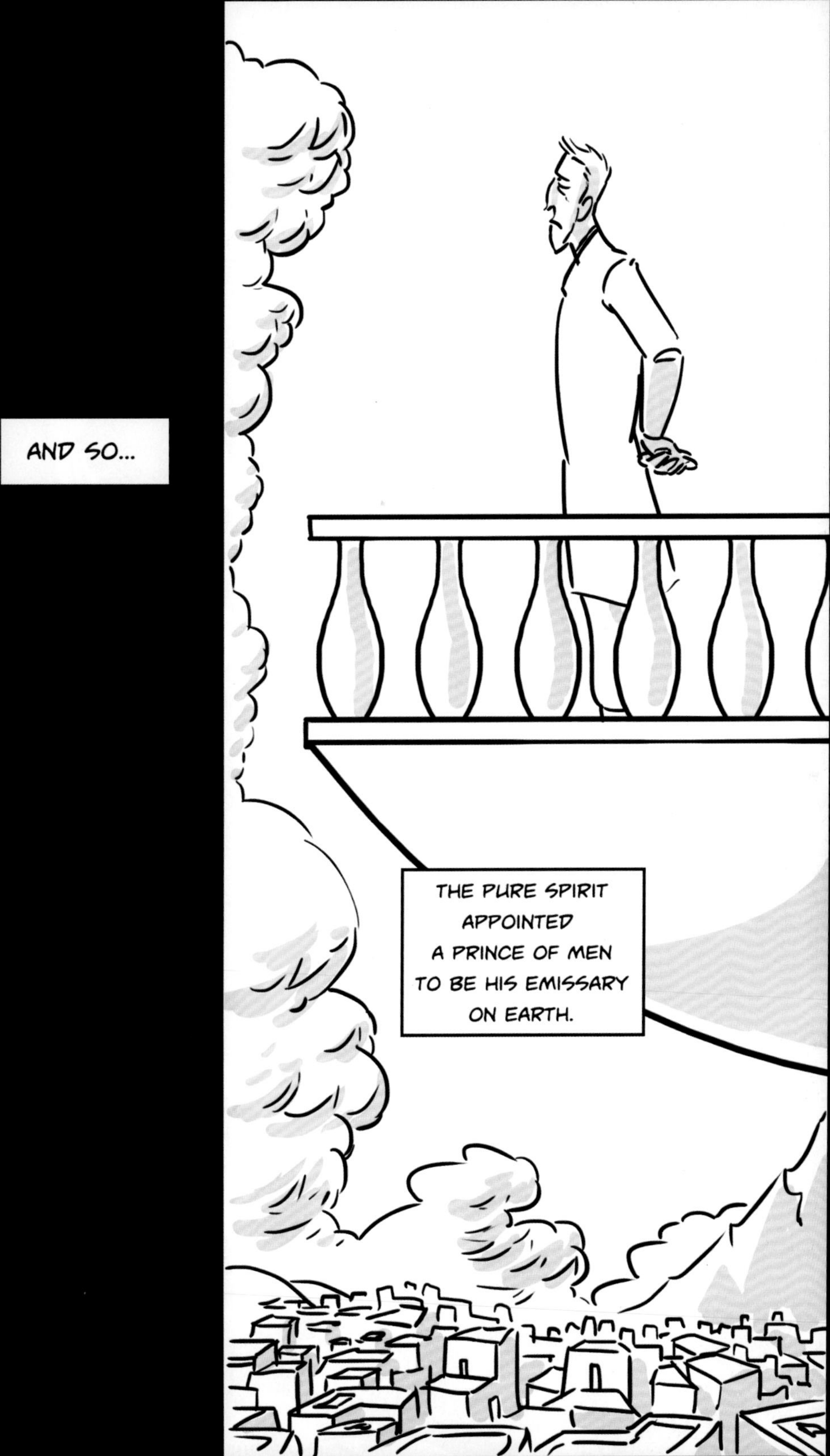
AND SO...
THE PURE SPIRIT APPOINTED A PRINCE OF MEN TO BE HIS EMISSARY ON EARTH.

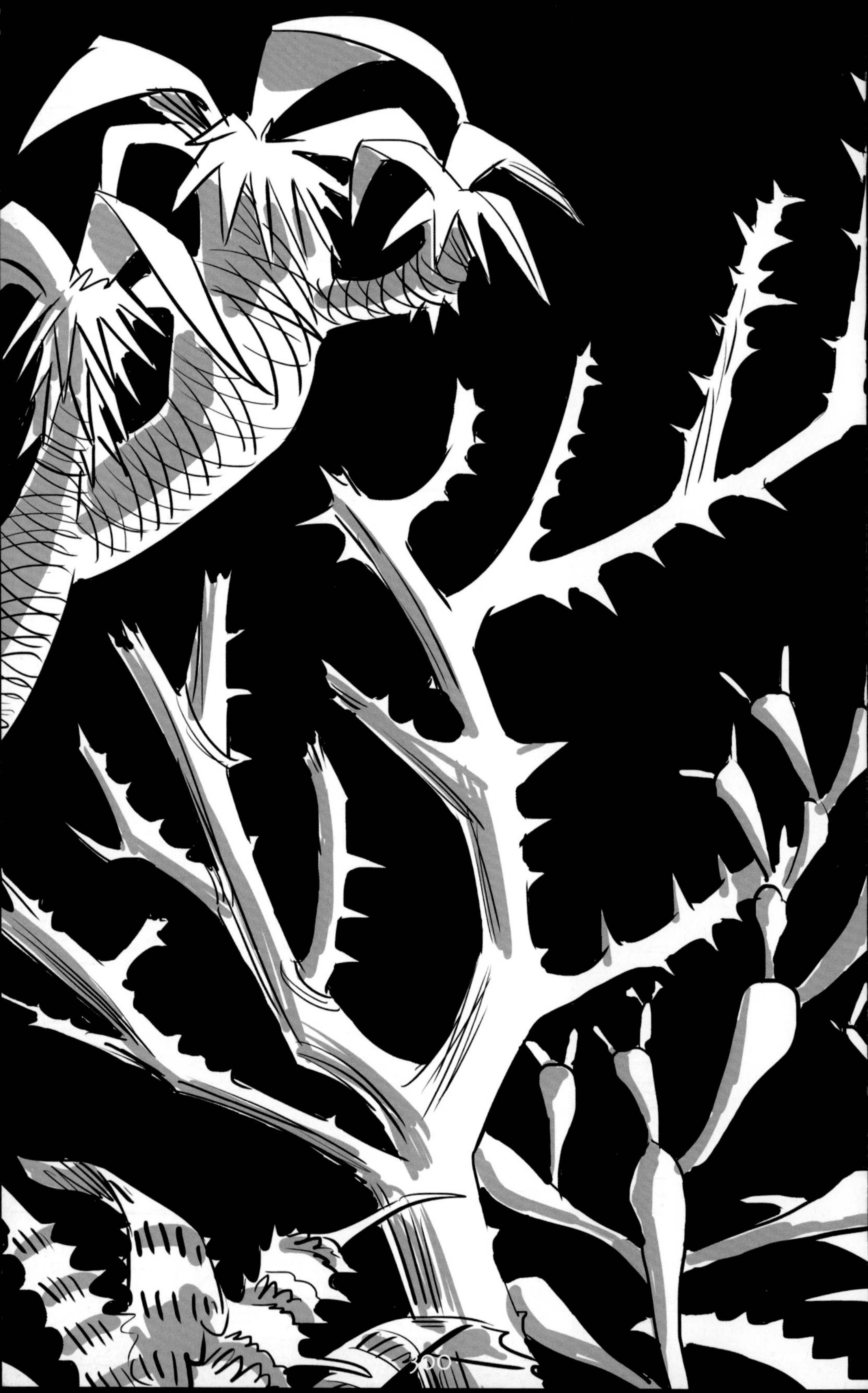

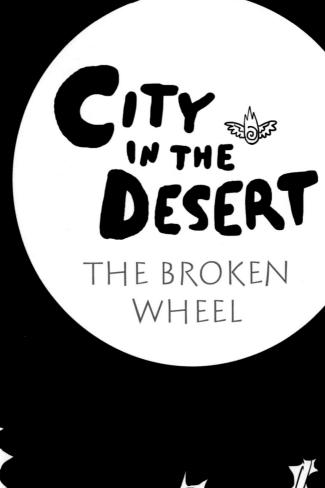

CITY IN THE DESERT

THE BROKEN WHEEL

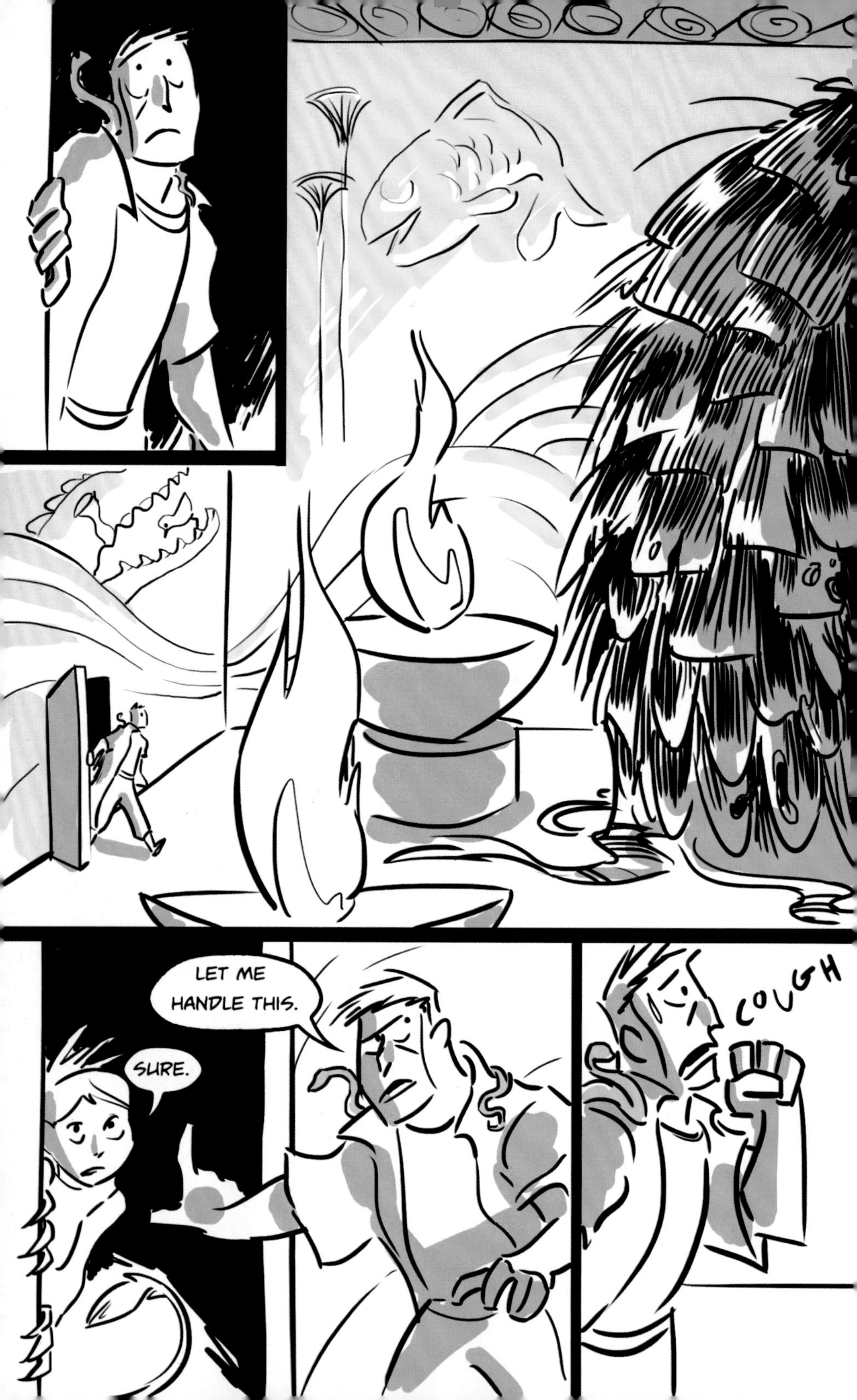
SURE.
LET ME HANDLE THIS.
COUGH

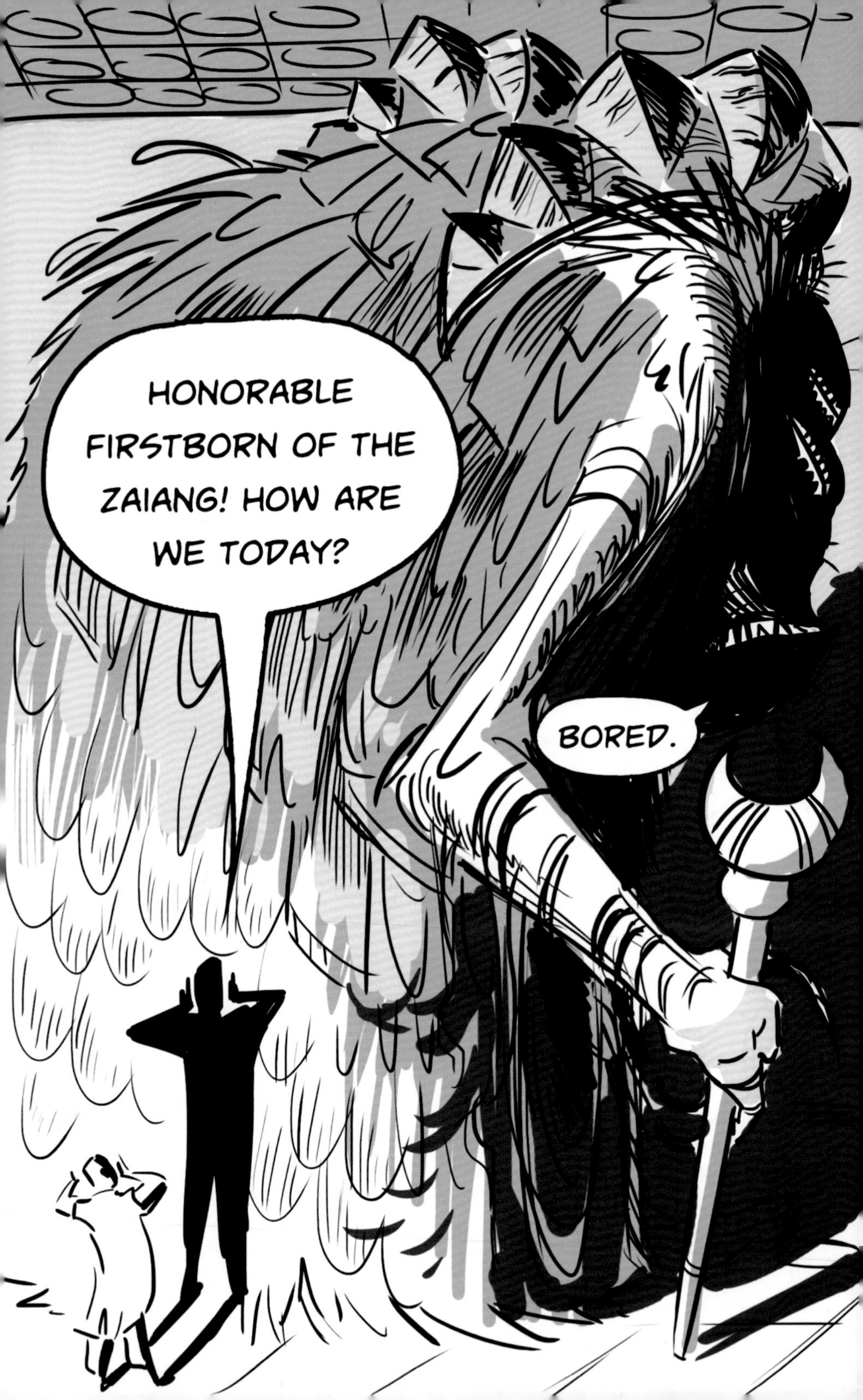
HONORABLE FIRSTBORN OF THE ZAIANG! HOW ARE WE TODAY?
BORED.

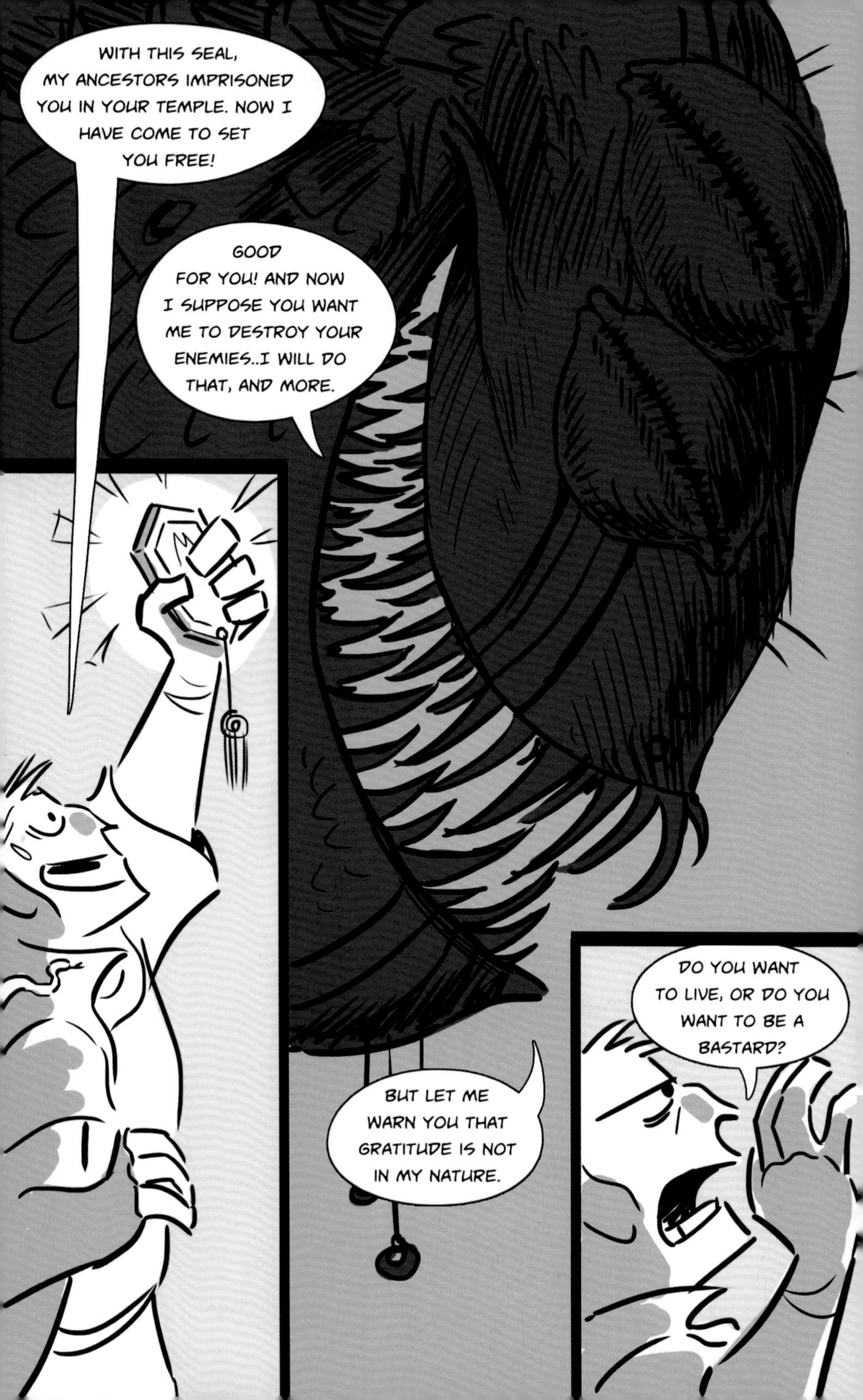
WITH THIS SEAL, MY ANCESTORS IMPRISONED YOU IN YOUR TEMPLE. NOW I HAVE COME TO SET YOU FREE!
GOOD FOR YOU! AND NOW I SUPPOSE YOU WANT ME TO DESTROY YOUR ENEMIES..I WILL DO THAT, AND MORE.
BUT LET ME WARN YOU THAT GRATITUDE IS NOT IN MY NATURE.
DO YOU WANT TO LIVE, OR DO YOU WANT TO BE A BASTARD?

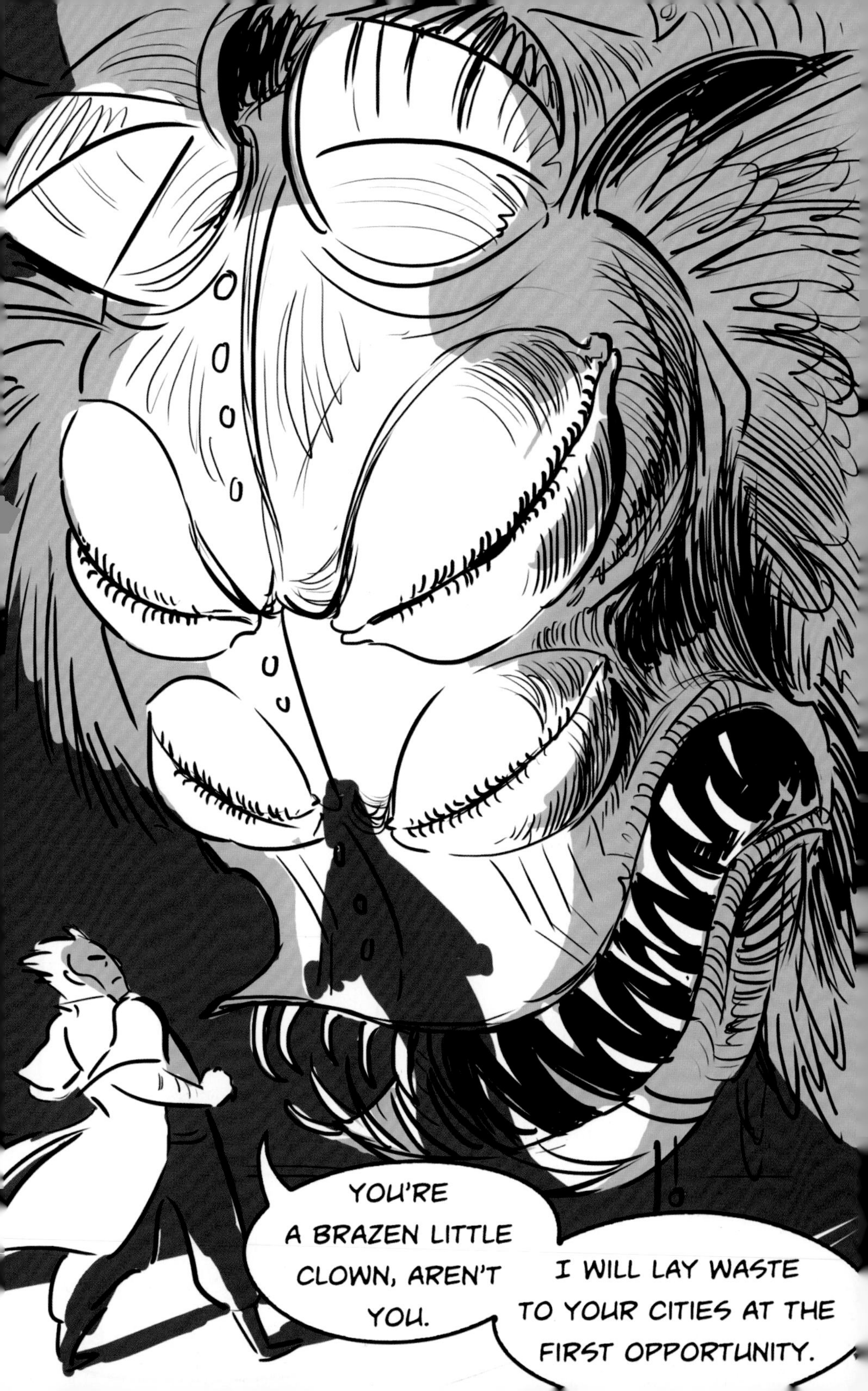
YOU'RE A BRAZEN LITTLE CLOWN, AREN'T YOU.
I WILL LAY WASTE TO YOUR CITIES AT THE FIRST OPPORTUNITY.

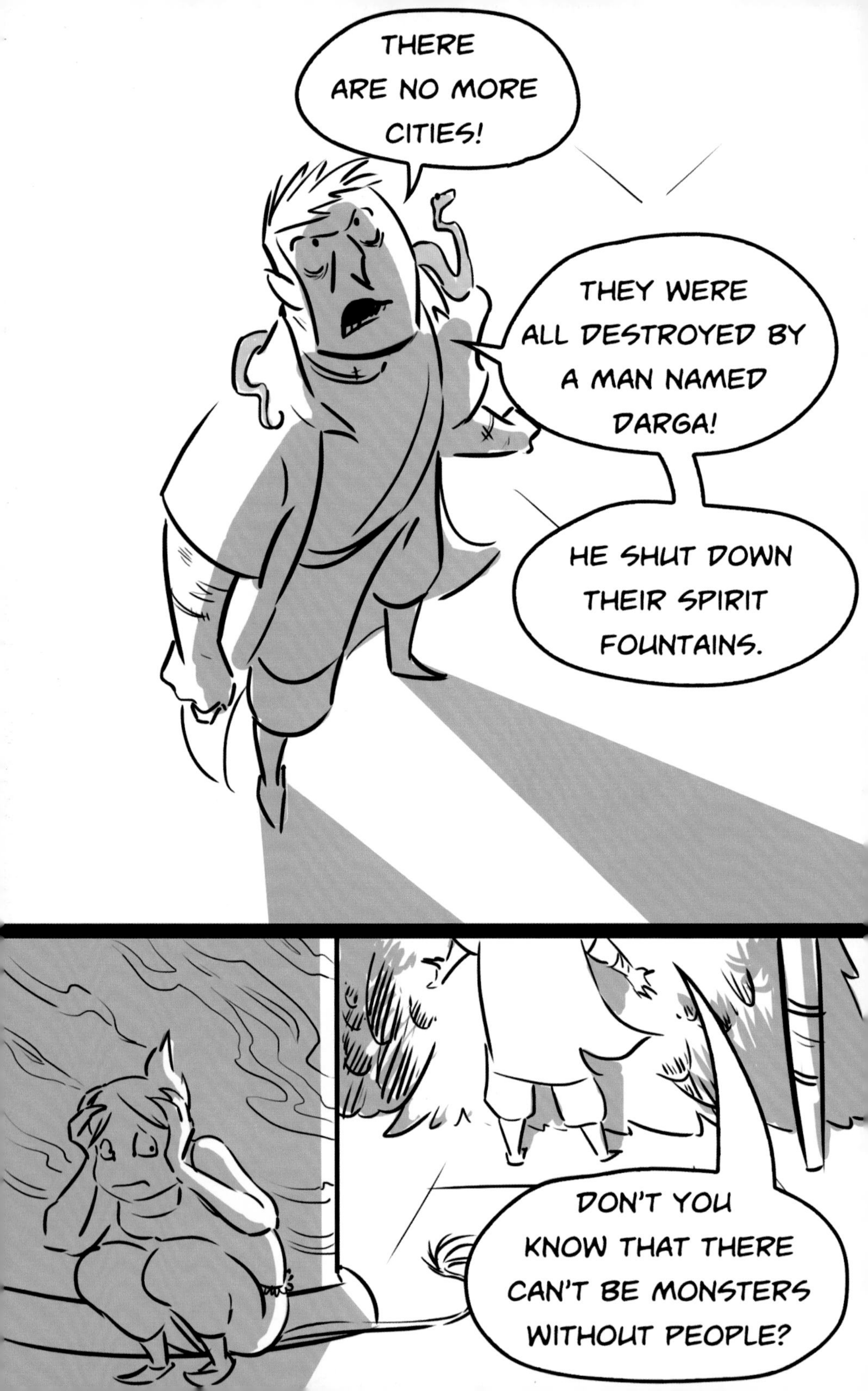
THERE ARE NO MORE CITIES!
THEY WERE ALL DESTROYED BY A MAN NAMED DARGA!
HE SHUT DOWN THEIR SPIRIT FOUNTAINS.
DON'T YOU KNOW THAT THERE CAN'T BE MONSTERS WITHOUT PEOPLE?

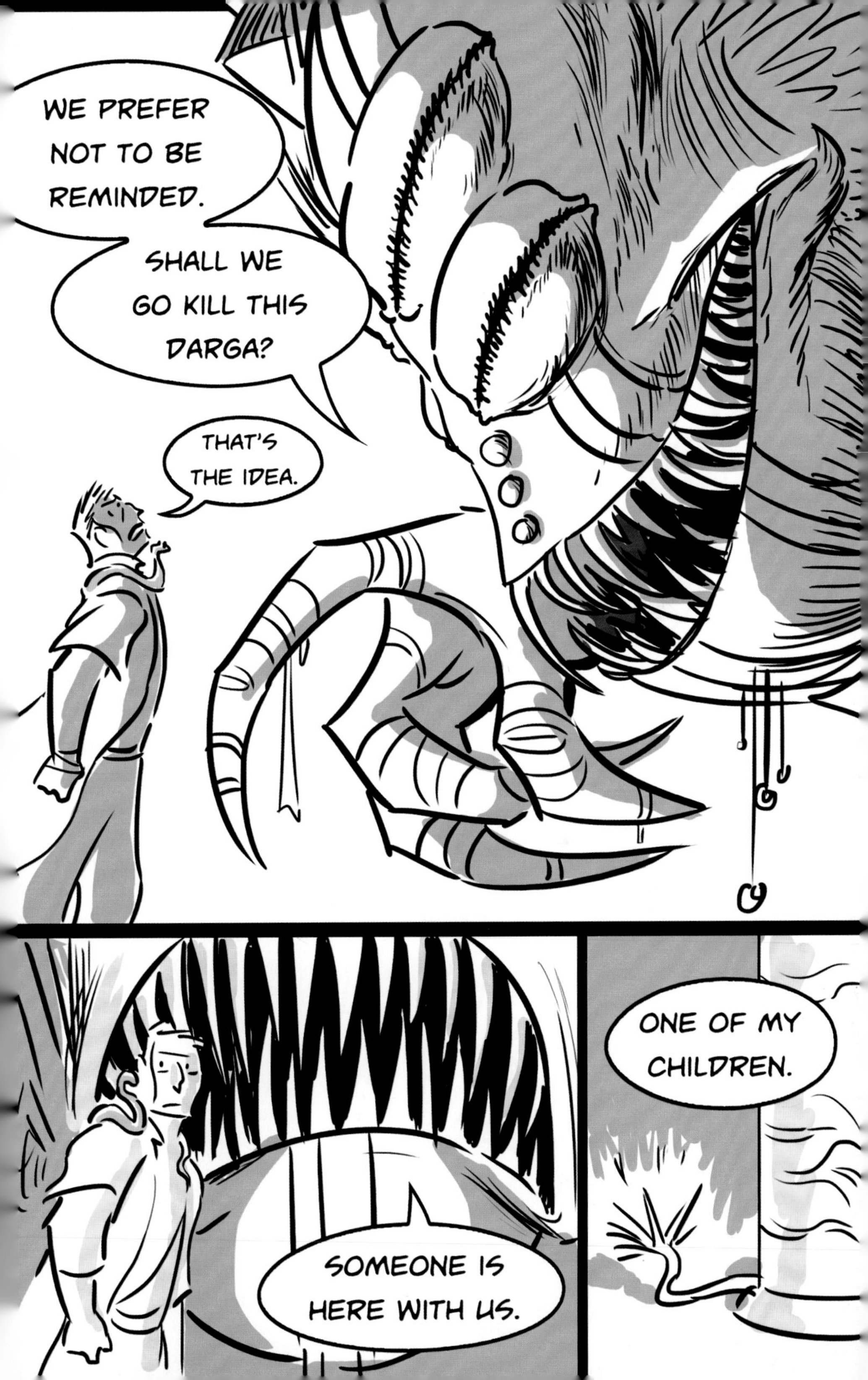
WE PREFER NOT TO BE REMINDED.
SHALL WE GO KILL THIS DARGA?
THAT'S THE IDEA.
SOMEONE IS HERE WITH US.
ONE OF MY CHILDREN.

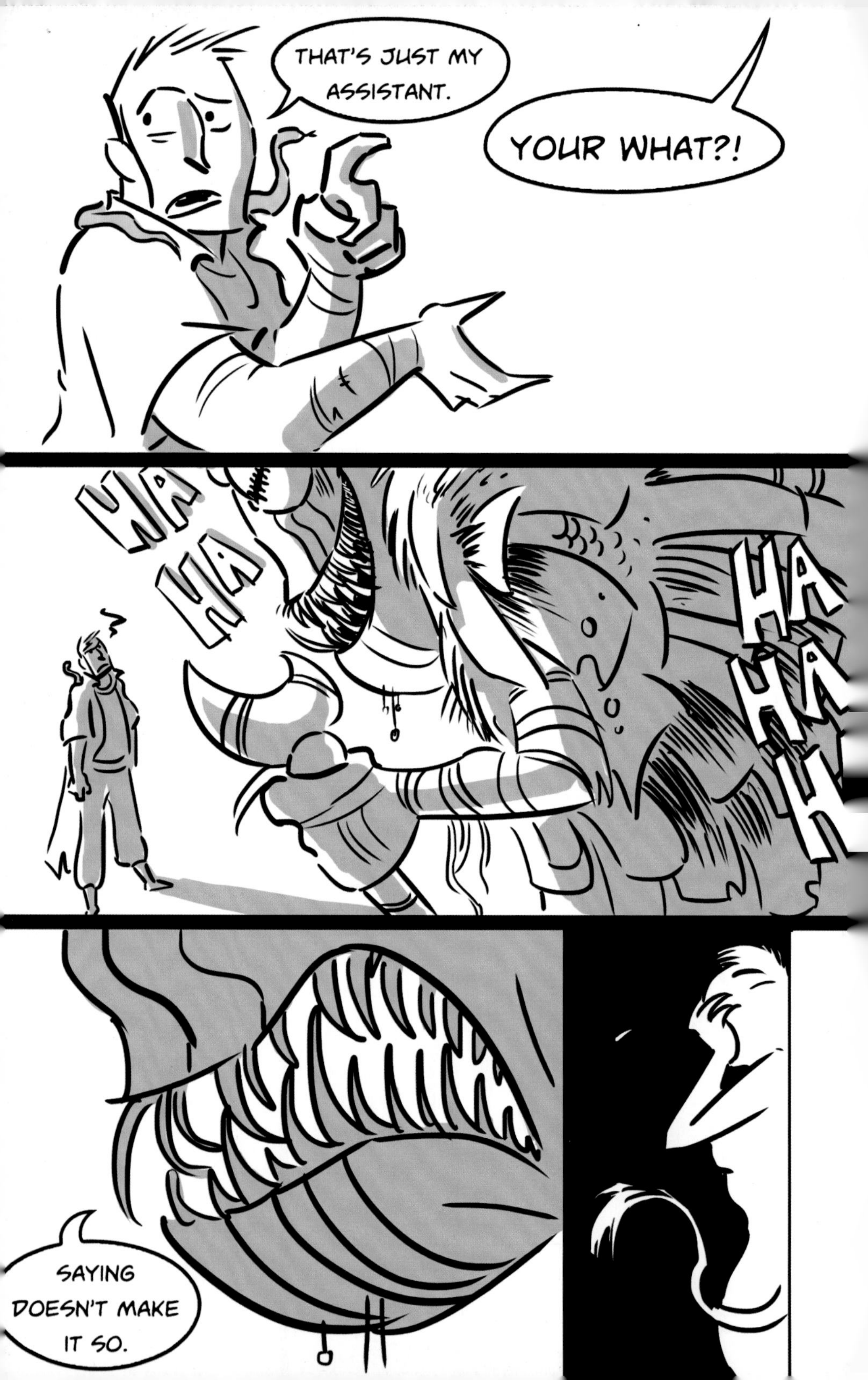
THAT'S JUST MY ASSISTANT.
YOUR WHAT?!
HA HA
HA HA HA
SAYING DOESN'T MAKE IT SO.

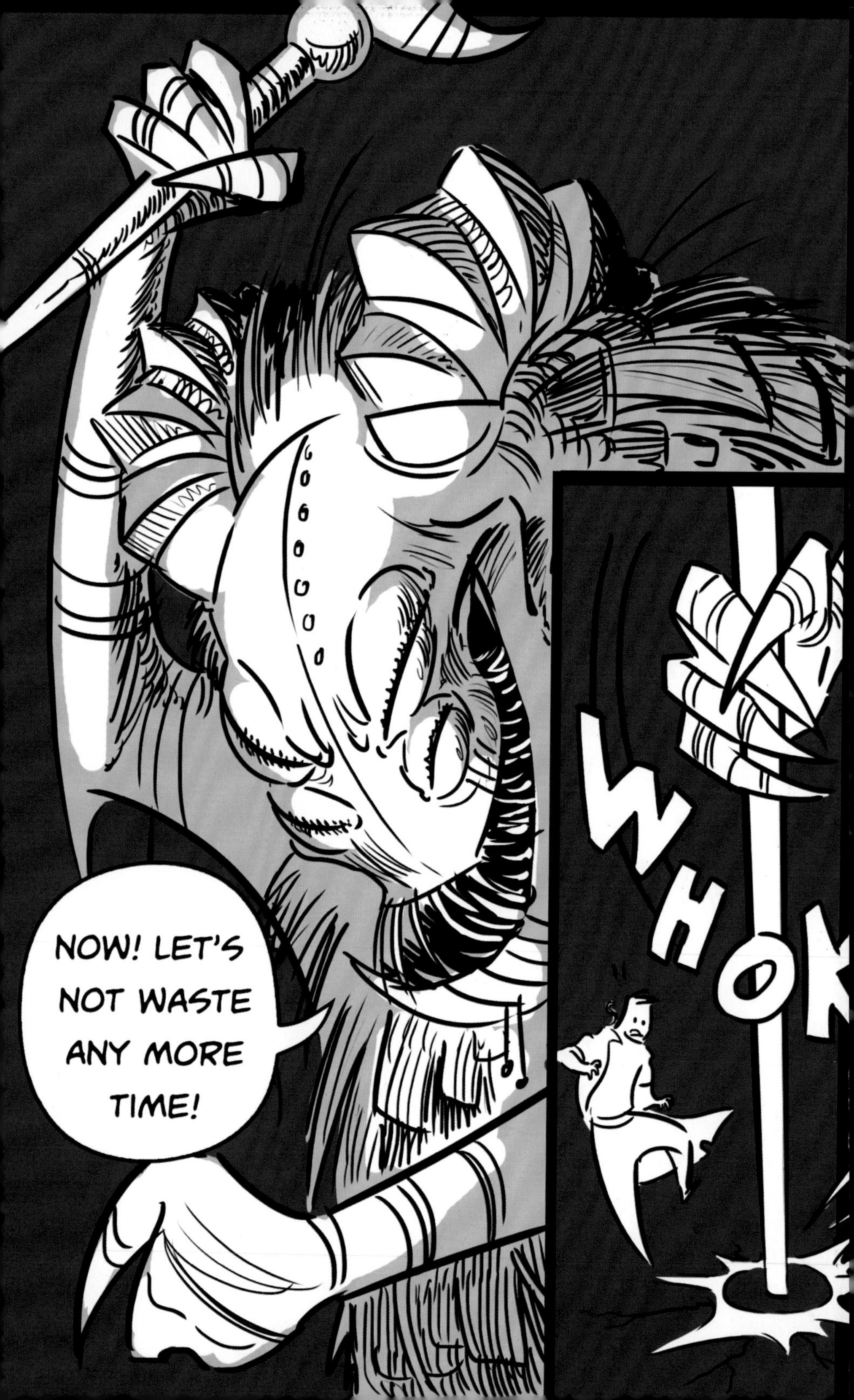
NOW! LET'S NOT WASTE ANY MORE TIME!
WHOK

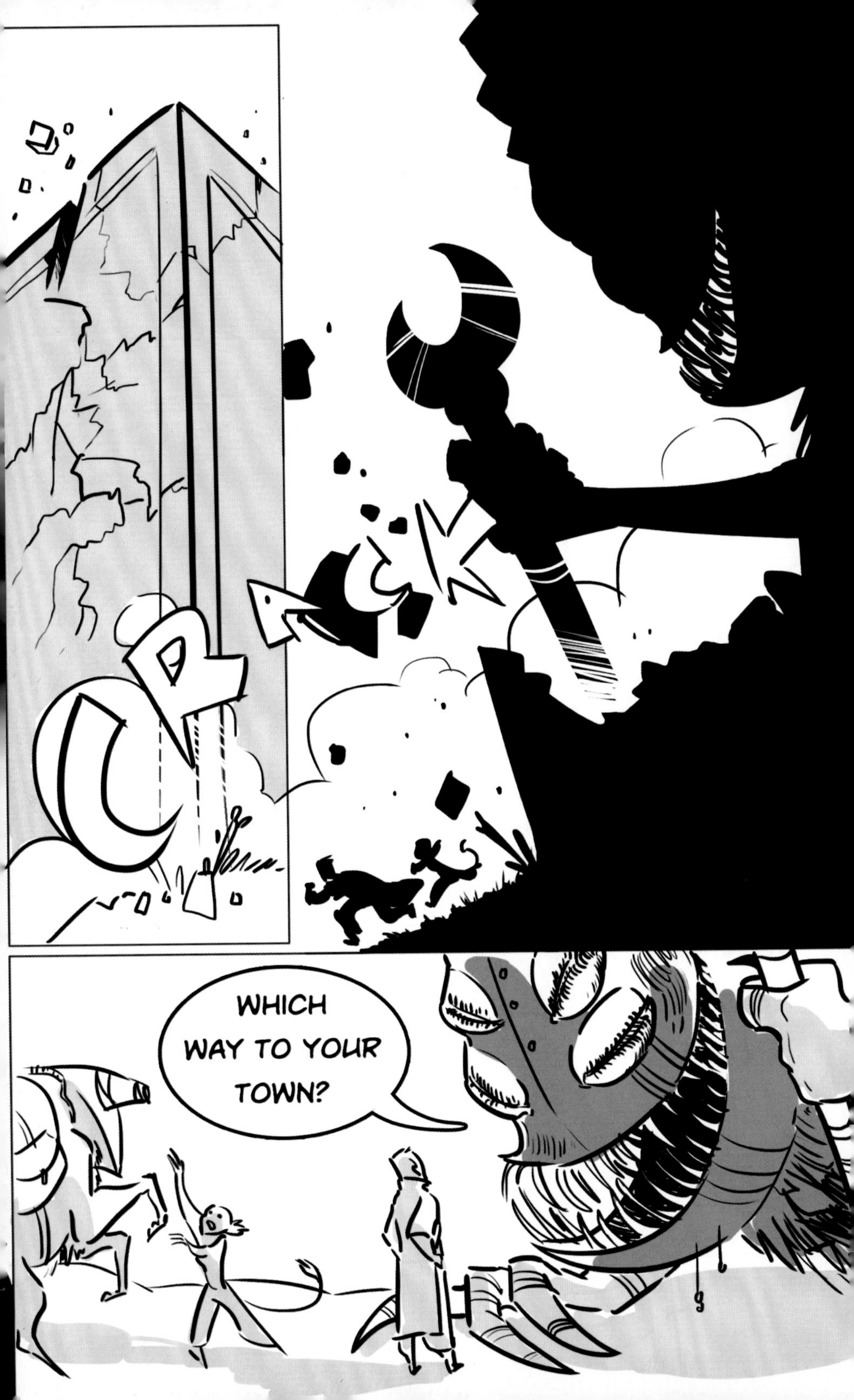
CRACK
WHICH WAY TO YOUR TOWN?

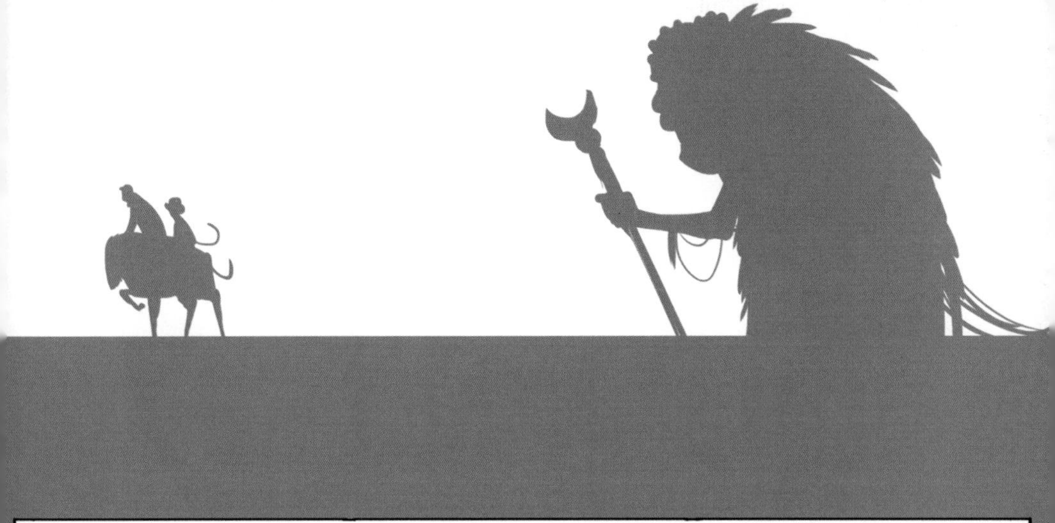

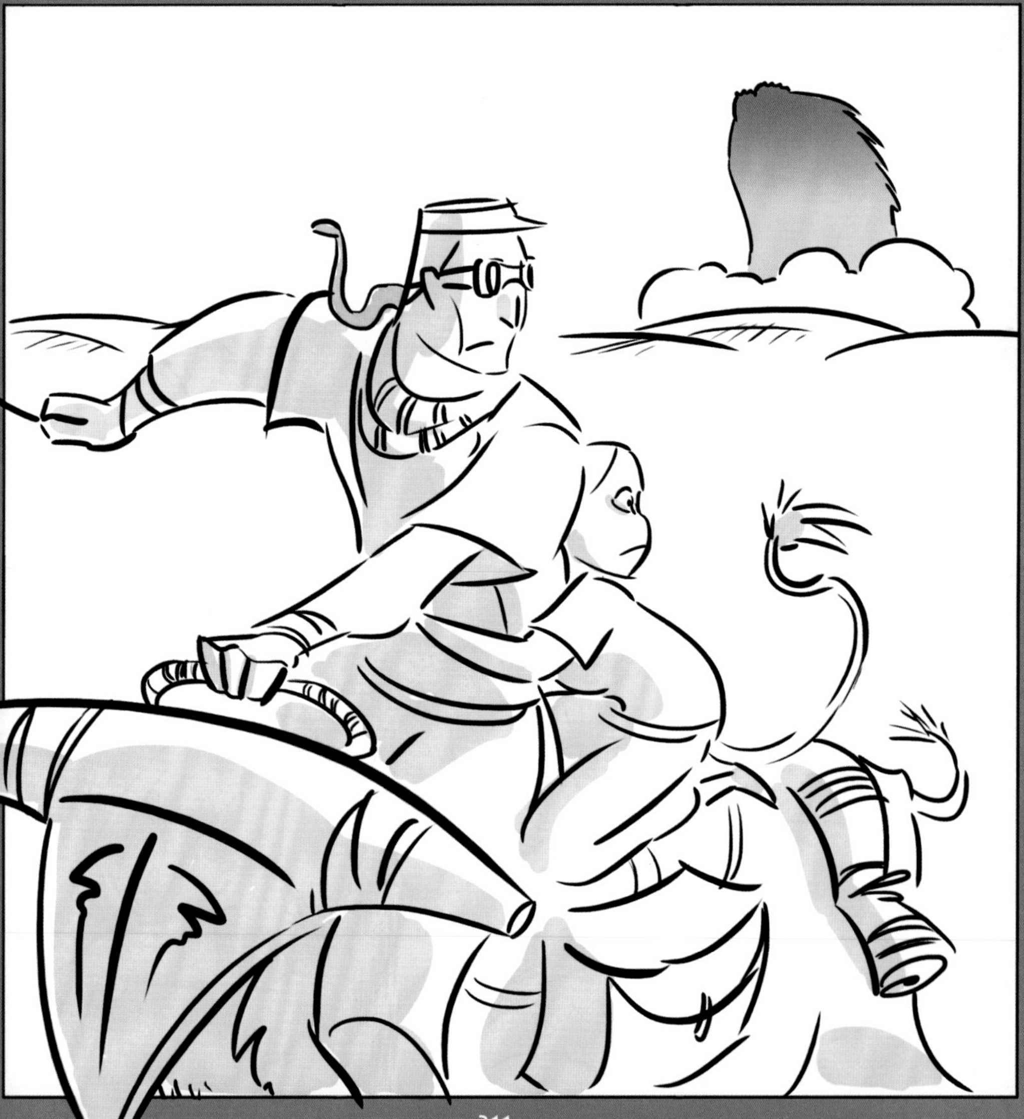

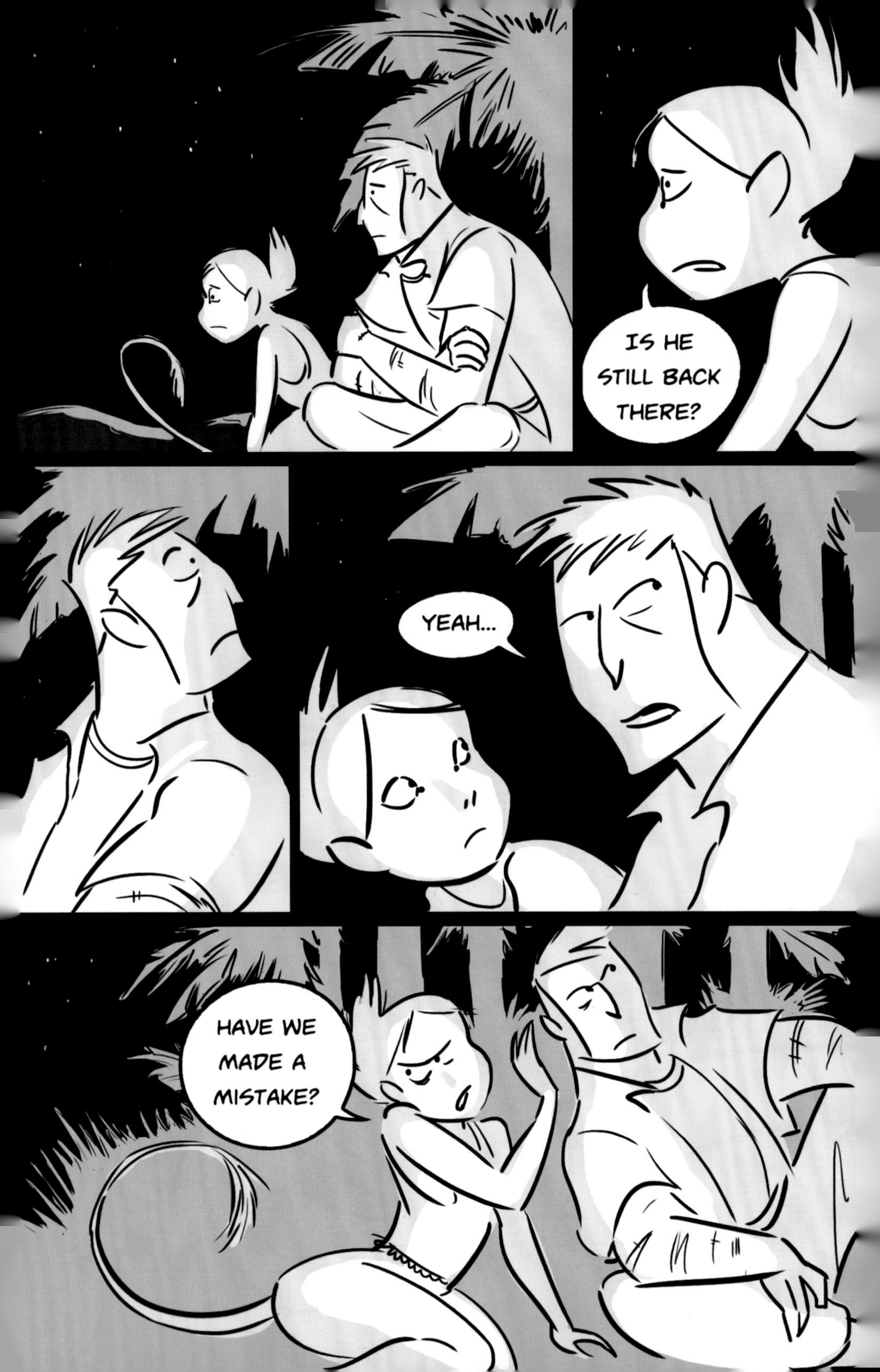
IS HE STILL BACK THERE?
YEAH...
HAVE WE MADE A MISTAKE?

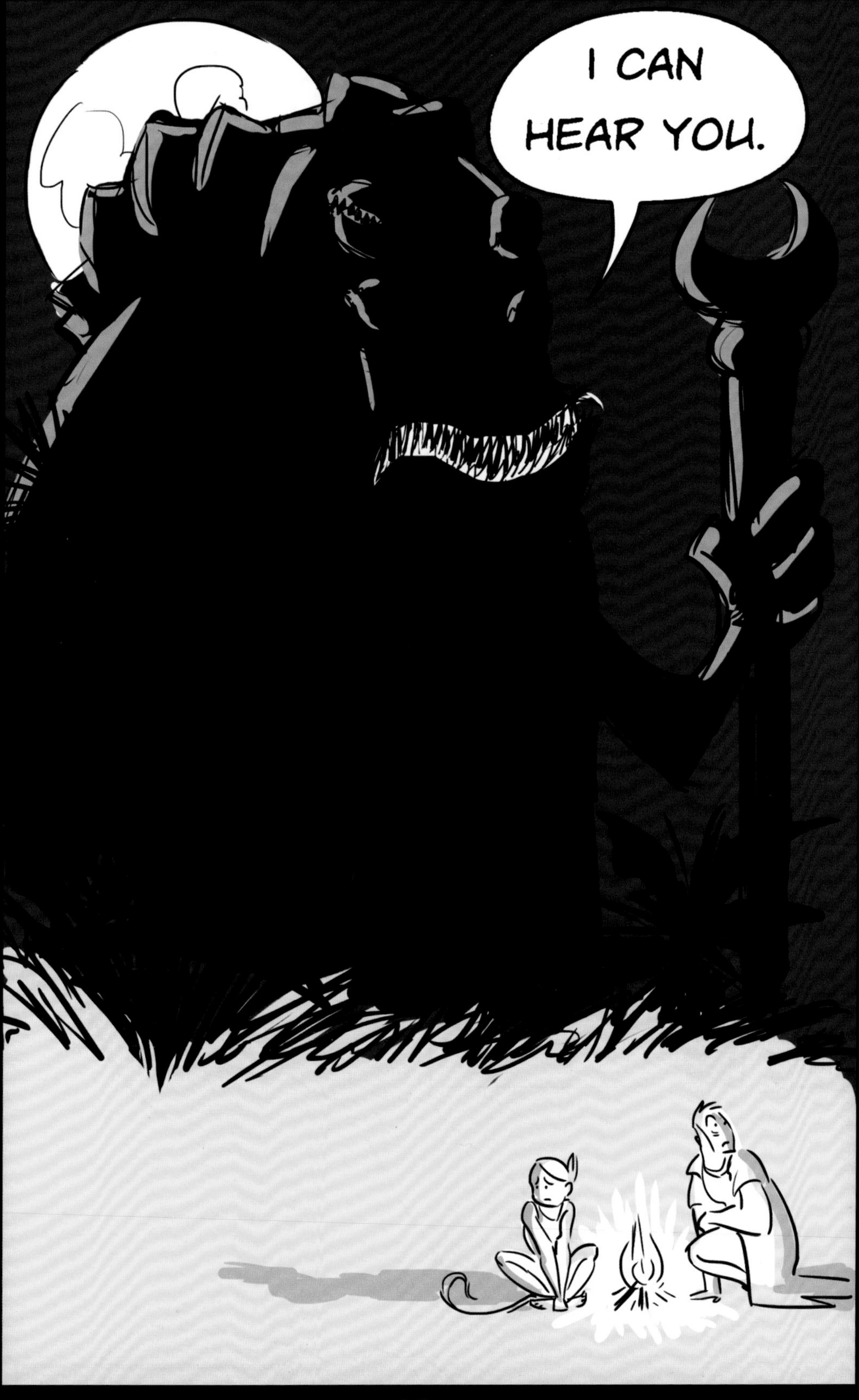
I CAN HEAR YOU.

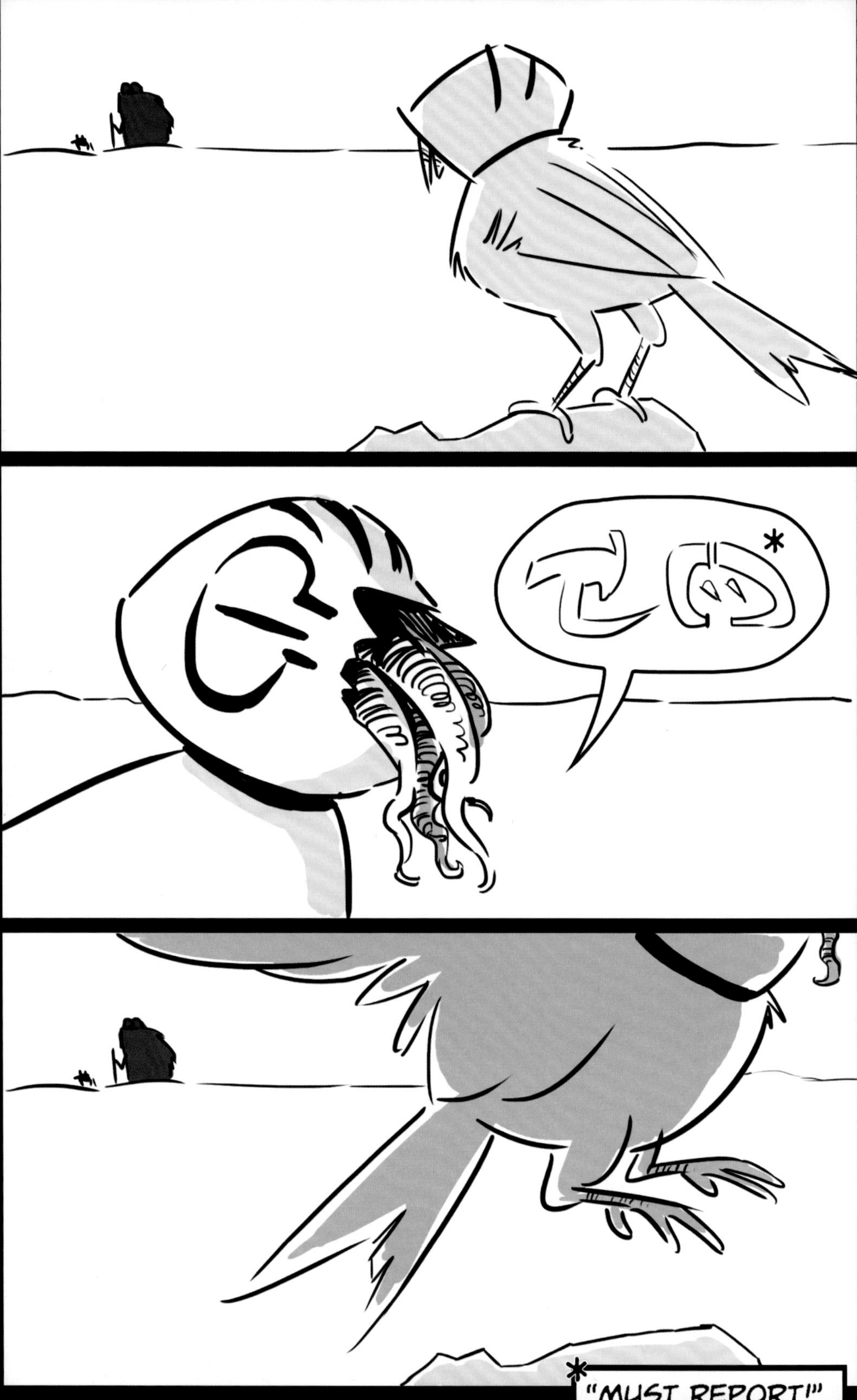
*
*"MUST REPORT!"

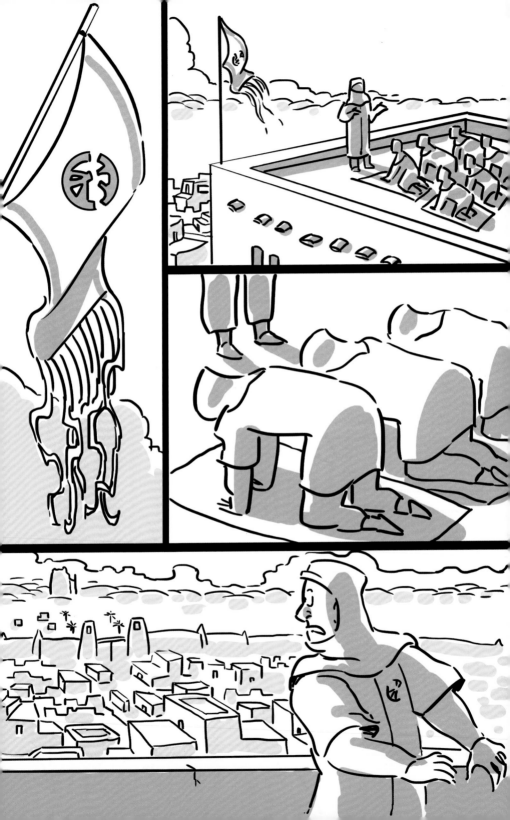

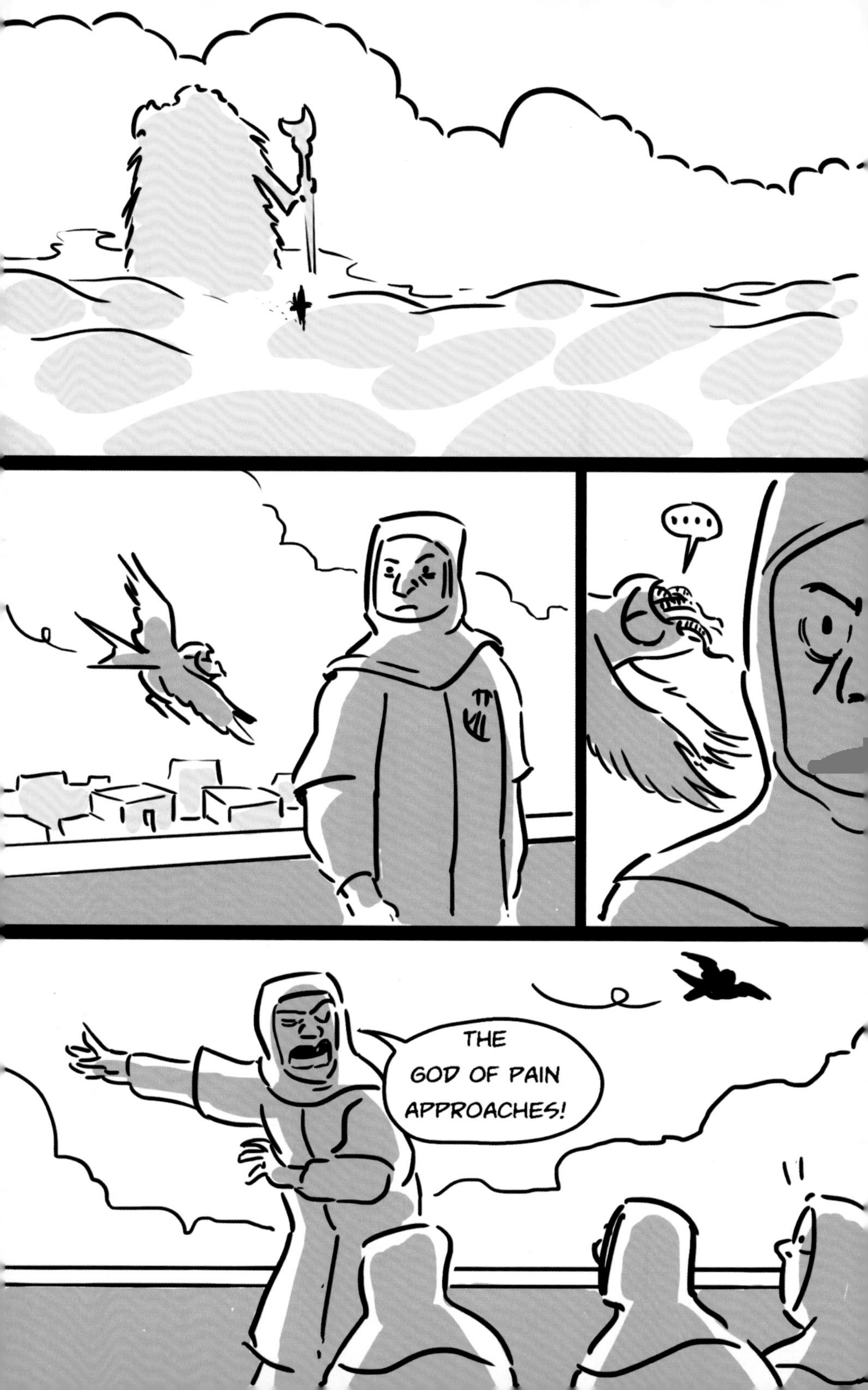
....
THE GOD OF PAIN APPROACHES!

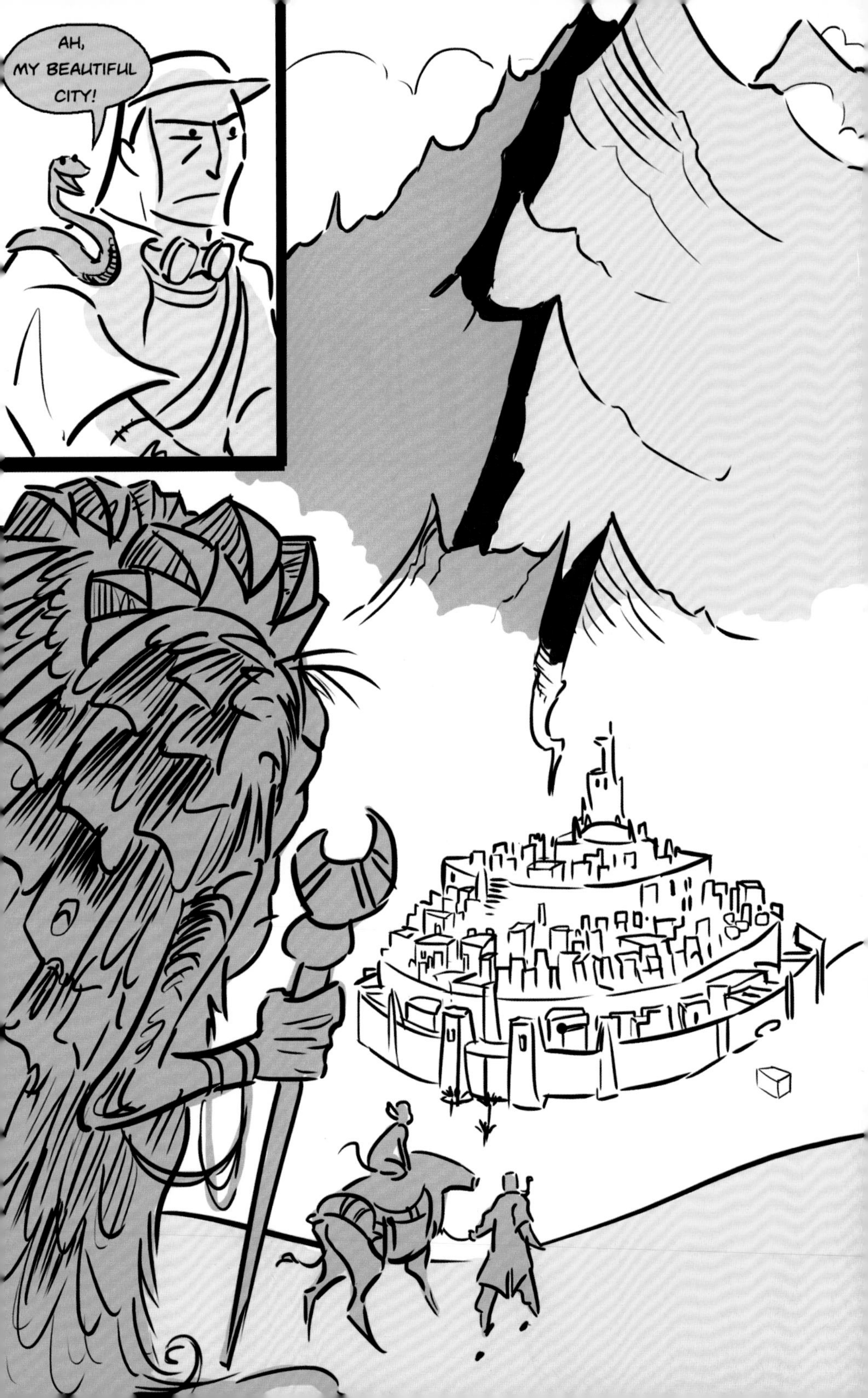
AH, MY BEAUTIFUL CITY!

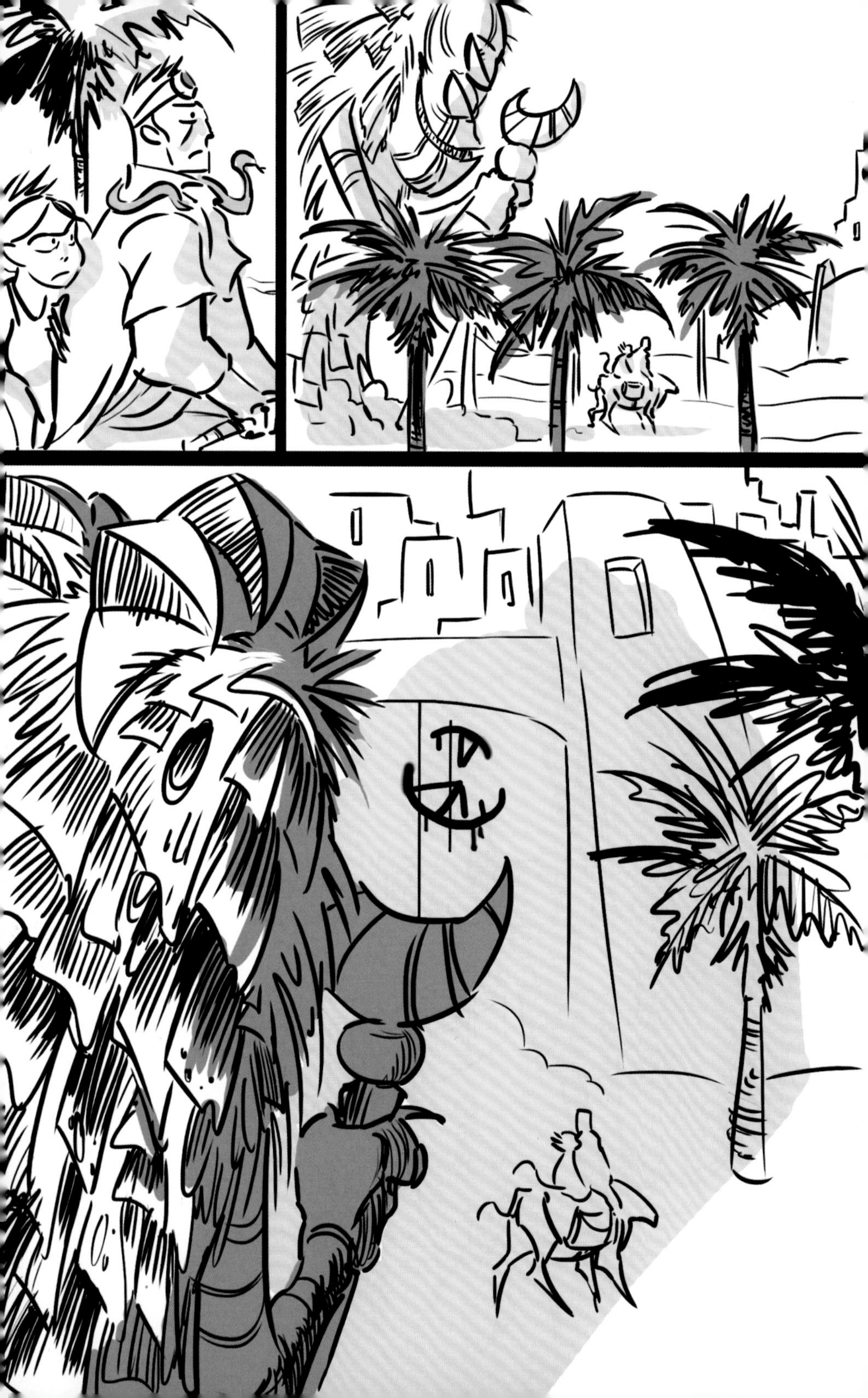

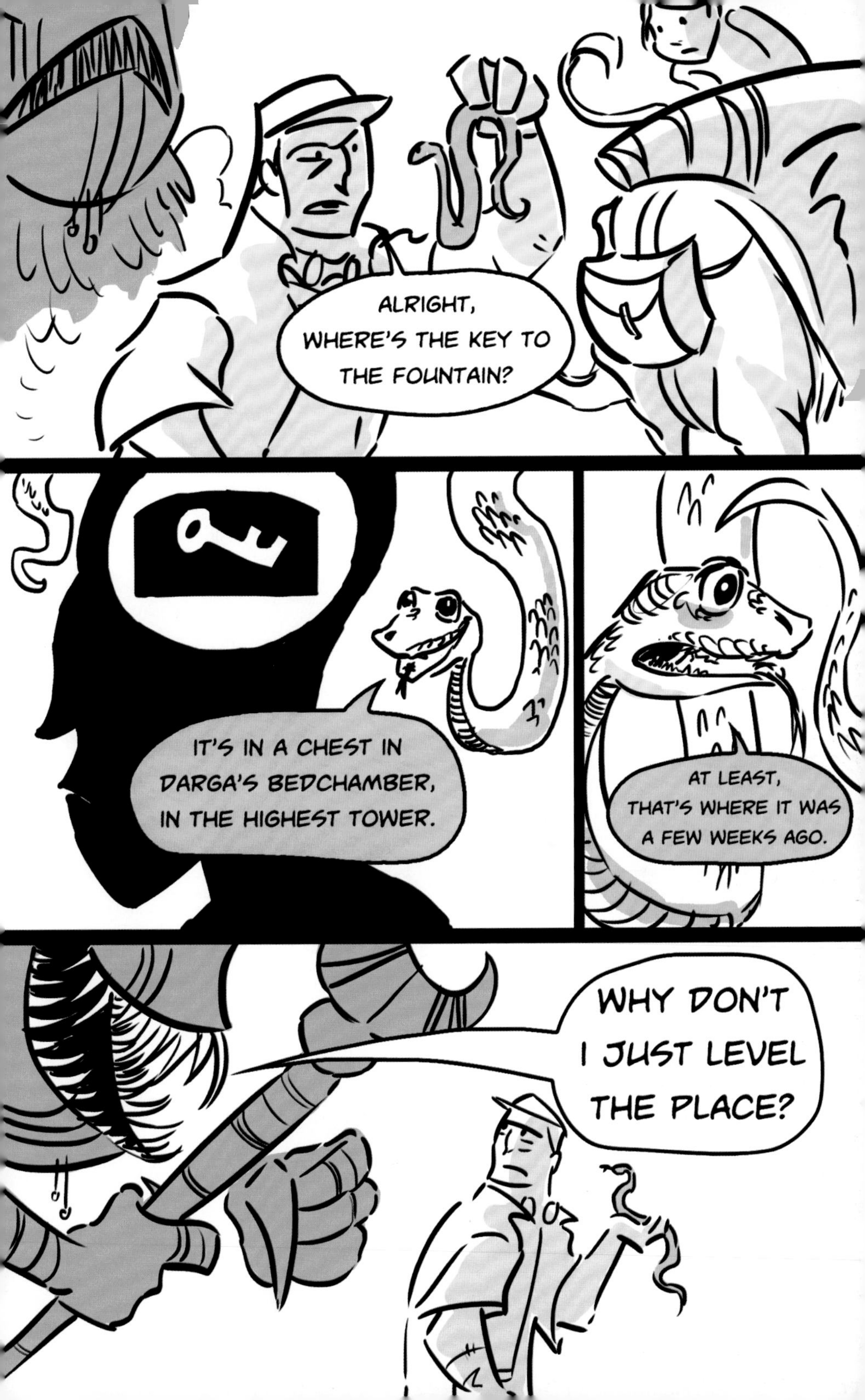
ALRIGHT, WHERE'S THE KEY TO THE FOUNTAIN?
IT'S IN A CHEST IN DARGA'S BEDCHAMBER, IN THE HIGHEST TOWER.
AT LEAST, THAT'S WHERE IT WAS A FEW WEEKS AGO.
WHY DON'T I JUST LEVEL THE PLACE?

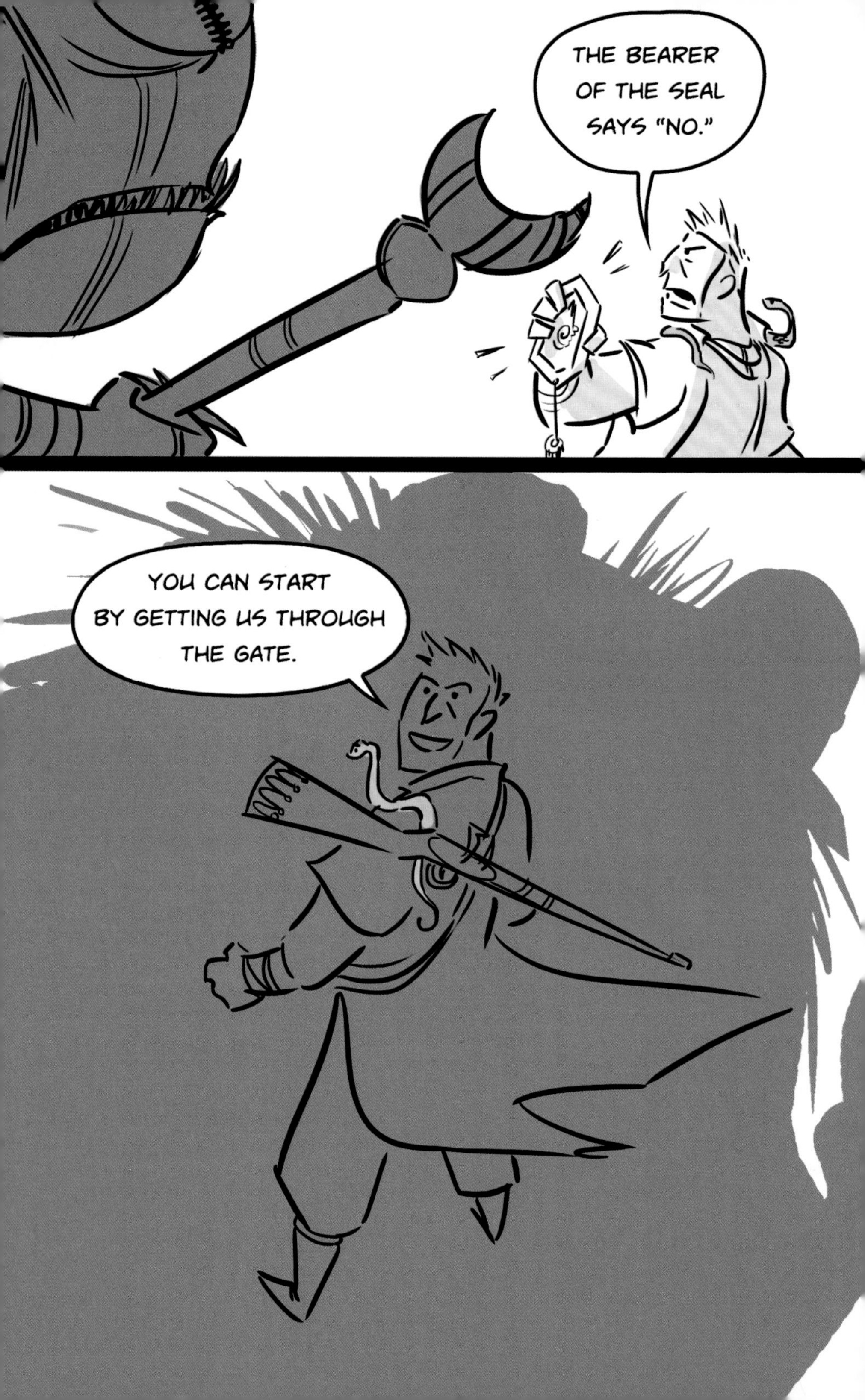
THE BEARER OF THE SEAL SAYS "NO."
YOU CAN START BY GETTING US THROUGH THE GATE.

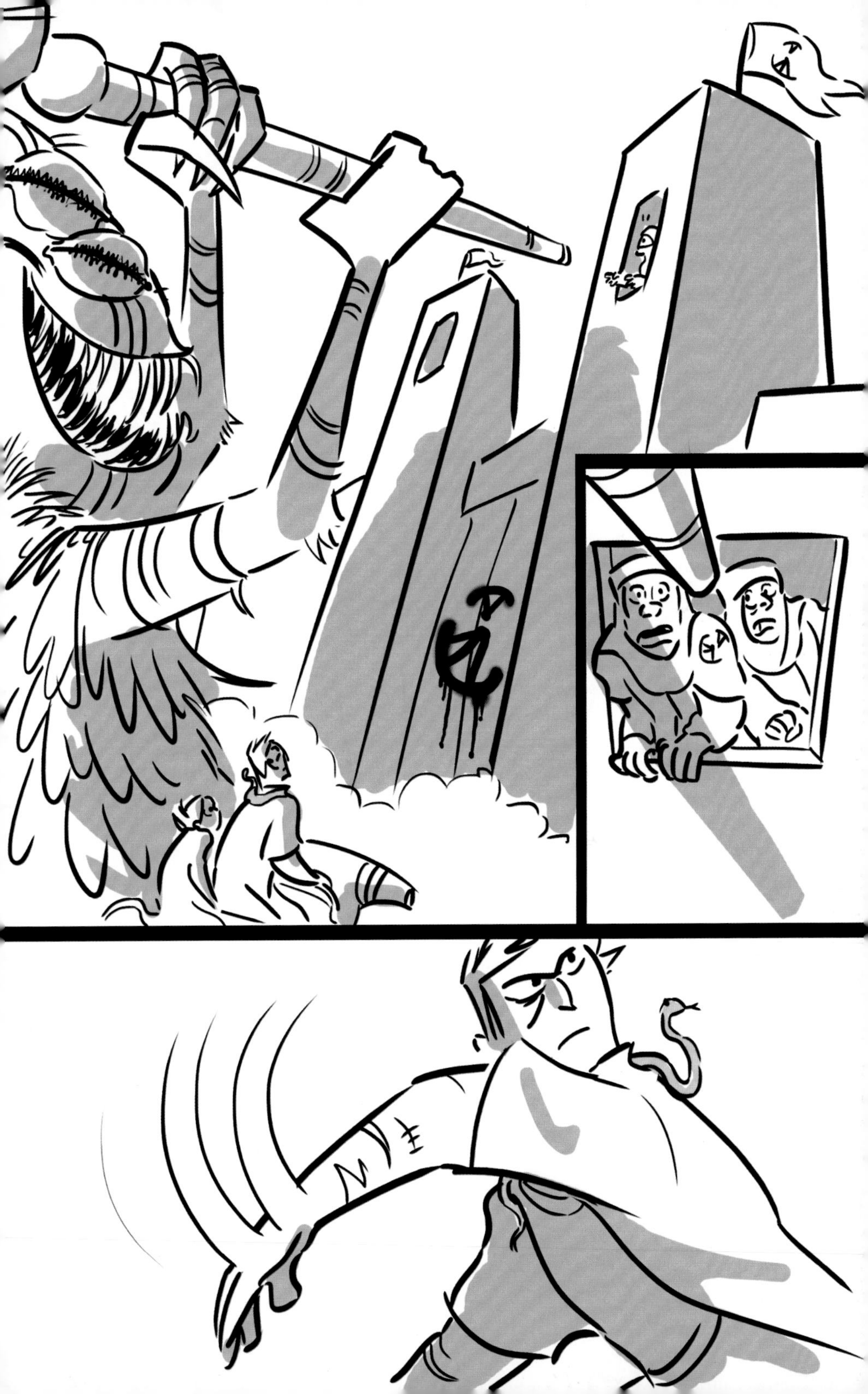

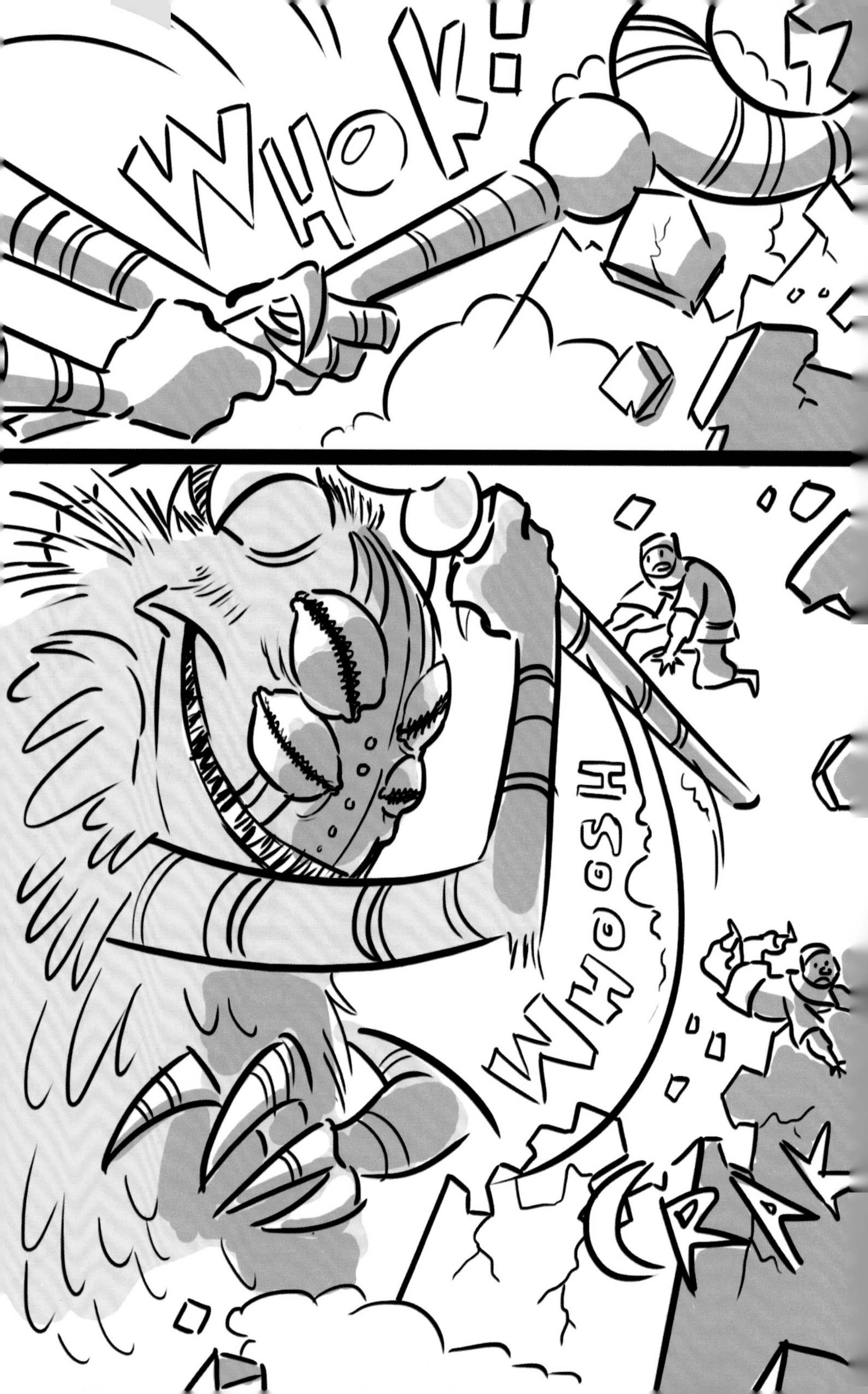
WHOK!
WHOOSH
CRAK

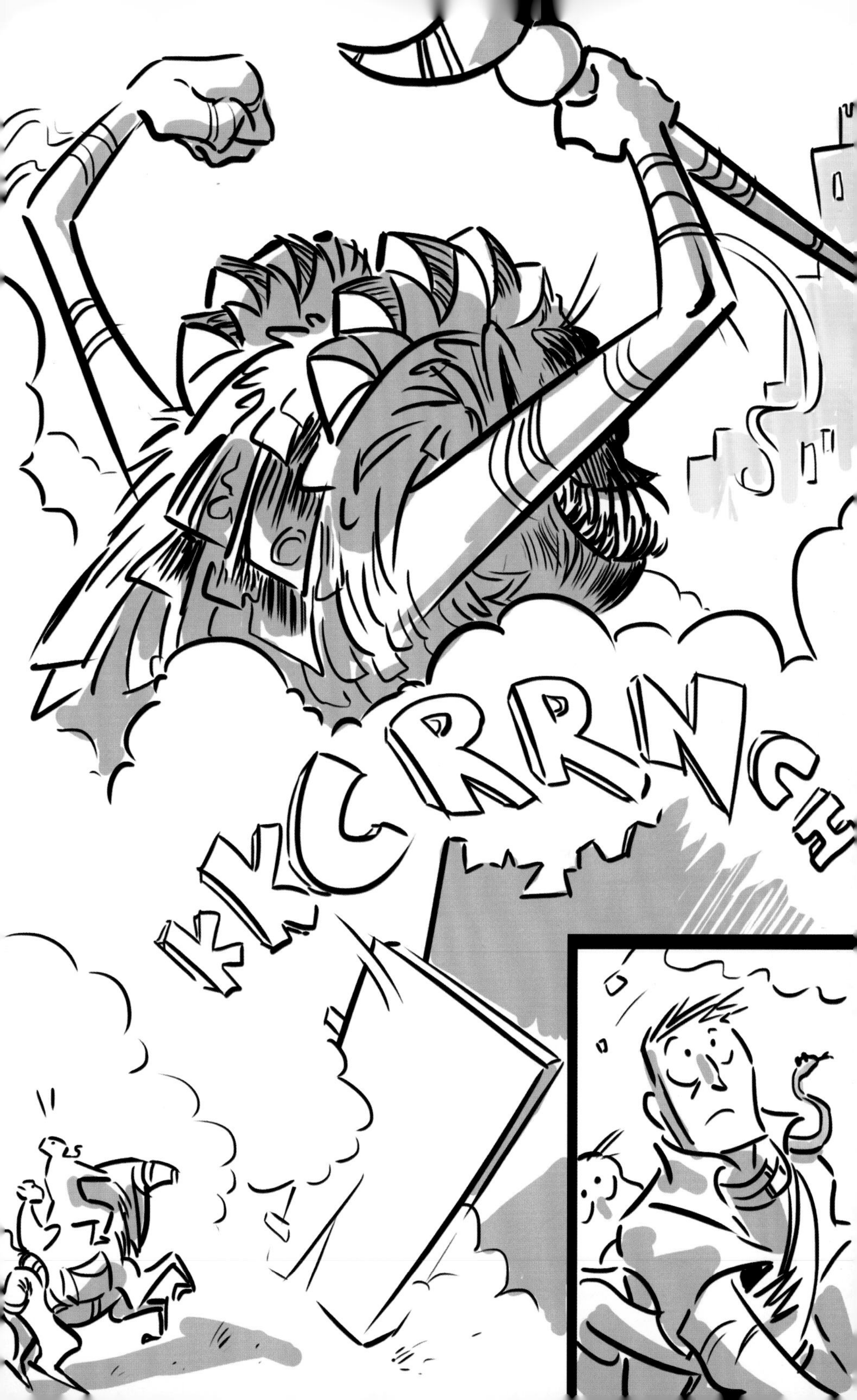
KKCRRNCH

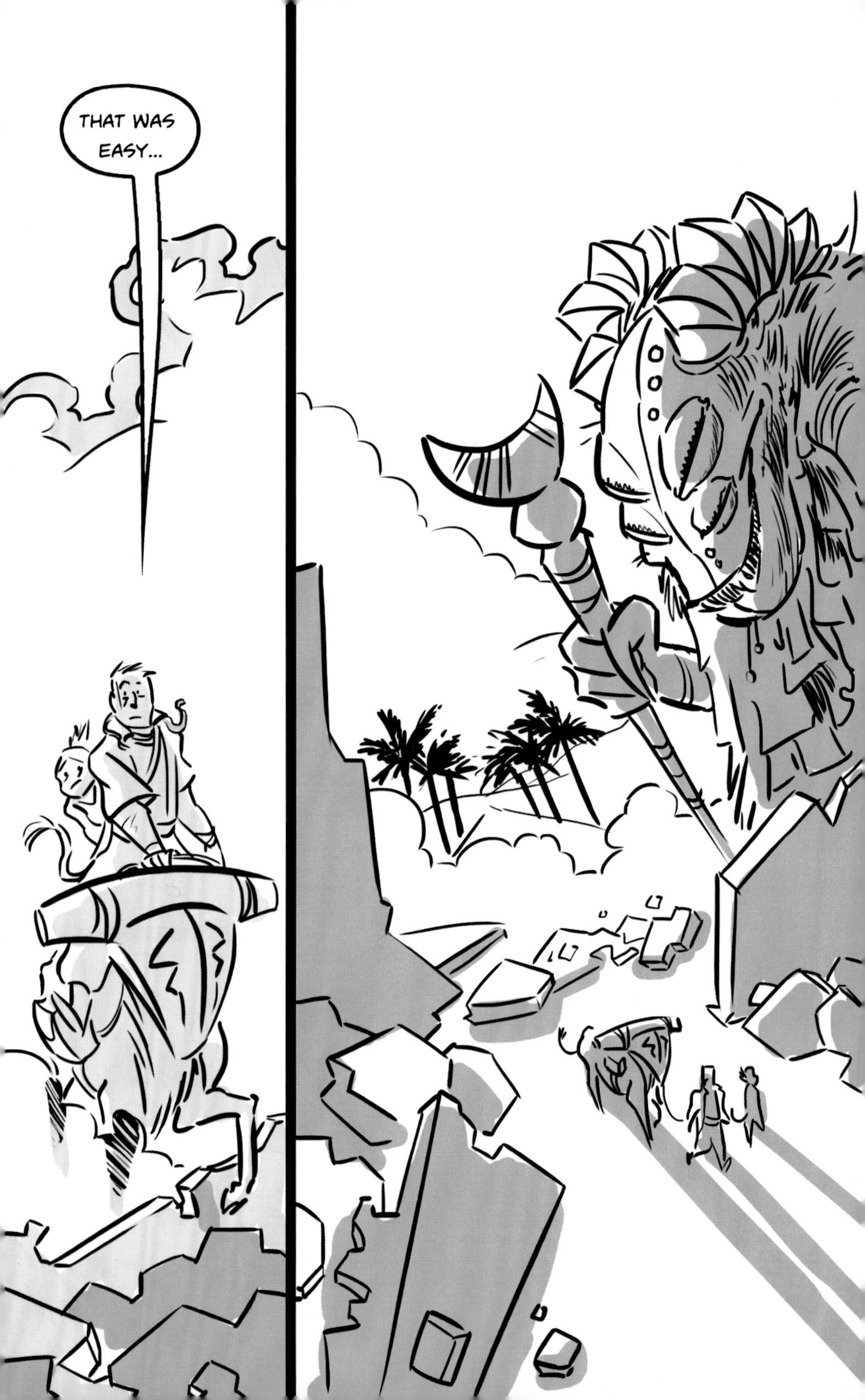
THAT WAS EASY...

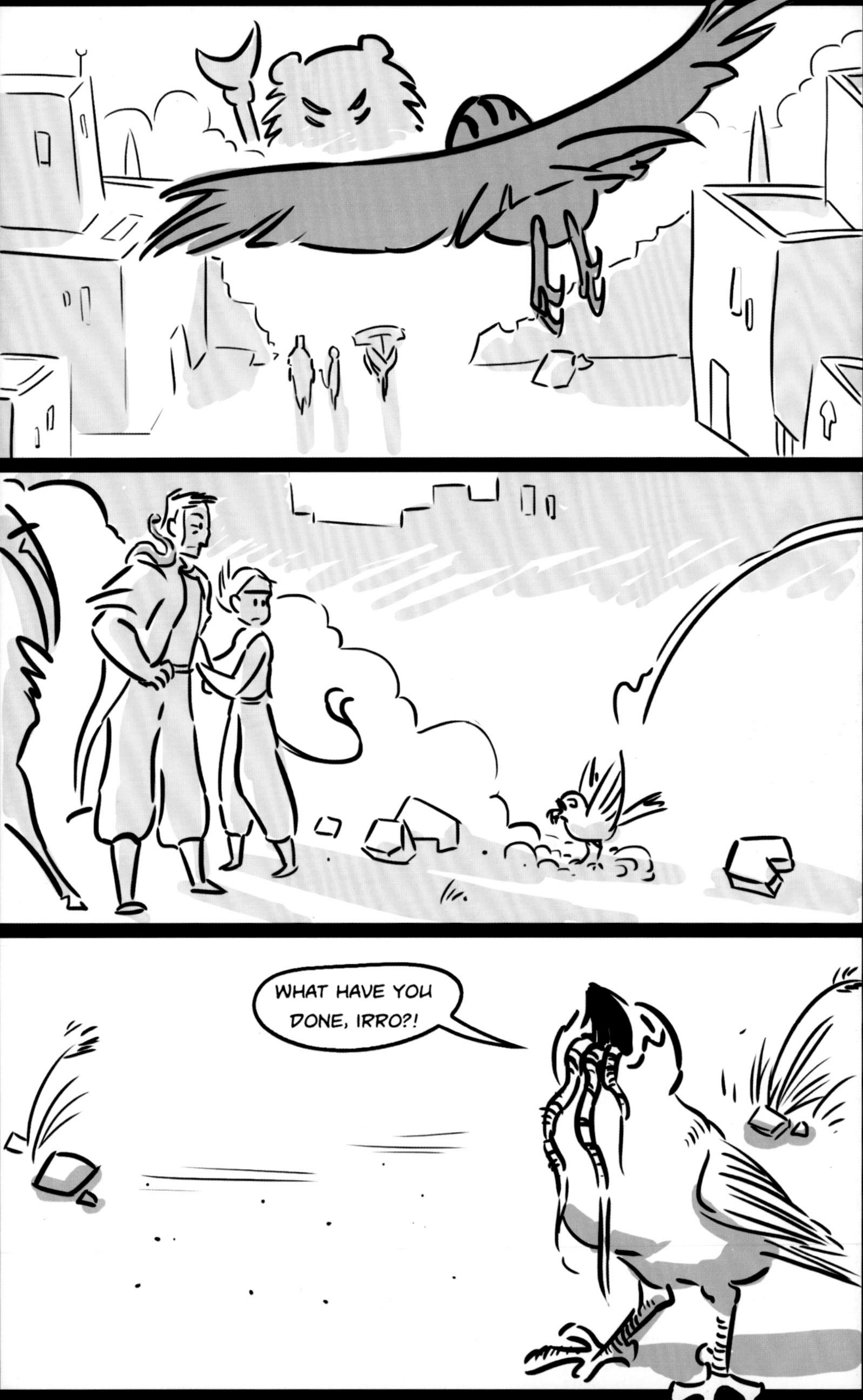
WHAT HAVE YOU DONE, IRRO?!

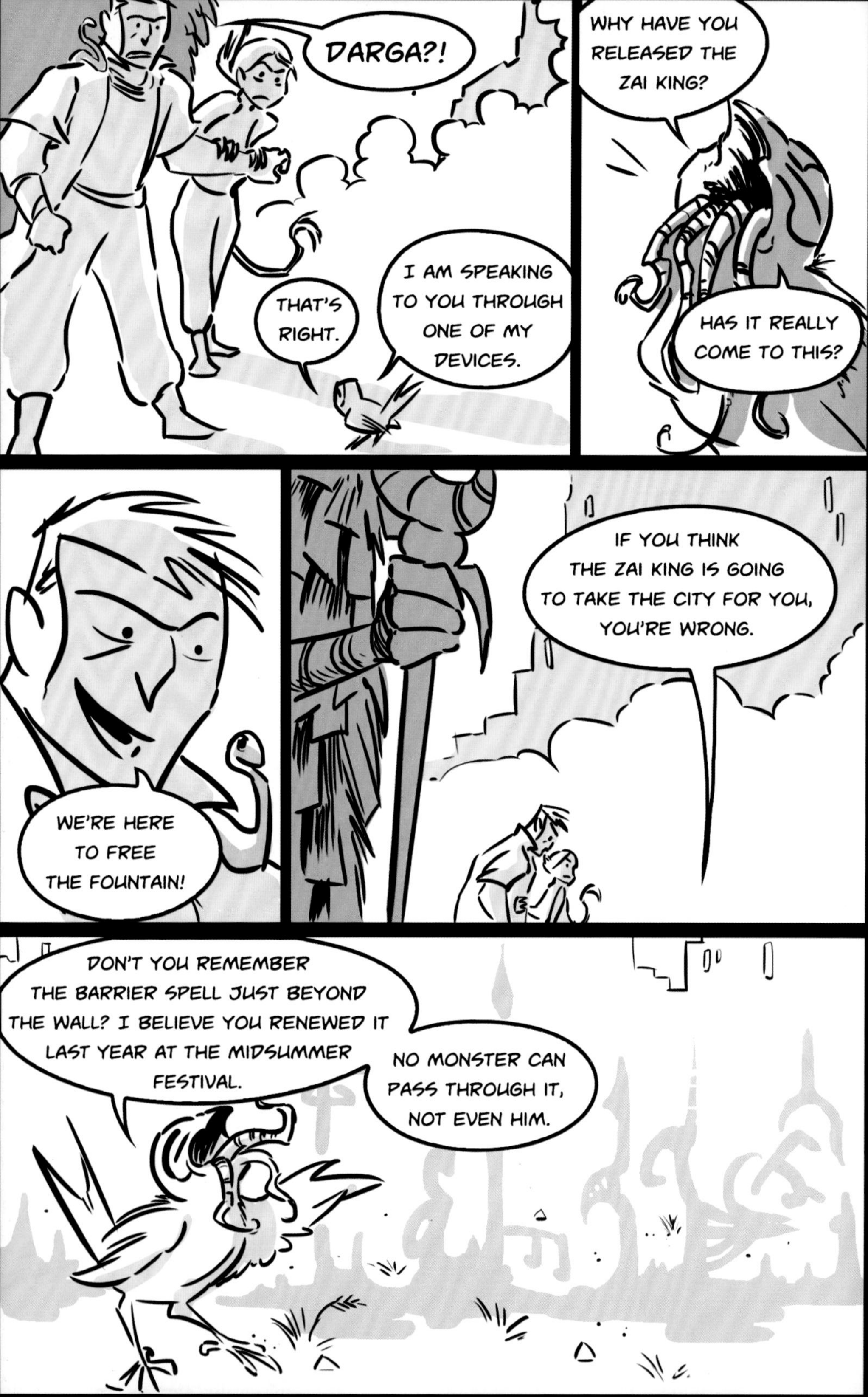
DARGA?!
THAT'S RIGHT.
I AM SPEAKING TO YOU THROUGH ONE OF MY DEVICES.
WHY HAVE YOU RELEASED THE ZAI KING?
HAS IT REALLY COME TO THIS?
WE'RE HERE TO FREE THE FOUNTAIN!
IF YOU THINK THE ZAI KING IS GOING TO TAKE THE CITY FOR YOU, YOU'RE WRONG.
DON'T YOU REMEMBER THE BARRIER SPELL JUST BEYOND THE WALL? I BELIEVE YOU RENEWED IT LAST YEAR AT THE MIDSUMMER FESTIVAL.
NO MONSTER CAN PASS THROUGH IT, NOT EVEN HIM.

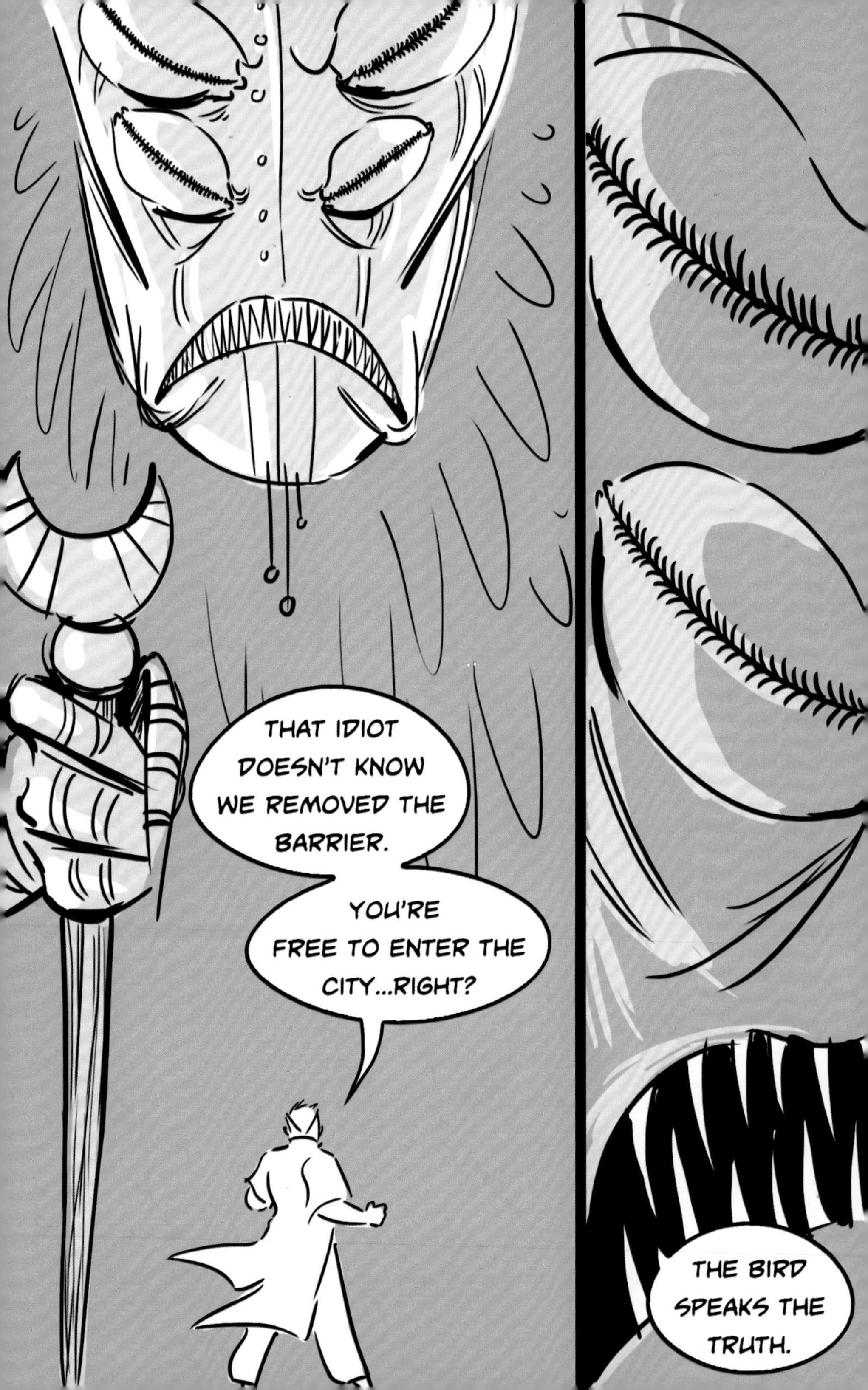
THAT IDIOT DOESN'T KNOW WE REMOVED THE BARRIER.
YOU'RE FREE TO ENTER THE CITY...RIGHT?
THE BIRD SPEAKS THE TRUTH.

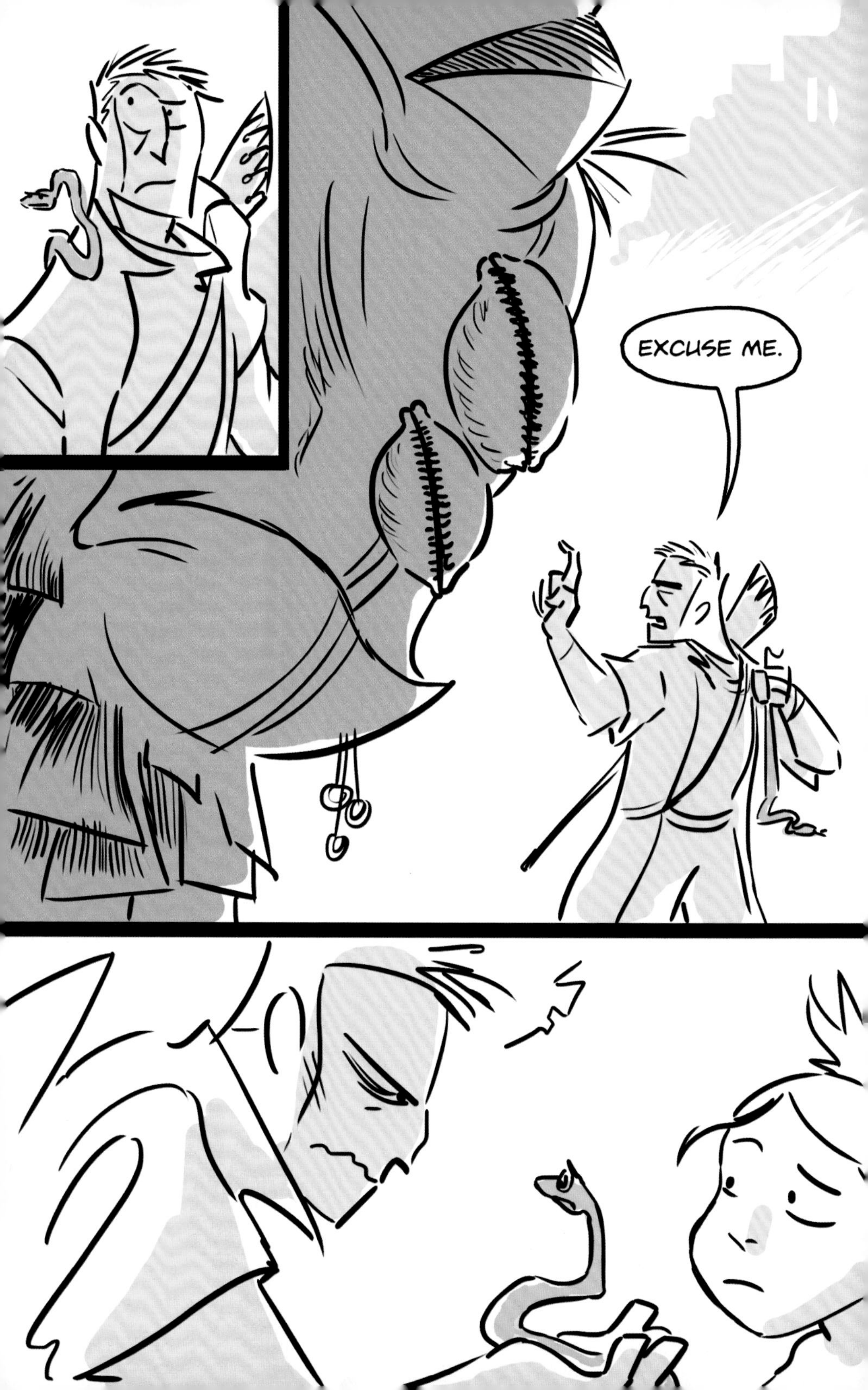
EXCUSE ME.

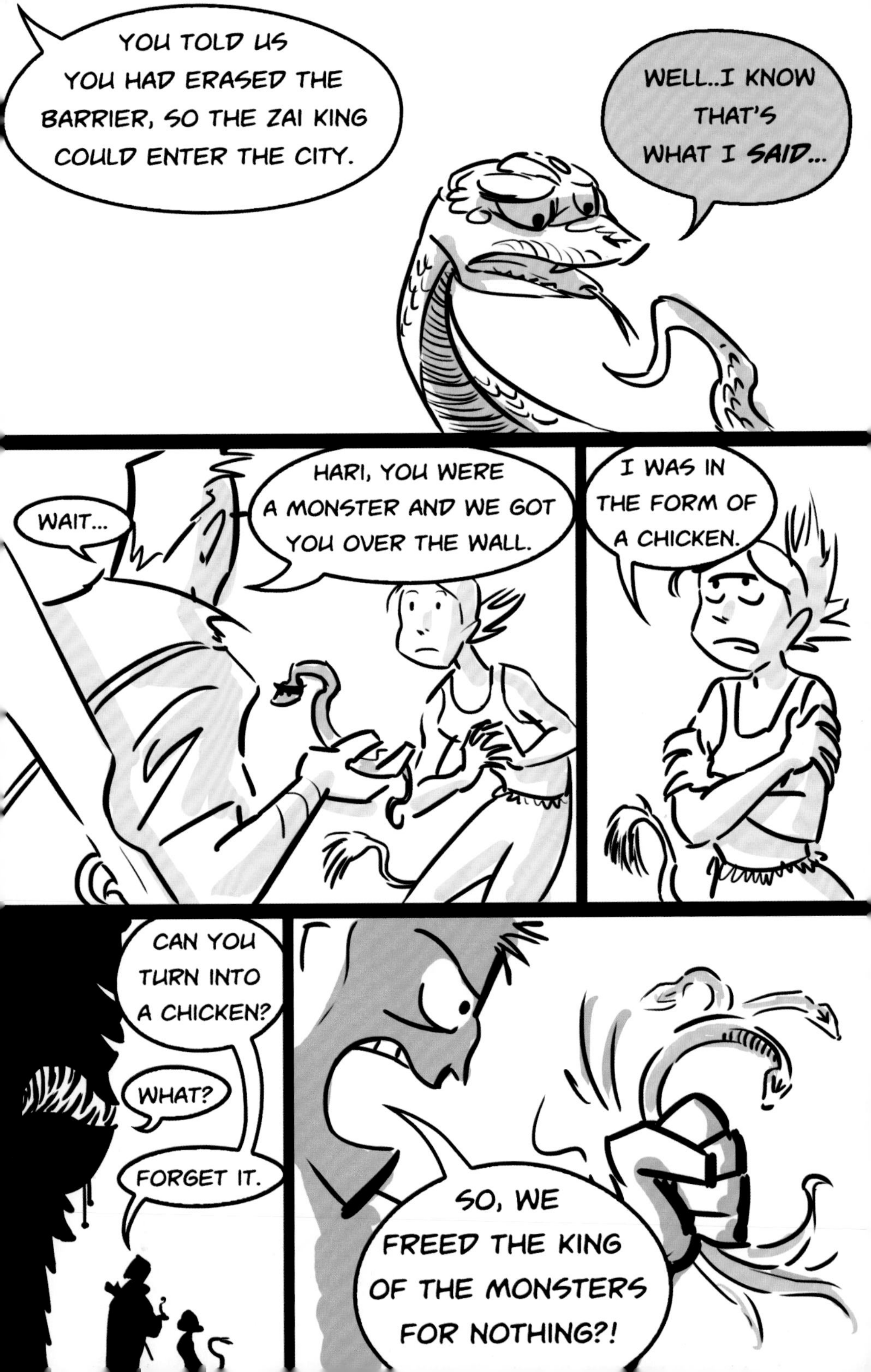
YOU TOLD US YOU HAD ERASED THE BARRIER, SO THE ZAI KING COULD ENTER THE CITY.
WELL..I KNOW THAT'S WHAT I **SAID**...
WAIT...
HARI, YOU WERE A MONSTER AND WE GOT YOU OVER THE WALL.
I WAS IN THE FORM OF A CHICKEN.
CAN YOU TURN INTO A CHICKEN?
WHAT?
FORGET IT.
SO, WE FREED THE KING OF THE MONSTERS FOR NOTHING?!

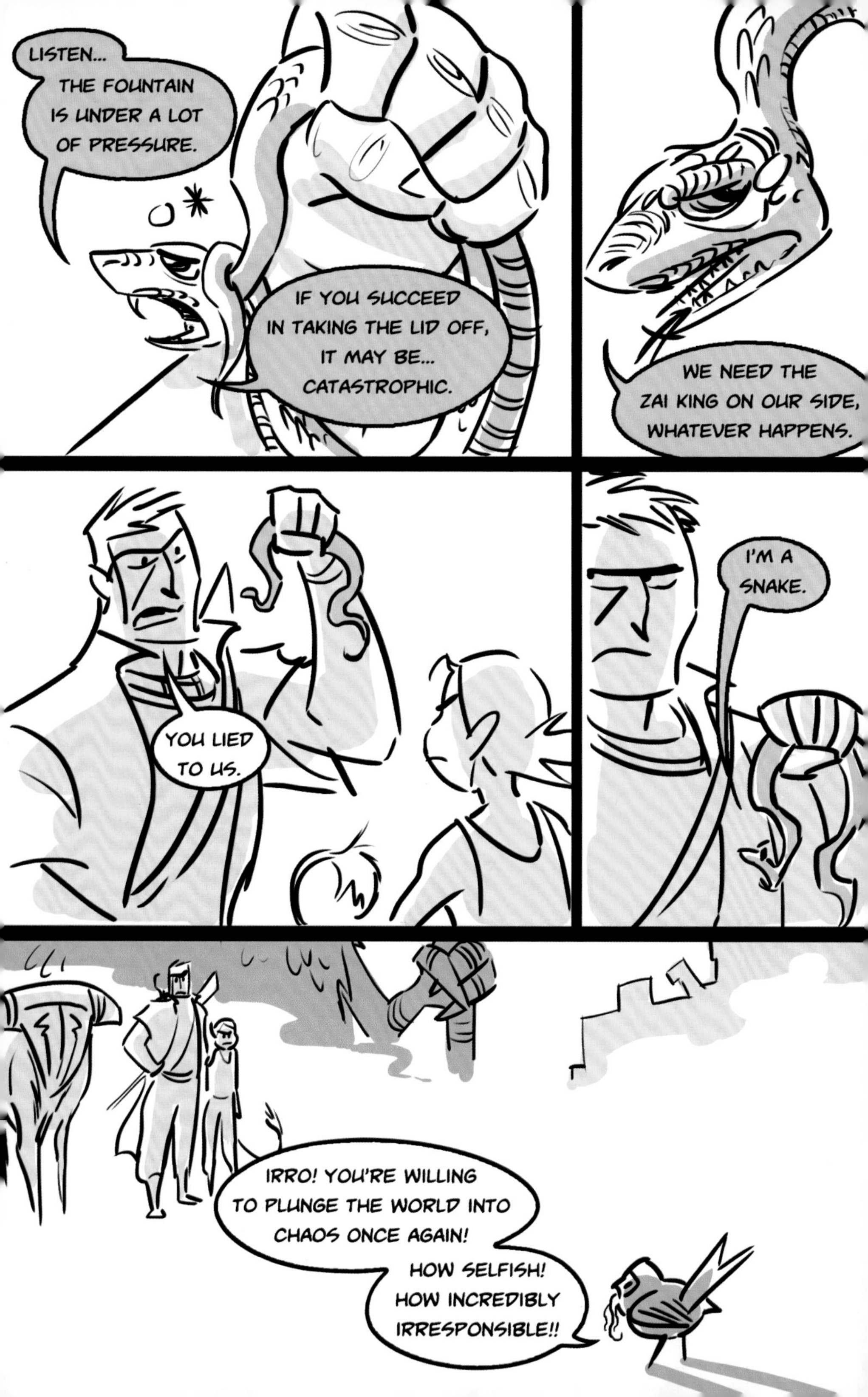
LISTEN...
THE FOUNTAIN IS UNDER A LOT OF PRESSURE.
IF YOU SUCCEED IN TAKING THE LID OFF, IT MAY BE... CATASTROPHIC.
WE NEED THE ZAI KING ON OUR SIDE, WHATEVER HAPPENS.
YOU LIED TO US.
I'M A SNAKE.
IRRO! YOU'RE WILLING TO PLUNGE THE WORLD INTO CHAOS ONCE AGAIN!
HOW SELFISH! HOW INCREDIBLY IRRESPONSIBLE!!

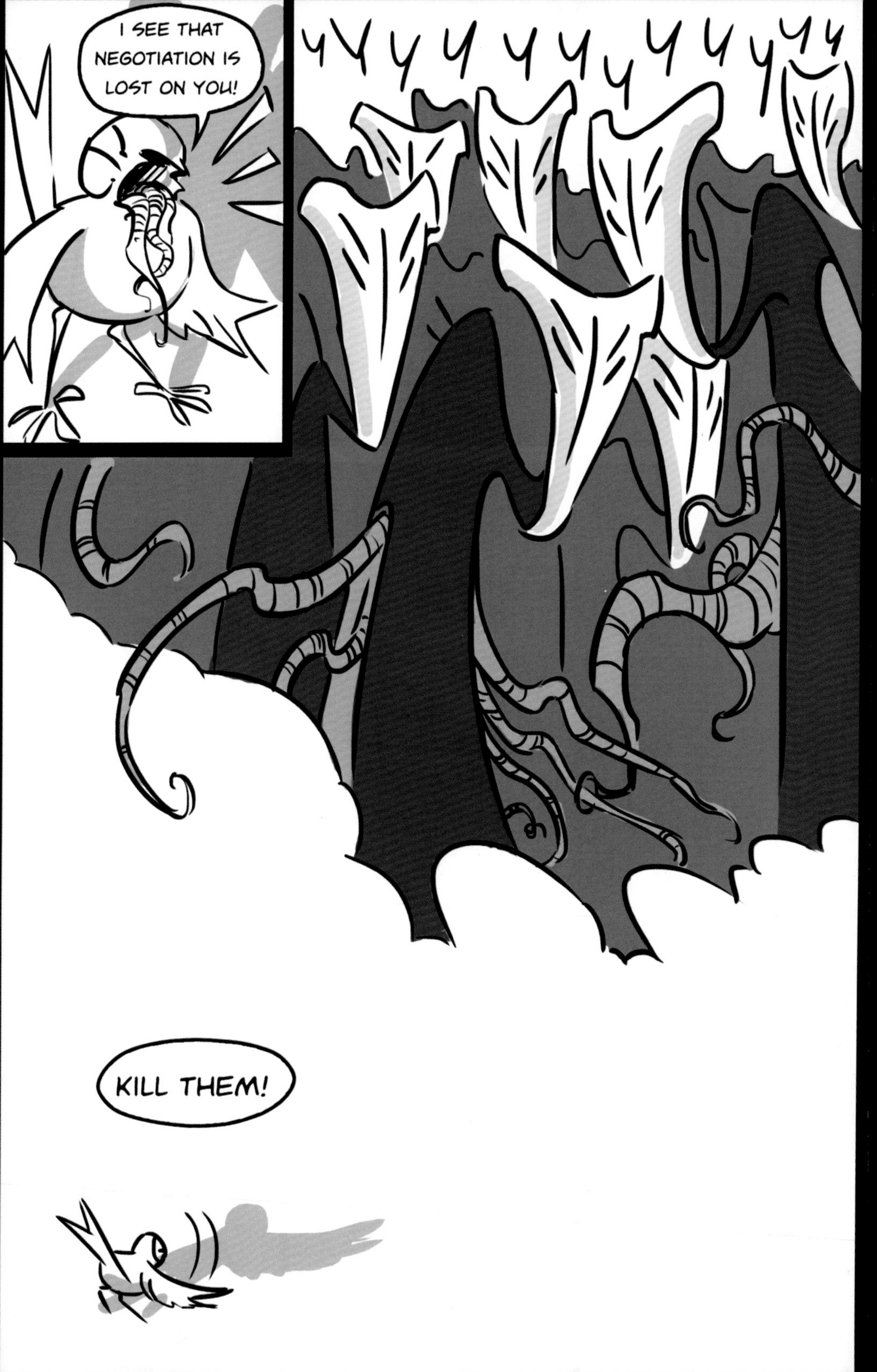
I SEE THAT NEGOTIATION IS LOST ON YOU!
KILL THEM!

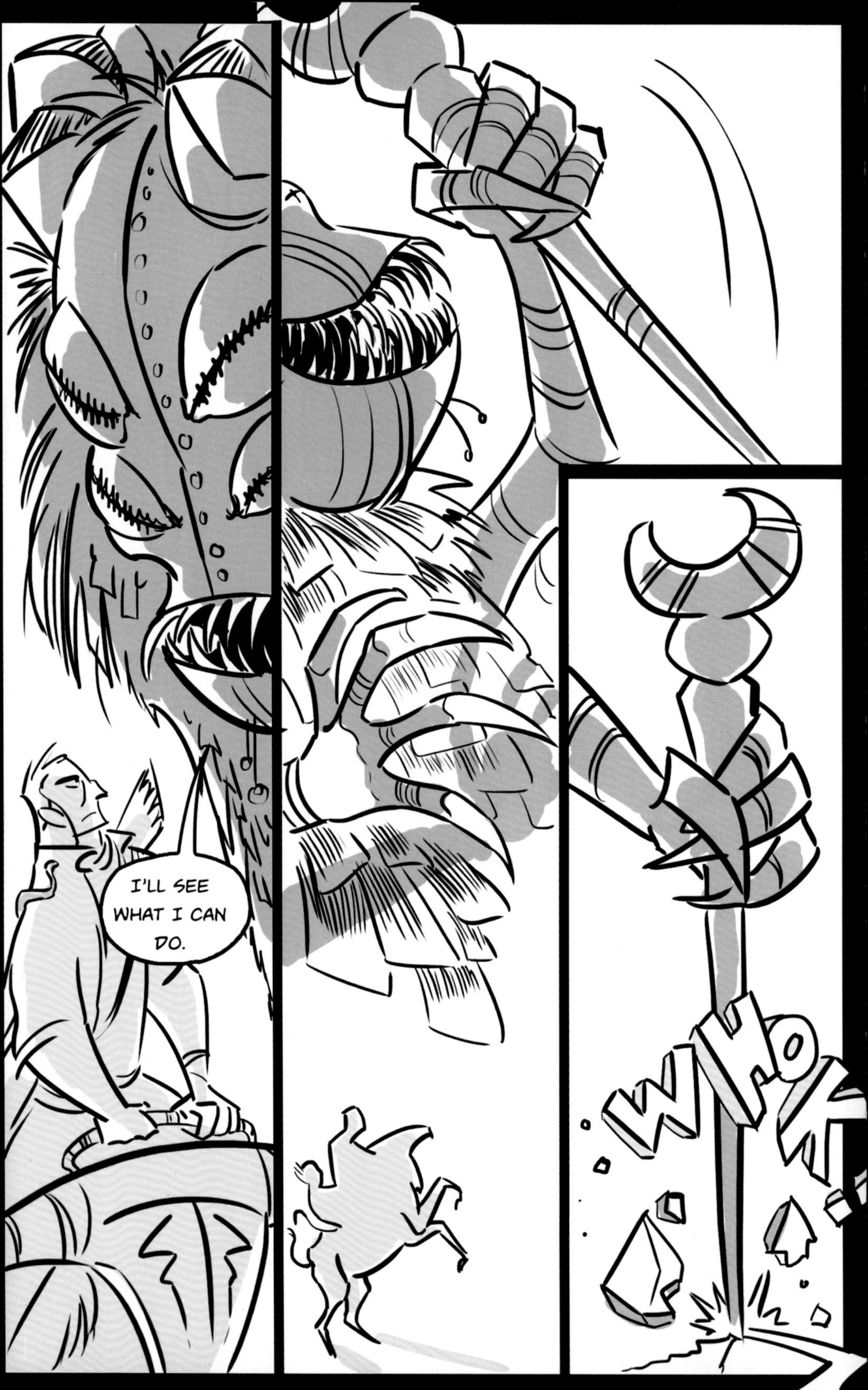
I'LL SEE WHAT I CAN DO.
WHOK

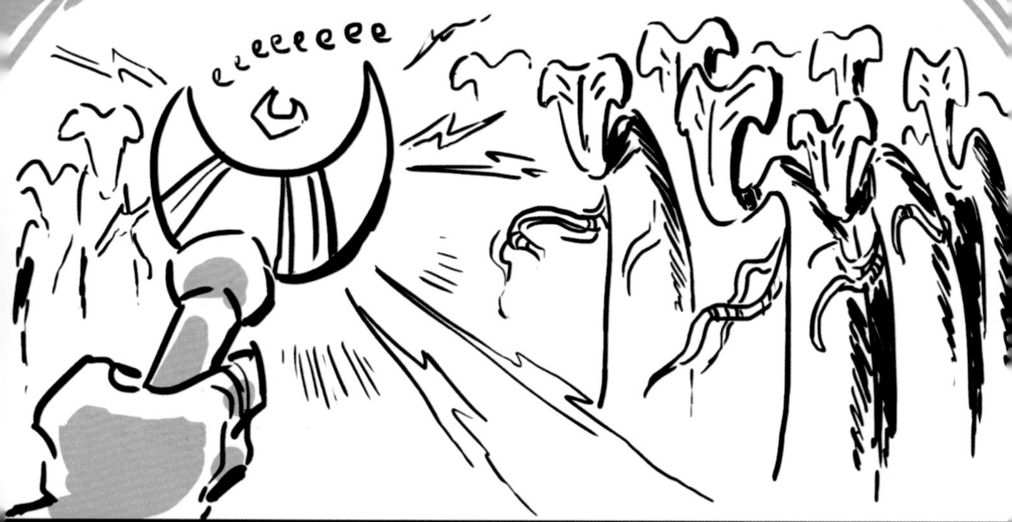
eeeeeeee

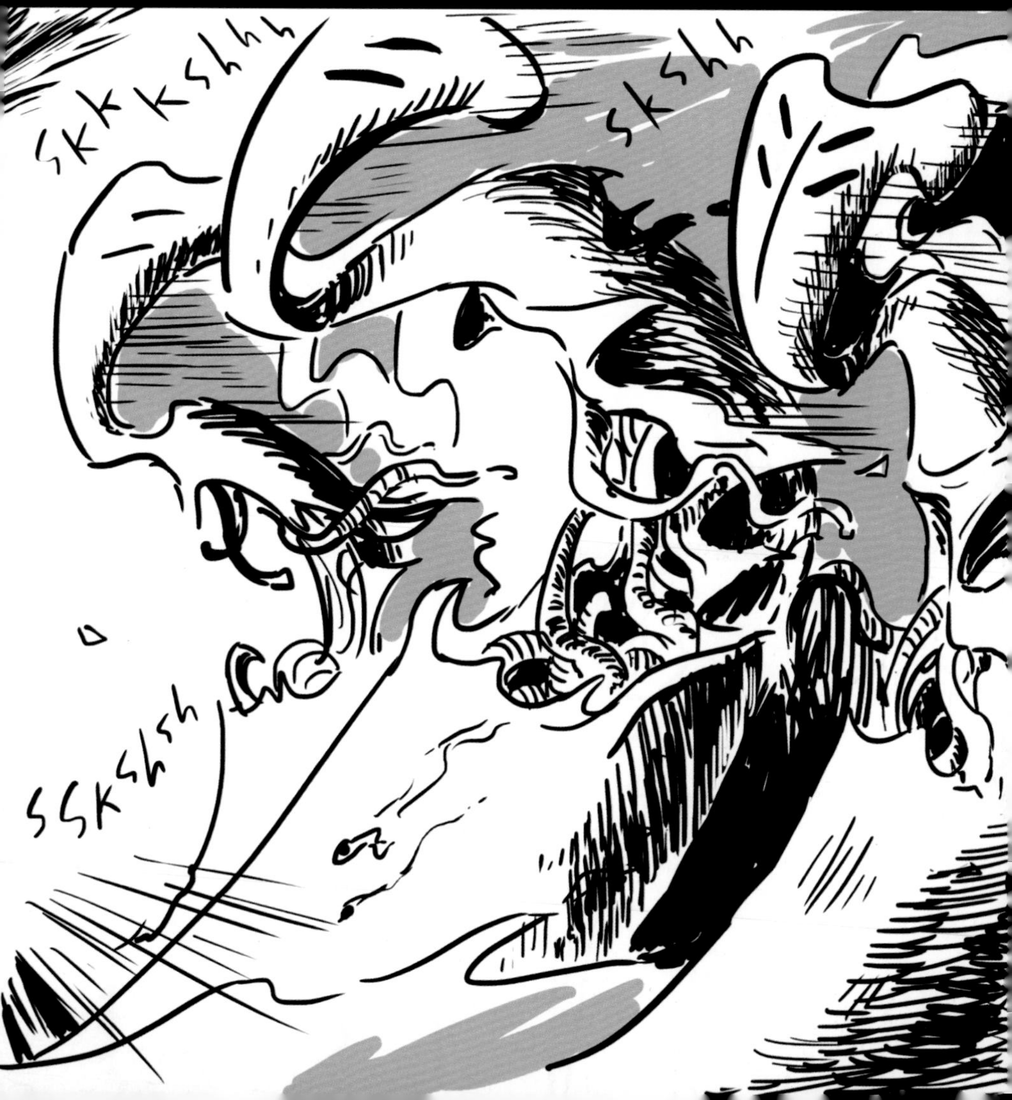
skkkshhh
skshh
sskshsh

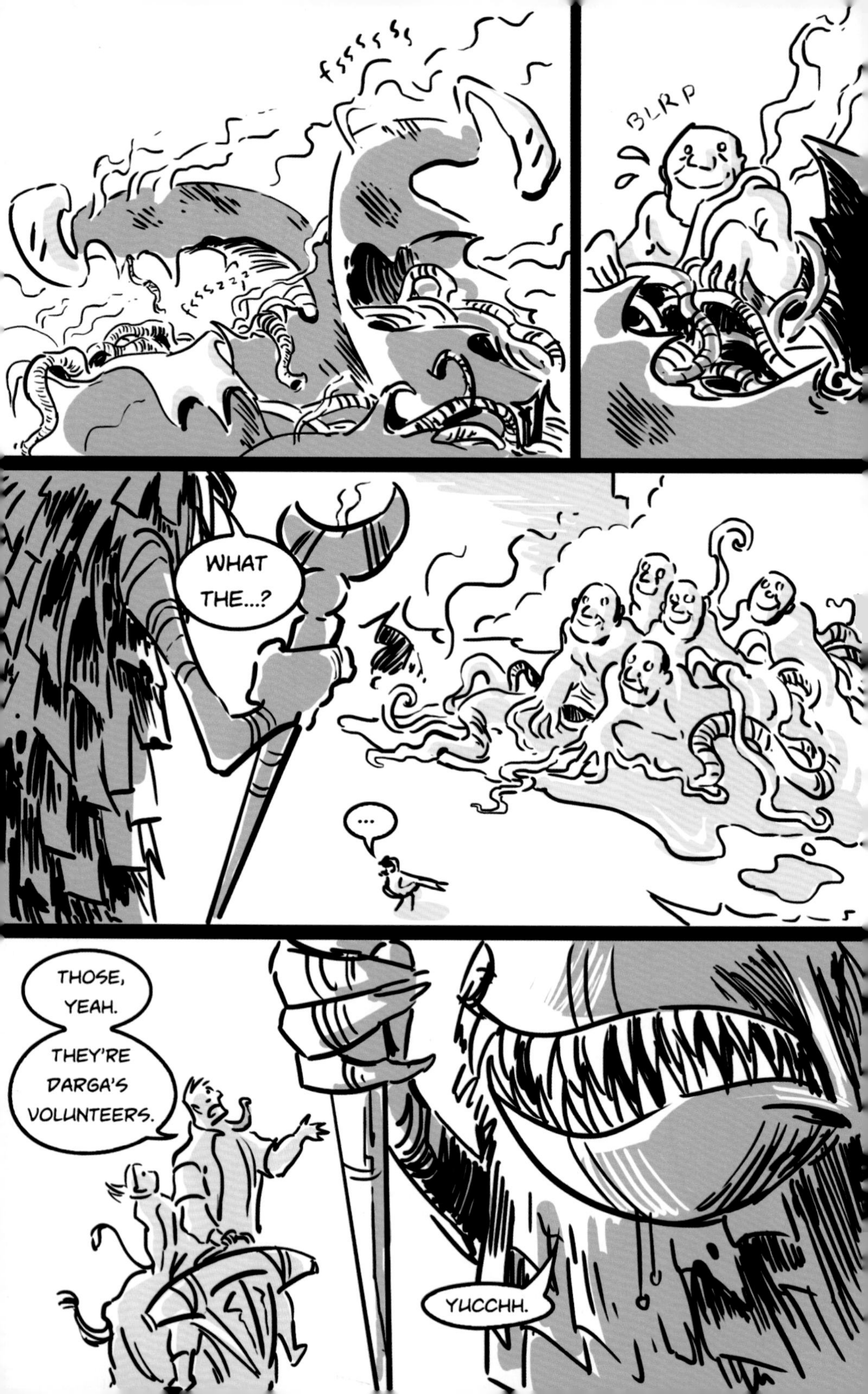
fssssss
fssszzzz
BLRP
WHAT THE...?
...
THOSE, YEAH.
THEY'RE DARGA'S VOLUNTEERS.
YUCCHH.

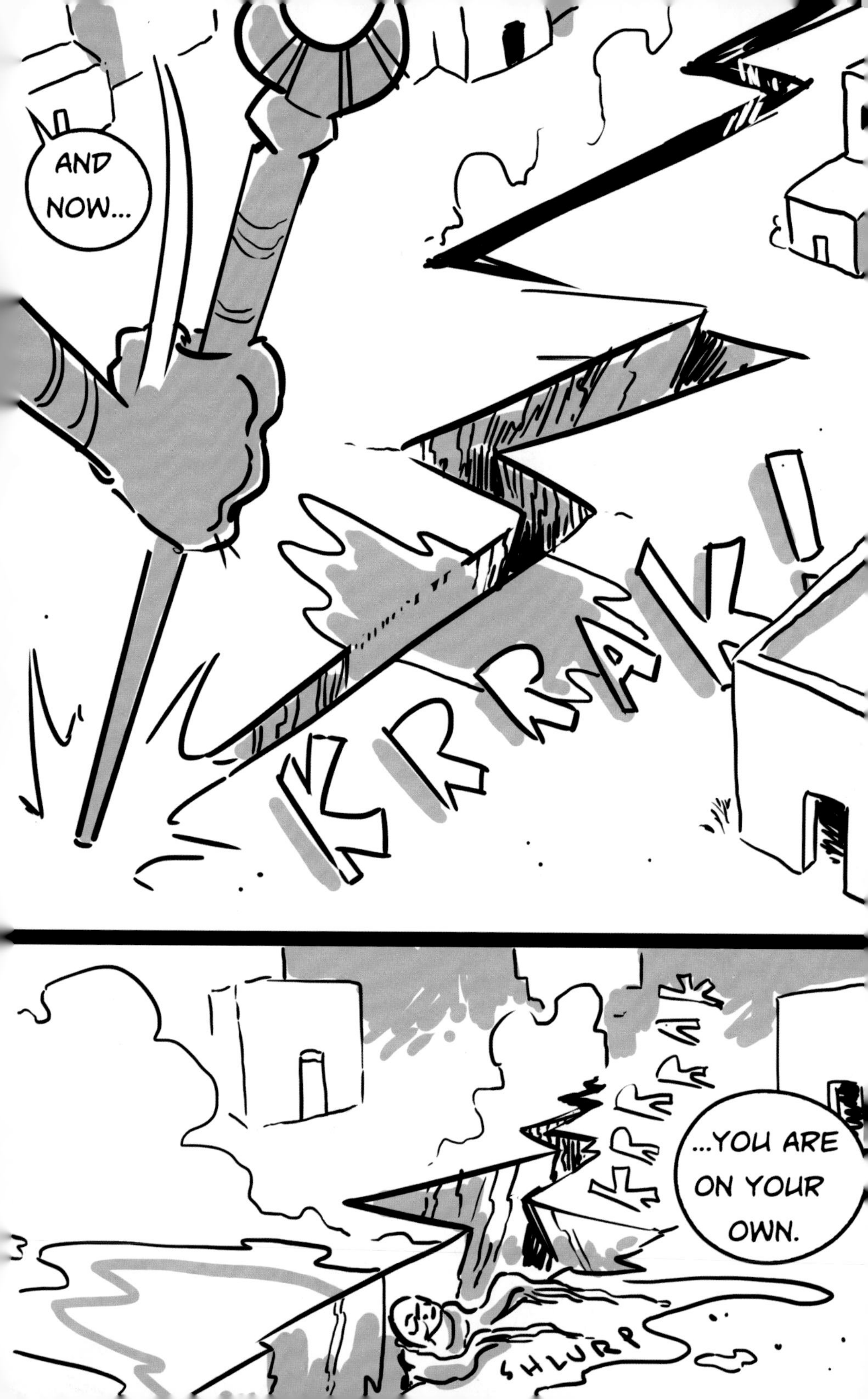
AND NOW...
KRRAK!
KRRAK!
...YOU ARE ON YOUR OWN.
SHLURP

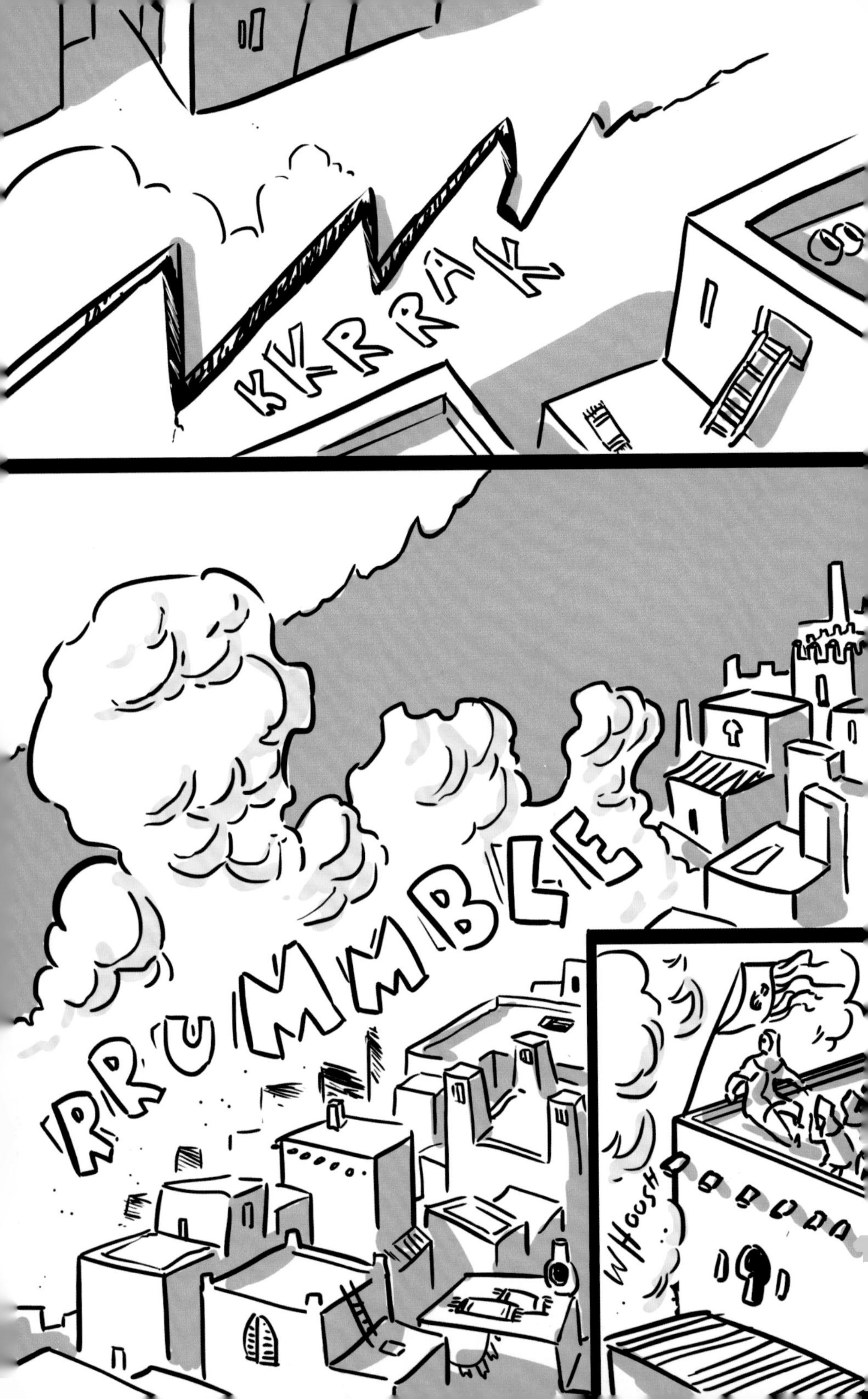
KKRRAK
RRUMMMBLE
WHOOSH

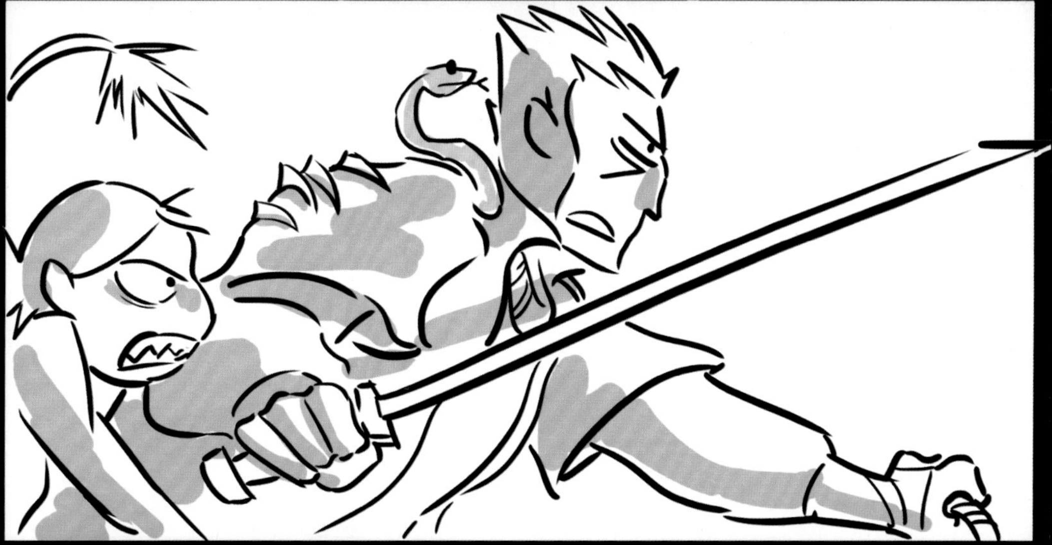
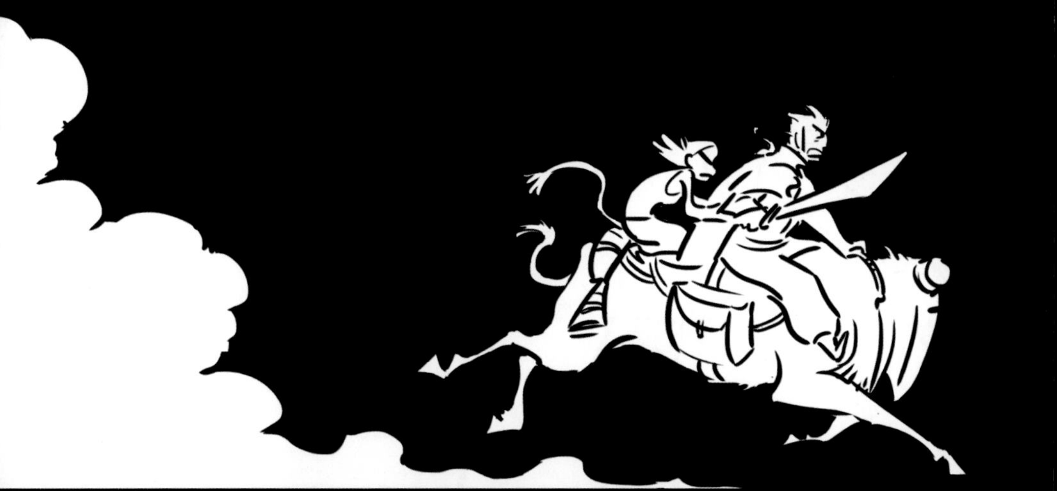
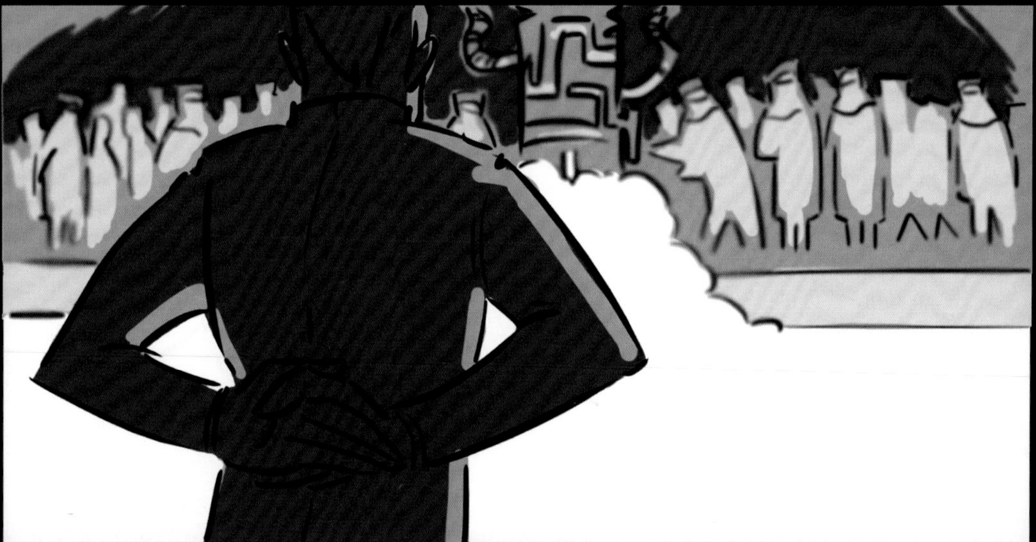

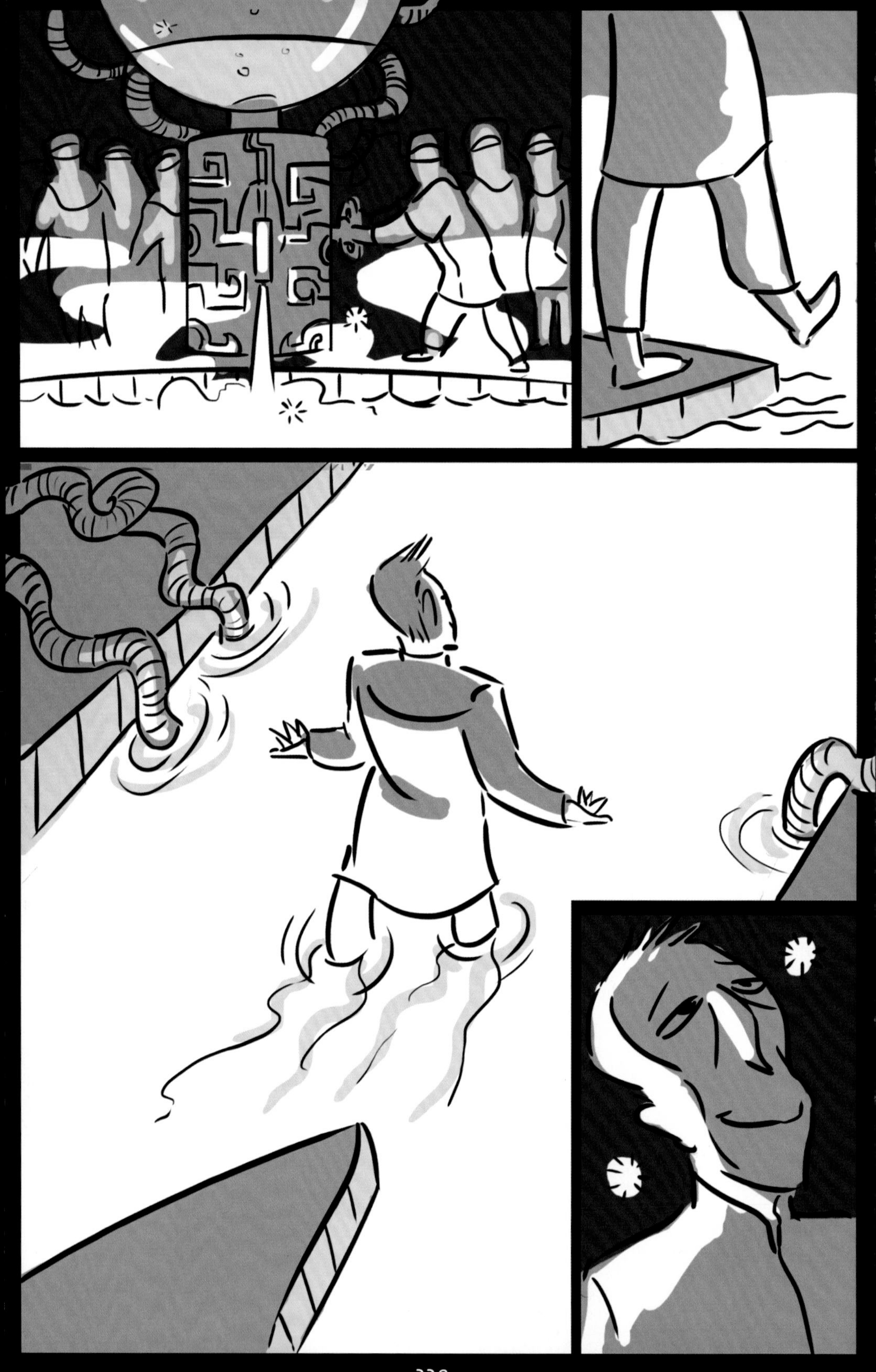

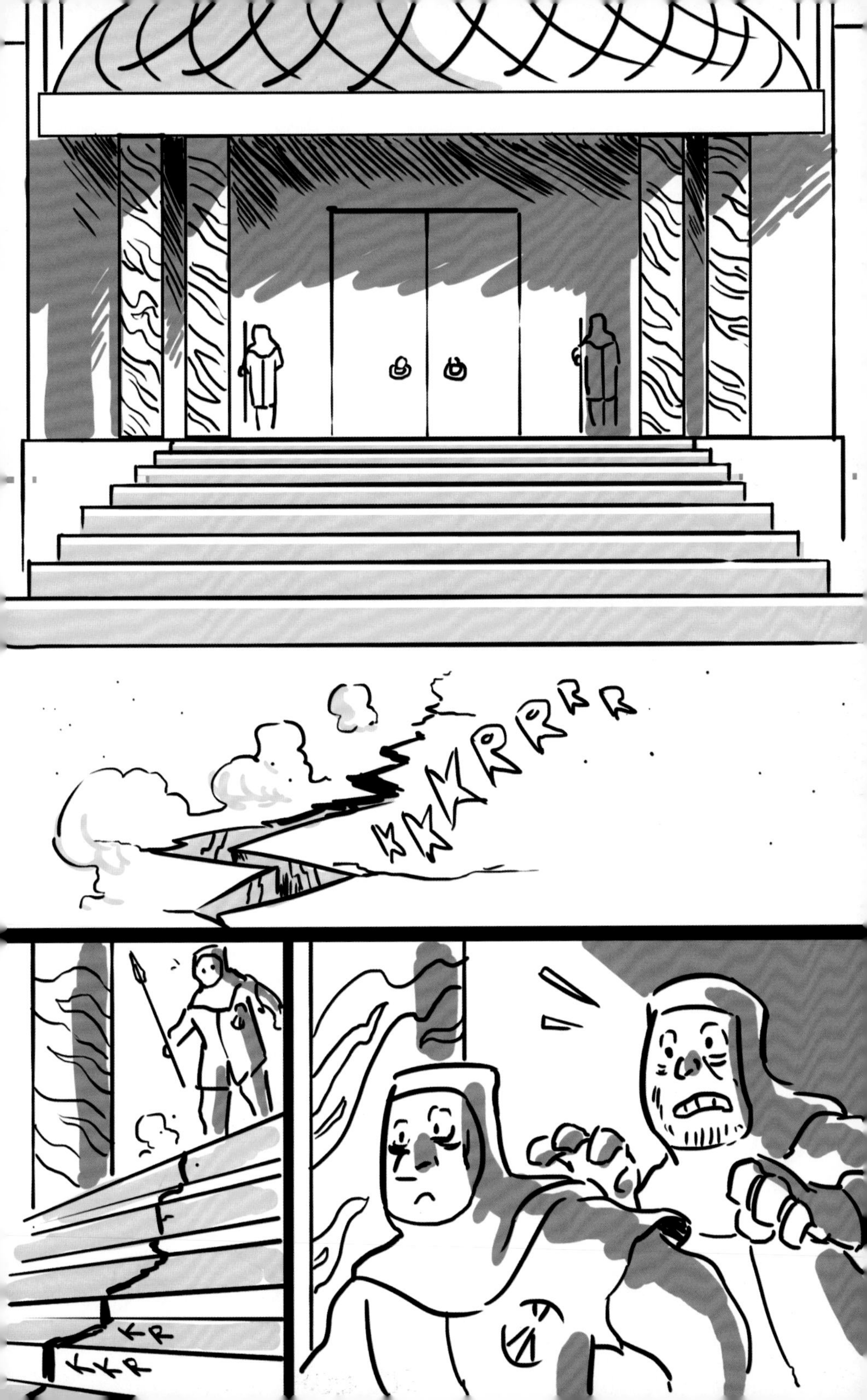
KKKRRRRR
KR
KKR

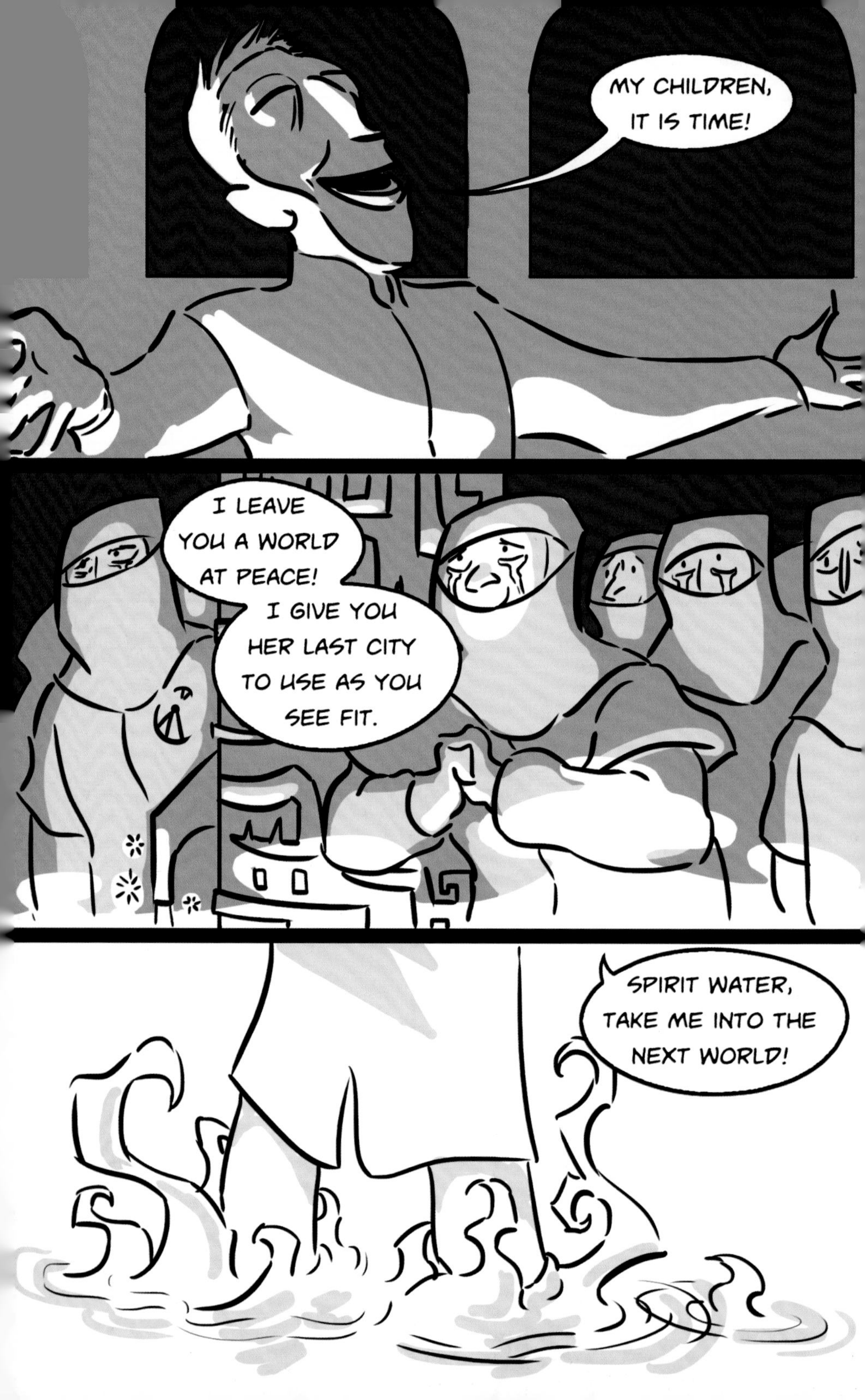
MY CHILDREN, IT IS TIME!
I LEAVE YOU A WORLD AT PEACE!
I GIVE YOU HER LAST CITY TO USE AS YOU SEE FIT.
SPIRIT WATER, TAKE ME INTO THE NEXT WORLD!

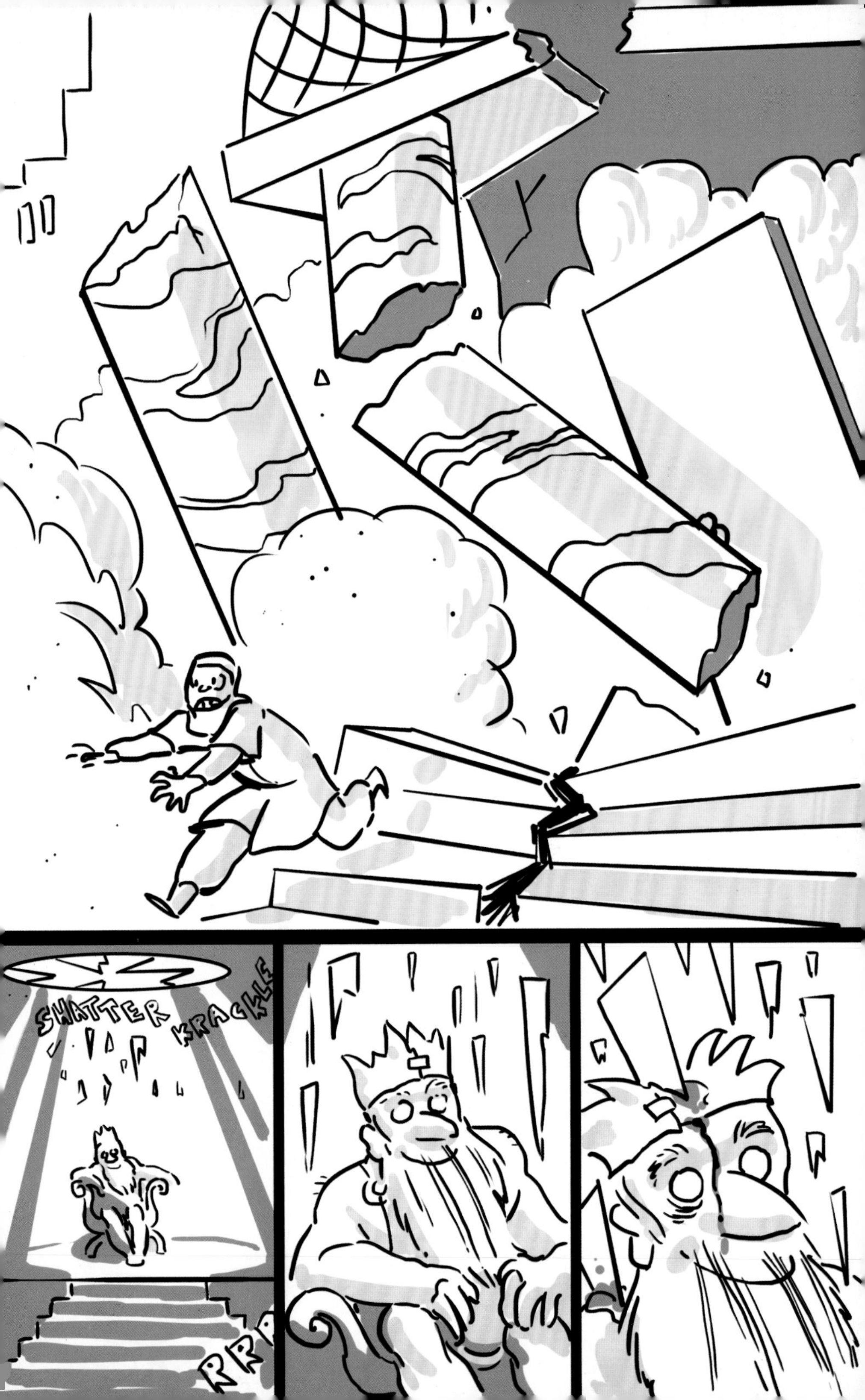
SHATTER
KRACKLE
RRR

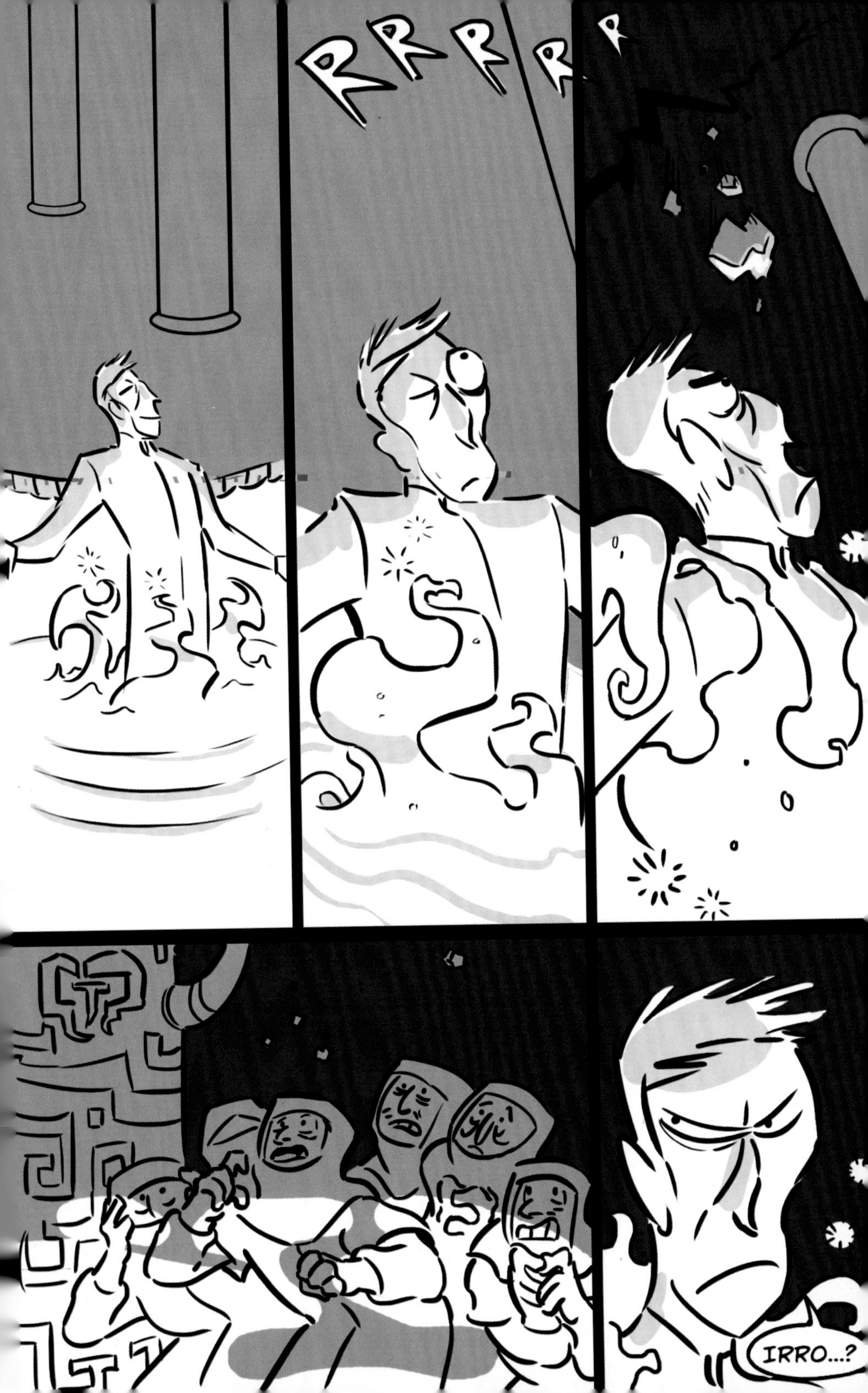
RRRRR
IRRO...?

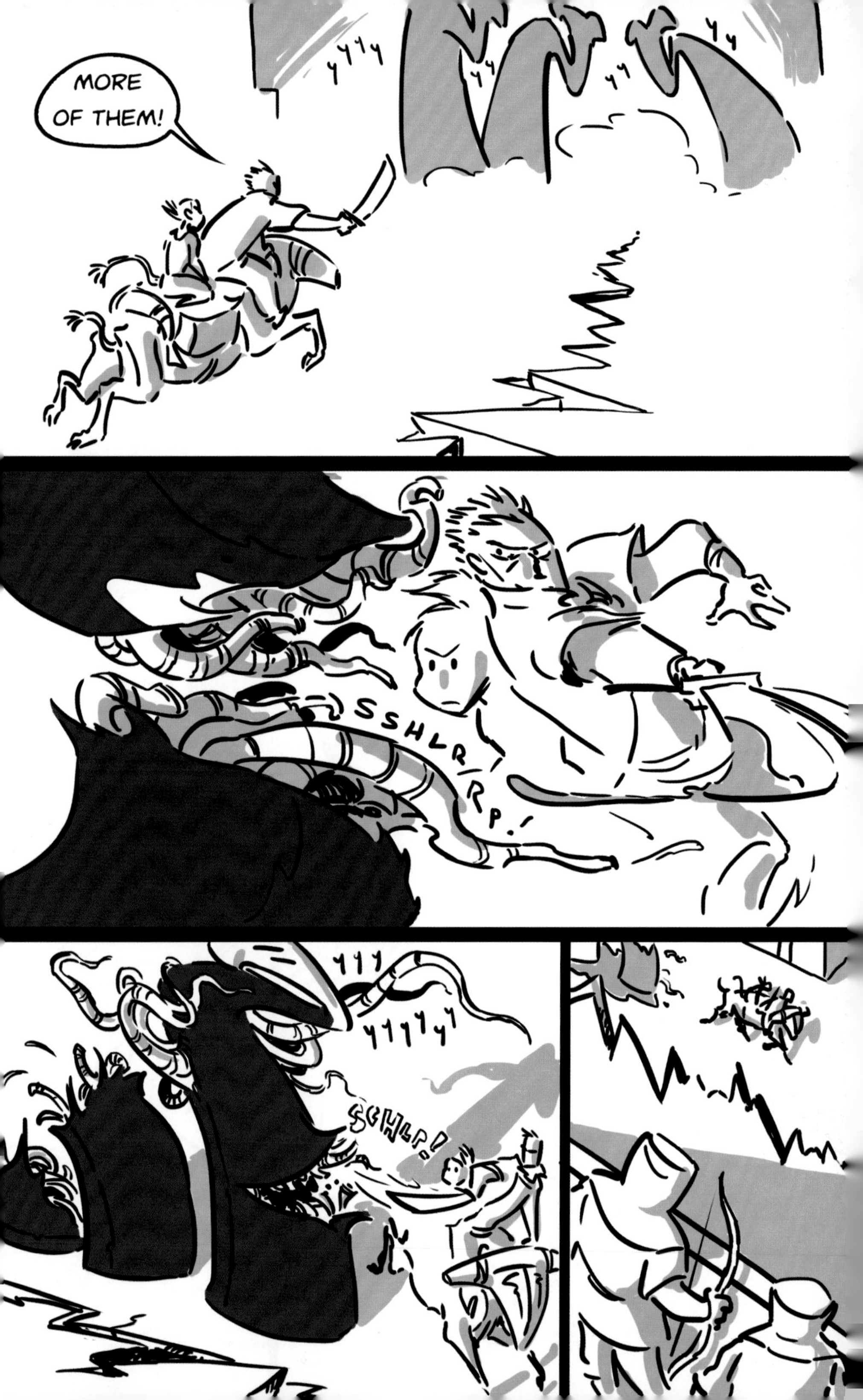
MORE OF THEM!
SSHLRRP!
SCHLP!

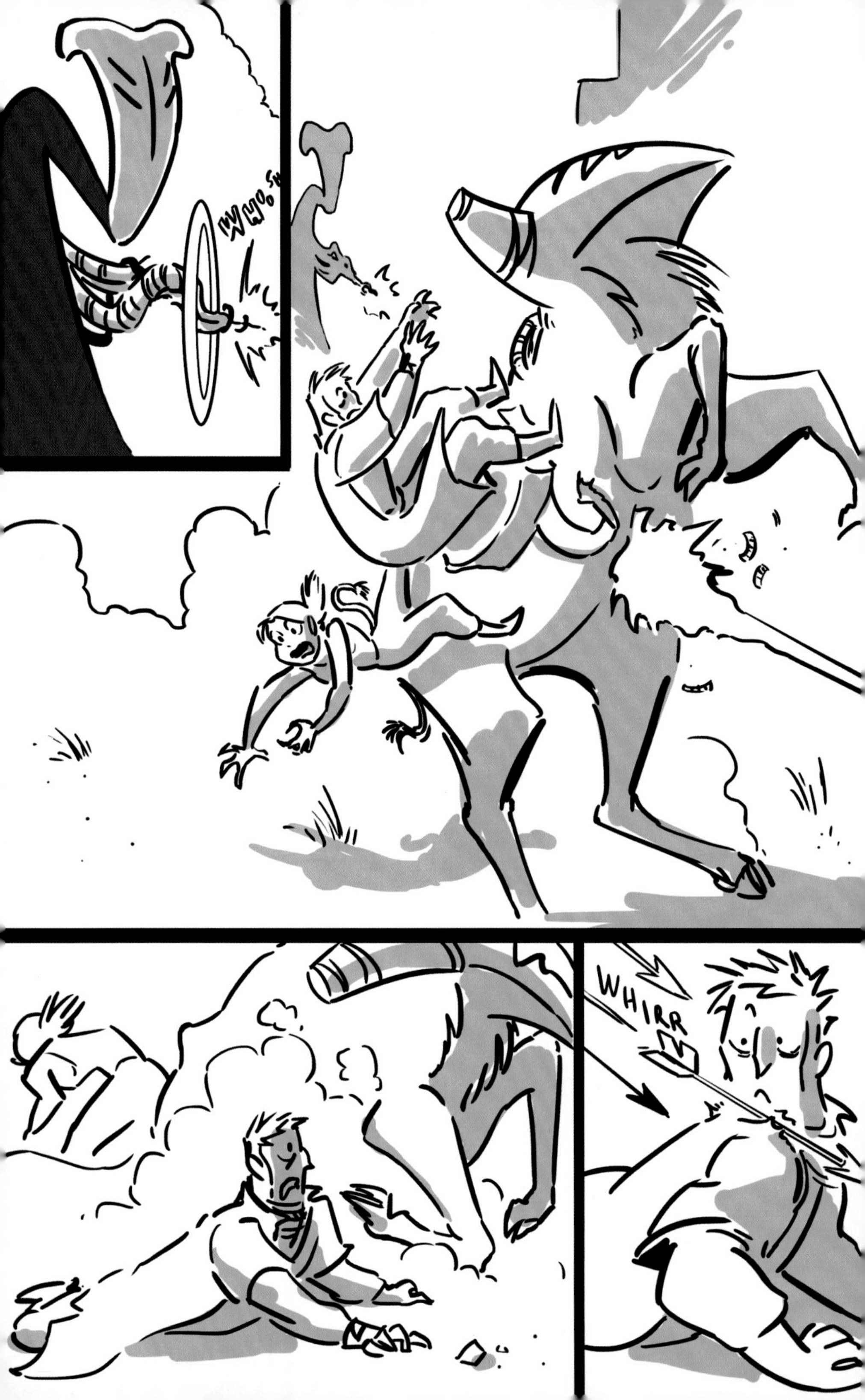
WHOOSH
WHIRR

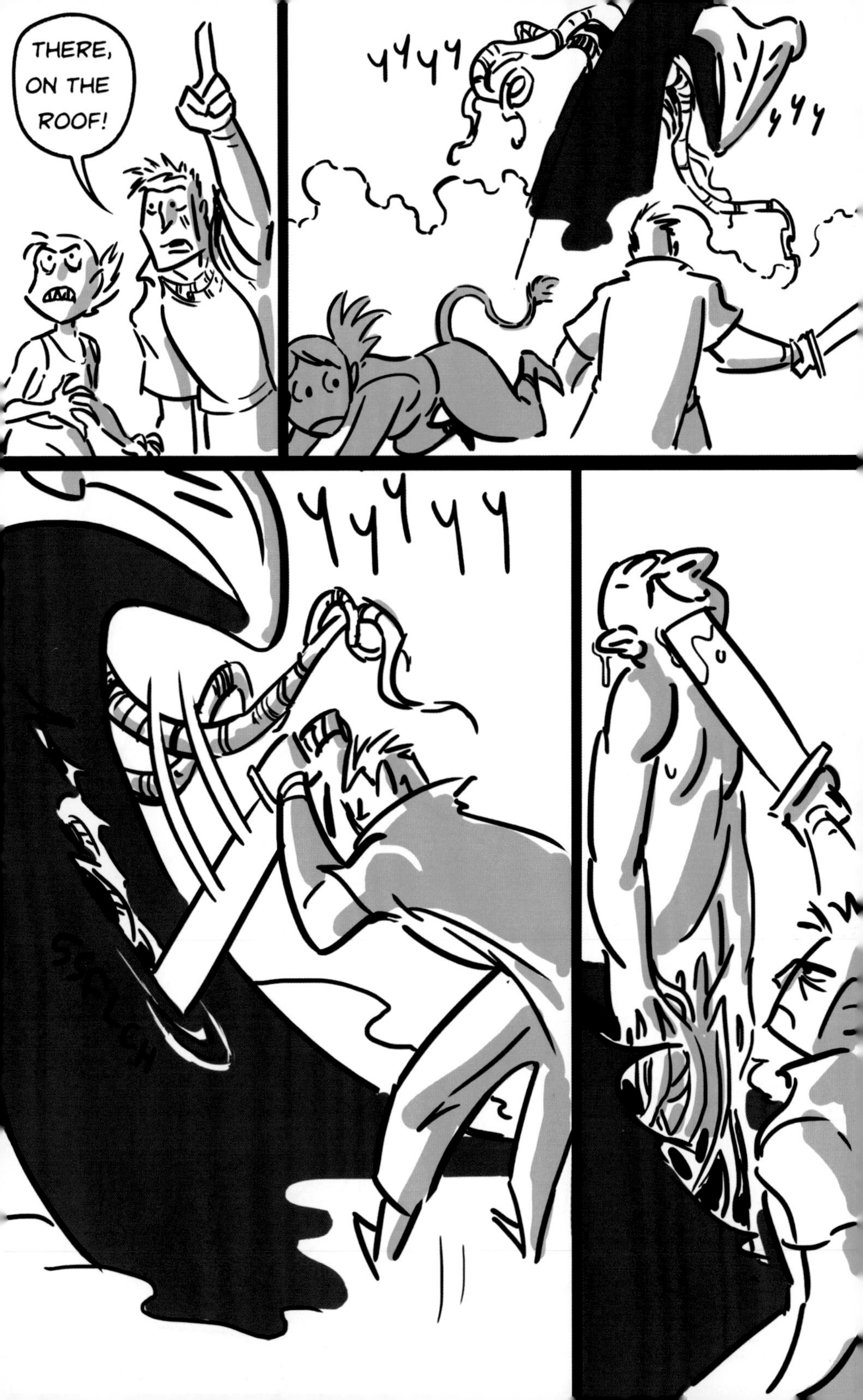
THERE, ON THE ROOF!
YYYY
YYY
YYYYY

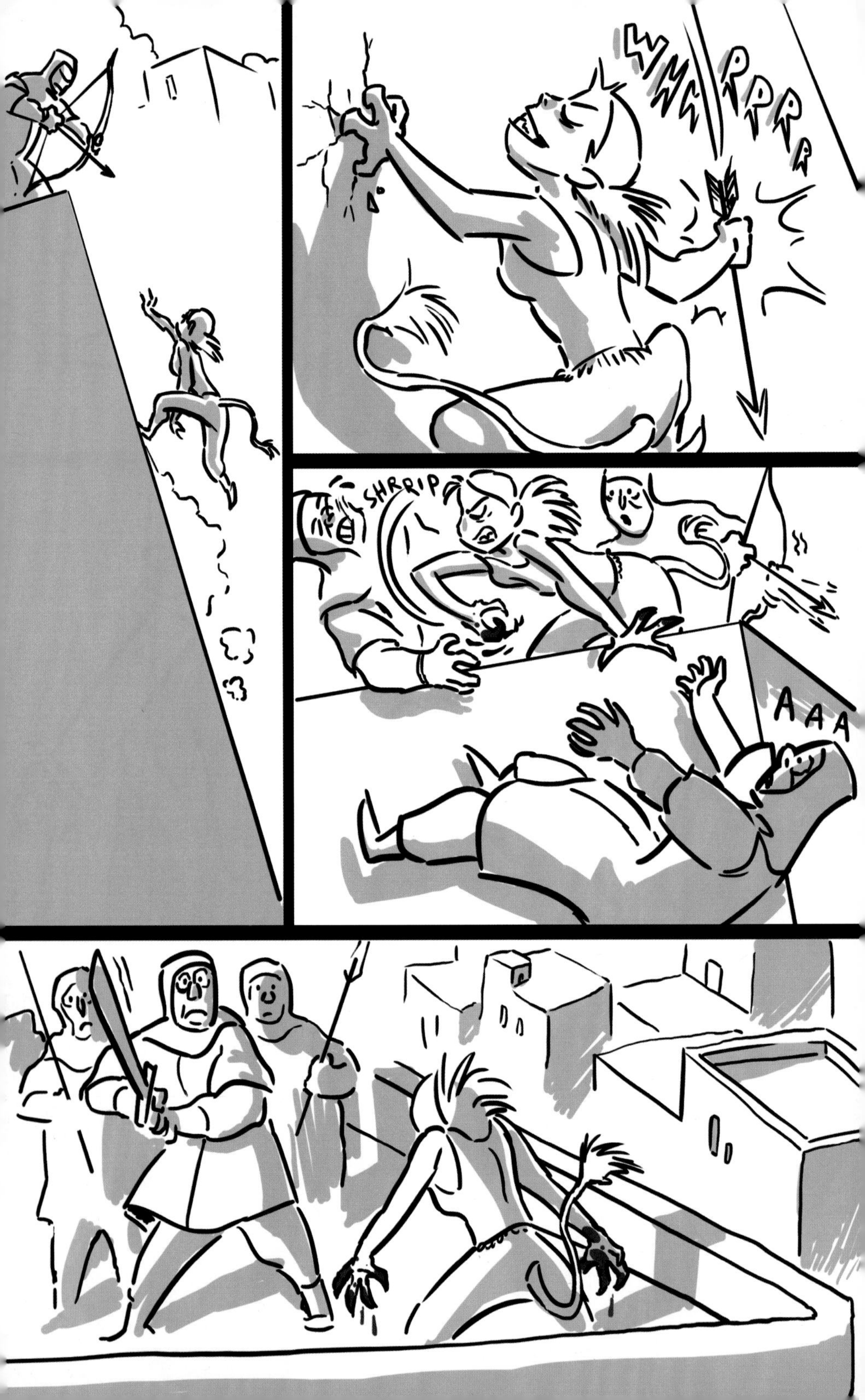
WHRRRRR
SHRRIP
AAA

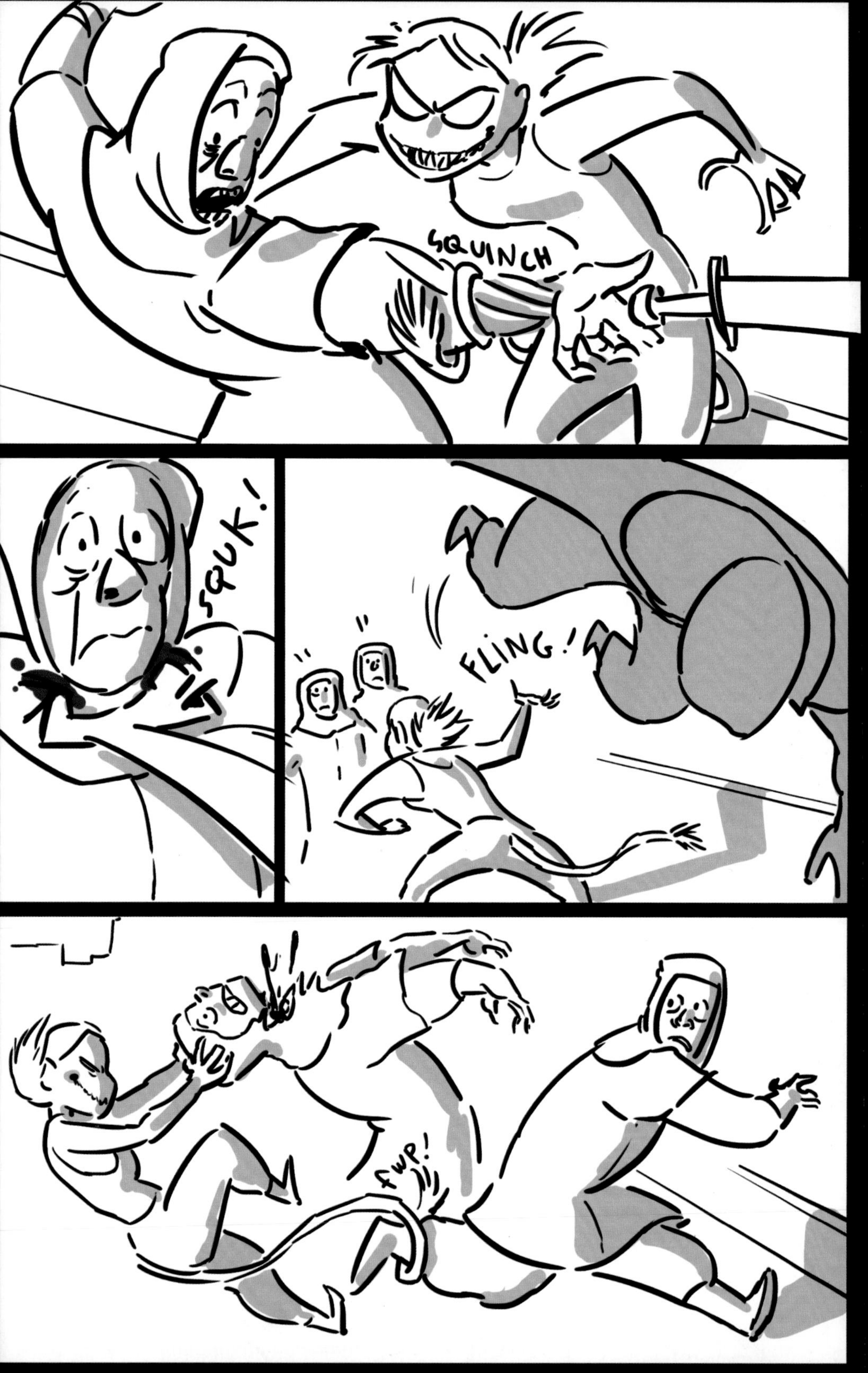
SQUINCH
SQUK!
FLING!
FWP!

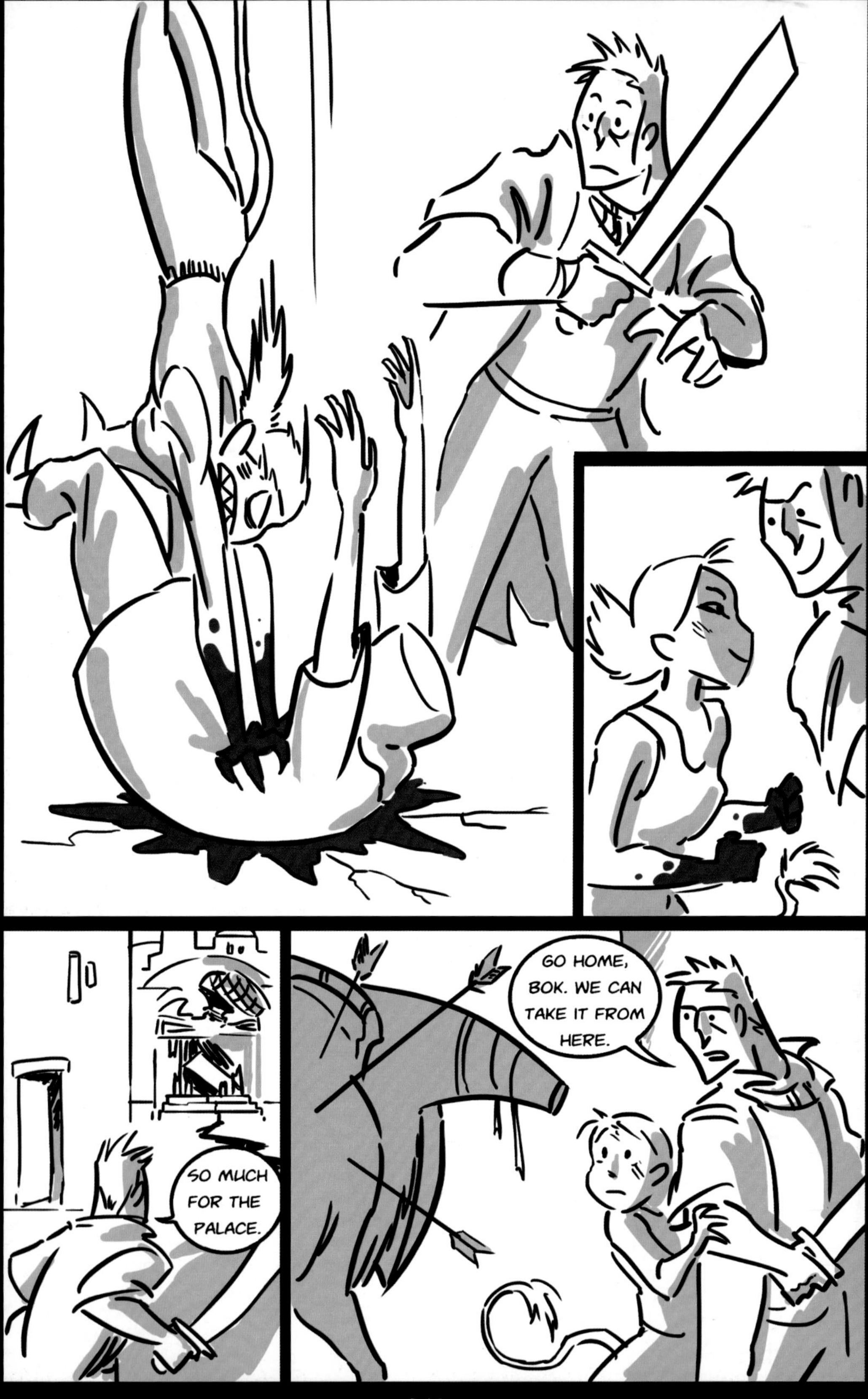
SO MUCH FOR THE PALACE.
GO HOME, BOK. WE CAN TAKE IT FROM HERE.

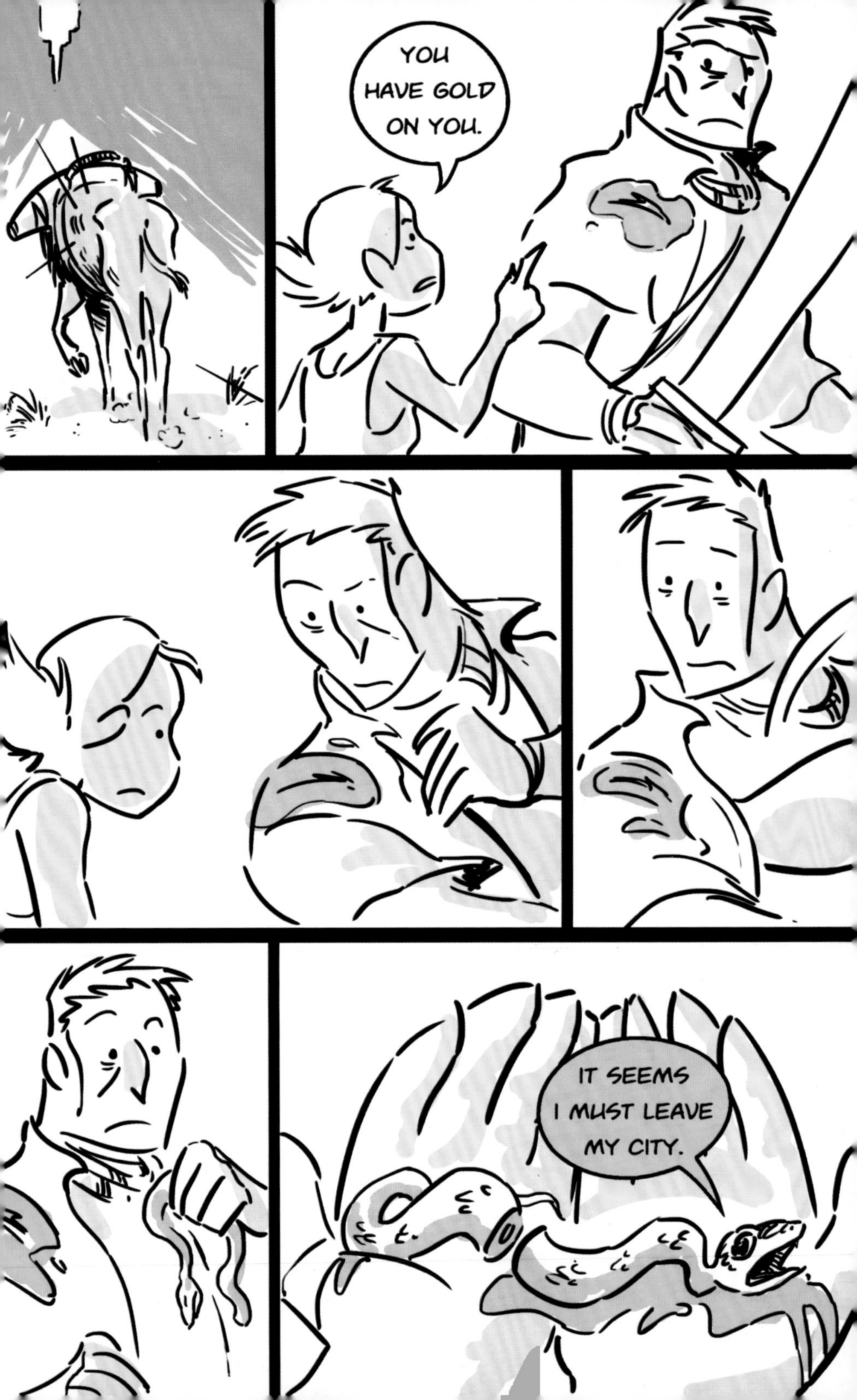
YOU HAVE GOLD ON YOU.
IT SEEMS I MUST LEAVE MY CITY.

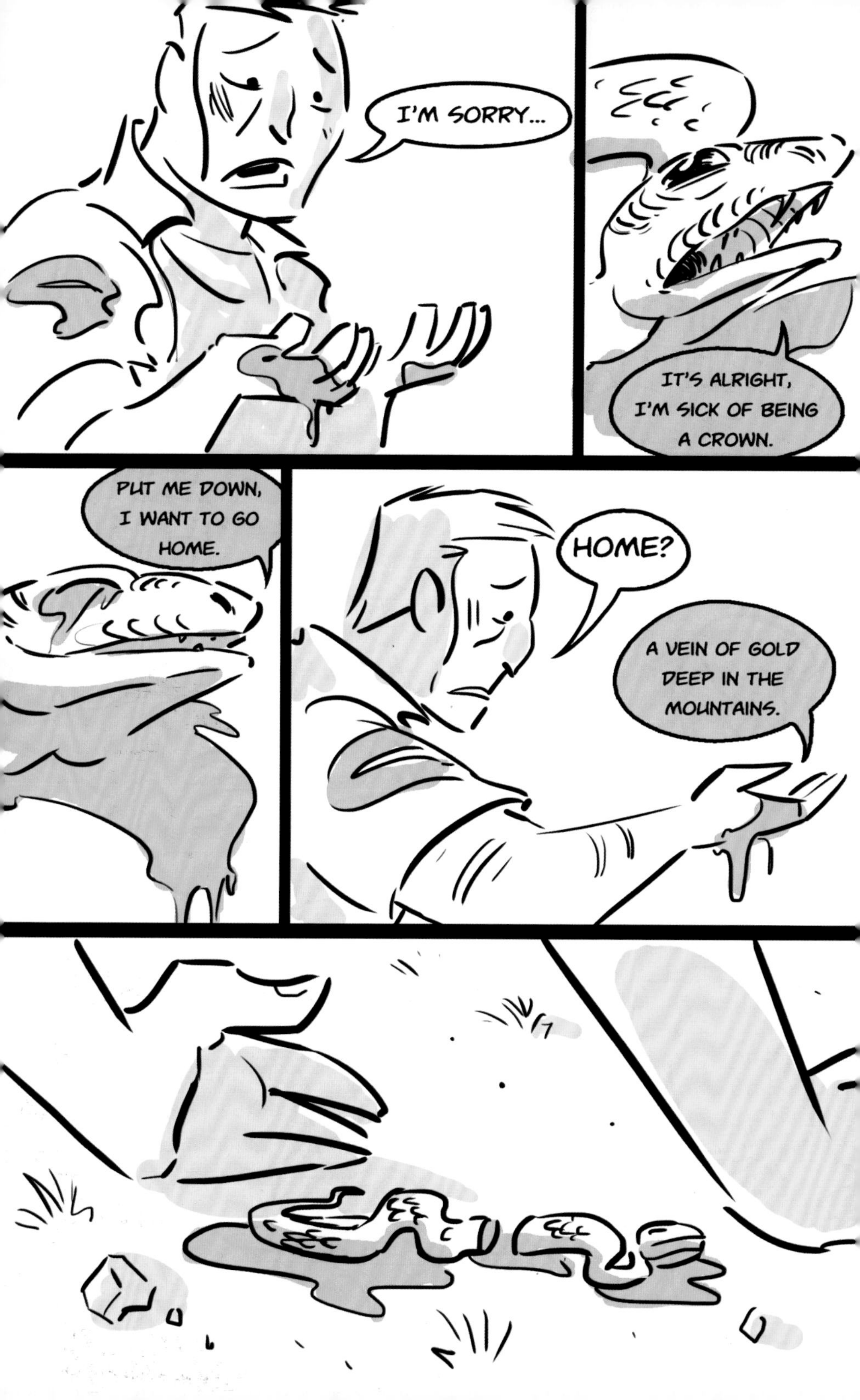
I'M SORRY...
IT'S ALRIGHT, I'M SICK OF BEING A CROWN.
PUT ME DOWN, I WANT TO GO HOME.
HOME?
A VEIN OF GOLD DEEP IN THE MOUNTAINS.

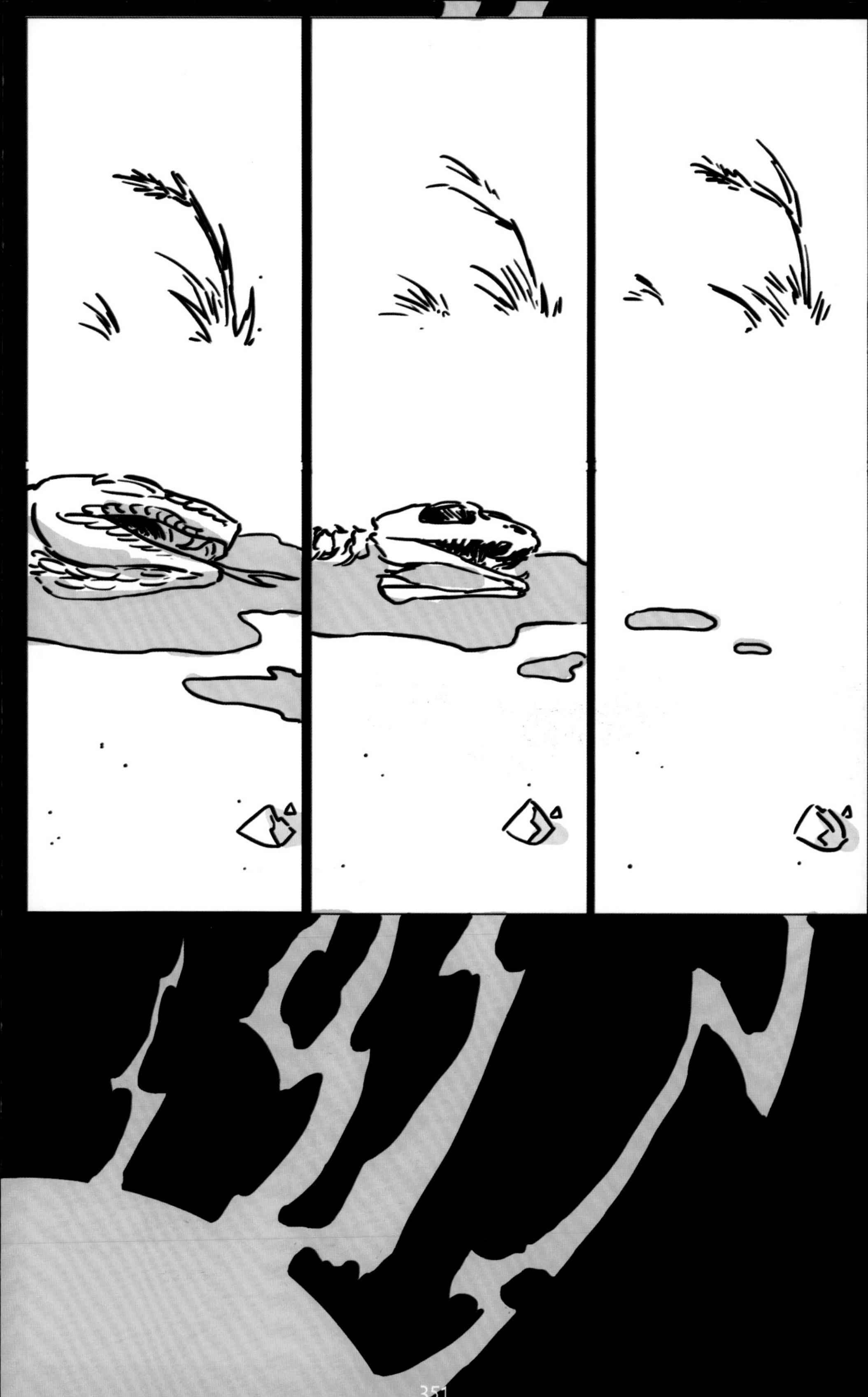

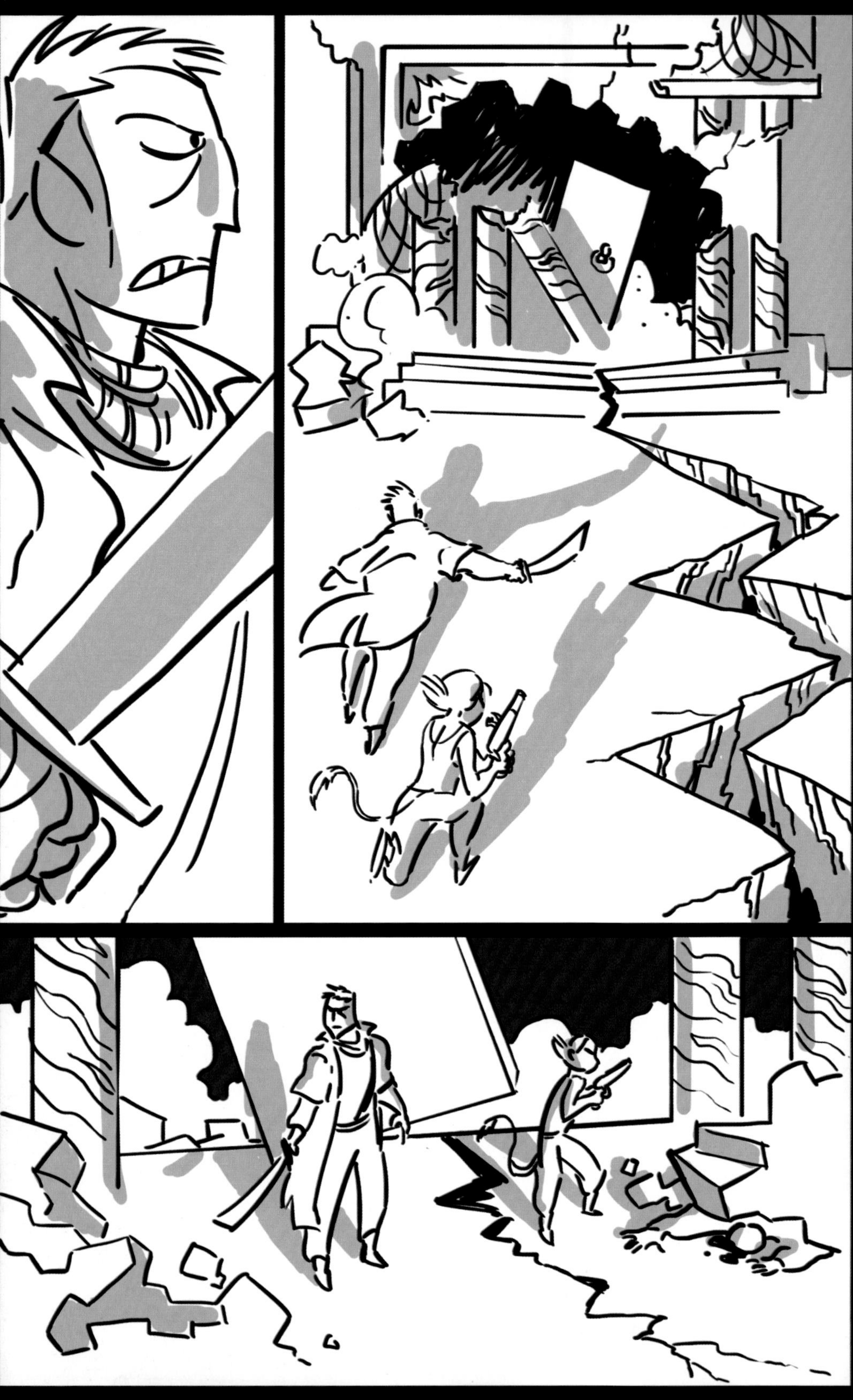

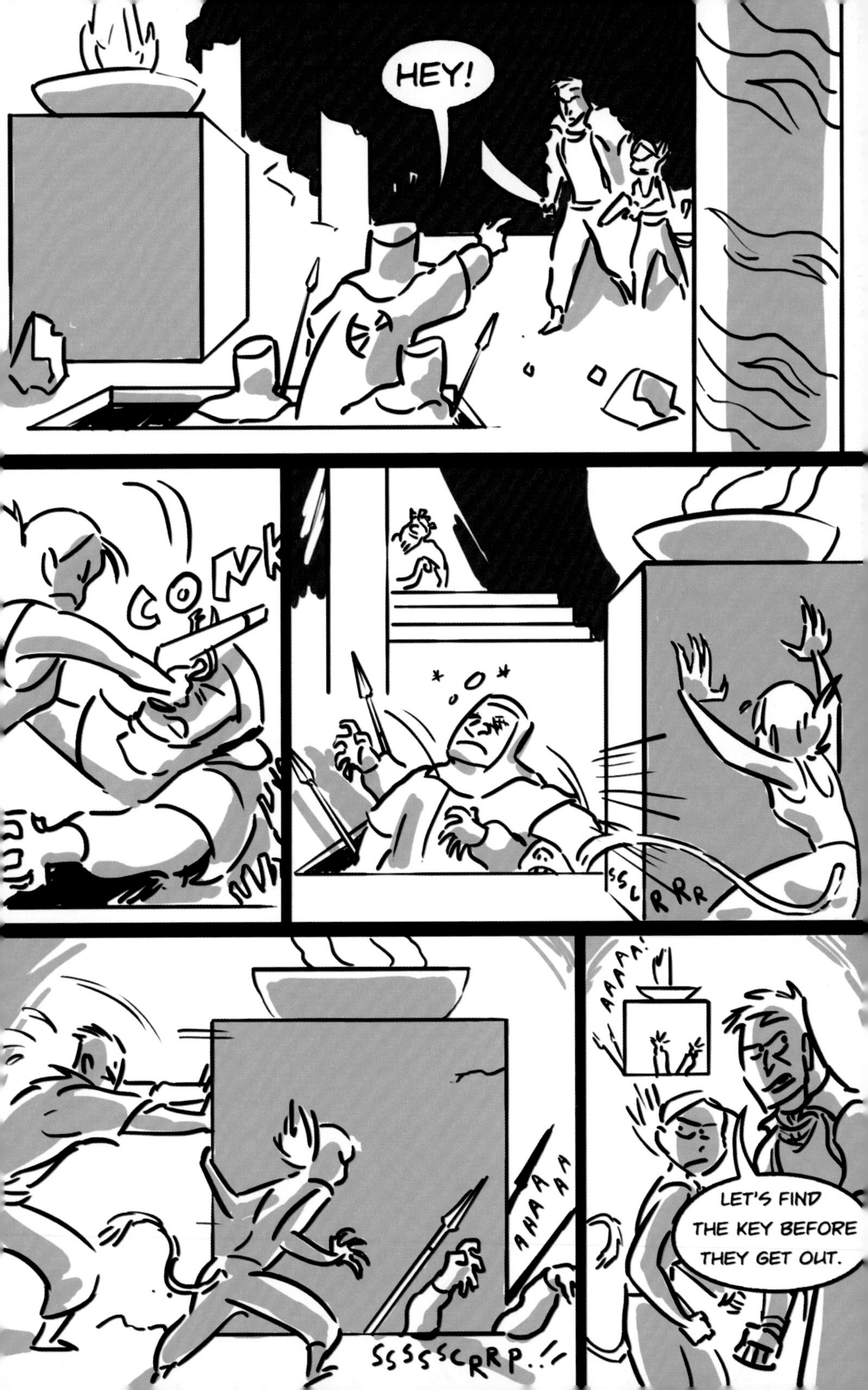
HEY!
CONK
SSCRRR
SSSSSSCRRP..!!
AAAAA
AAAAA!
LET'S FIND THE KEY BEFORE THEY GET OUT.

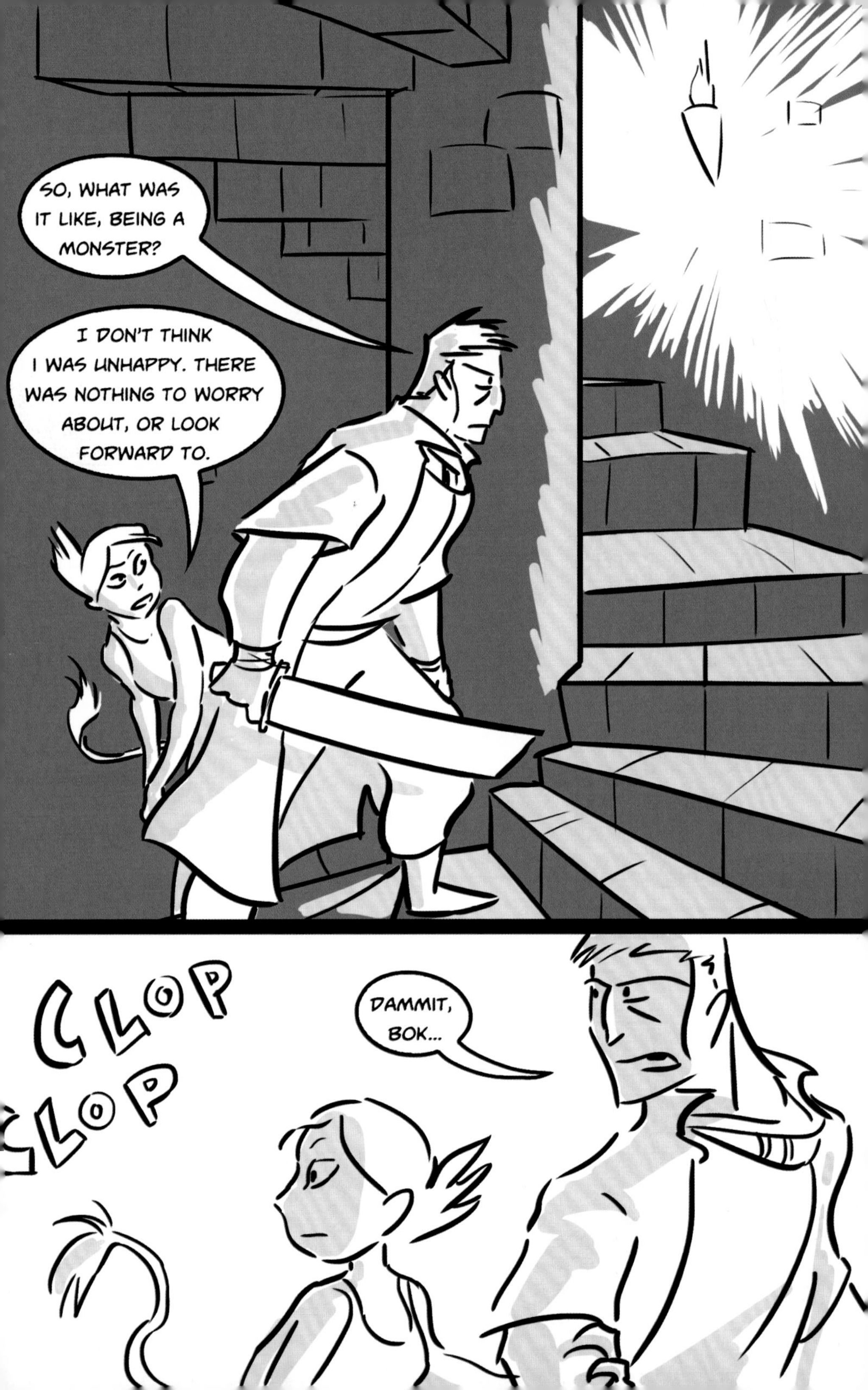
SO, WHAT WAS IT LIKE, BEING A MONSTER?
I DON'T THINK I WAS UNHAPPY. THERE WAS NOTHING TO WORRY ABOUT, OR LOOK FORWARD TO.
CLOP
CLOP
DAMMIT, BOK...

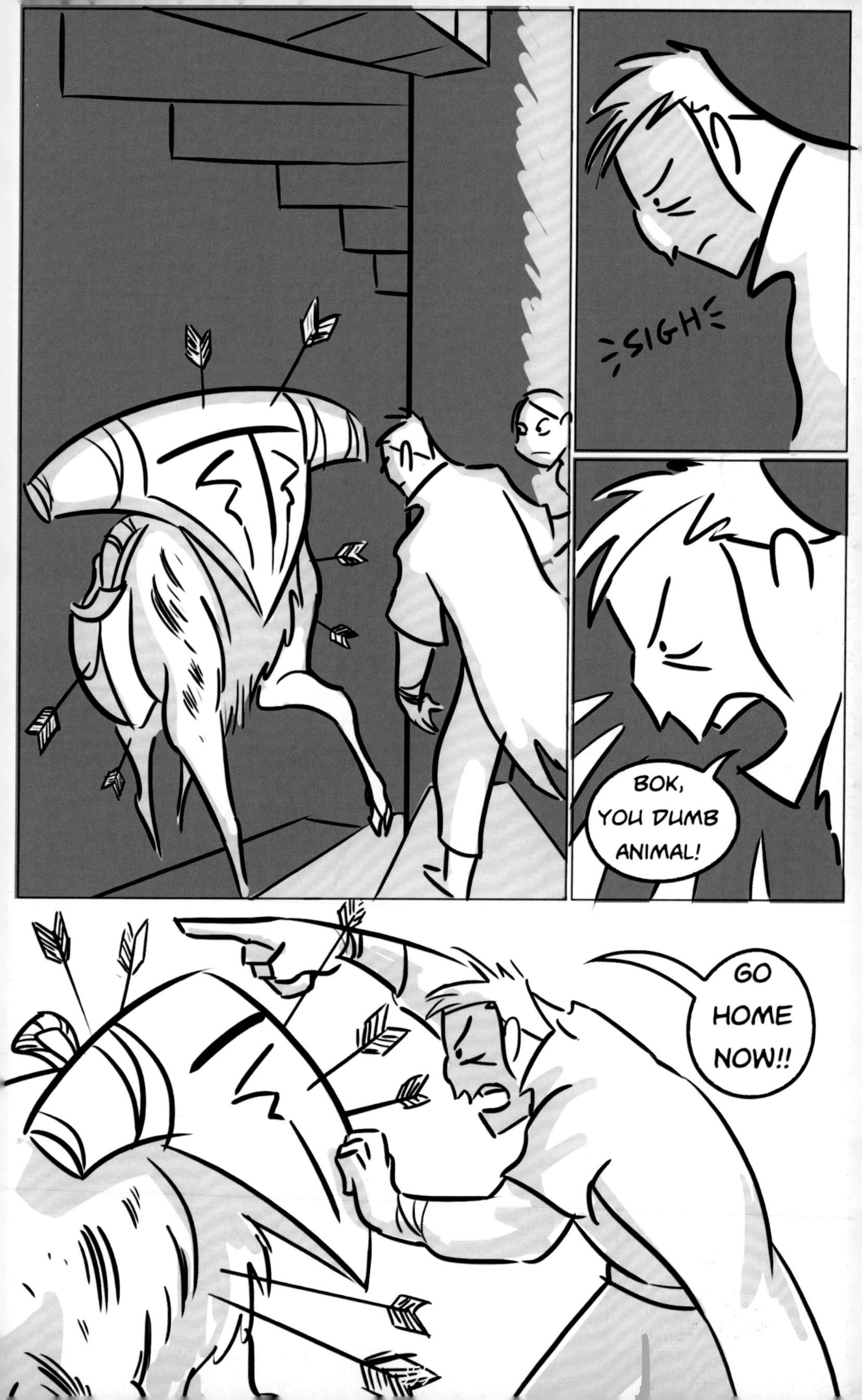
SIGH
BOK, YOU DUMB ANIMAL!
GO HOME NOW!!

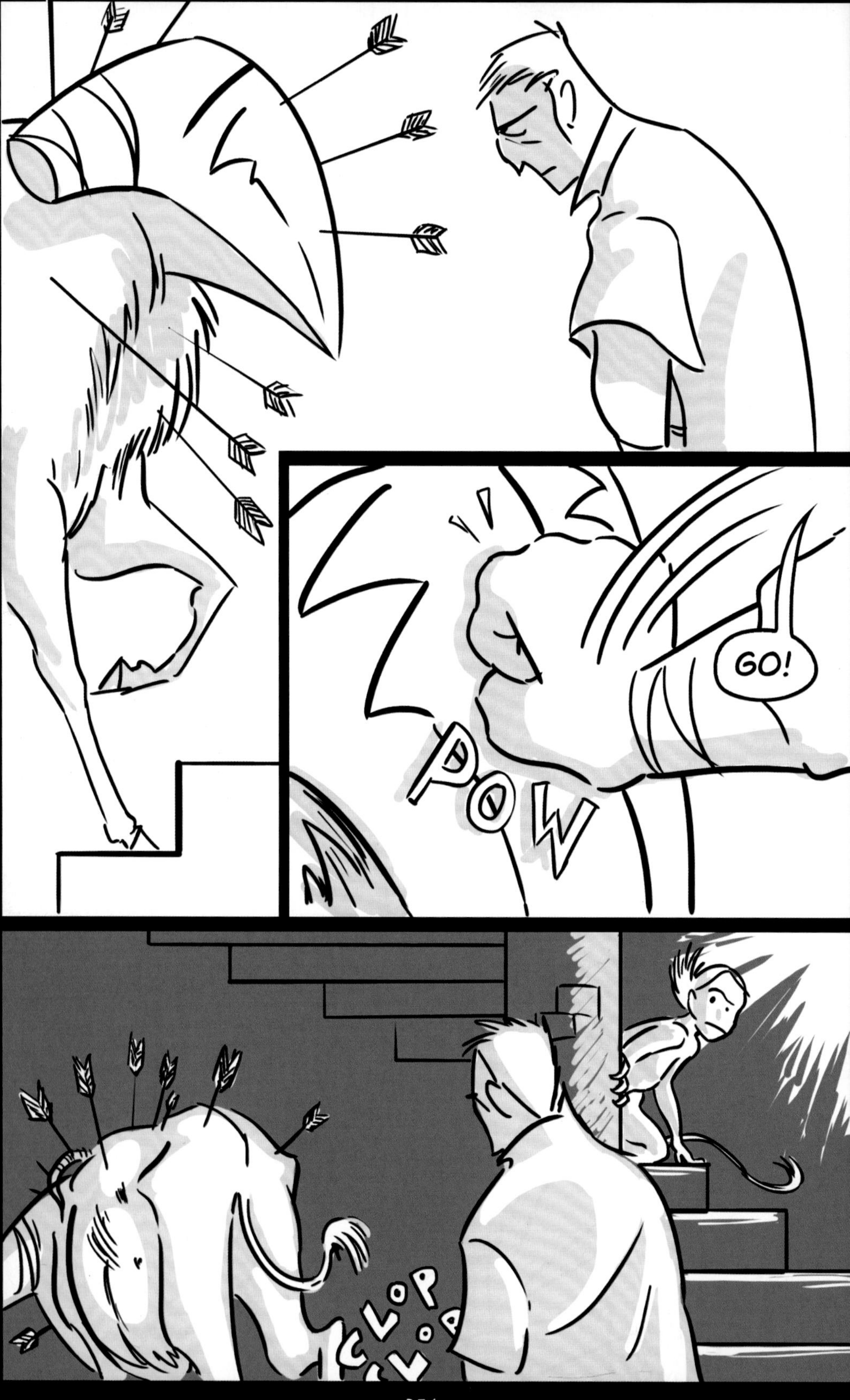
GO!
POW
CLOP
CLOP

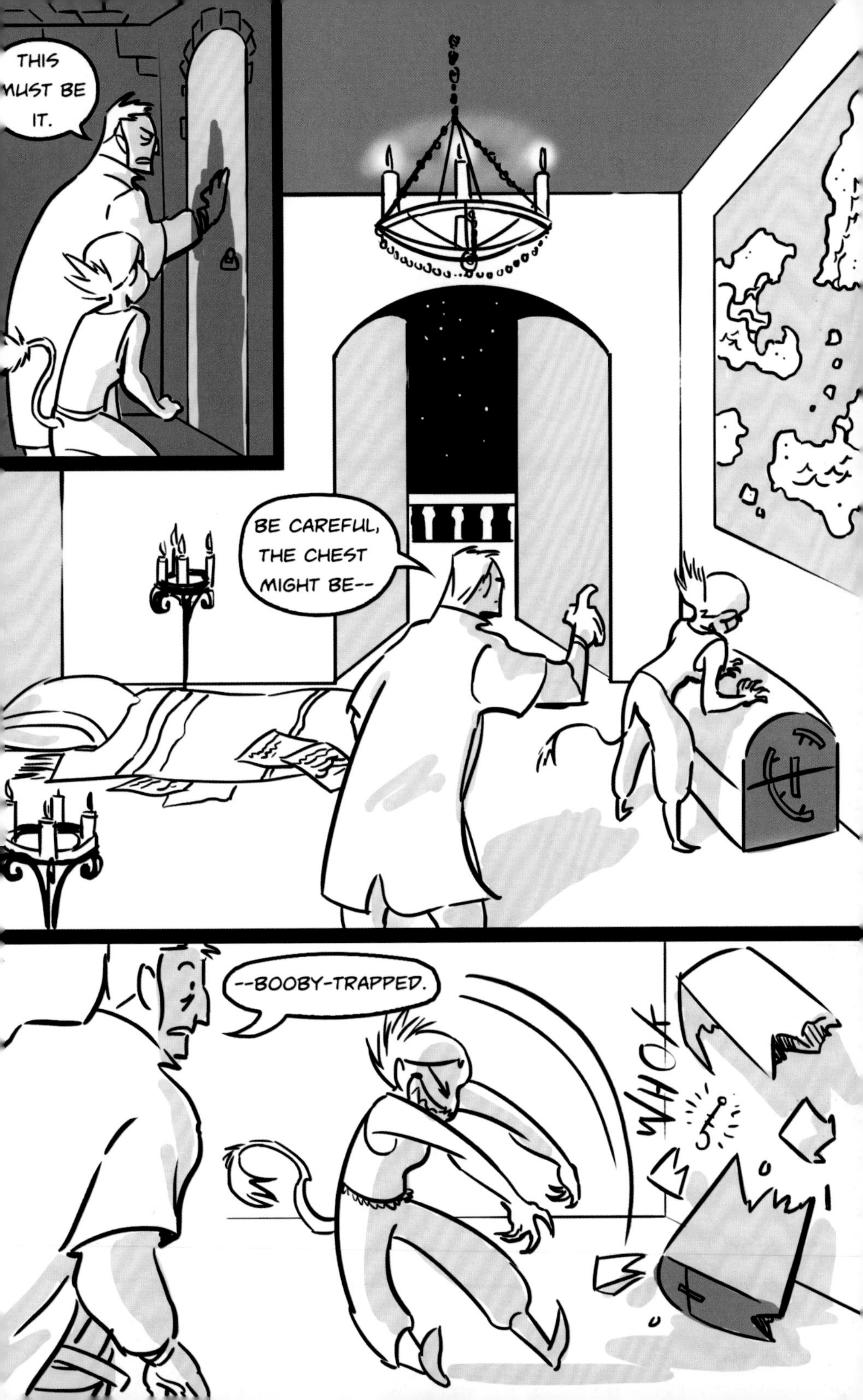
THIS MUST BE IT.
BE CAREFUL, THE CHEST MIGHT BE--
--BOOBY-TRAPPED.
WHOA

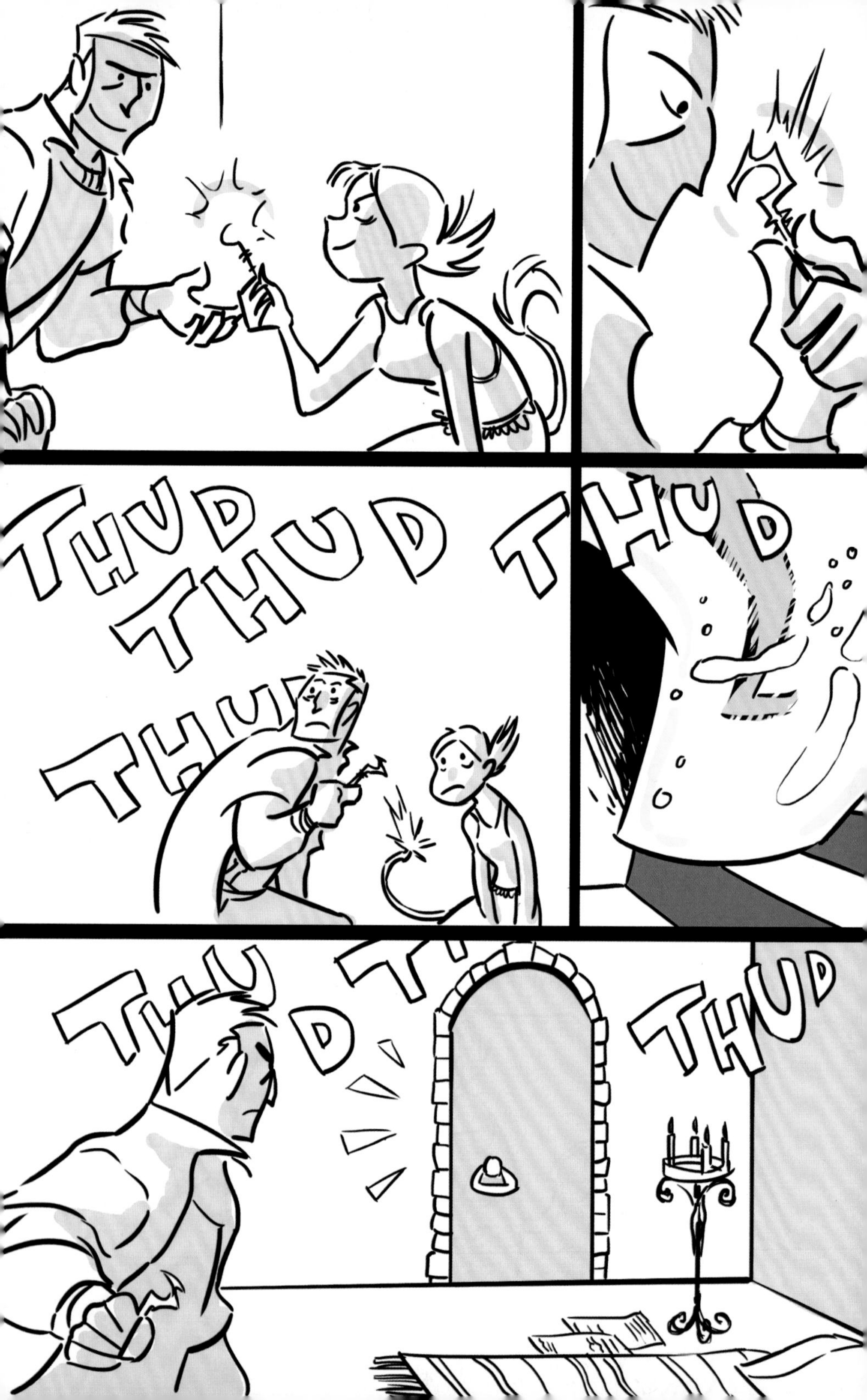
THUD
THUD
THUD
THUD

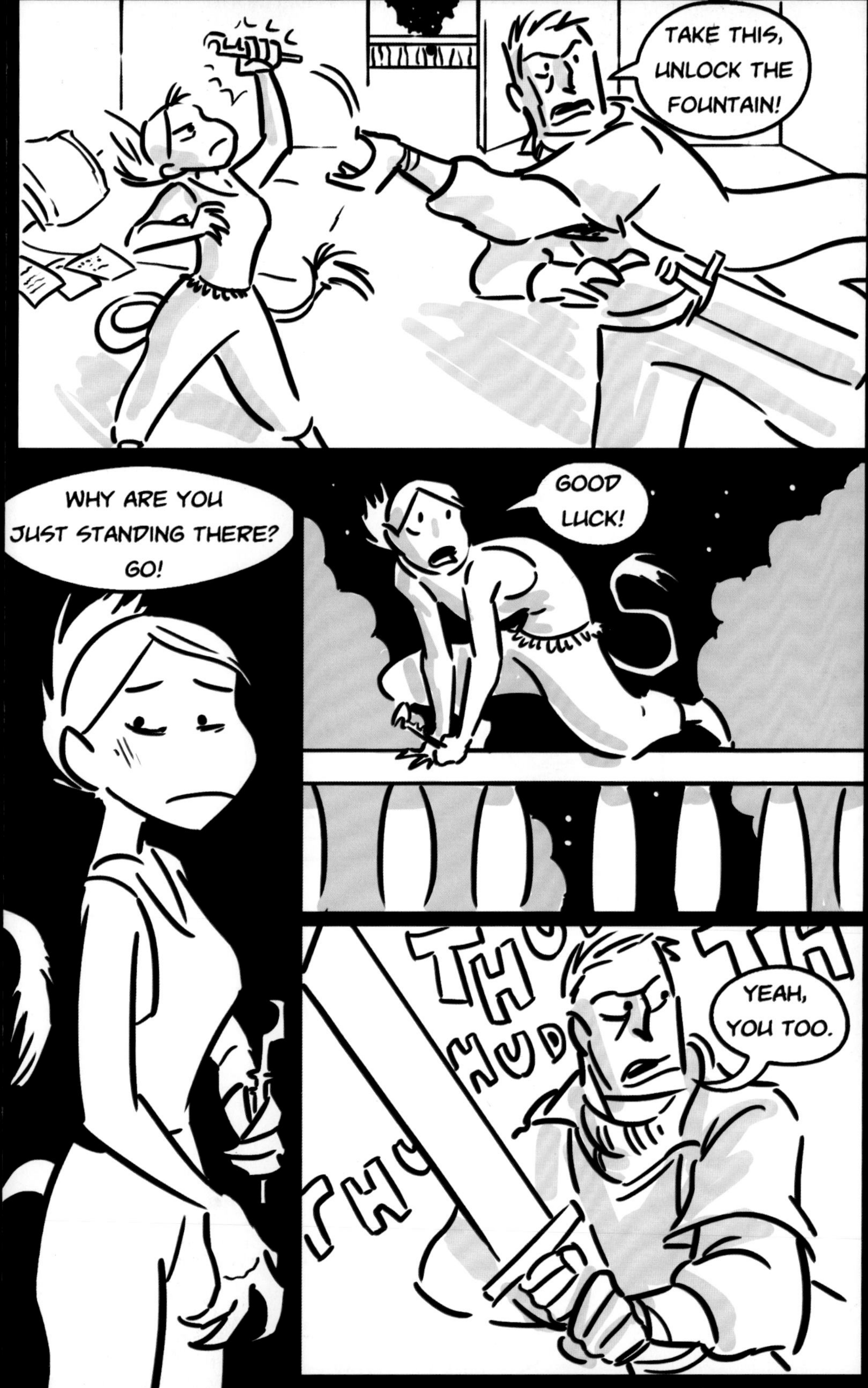
TAKE THIS, UNLOCK THE FOUNTAIN!
WHY ARE YOU JUST STANDING THERE? GO!
GOOD LUCK!
YEAH, YOU TOO.

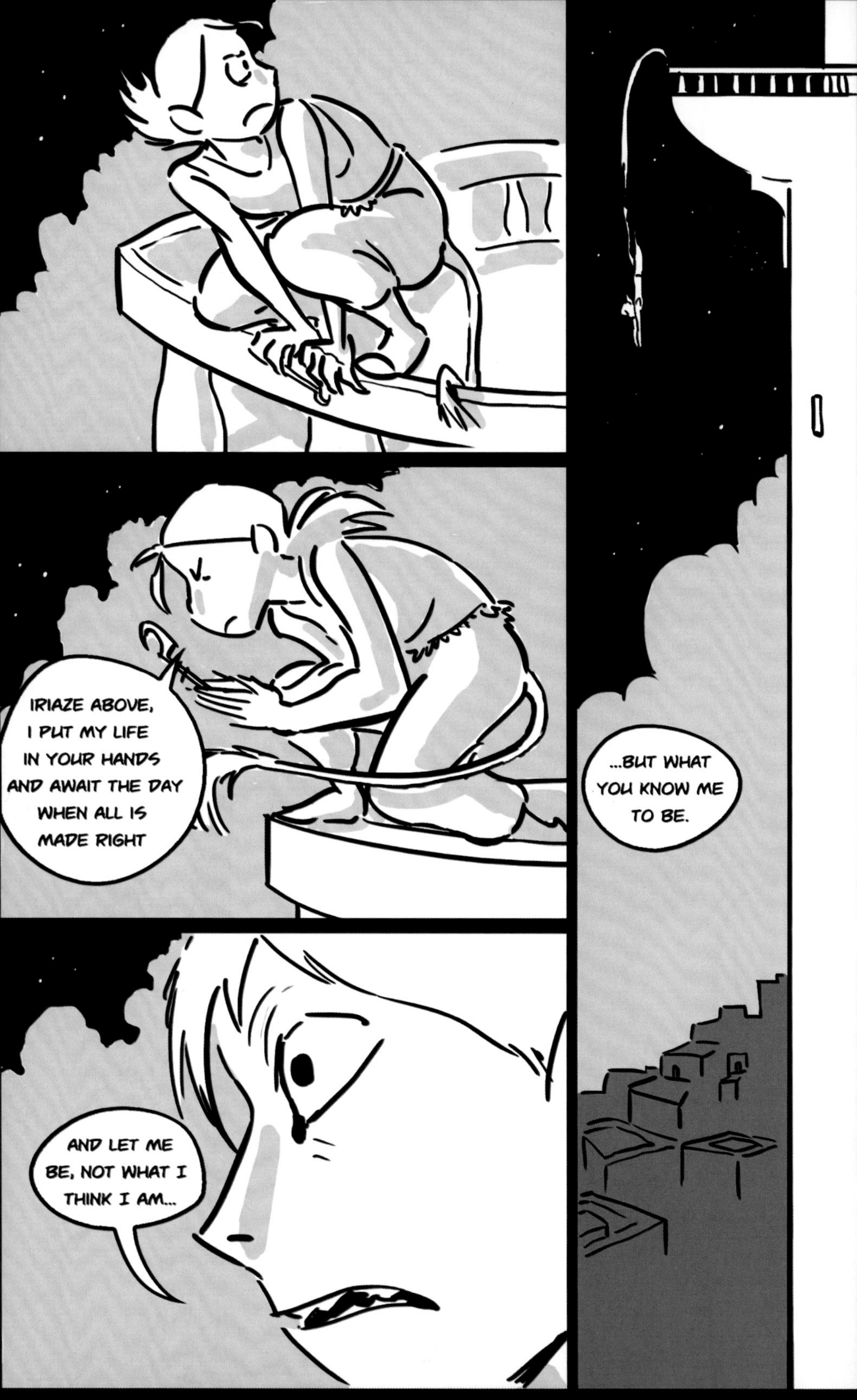
IRIAZE ABOVE, I PUT MY LIFE IN YOUR HANDS AND AWAIT THE DAY WHEN ALL IS MADE RIGHT
AND LET ME BE, NOT WHAT I THINK I AM...
...BUT WHAT YOU KNOW ME TO BE.

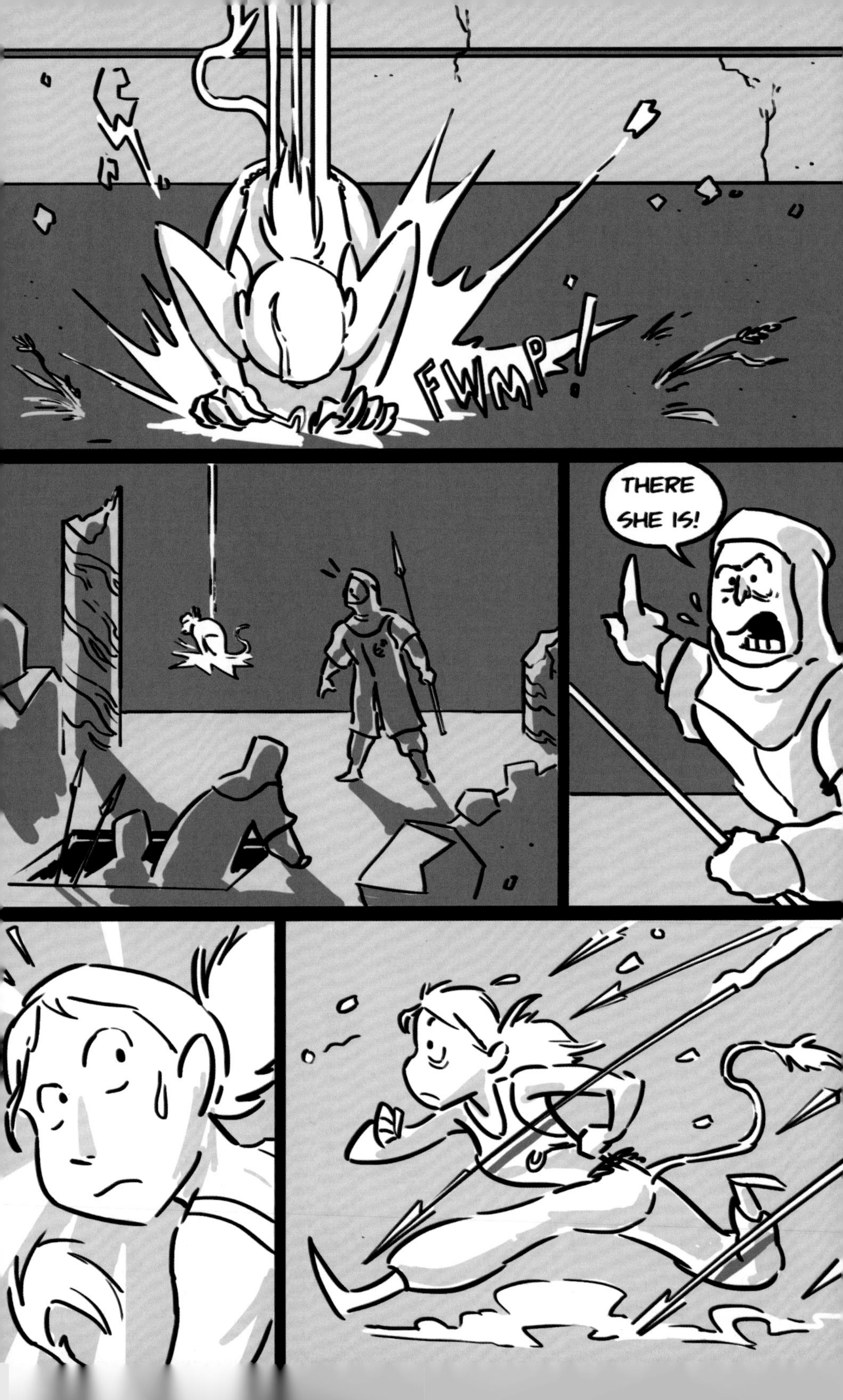
FWMP!
THERE SHE IS!

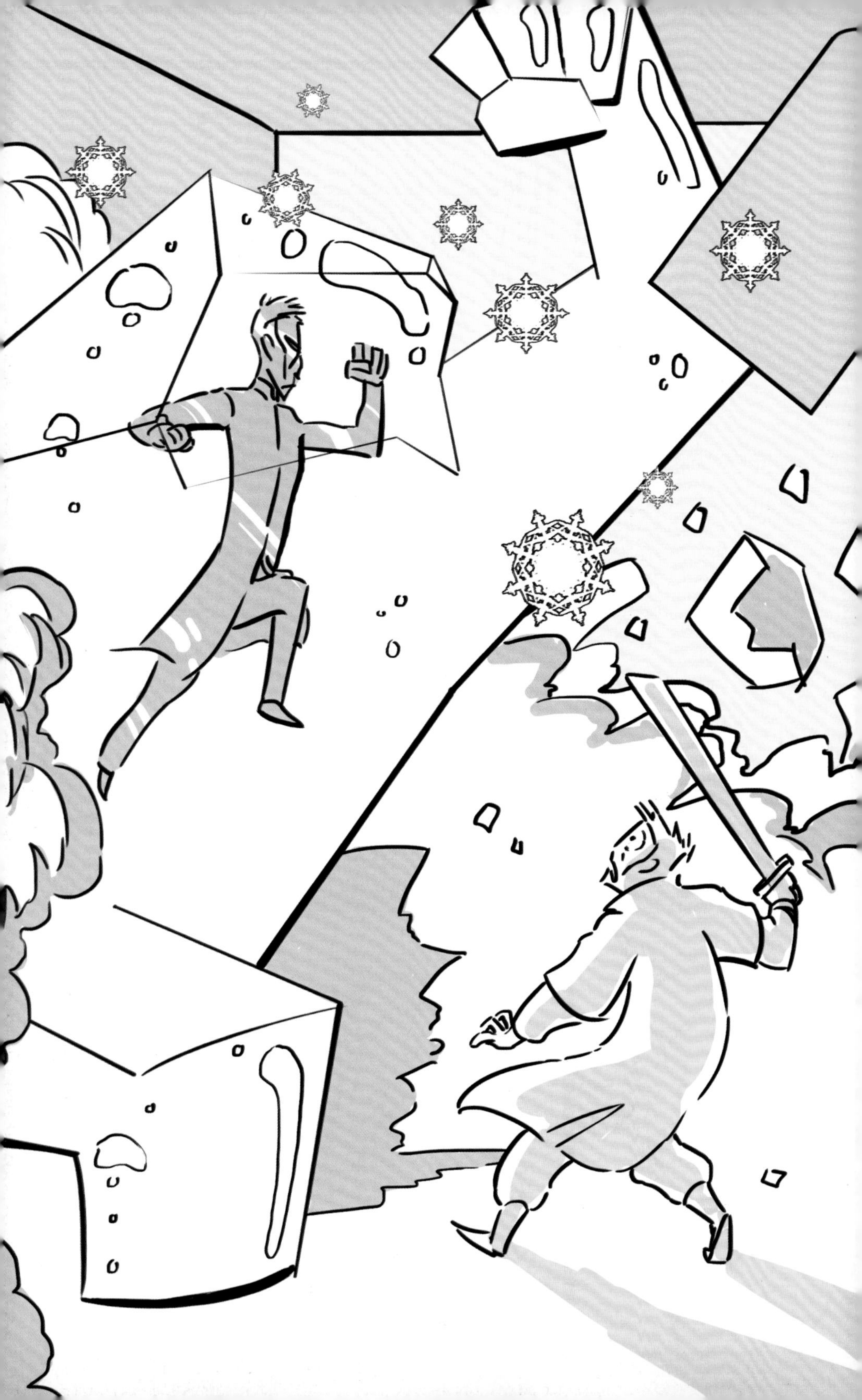

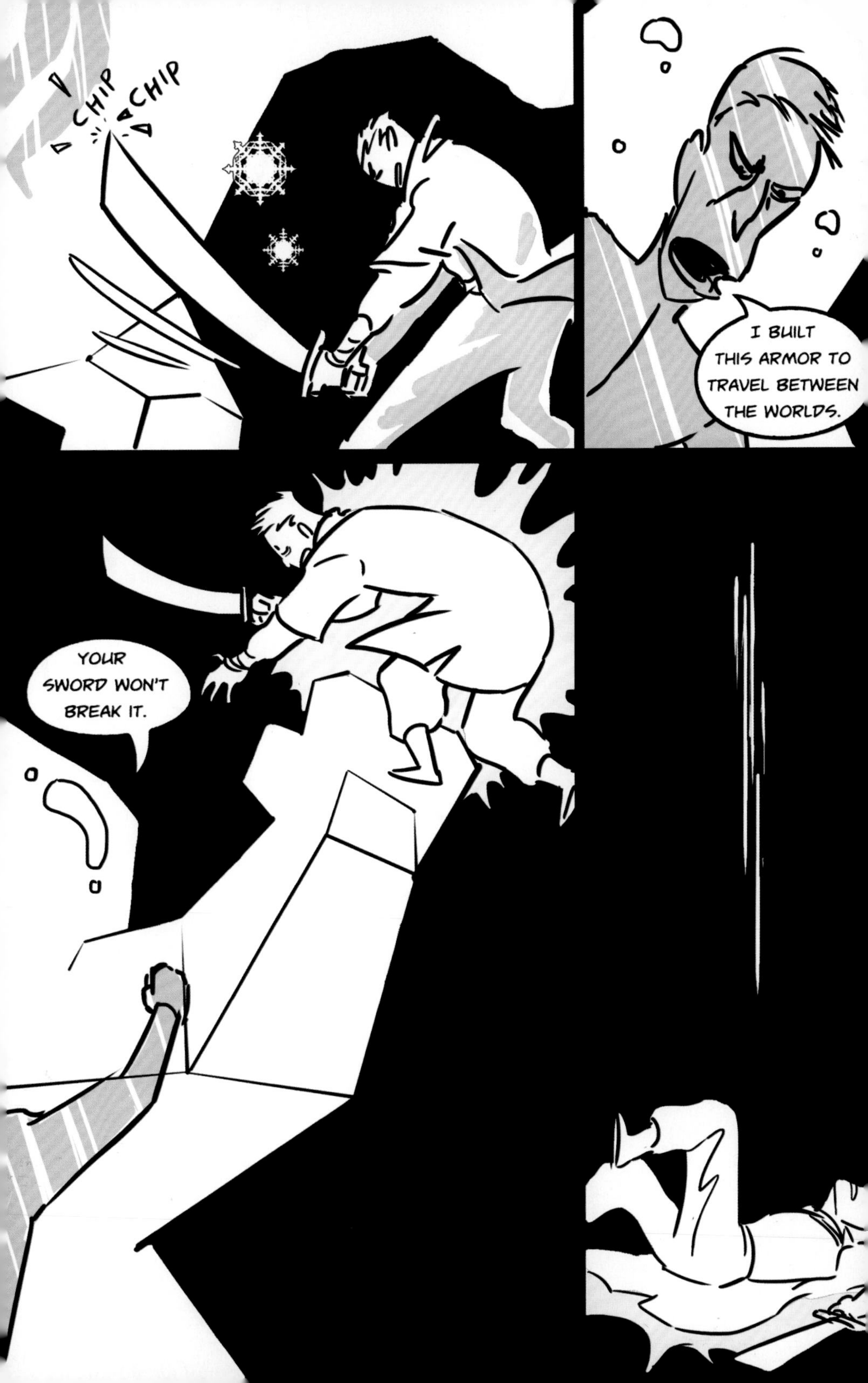
CHIP
CHIP
I BUILT THIS ARMOR TO TRAVEL BETWEEN THE WORLDS.
YOUR SWORD WON'T BREAK IT.

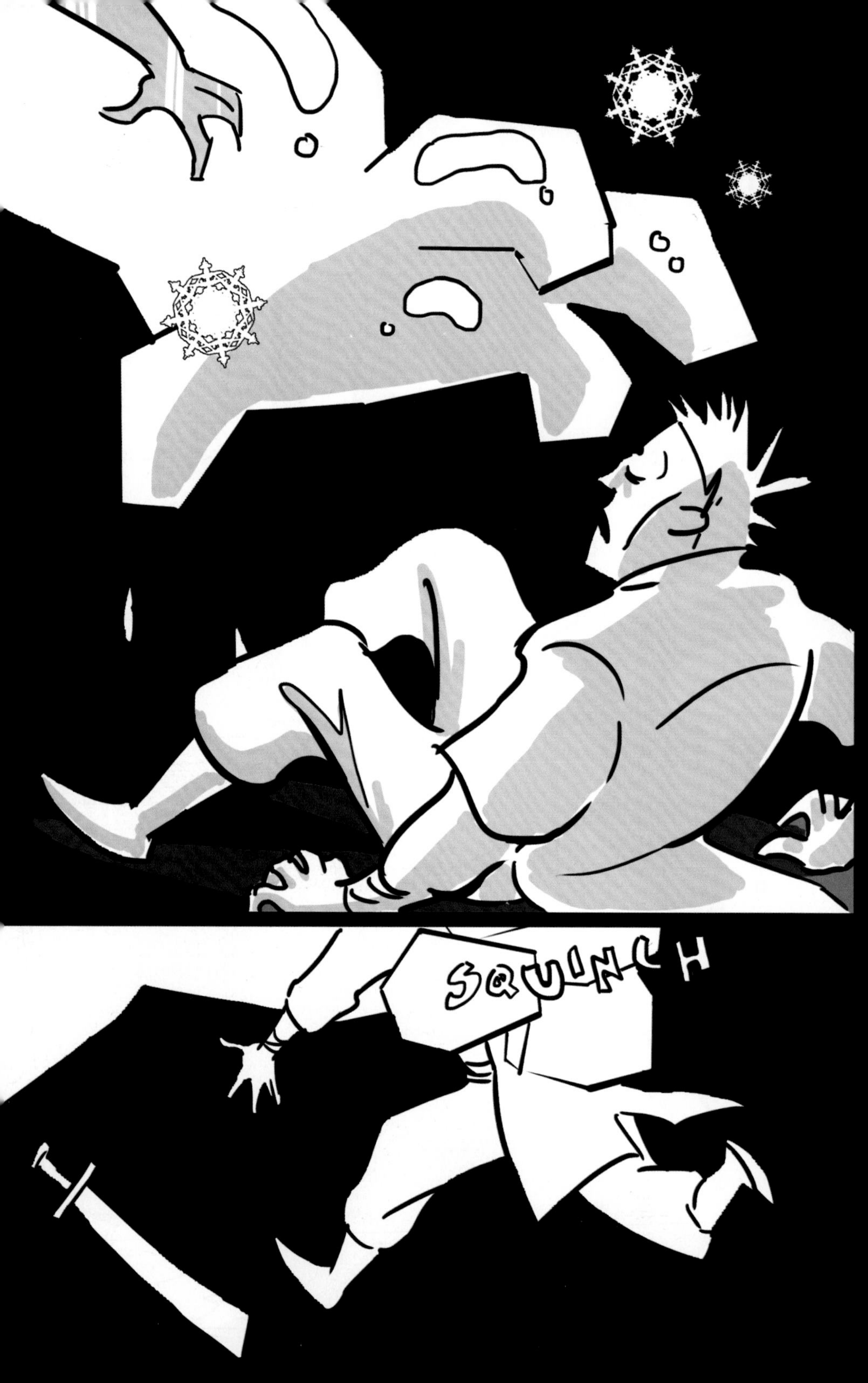
SQUINCH

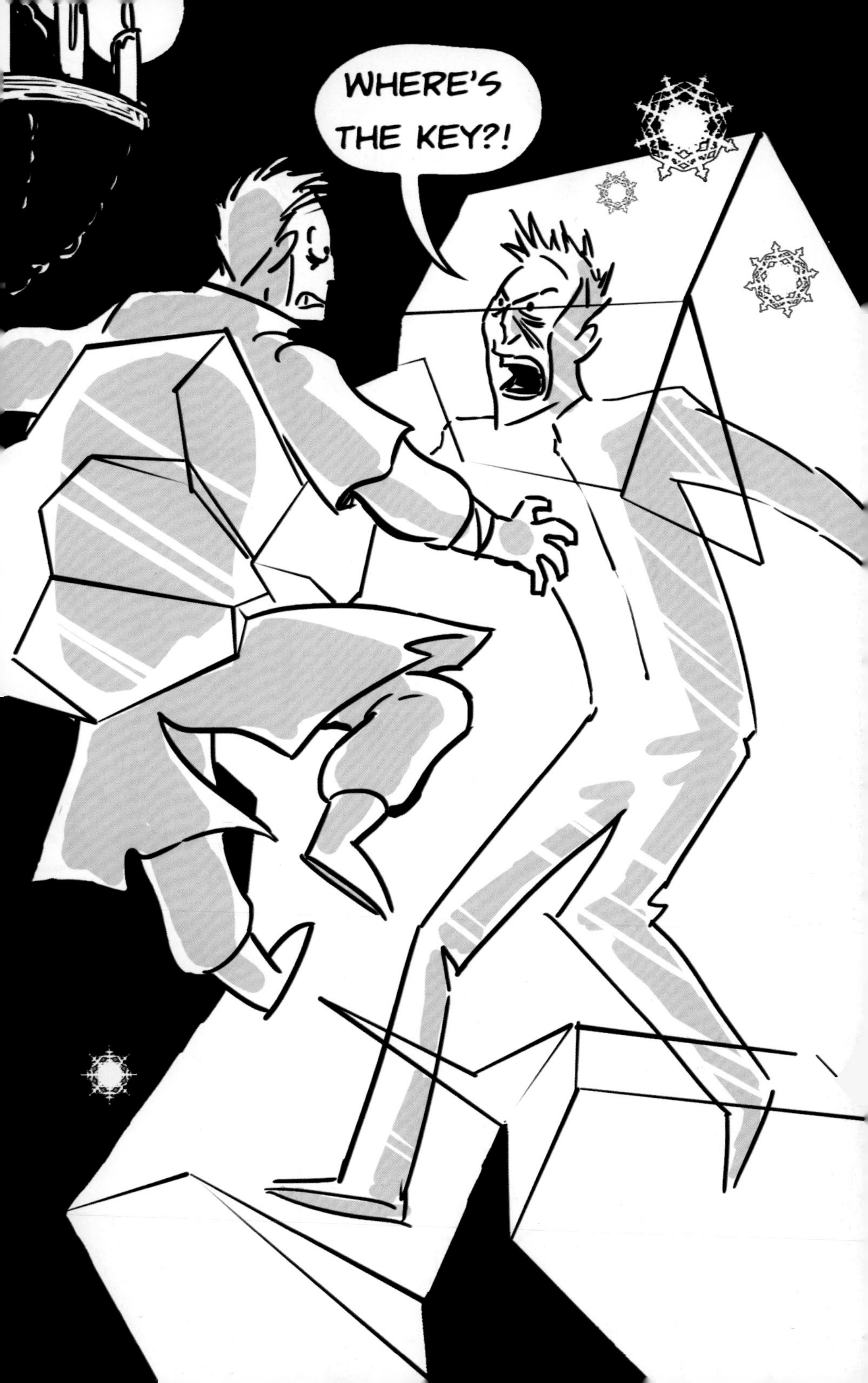
WHERE'S THE KEY?!

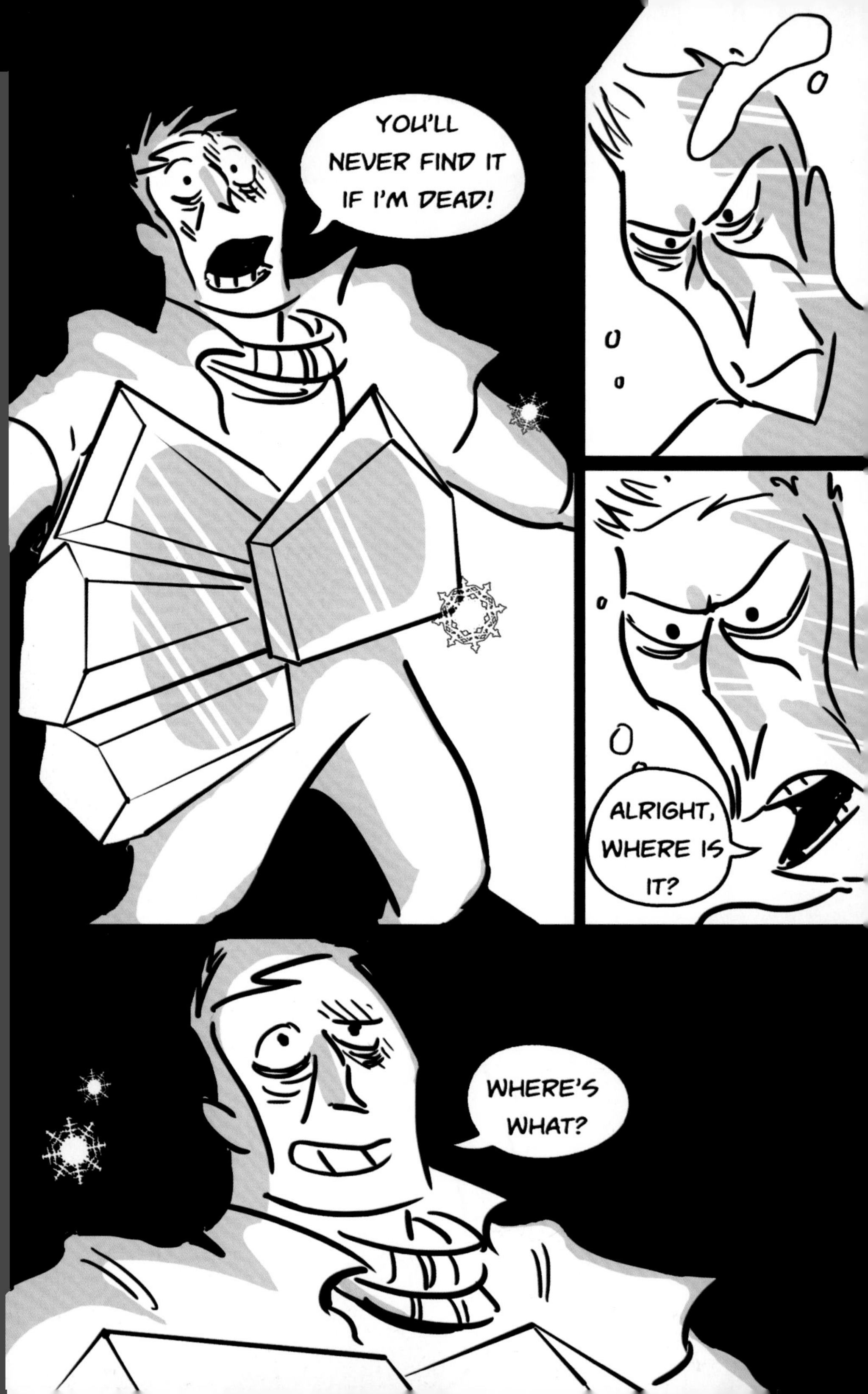
YOU'LL NEVER FIND IT IF I'M DEAD!
ALRIGHT, WHERE IS IT?
WHERE'S WHAT?

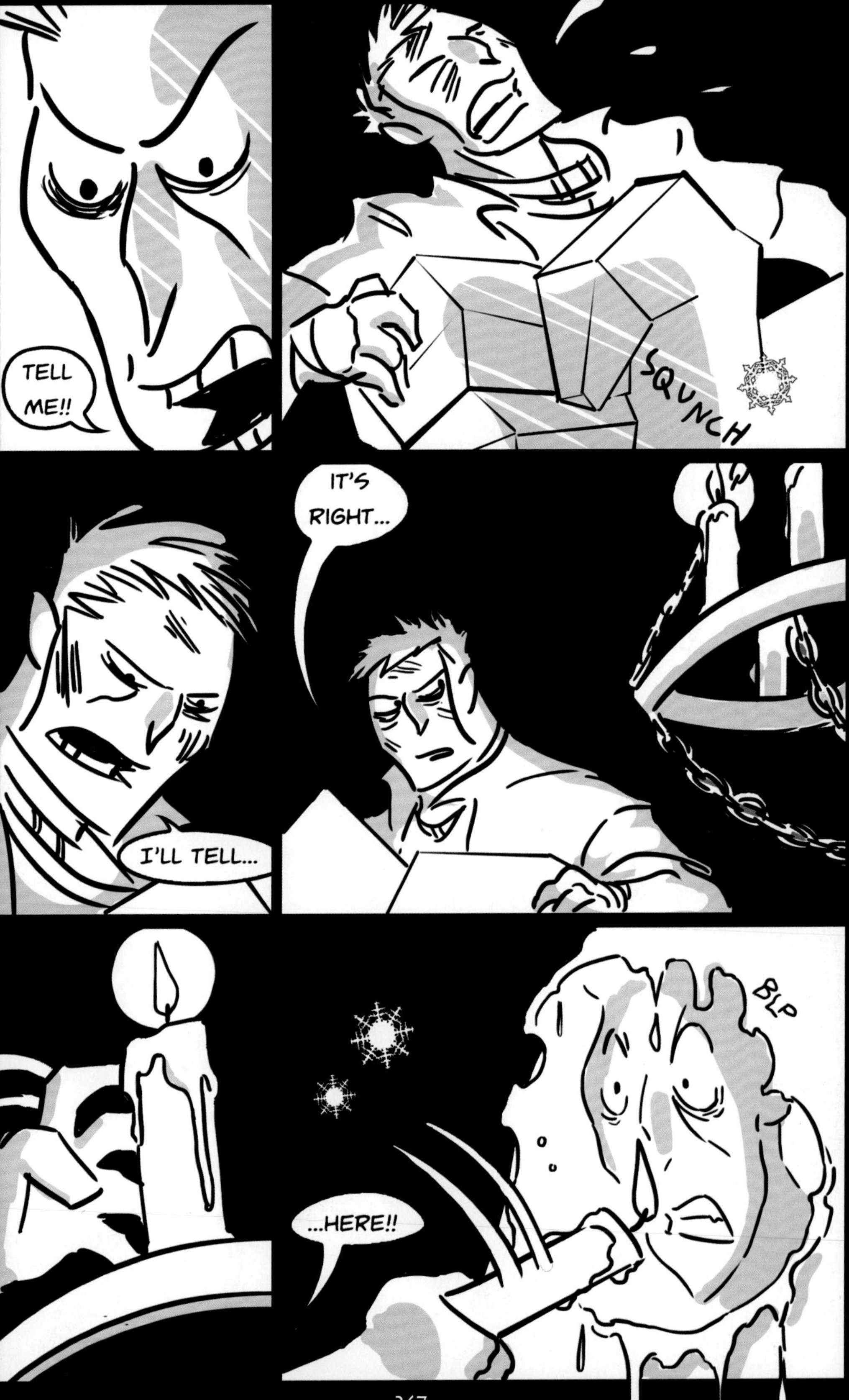
TELL ME!!
SQUNCH
IT'S RIGHT...
I'LL TELL...
...HERE!!
BLP

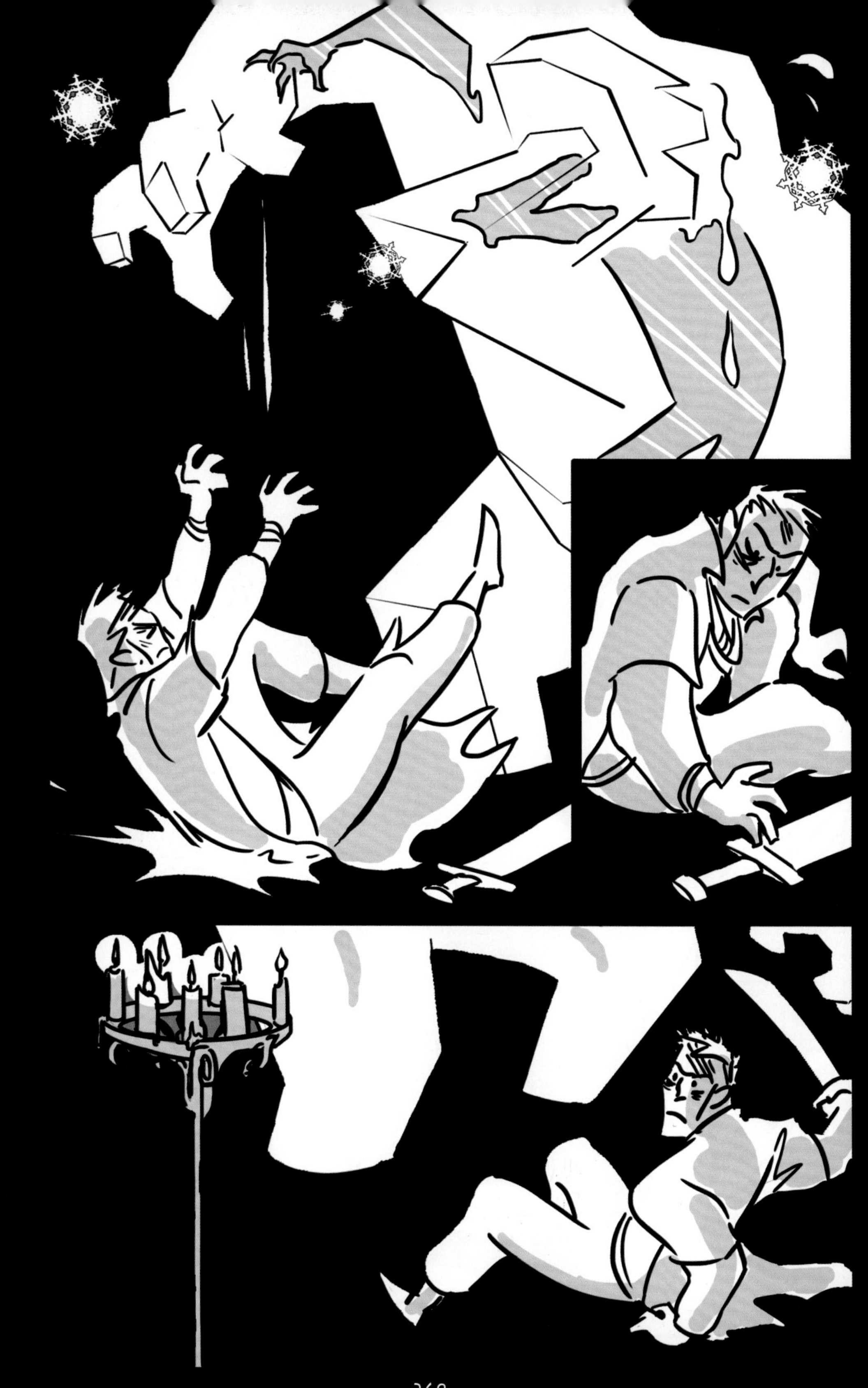

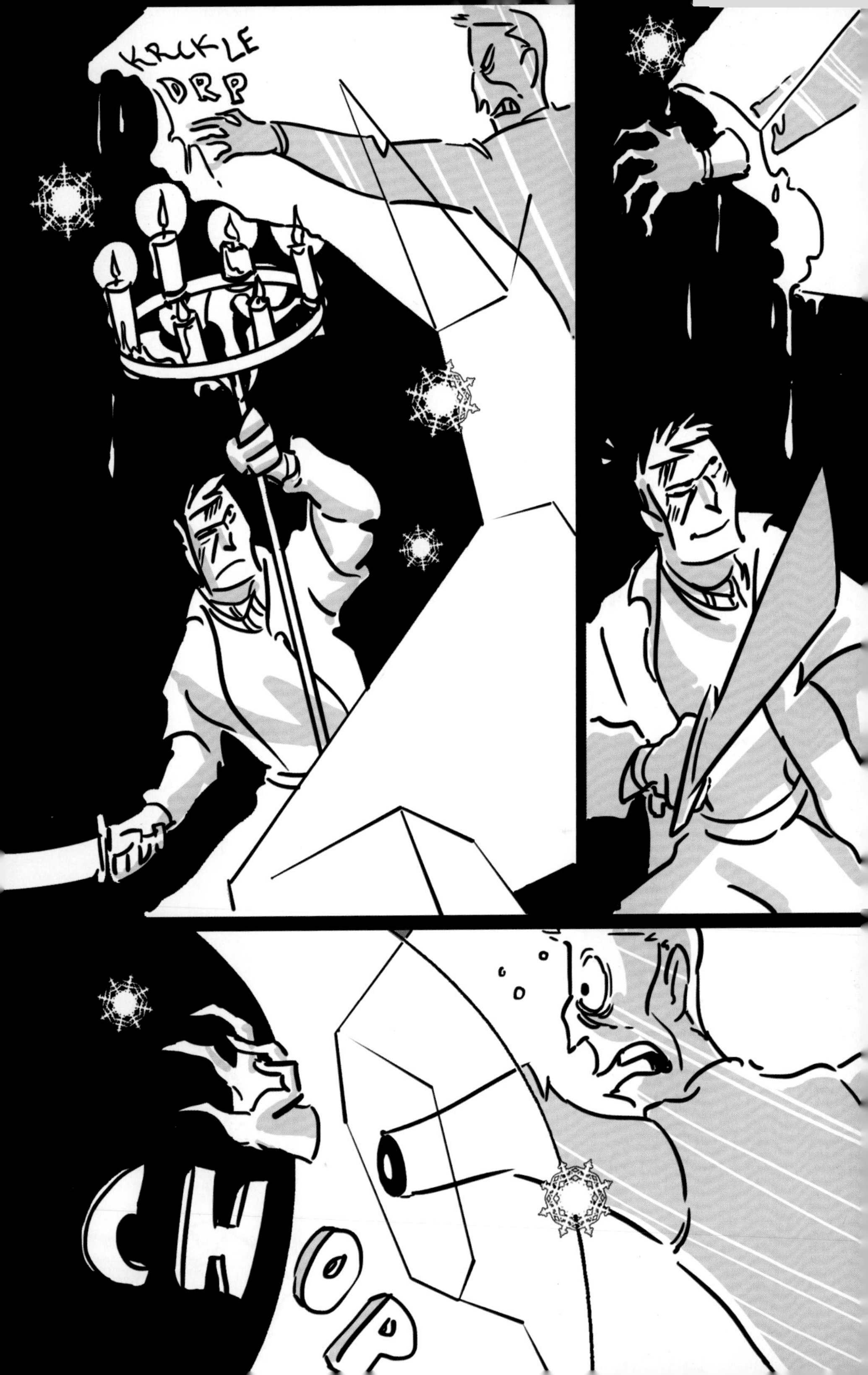
KRCKLE
DRP
CHOP

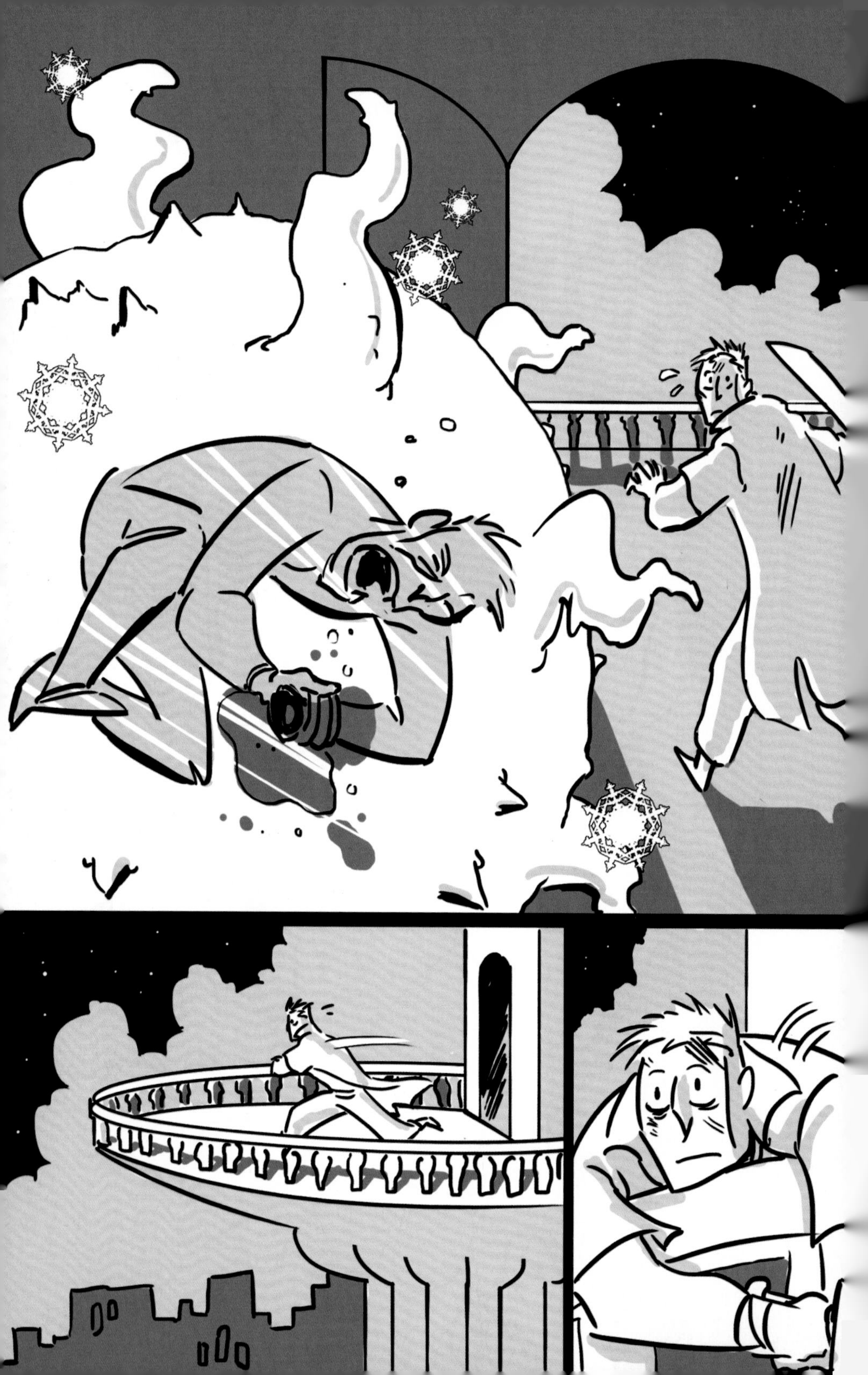

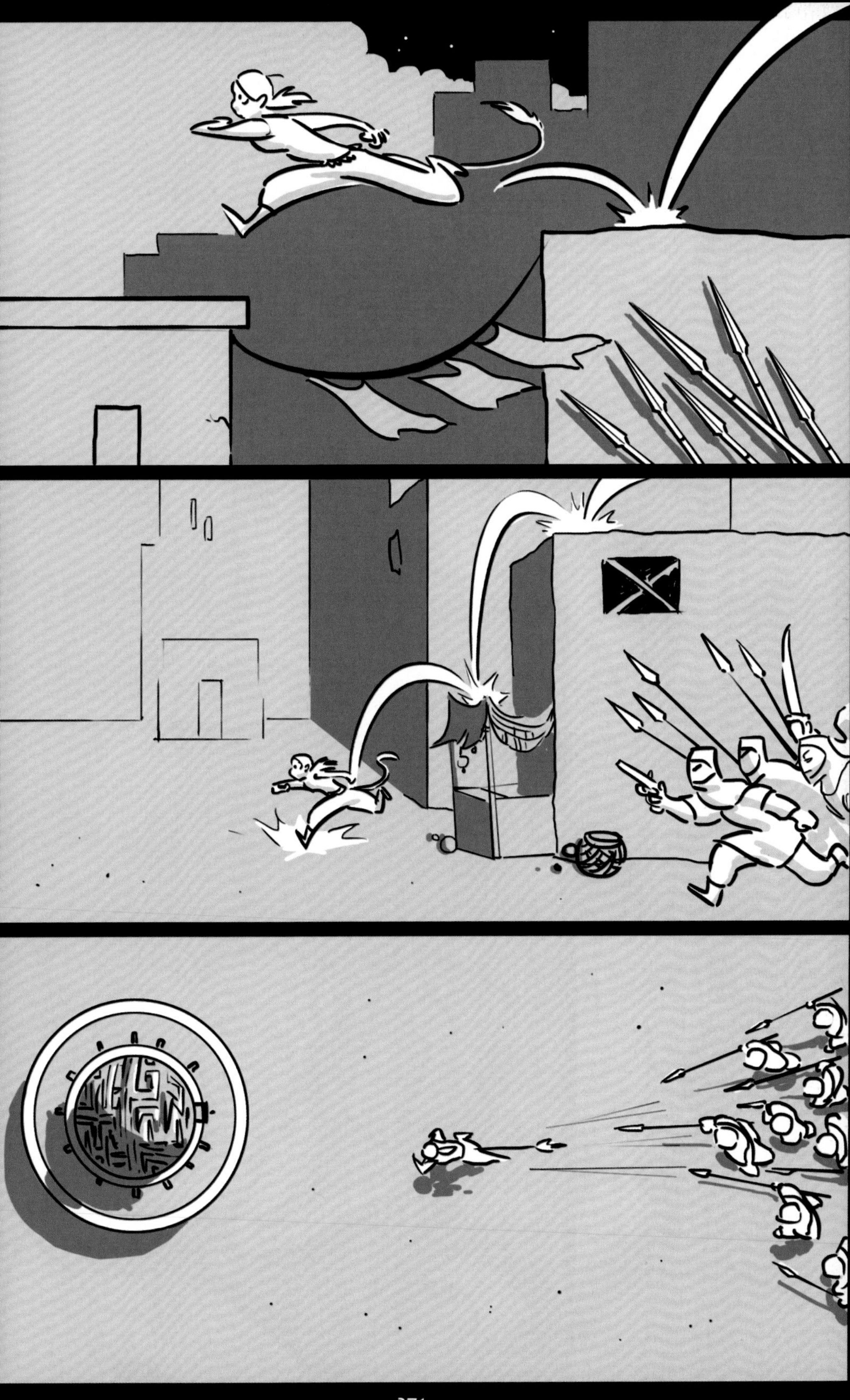

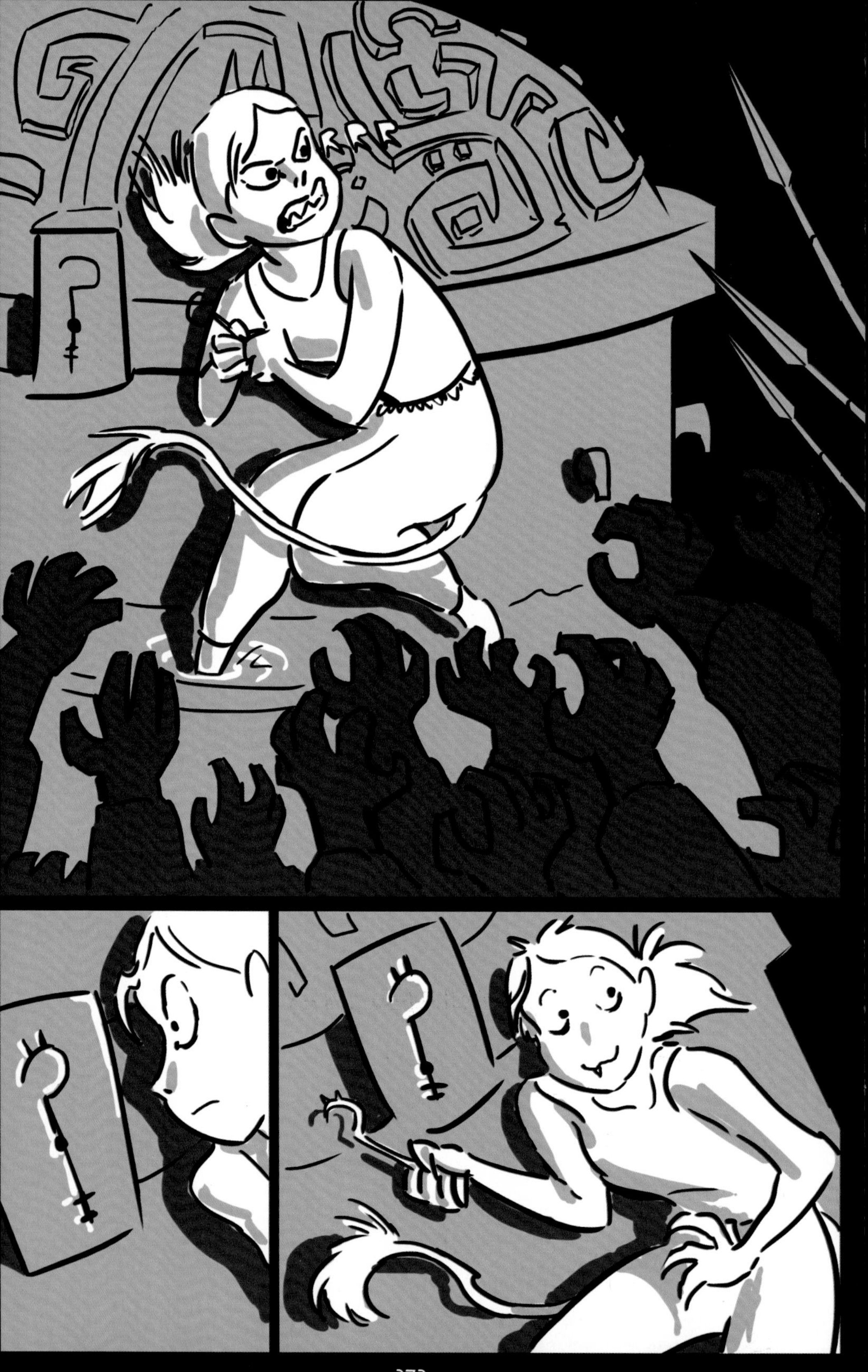
RRR

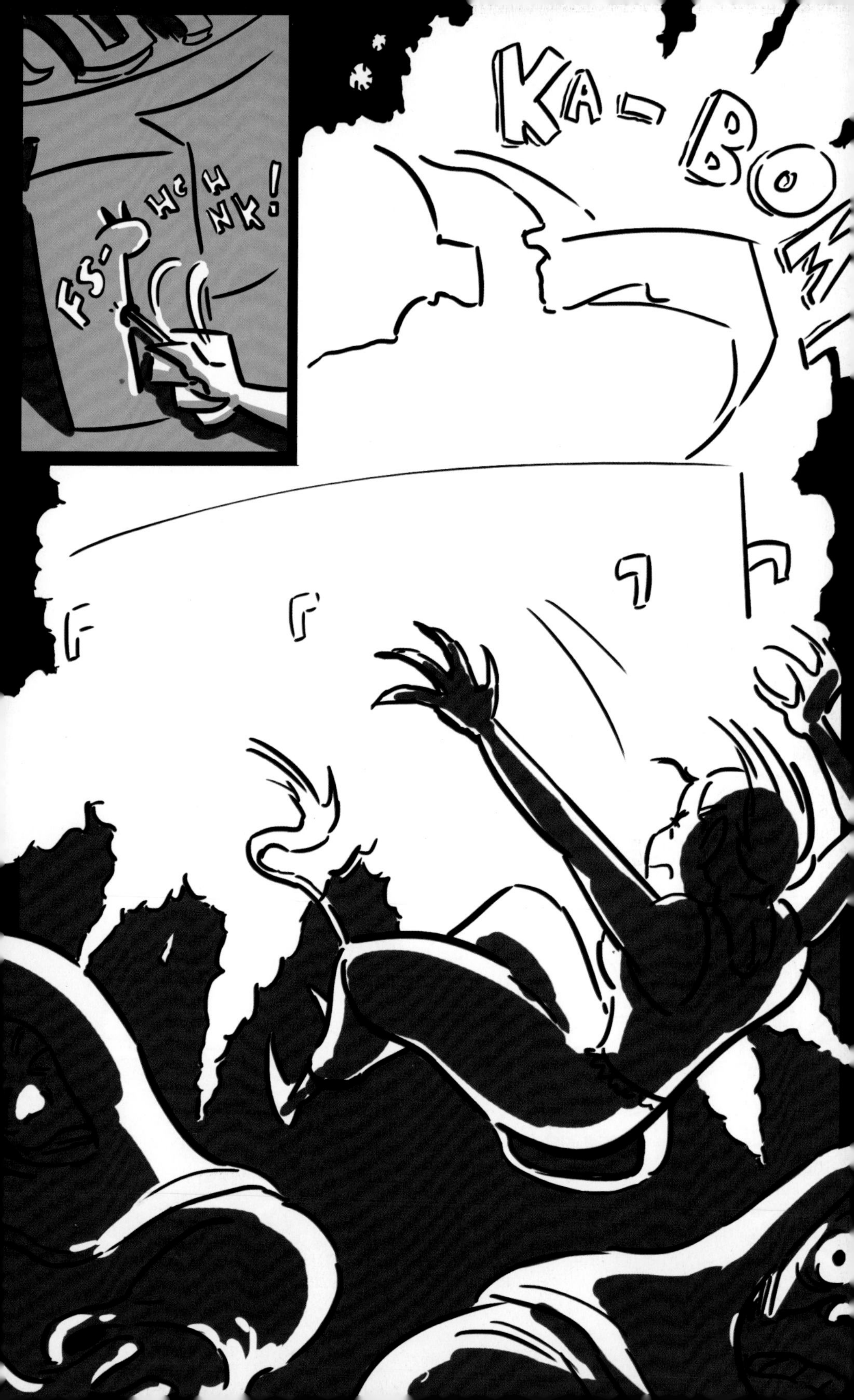
FS-HCH
HNK!
KA-BOM

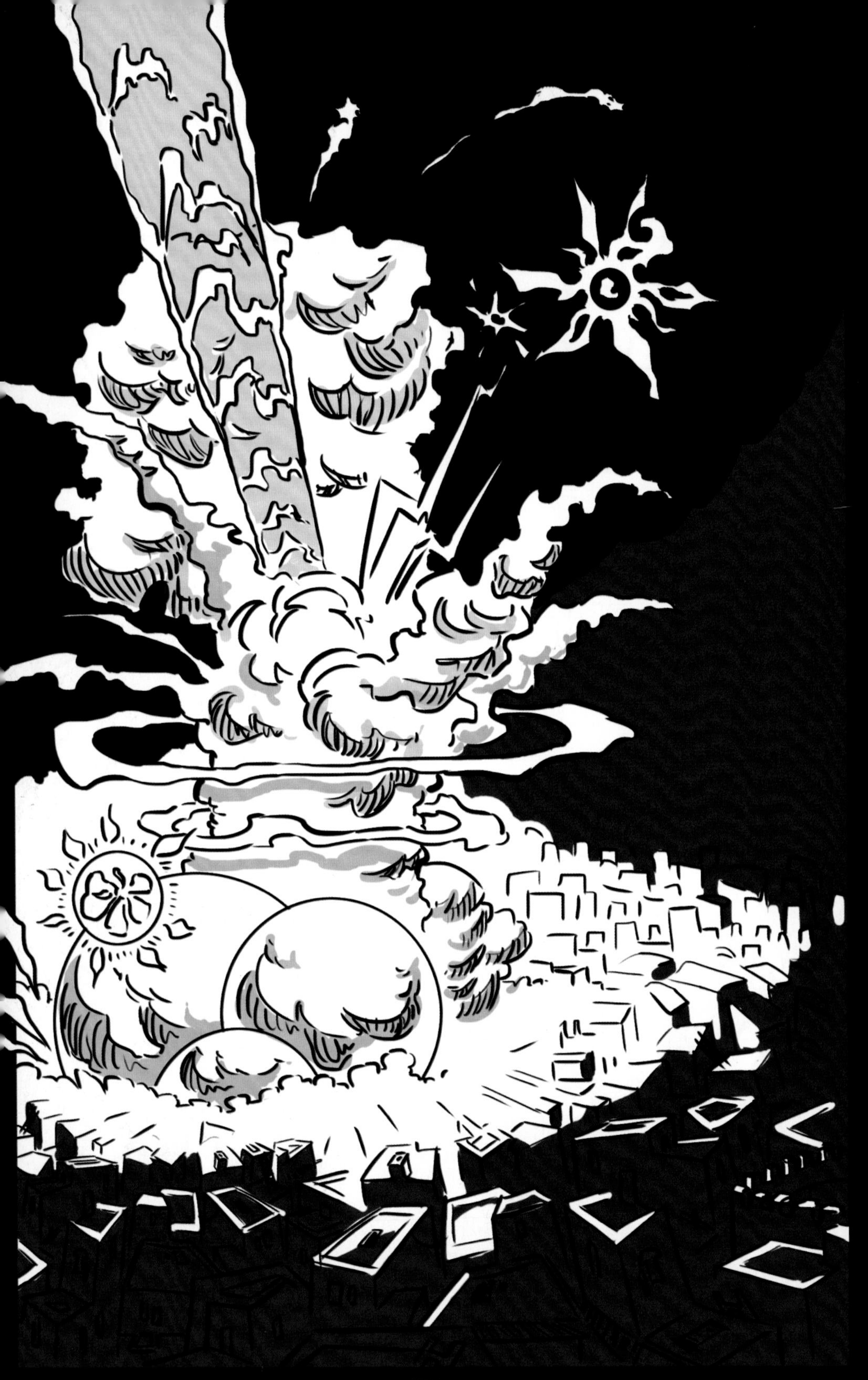

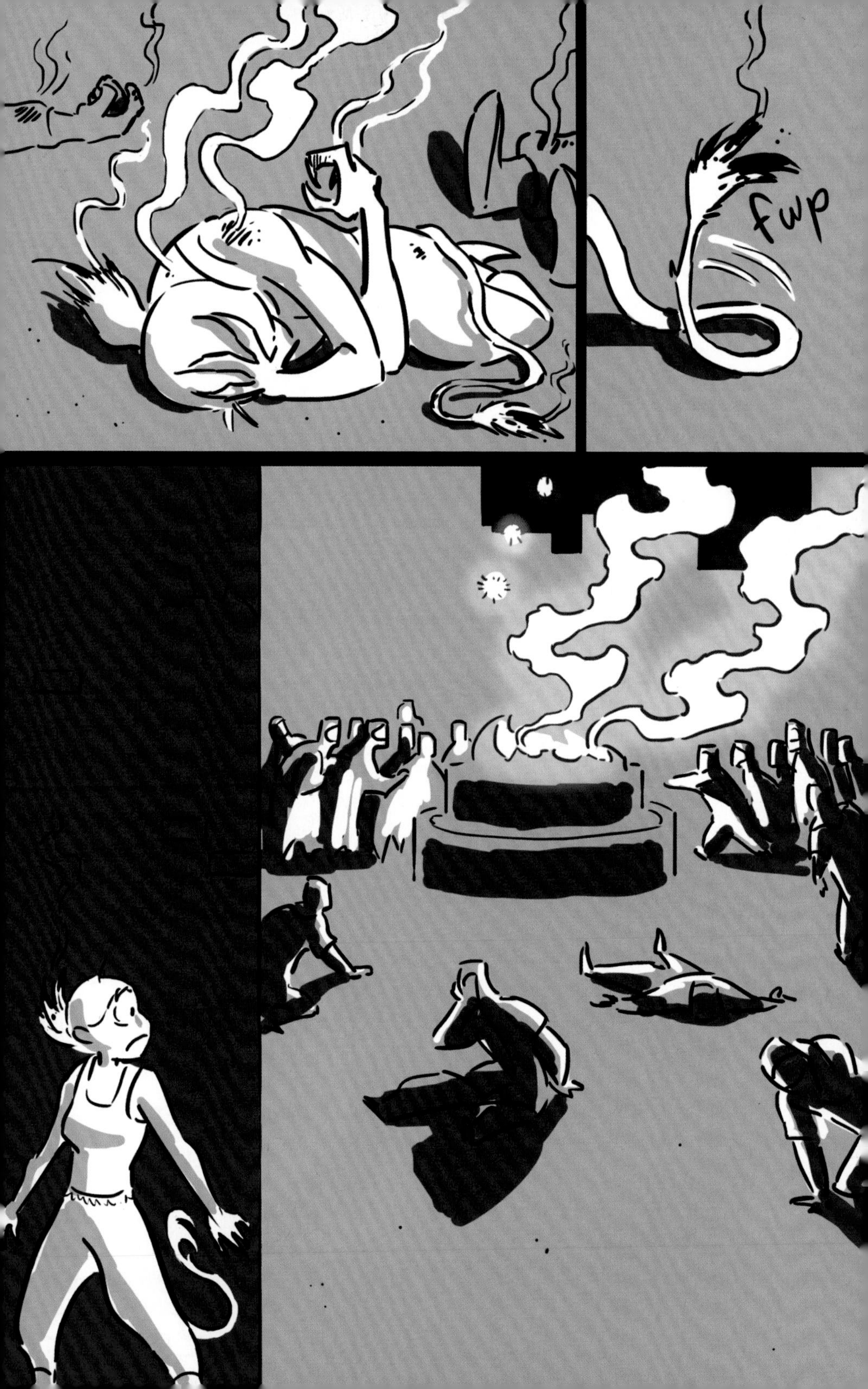
fwp

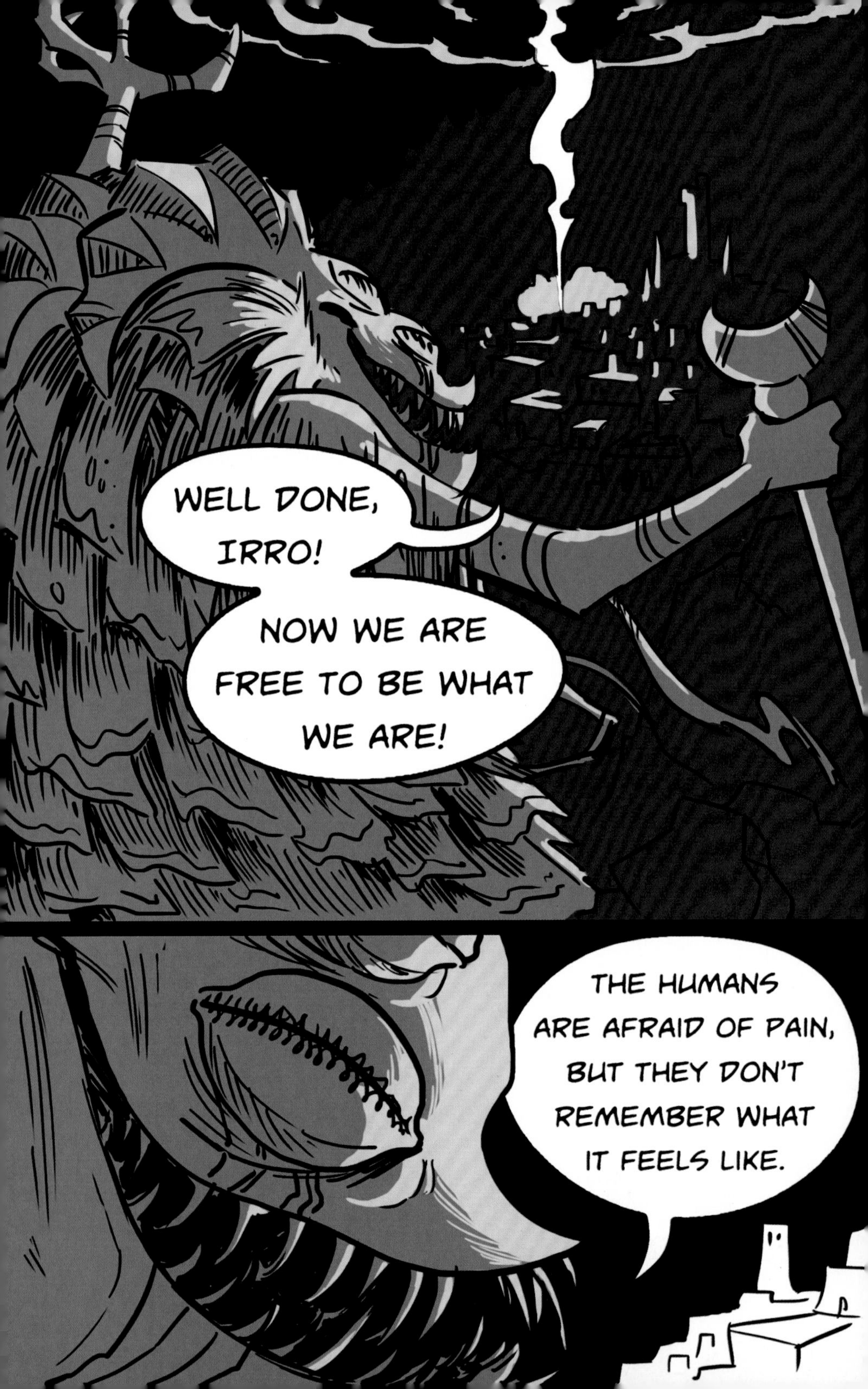
WELL DONE, IRRO!
NOW WE ARE FREE TO BE WHAT WE ARE!
THE HUMANS ARE AFRAID OF PAIN, BUT THEY DON'T REMEMBER WHAT IT FEELS LIKE.

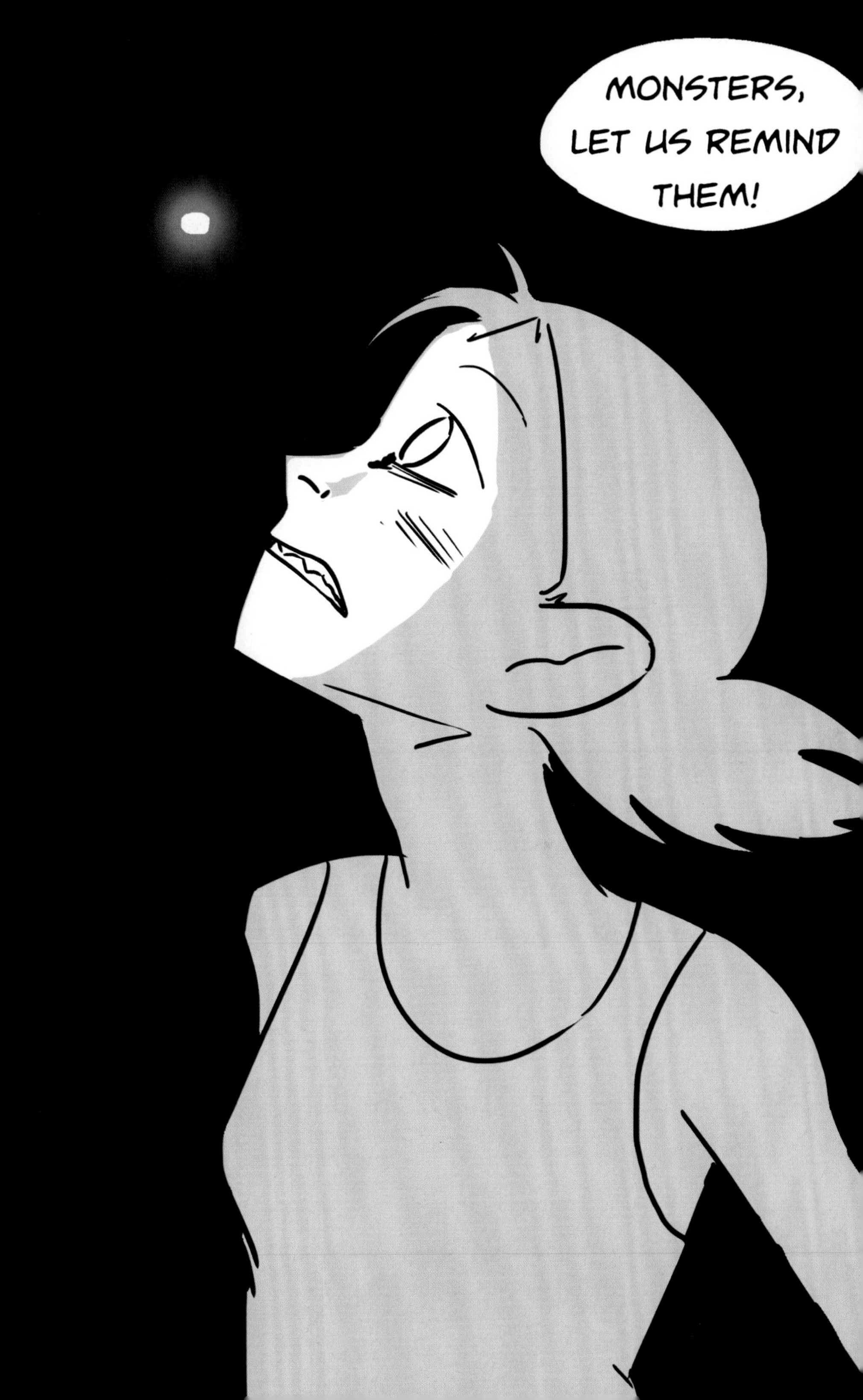
MONSTERS, LET US REMIND THEM!

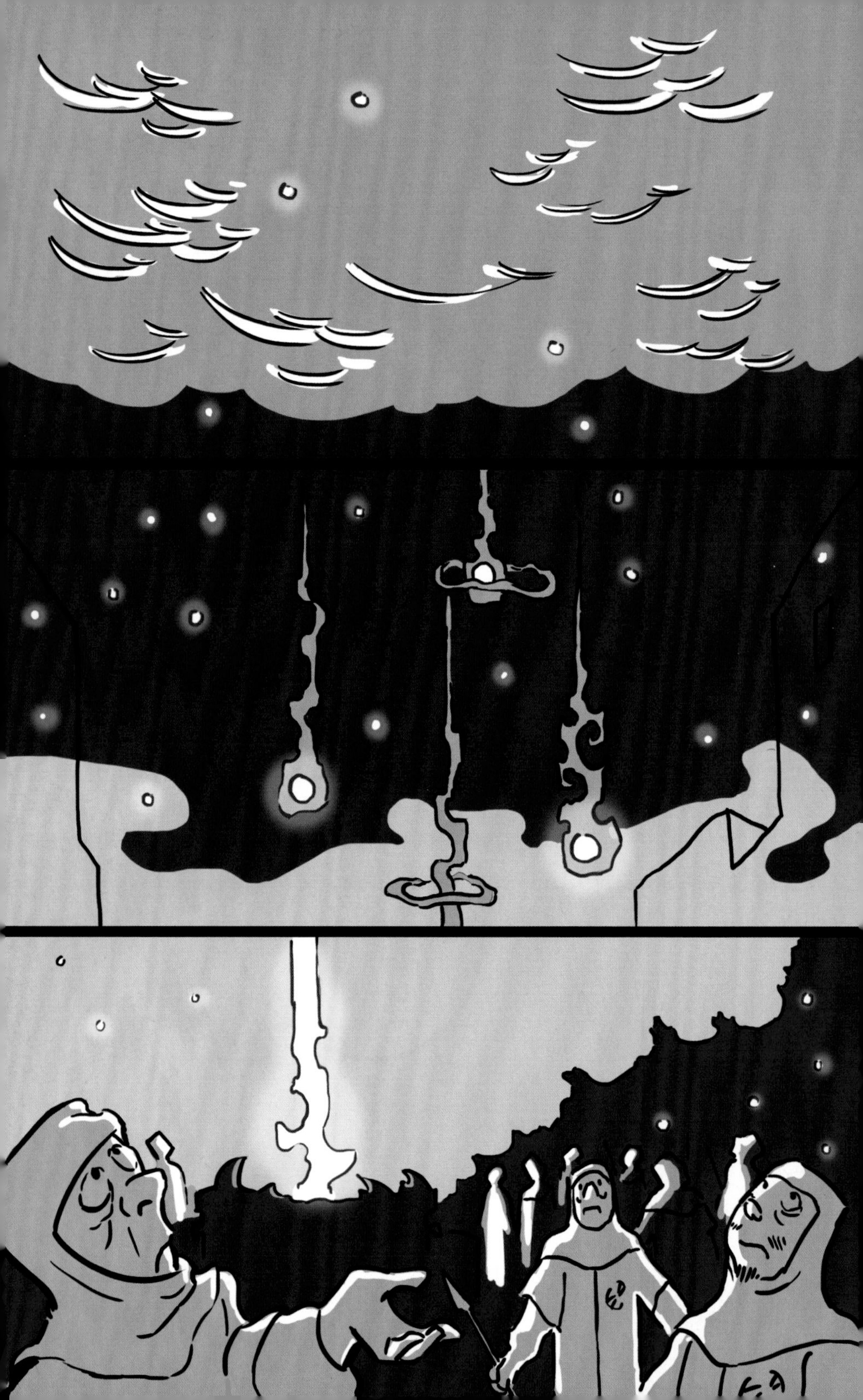

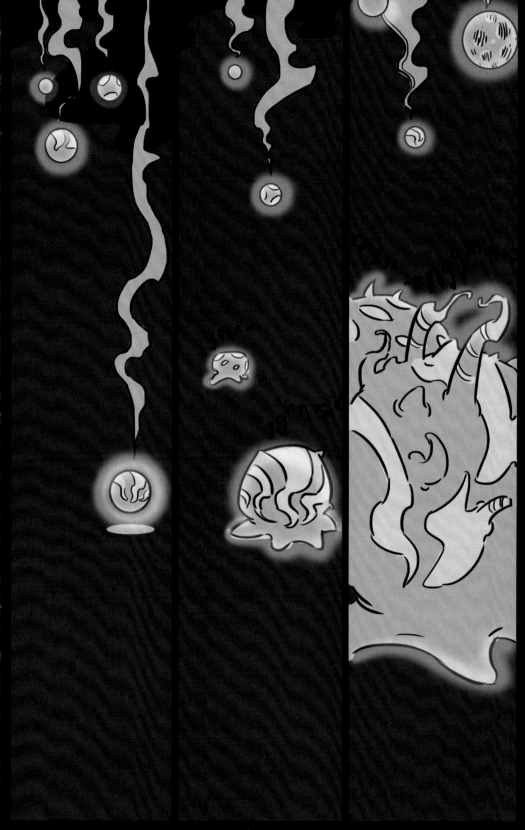

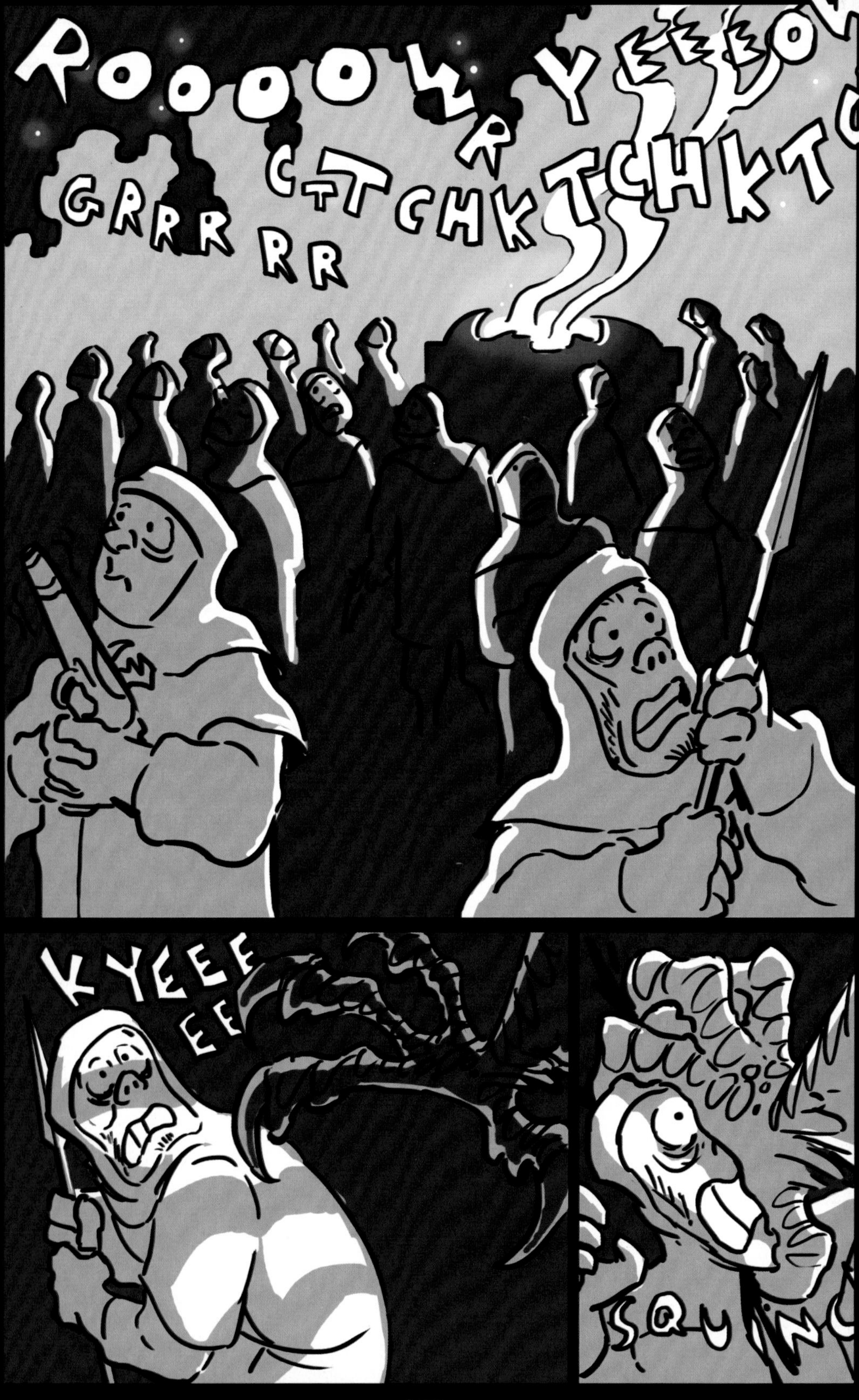
ROOOOWR
YEEEOW
CTTCHKTCHKT
GRRRRR
KYEEEEE
SQUNC

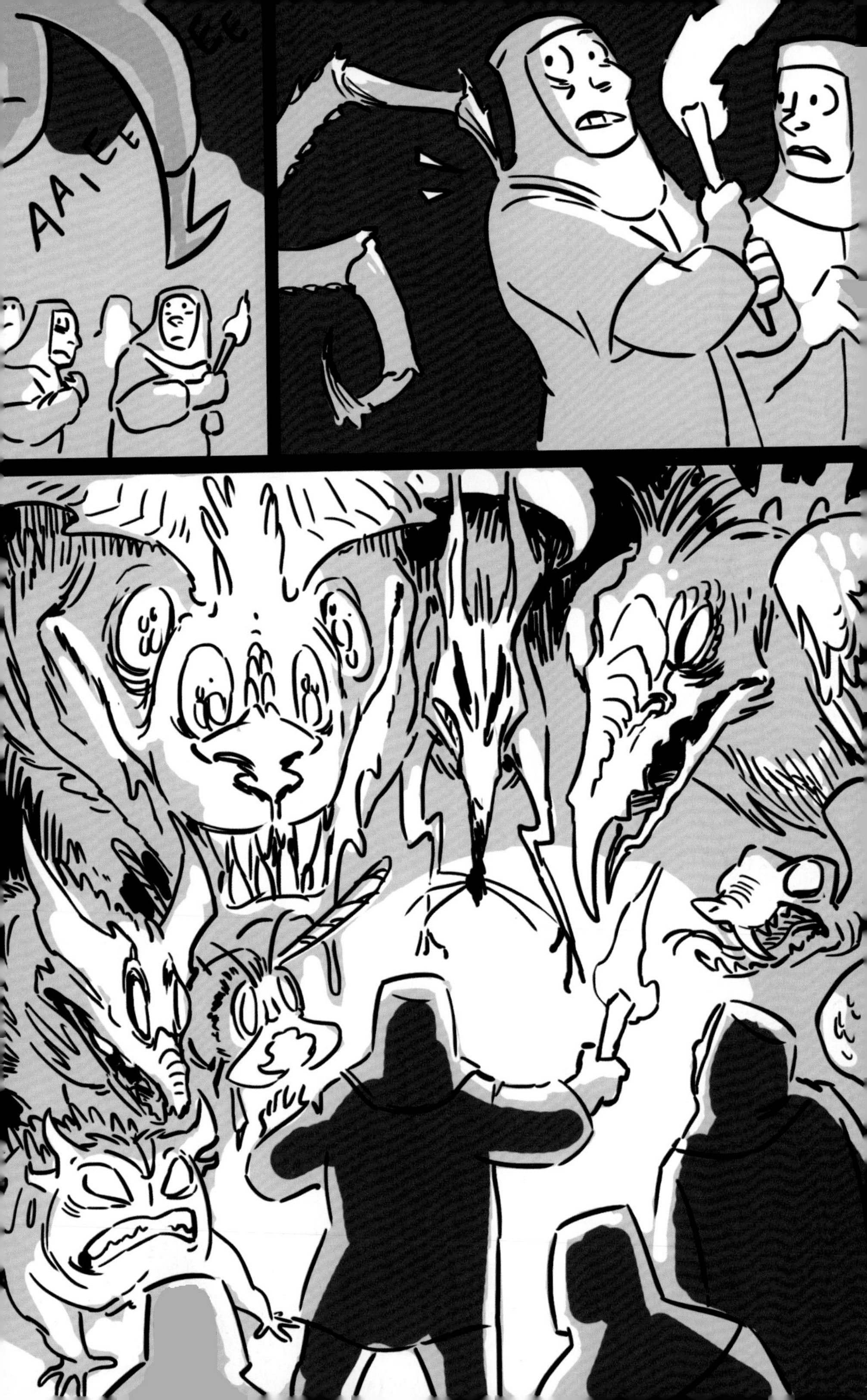
AAIEEEE

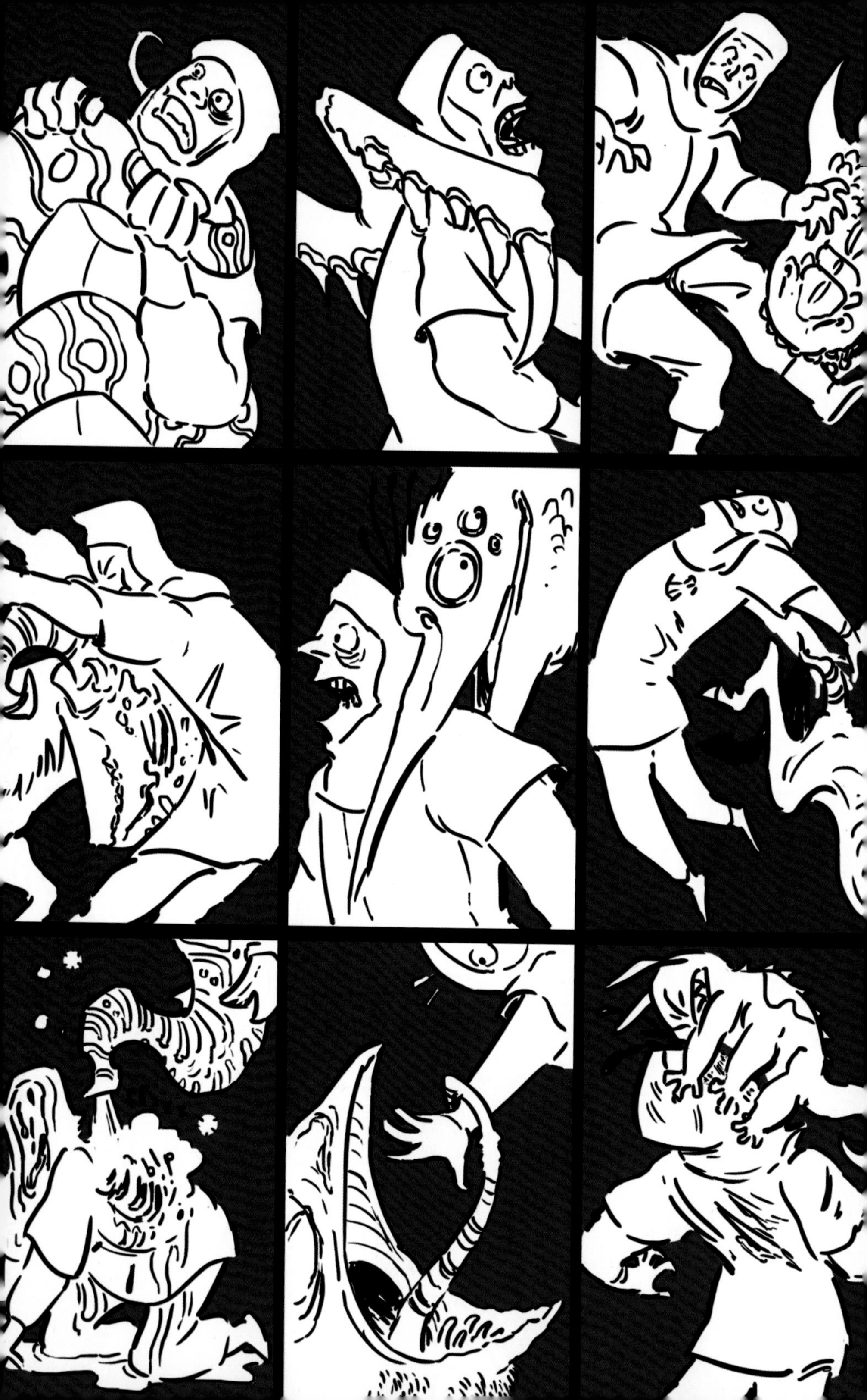
blp

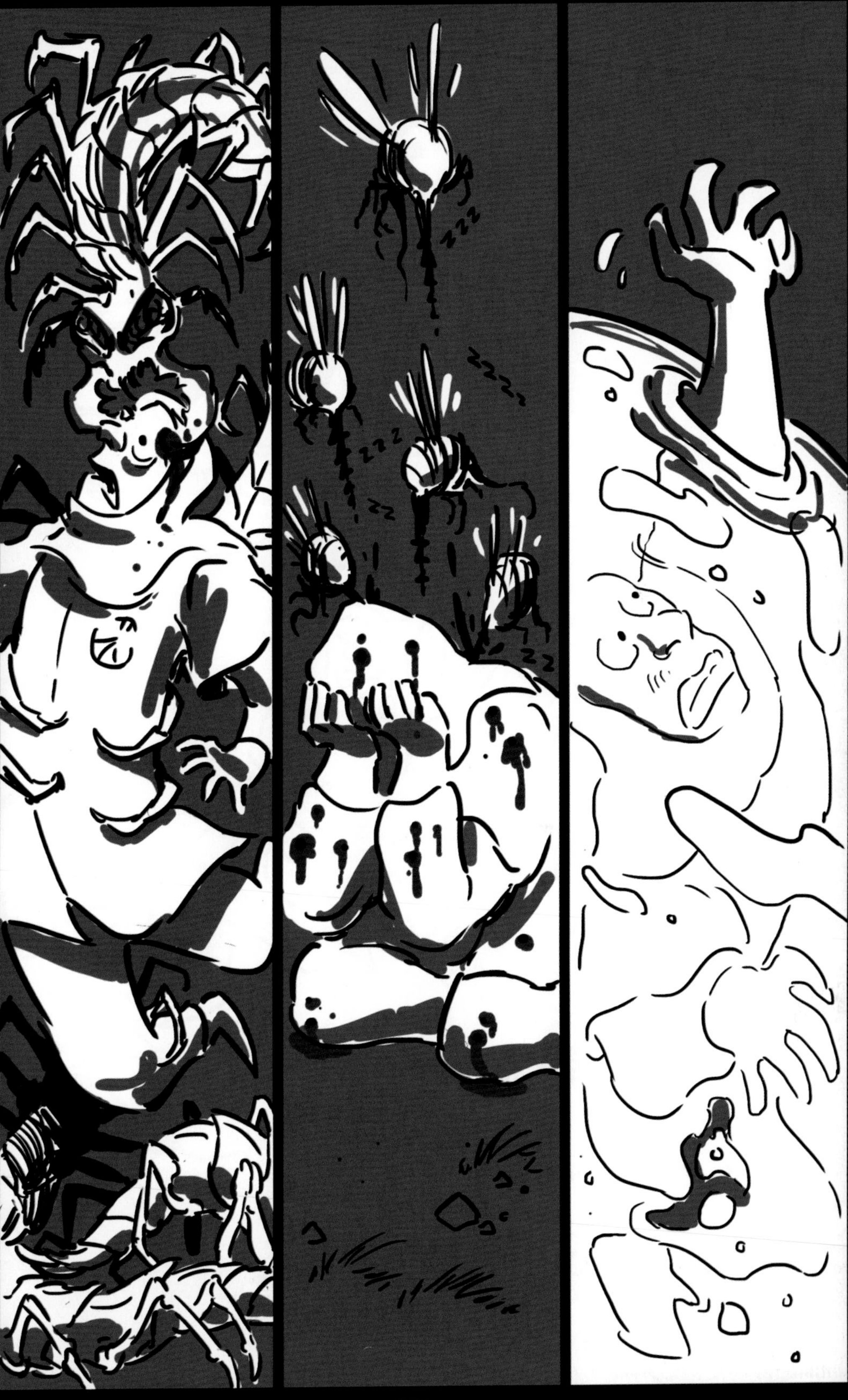

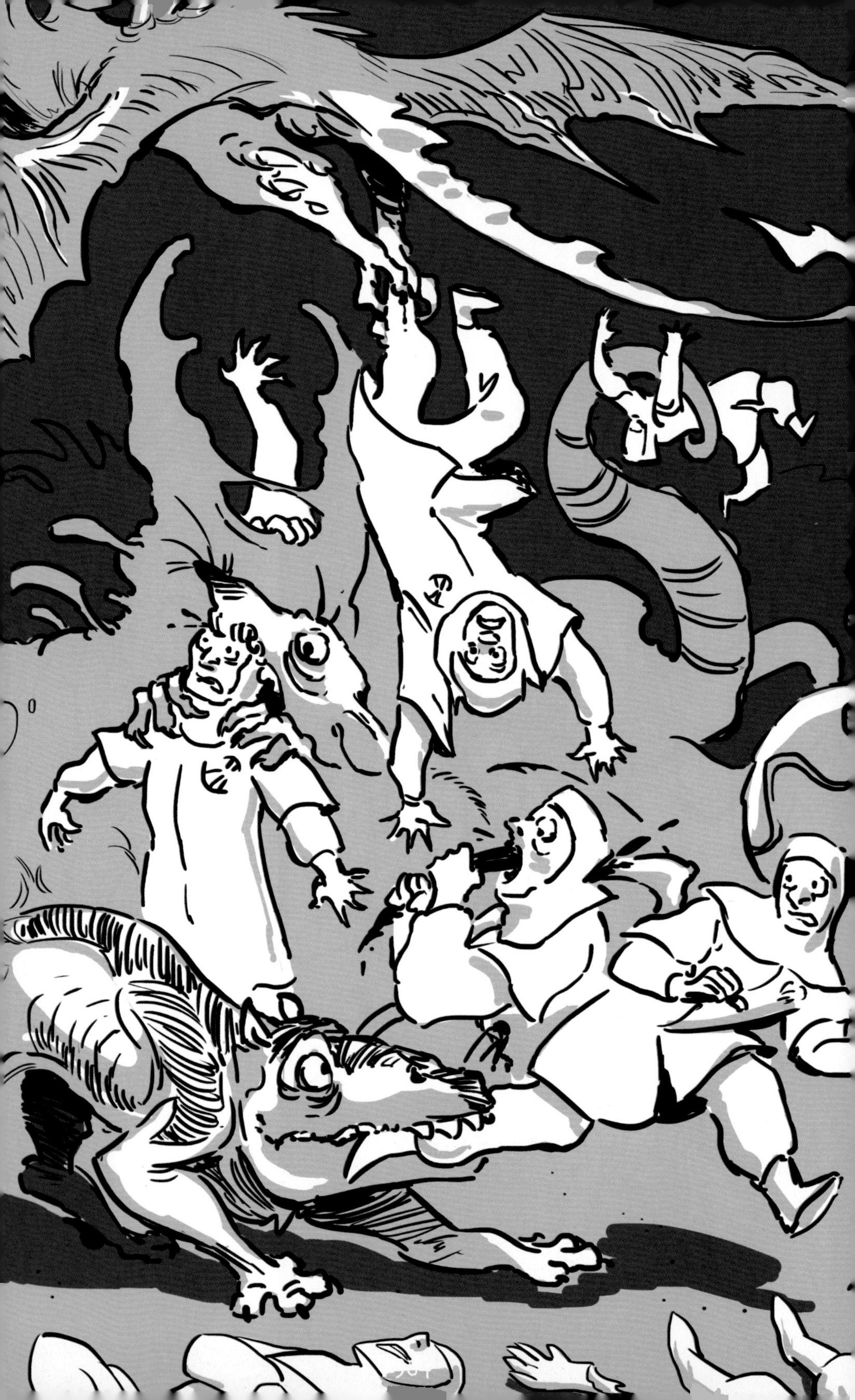

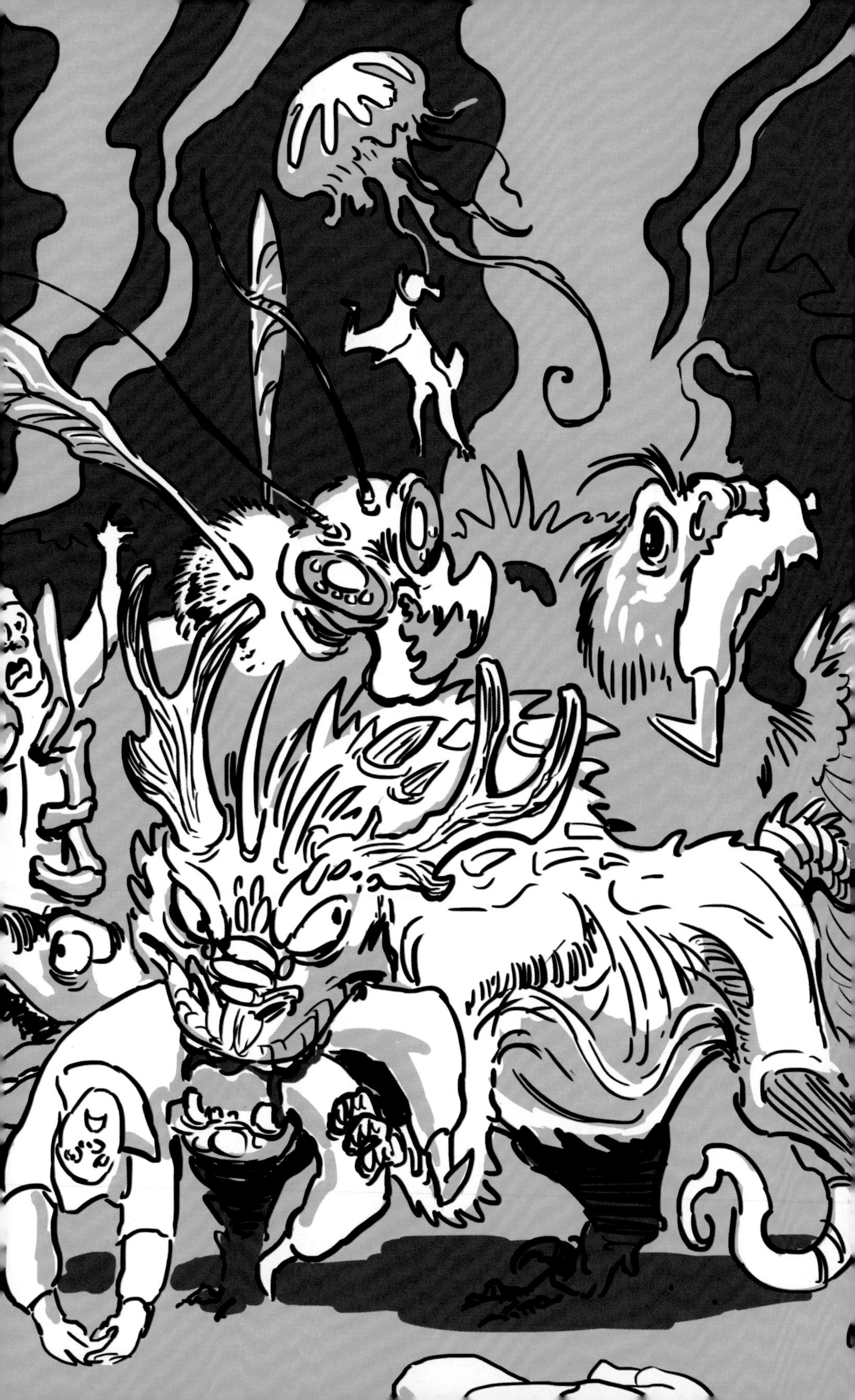

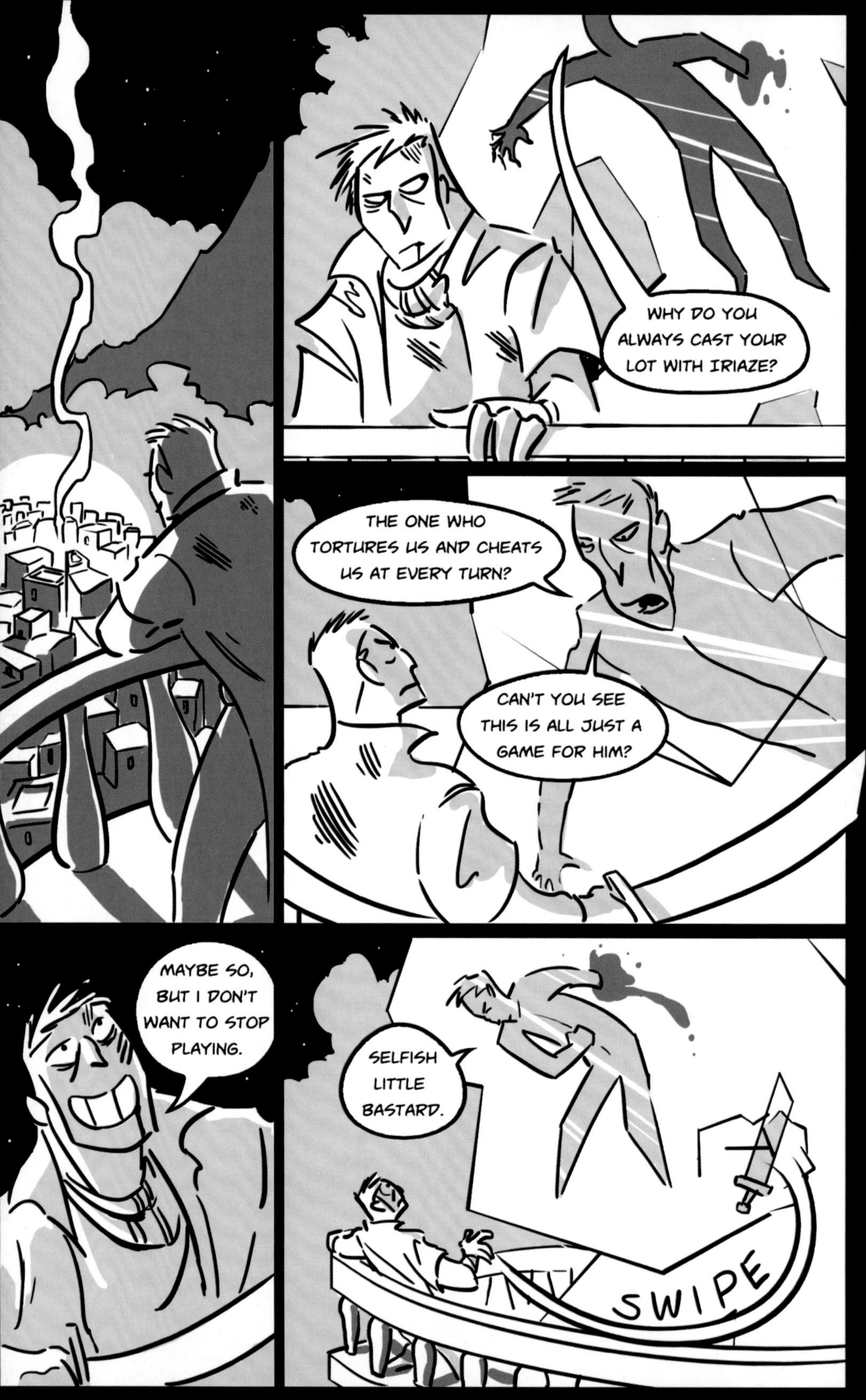
WHY DO YOU ALWAYS CAST YOUR LOT WITH IRIAZE?
THE ONE WHO TORTURES US AND CHEATS US AT EVERY TURN?
CAN'T YOU SEE THIS IS ALL JUST A GAME FOR HIM?
MAYBE SO, BUT I DON'T WANT TO STOP PLAYING.
SELFISH LITTLE BASTARD.
SWIPE

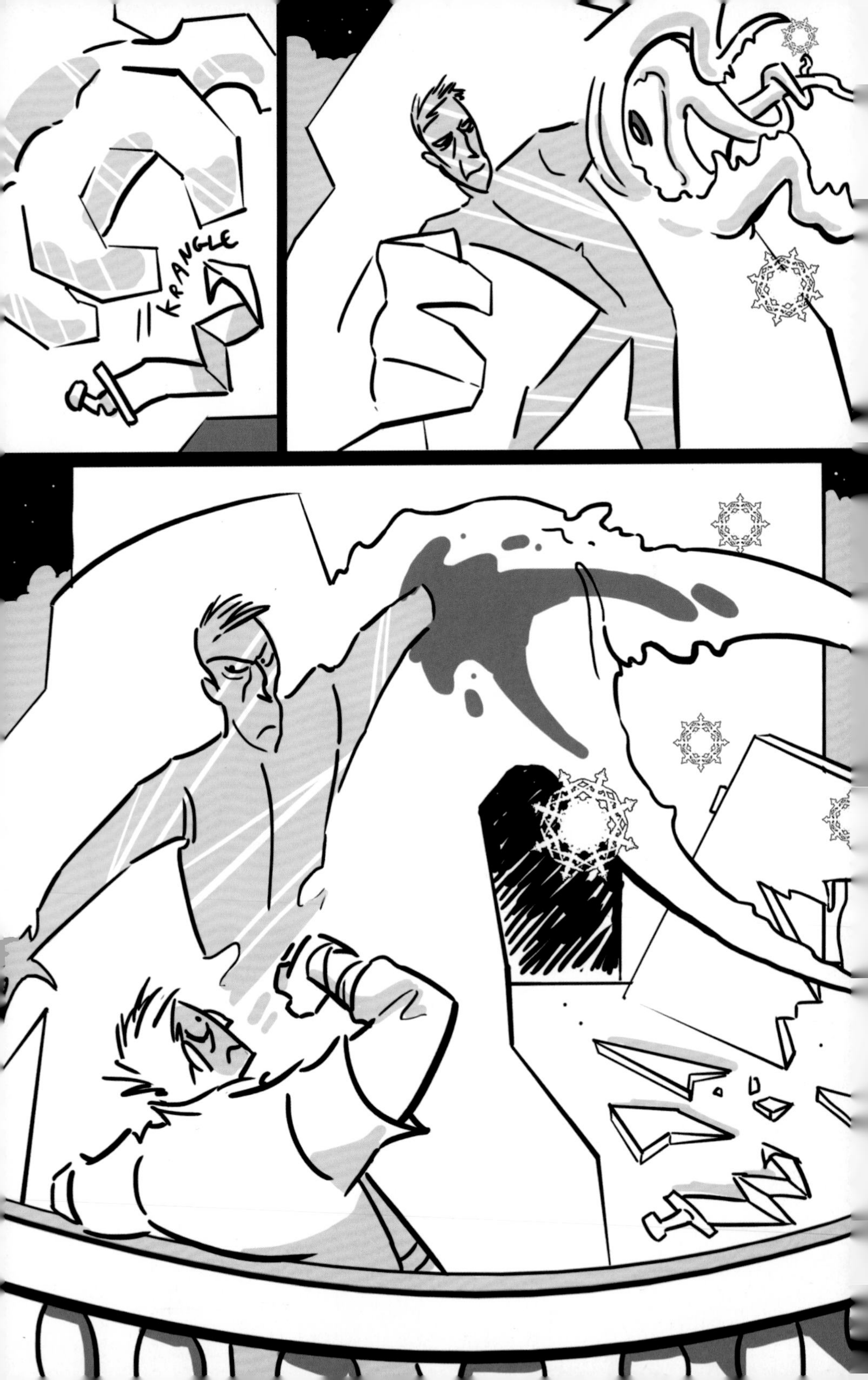
KRANGLE

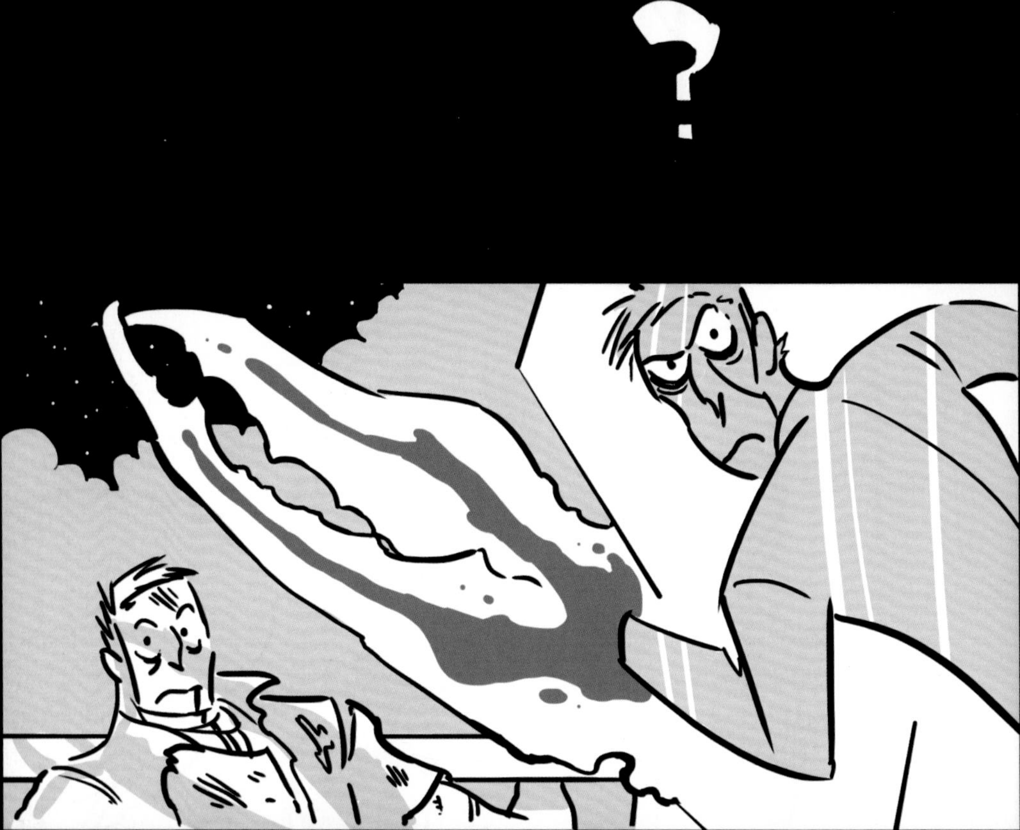
?

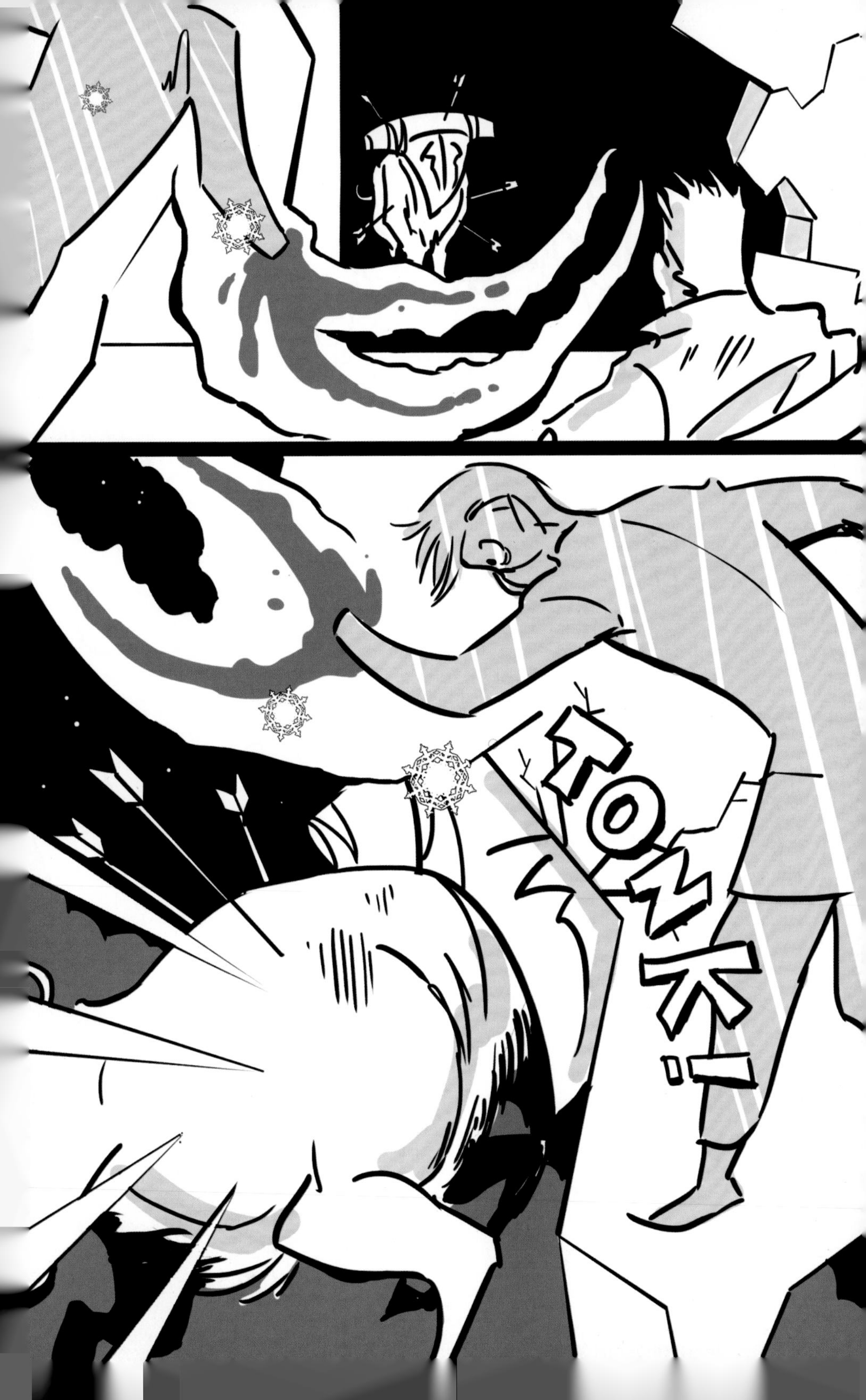
TONK!

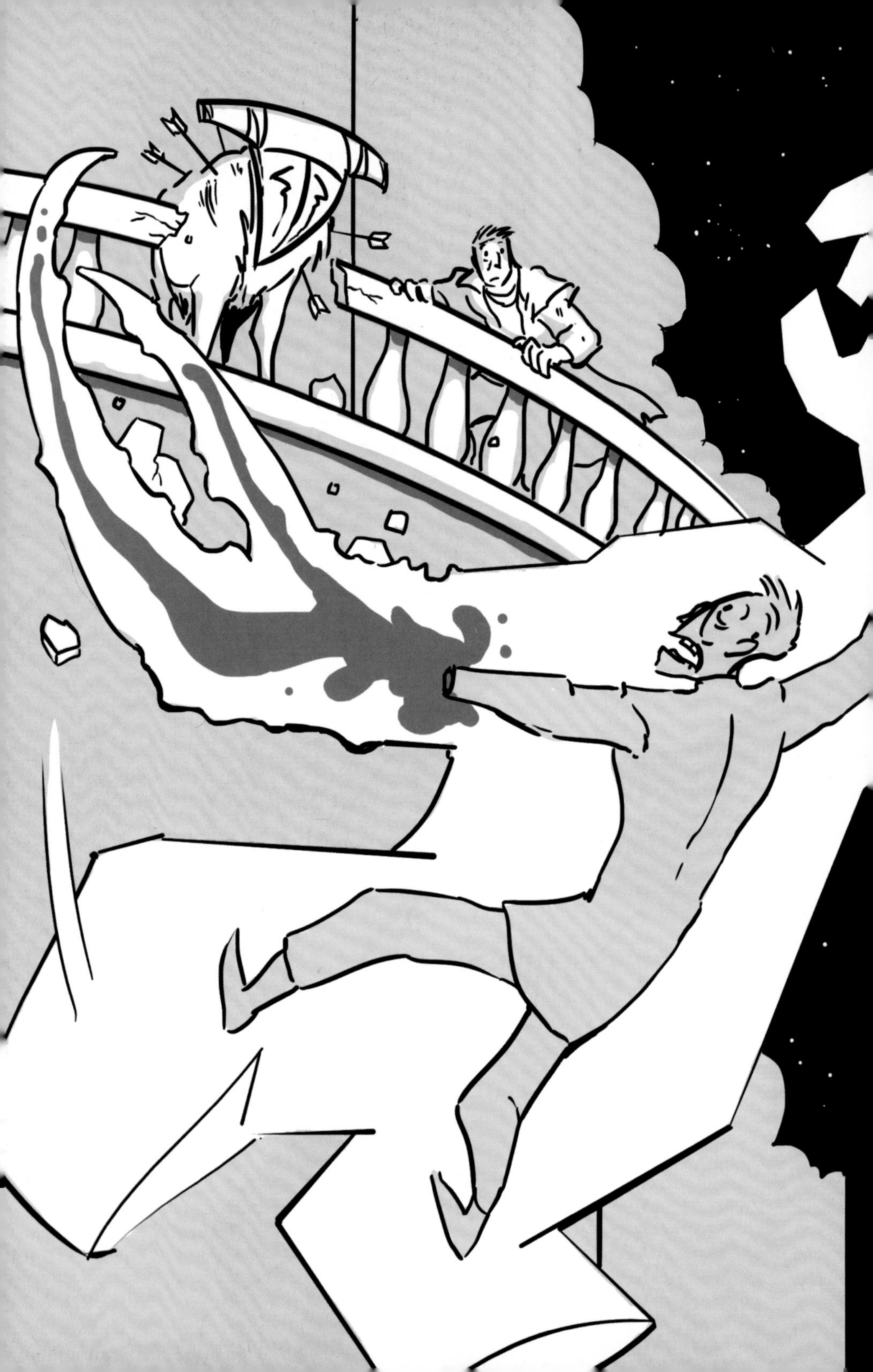

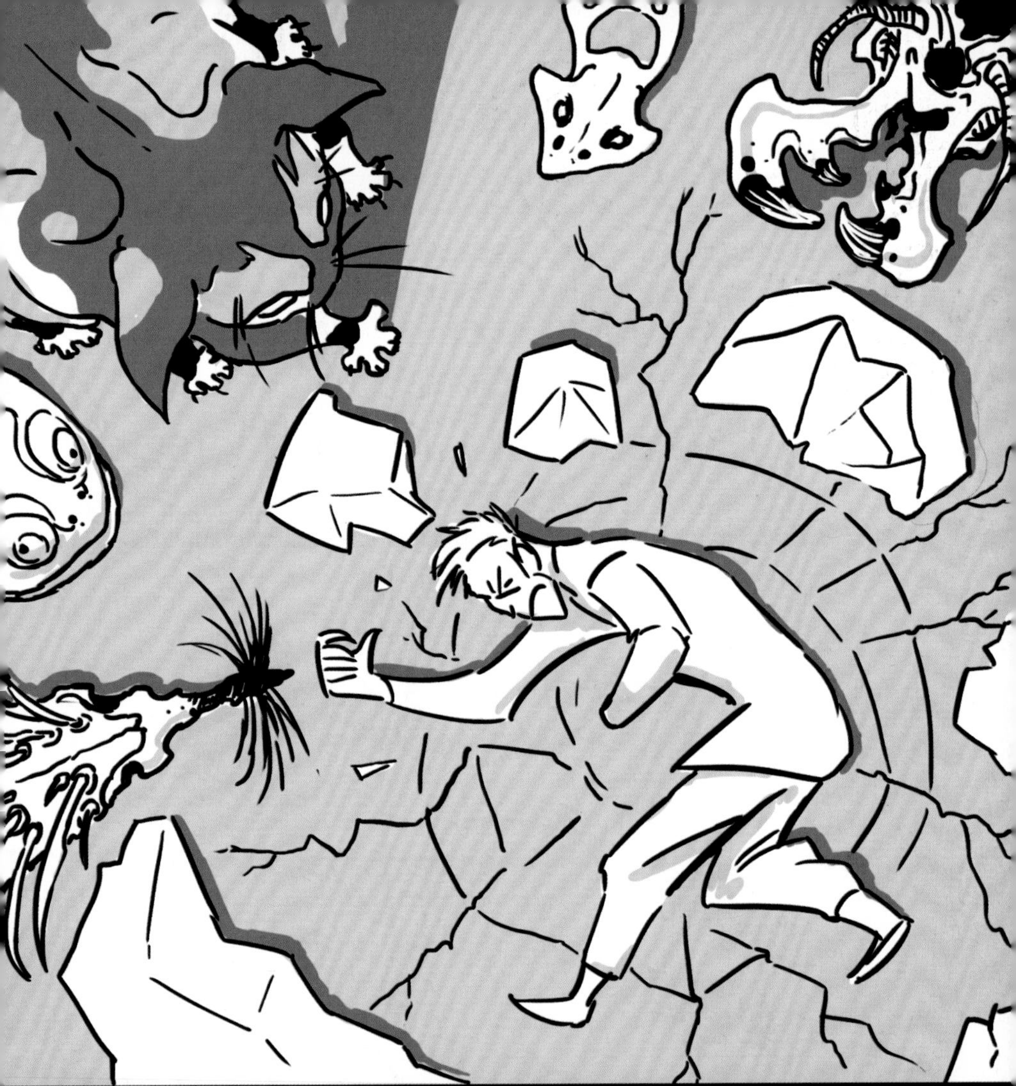

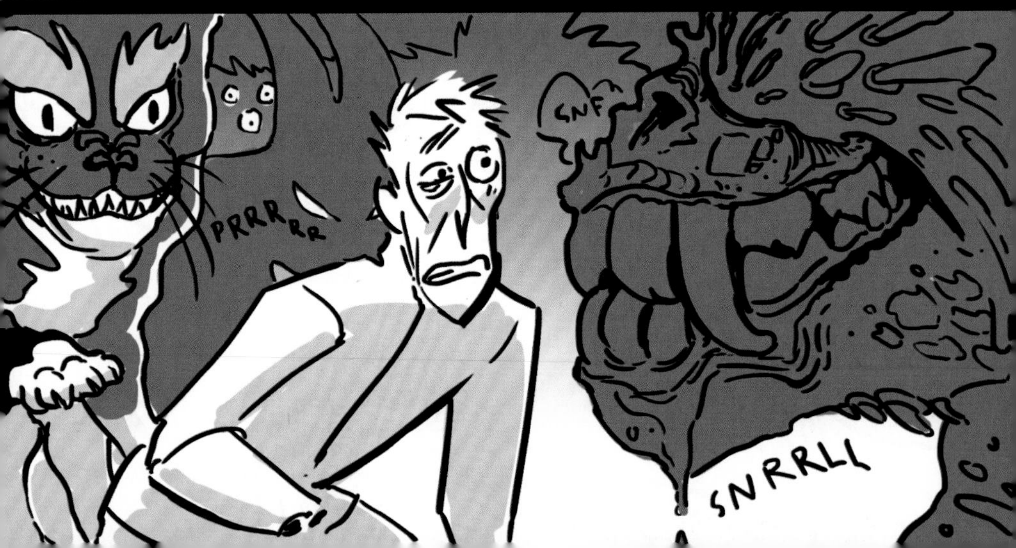
PRRRRR
SNF
SNRRLL

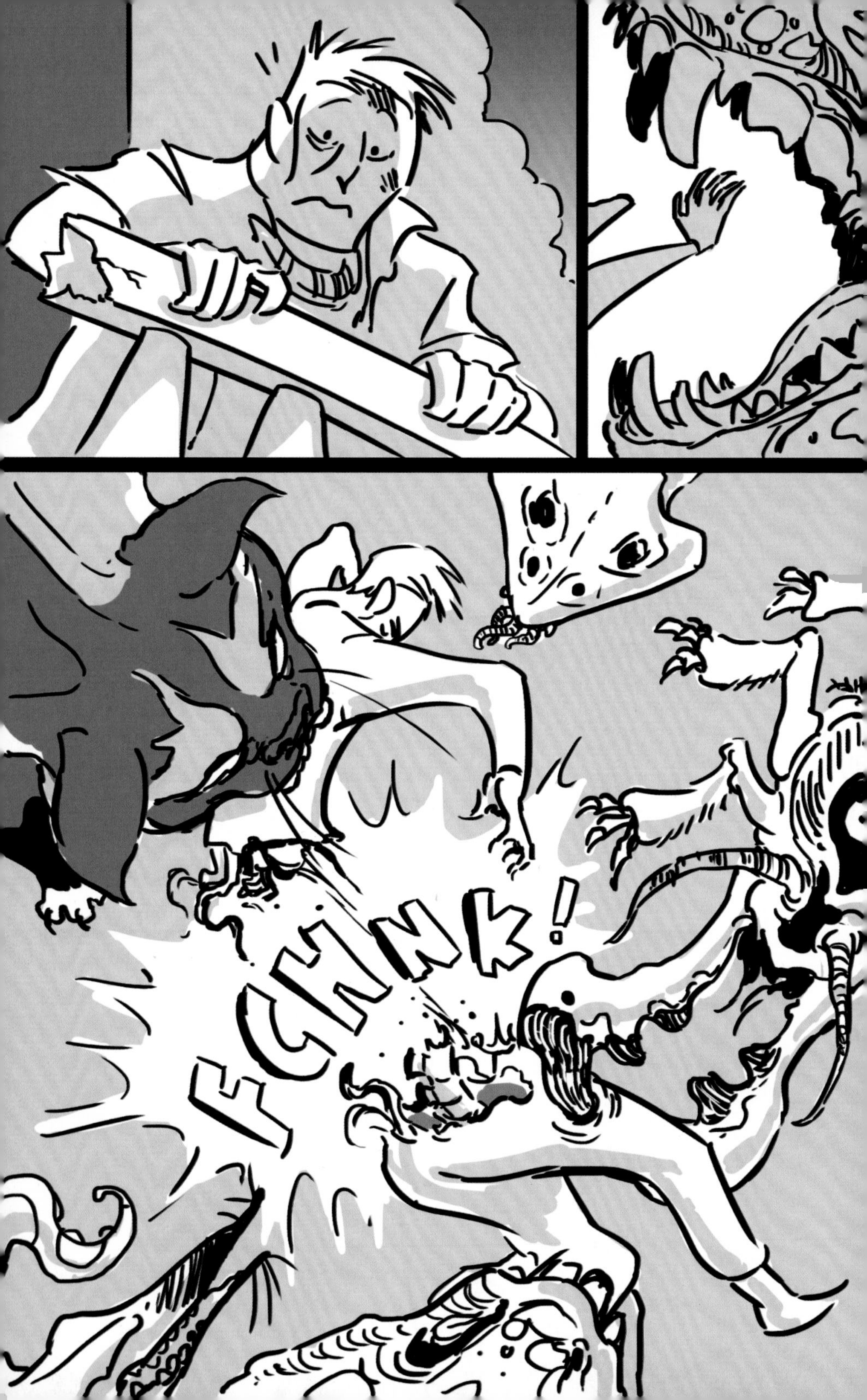
FCHNK!

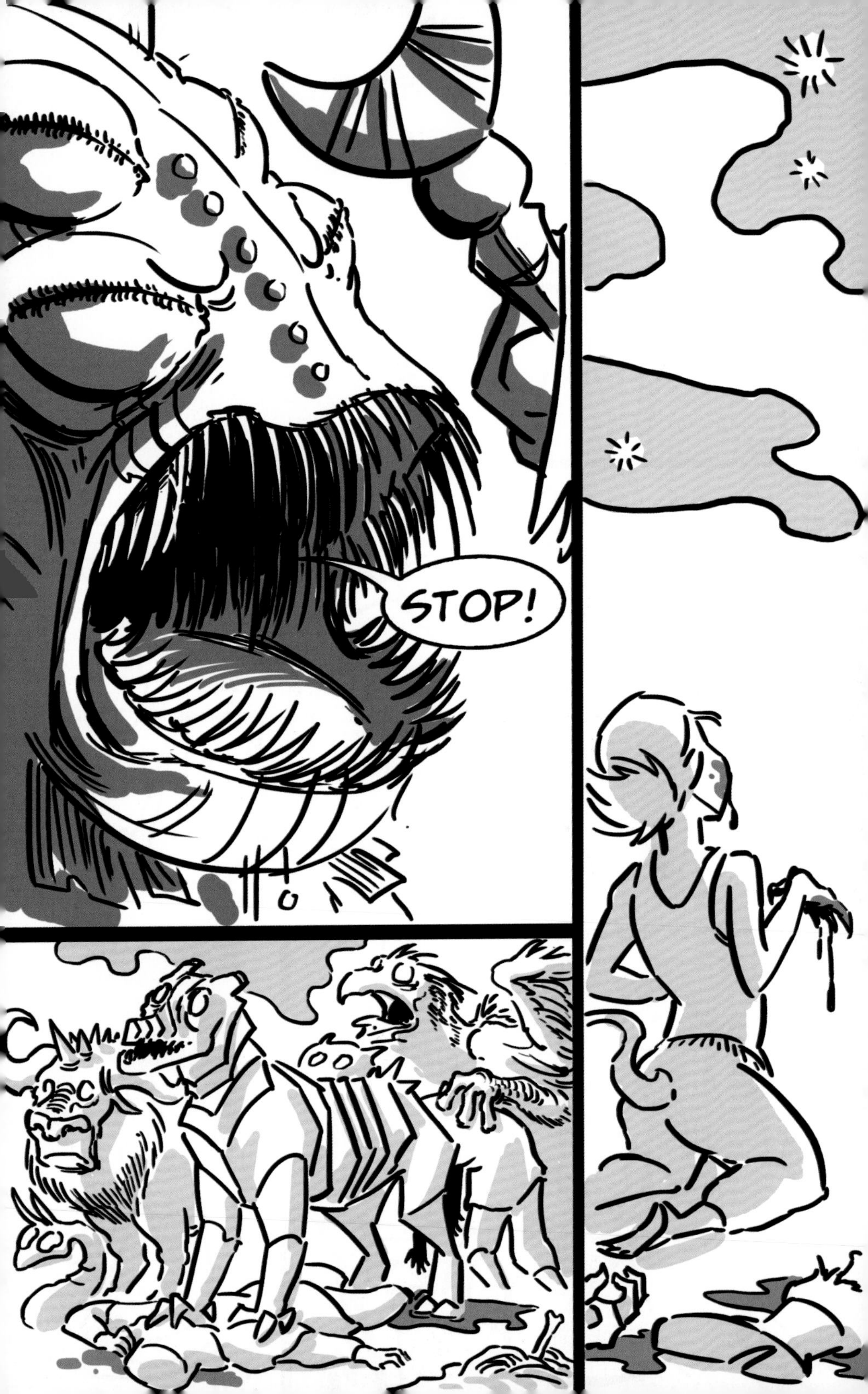
STOP!

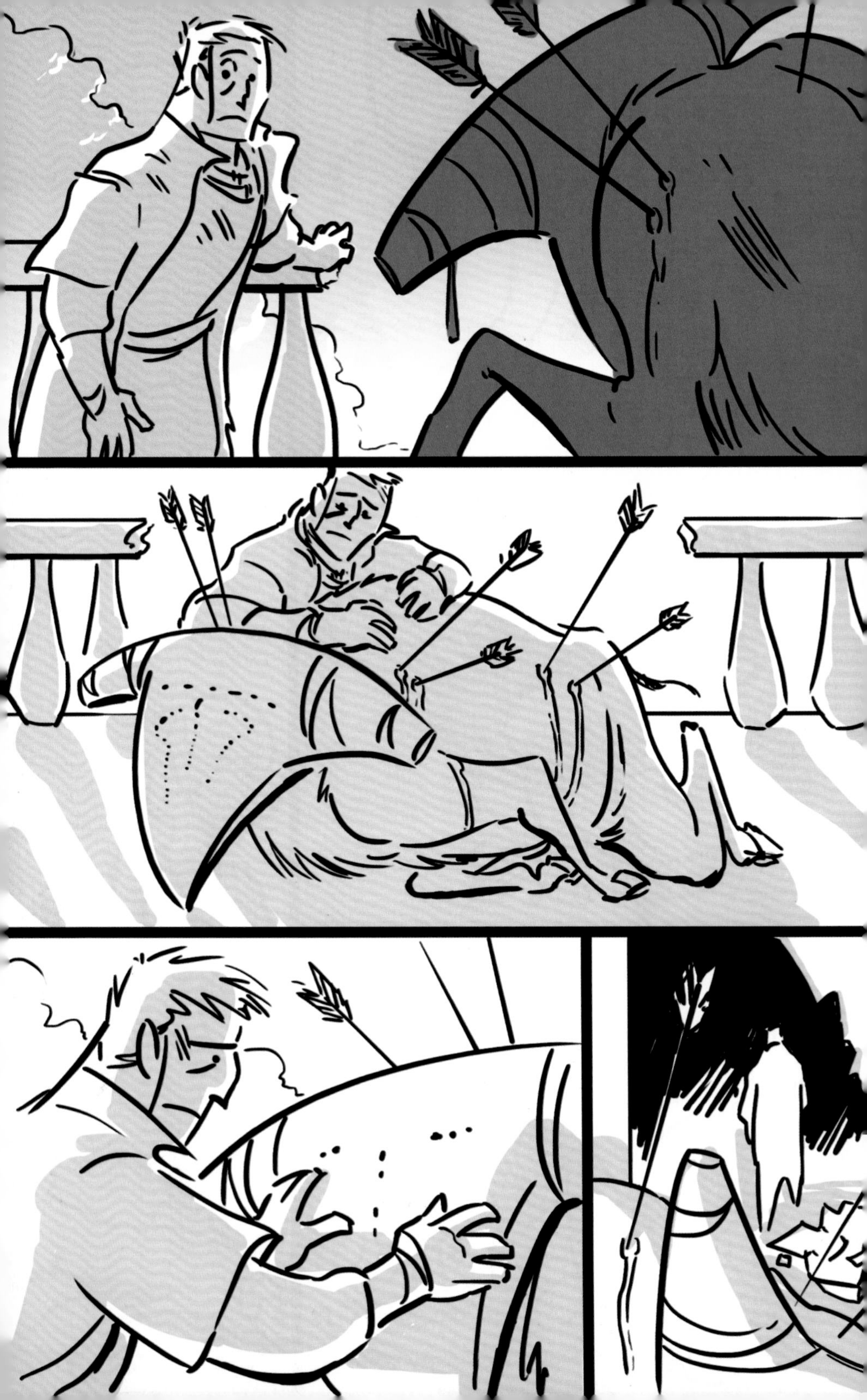

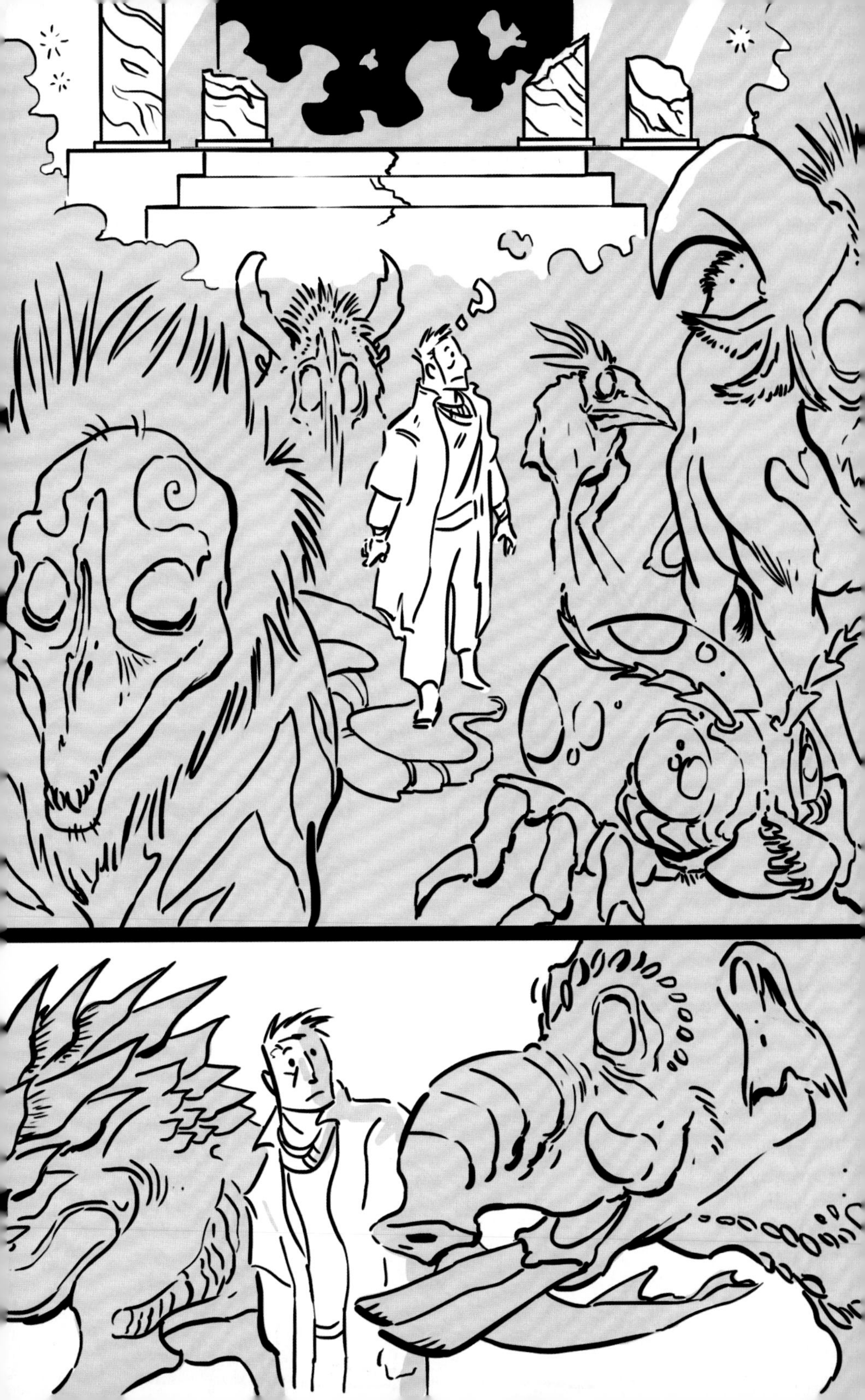

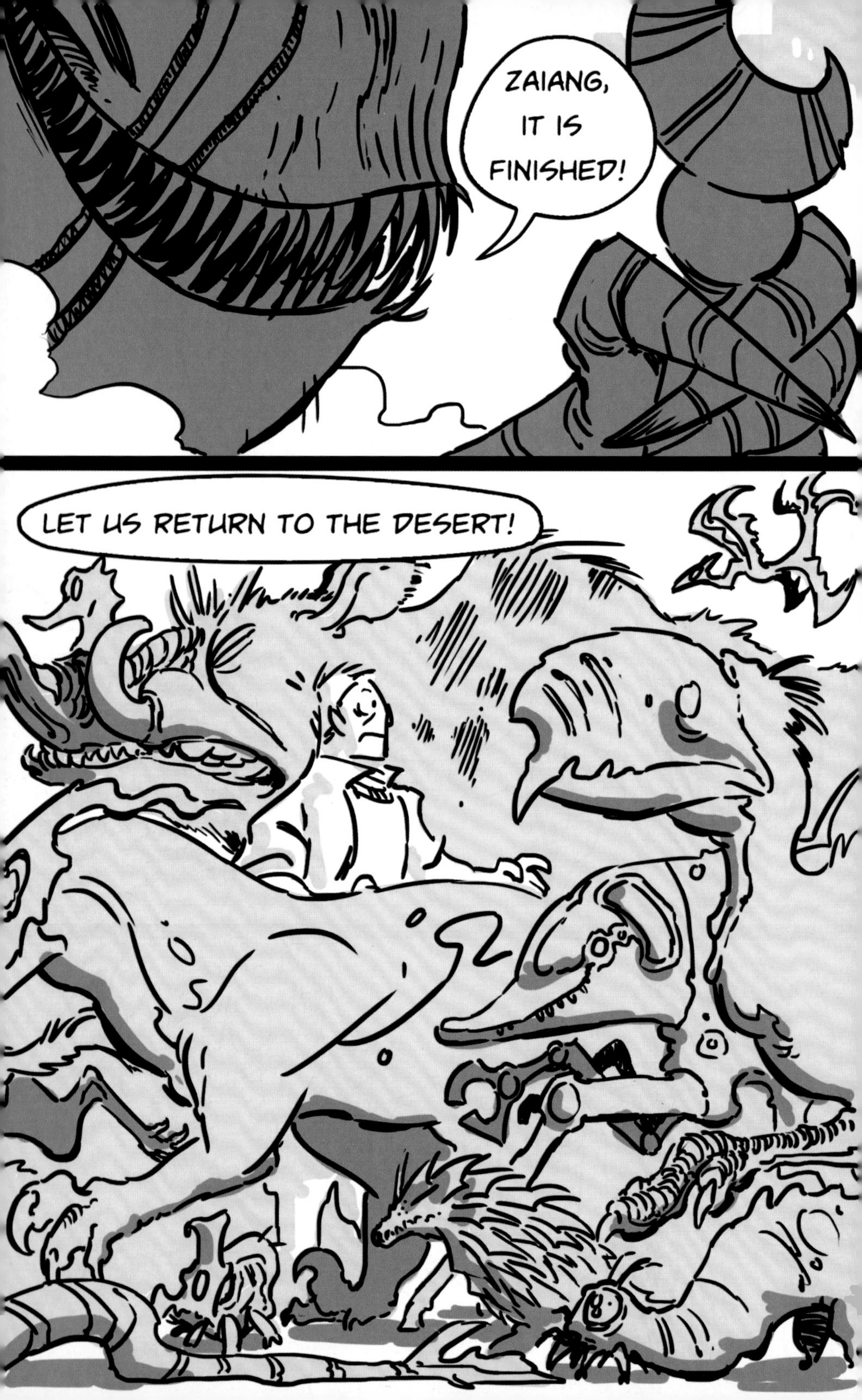
ZAIANG, IT IS FINISHED!
LET US RETURN TO THE DESERT!

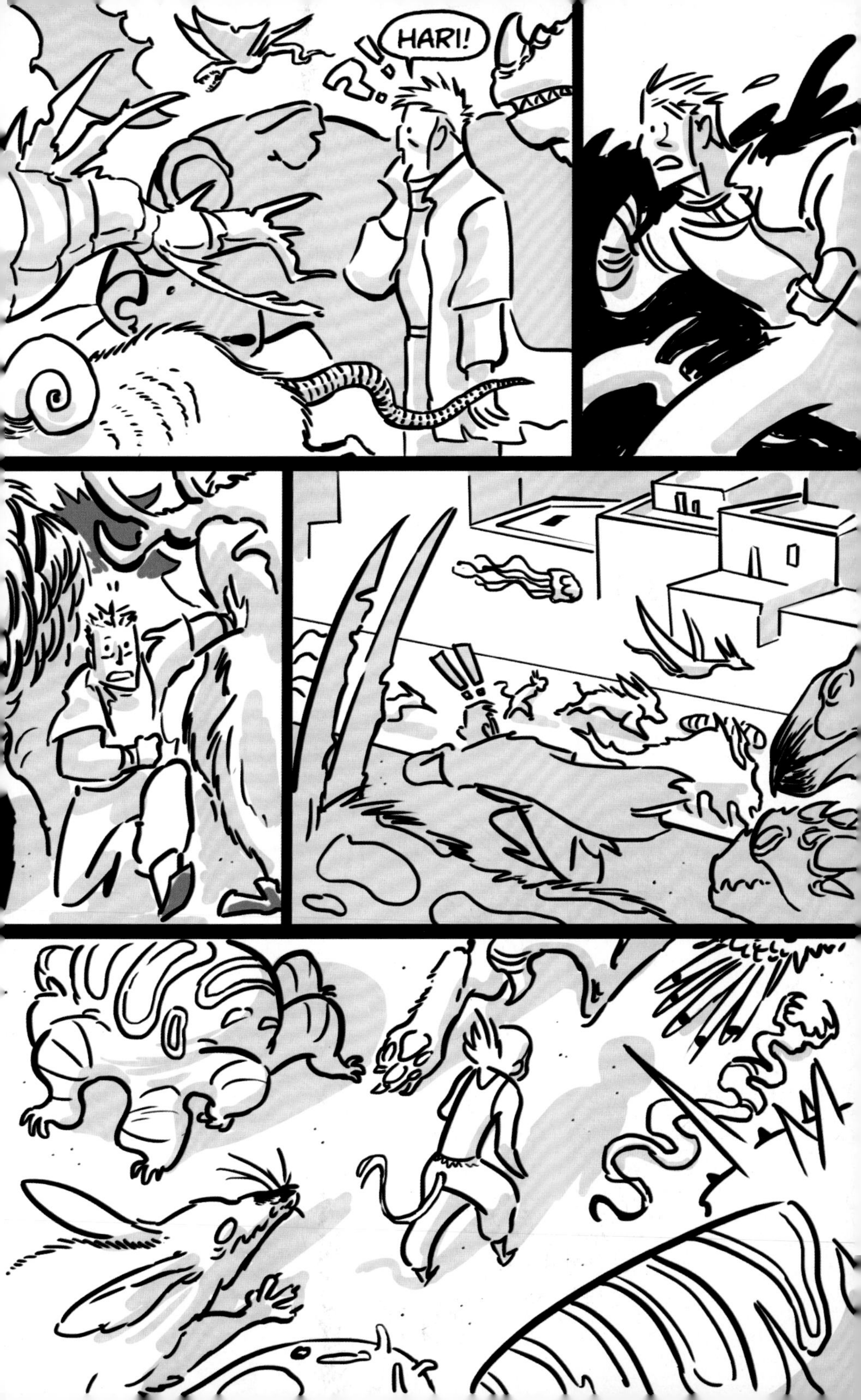
HARI!

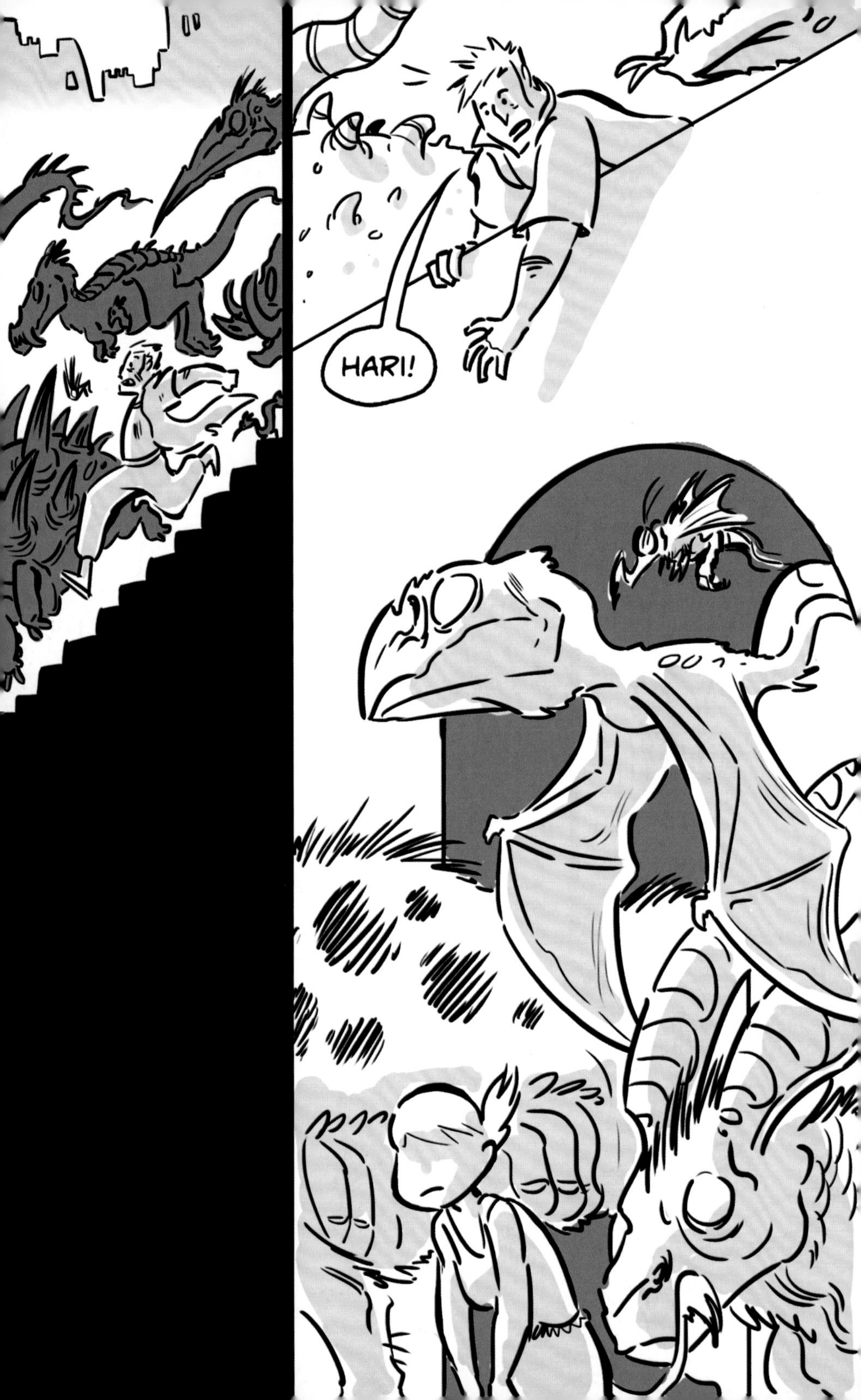
HARI!

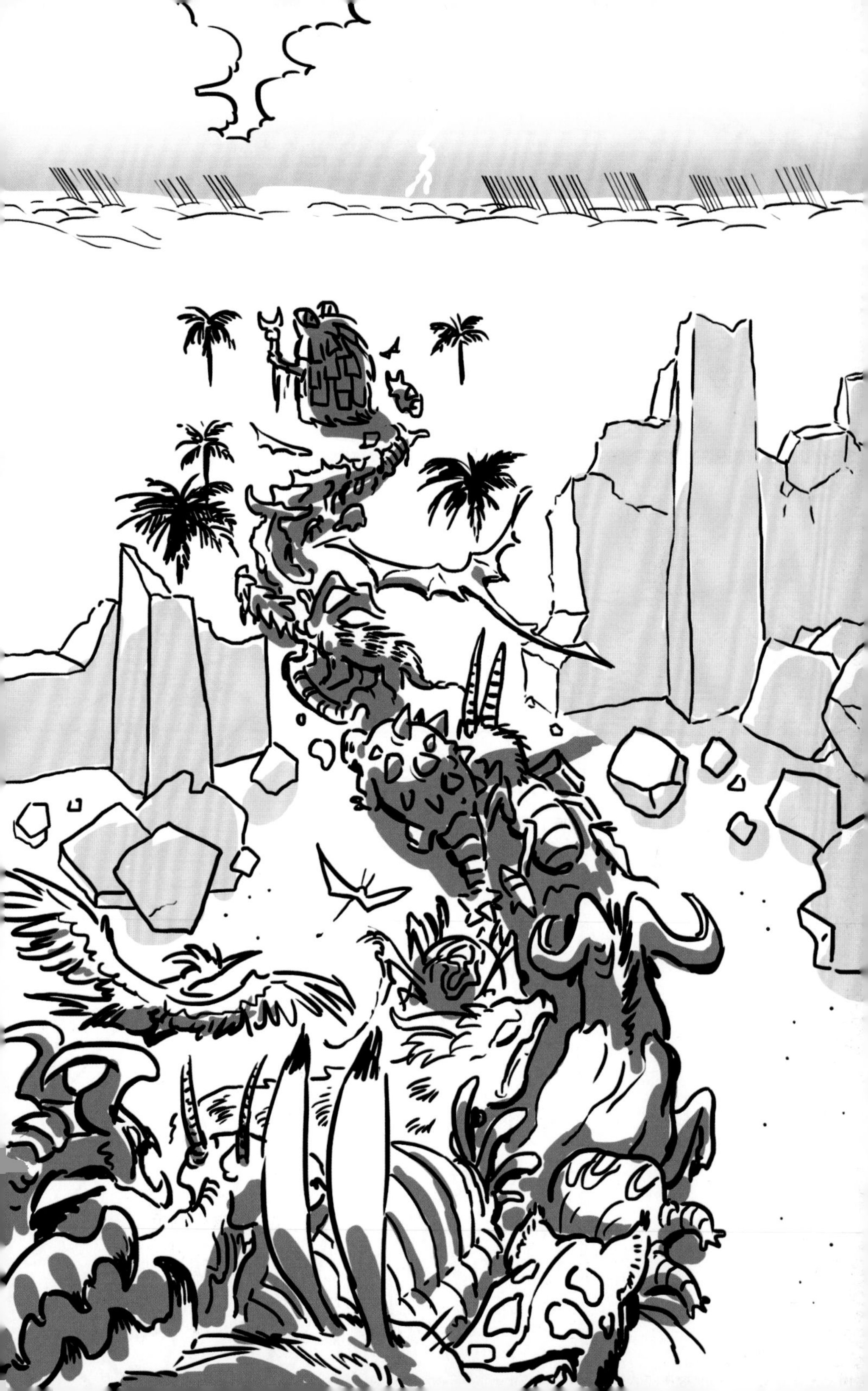

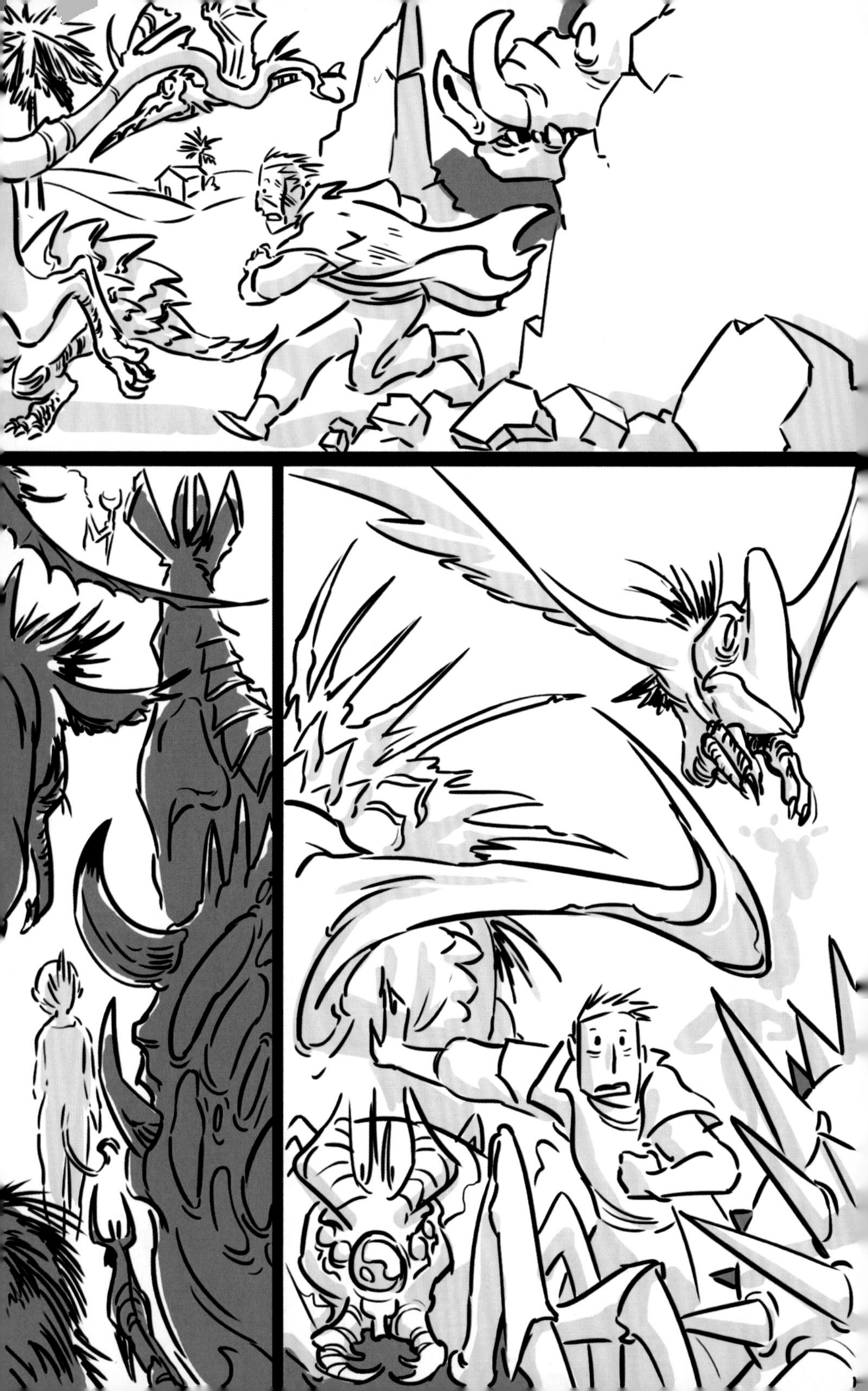

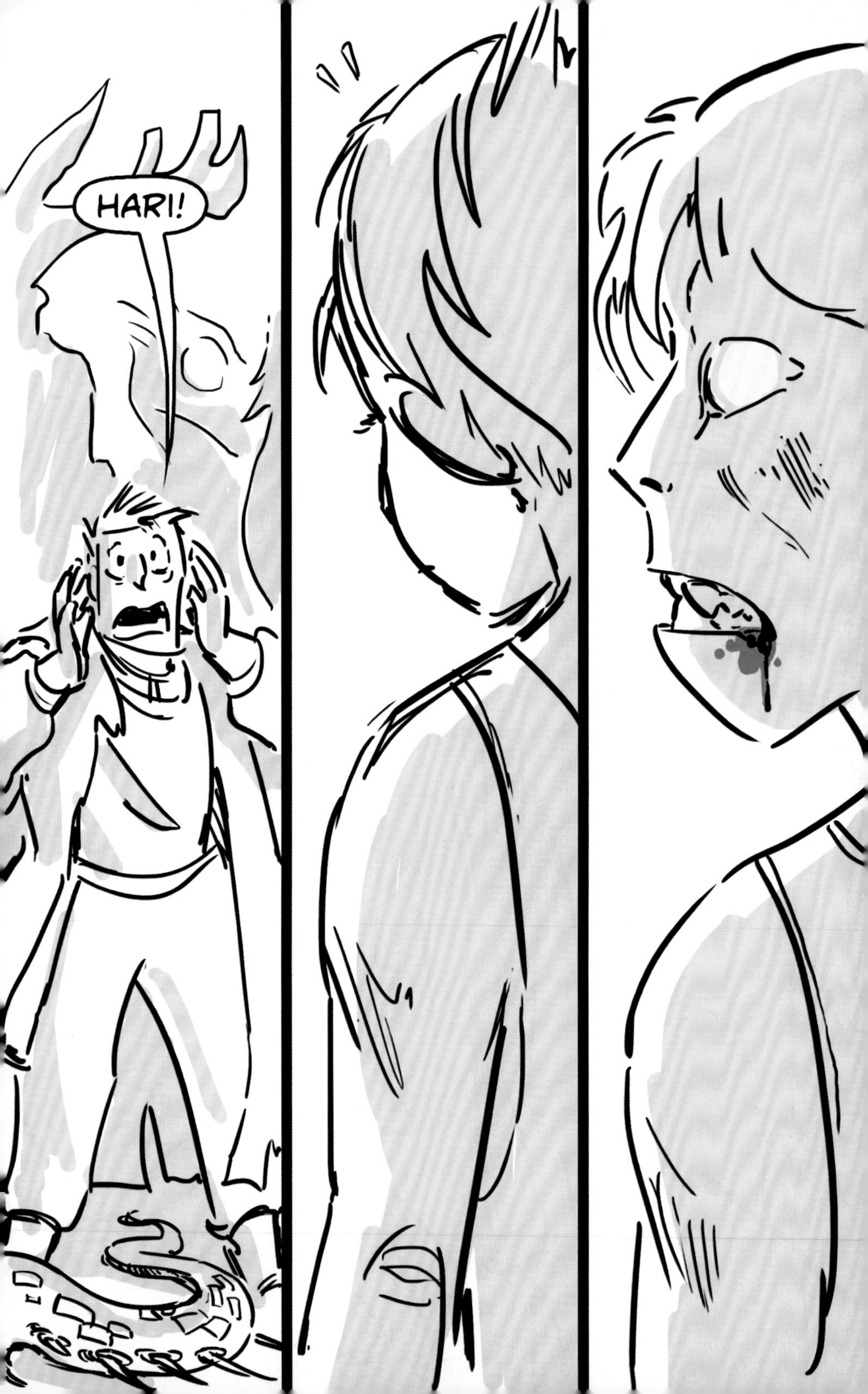
HARI!

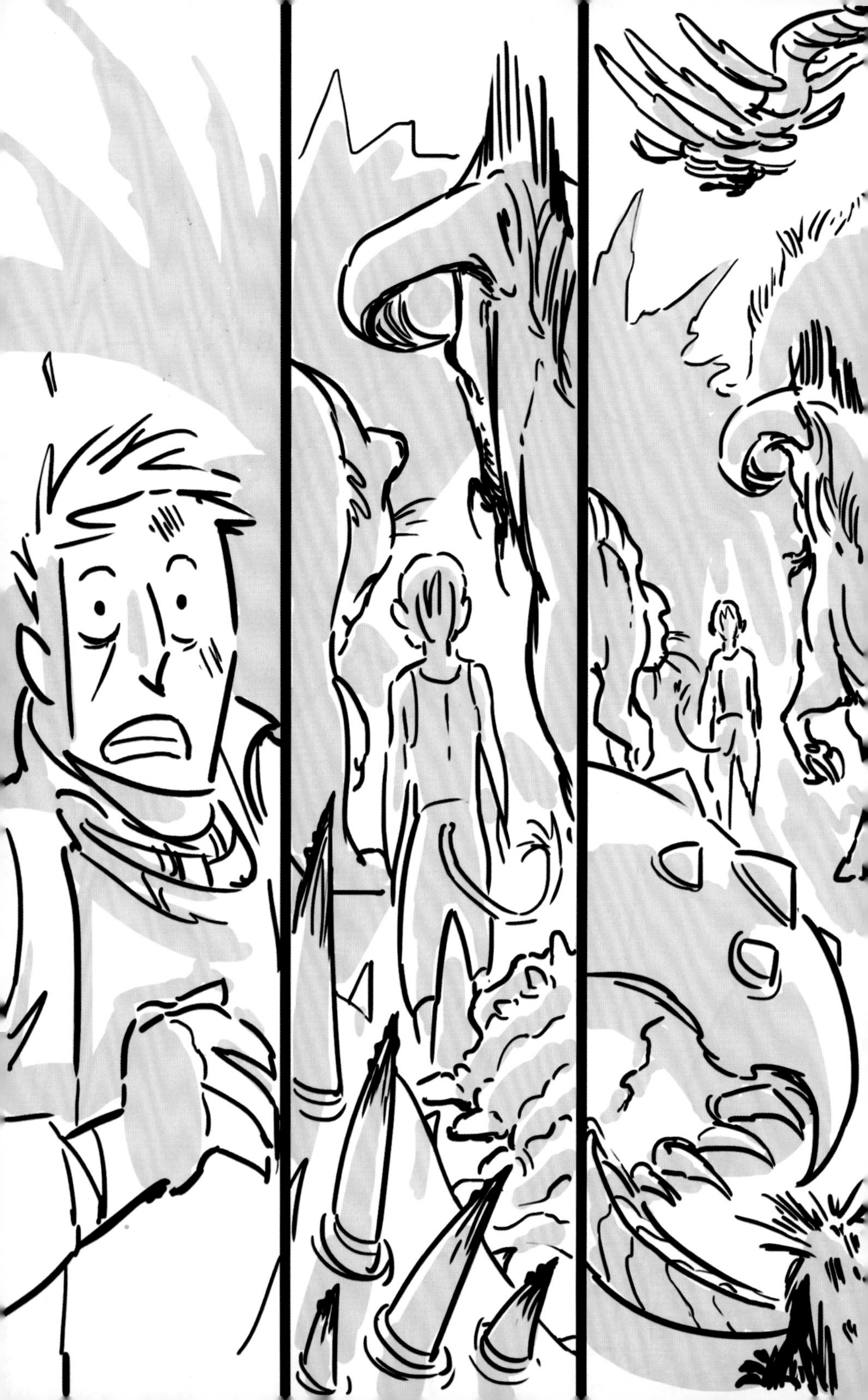

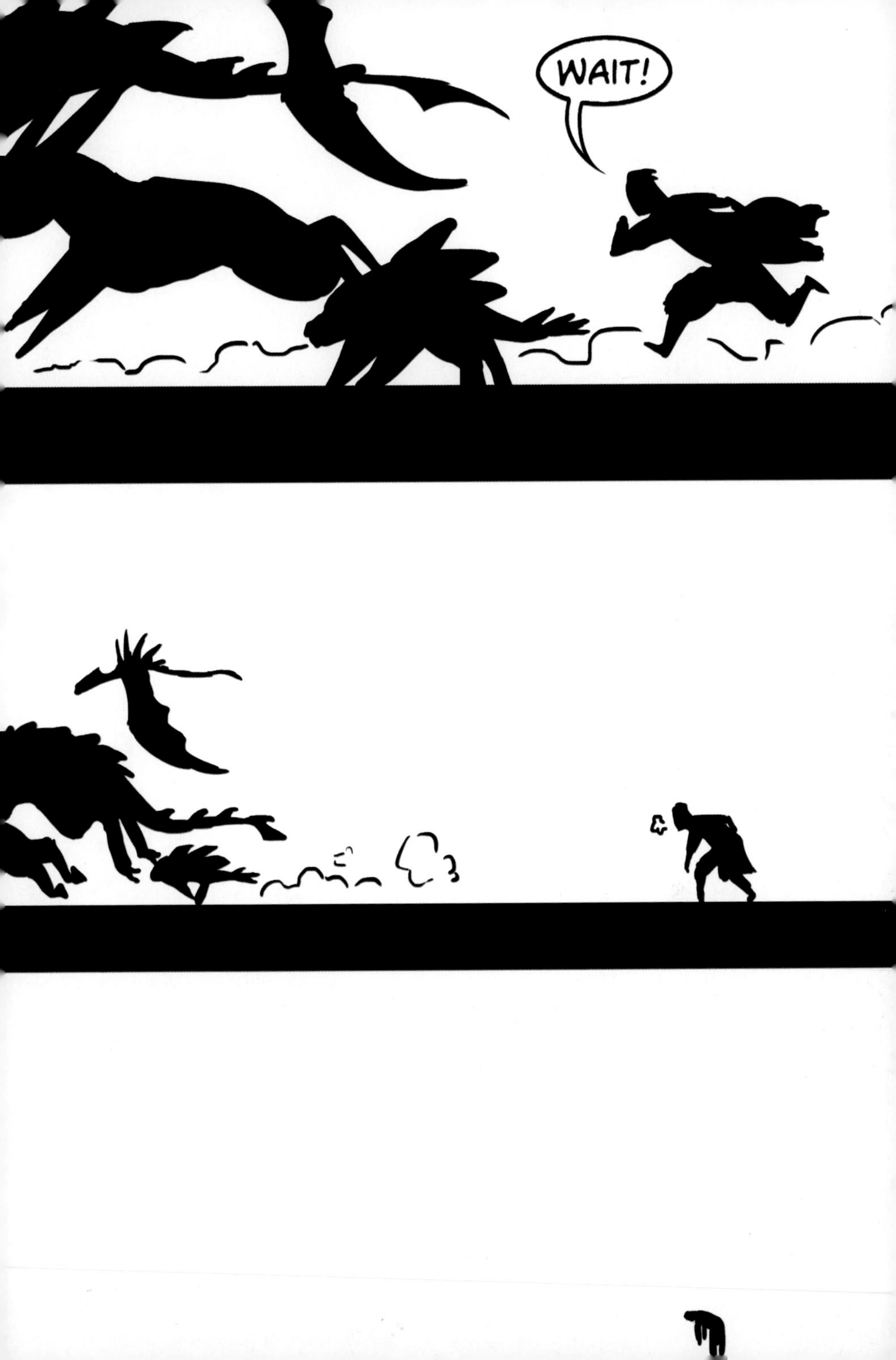
WAIT!

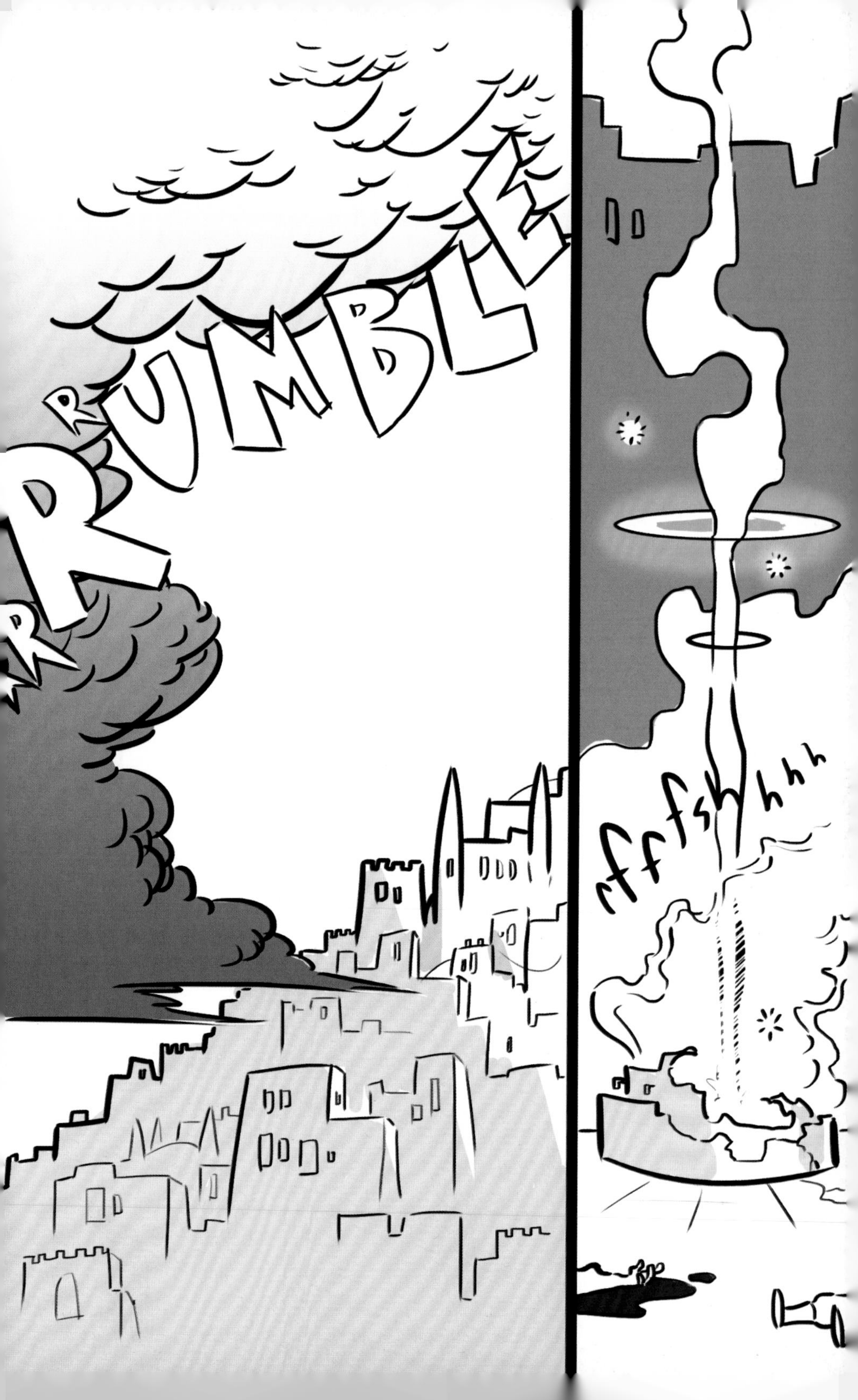
RRUMBLE
cffshhhh

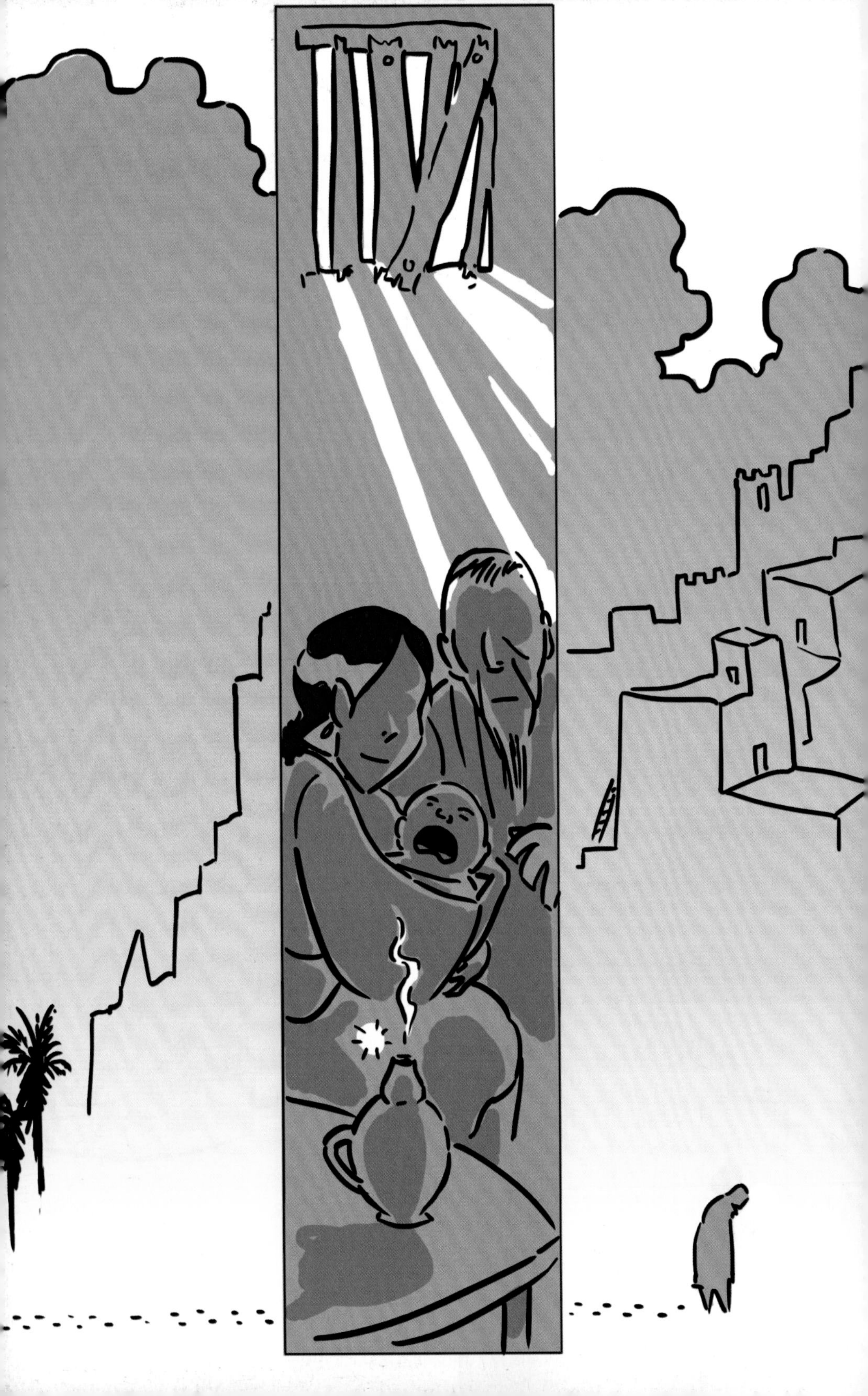

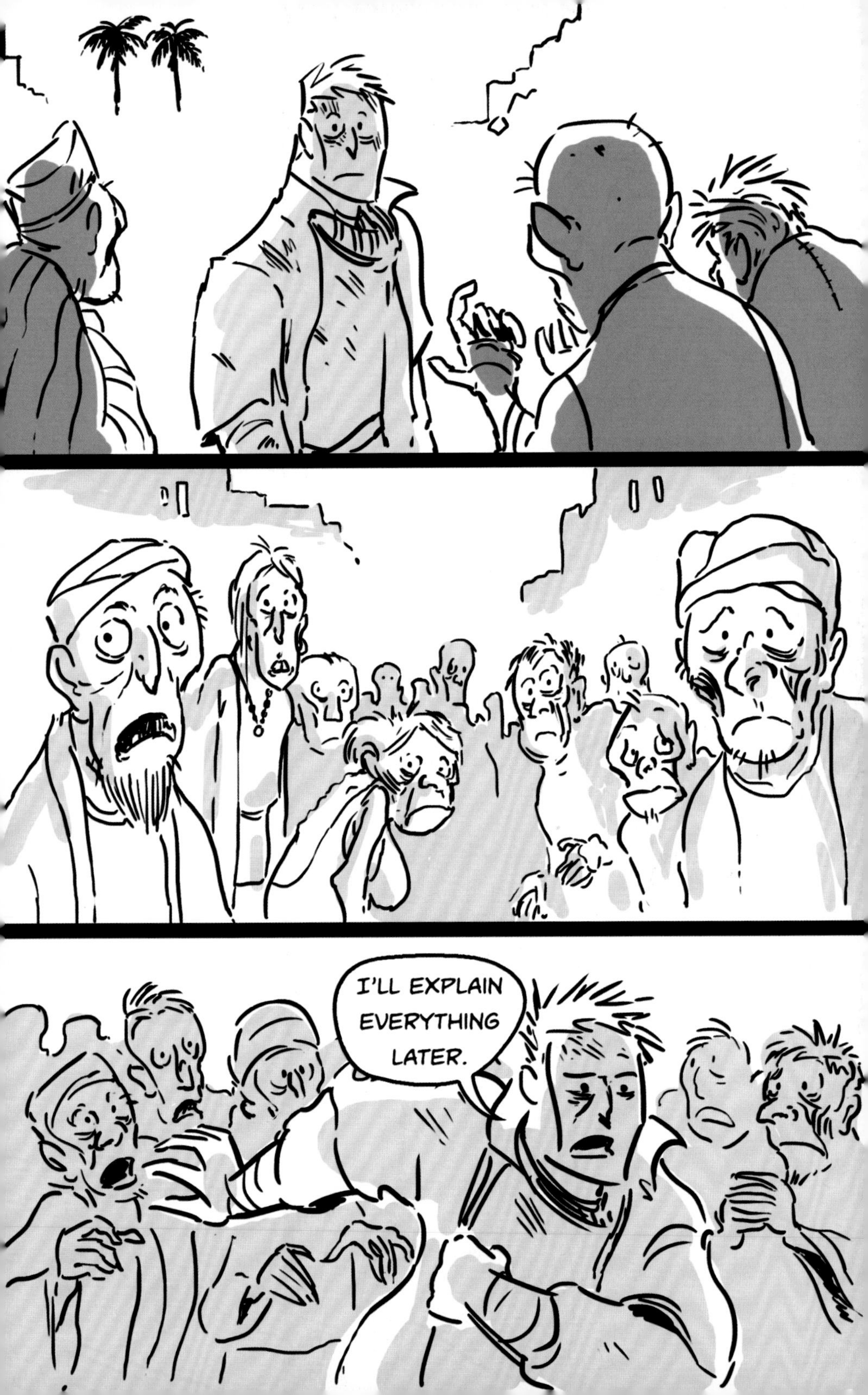
I'LL EXPLAIN EVERYTHING LATER.

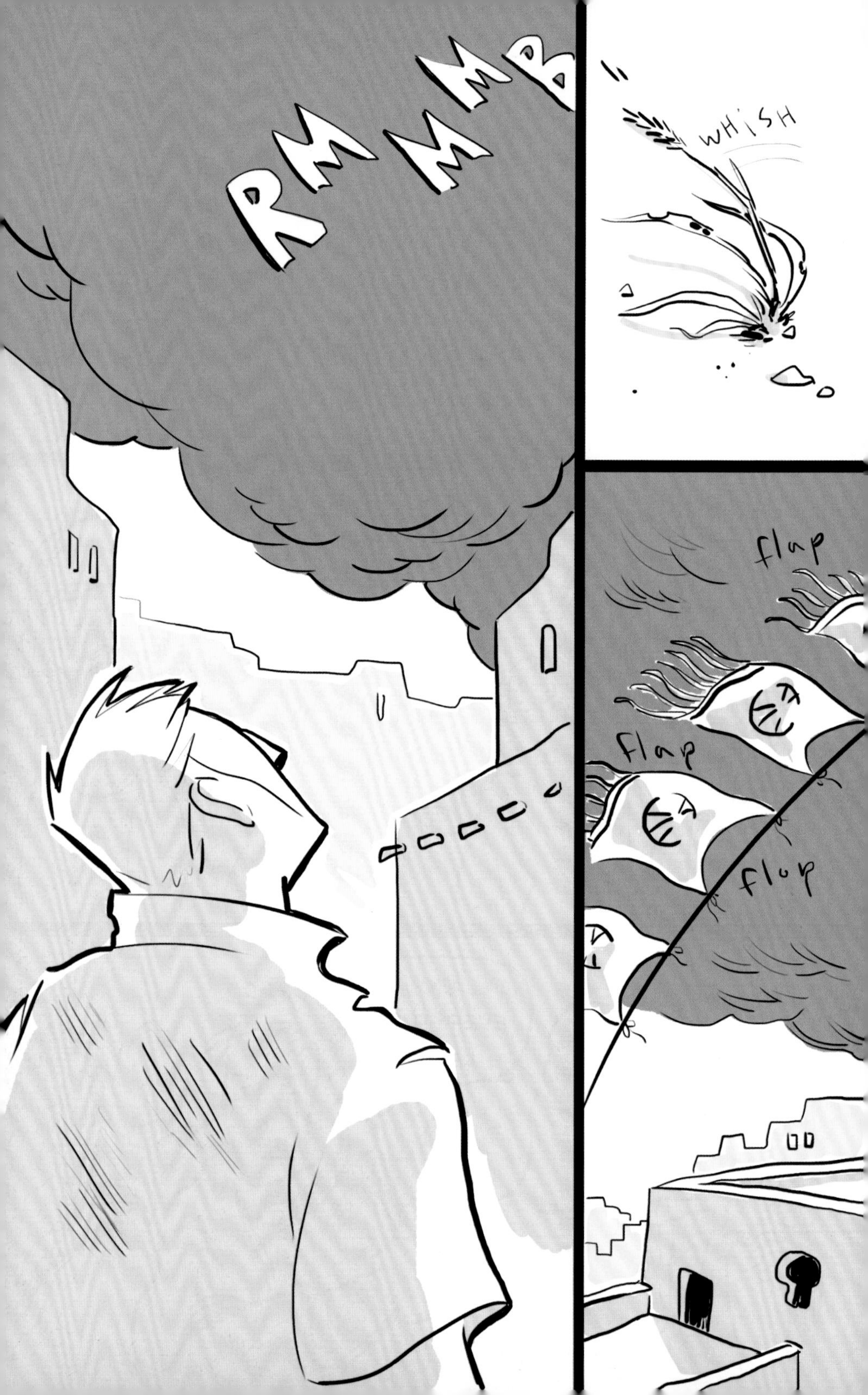
RMMMB
WHISH
flap
flap
flap

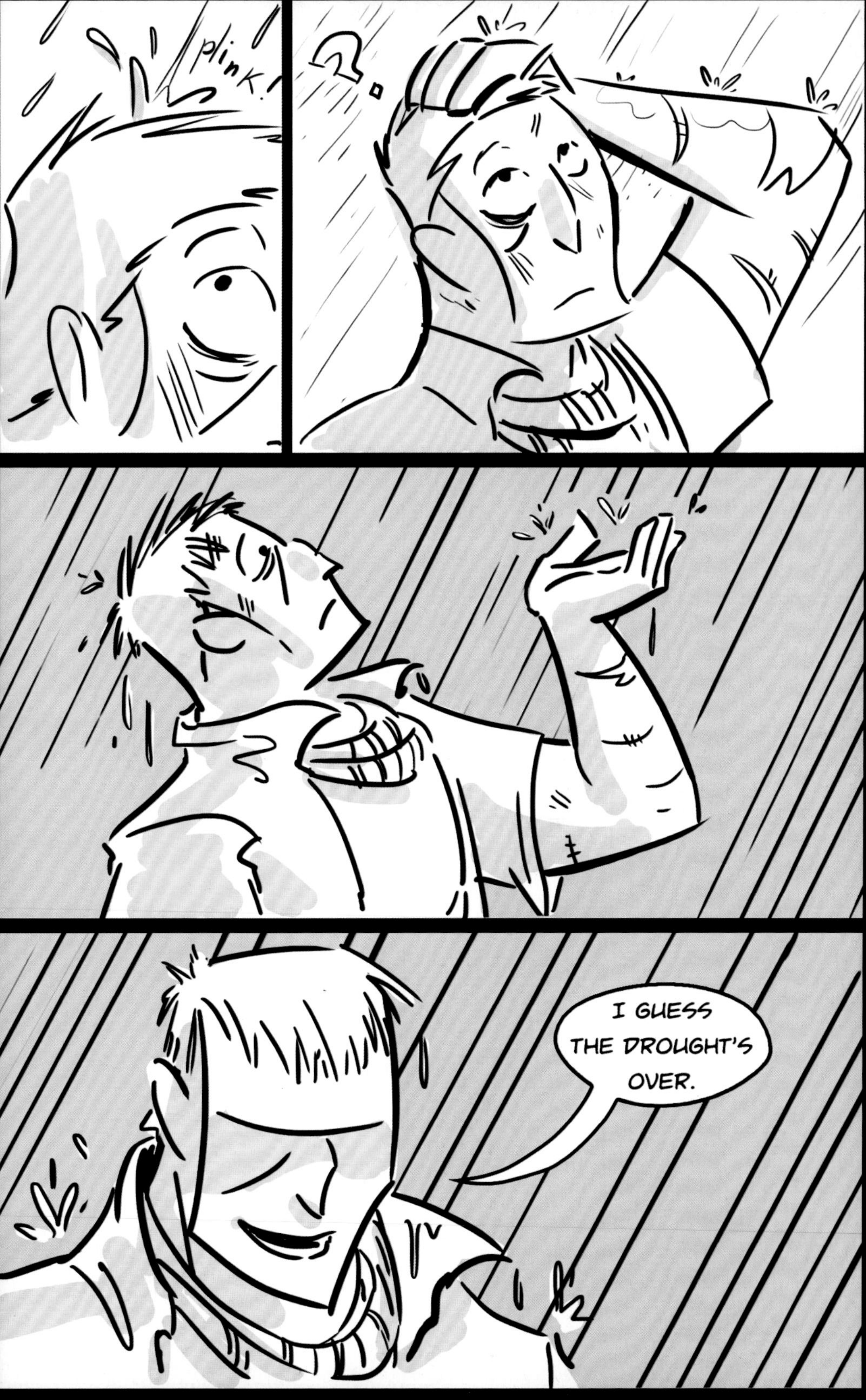
plink!
I GUESS THE DROUGHT'S OVER.

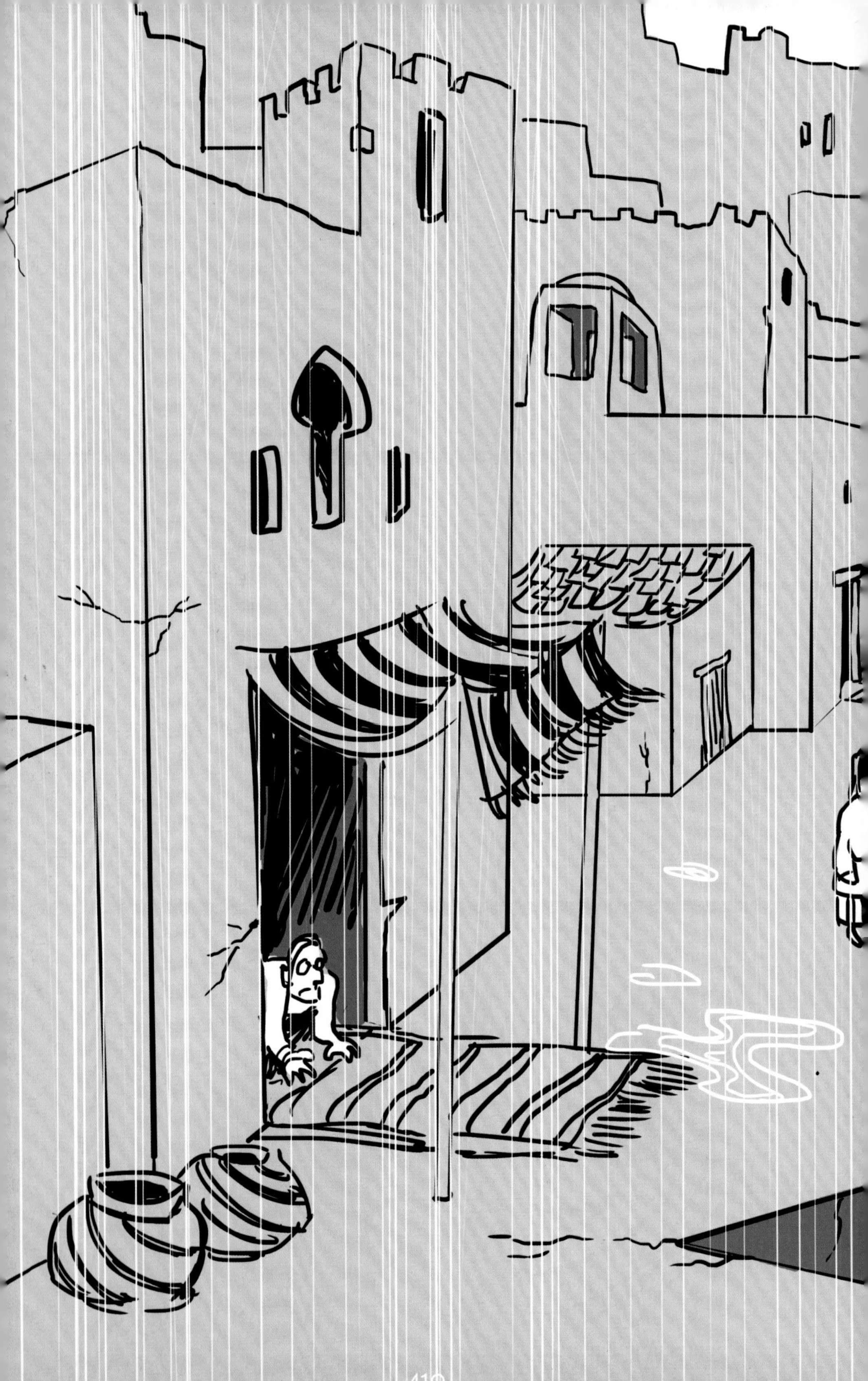

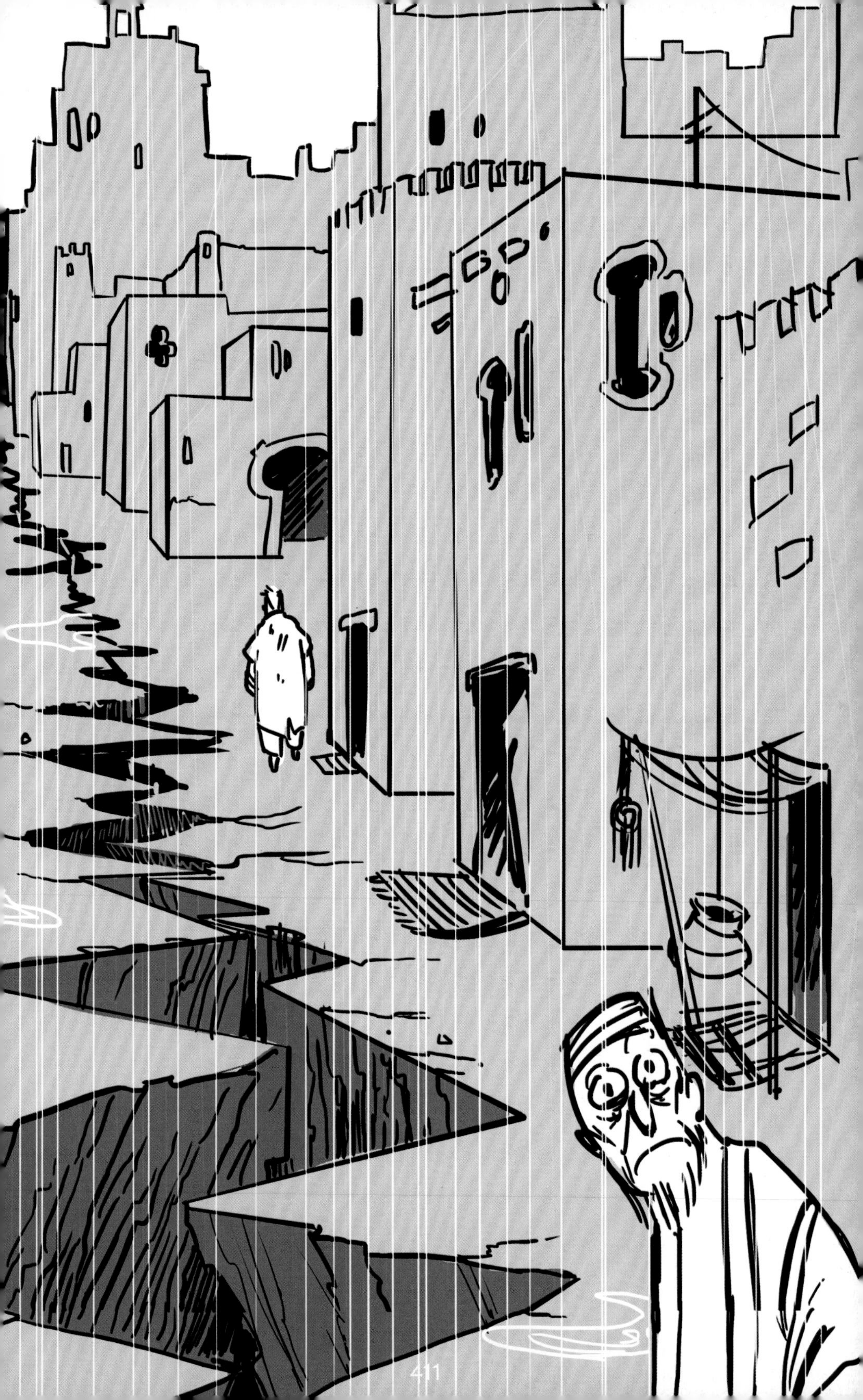

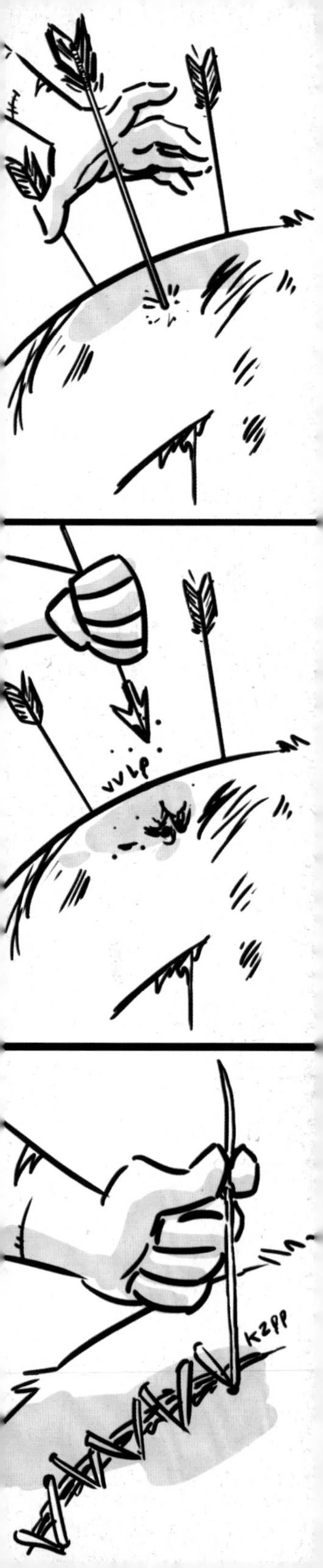
VVLP
KZPP

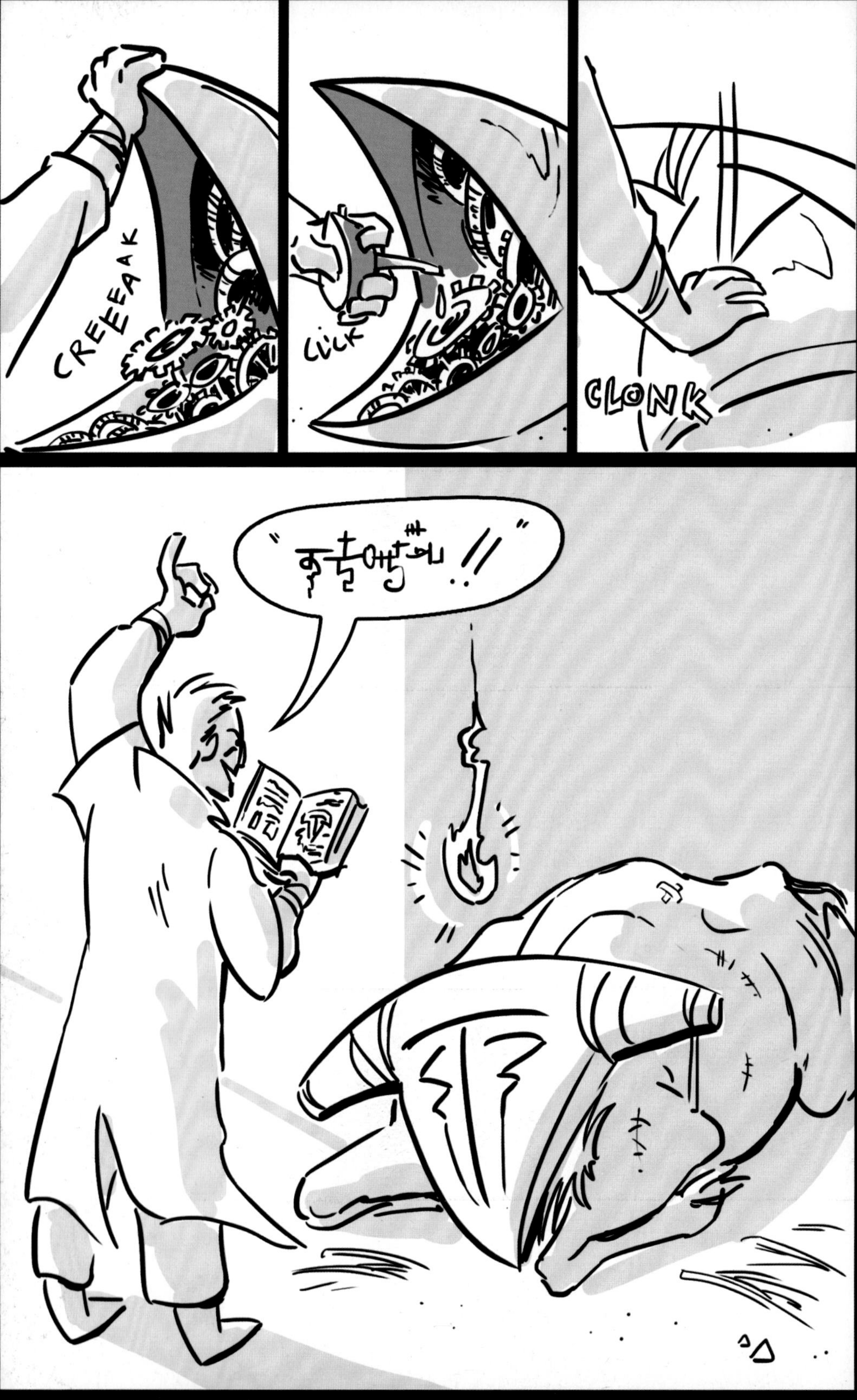
CREEEAAK
CLICK
CLONK

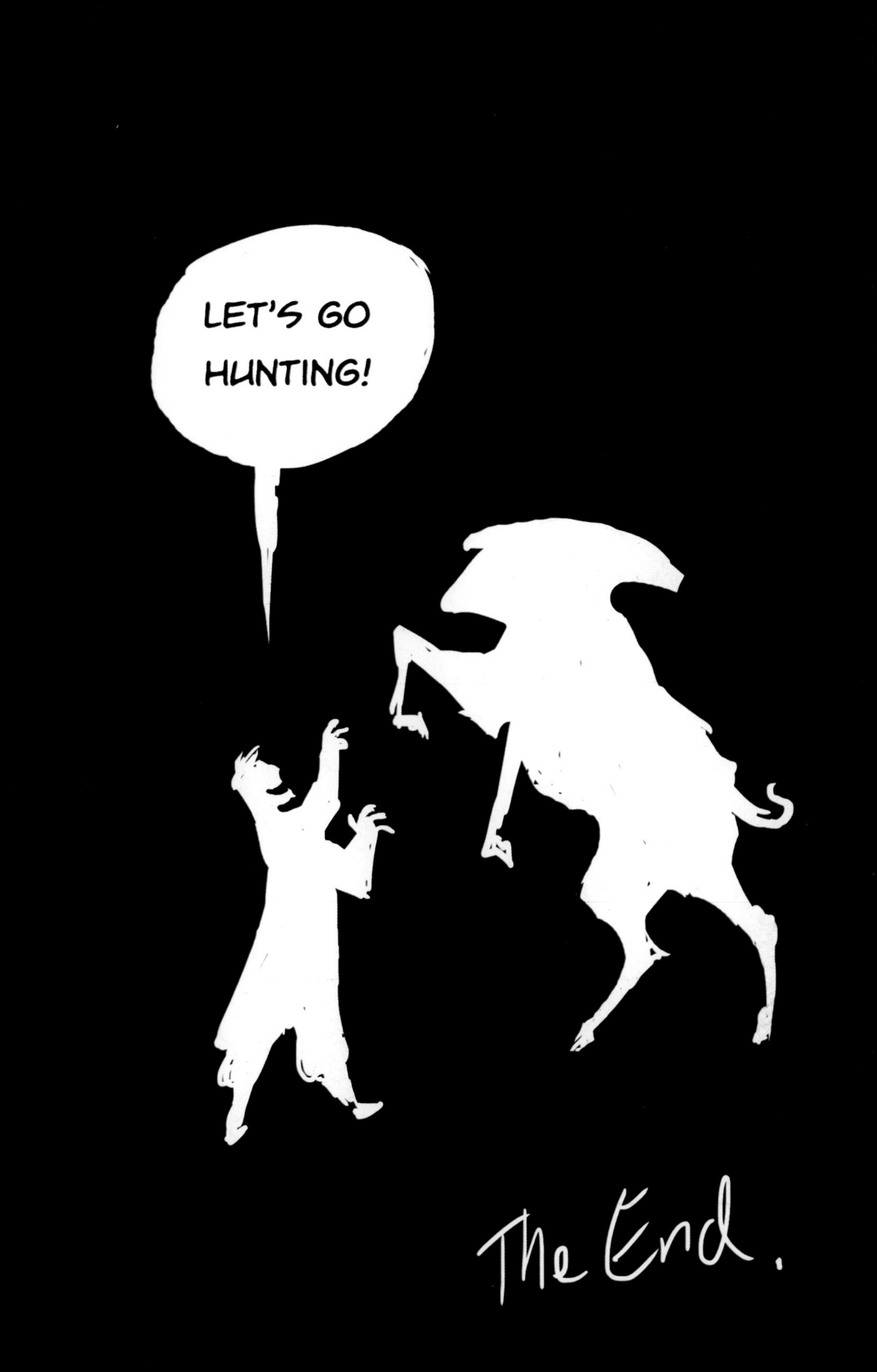
LET'S GO HUNTING!
The End.

" 'I LONG TO KILL THIS HNAKRA AS HE ALSO LONGS TO KILL ME. I HOPE THAT MY SHIP WILL BE THE FIRST AND I FIRST IN MY SHIP WITH MY STRAIGHT SPEAR WHEN THE BLACK JAWS SNAP. AND IF HE KILLS ME, MY PEOPLE WILL MOURN AND MY BROTHERS WILL DESIRE STILL MORE TO KILL HIM. BUT THEY WILL NOT WISH THAT THERE WERE NO HNERAKI; NOR DO I. HOW CAN I MAKE YOU UNDERSTAND, WHEN YOU DO NOT UNDERSTAND THE POETS? THE HNAKRA IS OUR ENEMY, BUT HE IS ALSO OUR BELOVED.' "

-CS LEWIS, OUT OF THE SILENT PLANET

SKETCHBOOK

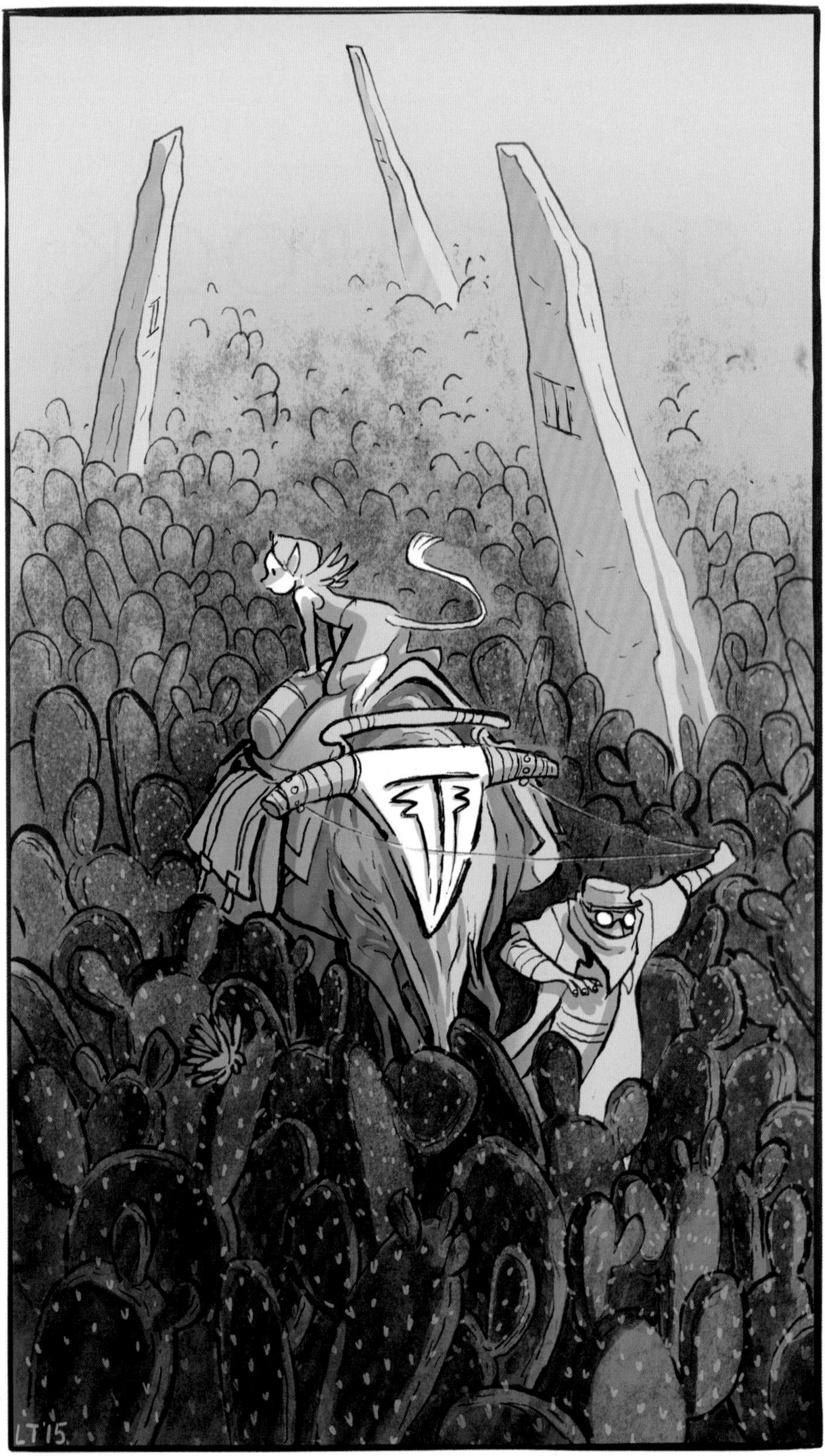
LT'15

LISSA TREIMAN

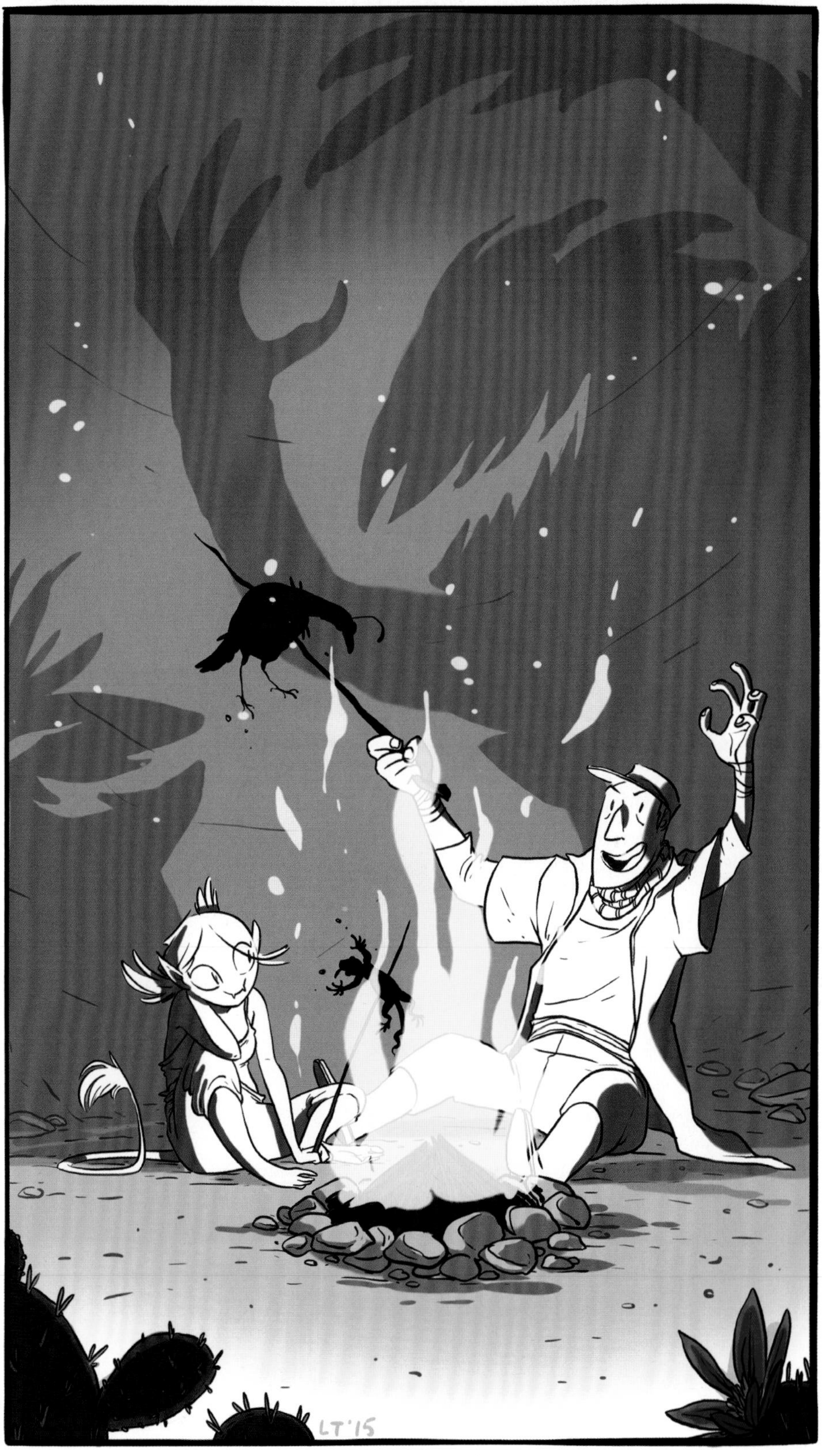
LT'15

LISSA TREIMAN

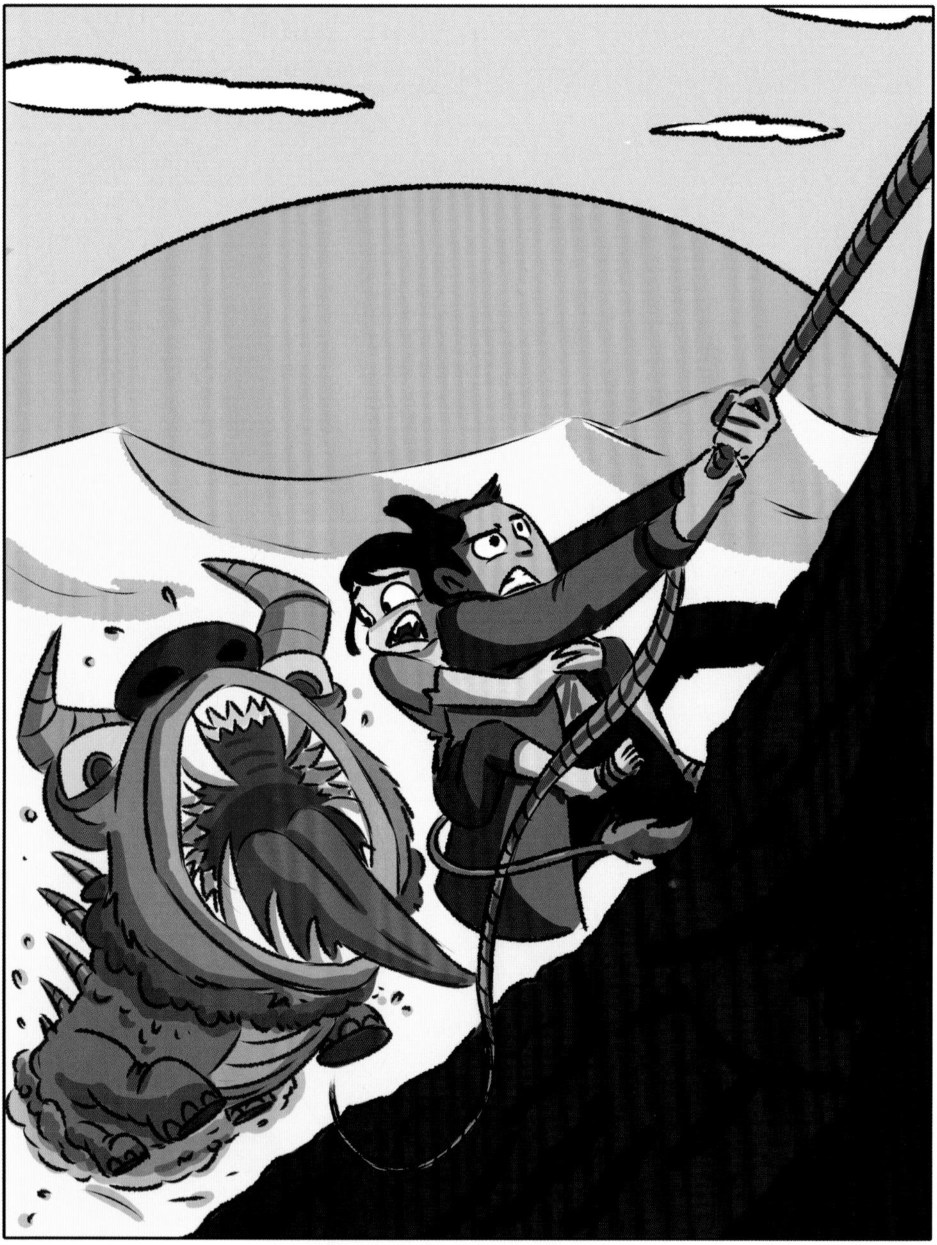

RANDEEP KATARI

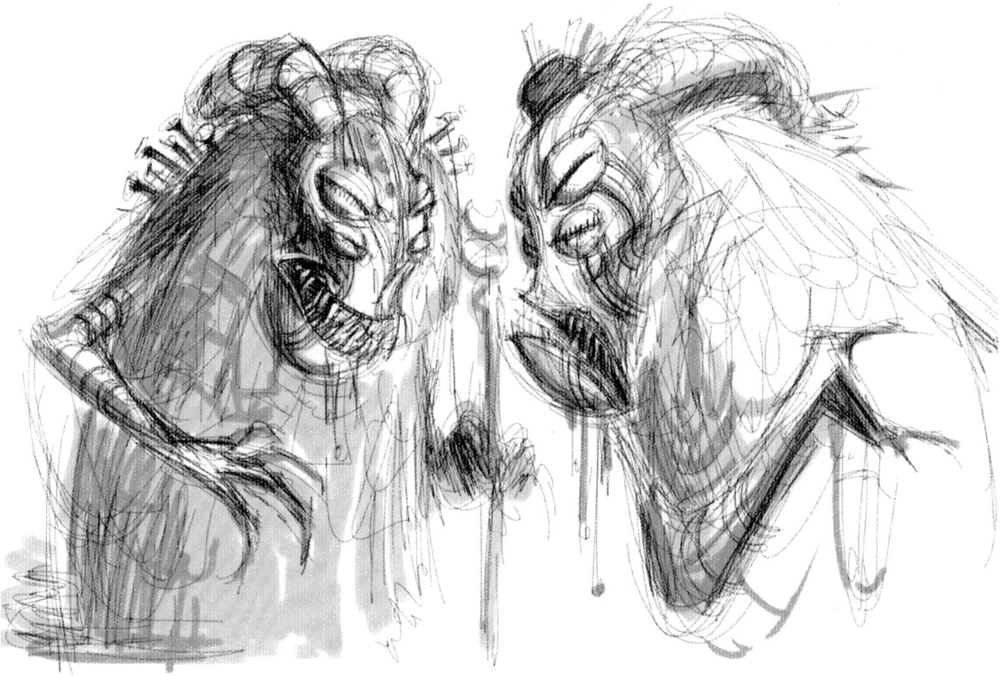

SOME SKETCHES OF THE ZAI KING.

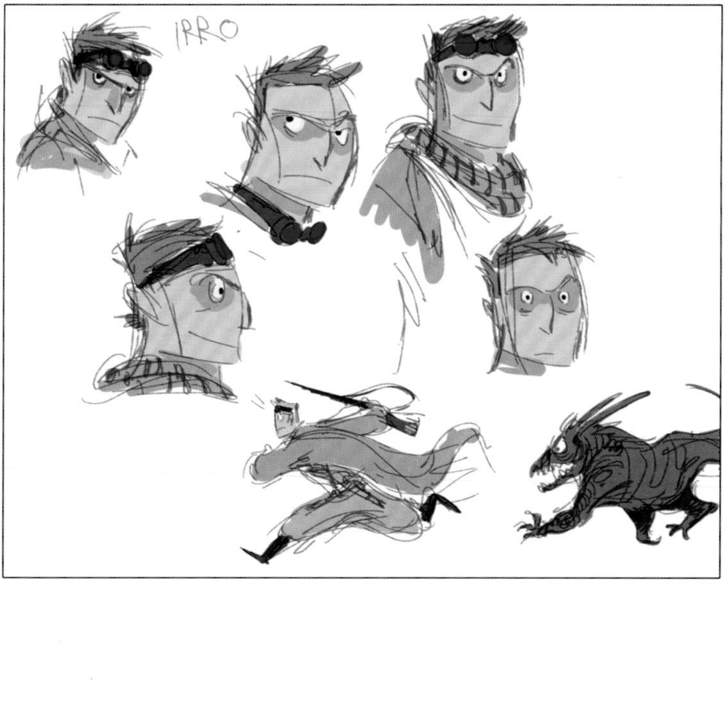
IRRO

IRRO HEADS!

IT'S TOUGH
BEING THE HIGH
PRIEST OF KEVALA

HARI,
THE BRATZ
VERSION.

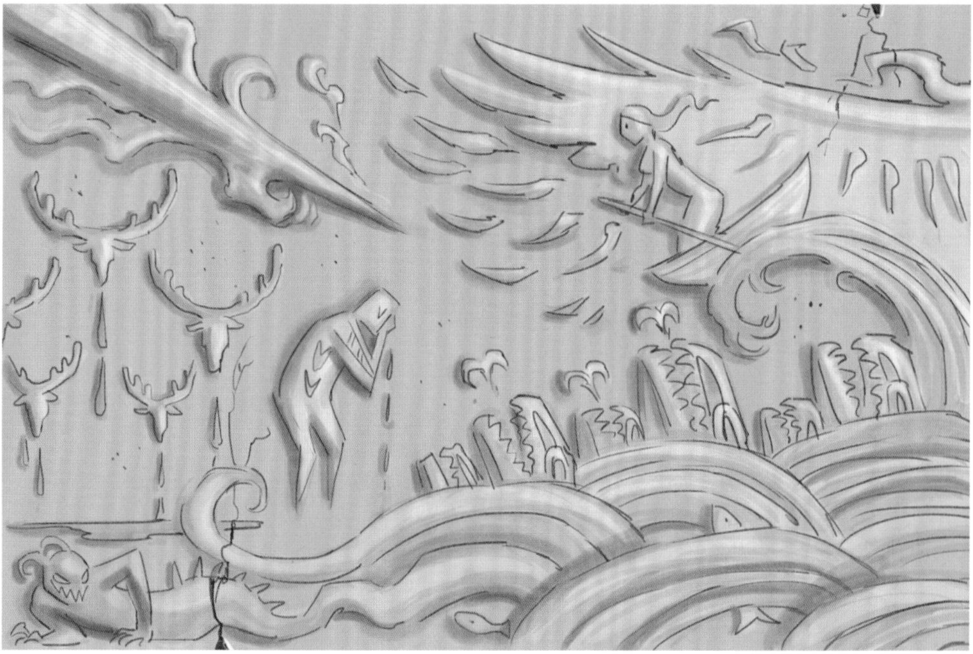

ENDPAPERS FOR VOLUME 1, POSSIBLY EXPLAINING THE ORIGIN OF WOMAN.

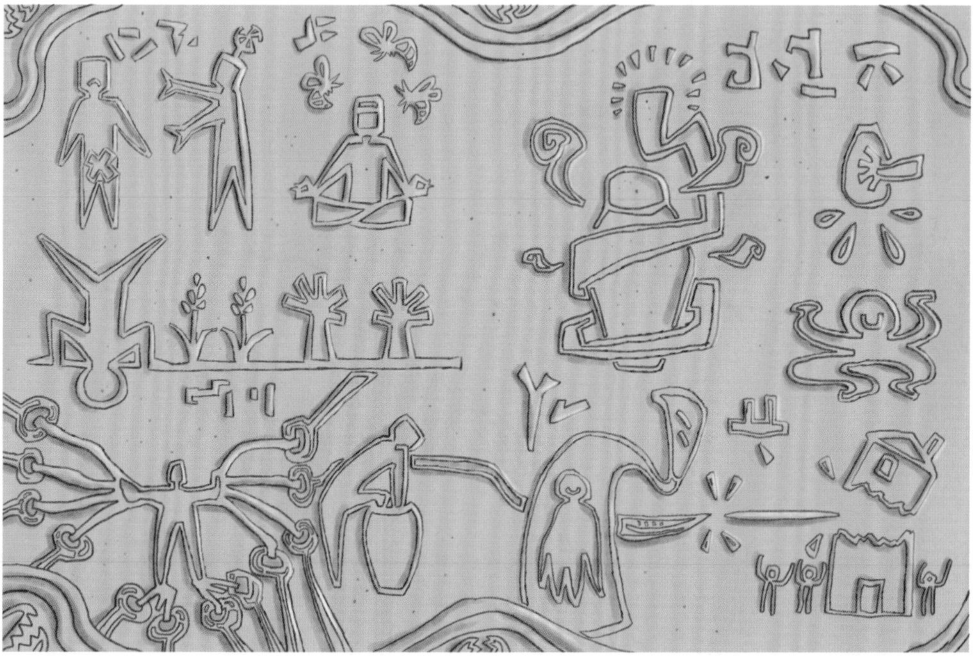

ENDPAPERS FOR VOLUME 2, A DIAGRAM OF THE YANTRA-MAKING PROCESS.

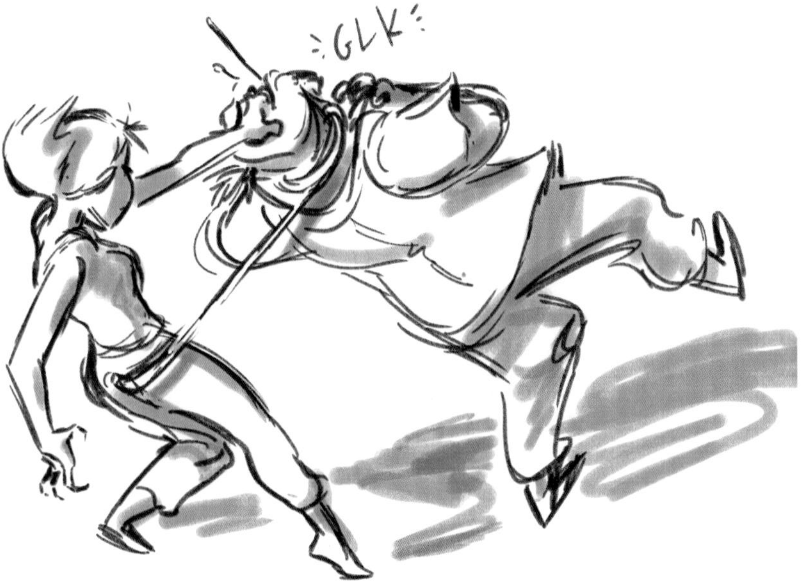
GLK

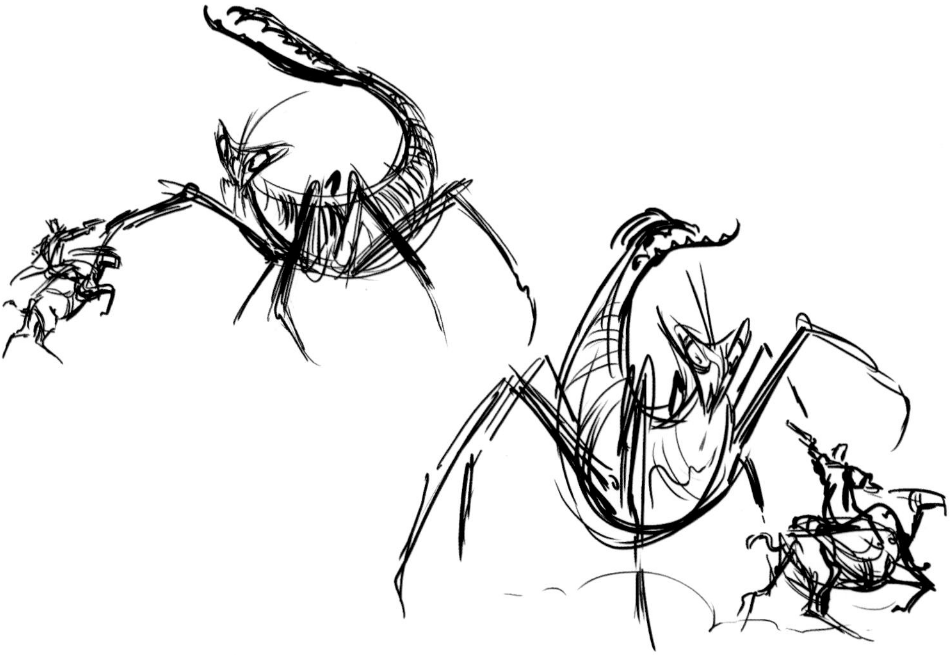

MORO ROGERS

MORO ROGERS LIVES IN DANA POINT CA
WITH HER HUSBAND JASON AND
GOZER THE CAT.

SPECIAL THANKS
TO MY HUSBAND AND PARENTS
FOR THEIR LOVE AND SUPPORT,
THE FOLKS AT ARCHAIA,
LISSA TREIMAN AND RANDEEP KATARI
FOR THEIR SWEET GUEST ART,
AND TO MY FRIEND MINKYU LEE
FOR HIS MUCH-NEEDED ADVICE AND CRITS.
ALSO TO GOD FOR MAKING SO MANY
WEIRD ANIMALS.

GRANT'S GOLDEN MOLE
(EREMITALPA GRANTI)